'The new *Routledge International Handbook of Early Literacy Education* is well-timed and rightly targeted at current cultural and linguistic super-diversity. The wide collection of chapters present new developments in old debates as well as new approaches to urgent social and cultural challenges. The broad overview of instruction methods in different languages, orthographies and education systems, is a rich and up-to-date resource for educators and researchers who wish to expand their knowledge and intervention repertoire.

The *Handbook* identifies several topics for research that need urgent attention, including the facilitative and problematic aspects of digital devices, also in view of linguistic super-diversity, the forms of oral language use in early childhood programs that support literacy development best and the role of bilingual children's first languages in second language literacy. Following these suggestions will strengthen early literacy education as an innovative international research and development program.'

– **Paul Leseman**, Professor of Education, Utrecht University, the Netherlands

'Global education is in dire need of scalable solutions to the crisis of learning. This stellar collection of the latest science that can inform strategies to foster literacy development is an important contribution. It will provide invaluable guidance to governments, NGOs and scholars worldwide on how to shift schooling from access to learning and truly fulfil the promise of education for all.'

– **Hirokazu Yoshikawa**, Courtney Sale Ross Professor of Globalization and Education, New York University, USA

'This is a timely and remarkable volume. Early childhood education is of global concern yet researchers have no comparable collection of solid empirical research. Chapters are written by exceptional authors, cover an astonishing number of countries, and deal with issues of pressing concern. It will play a pivotal role in facilitating conversation within the global early childhood community.'

– **David Dickinson**, Margaret Cowan Chair and Professor of Teacher Education, Department of Teaching and Learning; Associate Dean for Research and Strategic Planning, Peabody College, Vanderbilt University, USA

'This ambitious handbook includes contributions from early childhood educators from around the globe in a contemporary exploration of literacy in very different contexts. Led by internationally renowned scholars and emergent researchers it provides a comprehensive account of what early literacy development looks like in nations as diverse as New Zealand, Poland, India, USA, Norway, Canada, Israel, China, UK, Nordic and African countries and more. The wide representation of authors ensures that research which may not previously have been cited is included here. The volume tackles "hot topics" such as multi-literacies, phonemic awareness, vocabulary development as well as exploring seminal and current literature on continuing central areas in the early years, such as scaffolding, socio-economic disadvantage, bilingualism and so on. It will be a go-to resource for doctoral students and early childhood teacher educators as it provides a thorough, balanced discussion of key theories, debates and emergent themes in the field.'

– **Barbara Comber**, Research Professor, School of Education, University of South Australia

THE ROUTLEDGE INTERNATIONAL HANDBOOK OF EARLY LITERACY EDUCATION

The Routledge International Handbook of Early Literacy Education offers a pioneering overview of early literacy provision in different parts of the world and brings together interdisciplinary research evidence on effective literacy teaching to inform current and future practice and policy of early literacy. From the problem of identification of literacy difficulties in a particular learning context to supporting the provision of early literacy through digital media, the handbook deals with the major concerns and newest areas of interest in literacy research. With an international and future vision, it provides an accessible guide to the main debates and future trends in the global field of early literacy, and informs academics, policy-makers, practitioners, educators and students about innovative early literacy research methods and instruction.

The three sections and 30 ground-breaking chapters reflect a conceptual framework of questions asked by scholars and educators interested in looking beyond traditional definitions of literacy.

Part I provides contemporary insights collected by internationally renowned scholars on what literacy is, and what it can offer to young children in the twenty-first century.

Part II is a collection of detailed portraits of 14 countries, regions or language communities, and focuses on early literacy provision, practice and policy from across the world.

Part III outlines key interventions and research-endorsed practices designed to support home–school connections and children's reading and writing skills, as well as vocabulary, phonological awareness and narrative abilities, with examples drawn from various home, school and community environments.

All chapters promote discussion, critical analysis and questions for reflection and are written in jargon-free language in an easy-to-use themed format. This handbook is an indispensable reference guide for practising teachers and student teachers, especially those undertaking postgraduate qualifications, as well as early literacy researchers, policy-makers and school-based literacy leaders.

Natalia Kucirkova is Senior Research Fellow at University College London, UK.

Catherine E. Snow is Patricia Albjerg Graham Professor of Education at the Harvard Graduate School of Education, USA.

Vibeke Grøver is Professor of Education at the University of Oslo, Norway.

Catherine McBride is Professor of Psychology at The Chinese University of Hong Kong.

The Routledge International Handbook Series

A full list of titles in this series is available at:
www.routledge.com/series/HBKSOFED

THE ROUTLEDGE INTERNATIONAL HANDBOOK OF EARLY LITERACY EDUCATION

A Contemporary Guide to Literacy Teaching and Interventions in a Global Context

Edited by Natalia Kucirkova, Catherine E. Snow,
Vibeke Grøver and Catherine McBride

Routledge
Taylor & Francis Group

LONDON AND NEW YORK

First published 2017
by Routledge
2 Park Square, Milton Park, Abingdon, Oxon OX14 4RN

and by Routledge
711 Third Avenue, New York, NY 10017

Routledge is an imprint of the Taylor & Francis Group, an informa business

British Library Cataloguing in Publication Data
A catalogue record for this book is available from the British Library

Library of Congress Cataloging in Publication Data
Names: Kucirkova, Natalia, editor. | Snow, Catherine E., editor. | Grover, Vibeke, editor. | McBride-Chang, Catherine. editor.
Title: The Routledge international handbook of early literacy education / edited by Natalia Kucirkova, Catherine E. Snow, Vibeke Grover and Catherine McBride.
Description: New York : Routledge, 2017. |
Series: The Routledge
International Handbook Series
Identifiers: LCCN 2016043494 | ISBN 9781138787889 (hardback) | ISBN 9781315766027 (ebook)
Subjects: LCSH: Reading (Early childhood)—Cross-cultural studies.
Classification: LCC LB1139.5.R43 R68 2017 | DDC 372.4—dc23
LC record available at https://lccn.loc.gov/2016043494

ISBN: 978-1-138-78788-9 (hbk)
ISBN: 978-1-315-76602-7 (ebk)

Typeset in Bembo
by Keystroke, Neville Lodge, Tettenhall, Wolverhampton

Printed and bound in Great Britain by
TJ International Ltd, Padstow, Cornwall

CONTENTS

NOTES ON EDITORS

Natalia Kucirkova is a Senior Research Fellow at University College London, UK. Her research concerns innovative ways of supporting shared book reading, digital literacy and the role of personalization in early years. Her doctoral research inspired the development of the Our Story tablet/smartphone app. She is the founding convenor of the Children's Digital Books and Literacy Apps Special Interest Group of the United Kingdom Literacy Association. Her articles have appeared in *First Language*, *Computers & Education*, *Cambridge Journal of Education*, *Communication Disorders Quarterly* and *Learning, Media & Technology*.

Catherine E. Snow is the Patricia Albjerg Graham Professor at the Harvard Graduate School of Education. She has conducted research on first- and second-language acquisition and on the relation of language skills to literacy and to academic achievement. She has developed curricula for early childhood and middle-grade students, all focused on using oral discussion as a context for promoting literacy skills. She is past president of the International Association for the Study of Child Language and the American Educational Research Association, and holds visiting appointments at the University of Oslo and the University of Johannesburg.

Vibeke Grøver is a Professor of Education at the University of Oslo. She has conducted research on children's peer play, children's language use in a cross-cultural perspective and longitudinal relations between language exposure and vocabulary learning in language-minority children. Currently she is undertaking an intervention study of bilingual children and their language learning and text comprehension in urban, multi-ethnic preschools in Norway. She is a former dean at the Faculty of Educational Sciences at the University of Oslo and has been a visiting scholar at Harvard Graduate School of Education, New York University and UC Berkeley.

Catherine McBride is a Professor of Psychology at The Chinese University of Hong Kong. She specializes in developmental psychology, especially the development and impairment of reading and writing in children across cultures (on which she published the book *Children's Literacy Development*, Routledge, 2016). She is a Fellow of the Association for Psychological Science and Past President of the Society for the Scientific Study of Reading. She has served as the Associate Editor for four different journals and on the editorial boards of several others. She is currently working to establish a new Association for Reading and Writing in Asia (ARWA).

NOTES ON CONTRIBUTORS

María V. Acevedo is Assistant Professor of Early Childhood in the Department of Curriculum and Instruction at the University of Massachusetts, Boston. Her research explores the use of global literature and cultural artifacts to support young children's intercultural understanding and the portrayal of Latinos, especially Puerto Ricans, in multicultural literature. Her work in classrooms with early childhood educators and pre-service teachers focuses on story as a meaning-making process, education as inquiry and play as transformative experiences for young children. She has published in *Bookbird* and *Young Children*.

Ilgım Veryeri Alaca is Assistant Professor at Koc University, Media and Visual Arts Department, as well as a writer and illustrator of children's books. Her work explores transforming ecologies in book arts and their relation to creative thinking. She contributed to *The Routledge Companion to International Children's Literature* and *The Routledge Companion to Picturebooks*. Her articles have appeared in *Leonardo, International Journal of Education Through Art* and *Drawing: Research, Theory, Practice*.

Ann Anderson is a Professor in the Department of Curriculum and Pedagogy at the University of British Columbia. Her research and teaching are in mathematics education in the early years, parent mediation of young children's multi-literacies at home and family literacy. She researches the ways in which young children's multi-literacies are supported in families from diverse backgrounds, prior to and during primary school, and has ongoing collaborations with colleagues in family literacy. Her research is funded by the Social Sciences and Humanities Research Council of Canada. She has published in numerous journals in early childhood education and mathematics education.

Jim Anderson is a Professor of Early Literacy and Family Literacy at the University of British Columbia. He has also worked in the public school system as a classroom teacher, reading specialist, language arts consultant and assistant superintendent of curriculum and instruction. His research has been funded by the Social Sciences and Humanities Research Council (SSHRC) and other agencies. With colleagues, he is conducting a SSHRC-funded study of families' access to, and use of, digital tools in low-SES communities. He serves on the editorial board of several journals and on the Literacy Research Panel of the International Literacy Association.

Dorit Aram is a Professor and Head of the School Counseling Program in Tel Aviv University's School of Education. Her research focuses on adult–child literacy interactions and their implications for early literacy and socio-emotional development, in Hebrew and Arab communities. Addressing needs in special populations, her work examines these interactions in parent–child dyads of children with special needs and from low socio-economic backgrounds. She has conducted early interventions aimed at improving kindergarten and preschool teachers' as well as parents' mediation and children's early literacy and socio-emotional development.

Elżbieta Awramiuk is Associate Professor at the University of Bialystok in Poland. Her research concerns contemporary Polish, as well as language education and the psycholinguistics aspects of written communication (on which she has published the book *Lingwistyczne podstawy początkowej nauki czytania i pisania po polsku* [The linguistic aspects of initial reading and writing education in Polish], 2006). She is a Secretary of the International Association for Research in L1 Education (languages, literatures and literacies) (ARLE). She is on the editorial board of *L1 – Educational Studies in Language and Literature*.

Rukmini Banerji is currently the CEO of Pratham Education Foundation. From 2005 to 2014, she led the ASER (Annual Status of Education Report) in India. This is a nationwide annual household survey conducted in every rural district in India that generates estimates for basic reading and arithmetic. She also has extensive field experience in programme implementation and assessment in rural and urban India.

Margit Böck is Professor and Head, Institute of Teaching and Learning of German Language and Literature at the Alpen-Adria-Universität Klagenfurt, Austria. She is President of the Austrian Literacy Association. Between 1999 and 2012 she was closely involved with the Austrian PISA studies. Her publications cover gender and reading, issues of life worlds, information habitus and representation. Her present research interests are the literacy practices of young people in their 'everyday' life and in school, both face to face and in digital environments. She links this strongly with issues of equity and possibilities for learning in the widest sense.

Jeung-Ryeul Cho is a Professor of Psychology at Kyungnam University in South Korea. Her research concerns the word recognition of Korean Hangul among Korean adults, and reading and writing processes of Hangul among Korean children. She is one of the Korean scholars who specialize in Korean Hangul reading development and impairment. Her articles have appeared in *Journal of Educational Psychology*, *Scientific Studies of Reading, Reading and Writing* and *Dyslexia*. She is currently a member of SSSR and ARWA (Association for Reading and Writing in Asia).

John Everatt is a Professor of Education at the University of Canterbury, New Zealand. He has lectured on education and psychology programmes at universities in New Zealand and the UK, as well as supporting education-related projects in Arabia and other parts of the world. His research focuses on literacy acquisition and developmental learning difficulties (particularly dyslexia), including issues related to second-language literacy acquisition and biliteracy. His current work investigates relationships between literacy and language by considering the characteristics of different scripts and how these might lead to different manifestations of reading/writing problems.

Bente E. Hagtvet is Professor at the University of Oslo, Norway, where her field of expertise is children's oral and written language in typical and atypical development. Her special interest is reading difficulties and children's emergent literacy during the preschool years. She has published books and articles on topics related to children's early attempts to read and write in informal and play-oriented activities, and has led longitudinal as well as intervention studies on related issues (funded by the Norwegian Research Council), most recently a vocabulary intervention study including children in typical and delayed language development.

Rebecca Jesson is a Senior Lecturer in the Faculty of Education and Social Work at the University of Auckland. Her research interests focus on raising achievement in literacy in schools which serve diverse communities. Her work focuses on dialogic approaches to teaching, and the relationships between teaching and learning. Her projects include research and development in digital learning contexts in New Zealand as well as in communities across the Pacific.

Harriet Jisa is Professor Emeritus of Linguistics at the Université Lumière-Lyon 2 and member of the laboratory 'Dynamique du langage' (UMR 5596 – CNRS) and senior member of the Institut Universitaire de France. She received a PhD from the University of Southern California in 1985, a French Doctorat in 1989 and an Habilitation in 1992 from the Université Lumière-Lyon 2. Her research interests include language development in monolingual and bilingual children, the development of narrative competence and the impact of literacy on children's grammatical competence.

Bestern Kaani is a Lecturer in Educational Psychology and Special Education at The University of Zambia. His research focuses on understanding how linguistic characteristics, particularly orthographic transparency, affect the acquisition of reading skills among beginning readers in multilingual environments. He is also interested in cross-cultural variations and applications of traditional theories and models of intelligence in non-Western societies, especially in the developing world. In 2009, he was awarded the Developing Country Fellowship by the International Society for the Study of Behavioral Development (ISSBD). In addition to the ISSBD, he is also a member of the International Association of Cross-Cultural Psychology (IACCP).

Sylvia Chanda Kalindi is a Postdoctoral Fellow in the Psychology Department at The Chinese University of Hong Kong with expertise in developmental psychology. Her research focuses on how the environmental factors and parental writing support styles influence language and literacy development in monolingual and bilingual children across different cultures. She is also interested in the use of computer intervention to enhance the reading development of English-language learners identified to be at risk of reading difficulty.

Eiko Kato-Otani is President and a Professor of Osaka Jogakuin University. She received her EdD in language and literacy from Harvard University. Her research interests include children's language development as influenced by interaction with adults in home and preschool settings. She examines cultural differences between Japan and the US in home and preschool settings. She instructed kindergarten teachers using picture books on how young children can develop their language skills in 2008 as part of the projects of Osaka City Children and Youth Bureau.

Dorea Kleker is an early childhood educator and an instructor for the University of Arizona's early childhood teacher education programme (CREATE) where she teaches children's literature and early literacy courses. Working in Latino immigrant communities, her research has focused on cross-border teacher exchanges, cross-border narratives, intercultural understanding and teacher inquiry groups. She is currently exploring how using art and literature in classrooms and homes can build family–school relationships, promote learning from and with families, and support students' biliteracy development.

Graz˙yna Krasowicz-Kupis is Professor of Psychology at the Maria Curie Sklodowska-University in Lublin and at the Educational Research Institute in Warsaw, Poland. She specializes in developmental psychology and psycholinguistics, especially reading and writing development and disorders, as well as psychological assessment and diagnosis. She is the author of many books concerning these problems, including *Psychologia dysleksji* [The psychology of dyslexia] (2008) and *SLI i inne zaburzenia rozwoju je˛zykowego* [SLI and other disorders of language development] (2012). She has been the leader of several big projects on reading and spelling acquisition and dyslexia in Polish children aged 5–9.

Aylin C. Küntay is a Professor of Developmental Psychology at Koç University, Istanbul. Her research areas include early communicative and language development in young children with a focus on child-directed interaction in a cross-linguistic framework. She was appointed as the Prince Claus Chair for Development and Equity to Utrecht University in 2014, where she studied bilingual communicative development in a multicultural context. She served as the Acting Editor for the *Journal of Child Language* from 2011 to 2015 and the Associate Editor of *Turkish Psychology Journal* from 2002 to 2009.

Nonie Lesaux is Juliana W. and William Foss Thompson Professor of Education and Society at the Harvard Graduate School of Education. She leads a research programme that focuses on increasing opportunities-to-learn for students from diverse linguistic, cultural and economic backgrounds. Her work has earned her the William T. Grant Scholars Award and the Presidential Early Career Award for Scientists and Engineers, the highest honour given by the US government to young professionals beginning their independent research careers. She has served on the US Department of Education's Reading First Advisory Committee and on the Institute of Medicine and National Research Council's Committee on the Science of Children Birth to Age 8. Her research appears in numerous scholarly publications, and its practical applications are featured in three books: *Teaching Advanced Literacy Skills* (Guilford Press, 2016), *Cultivating Knowledge, Building Language: Literacy Instruction for English Learners in Elementary School* (Heinemann, 2015) and *Making Assessment Matter: Using Test Results to Differentiate Reading Instruction* (Guilford Press, 2011).

Wendy K. Mages is an Associate Professor at Mercy College, New York. Her research investigates the effect of educational strategies and contexts on language, cognitive and social development, with a particular emphasis on studying the arts as educational contexts. Her research has been published in journals such as *Review of Educational Research*, *NHSA Dialog: A Research-to-Practice Journal for the Early Childhood Field*, *Journal of Early Childhood Teacher Education*, *Research in Drama Education*, *Youth Theatre Journal* and the *International Journal of Education and the Arts*.

Allyssa McCabe, PhD, is Professor of Psychology at University of Massachusetts Lowell. She founded the journal *Narrative Inquiry* and has studied how narrative develops with age, the way parents can encourage narration and cultural differences in narration, as well as interrelationships between the development of narrative, vocabulary and phonological awareness (the Comprehensive Language Approach to acquisition of literacy). Her work has appeared in *Journal of Child Language*, *Developmental Psychology* and *Journal of Autism and Developmental Disorders*.

Her most recent books are *Chinese Language Narration: Culture, Cognition and Emotion* and *Spanish Language Narration: Culture, Cognition, and Emotion*.

Stuart McNaughton, PhD, is Professor of Education at the University of Auckland and Director of the Woolf Fisher Research Centre. He researches in children's literacy and language development, the design of effective educational programmes for culturally and linguistically diverse populations, and cultural processes in development. He consults on literacy and language curricula and educational interventions nationally and internationally. Recent appointments include Chief Education Scientific Advisor to the New Zealand government. He is a member of the International Literacy Association's Literacy Research Panel and an inductee in the Reading Hall of Fame.

Susana Mendive is an Associate Professor in the School of Education at the Pontificia Universidad Católica of Chile. Her research focuses on family and instructional factors affecting early language and literacy development and on evaluating the impact of related interventions. In the preschool teacher training programme she teaches Learning and Development in Early Years and Teaching and Learning of Early Language. In addition she is a member of the Early Childhood Learning, Teaching and Development research area in the doctoral programme. She has published in the *Journal of Educational Psychology*, *Early Education and Development* and *Infant Behavior & Development*.

Alejandra Meneses is an Associate Professor in the School of Education at the Pontificia Universidad Católica de Chile and member of the Didactics Department. She has had experience teaching grammar and literacy courses. Her research is focused on academic language development and its relation with literacy for learning, classroom interaction and text-based discussion for reading comprehension. She also has led for the last three years practice-based reform in the Universidad Católica Teacher Education programmes of Early Childhood, Elementary Education and High School Education. Her articles have appeared in *Applied Psycholinguistics*, *Reading Research Quarterly* and *Estudios de Psicología*.

Sonali Nag is a member of the Early Childhood and Primary School Programmes at The Promise Foundation and a Visiting Academic at the University of Oxford. Her research has shown how formal features of an orthography (e.g. its visual features, rules of representation) influence the weight of both lower level (e.g. visual complexity, visuo-motor complexity) and higher level (e.g. morphological features) processes throughout the early phases of literacy development. Her approach is multidisciplinary and straddles research, policy and practice. She has co-authored an evidence brief on literacy and foundation learning in developing countries.

Lea Nieminen, PhD, is a researcher in the Centre for Applied Language Studies, University of Jyvaskyla, Finland. Her main research interests are learning to read and write in L1 and L2 from cognitive and linguistic perspectives, assessment of literacy development, morphosyntactic development in early child language, and bilingual and bimodal language development. She has authored articles in several national and international journals, and published the co-authored book *The Diagnosis of Reading in a Second or Foreign Language* (Routledge, 2015). She also serves as an editor for the Finnish linguistic journal *Puhe ja kieli* (Speech and Language).

Lauren H. Pangle is an early childhood educator, currently teaching at the Museum School in Decatur, Georgia. She is Nationally Board Certified and has graduate degrees from Western

Oregon University and the University of Arizona in Language, Reading and Culture. Her interests include using children's literature to engage young children in reader response and inquiry-based learning. Her classroom is featured in *Literature for Young Children: Supporting Emergent Literacy, Ages 0–8* (7th edition).

Emily Phillips Galloway is an Assistant Professor at Vanderbilt University's Peabody School of Education. Before beginning her doctoral studies at the Harvard Graduate School of Education, she was a Michael Pressley Memorial Fellow at the Benchmark School in Media, PA where she taught adolescent struggling readers in grades 6, 7 and 8 and served as a reading specialist. Currently, her research explores the relationships between academic language development and reading skill in adolescent learners with a particular focus on English learners. Her work has been featured in *Reading Research Quarterly*, *Applied Psycholinguistics* and *Reading and Writing: An Interdisciplinary Journal*. With a commitment to advancing research-practice partnerships, she has also worked with teachers, school leaders and administrators in two of the largest urban districts in the United States. The fundamentals and lessons learned from this work are featured in a forthcoming book with Nonie Lesaux on leading advanced literacy instruction in linguistically diverse settings.

Victoria Purcell-Gates is Professor Emerita at the University of British Columbia where she held the Canada Research Chair in Early Childhood Literacy from 2004 to 2013. She has researched and written widely on the ways in which people within communities value and practise literacy. She currently lives in Berkeley, California, where she focuses on designing early literacy instruction that builds on young children's linguistic, cognitive, cultural and social models for reading and writing acquired within their home communities. She is a former president of the National Reading Conference and a member of the Reading Hall of Fame.

Harini Rajagopal is a doctoral student in the Department of Language and Literacy Education at the University of British Columbia. Her research interests are in the areas of early learning and literacies in transnational families and the institutions that these families engage with for education. She is particularly fascinated with the intersection of language, learning, identities and cultures, and is methodologically interested in multimodal perspectives, co-construction and reflexivity in research.

Ulla Richardson is a professor of technology-enhanced language learning in the Centre for Applied Language Studies, University of Jyväskylä, Finland. Her research falls into language acquisition, reading and writing skills in different languages and orthographies, dyslexia research, interventions and skill assessments, and evidence-based technology in language learning. She leads an interdisciplinary GraphoGame team who have developed the evidence-based GraphoGame learning environment (info.GraphoGame.com) for more than 20 languages to support learners in developing their reading skills. She has authored book chapters as well as articles in several journals including *Developmental Neuropsychology*, *Reading Research Quarterly*, *Journal of Experimental Child Psychology*, *Dyslexia* and *PNAS*.

Ana María Rodino is a researcher for the *State of Costa Rican Education Report* and a member of its Consulting Board. Within this nationwide biennial effort conducted by the Organization of Public University Rectors she has researched extensively on early childhood education and literacy development, preschool curricular reform and Costa Rican performance at PISA tests. She consults for UNICEF and is currently working on policy guidelines on early childhood and family education for the Ministry of Education. Her teaching, research and scientific and didactic publications in the language field focus on first- and second-language acquisition, reading and writing development, bilingualism and intercultural communication.

Deborah Wells Rowe is Professor of Early Childhood Education at Peabody College, Vanderbilt University. Her research focuses on how young children learn to write in preschool and primary grades classrooms. Recent work has explored how iPads and digital cameras can provide emergent bilinguals with opportunities for multimodal, multilingual composing. She is the author of the book *Preschoolers as Authors: Literacy Learning in the Social World of the Classroom* and numerous research articles. Her research on preschoolers' writing has been recognized with the International Literacy Association's Dina Feitelson Research Award. She is co-editor of the *Journal of Early Childhood Literacy*.

Elinor Saiegh-Haddad is a Professor of Linguistics at the English Linguistics and Literature Department, Bar-Ilan University, Israel. She specializes in literacy acquisition in bi-dialectal and bilingual contexts, particularly in literacy development in Arabic and the role of diglossia. She has published numerous papers on the topic and co-edited the volume *Handbook of Arabic Literacy* (Springer, 2014). She is actively involved in curriculum development and national testing in Israel, and is an advisor to the Israel Ministry of Education and UNESCO. She is a member of the editorial boards of two leading literacy journals: *Scientific Studies of Reading* and *Reading & Writing*.

Monique Sénéchal is a Professor of Psychology at Carleton University in Ottawa, Canada. In her research, she aims to understand better the interplay between oral and written language during the early phase of literacy acquisition. Moreover, she also studies how the family literacy environment might have a lasting influence on children's language and literacy skills.

Kathy G. Short is a Professor in Language, Reading and Culture at the University of Arizona with a focus on global children's and adolescent literature, literature circles, intercultural understanding and critical content analysis. She has co-authored many books, including *Teaching Globally: Reading the World through Literature*, *Essentials of Children's Literature*, *Creating Classrooms for Authors and Inquirers* and *Stories Matter: The Complexity of Cultural Authenticity in Children's Literature*. She is director of Worlds of Words, an initiative to build bridges across global cultures through children's literature, and is Past President of the National Council of Teachers of English.

Magdalena Smoczyńska is a psycholinguist, currently at the Educational Research Institute (Warsaw), formerly employed at the Jagiellonian University (Kraków). Most of her research concerns language acquisition in children. She authored the chapter 'Acquisition of Polish' in Dan Slobin (ed.), *The Crosslinguistic Study of Language Acquisition* (1985). In the last two decades her research has concentrated on language impairment. In a follow-up study of Polish late talkers she investigated the risk of SLI and dyslexia. She adapted MacArthur–Bates Communicative Development Inventories for Polish and co-authored a comprehensive language test for Polish children: *Test Rozwoju Językowego: TRJ* (2015).

Yuting Sun is a doctoral student at the Department of Human Development and Quantitative Methodology with a specialization in Educational Psychology at the University of Maryland. She received her master's degree at Tsinghua University. Her current research concerns children's relational reasoning, the ability to discern meaningful patterns within streams of information in naturalistic classroom settings, and its relationship with comprehension and achievement. She is also interested in early development of reading and writing in Chinese, especially how Chinese kindergarteners make use of orthographic knowledge in learning to read and write.

Aviva Sverdlov is a Lecturer at Shaanan Academic Religious Teachers' College, early childhood educational consultant and curriculum specialist. Her research focuses on kindergarten teachers' educational beliefs and practices. Previously she was a Supervisor at Preschool Educational Division and Curriculum Department at the Israeli Ministry of Education and was responsible for developing preschool curriculum and providing guidance on its implementation. She served as a coordinator of preschool curriculum committees that dealt with variety of educational areas, such as literacy, physical education, and science and technology education. She is co-author and editor of numerous guidebooks for preschool educators.

Liliana Tolchinsky is Emeritus Professor of Linguistics at the University of Barcelona and a Research Fellow in the Institute of Educational Sciences and head of the Consolidated Research Group on the Study of Linguistic Repertoire (GRERLI) at the University of Barcelona. The main focus of her research has been on later language development, developing literacy and its role in linguistic development. Besides publications in Spanish and several edited books and monographs on early literacy her work has appeared in *Journal of Pragmatics*, *First Language*, *Written Language and Literacy*, *Cognitive Development* and *Journal of Child Language*.

Shaher Banu Vagh is a Senior Research Fellow at the ASER Centre and Pratham Education Foundation. She holds an EdD in Human Development and Psychology from Harvard University. Her research explores the role of home environments and classroom practices in supporting children's language and literacy development and issues related to the assessment of literacy skills in the Akshara languages in multilingual settings. She is currently collaborating with Pratham colleagues to document effective practices in primary grade classrooms.

Ying Wang is a postdoc working on developmental psychology at the University of Michigan. She has a strong interest in literacy development and intervention, and children's cognitive and academic growth in early years. Her research is primarily focused on Chinese children's literacy development, bilingual children's language acquisition and the impact of child, family and schooling factors in children's cognitive and academic growth. Her articles have appeared in *Early Childhood Research Quarterly*, *International Journal of Behavioral Development*, *Applied Psycholinguistics* and *Reading and Writing*. She also serves as a member of the Society for Research in Child Development and the Society for the Scientific Study of Reading.

K. S. Richard Wong is an Assistant Professor in the Department of Early Childhood Education at the Education University of Hong Kong. His research concerns young children's language and cognitive development in early years. His academic articles have appeared in *Early Child Development and Care*, *Applied Psycholinguistics*, *Early Years* and *Early Years Education*.

Clare Wood is Professor of Psychology in Education at Coventry University and the Director of the Centre for Research in Psychology, Behaviour and Achievement. Her research interests over the last 20 years include the early identification and remediation of literacy difficulties in children, the relationships between speech and written language skills, and the educational potential of technology. Her work on the impact of text messaging on literacy skills has received widespread attention in the international media. In 2000 she was awarded the Reading/Literacy Research Fellowship by the International Reading Association and in 2006 she received the British Psychological Society's award for Excellence in the Teaching of Psychology. She is committed to developing more integrated theoretical accounts of literacy attainment and understanding the ecology of reading difficulties.

Li Yin is a Professor of Psycholinguistics at Tsinghua University, Beijing. She specializes in educational psychology (PhD at the University of Illinois at Urbana-Champaign, 2005), especially the development of reading and writing in young children. She is currently working on early diagnosis and intervention of Mandarin-speaking children (aged 2–7) at risk of reading and writing difficulties in mainland China. Her articles have appeared in *Psychological Science*, *Journal of Educational Psychology*, *Early Childhood Research Quarterly* and *Journal of Experimental Child Psychology*.

FOREWORD

Volumes on literacy education have long offered us sightings of the preoccupations of researchers and policy-makers. The stated aim of this collection is more ambitious: to 'offer new insights into children's literacy lives' – and it delivers.

One distinctive strength is a panorama that the chapters build up from both within and beyond the traditionally dominant monolingual, Anglo- and Western-centred view. We hear about a wide range of literacy achievements and challenges from the Germanic, Nordic, Romance, Arabic, Chinese and Akshara language families, and from colonial, indigenous and pluri-lingual readers, writers and educators in Latin America, Africa, the Middle East and New Zealand. While these views offer support for some aspects of the early literacy narrative that has come to us from familiar places, they challenge and, frankly, at times dismiss some long-cherished convictions.

The breadth of theoretical and methodological approaches is a further attraction. We see familiar psychological ideas and studies, now informatively and forcefully complemented by anthropological, literary and sociological work on expansive topics that rightly command such breadth – the politicized, online and globalized 'literacy lives' of young people.

For a field currently in danger of being corralled by tired, rudimentary or simplistic ideas and prescriptions, this collection has the potential to stimulate the commitment of a new generation of literacy researchers and practitioners, and to reinvigorate the efforts of the long-haulers.

Peter Freebody
University of Sydney, Australia

PART I

Contextualizing early literacy

High-quality early literacy education is essential for children to become active citizens, effective communicators and happy individuals.

Scholars and practitioners have been increasingly preoccupied with the question of how to foster early literacy in times of heightened global interactions, multiculturalism, multi-lingualism and migration across and within national borders. Early years classrooms in the twenty-first century have become very heterogeneous, with children of varied abilities, socio-cultural backgrounds and parental expectations. Many early years educators struggle with teaching the foundations of reading and writing in multilingual situations. This creates an acutely perceived need for more specific guidance on effective, culturally responsive and individualized early literacy instruction. In addition, today's children grow up in home and school environments that use a wide range of new, digitally mediated modes of communication, reading and writing. With a lacuna of cross-cultural guidance, future and current educators might be inadequately prepared to support effective multicultural and multi-media literacy provisions.

This handbook is a collection of original, carefully selected and reviewed chapters on early literacy practice and research across the world, representing policies and scholarship of the past two decades. The book aspires to offer new insights into children's literacy lives through the lens of international instruction models and past interventions and thus to add to current discussions on the topics of global, multicultural and digital literacy in the early years.

The chapters in the book provide key insights from studies of early literacy instruction and interventions, and position these alongside the status quo of early literacy education in different societies around the globe. While many studies of the impact of targeted literacy interventions (e.g. vocabulary interventions) are available in the research literature, these are rarely situated within the context of prevailing educational policies and practices, or related to other approaches for similar populations (e.g. teaching word attack). This handbook fills this gap by providing an overview of the valuable lessons learnt from a variety of approaches and perspectives focused on early literacy instruction and intervention.

Our aim was to contextualize the insights provided by past research, situate them within the broader context of early literacy education and provide a forum for discussion of the everyday issues surrounding literacy practice in classrooms in different parts of the world.

We also aimed to address past literacy research, acknowledging the concerns shared by both scholars and aspiring and current teachers worldwide, such as the best methods for literacy instruction, practice and policy for children from special populations, common standards and assessment policies. We hope to offer new insights into children's literacy lives by juxtaposing instruction models from different societies and designed for different languages. Lastly, our objective was to put together a basis for a shared understanding of the literacy challenges brought about by changes in the twenty-first century, characterized by multiculturalism and multi-literacies.

This book is interdisciplinary, with contributions from colleagues working in the fields of education, psychology, linguistics and sociology. It is intentionally international, with contributions from researchers working in many different countries (New Zealand, Germany, Austria, Nordic countries, Spain, France, Latin America, Poland, Turkey, Balkan countries, African countries, Israel, Arabic-speaking countries, Korea, Japan, China, Taiwan, Hong Kong and India) and language communities.

The handbook is organized in three parts, each introduced with a brief editorial orientation to the content. Part I outlines the principal theoretical paradigms that underlie past and present literacy research, and areas of dissent that have influenced policies for early literacy instruction, promotion and development across the globe. Although the principles underpinning past and present research are interwoven in the book, they are foregrounded within this section, so that the practices described in subsequent chapters can be situated within an understanding of research findings as well as the broader historical and social context. The section charts the scholars' changing perceptions of early literacy, and details the current global issues faced by early years practitioners.

Part II outlines provision of literacy in relation to the idiosyncrasies of the language and writing system in the individual countries covered by the authors. The authors describe national early literacy policies in relation to several key factors, including typological features of the language and orthography, the major curriculum models accommodating these, the national assessment and evaluation frameworks, provision of early literacy for children from special populations, availability of literacy resources, and current issues in fostering early reading and writing in the respective countries. As such, Part II presents the reader with various views on effective strategies to support young children's literacy and identifies gaps for future research. Importantly, the authors in this section establish a solid basis for comparative work in the global context of early literacy education.

Part III provides an overview of some of the key current themes in literacy research. Many of these chapters highlight one important area of literacy learning across cultures. The authors offer overviews of topics including writing, which is becoming more and more central to conceptualizations of literacy acquisition, phonological sensitivity, different approaches to stories and story-telling for children as well as their parents and teachers, vocabulary knowledge and recommended interventions for children at risk of reading difficulties by virtue of their language-learning difficulties. These chapters are useful for surveying a relatively broad gamut of literacy-learning issues, particularly because many of them take care to consider such issues in different countries, languages and scripts.

We now turn to Part I and highlight the excellent chapters in this first section. Chapter 1 lays the foundations for the work reported in subsequent chapters and allows the authors to revisit it as appropriate and connect to the work undertaken. Chapter 1 also pays attention to the enduring dimensions of literacy, such as the role of practitioners, parents and other children's educators who act as literacy teachers but also as makers and observers of young children's everyday literacy practices. The chapter addresses questions such as where and why literacy is important and reviews the key skills and qualities needed for early readers and writers (e.g. vocabulary, print skills or phonological awareness).

In Chapter 2 Ying Wang explores how early childhood education relates to literacy outcomes in young children, both concurrently and longitudinally. One issue is the nature of the early childhood education itself. Research on intensity, quality and type of schooling highlights how each of these factors matters for young children's preparation for literacy learning. Perhaps most fundamentally, those attending early childhood education programmes tend to make greater gains in early literacy skills than those who do not. In addition, Wang highlights how families can promote literacy at home, in cooperation with school-based programmes. Many cross-cultural studies demonstrate the importance of early training for both parents and teachers for facilitating children's early literacy development. Solid early childhood education in combination with some home-based literacy exposure provide the best overall support for young children for early literacy acquisition for all children, including those learning in multiple languages and those from economically disadvantaged backgrounds.

Chapter 3 by Emily Phillips Galloway and Nonie Lesaux addresses young bilingual learners and offers a developmental perspective focusing on exposure and opportunities to use either language in three periods from birth to the early elementary school years. Though the relationship between oral language skills and reading comprehension is fairly well established in monolingual children, there is still much we do not know regarding language and literacy relationships in young bilinguals, such as under what conditions cross-linguistic transfer may support literacy learning. Likewise, to disentangle the effects of socio-economic issues and instruction on bilingual learning, the chapter calls for research that takes into account the diversities of bilingual learners and instructional practices around the world, thus laying the ground for the presentation of literacy education in individual countries in Part II.

Natalia Kucirkova's chapter discusses four key features foregrounded by digital books and their role for early literacy: personalization, interactivity, haptic engagement and creativity. Drawing on a project dedicated to the exploration of affordances of digital books for young children, the chapter highlights the need for practitioners to seek synergies in children's digital and non-digital experiences and their commitment to support both. The chapter considers the possibility of using a community approach and expanding the place of public scholarship in children's use of new media. Overall, the chapter adds to the current academic inter-disciplinary discussions on the topics of global, multicultural and digital literacy (or 'twenty-first-century literacies').

Clare Wood's chapter brings together different research conceptualizations of what it means to read and write in a multicultural society, notably in light of the changes brought about by digital media in the twenty-first century. The chapter offers a critical perspective on the meaning of 'literacy' and 'texts' and concludes by redefining literacy. Traditional notions of literacy are revisited from the viewpoint of contemporary culture and technological innovation. The chapter provides an overview as well as a detailed consideration of particular studies that highlight the changes that have occurred to texts and to literacy in the past decade. The chapter calls for a re-examination of the multiple and complex ways in which children read and write in the twenty-first century, and suggests a new definition of literacy that would encompass these aspects.

Each of these chapters should be of particular interest to those seeking information on state-of-the-art theory and practice in relation to early childhood literacy learning.

1

EARLY LITERACY DEVELOPMENT AND INSTRUCTION

An overview

Catherine E. Snow

The goal of this chapter is to give an overview of what we know about literacy development in children up to age eight, as well as to introduce some topics for which more research is needed. We know that good readers have developed familiarity and automaticity with symbols used in their writing system and how those symbols represent sounds, as well as oral language skills strong enough to enable them to make sense of the words they are decoding. This full array of skills develops optimally when children have access to rich language and literacy experiences at home and in early education settings. Controversies persist about how early it is useful to introduce explicit literacy instruction, and the optimal balance in early literacy education between form-based and meaning-based instruction. The variety of approaches to literacy instruction implemented across different national education systems and different languages reveals both that a variety of approaches can work but also that some approaches, in particular those relying on rote memorization, generate a high risk of failure.

The goal of this introductory chapter is to give an overview of literacy development in children up to age eight. Literacy is the key survival skill for the twenty-first century, even more than in previous eras when it was possible to find employment and participate in public discourse with limited reading skills. Success in mastering literacy is greatly enhanced for some children by particular experiences and opportunities during early childhood. Research has generated lots of information about what those experiences and opportunities are: both a set of conditions that determine general good physical and mental health (clean water, appropriate nutrition, preventive medical care, protection from violence and other sources of extreme stress) and conditions that are more specifically supportive of literacy and cognitive development (freedom to play, rich language interactions with adults, access to literacy-infused activities mediated by adults). Many questions and challenges in ensuring these propitious circumstances remain, though, especially when we have to make decisions about actual practices to be implemented; when we consider the wide array of domestic circumstances into which children are born, and the variety of linguistic, social and educational settings in which they learn to read; when we review the disparities across groups within countries and across countries in the degree of success in literacy outcomes; and as we contemplate how even to define literacy in an era when digital forms of text and speech are crowding out traditional modes of distanced communication.

This chapter sets the stage for the chapters that follow, by reviewing some widely accepted claims about literacy development and instruction, previewing some of the variation that arises as a result of both national differences in the organization of early literacy education and language-related differences in the orthographies used to represent speech in print, and considering why we continue to have so much difficulty ensuring universal literacy despite the long history of relevant research and accumulated list of proven practices.

What we know

Fortunately, early literacy has been a target of research for a very long time, with the result that impressive amounts of knowledge about early literacy development and instruction have accumulated. Some widely accepted conclusions can, thus, be highlighted, with the reservation that these research findings have not yet all fully penetrated the worlds of policy and practice, where many myths and unproductive strategies may still hold sway.

Literacy is a human invention, one that has been around for a very long time but that has rarely been universally distributed. Now that literacy has become a prerequisite for successful participation in the modern, digitally mediated world of distanced communication and high information flow, ensuring universal access to it is a matter of social justice.

Literate forms of communication require a mechanism for rendering speech – an aural stream of phonemes – into print. The way that speech is represented in print is referred to as an *orthography* – a term that incorporates the script (e.g. Chinese characters vs. Japanese syllabaries vs. Semitic abjads or one of the Indo-European alphabets) as well as details of how the script is deployed (e.g. prioritizing one-to-one correspondence of sounds to symbols vs. prioritizing etymological information in the spelling). Different languages are well suited to particular orthographies (e.g. Japanese to the syllabary because the language has a limited set of possible syllables), but in principle any language could be represented in any orthography (see Table 1.1). English could, for example, be written using a syllabary, but because there are more than 15,000 distinct syllables in English (http://semarch.linguistics.fas.nyu.edu/ barker/Syllables/index.txt), it would be a tedious process to develop, teach and learn such a system. Similarly, Chinese could be written using the Roman alphabet (as it is when Pinyin is used), but the 26 letters would need to be supplemented with diacritics representing tones in order to disambiguate segmental homophones. And either English or Chinese could in principle be written using the Arabic script, but the omission of short vowels in the orthography would lead to considerable confusion about how to pronounce many words – confusion that is absent in Arabic because the vowel sequence is determined grammatically. Thus, to some extent orthographic choices are dictated by phonotactic and grammatical features of the language they represent.

Each of the language–orthography combinations offers its own learning challenges as well. It is easy to teach young children the principle of representing syllables with graphemes, because syllables are pronounceable and segmentable units. So children understand readily when told, for example, that '𝒪 says no'. The challenges are that there may be many visual forms to distinguish, and that representing syllables not in the language requires inventing a whole new system.

Alphabetic orthographies are more flexible, but can be much harder to 'break into' initially. Helping young children achieve the insight that letters represent phonemes rather

Table 1.1 The name *Barack Obama* as it is rendered in 13 widely used languages/orthographies

Name	Language
Barack Obama	English
ברק אובמה	Hebrew
باراك اوباما	Arabic
باراک اوباما	Urdu
ባራክ አባማ	Aramaic
Μπάρακ Ομπάμα	Greek
Барак Обама	Russian
巴拉克奥巴马	Chinese
バラック・オバマ	Japanese
बराक ओबामा	Hindi
ਬਰਾਕ ਓਬਾਮਾ	Punjabi
બરાક ઓબામા	Gujarati
บารัคโอบามา	Thai

than syllables can be difficult. That challenge is the one that leads to considerable emphasis in some instructional systems on explicitly teaching 'phonological awareness', the ability to treat oral word forms (in which successive phonemes in fact typically overlap and cannot be cleanly segmented) as a sequence of distinct sounds, by engaging in exercises like 'say frog without the fff' or 'let's blend the sounds, what does d-o-g say?'

There is now ample evidence that some training in phonological awareness is useful to children learning to read in alphabetic languages (National Early Literacy Panel, 2008). The form that training takes can vary. Standard approaches include practice in segmenting short words into onsets and rimes, e.g. d-og, l-og, c-og, f-og. While this approach works well in English, in Spanish it works better to segment into nucleus and coda, e.g. pa-n, pa-z, a fact reflected in the time-honoured syllabic approach to teaching reading in Spanish (i.e. teaching *ma-me-mi-mo-mu* as the basic units, rather than focusing on initial phonemes), and in the recurrent finding that phonemic awareness in Spanish is more closely related to spelling than to word reading (Denton et al., 2000; Manrique and Signorini, 1994). In Korean, like in Spanish, the nucleus-coda analysis of syllables is more natural than onset-rime, but Korean-speaking children need only learn to segment at the syllable level, because their alphabetic writing system highlights syllabic units rather than presenting the letters linearly (Kim 2007, 2008).

Most children learning alphabetic systems also need some explicit help to figure out which letters represent which sounds (though a small number of precocious readers intuit the relations themselves, bootstrapping information from letter names and from reading familiar, frequent words to figure out the larger system; e.g. Margrain, 2005; Stainthorp and Hughes, 2004). Both efficiency and the demands of age-graded schooling dictate that all children should be given the advantage of some explicit instruction in the details of how to read/spell words. The specific approach (i.e. the sequence of sounds/letters taught, whether one should start with short vowels or long ones, whether students should practise only with text they have already learned to decode or should be reading more challenging text from the start and how much time should be devoted to writing versus reading early in the process) varies greatly within and across countries/languages, as is clear from contrasting the various instructional strategies outlined in the second section of this volume.

Comprehending text requires that readers can connect print forms to meaning efficiently. Expending considerable effort to decode individual words impedes the construction of sentence or text meaning. A major goal of early reading instruction, then, is to ensure children have enough practice with reading that they can recognize many words automatically and thus read connected text at a rate sufficient to ensure comprehension. *Fluency* is the technical term that refers to reading aloud with adequate speed (about 60 words per minute by end of first grade in the USA), accurately, and with appropriate intonation, pauses and stress, when reading age-appropriate text. Expectations of speed increase through the first several years of schooling, and of course the texts that are read increase in difficulty over that same period. Oral reading fluency is a quick and easy measure of progress toward success in reading, one that is heavily relied on in widely used measures such as the DIBELS (Dynamic Indicators of Basic Early Literacy Skills; Kaminski and Good, 1996) and the closely related EGRA (Early Grades Reading Assessment; Gove and Cvelich, 2011), which has been promoted by Save the Children and USAID for international use. These measures become distractions, though, when they acquire high stakes and thus become a focus for instruction.

Giving all young students the chance to learn about print and how it relates to the phonological structure of words, and enough practice with reading to become fluent and accurate, will not ensure true literacy and academic success. In order to understand and learn from a text, students must know what the words in it mean, and must have the background knowledge the text presupposes, so they can fit new knowledge into a larger conceptual structure (Snow et al., 1998). It is entirely possible to learn to read accurately and fluently without access to meaning, as the activities in thousands of *madrasas* and *chedarim* testify, but if the goal of literacy education is access to learning, then rote memorization is not an effective approach.

Research studies have also generated considerable agreement about the features of young children's environments that generate better language skills, larger vocabularies and a richer knowledge base. These include access to a sufficient quantity of talk and opportunities for interaction with adults; some families and some early childhood classrooms offer dense language environments, whereas others provide much less language input or opportunities for conversation (Rowe, 2010). In addition to quantity of talk, quality of talk is important; varied vocabulary input that includes some relatively rare or sophisticated words (Tabors et al., 2001), conversation about abstract, challenging, non-here-and-now topics (de Temple, 2001; Mascareño et al., 2016), book sharing with attention to the language and the domains of knowledge being presented (Mol et al., 2009), pretend play as a source of hypotheticals and conditionals (Katz and Snow, 2000) and extended narratives and explanations (Grøver Aukrust and Rydland, 2011; Grøver Aukrust and Snow, 1998). Children who have had access to language interactions with these features are much better prepared to comprehend literate language, whether it is read aloud to them or they read it themselves.

In other words, there is now widespread agreement that learning vocabulary, developing oral language skills and acquiring knowledge are tasks to be tackled in early childhood and primary settings, and that they are just as important as the tasks of learning letters, sounds, decoding and fluency. Despite agreement on this as a principle, there remains considerable disagreement about relative emphasis and prioritization: How much time should be spent on each of the various tasks? How prominently should any of them figure in assessments?

Are some particularly important as gatekeepers to or as predictors of longer term literacy outcomes?

Areas of continuing contention

The chapters devoted to country portraits in the central section of this volume document enormous diversity in approaches to the practices and the organization of early childhood education and early literacy instruction. In some places literacy-related instruction begins as young as age 3, and in other places not till age 7. In some places mastering letter recognition and letter names is the first important task a child encounters, whereas in other places letter names are never taught, only letter sounds. In some early childhood programmes children begin writing before they can read, and in others writing is introduced only after word reading is well established. This list of differential practices and priorities could be much longer. To some extent, it reflects differences in culture – beliefs about young children and the goals of schooling; to some extent, it reflects the consequences of differences in languages and orthographies. In addition, though, these differences emerge from the unequal access of educators around the world to updated knowledge about the value of early childhood education and about the determinants of quality in early childhood and initial literacy classrooms.

In the English-speaking world the major disagreement within literacy has historically been between those who insist that a solid and systematic foundation of code-focused instruction (letter recognition, phonological awareness, phonics) is valuable for all children and crucial for many, and those who argue that most children will figure out the code on their own, that responsive instruction in letter–sound relationships is more effective than pre-planned systematic instruction, and that a rich literacy environment (frequent and regular experiences of being read to, discussing books, engaging in literacy-infused projects) will generate the best literacy outcomes. The 'great debate' (Chall, 1967) between phonics-based and meaning-based approaches has been analysed as particularly vitriolic for Anglophones because English has one of the world's deepest orthographies – i.e. a very complex set of multiple mappings from spelling to pronunciation, and from pronunciation to spelling. The phonics defenders argue that the complexity of the English orthography requires explicit, systematic teaching; the meaning defenders counter that the system is too complex and abstract to be taught explicitly to young children, who however are capable of inferring the rules with sufficient exposure and meaning-based support. While the phonics versus meaning debate has simmered down, and while educators agree in theory that both are important, there continues to be considerable variation in how much emphasis each of the components receives in the average early childhood classroom in the USA.

The fact is that many children can learn to read under either instructional regime. As noted above, some even learn to read with no instruction, surprising their parents as four-year-olds by asking questions at the breakfast table about the newspaper headlines! Others, in particular those with little exposure to literacy before school entry, no doubt benefit in efficiency and ease from a systematic presentation of how letters represent sounds, and from memorizing and practising the highly frequent words that deviate from strict decodability (so-called sight words, also taught as 'popcorn' words because they 'pop up all the time'). The challenge is that ultimately children need access both to code-focused and to meaning-focused skills, and that instructional approaches that prioritize the code for low-scoring readers (who are likely to come from less advantaged households) may inadvertently reduce their access to activities that support meaning-making. As a result, slightly better readers get more chances to read connected text, to encounter complex and stimulating text, and to talk about meaning, whereas struggling readers spend more time on worksheets designed to help them master the differences between long and short vowels or between SH and CH, displaying the essence of what Stanovich (1986) has referred to as the Matthew Effect – the rich getting richer while the poor progress more slowly.

These issues are somewhat less salient in languages with shallower orthographies, where knowing how to pronounce a word provides considerable certainty about its spelling and vice versa. Nonetheless, few orthographies are perfectly transparent. For example, considerable instructional time can be devoted to teaching correct spelling in French (where pronunciation is fully predictable but there are many alternative spellings of some sounds, leading to the ubiquitous *dictée* practice) and Spanish (where accents, diacritics and minor morphological variations in spelling take up considerable instructional time). Though Arabic and Hebrew are shallow orthographies when introduced to young children with full voweling, children will struggle with the unvoweled forms encountered a year or two later if there has been no attention to meaning (and the associated morphological and syntactic variants) in early instruction. In teaching Chinese, instruction focuses a lot on memorization of the appropriate shape, organization and stroke sequence for writing characters, but also provides young children with simplified forms for use in reading (the phonetic writing system called zhuyin fuhao in Taiwan, pinyin in China) and in their own writing. Thus, many instructional systems devise compromises between the code- and the meaning-focus.

A second area of continued controversy in the USA is the question of what sort of texts young readers should be practising with. Some educators and curriculum developers favour the use of 'decodable' texts, texts that avoid irregular, multisyllabic and low-frequency words, to promote fluency and a sense of success in reading. Hiebert, for example, argues that many reading curricula introduce new words and higher text difficulty too quickly, giving children too little practice to consolidate their word reading skills (Hiebert and Fisher, 2007; Hiebert and Mesmer, 2005). Others have argued that children need exposure to complex text if their own skills are to grow; this is a basic principle in the US Common Core State Standards, which emphasize that about 50 per cent of reading materials during the first grades should be above grade level. Chall (1977) also endorsed the use of challenging texts, arguing that US students' Scholastic Aptitude Test scores were predicted by the complexity of texts used in their classrooms, a conclusion echoed 20 years later by Hayes et al. (1996). The challenge for educators and curriculum designers is to find or devise reading texts that children can comprehend, but that at the same time stretch their language and analysis skills, and provide supports to ensure that children know how to attack those more difficult readings. Just providing more complex texts to low-level readers will not improve their comprehension skills!

An approach to early reading instruction that is unfortunately widespread in post-colonial schooling, and that might be seen as a solution to the challenge of finding appropriate level texts, involves memorization and recitation of text. This is a method frequently defaulted to when classes are very large, when children have limited access to their own reading or writing materials, when the medium of instruction is unfamiliar to many or all children (and sometimes only partially controlled by the teacher) and in places where teacher education is limited and unreformed. Rote memorization and choral recitation of text written on the blackboard do not add up to an effective or efficient method of teaching children to read – but even in these circumstances some children do figure out enough to make progress in what we would call real reading. The incentives to implement rote memorization are often located in the local assessment systems, which expect children to provide prepared, word-perfect responses to exam questions and which place little value on deeper understanding of what is read.

We can analyse these various kinds of disagreements as different examples of a single dimension: focus on short-term versus long-term outcomes. It is easy to understand that teachers or school leaders want their students to pass the end-of-year tests or meet the looming age-linked benchmarks. It is relatively straightforward and rewarding to teach young children phonological awareness or letter names, in large part because these are constrained skill domains and children can actually master them. Skill domains like vocabulary or narrative structure are much larger, less well-defined and thus less likely to reveal children's learning (Snow and Kim, 2006). They are, however, still crucial determinants of long-term literacy success, and likely to be domains of particular challenge for children at high risk of academic failure. So extra emphasis on the constrained skills for those children, at the cost of opportunities to develop language and knowledge, is almost certain to be counter-productive.

There is also considerable variation across schooling systems in the mechanisms used to assess literacy and determine whether children are on track to successful academic achievement. The widespread use of oral reading fluency as an early measure has been noted; in principle that measure is meant to be validated by also asking global comprehension questions about the passage read, but that step is often skipped. Some testing schemes put more emphasis on retelling or explaining the text read, using open-ended oral or written responses. Some schools avoid standardized tests completely for young children, preferring to assess their progress based on portfolios of their written work or of their contribution to small group projects (Davies and LeMahieu, 2003; Hanson and Gilkerson, 1999).

As noted above, post-colonial schooling systems incentivize rote memorization in part because the exams demand it. Assessment and school-improvement policies in the USA during the No Child Left Behind era similarly incentivized a focus on phonics and fluency skills, by identifying third grade as a key point at which to assess reading outcomes, and by promoting the use of assessments that relied on speed more than depth of processing. Policies intended to support children's literacy development can easily backfire if they are based on simplistic or misguided conceptualizations about literacy.

Conclusion

This chapter makes the point that we know quite a lot about literacy development and instruction, but at the same time our knowledge is far from equitably distributed over the domain. There is much more information available about literacy development and support in English than in other languages, about the acquisition of reading in the Roman script than in other alphabets, about alphabetic than other writing systems and about literacy instruction in relatively rich, First World countries than elsewhere. We know next to nothing about how children learn to read in hundreds of languages spoken in Asia and Africa, nor can we point to models for supporting teachers, designing curricular materials or organizing literacy instruction that are easily transported beyond the widely studied languages and countries.

We consider some overarching themes relevant to early literacy in the rest of this section of the volume, before turning to a set of country portraits designed to display something of the variety of challenges and approaches to literacy education around the world. The final chapter in this volume returns to the question of what we still need to know – seven issues that deserve particular attention from researchers and practitioners over the next ten years.

Finally, it is important to emphasize that early literacy development and instruction are crucial determinants of children's academic outcomes, but also that 'solving' all the issues and challenges of early literacy will not by itself be sufficient to ensure educational success for all. Children who read accurately and fluently after their first two–three years of school are on a path that augurs well, but still have much to learn if they are to master the literacy tasks of the twenty-first century. Getting early childhood literacy right is extremely important, and necessary, but then opens up the challenge of continued instruction to support analysis, critical reading and ongoing learning.

References

Chall, J. S. (1967). *Learning to Read: The Great Debate*. New York: Harcourt Brace.

Chall, J. (1977) An analysis of textbooks in relation to declining SAT scores. Educational Testing Service, Princeton, NJ.

Davies, A. and Le Mahieu, P. (2003). Assessment for learning: reconsidering portfolios and research evidence. In M. Segers, F. Dochy and E. Cascallar (eds), *Innovation and Change in Professional Education: Optimising New Modes of Assessment: In Search of Qualities and Standards* (pp. 141–169). Dordrecht: Kluwer Academic Publishers.

Denton, C., Hasbrouck, J., Weaver, L. and Riccio, C. (2000). What do we know about phonological awareness in Spanish? *Reading Psychology*, 21, 335–352. doi:10.1080/027027100750061958.

de Temple, J. (2001). Parents and children reading books together. In D. K. Dickinson and P. O. Tabors (eds), *Beginning Literacy with Language: Young Children Learning at Home and School* (pp. 31–51). Baltimore, MD: Brookes Publishing.

Gove, A. and Cvelich, P. (2011). *Early Reading: Igniting Education for All. A Report by the Early Grade Learning Community of Practice. Revised Edition*. Research Triangle Park, NC Research Triangle Institute.

Grøver Aukrust, V. and Rydland, V. (2011). Preschool classroom conversations as long-term resources for second language and literacy acquisition. *Journal of Applied Developmental Psychology*, 32(4), 198–207. doi:10.1016/j.appdev.2011.01.002.

Grøver Aukrust, V. and Snow, C. E. (1998). Narratives and explanations in Norwegian and American mealtime conversations. *Language in Society*, 27, 221–246.

Hanson, M. F. and Gilkerson, D. (1999). Portfolio assessment: more than ABC's and 123's. *Early Childhood Education Journal*, 27(2), 81–86.

Hayes, D., Wolfer, L. and Wolfe, M. (1996) Schoolbook Simplification and Its Relation to the Decline in SAT-Verbal Scores. Scholastic Aptitude Test.

Hiebert, E. H. and Fisher, C. W. (2007). The critical word factor in texts for beginning readers. *Journal of Educational Research*, 101(1), 3–11.

Hiebert, E. H. and Mesmer, H. (2005). Perspectives on the difficulty of beginning reading texts. In S. Neuman and D. Dickinson (eds), *Handbook of Research on Early Literacy* (Vol. 2, pp. 935–967). New York: Guilford Press.

Kaminski, R. A. and Good, R. H. (1996). Toward a technology for assessing basic early literacy skills. *School Psychology Review*, 25, 215–227.

Katz, J. and Snow, C. E. (2000). Language development in early childhood: the role of social interaction in different care environments. In D. Cryer and T. Harms (eds), *Infants and Toddlers in Out-of-Home Care* (pp. 49–86). Baltimore, MD: Paul H. Brookes.

Kim, Y.-S. (2007). Phonological awareness and literacy skills in Korean: an examination of the unique role of body-coda units. *Applied Psycholinguistics*, 28, 67–93. doi:10.1017.S014271640707004X.

Kim, Y.-S. (2008). Cat in a hat or cat in a cap? An investigation of developmental trajectories of phonological awareness for Korean children. *Journal of Research in Reading*, 31, 359–378. doi:10.1111/j.1467-9817.2008.00379.x.

Manrique, A. M. B. and Signorini, A. (1994). Phonological awareness, spelling and reading abilities in Spanish-speaking children. *British Journal of Educational Psychology*, 64, 429–439.

Margrain, V. G. (2005). Precocious readers: case studies of spontaneous learning, self-regulation and social support in the early years. Available from: http://hdl.handle.net/10063/481.

Mascareño, M., Snow, C. E., Deunk, M. I. and Bosker, R. J. (2016). Language complexity during read-alouds and kindergartners' vocabulary and symbolic understanding. *Journal of Applied Developmental Psychology*, 44, 39–51. doi:http://dx.doi.org/10.1016/j.appdev.2016.02.001.

Mol, S. E., Bus, A. G. and de Jong, M. T. (2009). Interactive book reading in early education: a tool to stimulate print knowledge as well as oral language. *Review of Educational Research*, 79, 979–1007. doi:10.3102/0034654309332561.

National Early Literacy Panel. (2008). *Developing Early Literacy: Report of the National Early Literacy Panel.* Washington, DC: National Institute for Literacy. Available from: www.nifl.gov/earlychildhood/NELP/NELPreport.html.

Rowe, D. W. (2010). Directions for studying early literacy as social practice. *Language Arts*, 88(2), 134–143.

Rowe, M. L. (2008). Child-directed speech in relation to socio-economic status, knowledge of child development and child vocabulary skill. *Journal of Child Language*, 35, 185–205.

Snow, C. E., Burns, S. and Griffin, P. (eds). (1998). *Preventing Reading Difficulties in Young Children.* Washington, DC: National Academy Press.

Snow, C. E. and Kim, Y.-S. (2006). Large problem spaces: the challenge of vocabulary for English language learners. In R. K. Wagner, A. Muse and K. Tannenbaum (eds), *Vocabulary Acquisition and its Implications for Reading Comprehension* (pp. 123–139). New York: Guilford Press.

Stainthorp, R. and Hughes, D. (2004). What happens to precocious readers' performance by the age of eleven? *Journal of Research in Reading*, 27, 357–372.

Stanovich, K. E. (1986). Matthew effects in reading: some consequences of individual differences in the acquisition of literacy. *Reading Research Quarterly*, 22, 360–407

Tabors, P. O., Snow, C. E. and Dickinson, D. K. (2001). Homes and schools together: supporting language and literacy development. In D. K. Dickinson and P. O. Tabors (eds), *Beginning Literacy with Language* (pp. 313–334). Baltimore, MD: Paul H. Brookes Publishing Co.

Weizman, Z. and Snow, C. E. (2001). Lexical input as related to children's vocabulary acquisition: effects of sophisticated exposure and support for meaning. *Developmental Psychology*, 37, 265–279.

2

THE ROLE OF EARLY CHILDHOOD EDUCATION IN PROMOTING EARLY LITERACY

Ying Wang

The view that early childhood education plays a key role in enabling children to learn to read and write is supported in both preschool settings and the home environment. This chapter provides a comprehensive review of the research on early childhood education, the home literacy environment and early literacy intervention programmes, as well as their relations to children's early literacy development. The chapter begins with a description of the importance of early childhood education in language and literacy learning. I further discuss how early childhood education influences children's literacy skills. The chapter also reviews home learning environment and the effects of early literacy intervention programmes across orthographies on early literacy acquisition. Finally, educational implications are provided for parents, caregivers/teachers and policy-makers. Overall, I argue that not only is early childhood education enrolment a key factor for early literacy development, but the programme's intensity, quality and type also play vital roles in children's early literacy acquisition. Further, home literacy environment and early interventions are also important for literacy development in the first years. For future, I anticipate that the mechanism by which early childhood education influences early language learning and their relationships with home literacy environment will be investigated in future studies among different age groups across the world.

Introduction

Early childhood is a critical and rapid period of development. Early childhood education (ECE) generally refers to the teaching of young children up to eight years. Prior research has shown that stronger language proficiency before formal schooling is linked to steeper growth in academic achievement (Burns and Helman, 2009; Geva, 2006; Halle et al., 2012; Sparks et al., 2014) and better socio-emotional skills, approaches to learning and prosocial skills as well as a lower likelihood of being a victim of aggression (Chang et al., 2007; Han et al., 2012). These factors in turn are related to subsequent trajectories of academic skills (Grimm et al., 2010; Li-Grining et al., 2010). There is strong continuity between the skills acquired during kindergarten and later academic performance. Kindergartners who enter school behind their peers remain so as they move through school (Lee and Burkham, 2002). However, children who enter kindergarten with well-prepared pre-reading skills are more likely to have academic success throughout school (Downer and Pianta, 2006; Lara-Cinisomo et al., 2008). Thus, early childhood education and early literacy skills prior to formal schooling are important foundations for subsequent literacy growth. The knowledge, skills and behaviours acquired during early childhood lay the foundation for lifelong learning and development.

Both human and animal studies highlight the critical importance of experiences in the earliest years of life for establishing the brain architecture that will shape future cognitive, social and emotional development, as well as physical and mental health (Knudsen et al., 2006; Sapolsky, 2004). Moreover, research on the malleability of cognitive abilities finds these skills to be highly responsive to environmental enrichment during the early childhood period (Nelson and Sheridan, 2011).

There is a positive relationship between receiving early childhood education (ECE) and language skills in both developed and developing countries (Engle et al., 2011; Rao et al., 2014; Sylva et al., 2006; Yoshikawa et al., 2013). Yoshikawa et al. (2013) summarized the short- and long-term benefits of early childhood education in the United States for cognitive/attainment, socio-emotional and health outcomes. They found that one to two years of centre-based ECE was associated with improvements in early language and literacy skills in three- and four-year-olds. Scientific evidence on the impact of ECE on early literacy development could also be found from the Head Start programme, which now provides comprehensive early childhood education to almost a million three- and four-year-old low-income children. After one academic year in the ECE programme, four-year-olds who enrolled in Head Start gained significantly more in six language and literacy areas than control-group children, with the effects ranging from .09 to .31 standard deviations (US Department of Health and Human Services, 2005). In contrast, there were few programme impacts on maths skills or on children's attention, socio-emotional or mental health problems.

In addition, home literacy environment and parental mediation also play an important and positive role in children's early literacy development and long-term language skills acquisition across orthographies (Farver et al., 2013; Korat et al., 2012; Levin and Aram, 2012; McBride-Chang et al., 2010; Neumann and Neumann, 2010; Niklas and Schneider, 2013; Reese et al., 2010). Thus, by promoting early language and literacy development, ECE may positively relate to children's longer-term development, especially for children in poverty, many of whom do not have access to adequate language and literacy experiences at home (Alexander et al., 1997; Wasik et al., 2006).

Better understanding of these issues is critical, because early childhood education plays a pivotal role in providing children with optimal environments for early language and literacy learning, and because children's later literacy skill and school achievement rely heavily upon early language and literacy skills.

The relation between ECE and early literacy

Constructivism is 'the process by which we observe, document, and interpret what children know, what they do, how they reason, and how the activities and instructional practices in the classroom facilitate or impede their learning' (Devries et al., 2002: 53). In other words, people learn by doing. Piaget (1985) viewed cognitive processes as continual construction and reorganization of knowledge, with the learner taking responsibility. According to Vygotsky

(1978), cognitive learning is a continual process that involves movement from a current intellectual level to a higher level (ZPD). Thus, a child as an active learner constructs his or her own knowledge. Teachers, caregivers and parents may help the child construct knowledge by providing new opportunities for learning and growth. Early childhood education that offers children quality learning opportunities and experiences gives children the knowledge necessary for early literacy skills.

Based on Bronfenbrenner's ecological systems framework, events occurring within specific settings affect children's development. Both family and preschool programmes constitute the child's early microsystem for promoting developmental outcomes (Bronfenbrenner, 2005). From a neuroscience perspective, many brain circuits are particularly sensitive to the influence of early experience during early life, and specific neural circuits are most plastic at this time. Experience during early childhood can have a significant and lasting impact on a range of important adult outcomes (Knudsen et al., 2006). Heckman (2006) also argued that life-cycle skill formation is a dynamic process in which early inputs strongly affect the productivity of later inputs. Early experience plays an important role in child, adolescent and adult achievement. Moreover, early mastery of language and literacy skills forms the foundations of later attainment.

The relation between ECE and early literacy skill has been a major area of research over the past few decades. ECE experience has been considered one of the most important predictors of school readiness and later academic achievement (Chien et al., 2010; Larson et al., 2015). Research regarding the effects of ECE on child development, particularly early language and literacy skills, mostly focuses on at least four fundamental parameters of the ECE experience: (a) attendance, (b) intensity, (c) quality and (d) type of care. Howes et al. (2008) found that pre-kindergarten children made small gains in standardized measures of language and literacy skills. The small gains may be related to the amount of time the child spends in the programme, the quality of instruction and the teacher to student ratio. Prekindergarten programmes that are not organized do not provide students with the tools necessary for kindergarten readiness (Hughes, 2010).

Attendance

As shown in large-scale national projects, ECE programme attendance has come to play a key role in the early literacy development of a majority of children in developed countries. For instance, by using data from Early Childhood Longitudinal Study-Kindergarten (ECLS-K), researchers have found that children who attended centre-based care demonstrated better reading skill after controlling for a wide range of background factors, such as family socioeconomic status (Loeb et al., 2007). The Longitudinal Study of Australian Children (LSAC; Australian Institute of Family Studies, N = 5,107) reported that participation in preschool programmes was associated with enhanced literacy skills in comparison to children not attending preschool programmes, but all the early academic benefits acquired from ECE programmes showed rapid fade-out by middle childhood (Claessens and Garrett, 2014; Smart et al., 2008). A longitudinal study of Australian children (LSAC) also demonstrated that children from disadvantaged groups were less likely to be using kindergarten than their peers. However, attendance in high-quality early childhood education and care (ECEC) has been shown to have a positive influence on young children's language development and life chances, especially for children from disadvantaged backgrounds (Wong et al., 2014). Moreover, using a large national sample from the Effective Pre-School and Primary Education

3–11 project in England, researchers found that preschool attendance has a positive and long-term impact on children's attainment in language and emergent literacy skills; the positive impact continued to influence outcomes throughout primary school, especially if it was of high quality (Taggart et al., 2015; Sylva et al., 2004).

Intensity

Intensity is defined as the numbers of hours per day/days per week of a given programme.

Clearly there is a need to move beyond assessing the effects of whether or not a child attends ECE on child literacy development to examining the effects of programme intensity on early literacy skills. The National Institute of Child Health and Human Development (NICHD) Study of Early Child Care in the USA found that both the intensity and duration of centre-based care affected children's language and literacy development. Longer hours of attendance were associated with greater language benefits (Loeb et al., 2007; Magnuson et al., 2007). Results from the ECLS-K indicated that children who attended full-time child-care programmes recorded greater gains in reading skills than those who attended part-time child-care (Votruba-Drzal et al., 2008).

The total time children spend in preschool also affects early literacy development. Children who started ECE at ages 2–3 showed greater gains in reading improvement than those who started when they were either below two or over three years (Loeb et al., 2007). Three-year-olds who received two years of ECE at the Chicago Child–Parent Centers showed higher language scores than those who only attended one year of the programme, but these group differences were no longer significant in first grade (Clements et al., 2004). Consistent with US studies, the Longitudinal Study of Australian Children (LSAC; N = 5,107) also found that greater duration and intensity of exposure to centre ECE settings predicted heightened language and literacy skills of children in first grade (Coley et al., 2015).

Quality

Quality of early childhood education traditionally has been defined and measured in two basic aspects – structural and process quality (Peisner-Feinberg and Yazejian, 2010; Vandell and Wolfe, 2000). Structural quality variables are the more basic and objectively measured aspects of quality, such as teacher education and credentials, teacher–child ratios and group size. Process quality represents the direct experiences of children in early childhood settings, and therefore requires more in-depth observation and standardized instruments to measure. Key aspects of process quality include the sensitivity and responsiveness of caregivers, the available learning materials and the interactions with the teacher and peers (Peisner-Feinberg et al., 2014). Evidence summarized by the 2008 National Early Literacy Panel report suggests that what one would observe in 'a really good preschool' (Neuman, 1999: 301) should be responsiveness to the strengths and needs of individual real children in the classroom, including, for example, playing with sounds in words, and engaging in meaningful and extended language interactions with the teacher (Lonigan and Shanahan, 2010).

ECE programmes are critically important for children's early literacy development, despite the fact that these programmes are not always implemented with high quality. Research has uncovered significant differences between early education programmes in how they work with children on language and literacy activities (Administration for Children and Families, 2003; Administration for Children, Youth, and Families, 2000; Gest et al.). Thus, in addition to attendance and intensity, programme quality also matters for children's early literacy development. Notably, large-scale studies in the United States have found that high-quality preschool care is related to better language and pre-academic outcomes at the end of the preschool period (Li et al., 2013). Analyses of data from children from low-income families in pre-kindergartens in 11 states indicate that the quality of instruction only predicts reading skills when instructional quality is high (Burchinal et al., 2010). The large-scale Effective Provision of Pre-school Education (EPPE) project in England also found strong, positive relationships between preschool quality and children's literacy skills (Sylva, Melhuish et al., 2011). In Denmark, based on a sample of 30,444 children, Bauchmuller et al. (2014) concluded that preschool quality significantly correlated with children's language skills.

Type

Research suggests that ECE affects children differently, depending on the types of ECE programmes, as well. Extensive evidence suggests that centre-based ECE programmes are related to small to moderate growth in children's literacy skills in comparison to informal ECE or parent care, particularly for children who enter ECE programmes with fewer resources and lower skills, such as children from low-income and low-education families (Gormley et al., 2005; Loeb et al., 2007; Magnuson et al., 2004; Morrissey, 2010; Votruba-Drzal et al., 2013). In addition, centre-based early education programmes have been found to be especially important for subgroups of children, for example children from immigrant families. Votruba-Drzal et al. (2015) demonstrated clear associations between centre-based early education programmes attendance and heightened reading and expressive language skills for children of immigrants in comparison to children of non-immigrant parents. Compared to informal relative care and home-based early education and care (EEC) settings, centre-based ECE tends to provide more highly trained caregivers, peer interaction opportunities, and structured and varied language curricula. Centre programmes also tend to score higher on measures of process quality, which assess factors such as the quality of language interactions, learning materials and experiences, and organization (Dowsett et al., 2008; Fuller et al., 2004; Maccoby and Lewis, 2003).

Family influence on children's literacy skills

During the early years, family is perhaps the most influential environment for children's development. The home literacy environment influences aspects of children's early literacy development such as reading recognition, vocabulary knowledge, print knowledge and reading interests (Farver et al., 2013; Roberts et al., 2005; Sylva, Chan et al., 2011; Weigel et al., 2006). Storybook exposure independently explains children's oral-language skills of vocabulary and listening comprehension, which in turn directly relate to children's reading in grade 3 (Sénéchal and LeFevre, 2002). In contrast, parent teaching of reading and writing explains children's written-language skills, which influence their subsequent reading skills (Sénéchal and LeFevre, 2002). Lin et al. (2009) showed that maternal mediation of writing was uniquely associated with Chinese-word-reading skill. For children from low-socioeconomic status (SES) families, data from the Head Start programme showed that the home learning environment mediates the association between SES and children's emergent literacy competence (Foster et al., 2005).

In addition to the correlational studies, several experimental studies have also suggested causal relations between parent–child reading activity and children's literacy skills. Dialogic reading, for example, is a special parent–child reading method that involves high levels of interactions between parents and children when they share a book together (Whitehurst et al., 1988). It aims to empower children to become storytellers themselves, or at least to talk a lot about the stories they are sharing with their parents/caregivers. For example, they are encouraged to relate their own experiences and ideas to the books. Researchers (e.g. Chow et al., 2008; Whitehurst et al., 1994; Whitehurst et al., 1999) have shown that after 8–12 weeks, children in the group whose parents practised the dialogic reading technique tend to demonstrate stronger vocabulary knowledge than those whose parents simply read the stories in a traditional way. Aram and Levin (2004) also demonstrated that mothers' strategies for promoting word-writing in their preschoolers at home are linked to subsequent reading and writing performance in children 2.5 years later, even controlling for previous writing skills. This suggests that parent–child joint literacy activity is essential for early literacy development. Lin et al. (2009) also showed that more analytic strategies, including attention to morphological and orthographic features within Chinese characters in mother–child joint activities, were linked to better Chinese-word reading among kindergarteners. Neuman (1999) further suggested that young children need not only rich and diverse reading materials, but that these need to be interactively shared with more knowledgeable others, in order to acquire the complex set of attitudes, skills and behaviours associated with early literacy development.

Recently, home literacy environment has been investigated in a broader way. The Baltimore Early Childhood Project aimed to investigate the relations between children's home experiences, including parental beliefs, recurrent activities and interactive processes, and their early literacy development. Sonnenschein et al. (2010) found that parental beliefs and enjoyable interactions with their children in reading activities influence children's early literacy development. They also showed that children whose literacy skills improved during early elementary school more frequently participated in daily and varied reading activities at home, went to the library and played with educational toys.

Hence, the important roles of home learning environment and parental beliefs in early years in promoting their children's literacy development should be noted. These can even narrow literacy gaps at an initial stage. Practically, these findings have implications for ways to assist parents in facilitating their children's early literacy development.

Early literacy instruction and interventions

Early literacy development is influenced by various aspects of early childhood education, including play and learning activities, the language-learning environment, and interactions between experienced adults and young children. Early literacy instruction and interventions have powerful influences on literacy development prior to school entry. Existing intervention programmes in relation to children's early literacy development mainly include (1) reading activities focused on print; (2) environmental print exposure; (3) combined programmes of literacy activity and language knowledge.

Reading activities focused on print acquisition emphasize incorporating print awareness, including words in print, print recognition and letter/character knowledge, into reading activities and daily routines. Justice and Ezell (2002) carried out English book-reading sessions in small groups to stimulate preschool children's print awareness for eight weeks, and they found that three–five-year-old children who participated in print-focused shared reading sessions had a greater increase in print and word awareness than those in the control group who experienced picture-focused reading. This finding implies that direct and adult-mediated interventions focused on printed words stimulate young children's print awareness and alphabetic knowledge. The evidence supports the idea that training programmes that focus on print and letter knowledge during storybook reading are beneficial to children's print awareness related to early reading and writing skill. Even though print concepts are not the main or typical part of storybook reading, explicitly introducing print knowledge within books, including the position and size of print, print directionality, and font types and sizes, will effectively enhance children's early literacy skills.

Environmental print exposure during early literacy instruction can further enhance children's print awareness and perhaps their literacy skills. Justice and Pullen's study (2003) indicated that a child's understanding of print concepts is one of the necessary foundations for reading and writing. As an important extrinsic factor, a print-rich environment is helpful for children's print awareness. In a 20-month-long programme, Yaden et al. (2000) created a rich literacy environment with many books, reading activities, writing centres and book-lending library for English-speaking and Spanish-speaking preschoolers. Children in this programme outscored their peers on letter and word concepts, print awareness and letter recognition. Neuman (1999) also examined the impact of a one-year comprehensive programme involving rich literacy activities and external factors in economically disadvantaged preschool children. Results supported the idea that the physical environment of the classroom, literacy-related interactions between teachers and children, and storybook reading activities enhance young children's literacy development. These integrated programmes usually last for a long time and are targeted to more disadvantaged children. In a broader perspective, Larson and Marsh (2007) indicated that children could learn skills through everyday literacy events, such as others' conversations, as well as reading street signs and store lists.

Combined programmes of literacy activity and language knowledge focus on both literacy activities and metalinguistic knowledge in literacy instruction. Researchers found that combined training programmes significantly promoted children's early literacy skills. Moreover, the younger children gained significantly more than the older children on receptive vocabulary. This suggests that even very young children can benefit from intensive programme focusing on both writing and language skills (Aram and Biron, 2004). A recent longitudinal study conducted by Levin and Aram (2012) also found significant effects of home-based combined writing mediation on kindergarteners' literacy skills. In their study, parents who were instructed in specific training implemented different intervention programmes on their children for seven weeks. The results indicated that the writing programme that combined an interactive writing activity with letter knowledge and phonological awareness significantly improved five-year-old kindergarteners' writing and alphabetic skills in Hebrew. Overall, the series of Hebrew intervention programmes demonstrated that combined programmes consisting of intensive writing activities, related letter knowledge and phonological awareness have an effective influence on young children's early literacy skills, even in the long term. Similar effects were found in Chinese literacy acquisition. In one study, Chinese kindergarteners in combined groups of writing practice and morphological awareness outperformed other groups on word writing and orthographic awareness (Wang and McBride, unpublished).

In general, literacy intervention programmes that combine several skills tend to yield stronger results than do those that focus on fewer skills. For example, Ball and Blachman (1991) found that a combined programme of letter sound, letter name and phonemic segmentation significantly improved early reading and spelling skills of kindergarteners. In contrast, the other programme, focused on letter sound and letter names alone, failed to significantly improve the early reading or spelling skills of kindergarten children, as compared with the control group. Some longitudinal studies have also found that low-SES preschoolers from

Head Start participating in a combined programme of dialogical reading and phonemic awareness at home and school showed significant progress on a wide range of literacy skills such as print concepts, name writing and PPVT, and the positive effects on writing skill lasted over one year (e.g. Whitehurst et al., 1999). For children at risk for reading and writing disability, researchers have also found that combined programmes tend to yield better literacy learning over time. For example, Schneider et al. (2000) compared the effects of three kindergarten training programmes on children at risk for dyslexia. Findings showed that the 20-week combined training of phonological awareness and letter knowledge produced the strongest effects on reading and spelling skills in Grades 1 and 2. Children at risk in the combined training group even showed no difference as compared with those in the control group in spelling both in the post-test and delayed post-test (four months later).

Early literacy acquisition, thus, sometimes includes intensive and systematic training that involves print knowledge, metalinguistic knowledge and literacy practice. Moreover, long-term comprehensive programmes that involve various literacy-related activities and a print-rich environment also have positive effects on children's literacy acquisition.

Educational implications and future research directions

Based on the scientific evidence, I offer three major educational implications. First, it is recommended that children attend a high-quality ECE programme prior to formal schooling. This will not only benefit children's early literacy skill, but also subsequent academic achievement. ECE programme standards and professional development should be put into place given that early education programmes tend to have a significant impact on children. Second, in addition to quality preschool settings, home literacy environment and parental beliefs are important in children's literacy development. I recommend that parents and caregivers consider children's early literacy development (especially before the beginning of formal schooling) and seek opportunities to introduce letter and print knowledge in developmentally appropriate ways at home. Third, early childhood educators and the instructional practices they employ are vital for reducing the literacy developmental gaps of children from economically disadvantaged families or those at risk for learning difficulties.

This chapter calls for three considerations for future research. First, it would be helpful to have a larger and more representative population that is typically studied in research studies. Second, controlled intervention studies and observational methods would enhance the conclusions drawn from studies using correlational approaches. Finally, it may also be beneficial to carry out longitudinal studies to see how children who enter ECE below benchmark in early literacy skills perform throughout their school years.

References

Administration for Children and Families. (2003). Head Start Family and Child Experiences Survey (FACES). Retrieved 1 January 2005, from Administration for Children and Families website: www.acf.hhs.gov/programs/opre/hs/faces/.

Administration for Children, Youth, and Families. (2000). FACES findings: New research on Head Start program quality and outcomes. Washington, DC: U.S. Department of Health and Human Services.

Alexander, K. L., Entwisle, D. R. and Horsey, C. S. (1997). From first grade forward: Early foundations of high school dropout. *Sociology of Education*, 87–107.

Aram, D. and Biron, S. (2004). Joint storybook reading and joint writing interventions among low SES preschoolers: Differential contributions to early literacy. *Early Childhood Research Quarterly*, *19*(4), 588–610.

Aram, D. and Levin, I. (2004). The role of maternal mediation of writing to kindergartners in promoting literacy in school: A longitudinal perspective. *Reading and Writing*, *17*(4), 387–409.

Ball, E. W. and Blachman, B. A. (1991). Does phoneme awareness training in kindergarten make a difference in early word recognition and developmental spelling? *Reading Research Quarterly*, *26*(1), 49–66.

Bauchmüller, R., Gørtz, M. and Rasmussen, A. W. (2014). Long-run benefits from universal high-quality preschooling. *Early Childhood Research Quarterly*, *29*(4), 457–470.

Bronfenbrenner, U. (2005). *Making Human Beings Human: Bioecological Perspectives on Human Development*. Thousand Oaks, CA: Sage.

Burchinal, M., Vandergrift, N., Pianta, R. and Mashburn, A. (2010). Threshold analysis of association between child care quality and child outcomes for low-income children in pre-kindergarten programs. *Early Childhood Research Quarterly*, *25*(2), 166–176.

Burns, M. K. and Helman, L. A. (2009). Relationship between language skills and acquisition rate of sight words among English language learners. *Literacy Research and Instruction*, *48*(3), 221–232.

Chang, F., Crawford, G., Early, D., Bryant, D., Howes, C., Burchinal, M. et al. (2007). Spanish-speaking children's social and language development in pre-kindergarten classrooms. *Early Education and Development*, *18*(2), 243–269.

Chien, N. C., Howes, C., Burchinal, M., Pianta, R. C., Ritchie, S., Bryant, D. M. et al. (2010). Children's classroom engagement and school readiness gains in prekindergarten. *Child Development*, *81*(5), 1534–1549.

Chow, B. W. Y., McBride-Chang, C., Cheung, H. and Chow, C. S. L. (2008). Dialogic reading and morphology training in Chinese children: Effects on language and literacy. *Developmental Psychology*, *44*, 233–244.

Claessens, A. and Garrett, R. (2014). The role of early childhood settings for 4–5 year old children in early academic skills and later achievement in Australia. *Early Childhood Research Quarterly*, *29*(4), 550–561.

Clements, M. A., Reynolds, A. J. and Hickey, E. (2004). Site-level predictors of children's school and social competence in the Chicago Child–Parent Centers. *Early Childhood Research Quarterly*, *19*(2), 273–296.

Coley, R. L., Lombardi, C. M. and Sims, J. (2015). Long-term implications of early education and care programs for Australian children. *Journal of Educational Psychology*, *107*(1), 284–299.

Devries, R. et. al. (2002). *Developing Constructivist Early Childhood Curriculum*. New York: Teachers' College Press.

Downer, J. T. and Pianta, R. C. (2006). Academic and cognitive functioning in first grade: Associations with earlier home and child care predictors and with concurrent home and classroom experiences. *School Psychology Review*, *35*(1), 11–30.

Dowsett, C. J., Huston, A. C., Imes, A. E. and Gennetian, L. (2008). Structural and process features in three types of child care for children from high and low income families. *Early Childhood Research Quarterly*, *23*(1), 69–93.

Engle, P. L., Fernald, L. C., Alderman, H., Behrman, J., O'Gara, C., Yousafzai, A. et al. (2011). Strategies for reducing inequalities and improving developmental outcomes for young children in low-income and middle-income countries. *The Lancet*, *378*(9799), 1339–1353.

Farver, J. A. M., Xu, Y., Lonigan, C. J. and Eppe, S. (2013). The home literacy environment and Latino head start children's emergent literacy skills. *Developmental Psychology*, *49*(4), 775–791.

Foster, M. A., Lambert, R., Abbott-Shim, M., McCarty, F. and Franze, S. (2005). A model of home learning environment and social risk factors in relation to children's emergent literacy and social outcomes. *Early Childhood Research Quarterly*, *20*(1), 13–36.

Fuller, B., Kagan, S. L., Loeb, S. and Chang, Y. W. (2004). Child care quality: Centers and home settings that serve poor families. *Early Childhood Research Quarterly*, *19*(4), 505–527.

Gest, S. D., Holland-Coviello, R., Welsh, J. A., Eicher-Catt, D. L. and Gill, S. (2006). Language development subcontexts in Head Start classrooms: Distinctive patterns of teacher talk during free play, mealtime, and book reading. *Early Education and Development*, *17*(2), 293–315.

Geva, E. (2006). Learning to read in a second language: Research, implications, and recommendations for services. *Encyclopedia on Early Childhood Development*, online resource. Montreal Quebec: Centre of Excellence for Early Childhood Development. www.child-encyclopedia.com/documents/GevaANGxp.pdf.

Gormley Jr, W. T., Gayer, T., Phillips, D. and Dawson, B. (2005). The effects of universal pre-K on cognitive development. *Developmental Psychology*, *41*(6), 872–884.

Grimm, K. J., Steele, J. S., Mashburn, A. J., Burchinal, M. and Pianta, R. C. (2010). Early behavioral associations of achievement trajectories. *Developmental Psychology*, *46*(5), 976–983.

Halle, T., Hair, E., Wandner, L., McNamara, M. and Chien, N. (2012). Predictors and outcomes of early versus later English language proficiency among English language learners. *Early Childhood Research Quarterly*, *27*(1), 1–20.

Han, W. J., Lee, R. and Waldfogel, J. (2012). School readiness among children of immigrants in the US: Evidence from a large national birth cohort study. *Children and Youth Services Review*, *34*(4), 771–782.

Heckman, J. J. (2006). Skill formation and the economics of investing in disadvantaged children. *Science*, *312*(5782), 1900–1902.

Howes, C., Burchinal, M., Pianta, R., Bryant, D., Early, D., Clifford, R. and Barbarin, O. (2008). Ready to learn? Children's pre-academic achievement in pre-kindergarten programs. *Early Childhood Research Quarterly*, *23*(1), 27–50.

Hughes, J. N. (2010). Identifying quality in preschool education: Progress and challenge. *School Psychology Review*, *39*(1), 48–53.

Justice, L. M. and Ezell, H. K. (2002). Use of storybook reading to increase print awareness in at-risk children. *American Journal of Speech-Language Pathology*, *11*(1), 17–29.

Justice, L. M. and Pullen, P. C. (2003). Promising interventions for promoting emergent literacy skills three evidence-based approaches. *Topics in Early Childhood Special Education*, *23*(3), 99–113.

Knudsen, E. I., Heckman, J. J., Cameron, J. L. and Shonkoff, J. P. (2006). Economic, neurobiological, and behavioral perspectives on building America's future workforce. *Proceedings of the National Academy of Sciences*, *103*(27), 10155–10162.

Korat, O., Arafat, S. H., Aram, D. and Klein, P. (2012). Book reading mediation, SES, home literacy environment, and children's literacy: Evidence from Arabic-speaking families. *First Language*, *33*(2), 132–154.

Lara-Cinisomo, S., Fuligni, A. S., Ritchie, S., Howes, C. and Karoly, L. (2008). Getting ready for school: An examination of early childhood educators' belief systems. *Early Childhood Education Journal*, *35*(4), 343–349.

Larson, J. and Marsh, J. (2007). *Making Literacy Real: Theories and Practices for Learning and Teaching*. Los Angeles: Sage Publications.

Larson, K., Russ, S. A., Nelson, B. B., Olson, L. M. and Halfon, N. (2015). Cognitive ability at kindergarten entry and socioeconomic status. *Pediatrics*, *135*(2), e440–e448.

Lee, V. E. and Burkam, D. T. (2002). *Inequality at the Starting Gate: Social Background Differences in Achievement as Children Begin School*. Washington, DC: Economic Policy Institute.

Levin, I. and Aram, D. (2012). Mother–child joint writing and storybook reading and their effects on kindergartners' literacy: an intervention study. *Reading and Writing*, *25*(1), 217–249.

Li, W., Farkas, G., Duncan, G. J., Burchinal, M. R. and Vandell, D. L. (2013). Timing of high-quality child care and cognitive, language, and preacademic development. *Developmental Psychology*, *49*(8), 1440–1451.

Li-Grining, C. P., Votruba-Drzal, E., Maldonado-Carreño, C. and Haas, K. (2010). Children's early approaches to learning and academic trajectories through fifth grade. *Developmental Psychology*, *46*(5), 1062–1077.

Lin, D., McBride-Chang, Aram, D., Levin, I., Cheung, R. Y. M. and Chow, Y.-Y. (2009). Maternal mediation of writing in Chinese children. *Language and Cognitive Processes*, *24*(7–8), 1286–1311.

Loeb, S., Bridges, M., Bassok, D., Fuller, B. and Rumberger, R. W. (2007). How much is too much? The influence of preschool centers on children's social and cognitive development. *Economics of Education Review*, *26*(1), 52–66.

Lonigan, C. J. and Shanahan, T. (2010). Developing early literacy skills things we know we know and things we know we don't know. *Educational Researcher*, *39*(4), 340–346.

Maccoby, E. E. and Lewis, C. C. (2003). Less day care or different day care? *Child Development*, *74*(4), 1069–1075.

Magnuson, K. A., Meyers, M. K., Ruhm, C. J. and Waldfogel, J. (2004). Inequality in preschool education and school readiness. *American Educational Research Journal*, *41*(1), 115–157.

Magnuson, K. A., Ruhm, C. and Waldfogel, J. (2007). Does prekindergarten improve school preparation and performance? *Economics of Education Review*, *26*(1), 33–51.

McBride-Chang, C., Chow, Y. Y. and Tong, X. (2010). Early literacy at home: General environmental factors and specific parent input. In D. Aram and O. Korat (eds), *Literacy Development and Enhancement Across Orthographies and Cultures* (pp. 97–109). New York: Springer.

Nelson, C. A. and Sheridan, M. A. (2011). Lessons from neuroscience research for understanding causal links between family and neighborhood characteristics and educational outcomes. In G. Duncan and R. Murnane (eds), *Whither Opportunity? Rising Inequality, Schools, and Children's Life Chances* (pp. 27–46). New York: Russell Sage Foundation.

Neumann, M. M. and Neumann, D. L. (2010). Parental strategies to scaffold emergent writing skills in the pre-school child within the home environment. *Early Years*, *30*(1), 79–94.

Neuman, S. (1999). Books make a difference: A study of access to literacy. *Reading Research Quarterly*, *34*(3), 286–311

Niklas, F. and Schneider, W. (2013). Home literacy environment and the beginning of reading and spelling. *Contemporary Educational Psychology*, *38*(1), 40–50.

Peisner-Feinberg, E. S. and Yazejian, N. (2010). Research on program quality: The evidence base. In P. W. Wesley and V. Buysse (eds), *The Quest for Quality: Promising Innovations for Early Childhood Programs* (pp. 21–45). Baltimore, MD: Paul H. Brookes.

Piaget, J. (1985). *The Equilibration of Cognitive Structures: The Central Problem of Intellectual Development*. Chicago: University of Chicago Press.

Rao, N., Sun, J., Wong, J. M. S., Weekes, B., Ip, P., Shaeffer, S. et al. (2014). *Early Childhood Development and Cognitive Development in Developing Countries: A Rigorous Literature Review*. Department for International Development (DFID), UK Government.

Reese, E., Sparks, A. and Leyva, D. (2010). A review of parent interventions for preschool children's language and emergent literacy. *Journal of Early Childhood Literacy*, *10*(1), 97–117.

Roberts, J., Jergens, J. and Burchinal, M. (2005). The role of home literacy practices in preschool children's language and emergent literacy skills. *Journal of Speech, Language, and Hearing Research*, *48*(2), 345–359.

Sapolsky, R. (2004). Mothering style and methylation. *Nature Neuroscience*, *7*(8), 791–792.

Schneider, W., Roth, E. and Ennemoser, M. (2000). Training phonological skills and letter knowledge in children at risk for dyslexia: A comparison of three kindergarten intervention programs. *Journal of Educational Psychology*, *92*(2), 284.

Sénéchal, M. and LeFevre, J. A. (2002). Parental involvement in the development of children's reading skill: A five-year longitudinal study. *Child Development*, *73*(2), 445–460.

Smart, D., Sanson, A., Baxter, J., Edwards, B. and Hayes, A. (2008). *Home-to-School Transitions for Financially Disadvantaged Children* (Final Report). Melbourne: Australian Institute of Family Studies.

Sonnenschein, S., Baker, L. and Serpell, R. (2010). The Early Childhood Project: A 5-year longitudinal investigation of children's literacy development in sociocultural context. In D. Aram and O. Korat (eds), *Literacy Development and Enhancement Across Orthographies and Cultures* (pp. 85–96). New York: Springer.

Sparks, R. L., Patton, J. and Murdoch, A. (2014). Early reading success and its relationship to reading achievement and reading volume: Replication of '10 years later'. *Reading and Writing*, *27*(1), 189–211.

Sylva, K., Chan, L. L., Melhuish, E., Sammons, P., Siraj-Blatchford, I. and Taggart, B. (2011). Emergent literacy environments: Home and preschool influences on children's literacy development. In S. Neuman and D. Dickinson (eds), *Handbook of Early Literacy Research* (pp. 189–199). New York: Guilford.

Sylva, K., Melhuish, E., Sammons, P., Siraj-Blatchford, I. and Taggart, B. (2011). Pre-school quality and educational outcomes at age 11: Low quality has little benefit. *Journal of Early Childhood Research*, *9*(2), 109–124.

Sylva, K., Melhuish, E., Sammons, P., Siraj-Blatchford, I., Taggart, B., Smees, R. et al. (2004). *The Effective Provision of Pre-School Education (EPPE) Project*. DfES report.

Sylva, K., Siraj-Blatchford, I., Taggart, B., Sammons, P., Melhuish, E., Elliot, K. and Totsika, V. (2006). Capturing quality in early childhood through environmental rating scales. *Early Childhood Research Quarterly*, *21*, 76–92.

Taggart, B., Sylva, K., Melhuish, E., Sammons, P. and Siraj, I. (2015). Effective pre-school, primary and secondary education project (EPPSE 3–16+): How pre-school influences children and young people's attainment and developmental outcomes over time. Research Brief. UCL Institute of Education, University College London, Birkbeck, University of London and University of Oxford.

US Department of Health and Human Services, Administration for Children and Families (2005). *Head Start Impact Study: First Year Findings*. Washington, DC.

Vandell, D. and Wolfe, B. (2000). *Child Care Quality: Does It Matter and Does It Need to Be Improved?* (Vol. 78). Madison, WI: Institute for Research on Poverty.

Votruba-Drzal, E., Coley, R. L., Collins, M. and Miller, P. (2015). Center-based preschool and school readiness skills of children from immigrant families. *Early Education and Development*, *26*(4), 549–573.

Votruba-Drzal, E., Coley, R. L., Koury, A. S. and Miller, P. (2013). Center-based child care and cognitive skills development: Importance of timing and household resources. *Journal of Educational Psychology*, *105*(3), 821–838.

Votruba-Drzal, E., Li-Grining, C. P. and Maldonado-Carreño, C. (2008). A developmental perspective on full- versus part-day kindergarten and children's academic trajectories through fifth grade. *Child Development*, *79*(4), 957–978.

Vygotsky, L. (1978). Interaction between learning and development. *Readings on the Development of Children*, *23*(3), 34–41.

Wang, Y. and McBride, C. (2015). Beyond copying: A comparison of multi-component interventions on Chinese early literacy skills. Unpublished manuscript.

Wasik, B. A., Bond, M. A. and Hindman, A. (2006). The effects of a language and literacy intervention on Head Start children and teachers. *Journal of Educational Psychology*, *98*(1), 63–74.

Weigel, D. J., Martin, S. S. and Bennett, K. K. (2006). Mothers' literacy beliefs: Connections with the home literacy environment and pre-school children's literacy development. *Journal of Early Childhood Literacy*, *6*(2), 191–211.

Whitehurst, G. J., Arnold, D. S., Epstein, J. N., Angell, A. L., Smith, M. and Fischel, J. E. (1994). A picture book reading intervention in day care and home for children from low-income families. *Developmental Psychology*, *30*(5), 679–689.

Whitehurst, G. J., Falco, F. L., Lonigan, C., Fischel, J. E., DeBaryshe, B. D., Valdez-Menchaca, M. C. et al. (1988). Accelerating language development through picture- book reading. *Developmental Psychology*, *24*, 552–558.

Whitehurst, G. J., Zevenbergen, A. A., Crone, D. A., Schultz, M. D., Velting, O. N. and Fischel, J. E. (1999). Outcomes of an emergent literacy intervention from Head Start through second grade. *Journal of Educational Psychology*, *91*(2), 261–272.

Wong, S., Harrison, L., Rivalland, C. and Whiteford, C. (2014). Utilisation of early childhood education and care services in a nationally representative sample of Australian children: A focus on disadvantage. *Australasian Journal of Early Childhood*, *39*(2), 60–69.

Yaden, D. B., Tam, A., Madrigal, P., Brassell, D., Massa, J., Altamirano, L. S. and Armendariz, J. (2000). Early literacy for inner-city children: The effects of reading and writing interventions in English and Spanish during the preschool years. *The Reading Teacher*, *54*(2), 186–189.

Yoshikawa, H., Weiland, C., Brooks-Gunn, J., Burchinal, M., Espinosa, L., Gormley, W. et al. (2013). *Investing in Our Future: The Evidence Base on Preschool Education*. New York: Foundation for Child Development and Ann Arbor, MI: Society for Research in Child Development.

3

A MATTER OF OPPORTUNITY

Language and reading development during early childhood for dual-language learners

Emily Phillips Galloway and Nonie Lesaux

In this chapter, we offer an overview of the early literacy development of young dual-language learners (DLLs) – children whose home language differs from the societal language and who represent a large and growing segment of the school-aged population in industrialized nations. We focus on the sociopolitical context of the United States where educational practices and policies have been largely designed with monolingual English-speaking children in mind, but where schools are increasingly serving multilingual children. While speaking two or more languages has been shown to facilitate heightened development in some cognitive and early literacy skills, especially phonemic and metalinguistic awareness, at scale, there is a paradox to be addressed. While some DLLs develop their literacy skills to the same levels as their majority-culture, monolingual peers, on average, achievement data suggest that these readers struggle to attain English literacy skills to age-appropriate levels even after many years of schooling. To make visible the types of language interactions that must be fostered as part of early literacy initiatives that attempt to address this paradox, we focus on three developmental periods in this chapter: from birth to preschool entry (age 0–3); the preschool years (age 3–5); and the early elementary school period from kindergarten to grade 3 (age 5–8). For each, we highlight a key context of language and literacy development: the family and community (0–3); the preschool classroom where children engage in play with peers and teachers that builds language skills (3–5); and the elementary school classroom where children participate in formal literacy instruction (5–8). In each context, we underscore the 'inputs' – opportunities to be exposed to and to participate in language interactions – that foster DLLs' oral language and literacy development ('outputs').

In this chapter, we offer an overview of what we know about early literacy development of young dual-language learners (DLLs) – children whose home language differs from the societal language and who represent a large and growing segment of the school-aged population in industrialized nations. In providing the overview, we focus on the socio-political context of the United States where educational practices and policies have been largely designed with monolingual English-speaking children in mind, but where schools are increasingly serving multilingual children. While speaking two or more languages has been shown to facilitate heightened development in some cognitive (e.g., executive functioning, Calvo & Bialystok, 2014) and early literacy skills, especially phonemic and metalinguistic awareness (Yoshida, 2008), at scale, there is a paradox to be addressed. While some DLLs develop their literacy skills to the same levels as their majority-culture, monolingual peers, on average, achievement data suggest that these readers struggle to attain English literacy skills to age-appropriate levels even after many years of schooling (Kieffer, 2011; Mancilla-Martinez & Lesaux, 2011). Indeed, it appears that in the USA and other Western industrialized nations, DLLs' low achievement is about more than language learning; their difficulties are linked, in part, to the influences of poverty on development. To this end, many DLLs' majority-culture peers growing up in low-income households show similar academic profiles (Kieffer, 2011; Lesaux & Kieffer, 2010). For educators and policymakers the goal must be two-fold: (1) to understand the developmental processes through which children acquire two (or more) languages and how these experiences influence early literacy development; and (2) to understand the overlap in the early learning and academic needs of DLLs and their monolingual peers. With this knowledge, educators and policymakers might envision how the language-learning contexts (preschool classrooms, childcare settings, homes, communities) where young DLLs (and their monolingual English peers) are educated can better support their future participation in the K-12 classroom, the workplace and society.

Chapter outline

Given that language development is cumulative and takes different forms at different ages and stages, and because the contexts in which children are exposed to language and literacy expand throughout early childhood, we focus on three developmental periods in this chapter: from birth to preschool entry (age 0–3), the preschool years (age 3–5) and the early elementary school period from kindergarten to grade 3 (age 5–8). For each, we focus on a key context of language and literacy development: the family and community (0–3); the preschool classroom where children engage in play with peers and teachers that builds language skill (3–5); and the elementary school classroom where children participate in formal literacy instruction (5–8). In each context, we highlight the 'inputs' – opportunities to be exposed to and to participate in language interactions – that foster DLLs' oral language and literacy development ('outputs'). In so doing, we hope to make visible the types of language interactions that must be fostered as part of early literacy initiatives that target this population. In our discussion of early elementary school literacy learning we focus on reading development; research on DLLs' writing skill development is very limited and does not support synthesis.

In addition, given the purpose of the volume and today's demographic data, we focus on the children who are members of the two largest and fastest growing subpopulations of second-language learners in US schools and in other industrialized nations with a rich history of immigration: students who immigrated before kindergarten and children of immigrants born in the country in which they are being educated (Hernández et al., 2008). We also place an emphasis on research conducted with children negotiating Spanish and English, children who constitute 72 per cent of the DLL population, and a population that is expected to grow rapidly over the next ten years in the USA (Aud et al., 2011). We conclude this chapter by suggesting future research avenues that might further describe the nature of biliteracy development in young children.

From birth to preschool entry (0–3): bilingual development during infancy and toddlerhood

Typical language development – in any language – begins at birth (see Figure 3.1 for milestones) and the maxim that 'more language exposure is linked with more language learning' holds for both monolingual and bilingual populations (Song et al., 2012 for a discussion). This exposure may occur via interactions with caregivers/family – considered the primary mechanism – and with the wider community (e.g. at the park, public transportation, grocery store).

Language development in the home or child-care setting

In any language, the *quantity* and *quality* of a caregiver's speech directed at the child influences language development. 'Quantity' refers to both the amount of language a child is exposed to *and* to the relative exposure to each language, for instance Spanish and English. Unsurprisingly, a number of studies now document the strong relationship between the frequency with which young DLLs (e.g. age 30 months) have been exposed to Spanish and English and their phonological, grammatical and vocabulary skills in each of these languages (Hindman and Wasik, 2015; Hoff et al., 2012; Parra et al., 2011). Because they are acquiring words in two or more languages, these children may well experience less overall input in *each* language, despite being exposed to an equal (or greater) number of words than a monolingual infant (Hoff et al., 2012). This balance of language exposure appears to influence productive and receptive language skills. For example, Hoff and colleagues find that by 30 months of age, toddlers showed greater relative skill in producing the language they heard more often than in comprehending it – a trend that was reversed for the language they heard less frequently (Hoff et al., 2014).

Defining what we mean by 'the quality of language inputs' is a much more complex endeavour than defining quantity. In brief, research suggests that high-quality language is: directed at the child and in response to her behaviour, and includes a diversity of words, phrases and sentence structures (Ramírez-Esparza et al., 2014; Rowe, 2012). The diversity of the caregiver's speech (i.e. using many different types of words and grammatical structures) and the frequency with which she uses these words and structures therefore contributes to gains in a bilingual toddler's vocabulary size and syntactic skill in the first and second language (Parra et al., 2011).

As we might expect, there are differences in young DLLs' individual rates of language learning and proficiency, some of which is about normal variation, and some of which in fact mirrors patterns of social division in the USA (Rowe et al., 2012; Weisleder and Fernald, 2014). Research demonstrates that children growing up in low socioeconomic status (SES) households are, on average, exposed to less child-directed, complex and diverse language; and, by age 3, have smaller vocabularies (Hoff, 2013). These differences are of practical significance for DLLs in the USA, who are disproportionately growing up in poverty and for whom recent research shows variation in the quality of their language experiences. For example, in a study of 29 low-SES Spanish-speaking families followed over a single day, amounts of child-directed speech differed radically: one caregiver spoke more than 12,000 words to an infant while another used only 670 words (Weisleder and Fernald, 2014). And other research reminds us that older siblings of infants and toddlers are sources of language exposure; in Spanish-speaking families where school-aged siblings are enrolled in English-speaking elementary schools, toddlers are exposed to more English (Bridges and Hoff, 2014).

Language development in the community

We use the term 'community' to refer to people outside of a child's immediate circle of caregivers and household members – store clerks, librarians and other children's parents and siblings that a given child may interact with on a day-to-day basis. While a number of studies have shown that infants and young children are 'selective learners' and resist information provided by speakers with a foreign accent (Buttelmann et al., 2013), this may not be the case for infants growing up in more diverse communities. Howard and colleagues found that 19-month-olds from monolingual, English-speaking homes who were often exposed to linguistic diversity in their neighbourhoods (e.g. parks, bus rides, grocery stores) were more likely to imitate the actions of a Spanish speaker, signalling an openness to learning from those who did not share their language background (Howard et al., 2014). In contrast to learning from caregivers through direct interaction, this study and others suggest that infants and toddlers may *also* be able to learn through 'overheard speech' (Gampe et al., 2012) and by observing others (Gaskins and Paradise, 2010). While not without controversy, this research points to the need for additional studies that would explore how neighbourhood characteristics shape language-learning opportunities for very young DLLs.

Summary: language exposure the homes and the community

The contexts in which young children are acquiring language are diverse, and the child's exposure to one or more languages varies. Given this, bilingualism can be conceptualized as a continuum of proficiency in a first and second language that begins when an infant is exposed to an additional language. From this perspective, children entering preschool classrooms bring a range of language resources that can be leveraged as they develop literacy skills; however, even conversationally proficient children – whether in a first or second language – require additional language development to support literacy skills.

Early childhood education settings (3–5): bilingual and biliterate development during the preschool years

From age 3 to 5, young DLLs are not only acquiring language orally – they are also beginning to map sounds from spoken language to the written word, and to realize the function of print as emerging readers and writers (Figure 3.2 describes typical development). For DLLs, oral language, phonological awareness and print knowledge – all targets in a high-quality preschool classroom – are strong and independent predictors of later reading skill (Puranik et al., 2011). However, US Census data suggests that DLLs are underrepresented in preschool and centre-based childcare, with the children of undocumented immigrants posting the lowest levels of enrolment (Yoshikawa and Kalil, 2011).

While early education offers a mechanism for supporting young DLLs' early literacy development, if preschools are to support DLLs, there is much work to do, particularly for those children growing up in poverty. Studies conducted with DLLs (mostly Spanish-speaking) in English-dominant Head Start classrooms suggest that while, on average, they make gains in English vocabulary – at rates that outpace some monolinguals – they nevertheless demonstrate English vocabulary skills far below their English-speaking peers in the US upon preschool completion (Hindman and Wasik, 2015; Lonigan et al., 2013). In the domain of instruction, this suggests that much more attention to language development is needed. While an appealing approach is to simply teach English vocabulary, Hindman and Wasik

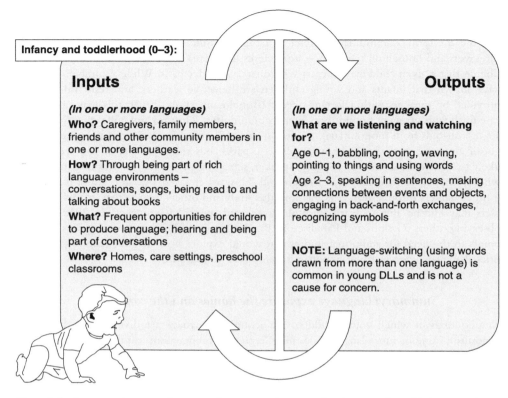

Infancy and toddlerhood (0–3):

Inputs

(In one or more languages)

Who? Caregivers, family members, friends and other community members in one or more languages.

How? Through being part of rich language environments – conversations, songs, being read to and talking about books

What? Frequent opportunities for children to produce language; hearing and being part of conversations

Where? Homes, care settings, preschool classrooms

Outputs

(In one or more languages)

What are we listening and watching for?

Age 0–1, babbling, cooing, waving, pointing to things and using words

Age 2–3, speaking in sentences, making connections between events and objects, engaging in back-and-forth exchanges, recognizing symbols

NOTE: Language-switching (using words drawn from more than one language) is common in young DLLs and is not a cause for concern.

Figure 3.1   Language inputs and outputs that support language development from birth to age three for DLLs

(2015) suggest that this is an oversimplification given their finding that Spanish-speaking four-year-olds also demonstrated low levels of knowledge of Spanish vocabulary. This evidence points towards a broader need for this population to be exposed to rich content and ideas – to keep knowledge building at the core of any language-learning instruction (see also Pinkham et al., 2012). The importance of language development during the preschool years is underscored by the finding that those DLLs who are considered English proficient upon school entry keep pace with their monolingual English peers in kindergarten and beyond (Halle et al., 2012). Therefore, the question of *how* to create these classrooms rich in language-learning opportunity is a crucial one.

Language exposure in the preschool classroom: teachers' inputs

Children's opportunities for extended talk with educators, particularly talk that goes beyond the 'here and now' and includes the opportunity for back-and-forth conversation, is the single most important element of the preschool language learning environment. However, in preschool classrooms with high numbers of DLLs who are at risk for later reading difficulties, these opportunities may be infrequent (Cheatham et al., 2015). For example, in a study conducted in a large Head Start programme in a semi-urban area serving large numbers of Latino children, Jacoby and Lesaux (2014) found that language interactions where children were afforded multiple conversation turns and discussed topics beyond those in the immediate environment (e.g. engaging in pretend play or narrating a past event) comprised only 22 per cent of all observed lessons. Consistent with prior studies (Dickinson et al., 2008) most teacher–child interactions demanded and/or resulted in one-word answers from children. Shedding light on promising levers for improvement, the authors found that some instruc-tional formats, particularly those involving small group, teacher-led activities, were more likely to elicit extended talk from the young DLLs in the study – talk that is related to later reading achievement (Dickinson et al., 2008; Jacoby and Lesaux, 2014).

While the studies in this area have traditionally focused exclusively on language *inputs*, researchers are also increasingly attending to the impact of children's language *outputs* on their own language development. For instance, Bohman et al. (2010) in a large-scale study with 757 children found that language exposure alone did not exert as much of an impact on DLLs' pre-kindergarten and kindergarten English and Spanish language development as did children's language usage (output) and exposure (input) combined. The authors also found that these relationships were not stable over time: input is important as a child first begins to use a language, but amount of language output is important for developing language over time.

Promoting language during the preschool years: a cautionary tale

The ways in which early educators and preschool teachers design language-learning oppor-tunities for, and interact with, young DLLs may depend greatly on their own understanding of second-language acquisition. Theories describing the stages of language development for DLLs have long included a 'silent period' or stage (also referred to as 'non-verbal', 'receptive' or 'pre-productive' phase) in which the child elects to produce no (or very little) oral lan-guage as she begins to acquire the language of the classroom. Many policies and practices in early childhood education have been shaped by the idea that *all* children acquiring a second language pass through this stage (Le Pichon and de Jonge, 2015; Roberts, 2014). Many educators therefore do not expect DLLs to produce language upon classroom entry and may not place DLLs in situations where language production is necessary (Roberts, 2014). However, it is not clear that there is a lock-step progression, or that all DLLs experience a silent period. Therefore, educators should consistently provide children with rich language inputs, and supported opportunities for outputs (Le Pichon and de Jonge, 2015), while they are acquiring familiarity with the language of the classroom (see Figure 3.2).

Elementary schooling (5–8): DLLs' reading development in the first years of formal schooling

As beginning readers, young children in the early elementary grades are acquiring many of the specific skills and competencies that make up this thing called 'reading'. At the same time, many DLLs must also rapidly acquire English-language skills. We turn in this section to focus explicitly on the research that examines DLLs' reading development in classroom settings where monoliteracy is the norm, which is the case in most US schools (for a description of typical development, see Figure 3.3).

Becoming a reader: developing code and meaning-based skills

In this section, we focus on two broad sets of skills and competencies. One set, 'code-based skills', revolves around the skills and competencies needed to read the words on the page

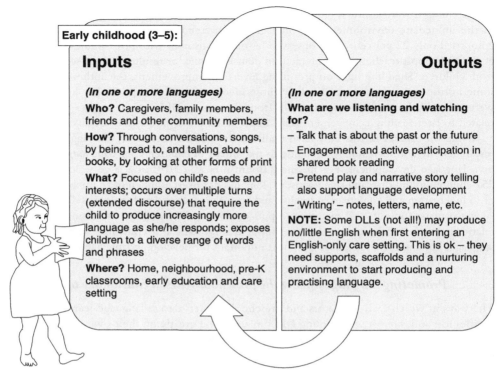

Early childhood (3–5):

Inputs

(In one or more languages)

Who? Caregivers, family members, friends and other community members

How? Through conversations, songs, by being read to, and talking about books, by looking at other forms of print

What? Focused on child's needs and interests; occurs over multiple turns (extended discourse) that require the child to produce increasingly more language as she/he responds; exposes children to a diverse range of words and phrases

Where? Home, neighbourhood, pre-K classrooms, early education and care setting

Outputs

(In one or more languages)

What are we listening and watching for?

– Talk that is about the past or the future

– Engagement and active participation in shared book reading

– Pretend play and narrative story telling also support language development

– 'Writing' – notes, letters, name, etc.

NOTE: Some DLLs (not all!) may produce no/little English when first entering an English-only care setting. This is ok – they need supports, scaffolds and a nurturing environment to start producing and practising language.

Figure 3.2   Language inputs and outputs that support language and literacy development during early childhood for DLLs

and the other, 'meaning-based skills', around the skills and competencies needed to understand what children are reading.

Code-based skills

For all children learning to read, whether monolingual or bilingual, phonological processing skills, one's ability to work with and process the sounds of the language, are central to the development of accurate and efficient word reading. For the DLLs, phonological awareness is likely to be language specific at the onset, i.e. working with the sounds of her own language. However, as the child comes to understand how sounds are related to printed letters, this metalinguistic knowledge that printed words are representations of sounds and map to words in oral language can be transferred from one language to another (López, 2012; Yoshida, 2008). What may not transfer, depending on the similarity between the child's language systems (e.g. Spanish and Czech have little in common), are the language-specific spelling patterns (for additional discussion on transfer, see the following sections). If phonics instruction is adequate, by the end of second grade in school settings, both DLLs and their native English-speaking peers should show mastery or near-mastery of grade-level word reading skills.

Meaning-based skills

There is often a gap between DLLs' ability to read the words on the page and ability to make meaning from text (Mancilla-Martinez and Lesaux, 2011), especially over time, as texts become more complex. These differences are due in large part to the nature of these skills; code-based skills are discrete, highly susceptible to instruction and can be taught to achieve mastery (for a discussion see Chapter 23 in this volume). In contrast, meaning-related skills (such as having the relevant background knowledge and linguistic knowledge to make sense of a text, sometimes called academic language) are not mastery-oriented and cannot be taught in a short period of time (Snow and Uccelli, 2009).

Outside of their distinct nature, why do these meaning-based skills pose a particular challenge for DLLs? In short, most meaning-related skills hinge on language comprehension. In particular, DLLs' oral language, vocabulary and listening comprehension skills in English tend to be underdeveloped compared to those of their monolingual peers, especially those growing up in middle-income families. This is not to suggest that these skills do not follow linear trends or that DLLs are not experiencing language growth over time; in fact, mirroring trends identified among preschool DLLs, Mancilla-Martinez and Lesaux (2011) found that from age 4.5 through middle-school entry, Spanish-speaking DLLs' oral language skills (including vocabulary) grew at a rate that exceeded the monolingual norm. However, despite this rate of growth, these students, who entered school with vocabulary levels that were far below their English-speaking counterparts, were not able to 'catch up' (Mancilla-Martinez and Lesaux, 2011) under typical instructional circumstances, which involve limited focus on developing language skills and competencies. This is also the case for many of their monolingual peers growing up in poverty.

We noted at the outset of this chapter that bilingualism is often associated with higher cognitive functions and we don't want to lose that thread in our discussion of underdeveloped language and literacy skills. It appears that bilingual readers use all language and cognitive resources acquired in both a first and second language when they read and write (Hopewell and Escamilla, 2014). For instance, when reading in English a student might encounter the name, Nina, to refer to the main character. If the child is a Spanish speaker, she may, at first, read the word as '*niña*' (meaning 'girl' in Spanish), and interpret the sentence to be about a girl rather than about the character, Nina. She will have to 'override' these Spanish-language resources (a process that occurs instantaneously) and access those she has developed in English both to decode the word and to understand the sentence, a task that draws on her executive functioning skills. It is this recursive moving between languages that is thought to lead to increased executive functioning skills (and slightly slower performances on some language tasks) among DLLs.

Language and literacy exposure in the elementary classroom

While simply reading text has long been thought to be a critical mechanism for language and vocabulary development (Stanovich and Cunningham, 1993), this relationship may not be so straightforward for DLLs and for many of their peers who are academically vulnerable. That is, acquiring language from text requires an age-appropriate level of text comprehension, which, in turn, depends on having adequate knowledge of the text's language. Only as students become able readers do they acquire language and knowledge from text. Yet, though conversationally proficient, many DLLs have had little opportunity to acquire the language found in texts – language known as 'academic language', in either a first or additional language (Scarcella,

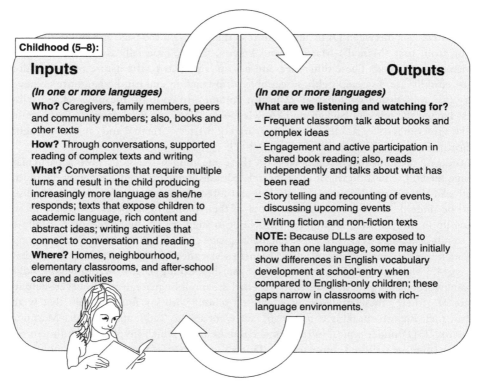

Childhood (5–8):

Inputs

(In one or more languages)

Who? Caregivers, family members, peers and community members; also, books and other texts

How? Through conversations, supported reading of complex texts and writing

What? Conversations that require multiple turns and result in the child producing increasingly more language as she/he responds; texts that expose children to academic language, rich content and abstract ideas; writing activities that connect to conversation and reading

Where? Homes, neighbourhood, elementary classrooms, and after-school care and activities

Outputs

(In one or more languages)

What are we listening and watching for?

– Frequent classroom talk about books and complex ideas

– Engagement and active participation in shared book reading; also, reads independently and talks about what has been read

– Story telling and recounting of events, discussing upcoming events

– Writing fiction and non-fiction texts

NOTE: Because DLLs are exposed to more than one language, some may initially show differences in English vocabulary development at school-entry when compared to English-only children; these gaps narrow in classrooms with rich-language environments.

Figure 3.3 Language inputs and outputs that support language and literacy development from age five to eight in DLLs

2003; Uccelli et al., 2015). Academic language skill includes knowledge of vocabulary; but it also includes an awareness of sentence structures, words used to link ideas and create cohesion in texts (connectives), awareness of how texts are organized and the ability to manipulate words by shifting their grammatical categories (morphology) (for additional discussion see Uccelli et al., 2015).

Given their challenges accessing texts, classroom talk is the cornerstone of a language-building approach for DLLs. In our own work, we have found that supporting teachers to make use of more diverse and complex vocabulary can be accomplished by providing them with professional development that emphasizes the centrality of classroom discussion to student achievement, as well as with instructional materials that emphasize the use and instruction of complex academic language (Gámez, 2015; Lesaux et al., 2014). By selecting topics and texts that require the use of complex language to discuss, teachers and students are compelled to use this language when speaking and writing. Figure 3.3 outlines language inputs and opportunities for language use that support literacy development for DLLs and their monolingual classmates.

Implications for policy, practice and research

To draw out the implications of the extant research base for policy and practice and next steps in research, we necessarily start by reminding the reader that the story of DLLs in the

USA is not a straightforward one. That is, while research has documented initial gaps in depth and breadth of vocabulary knowledge in DLL children (Bialystok et al., 2005) compared to national norms, explaining this gap is challenging because research has only recently begun to parse the effects of SES from the effect of growing up learning two or more languages.

Disentangling the effects of low-SES and dual/second language learning

More research that aims to explain the relationships between and among DLL status and low SES is needed. For now, however, there are important implications for practice; that is, while we have typically focused on the needs of DLLs separate from the needs of their monolingual peers, emerging research suggests that there are substantive and practical reasons to consider classroom-level efforts to improve language and literacy outcomes – rather than relying on intervention targeting subgroups. For example, using the nationally representative ECLS-K dataset, Kieffer (2011) demonstrated that kindergarten DLLs showed similar trajectories in reading through fifth grade, and similarly low-performance levels, as English speakers from homes at comparable socioeconomic levels. Conversely, limited but insightful research suggests that when comparing the vocabulary learning trajectories of DLLs and monolingual children all of middle SES, DLLs can achieve the same levels of vocabulary through the elementary school years (Umbel et al., 1992).

Theorizing the design of interventions that enrich language environments

As we continue to focus on unanswered questions, we also remind ourselves that at each developmental stage, hearing and producing language (inputs and outputs) matter greatly and have significant implications for how we educate caregivers and teachers about these relationships. Of particular interest are interventions that have sought to shape educators' and parents' understanding of children's language development as a mechanism to enrich children's language-learning contexts, with a particular focus on the back-and-forth exchange that is so important (see Han et al., 2014; Landry et al., 2014; Rowe, 2012). That is, supporting adults to respond to children as they begin to produce language and fostering adults' skills to engage children in extended conversations are particularly important and fruitful avenues for preparing DLLs to become readers and writers. There are many questions to be answered about *how* to support these adults. For example: What intensity and type of intervention best supports parents and educators of DLLs? What additional adult-level factors must be considered for a school-based intervention targeting DLLs' language and literacy development to succeed at scale?

Clarifying the importance of fluent language models

As we consider supporting the large and growing population of DLLs to develop strong early literacy skills, we are mindful that, over the years, parents and early educators providers have received conflicting messages about which language(s), native and/or English, should be employed to prepare children for school. In fact, it is well established that children's language acquisition in any language depends primarily upon a strong foundation – what's most important is for children to have caregivers who use high-quality language, irrespective of the language itself (Place and Hoff, 2011). When speaking in a native language, parents appear to use more diverse language with their young children than when using a second language (Hoff et al., 2014). However, given the sociopolitical context of the USA, a common practice has been for caregivers, who want the best for their child, to focus on providing English exposure − even if they are not native English speakers − leading to a loss or stagnation of the child's native language development and compromised opportunities for extended talk due to the caregiver's developing English (Hammer et al., 2009). Indeed, in the press to support young DLLs' early literacy skills, a knowledge-building approach to language development − one that places extended conversations about concepts and facts and in turn builds language that maps to the texts used in the elementary grades, as early as kindergarten − is crucial. In turn, this means supporting adults to use the language − native or otherwise − that will best facilitate and provide such learning opportunities.

Understanding the relationship between cross-linguistic transfer and literacy

Finally, we note that the question of how to support today's DLLs hinges to some degree on how we understand the relationship between the languages a child has acquired. The concept of transfer − of leveraging linguistic knowledge, both conceptual and phonological, from a first language to learn an additional language − is worth a brief discussion. Some empirical work suggests that Spanish–English DLLs who know more vocabulary in Spanish (vocabulary breadth) often know more vocabulary in English (Uccelli and Páez, 2007), and are more apt to demonstrate skill in decoding and comprehending English texts (Proctor et al., 2012). Nevertheless, other work has failed to identify these relationships (Hammer et al., 2014). For example, Gottardo and Mueller (2009) found that later English reading comprehension was only supported by English vocabulary skills, not by these skills in Spanish. In the realm of interventions, we also note that Spanish instruction is strongly linked with vocabulary learning in Spanish, but appears not to influence English vocabulary skills, speaking skills or reading proficiency (Cena et al., 2013). In part, these differences are likely an artifact of the diverse numbers of measures used, the differences in the samples (age, language proficiency levels, SES) and in the design of the study (some were longitudinal, others cross-sectional) (Goodrich et al., 2013). It may also be the case that cross-linguistic transfer only impacts on reading comprehension skills when the learner has reached a 'threshold' of first and second ability (Leider et al., 2013). Given this, questions remain about which linguistic skills show evidence of transfer at which developmental periods, and for which learners.

Conclusion

The growth of the DLL population in the United States and in other industrialized nations offers opportunities for creating a citizenry where a diversity of languages and cultures coexist; but also presents challenges for an educational system that has been designed around monolingual learners. While adult–child interactions that develop language and literacy differ in type and texture across development, we emphasize the fundamental role of language inputs and outputs at all stages and ages. Whether at home or in the classroom, DLLs' literacy achievement hinges to an extent on rich opportunities to hear and to produce oral and written language in a first and/or additional language.

References

Aud, S., Hussar, W., Kena, G., Bianco, K., Frohlich, L., Kemp, J. and Tahan, K. (2011). U.S. Department of Education, National Center for Education Statistics. The condition of education 2011 (NCES 2011-033). Washington, DC: U.S. Government Printing Office.

Bialystok, E., Luk, G. and Kwan, E. (2005). Bilingualism, biliteracy, and learning to read: Interactions among languages and writing systems. *Scientific Studies of Reading, 9*(1), 43–61.

Bohman, T. M., Bedore, L. M., Peña, E. D., Mendez-Perez, A. and Gillam, R. B. (2010). What you hear and what you say: Language performance in Spanish English bilinguals. *International Journal of Bilingual Education and Bilingualism, 13*(3), 325–344.

Bridges, K. and Hoff, E. (2014). Older sibling influences on the language environment and language development of toddlers in bilingual homes. *Applied Psycholinguistics, 35*(2), 225–241.

Buttelmann, D., Zmyj, N., Daum, M. and Carpenter, M. (2013). Selective imitation of in- group over out-group members in 14-month-old infants. *Child Development, 84*(2), 422–428.

Calvo, A. and Bialystok, E. (2014). Independent effects of bilingualism and socioeconomic status on language ability and executive functioning. *Cognition, 130*(3), 278–288.

Cena, J., Baker, D. L., Kame'enui, E. J., Baker, S. K., Park, Y. and Smolkowski, K. (2013). The impact of a systematic and explicit vocabulary intervention in Spanish with Spanish-speaking English learners in first grade. *Reading and Writing, 26*(8), 1289–1316.

Cheatham, G. A., Jimenez-Silva, M. and Park, H. (2015). Teacher feedback to support oral language learning for young dual language learners. *Early Child Development and Care, 185*(9), 1452–1463.

Dickinson, D. K., Darrow, C. L. and Tinubu, T. A. (2008). Patterns of teacher–child conversations in head start classrooms: Implications for an empirically grounded approach to professional development. *Early Education and Development, 19*(3), 396–429.

Gámez, P. B. (2015). Classroom-based English exposure and English Language Learners' expressive language skills. *Early Childhood Research Quarterly, 31*, 135–146.

Gampe, A., Liebal, K. and Tomasello, M. (2012). Eighteen-month-olds learn novel words through overhearing. *First Language, 32*(3), 385–397.

Gaskins, S. and Paradise, L. (2010). Learning through observation in daily life. In D. F. Lancy, J. C. Bock and S. Gaskins (eds), *The Anthropology of Learning in Childhood*. Walnut Creek, CA: AltaMira Press.

Goodrich, J. M., Lonigan, C. J. and Farver, J. M. (2013). Do early literacy skills in children's first language promote development of skills in their second language? An experimental evaluation of transfer. *Journal of Educational Psychology, 105*(2), 414–426.

Gottardo, A. and Mueller, J. (2009). Are first-and second-language factors related in predicting second-language reading comprehension? A study of Spanish-speaking children acquiring English as a second language from first to second grade. *Journal of Educational Psychology, 101*(2), 330–344.

Halle, T., Hair, E., Wandner, L., McNamara, M. and Chien, N. (2012). Predictors and outcomes of early versus later English language proficiency among English language learners. *Early Childhood Research Quarterly, 27*(1), 1–20.

Hammer, C. S., Davison, M. D., Lawrence, F. R. and Miccio, A. W. (2009). The effect of maternal language on bilingual children's vocabulary and emergent literacy development during Head Start and kindergarten. *Scientific Studies of Reading, 13*(2), 99–121.

Han, M., Vukelich, C., Buell, M. and Meacham, S. (2014). Beating the odds: A longitudinal investigation of low-income dual-language and monolingual children's English language and literacy performance. *Early Education and Development, 25*(6), 841–858.

Hernandez, D. J., Denton, N. A. and Macartney, S. E. (2008). Children in immigrant families: Looking to America's future. Social Policy Report. *Society for Research in Child Development, 22*(3), 3–23.

Hindman, A. H. and Wasik, B. A. (2015). Building vocabulary in two languages: An examination of Spanish-speaking dual language learners in Head Start. *Early Childhood Research Quarterly, 31*, 19–33.

Hoff, E. (2013). Interpreting the early language trajectories of children from low-SES and language minority homes: Implications for closing achievement gaps. *Developmental Psychology, 49*(1), 4–14.

Hoff, E., Core, C., Place, S., Rumiche, R., Señor, M. and Parra, M. (2012). Dual language exposure and early bilingual development. *Journal of Child Language, 39*(1), 1–27.

Hoff, E., Welsh, S., Place, S. and Ribot, K. M. (2014). Properties of dual language input that shape bilingual development and properties of environments that shape dual language input. *Input and Experience in Bilingual Development, 13*, 119–140.

Hopewell, S. and Escamilla, K. (2014). Biliteracy development in immersion contexts. *Journal of Immersion and Content-Based Language Education, 2*(2), 181–195.

Howard, L. H., Carrazza, C. and Woodward, A. L. (2014). Neighborhood linguistic diversity predicts infants' social learning. *Cognition, 133*(2), 474–479.

Jacoby, J. W. and Lesaux, N. K. (2014). Support for extended discourse in teacher talk with linguistically diverse preschoolers. *Early Education and Development, 25*(8), 1162–1179.

Kieffer, M. J. (2011). Converging trajectories reading growth in language minority learners and their classmates, kindergarten to grade 8. *American Educational Research Journal, 48*(5), 1187–1225.

Landry, S. H., Zucker, T. A., Taylor, H. B., Swank, P. R., Williams, J. M., Assel, M. et al. (2014). Enhancing early childcare quality and learning for toddlers at risk: The responsive early childhood program. *Developmental Psychology, 50*(2), 526–541.

Le Pichon, E. and de Jonge, M. (2015). Linguistic and psychological perspectives on prolonged periods of silence in dual-language learners. *International Journal of Bilingual Education and Bilingualism, 19*(4), 426–441.

Leider, C. M., Proctor, C. P., Silverman, R. D. and Harring, J. R. (2013). Examining the role of vocabulary depth, cross-linguistic transfer, and types of reading measures on the reading comprehension of Latino bilinguals in elementary school. *Reading and Writing, 26*(9), 1459–1485.

Lesaux, N. K. and Kieffer, M. J. (2010). Exploring sources of reading comprehension difficulties among language minority learners and their classmates in early adolescence. *American Educational Research Journal, 47*(3), 596–632.

Lesaux, N. K., Kieffer, M. J., Kelley, J. G. and Harris, J. R. (2014). Effects of academic vocabulary instruction for linguistically diverse adolescents evidence from a randomized field trial. *American Educational Research Journal, 51*(6), 1159–1194.

Lonigan, C. J., Farver, J. M., Nakamoto, J. and Eppe, S. (2013). Developmental trajectories of preschool early literacy skills: A comparison of language-minority and monolingual-English children. *Developmental Psychology, 49*(10), 1943–1957.

López, L. M. (2012). Assessing the phonological skills of bilingual children from preschool through kindergarten: Developmental progression and cross-language transfer. *Journal of Research in Childhood Education, 26*(4), 371–391.

Mancilla-Martinez, J. and Lesaux, N. K. (2010). Predictors of reading comprehension for struggling readers: The case of Spanish-speaking language minority learners. *Journal of Educational Psychology, 102*(3), 701–711.

Mancilla-Martinez, J. and Lesaux, N. K. (2011). The gap between Spanish speakers' word reading and word knowledge: A longitudinal study. *Child Development, 82*(5), 1544–1560.

Parra, M., Hoff, E. and Core, C. (2011). Relations among language exposure, phonological memory, and language development in Spanish–English bilingually developing 2-year-olds. *Journal of Experimental Child Psychology, 108*(1), 113–125.

Pinkham, A. M., Kaefer, T. and Neuman, S. B. (eds). (2012). *Knowledge Development in Early Childhood: Sources of Learning and Classroom Implications.* New York: Guilford Press.

Place, S. and Hoff, E. (2011). Properties of dual language exposure that influence 2-year-olds' bilingual proficiency. *Child Development, 82*(6), 1834–1849.

Proctor, C. P., Silverman, R. D., Harring, J. R. and Montecillo, C. (2012). The role of vocabulary depth in predicting reading comprehension among English monolingual and Spanish–English bilingual children in elementary school. *Reading and Writing, 25*(7), 1635–1664.

Puranik, C. S., Lonigan, C. J. and Kim, Y. S. (2011). Contributions of emergent literacy skills to name writing, letter writing, and spelling in preschool children. *Early Childhood Research Quarterly, 26*(4), 465–474.

Ramírez-Esparza, N., García-Sierra, A. and Kuhl, P. K. (2014). Look who's talking: Speech style and social context in language input to infants are linked to concurrent and future speech development. *Developmental Science, 17*(6), 880–891.

Roberts, T. A. (2014). Not so silent after all: Examination and analysis of the silent stage in childhood second language acquisition. *Early Childhood Research Quarterly, 29*(1), 22–40.

Rowe, M. L. (2012). A longitudinal investigation of the role of quantity and quality of child-directed speech in vocabulary development. *Child Development, 83*(5), 1762–1774.

Rowe, M. L., Raudenbush, S. W. and Goldin-Meadow, S. (2012). The pace of vocabulary growth helps predict later vocabulary skill. *Child Development, 83*(2), 508–525.

Scarcella, R. (2003). Academic English: A conceptual framework (University of California Linguistic Minority Research Institute Technical Report 2003–1). Irvine, CA: University of California.

Snow, C. E. and Uccelli, P (2009). The challenge of academic language. In D. R. Olson and N. Torrance (eds), *The Cambridge Handbook of Literacy* (pp. 112–133). New York: Cambridge University Press.

Song, L., Tamis-LeMonda, C. S., Yoshikawa, H., Kahana-Kalman, R. and Wu, I. (2012). Language experiences and vocabulary development in Dominican and Mexican infants across the first 2 years. *Developmental Psychology, 48*(4), 1–18.

Stanovich, K. E. and Cunningham, A. E. (1993). Where does knowledge come from? Specific associations between print exposure and information acquisition. *Journal of Educational Psychology*, *85*(2), 211–229.

Uccelli, P. and Páez, M. M. (2007). Narrative and vocabulary development of bilingual children from kindergarten to first grade: Developmental changes and associations among English and Spanish skills. *Language, Speech, and Hearing Services in Schools*, *38*(3), 225–236.

Uccelli, P., Galloway, E. P., Barr, C. D., Meneses, A. and Dobbs, C. L. (2015). Beyond vocabulary: Exploring cross-disciplinary academic-language proficiency and its association with reading comprehension. *Reading Research Quarterly*, *50*(3), 337–356.

Umbel, V. M., Pearson, B. Z., Fernández, M. C. and Oller, D. K. (1992). Measuring bilingual children's receptive vocabularies. *Child Development*, *63*(4), 1012–1020.

Weisleder, A. and Fernald, A. (2014). Talking to children matters early language experience strengthens processing and builds vocabulary. *Psychological Science*, *24*(11), 2143–2152.

Yoshida, H. (2008). The cognitive consequences of early bilingualism. *Zero to Three*, *29*(2), 26–30.

Yoshikawa, H. and Kalil, A. (2011). The effects of parental undocumented status on the developmental contexts of young children in immigrant families. *Child Development Perspectives*, *5*(4), 291–297.

4

NEW LITERACIES AND NEW MEDIA

The changing face of early literacy

Natalia Kucirkova

This chapter addresses the possibility of connecting children's print-based literacy experiences with technology-mediated interactions. The concept of new literacies is introduced in light of the implications for young children's consumption and creation of digital texts. Four key features brought to the fore with new media – personalization, creativity, haptic feedback and interactivity – are discussed in detail, to prompt a broader outlook on the enduring key issues in early years literacy education.

Unlike generations before them, today's children can engage with texts in various forms and formats and can become part of a story experience in various multimodal, hybridized ways. In addition to physical books, children's texts and narratives are available on several devices (e.g. iPads, Kindles, Wiis, Xboxes), with each platform affording a different experience of stories, text and narrative.

The emergence of new reading platforms (such as Kindles and iPads) on the market in the early 2000s has been accompanied by an emergence of new terms to describe their affordances and accompanying practices. The so-called 'new media' encompass a variety of functions and possibilities with new technologies, including those for reading and writing, and the term 'new literacies' is used to describe the range of digital, multimodal ways of meaning-making with texts in the twenty-first century. I begin this chapter by specifying what new media and new literacies mean in the context of early literacy and discuss the old dichotomized view of positive and negative influences of new media on children's early language and literacy development. This brings to the fore four issues accentuated through new media and emergent research on their benefits: personalization, creativity, haptic feedback and interactivity. I discuss each feature in detail, with emphasis placed on the extent to which they constitute new objects of study and practical concern. I outline how the focus on specific affordances of new media for specific kinds of literacy can cultivate a broader outlook on the overall merit of technologies for children's reading and writing. The chapter concludes with an outline of the additional work necessary to come to a better understanding of the affordances of new *and* old media for children's literacy now, and in the future.

New media

Since the early 2000s, children's books have begun to emerge on iPads as storybook apps or ibooks and on various Android tablets and smartphones as digital or enhanced e-books. National surveys in Western countries indicate that increasingly young children are accessing texts and narratives in digital in addition to printed format. In the UK, data from Ofcom (2013) suggest that 39 per cent of three- and four-year-old children now use a tablet computer at home. In the USA, the percentage of children who have read an e-book increased across all age groups between 2010 and 2014 (25 per cent vs. 61 per cent; Scholastic, 2014). In Australia, 45 per cent of eight-year-olds use screen-based media for longer than two hours a day (Houghton et al., 2015). These numbers increase year on year and over the globe. Some large-scale initiatives (e.g. One Laptop per Child; see Negroponte et al., 2006) have brought digital books to the developing world, contributing to the rise in availability and increased use of new technologies among young children outside the USA or UK. In addition, the price of mobile phones and simple tablets has gone down significantly, allowing for a widespread use of mobile technologies on a global scale. Availability and accessibility ought not to be confused with quality of interaction. There is evidence that even in developed countries such as the USA, there are the so-called access and participation gaps in low-income families (Rideout and Katz, 2016), which constrain the quality of interaction and educational benefits derived from children's engagement with technologies. In developing countries, the complexity of merging the knowledge of the West with the physical infrastructure of the developing world often means that the benefits are often not evident or sustained (Kraemer et al., 2009). What remains a fact is that increasingly young children are engaging with texts and narratives in a digital format, that this is a trend across the world and that it has implications for their early literacy.

What is also clear is that the technology development is advancing at a rate faster than at any time in history. Researchers cannot leapfrog over old infrastructure models in schools and research institutions. Consequently, there is a growing gap between practice and research in relation to new technologies in all areas, including early literacy (Robb et al., 2011). Teachers and caregivers are regularly 'bombarded' with conflicting advice concerning whether and how to use new media with young children and often, in the absence of empirically based guidelines, they tend to follow advice from technology journalists rather than researchers. Inadvertently, this may lead to the introduction of inconsistencies into practice and the neglect of important functions of technology for young children's development (Brooker and Siraj-Blatchford, 2002). It has also led to several myths developed around the benefits and limitations of new media, including the popular notion that new media bring unprecedented opportunities which can revolutionize education (see Selwyn, 2007 for a discussion on this topic). While it is true that the devices and forms of education delivery are new (for example, iPads have been on the market since 2010), what is often not new are the *ways* in which these new tools are used in school settings. Several reports document that in many school settings, teachers use new media in the same way as they used their old media, a challenge all too familiar to technology researchers and educators (Crook, 1998, 2001).

This leads us to the question of what new media actually mean and the importance of specifying what is *new* about them: is it the new way of representing content or is it the actual usage? In the case of early literacy, are new media 'new' because, for example, they represent stories as interactive short films specifically designed for iPads? Or are they new because the way we read these stories is fundamentally different from our previous way of engaging with stories? In these reflections, it is important to specify whether we focus on the specific technology underlying the media or its actual usage or its context of use. As for the technology underlying or generating new media, the following platforms have become available since the early 2000s: smartphones and tablets, wearable technologies (e.g. activity trackers) and augmented reality technologies. When thinking about the usage of these new technologies, the many media supported by the technology include 'computer and video games (both casual and serious types), virtual reality environments, social networks, web sites, mobile devices, blogs, and podcasts' (Kron et al., 2010: 2). In terms of context of use, new media can be used for various purposes in various environments, including home and school or formal and informal learning contexts (see Falloon and Khoo, 2014).

In this chapter, the focus is on the purpose of nurturing children's early literacy skills (in their traditional as well as contemporary sense), and on media use in children's homes and schools. Given this focus, I selectively focus on literature that is built around children's digital books, available on a range of platforms, supporting various usage patterns in various contexts.

Children's digital books

Children's digital books range from multimodal digital displays of traditional stories to highly interactive new story experiences. Often called e-books and apps, digital books can be accessed on portable touch-screen technologies (tablets, smartphones, mini tablet computers) or simple e-readers (Kindles, Nooks or Leapsters). These devices can display a given text or story in sound, pictures and text, with a varying degree of customization and personalization options. Depending on the interactivity embedded in a specific digital book, there are varying degrees of nurturing a child's creativity, imagination, hands-on experiences and intrinsic motivation to read. This chapter focuses specifically on the digital books that display the narrative in a multimodal way (i.e. pictures, text and sound) and with which children can interact via touch, in addition to sound and visual mode of interaction.

Before I delve into the potential of such digital books for supporting children's literacies, it is important to acknowledge the current debate about their appropriateness for young children. Digital books are part of the new frontier of technologies which are often scrutinized for their value and developmentally appropriate content. The current research and policy consensus is that for children under the age of two, there is little additional benefit of using digital books instead of physical books (see Brown, 2015). For children aged two years above, there is no officially agreed minimal age of use, with very contrasting views in terms of whether technology helps (e.g. Wolfe and Flewitt, 2010), damages (e.g. Greenfield, 2004) or enriches (Plowman et al., 2010) children's early learning. The stance taken in this chapter is that given the ubiquity and frequent use of technology among children of preschool age, the question of whether children's digital books are good or bad is essentially beside the point. Digital books should not replace but enrich children's literacy experiences. The age at which digital books are introduced to an individual child depends on the child's abilities and family preferences. The real question then is how we can effectively integrate digital with traditional reading resources. Before attempting to answer this question, it is important to agree on a definition of new literacy or new literacies.

New literacies

As other chapters in the book have indicated, the definition of literacy is in the process of flux, with concepts such as multiliteracies (Cazden et al., 1996), digital literacy

(Merchant, 2007), information literacy (Eisenberg et al., 2004) and new literacies (Street, 1998) extending the traditional definition of literacy (see Clare Wood's chapter in this volume). The key issue that draws these various concepts together is the attempt to understand the multitude of ways in which today's children engage with text presented on digital platforms. To engage with text and narrative represented in multiple forms and formats requires a wider set of skills than to engage with text in the print format. Therefore, 'literacies' in the plural rather than 'literacy' in the singular helps keep the focus on the multiple ways in which children make meaning of texts represented on various platforms available to them. These literacies encompass a range of competencies, including touch-typing and navigating through a complex landscape of textual, visual and audio meanings, as well as interfaces activated through various kinds of finger swipes, clicks and taps. Thanks to advanced logographic and haptic navigation options in some of the devices (e.g. the latest iPad version), increasingly young children can lead complex literacy lives without the ability to spell or decode. In addition, the digital medium allows manipulation through drawing (aka visual texts) and/or recording (aka spoken texts), which makes it easier for young children to manage specific book functions and access content from within, as well as outside, their favourite titles. Moreover, considering the recent trends in the app development for adult users, it is likely that gesture and simple sounds will become important engagement mechanisms for young children who might not be able to, or who choose not to, manipulate digital books through speech or tapping.

Despite the wider recognition of multiple literacies, when it comes to digital books and new technologies more generally, there is often a tendency to plummet into black-and-white thinking about the role of print versus digital books rather than their synergistic potential for innovation. As mentioned, the danger of such an approach is that it creates a conflict between research and practice and confusion for parents/educators. Children's digital books are a hybrid of previous and new media (Kucirkova, 2014b) and separating them might create disjoint experiences for the children. In contrast, keeping the digital and print books, with their benefits and limitations, together can create a spectrum of possibilities for innovation. In particular, if researchers approach new literacies from the point of view of new as well as old media, they could catalyse innovative research which contributes to a synergistic and more holistic curriculum of early literacy. Thus, if we wish to foster children's current and future literacy skills, we need to be 'mindful of issues related to the evaluation of new and traditional literacy practices' (Kucirkova, 2013).

Thus far, the potential of digital books to support children's early literacy has been divided into investigations preserving traditional theoretical frameworks of literacy and those following the newer definition of new literacies. Similarly in school contexts, the focus has been on traditional literacy skills while in children's homes book engagement often takes place with new literacies. Traditional literacy practices include writing development, phonological abilities, independent reading (Labbo, 2006) and traditional outcome measures related to shared reading include story comprehension or vocabulary development (see Chapter 22). There is a growing body of evidence concerned with the benefits of digital book reading measured according to traditional literacy practices and outcome measures (see, e.g. Korat and Shamir, 2012; Parish-Morris et al., 2013). Also, there seems to be ample official guidance concerning how teachers or caregivers can support children's development for traditional (e.g. Dickinson and De Temple, 1998) or new literacies (e.g. Revelle et al., 2007). What is currently missing in the literature is advice on how to use digital and print books to nurture children's traditional as well as new literacy skills. Also, how can digital and print books *jointly* support children's traditional literacy skills as well as their *new* literacies?

If we wish to understand how print and digital books support traditional (e.g. reading and writing in print media) as well as new literacies (e.g. navigating digital interactive books), we need to become more nuanced in the way we think about the main features of digital books and about the ways in which they might enrich rather than disrupt or replace previous formats. Given that literacies are multifaceted, we need to explore multiple forms of engagement and identify the common features that cut across the boundaries between new and old media and new and old literacies. The current thinking is to direct practice and research more towards a synergistic understanding of digital books and, in the remainder of the chapter, I outline how it can be further developed. I begin with a short overview of how such an understanding came about in my own work.

Key features of children's digital books

In 2014, I became involved in a project between Book Trust (the UK's largest literacy charity) and The Open University (my home institution at that time), which aimed to identify the key facets of children's engagement with digital books and offer a 'partnership' approach for digital and print books (Kucirkova, 2014a). As part of the project, we ran several workshops and focus groups with teachers and children under the age of eight across the UK, with the aim of identifying the key influences of digital books on the child–caregiver shared reading experience and children's budding literacy. We were keen to crowdsource ideas and keep the dialogue open to practitioners and parents worldwide. The project was therefore accompanied by a series of research blogs freely accessible on the Booktrust website with the possibility to comment on content (www.booktrust.org.uk/).

In these research blogs, I documented the teachers' and children's perspectives which we collected throughout the project, and summarized literature and current thinking around some key issues in relation to the use of digital books with preschoolers. I share here some of the main points from these blogs, which revolved around the key defining features of digital books and their influences on early and new literacy. There were four main features that were highlighted in these discussions and that are particularly relevant for early literacy development: personalization, creativity, haptic feedback and interactivity.

Personalization

A comparison of key features of print books, simple electronic books available for desktop computers and highly interactive digital books available for tablets reveals that they share many similarities. However, their key difference is personalization, or the possibility to personalize a narrative to a child's needs, preferences and interests. For digital interactive books personalization is available via multimedia and increasingly also connected to augmented and virtual reality.

Although in practice, customization and personalization are often used interchangeably, there is an important conceptual difference between the two. Children's digital books can be *customized* in terms of their display. For example, an image can be made bigger or the font can be enlarged. Children's digital books available for tablets and iPads can be *personalized* in terms of their multimodal content. For instance, children can insert their own voice-overs to accompany a given text, or they can add their 'selfies' to the illustrations of a favourite story. Clearly, children are likely to be more motivated to engage with books that feature content they have created themselves or others have created specifically for them. For instance, a child is more likely to engage with a digital book that features a recording of their parent than a pre-recorded automated voice. It is also clear, however, that adding the user's own contents may exert a motivational influence that is not related to literacy but to other aspects of a child's early development, such as self-esteem or self-awareness (Demoulin, 1999, 2001). In addition, the sensitive nature of children's marketization and the growing commercial interest in personalizable products (Arora et al., 2008) make it important for adults to support and carefully navigate the personalization options *together with* the children. Considering the wider context of personalized books, it is no secret that personalization is also a powerful marketing tactic, with many products and services tailored to appeal to young children. Adults therefore need to help children strike a judicious balance between personalized and non-personalized stories, given that children need both for holistic education.

It is also important that teachers, parents and other caregivers and educators reflect on the extent to which children create their own stories or merely select pre-established story elements. Apps with pre-established story templates, story characters or customizable voice-overs may be engaging or entertaining but, in terms of honouring children's voices, they are merely guiding children's story-making in accordance with the publisher/app producer. What is important to bear in mind is the difference between genuine and superficial personalization options. Open-ended story apps, such as tablet book-making applications (e.g. My Story™, Our Story™, Book Creator™), enable children to create stories based on their own texts, pictures or sounds. The more children add their own story extensions, the more they can become empowered (Harrison, 2003) and engaged in the story (Kucirkova et al., 2012). However, the more a book is personalized, the more it means that children can become self-centred in their speech when they talk about the books' contents with an adult (Kucirkova et al., 2014a). Sénéchal in this volume outlines how children acquire new vocabulary from books, which underlies the importance of rich text and new vocabulary in children's books.

Again, the importance of careful guidance provided by parents or educators is paramount here as adults can use a number of interactive techniques to guide the child through the book experience. Decades of research on effective reading with young children and *print* books show that children whose parents ask questions during book reading and link the content to their lives as well as wider concepts benefit more from the reading experience (DeBaryshe, 1995) and have improved literacy (Senechal and LeFevre, 2002). Personalization is thus a feature that has become more dominant with digital books given the varied personalization options these offer, but its role in the reading experience has not changed: to motivate the child and to ensure that children become aware of the connections between the story contents and their own and others' lives.

Creativity

Creativity has become one of the key considerations when trying to ascertain whether a digital book is of value to young children (see, e.g., Children's Technology Review http://childrenstech.com/blog/archives/tag/creativity). Creativity is a complex and somehow elusive phenomenon, often used to describe the ability to think about new ways of solving a problem or finding an alternative route to reach an end goal (Goleman et al., 1992). As Young (1985) points out, some believe that creativity is a gift, while others consider it a skill that can be nurtured and developed with the right amount of support and guidance from others. A key component of Craft's (2005) definition of creativity is the capacity to envision solutions that move from 'what is' to 'what might be'. Craft (2001) coined the term 'possibility thinking' which covers the various kinds of dispositions related to creativity, including children's capacity to ask questions, play, immerse themselves in an activity, imagine alternative solutions, make connections, take risks and generate innovative ideas. To facilitate children's possibility thinking at home and in schools, educators and caregivers need to provide children with opportunities for exploratory and combinatory play and facilitate environments that foreground 'the combination of relevance, ownership and control' (Jeffrey and Craft, 2004).

In a study with 40 preschoolers, Kucirkova and colleagues (Kucirkova et al., 2014b) compared children's use of exploratory talk (which includes asking questions and providing reasons; see Mercer and Wegerif, 1999) with open-ended versus closed digital books. Quantitative and qualitative indices of children's engagement suggested that with open-ended digital books where children could add their own texts, sounds and pictures, children used more exploratory talk. Joint problem-solving and collaborative engagement was also apparent when children were given the opportunity to add their own captions to digital photographs. It thus seems to be the case that digital books which do not limit children's story-expression through template-based approaches are more likely to support children's collaboration with others and their discussion of ideas and possibilities.

This is not dissimilar from research with print books and hand-written texts, where numerous studies showed that learning contexts that are open to building upon the expertise of children and that incorporate different forms of text and different kinds of knowledge are more likely to develop and capitalize upon creative and productive educational curricula (Chappell et al., 2012; Cremin et al., 2013).

Haptic representation

When thinking about new literacies facilitated with new media, we need to reflect on the role of touch and the extent to which haptic engagement with digital books is different from children's experiences with a print book and what this difference might mean for children's early literacy. Research conducted with traditional books found that when it comes to book reading and young children, touch is extremely important to enrich the reading experience. The so-called touchy-feely books with animals' fur, ribbons or small mirrors, or the little holes in peekaboo books, have been designed to support young children's physical exploration of various textures and sizes and help develop their fine motor skills (Henderson and Peholski, 2006). The touch-interactive elements in the book are crucial to enable children to develop general as well as book-specific fine motor skills, including page-turning and positioning the book at a good angle for viewing/reading (Harms et al., 1998). As such, children who are given the opportunity to manipulate objects and experience their textures can often demonstrate implicit knowledge that they may not yet be able to verbalize.

As I discussed with teachers and on the Book Trust blogs, with digital books a gentle touch initiates a very different response than one could expect from a non-digital object. Although the surface and texture is the same for all digital books (i.e. that of a tablet or e-reader), it generates a different response when tapped or touched. For instance, touching the right corner of one digital book may link children to the next page. In another digital book, a circular movement with a finger may activate a pre-recorded voice-over for their favourite book character. In another e-book, sliding a button may activate the 'buy more' button for purchasing new clothes for their book avatars. Parents, educators and other caregivers can help children to distinguish the complex consequences resulting from touching or tapping a 'hot spot' in a digital book, and point them towards resources where touching a specific item is also educationally rewarding. Haptic manipulation of digital skills is thus becoming a new kind of 'digital literacy skill', which gets more complex as children encounter different touch-manipulatable digital texts and interact with different touch-screen technologies.

For children with special educational needs, the possibility to interact with a digital book through touch is a particularly valuable way of communicating their feelings around a story and self-managing the experience. Flewitt et al. (2014) examined how the gestural and sensory experience of touch can enable young learners with moderate to complex physical and/or cognitive disability to engage in independent engagement with digital books. In a case study with a diverse group of students aged 3 to 19 years with a range of complex learning difficulties, we found that the sensory and kinaesthetic experience of human touch enhanced the students' motivation, control and independence when engaged in literacy endeavours with digital books, notably if these allowed them to freely communicate their feelings. For instance, when children in the class created book covers for their self-made digital stories, they used various advanced features provided by the tablet (e.g. checking for potential grammatical errors with the spell checker, experimenting with font and colour options), using their fingertips to drag each element around the screen. This would not be possible with traditional literacy resources which do not afford this level of aesthetic appraisal of a piece of text and the corresponding literacy engagement options through touch.

Thus, although the role of haptic engagement in children's typical early literacy engagement has been by and large under-theorized, its role in new literacies and new media is becoming more important (see Mackey, 2016).

Interactivity

Another feature brought to the fore with the digital medium is interactivity. Interactivity refers to the child's interactivity with the text, and the potential interactivity between a child and adult as they read the text together. While with print books, interactivity was mainly of a physical nature, the way digital books interact with the emerging reader is different. As others have pointed out (Cordero et al., 2015), interactivity or physical engagement with a book are not novel features belonging to digital books only – they have been embedded in different forms in print books before. What is new is their representation in the digital book and the potential impact they could have on the child and their literacy development. With print books, children have long been able to interact with pop-up books such as *Pretty Polly* (Bingham and Nesbit, 1897), or in question-and-answer books (e.g. *Don't Let the Pigeon Drive the Bus*, Willems, 2003). Digital books offer educational interactivity features, for instance scaffolding for the emerging reader (e.g. highlighting the text when each word is read aloud) or let the child choose independently how to advance the story (e.g. by choosing alternative story endings). This could be facilitated by the adult when reading a book, so the child is more independent with an interactive digital book. In addition, augmented reality apps, which overlay digital elements on to real objects as viewed (through the device's camera) on the screen, allow children to interact with the story in a three-dimensional multimodal and multi-media way.

Emergent research with digital books shows that there is a fine line between interactive features engaging children and distracting them from the book. Kim (2014) compared parent–child interaction when reading print, digital and handheld electronic storybooks. Systemic functional linguistics (SFL) showed that the talk of 20 parent–child dyads was different across the contexts, with some digital features of the electronic and digital books supporting more technology-oriented talk rather than talk concerned with the meaning of the stories. With too much interactivity, children spend the reading time playing the game or engaging with the interactive features and miss many of the educational elements embedded in high-quality children's books. These findings are not dissimilar from findings yielded by research concerned with print books. An important study by Ganea et al. (2008) indicates that learning (as measured by how well 15- and 18-month-olds can extend newly learned labels both from pictures to objects and from objects to pictures) from print picture books is facilitated if the books are simple and non-manipulable and contain realistic illustrations.

Bus et al. (2015) and Takacs et al. (2015) reviewed the effects of interactivity in enhanced digital books as well as simpler e-books for desktop PCs and found that, overall, interactive features like games, hotspots and dictionaries embedded in books, impede children's performance on tests of vocabulary and story comprehension. However, some interactive features, such as animated pictures, music and sound effects, which are compatible with the story, were found to be beneficial for children's story comprehension and expressive vocabulary. Thus, interactivity can be beneficial to children's learning from digital books (when evaluated from the perspective of traditional reading skills), but it is important to differentiate the various kinds of interactivity available and their alignment with the storyline.

This research also highlights that interactivity is a two-way variable; that it affects the child in terms of independent as well as shared book reading. While there are interactivity options embedded in the book, research also needs to be mindful of the child's interactive engagement with the adult reading the book with him or her. As we know from research with print books, the social aspect of reading books with adults or with an older child is vitally important to children's language development (Snow, 1976, 1993). When children are learning to read from digital books with embedded feedback, the parent–child dynamic is affected which may have important learning implications. In 2013, Parish-Morris et al. explored the differences between reading styles when parents and children read a print book as compared to a story presented on a children's touch-sensitive electronic console book. The more electronic features there were in the book, the less parents engaged in supportive reading styles and the lower the children's overall story comprehension. When thinking about interactivity, it is therefore crucial to consider not only its influence on a child's independent engagement but also its effects on parent–child joint interaction.

Future directions

Digital books foreground several features of early literacy engagement which are becoming the focus of research concerned with new as well as traditional forms of book reading with young children. If researchers and practitioners engage in questions around how the new features of digital books can complement learning from the printed page, they can move closer to a considered dialogue around potential benefits and limitations of digital books on children's emergent literacy in the novel as well as traditional sense. One should also bear in mind that there is some overlap between old and new practices and therefore scope to combine some of the educational outcomes and children's skills, for example engagement with the material or critical thinking (Grisham et al., 2014).

Given the newness of the medium, the benefits/limitations analysis remains by and large hypothetical. However, given the urgency of the need to inform practitioners and children's parents about the usefulness of these tools for young children, I provide some practical points below that could be considered by practitioners and policy-makers. These are based on several consensus statements and recommendations in the literature as well as on theoretical and expert opinion.

Practical implications

On a daily basis, practitioners and caregivers are faced with the question of which digital book to offer to their child, which digital reading platform to invest in and how to align it with specific curricular objectives or their child's specific needs. What are the key considerations for book and reading platform use with young children in light of their developing literacy skills?

The potential benefits of digital books on young children's early literacy are several: interactive digital books can provide an impetus for parents to interact with children in ways that could be mutually enjoyable and beneficial. The technology means that storybook apps offer a means to decrease the asymmetry of adults reading and children listening, instead providing opportunities for both parent and child to jointly discover meaning embedded in an app or e-book. On a wider level, the global market for digital books offers the potential for a much easier production of international variants of the same book. Digital storybooks can more effectively connect remote communities and bring local stories to global audiences. With easy personalization options embedded in many digital books, children can become book authors but also book heroes with a few taps. Parents can create stories together with their children, incorporating photos of family members or audio-recordings. Some basic customization features (such as enlarging the text or changing the background colour) make engagement easier for those who are not confident readers. Similarly, for children with attention difficulties, feedback embedded in the digital books may help capture their attention and thus motivate them to engage with a piece of text.

However, at the time of writing this chapter, we are far from realizing this potential of digital books. Research is predominantly concerned with traditional outcome measures of book reading and there is a very limited range of quality texts designed for the digital multimedia format. In research, we need to be asking more ambitious questions around children's individual and shared reading engagement with digital books, how this dovetails with their engagement with physical books and impacts their development of reading, writing, language, story comprehension *as well as* their haptic engagement, awareness of personalization options, ability to navigate interactive features and be creative. When supporting children's reading for pleasure or reading for enjoyment, we need to be mindful of the six key facets of engagement brought to fore with digital books: affective, creative, interactive, shared, sustained and personalized reading engagements (Kucirkova et al., 2015b). These facets do not only support children's reading for pleasure but are also aligned with the '4Ps of digital childhood' – plurality of identities (people, places, activities, literacies), possibility-awareness (of what might be invented, of access options, of learning by doing and of active engagement), playfulness of engagement (the exploratory drive) and participation, which Craft (2011: 33) theorized as the key features of changing childhood and youth in the digital revolution.

Currently, and disappointingly, too many children's e-books seem to compromise well-established book principles for the sake of novelty. There are children's book apps that are very 'game-like' (full of entertainment features) but supplemented with only formulaic text. At the other end of the spectrum, we have digital books that are very text-heavy, with only a few engaging features. In addition, far too many decisions in the children's digital book market are dictated by cost rather than the affordances of the various media currently available, and the creative potential for children's learning and enjoyment. Therefore, practitioners and parents need to be aware of some important limitations of new media. While in some instances augmented reality apps can enhance a story experience, in others they may take away the impetus for a child's own imagination. Personalized digital books can be both motivating and great fun – but too much personalization may become self-absorbing. Similarly, while digital books with several interactive features can involve and empower children, too many bells and whistles may simply overwhelm them. There is also a real concern among educators that innovative digital experiences with text at home are radically different from children's experiences with texts at school, which might divide instead of connect their home–school lives.

Practitioners play a vital role in ensuring that the benefits and limitations of digital books are adequately understood and shared with children. They also play a crucial role in helping children to balance their interactions with print and digital media. Currently, the guidance on how to merge digital with print books to support old as well as new literacies is very limited. It is important that children's 'reading diet' includes both and merges practices and skills necessary for children's meaningful engagement. Many teachers develop their own strategies to achieve a healthy balance. For instance, in our project (Kucirkova et al., 2015a), the teachers employed digital books to support children's hand-writing skills: teachers used digital pictures and digital recordings as stimuli for the writing activity. To teach children different genres, they used the digital books with editable text. For instance, children inserted a caption below a photograph in the digital book or added a typed label to their own digital drawings. As such, they became aware of the various affordances of the different media and how they can be used in different contexts, fulfilling different purposes.

Future research directions

In an increasingly globalized world and in the context of fluid notions of literacy, one of the most important future research directions is community literacy which brings together cross-generational and cross-cultural perspectives (see the seminal work of Gonzales et al., 2013). A community approach can ensure that new literacies become a shared concern among old and young. All too often, elderly members of the community, including children's grand-parents and senior teachers, hesitate to become part of technology-mediated activities. Part of their hesitation follows naturally from some of the rhetoric that has surrounded the discussion of 'digital natives'. Prensky (2001) and followers speak of younger generations in terms of digital natives as if they come naturally to new technologies. While this might be helpful to highlight young children's natural disposition to confidently approach and easily manipulate touch-screen devices, the language of 'digital natives' and 'digital immigrants' implies a divide and a homogeneous group of children. This shifts the focus to what separates the older and younger generation rather than looking for points of conjunction and often leads to the perception that all children are digitally savvy and skilled. If we focus on specific features of digital and print books, such as personalization, creativity, haptic feedback and interactivity, that is features that are relevant to children's current and past literacies, we are more likely to recognize commonalities across practices and populations.

A community approach to the study of digital books implies synergy between old and new forms of engagement with texts and, in addition, a collaborative stance among all stakeholders. It is only through collaboration and high-quality public scholarship that we can strengthen the ties between academia and book producers (or software designers) and between teachers and policy-makers. To fast forward the gap between available research evidence and the range of digital books advertised as educational and marketed for young children (Shuler, 2009), the principal stakeholders need to closely collaborate with each other. In this collaboration, we need to ensure that media released on the market fulfil criteria of effective interaction, support effective learning practices and, crucially, that the child's voice is foregrounded.

If we position the reader, that is the child, at the centre of all discussions and decisions, the potential for innovation is enormous: there could be greater democratization of literacy ownership, with more children authoring the story contents and the potential for more printed stories to originate and propagate in multilingual and multicultural communities (Kucirkova, 2016). This would also imply a greater variety of formats and forms, given that children, just as adults (Zhang and Kudva, 2014), can use digital and paper-based books for different purposes (O'Donnell and Hallam, 2014). For digital books in particular, children's contribution would be critical, given that children understand and use technology differently than adults. The tradition of involving children in research and product development is not new (see Kellett, 2005), but digital books and comparable technologies highlight its need and offer several novel possibilities for its realization.

In conclusion, new media is a broad concept which, in relation to supporting children's early literacy, includes digital books and their use in home and school context. Digital books can be deployed to support children's new literacies, such as meaning making with multimedia representation of texts and narratives. Although the term 'new' implies novelty, it would be more accurate to think of these tools and practices as foregrounding certain new features. A community-oriented, collaborative stance towards the role of new features in children's development of traditional and new literacies can illuminate the conditions in which individual children benefit most.

References

Arora, N., Dreze, X., Ghose, A., Hess, J. D., Iyengar, R., Jing, B. and Zhang, Z. J. (2008). Putting one-to-one marketing to work: Personalization, customization, and choice. *Marketing Letters, 19*(3–4), 305–321.

Bingham, C and Nesbit, E (1897) *Pretty Polly, A Novel Panorama Picture Book.* London: Ernest Nister.

Brooker, L. and Siraj-Blatchford, J. (2002). 'Click on Miaow!': How children of three and four years experience the nursery computer. *Contemporary Issues in Early Childhood, 3*(2), 251–273.

Brown, A., Shifrin, D. L. and Hill, D. L. (2015). Beyond 'turn it off': How to advise families on media use. *AAP News, 36*(10), 54–54.

Bus, A. G., Takacs, Z. K. and Kegel, C. A. (2015). Affordances and limitations of electronic storybooks for young children's emergent literacy. *Developmental Review, 35*, 79–97.

Cazden, C., Cope, B., Fairclough, N., Gee, J., Kalantzis, M., Kress, G. and Nakata, M. (1996). A pedagogy of multiliteracies: Designing social futures. *Harvard Educational Review, 66*(1), 60–92.

Chappell, K., Craft, A. R., Rolfe, L. and Jobbins, V. (2012). Humanizing creativity: Valuing our journeys of becoming. *International Journal of Education & the Arts, 13*(8). Retrieved December 2015 from www.ijea.org/v13n8/.

Cordero, K., Nussbaum, M., Ibaseta, V., Otaíza, M. J., Gleisner, S., González, S. and Carland, C. (2015). Read Create Share (RCS): A new digital tool for interactive reading and writing. *Computers & Education, 82*, 486–496.

Craft, A. (2001). Little 0 creativity. In A. Craft, B. Jeffrey and M. Leibling (eds), *Creativity in Education* (pp. 45–62). London: A&C Black.

Craft, A. (ed.). (2005). *Creativity in Schools: Tensions and Dilemmas.* London: Psychology Press.

Craft, A. (2011). *Creativity and Education Futures: Learning in a Digital Age.* Stoke-on-Trent: Trentham Books.

Cremin, T., Chappell, K. and Craft, A. (2013). Reciprocity between narrative, questioning and imagination in the early and primary years: Examining the role of narrative in possibility thinking. *Thinking Skills and Creativity, 9*, 135–151.

Crook, C. (1998). Children as computer users: The case of collaborative learning. *Computers & Education, 30*(3), 237–247.

Crook, C. (2001). The social character of knowing and learning: Implications of cultural psychology for educational technology. *Journal of Information Technology for Teacher Education*, *10*(1–2), 19–36.

DeBaryshe, B. D. (1995). Maternal belief systems: Linchpin in the home reading process. *Journal of Applied Developmental Psychology*, *16*(1), 1–20.

Demoulin, D. F. (1999). A personalized development of self-concept for beginning readers. *Education*, *120*(1), 14.

DeMoulin, D. F. (2001). The hidden value of personalization and rhyme in reading. *Reading Improvement*, *38*(3), 116–118.

Dickinson, D. K. and De Temple, J. (1998). Putting parents in the picture: Maternal reports of preschoolers' literacy as a predictor of early reading. *Early Childhood Research Quarterly*, *13*(2), 241–261.

Eisenberg, M. B., Lowe, C. A. and Spitzer, K. L. (2004). *Information Literacy: Essential Skills for the Information Age*. Westport, CT: Greenwood.

Falloon, G. and Khoo, E. (2014). Exploring young students' talk in iPad-supported collaborative learning environments. *Computers & Education*, *77*, 13–28.

Flewitt, R.S., Kucirkova, N. and Messer, D. (2014) Touching the virtual, touching the real: iPads and enabling literacy for students with learning disabilities. *The Australian Journal of Language and Literacy*, Special Issue, *37*(2), 107–116.

Ganea, P. A., Pickard, M. B. and DeLoache, J. S. (2008). Transfer between picture books and the real world by very young children. *Journal of Cognition and Development*, *9*(1), 46–66.

Goleman, D., Kaufman, P. and Ray, M. L. (1992). *The Creative Spirit*. New York: Dutton.

González, N., Moll, L. C. and Amanti, C. (eds). (2013). *Funds of Knowledge: Theorizing Practices in Households, Communities, and Classrooms*. Abingdon: Routledge.

Greenfield, S. (2004). *Tomorrow's People: How 21st-Century Technology Is Changing the Way We Think and Feel*. London: Penguin.

Grisham, D.l., Lapp, D., Wolsey, T. D. and Vaca, J. (2014). Combining print and visual information via eposters: generating and displaying learning. *JSC*, *5*(1), 59–75.

Harms, T., Clifford, R. M. and Cryer, D. (1998). *Early Childhood Environment Rating Scale*. New York: Teachers College Press.

Harrison, C. (2003). *Understanding Reading Development*. London: Sage.

Henderson, A. and Pehoski, C. (eds) (2006). *Hand Function in the Child: Foundations for Remediation*. St Louis, MO: Elsevier Health Sciences.

Houghton, S., Hunter, S. C., Rosenberg, M., Wood, L., Zadow, C., Martin, K. and Shilton, T. (2015). Virtually impossible: Limiting Australian children and adolescents daily screen based media use. *BMC Public Health*, *15*(1). Available only online, doi:10.1186/1471-2458-15-5.

Jeffrey, B. and Craft, A. (2004). Teaching creatively and teaching for creativity: Distinctions and relationships. *Educational Studies*, *30*(1), 77–87.

Kellett, M. (2005). *How to Develop Children as Researchers: A Step by Step Guide to Teaching the Research Process*. London: Sage.

Kim, J. E. (2014). Parent–child shared reading: The affordances of print, digital, and hand-held electronic storybooks. Doctoral dissertation, University of British Columbia, Vancouver.

Korat, O. and Shamir, A. (2012). Direct and indirect teaching: Using e-books for supporting vocabulary, word reading, and story comprehension for young children. *Journal of Educational Computing Research*, *46*(2), 135–152.

Kraemer, K. L., Dedrick, J. and Sharma, P. (2009). One laptop per child: Vision vs. reality. *Communications of the ACM*, *52*(6), 66–73.

Kron, F. W., Gjerde, C. L., Sen, A. and Fetters, M. D. (2010). Medical student attitudes toward video games and related new media technologies in medical education. *BMC Medical Education*, *10*(1), 10–50.

Kucirkova, N. (2013). Children's interactions with iPad books: Research chapters still to be written. *Frontiers in Psychology*, *4*, 1–3. Available from www.ncbi.nlm.nih.gov/pmc/articles/PMC3871707/.

Kucirkova, N. (2014a). Booktrust Research Blogs documenting the Open University–Booktrust Research Project, www.booktrust.org.uk/d/news-and-blogs/blogs/booktrust/author/562/.

Kucirkova, N. (2014b). Shiny APpy children, *The Guardian*. Available from www.theguardian.com/science/head-quarters/2014/dec/15/shiny-appy-children.

Kucirkova, N. (2016). Personalisation: A theoretical possibility to reinvigorate children's interest in storybook reading and facilitate greater book diversity. *Contemporary Issues in Early Childhood*, 17(3), 304–316.

Kucirkova, N., Littleton, K., AirWatch, Aerohive and Swallowfield Lower School (2015a) The 'Remember' Project: Using mobile technologies for community story creation. Paper presented at the London Book Fair, London.

Kucirkova, N., Littleton, K. and Cremin, T. (2015b). Young children's reading for pleasure with digital books: Six key facets of engagement. *Cambridge Journal of Education*. doi:10.1080/0305764X.2015.1118441.

Kucirkova, N., Messer, D. and Sheehy, K. (2014a). The effects of personalization on young children's spontaneous speech during shared book reading. *Journal of Pragmatics*, 71, 45–55, doi:http://dx.doi.org/10.1016/j.pragma.2014.07.007.

Kucirkova, N., Messer, D., Sheehy, K. and Fernandez-Panadero, C. (2014b). Children's engagement with educational iPad apps: Insights from a Spanish classroom, *Computers & Education*, 71, 175–184.

Kucirkova, N., Messer, D. and Whitelock, D. (2012) Parents reading with their toddlers: The role of personalization in book engagement. *Journal of Early Childhood Literacy*, 13(4), 445–470.

Labbo, L. D. (2006). Literacy pedagogy and computer technologies: Towards solving the puzzle of current and future classroom practices. *Australian Journal of Language and Literacy*, 29(3), 199–210. Available from: www.alea.edu.au/site-content/publications/documents/ajll/Labbo.pdf.

Mackey, M. (2016). Literacy as material engagement: the abstract, tangible and mundane ingredients of childhood reading. *Literacy*, 50(3), 166–172.

Mercer, N. and Wegerif, R. (1999). Is 'exploratory talk' productive talk? In K. Littleton and P. Light (eds), *Learning with Computers: Analysing Productive Interaction* (pp. 79–102). London: Psychology Press.

Merchant, G. (2007). Writing the future in the digital age. *Literacy*, 41(3), 118–128.

Negroponte, N., Bender, W., Battro, A. and Cavallo, D. (2006). One laptop per child. Video resource available from: http://one.laptop.org/about/mission.

O'Donnell B. and Hallam S. (2014). Read for my school: Digital versus paper books. Paper presented at the London Book Fair Conference, London.

Ofcom (2013). UK Communications Market Report, UK Mobile Phone Usage Statistics, London.

Parish-Morris, J., Mahajan, N., Hirsh-Pasek, K., Golinkoff, R. M. and Collins, M. F. (2013). Once upon a time: Parent–child dialogue and storybook reading in the electronic era. *Mind, Brain, and Education*, 7(3), 200–211.

Plowman, L., Stephen, C. and McPake, J. (2010). *Growing up with Technology: Young Children Learning in a Digital World*. London: Routledge.

Prensky, M. (2001). Digital natives, digital immigrants part 1. *On the Horizon*, 9(5), 1–6.

Revelle, G., Reardon, E., Green, M. M., Betancourt, J. and Kotler, J. (2007). The use of mobile phones to support children's literacy learning. In Y. de Kort, W. IJsselsteijn, C. Midden, B. Eggen and B. J. Fogg (eds), *Persuasive Technology* (pp. 253–258). Berlin: Springer.

Rideout, V. and Katz, V. (2016) Opportunity for all? Technology and learning in lower-income families. New York: Joan Ganz Cooney Centre. Available from: www.joanganzcooneycenter.org/publication/opportunity-for-all-technology-and-learning-in-lower-income-families/.

Robb, M., Takeuchi, L. and Kotler, J. (2011). Always connected: The new digital media habits of young children. Joan Ganz Cooney Center at Sesame Workshop. Available from: www.joanganzcooneycenter.org/.

Scholastic (2014) Kids & Family Reading Report™. Available from: www.scholastic.com/readingreport/about.htm.

Selwyn, N. (2007). Curriculum online? Exploring the political and commercial construction of the UK digital learning marketplace. *British Journal of Sociology of Education*, 28(2), 223–240.

Sénéchal, M. and LeFevre, J. A. (2002). Parental involvement in the development of children's reading skill: A five-year longitudinal study. *Child Development*, 73(2), 445–460.

Shuler, C. (2009). iLearn: A content analysis of the iTunes App Store's Education Section. New York: Joan Ganz Cooney Center at Sesame Workshop.

Snow, C. E. (1993). Families as social contexts for literacy development. *New Directions for Child and Adolescent Development*, 1993(61), 11–24.

Snow, C., Arlman-Rupp, A., Hassing, Y., Jobse, J., Joosten, J. and Vorster, J. (1976). Mothers' speech in three social classes. *Journal of Psycholinguistic Research*, 5(1), 1–20.

Street, B. (1998). New literacies in theory and practice: What are the implications for language in education? *Linguistics and Education, 10*(1), 1–24.

Takacs, Z. K., Swart, E. K. and Bus, A. G. (2015). Benefits and pitfalls of multimedia and interactive features in technology-enhanced storybooks a meta-analysis. *Review of Educational Research.* doi:10.3102/0034654314566989.

Willems, M. (2003), *Don't Let the Pigeon Drive the Bus.* New York: Disney-Hyperion.

Wolfe, S. and Flewitt, R. (2010). New technologies, new multimodal literacy practices and young children's metacognitive development. *Cambridge Journal of Education, 40*(4), 387–399.

Young, J. G. (1985). What is creativity? *The Journal of Creative Behavior, 19*(2), 77–87.

Zhang, Y. and Kudva, S. (2014). E-books versus print books: Readers' choices and preferences across contexts. *Journal of the Association for Information Science and Technology, 65*(8), 1695–1706.

5

EARLY LITERACY PRACTICE

More than just knowing how to read and write

Clare Wood

In this chapter I discuss how we as an adult community, concerned with supporting children's learning, define, use and understand what literacy is, and what it looks like in the early years. Attention is paid to the impact of digital technologies on early literacy development, the tensions between school assessment and everyday reading practices as well as the disconnection between literacy in formal and informal contexts in relation to children's writing. The key challenges brought about by technology to traditional forms of literacy result in a proposed redefinition of what we mean by reading and writing in the twenty-first century.

In this chapter I will present an overview of how we understand and use the term 'literacy', and what the implications of these uses are for the young children whose literacy development we are seeking to study, support and assess. A re-examination of this term is necessary because of the transformation of 'text' that has occurred as a result of the wide ranging use of digital media to resource communication, and therefore teaching and learning. As Angela McFarlane (2014: 7) put it: 'The long-anticipated era of ubiquitous computing has finally arrived. Predicted, lauded and longed for, the day when every learner can have a powerful computing device in their hand is here.'

Such technology affords parents and early years educators a range of new ways to engage children with text and meaning-making. However, this potential for transformation of early years practice, and the evolution of 'digital childhoods', has been met with concern and discussion of how to to restrict children's access to technology during this sensitive developmental period. But before we move too far down this route, it is helpful to remind ourselves what literacy really is, to think about how this has been broadened and deepened by increased access to technology, and to reflect on our responsibilities as adults to enable young children to become truly literate, in all senses of the word.

What do we mean by 'literacy'?

Literacy is more than just knowing how to read and write, although this is the way that the term is most commonly understood, and written language skills remain at the heart of children's educational success and failure. However, true literacy encompasses much more. It involves the use of language more broadly, to include oral communication and comprehension skills. Literacy also includes the skilled understanding and use of 'symbols' more generally, and so an awareness of how to 'read' refers not just to the procedural ability to decode graphemes on a page or screen, but also an ability to read the intended meaning of the 'author'. This often extends beyond the use of words on a page, but also the use of other cultural symbols, signs and gestures. Literacy, crucially, also involves the successful application of these skills. For example, someone might be able to decode a text, comprehend its meaning and write a response, but a literate individual knows how to apply these skills in a real world context to enable him or her to function successfully and behave appropriately, being sensitive to cultural norms that are relevant to that context. To be literate therefore also implies real-world, practical competence (as in the case of being 'computer literate', or more recently 'digitally literate'). This is an important distinction, which flags a tension between cognitively driven definitions of what literacy is (and how it might be assessed) and how literacy functions for individuals in the context of the demands of their daily lives. Wells (2012: 2) articulates this most clearly:

> For some theorists literacy can best be understood in terms of skills which are relatively context free, that is they work wherever you use them. For others, literacy needs to be understood in terms of the social practices in which it is embedded and in terms of the ideologies which sustain those practices.

Wells (2012) argues that literacy is powerful for four reasons. First, it provides literate individuals access to endless texts. Second, it permits the representation of knowledge that makes extended reasoning possible (and therefore higher reasoning and theorizing). Third, it increases human capabilities and capacities, especially with respect to cultural activity. Finally, it provides an essential foundation for other domains that are important for the development of our society, such as science and mathematics. In this way literacy is more than just a skill set or a group of activities. It is a cultural tool that permits users to engage with cultural resources, to create new ones and ultimately to transform the nature of the cultures and societies that they participate in.

Theoretically driven notions of literacy have broadened over the last 25 years in particular. For example, the New Literacy Studies movement recognized the need for multiple literacies that were necessarily situated in social, cultural and political contexts. Through this movement literacy was seen as being about meaning-making and multiple ways of knowing (Gee, 1990) and was heavily informed by social constructivist models of teaching and learning. Technology has contributed to the development of such theoretical debates (e.g. Lankshear and Knobel, 2003). In this conceptualization technology enables multiple literacies, presenting readers with multimodal texts. The New Literacy Studies movement identified a gap between cultural practices around 'text' in the home and those enacted in the classroom, but Maybin (2007) has also identified that *literacies-in-practice* can occur, where accepted and unconventional/ unrecognized literacy coexist. Moreover, Merchant's (2009) work has used the features of Web 2.0 to explore the idea that knowledge becomes socially constructed through identity and shared online cultures and practices. To participate in such activity, to make meaning, to co-construct knowledge, children need to be digitally literate. Without this, they risk becoming disenfranchised from the knowledge society.

A further philosophical approach to understanding what we mean by literacy is articulated within Multiple Literacies Theory (Cole and Masny, 2012). This Deleuzian-inspired view (i.e. based on the ideas of French philosopher Gilles Deleuze) attempts to map simultaneously the complexities of literacy rather than emphasizing one aspect of the construct over that of another. Moreover, according to this approach, thinking is conceptualized as experiences of becoming, rather than manipulating or reflecting on representations of knowledge. Thinking is something that happens to us rather than something that we 'do'; we have no conscious control over it. In line with this, reading is seen as a process of becoming, and the idea of reading as interpreting and representing text is problematized (Masny, 2012). This aspect of becoming literate (that is, of becoming ourselves) and that it is ongoing and necessarily bound up with other experiences and cognitions that rupture our consciousness is something that, although more philosophically driven, is an under-articulated aspect of what becoming literate (as opposed to *being* literate) is about. It opens up the act of reading, and of becoming literate, to all aspects of our environmental and internal experience, past and present. The idea of some things being more conducive to effective literacy than others, or of literacy being something that adults can control or manipulate, is rejected by such notions.

My own theoretical orientation to what it means to be (or become) literate lies somewhere between these different ideological positions. As a psychologist who has studied the acquisition of reading, I have been trained in the tradition of 'literacy' meaning only written language skills, and the belief that these are cognitive activities and behaviours that are open to assessment, albeit imperfectly. In addition, my own stance is that literacy is multifaceted and complex in the ways described earlier, and that the digital saturation of childhood means that literacy itself is in transition. Reading and writing remains at its heart, as without these it is difficult to fully engage with multimodal texts, but clearly they do not encompass all the forms of literate experience children in the early years are now exposed to. Within this I recognize technology as affording children increased and more varied interactions with images and symbols, and that children come to interpret their interactions with 'text' (of whatever kind) in the context of prior contact with similar resources and activities.

Consider the following example. My daughter, between the ages of two and three years, used my smartphone to access apps which were intended to provide age-appropriate educational activity. One app presented her with a choice of story based on a familiar television series. To navigate her choice of story, she swiped her finger to the left or right to 'turn the page' to the next story choice. In this way she was bringing two different literate practices to bear – the experience of turning a page when faced with a 'book' but also the motion of swiping the screen, which is an action she recognized as valid from using the smartphone in other ways. She then tapped to select that story, and had to tap again one of two buttons, both labelled with text, to indicate whether she wanted the story to be read to her, or whether she or the adult with her would read the text. My daughter could not 'read' the text on these buttons in the traditional sense of the word, but she had learned through trial and error what each one meant, and knew which one to tap to access the function which was appropriate to her needs at that moment (either because she wanted to interact with the story independently or because she wanted to use the app to resource a shared interaction with an adult). Within the stories the illustrations did more than just illustrate the story; they invited the reader to participate in the events of the story in order to move it on. To interact successfully with the text, the reader had to attend to the story and map vocabulary on to the images on the screen to know how to perform the interactions that would result in the next page becoming available to view. Often the instructions regarding what to do next relied on inferences being drawn. Even in terms of simple navigation, my preschool child had to learn to associate the end of the text with the appearance of a red arrow, and to realize that the arrow meant 'move on'. This was never provided as an explicit instruction.

I am not a digital technology evangelist, but there is clearly an art to constructing these environments with a degree of looseness which allows for self-teaching/trial and error learning, and also for shared interaction with adults or peers. One of the concerns raised around the use of digital technology is that the features that enable children to engage with it independently of adult support could result too easily in socially isolated learning. This is problematic if you believe, as I do, that making meaning from texts is based on co-construction and is necessarily socially situated. The lone child engaging with text undergoes a more impoverished experience and understanding of that text without some form of shared discourse around it. It is the responsibility of adults in the early years to model how to engage in shared interactions around such resources in the early years, when children are not yet literate enough to engage with online communities that could support collaborative learning online. As noted earlier, children approach educational technology with their prior experiences of similar resources foremost in their minds (e.g. see Wood et al., 2005). In this way, if children's typical experience of using digital resources (or seeing them used) is solitary, or competitive rather than collaborative, then this is how they will expect to use them to resource their education experiences. This is why it is important that parents model the sharing and discussion of digital texts in their own use of such media. The tablet or smartphone should represent a hub for shared engagement and discussion of what is presented, rather than a private and personal experience of reading or other engagement. The extreme phenomenon of the *hikikomori* in Japan, teenagers and young adults who have retreated from human contact to engage with technology in an isolated manner, serve to remind us that if we do not draw technology into shared human spaces, it can be used to resource a completely asocial form of engagement.

The formalization of literate practices

Several threats to literacy emerge when we reflect on literacy's position as an activity that is 'owned' (authenticated) by adults and educational systems. The first is that what is taught as literacy in formal contexts like primary schools and even early years settings may be narrower than what young people need to be competent in to function successfully in different arenas. The second threat to literacy is that the teaching of literacy necessarily focuses on what is assessed, which in turn reinforces the 'need' to teach a narrow form of literacy as some forms of literacy are easier to operationalize and quantify than others (e.g. can the child 'read' his/her name vs. evidence of creative engagement with language). In this way literacy is defined by what goes on in the classroom or, rather, what is taught and assessed within a curricular framework. Literate activities that fall outside of these assessed activities are less likely to be valued or prioritized, and may even be perceived as undesirable (Maybin, 2013).

Janet Maybin (2013) has examined the tensions between how reading is defined and assessed at school, and how literacy is enacted by children in behaviour that is not visible in terms of conventional literacy activities. For example, she noted that PIRLS acknowledges a broader definition of what literacy is than what is actually assessed.

If we look at the current 2016 Progress in International Reading Literacy Study (PIRLS) assessment framework, reading is defined as follows:

> Reading literacy is the ability to understand and use those written language forms required by society and/or valued by the individual. Readers can construct meaning from texts in a variety of forms. They read to learn, to participate in communities of readers in school and everyday life, and for enjoyment.
>
> *(Mullis et al. 2015: 12)*

However, in the PIRLS assessment this is operationalized as reading for two purposes: reading for 'literary experience' and reading 'to acquire and use information'. Comprehension processes are assessed as a child's ability to:

- focus on and retrieve explicitly stated information;
- make straightforward inferences;
- interpret and integrate ideas and information; and
- evaluate and critique content and textual elements.

Maybin makes the point that frameworks like the PIRLS may recognize the creative, expressive and experiential aspects of reading in their definitions, but when they operationalize reading for the purposes of assessment, the range of skills under consideration and the use of resources to foster literate activity is much narrower. For example, if we look at the 2016 framework assessment, there is no operationalization of 'participation in communities of readers' which is identified as the third function of reading. Instead, this kind of framework 'silences children's voices, restricts their creativity and does not allow enough time to stimulate their imagination . . . literature is reduced to a resource for teaching the linguistic and textual features of written genre' (2013: 60).

Maybin (2013) examined children's spontaneous literacy activities: one in relation to children's discussion of an episode of *EastEnders* (a UK serial drama) and another in relation to playful but 'unofficial' engagement with a poem that was the focus of a lesson at school. In both cases the children's activity (as a result of being playful, fragmented and located in talk) is presented as activity that would been seen by the teacher as unrelated to literacy-related learning outcomes. However, Maybin's analysis shows how these episodes of talk map on to formal understandings of literacy in terms of the PIRLS and National Curriculum definitions of literacy.

> Imagination, emotional and moral engagement, critique, humour and fun are all important aspects of these children's spontaneous responses to texts. Yet none of these dimensions of reading are easily reduced to testable items within the current assessment regime which dominates classrooms, nor are they captured in PIRLS tests or questionnaires . . . [official models of literacy] run the risk of promulgating a reductive, impoverished form of reading which fails to match up to pupils' natural propensity and aptitude for collaborative, creative and rewarding readings of many different kinds of texts.
>
> *(p. 66)*

There is a similar example of a disconnection between literacy in formal and informal contexts in relation to children's writing, if we consider the example of children's writing in digital contexts, such as in text messages (SMS) or on social media. In such contexts (recall 'participation in communities of readers . . . in everyday life' from Mullis et al., 2015) children are observed to use 'textisms' – a form of digital slang that uses alternative spellings and punctuation conventions (e.g. see Wood, Meacham et al., 2011; Wood et al., 2014). The majority of textisms are phonetic in nature (e.g. c u 2nite), and research has shown that there is no negative relationship between writing in this way and the children's understanding of conventional spelling or grammar (Wood, Meacham et al., 2011; Wood et al., 2014). In fact, the data suggest that textism use may be supporting children's spelling development (Wood, Meacham et al., 2011; Wood, Jackson Hart et al., 2011). However, children's informal digital writing is rejected as a form of legitimate literate practice, and is characterized as damaging both for the individual child (see Woronoff, 2007) and language itself (Humphries, 2007).

The way in which literate behaviour is quantified and assessed seems to drive what is valued in terms of children's literate experiences. Although the Maybin example was focused on primary school children aged 10–11 years, and the texting research has similarly examined children aged 8 years or older, the principles of Maybin's argument remain applicable to early years domains. To illustrate this, Figure 5.1 summarizes the impact of operationalizing literacy for assessment purposes on our functional understanding of what literacy 'is' in early years settings.

In the top box of Figure 5.1 I have selected the Marsh and Hallet (2008) definition of what literacy curriculum provision should encompass as an example of one that explicitly recognizes the wider context and purpose of literacy. Below this are the behavioural indicators of progress that are provided to UK early years practitioners to help them to understand what this might look like if children are making 'expected' progress for their age (Early Education, 2012). I have focused on the expected behaviours for reading and writing, as the Early Years Foundation Stage framework defines literacy as reading and writing. Language and communication (speaking and listening) are presented as separate from 'literacy', as are 'understanding the world' and 'expressive arts and design'. Some reference is made to technology in relation to understanding the world, and expressive arts, but it is notable that engagement with such tools is not linked to 'traditional' literate practices in the behavioural milestones listed.

In the final box for Figure 5.1, we can see how this narrowly defined list of behavioural indicators is further reduced to the achievement of assessment targets at around the age of five years. These targets further focus the achievement of literate activity in the early years as 'reading as decoding and comprehending simple text' and writing as the application of phonics rules to generate attempts at writing that although inaccurate, should be understandable. No mention is made of other forms of symbolic understanding or use. The contribution of others in literate interactions is restricted to being a marker of how successfully the child has managed to write a sentence, or a faceless target for a child to re-tell a story to. There is no mention of collaborative communication or extra-curricular/home practices.

Does technology impact early literacy learning?

Hsin et al. (2014) conducted a systematic review of the literature published between 2003 and 2013 that examined the impact of technology on children's learning. From this they noted that the available data on the influence of technology on children's learning in relation to language and literacy was ambivalent: 26 studies showed a positive impact, only one showed a negative impact, 16 observed no influence and a further 32 fell into the category of 'it depends'. They identified a number of factors that influenced whether or not children's learning was influenced by technology use. They noted that effects were generally better for older rather than younger children, but also that the children's prior knowledge and use of a computer in the home could impact what they learned. Prior knowledge of the domain under instruction was a double-edged sword. That is, Levy (2009) observed that children's prior exposure to reading activities as reading print books constrained children's ability to read multimodal computer texts. We also saw this in some of our own research, where there was evidence of children importing linear reading practices in their use of talking books which had embedded activities (Wood, 2005). The review noted that the more time spent using an intervention involving talking books, the better the outcomes.

Definition – The Spirit of Early Years Literacy

… offer a broad and rich language and literary curriculum to young children, the importance of recognizing literacy as a social and cultural practice, and, thus, ensure curricular links to the wider world and the need to engage children as active participants in

'Expected' Literacy Behaviours (taken from Early Education, 2012)

Birth to 11 months

Enjoys looking at books and other printed material with familiar people.

8–20 months

Handles books and printed material with interest.

16–26 months

Interested in books and rhymes and may have favourites.

22–36 months

Has some favourite stories, rhymes, songs, poems or jingles. • Repeats words or phrases from familiar stories. • Fills in the missing word or phrase in a known rhyme, story or game, e.g. 'Humpty Dumpty sat on a …'. Distinguishes between the different marks they make.

30–50 months

Enjoys rhyming and rhythmic activities. • Shows awareness of rhyme and alliteration. • Recognizes rhythm in spoken words. • Listens to and joins in with stories and poems, one-to-one and also in small groups. • Joins in with repeated refrains and anticipates key events and phrases in rhymes and stories. • Beginning to be aware of the way stories are structured. • Suggests how the story might end. • Listens to stories with increasing attention and recall. • Describes main story settings, events and principal characters. • Shows interest in illustrations and print in books and print in the environment. • Recognizes familiar words and signs such as own name and advertising logos. • Looks at books independently. • Handles books carefully. • Knows information can be relayed in the form of print. • Holds books the correct way up and turns pages. • Knows that print carries meaning and, in English, is read from left to right and top.

Assessment Targets

(Early Years Foundation Stage Statutory Early Learning Goals, to be achieved by age 5 years)

Reading: children read and understand simple sentences. They use phonic knowledge to decode regular words and read them aloud accurately. They also read some common irregular words. They demonstrate understanding when talking with others about what they have read.

Writing: children use their phonic knowledge to write words in ways which match their spoken sounds. They also write some irregular common words. They write simple sentences which can be read by themselves and others. Some words are spelt correctly and others are phonetically plausible.

Figure 5.1   Understandings of literacy in early years education

Overall the Hsin et al. (2014) review does not paint technology use as a threat, but its benefits are often context-driven, and are greater for older children. Taken together this evidence could suggest that perhaps early years educators should continue with a focus on traditional literate experiences and leave the development of digitally mediated engagement with texts for the school years. However, to agree with this interpretation is to focus on the construction of digital media as something which needs to 'outperform' traditional literacy resources before it can be considered to have value. To do this is to ignore the everyday context in which children are growing up. In the home, the early years of children are now digitally saturated – even in low-income homes the presence of digital media can be observed (Ofcom, 2012, 2015). The question should not be 'Is this better than a traditional approach to resourcing literate activity?', but 'Does this way of resourcing literate activity represent a threat or an opportunity?' The evidence would suggest that digital media do represent a pervasive feature of contemporary childhood that can be used to resource literacy in positive ways just as traditional print media can. There does, however, appear to be a mismatch between home literacy practices that can and do include the full range of texts, and how literacy is enacted in early years settings.

The challenges

Parents are advised to restrict children's screen time, to be on their guard regarding the threats posed by digital media as a key component of 'toxic childhood' (Palmer, 2006). The emphasis on threat limits an awareness of the affordances of technology.

Adults can feel threatened by children's use of digital media and technology because it enables and it is 'democratic': that is, digital media allow children to communicate their own messages in their own way. This might be through the use of images, or in older children through being able to write using an orthographic system of their own collective design (textspeak, see Plester et al. 2009; Wood et al., 2011; Wood et al., 2014 for examples). In this world, adults are not required to determine or authenticate the 'correct' response: it is a creative domain in which children can assume the role of storyteller before they can write. Or as Ohler (2013: 4) has put it: 'The digital revolution in a sentence: finally, we all get to tell our own story in our own way.'

The beauty of this for parents and early years practitioners is that children from a very young age are facilitated by such technology to participate in literate practices in a more developed way than ever before. In particular, they can author 'texts' long before they are able to form letters with a pen or spell words. As Kucirkova et al. (2014) have shown, both story-book and 'non-literacy' related apps afford young children opportunities for educationally meaningful talk, joint problem-solving and collaborative activity.

Technology is a resource like any other: books, pictures, pens, audio, video or language. Like all resources, on their own they deliver potential learning but the resource itself does not instruct. A book does not teach the child to read. The picture does not convey meaning or experiences. Pens do not write. Computers do not harm or facilitate learning as a function of their sophistication. Televisions do not educate or reduce IQs by their mere existence. It is how they are used to resource literacy that is critical. The issue is that digital media, by virtue of its increased interactivity and design features, enables a level of independent use by children which traditional print resources struggle to achieve. As noted earlier, if children come to observe and experience the use of digital resources as highly personalized and individualized (see Chapter 3 in this book) then this is how they will come to use them as a literacy resource. To unlock their potential they need to be the focus of joint attention and shared experience. Literacy is about communication and language, and communication and language are about interaction and shared understandings. It is not about books or pens any more than it is about computers and smartphones. It is about how these technologies are used and shared, how communities see them as resources.

Adults can construct digital technologies as problematic for resourcing literacy, but why? This concern may be a valid one if the early years practitioner (or parent) lacks confidence about how to interact around these resources. Is it not the technology that is the problem, but the lack of cultural practices regarding how and when to share technology with children. We have well-established cultural practices around shared book reading and a general appreciation of its importance for literacy development. We do not yet have a common set of practices regarding how to share digital texts in the same way. This is evident from the recent responses to the National Literacy Trust Early Years Survey (Formby, 2014), which also found that only 23.7 per cent of early years practitioners thought that there was a place for touch-screen technology in early years settings, and there was higher incidence of this attitude in early years settings that had been evaluated as 'outstanding' in relation to settings where provision was seen as suboptimal. The value of digitally mediated literacy may be perceived to be lower in contexts where there is less of an imperative to engage with it.

Technology aside, the other issue that arises from the valuing of some forms of literacy over others is that adults and professionals who care for preschool children may limit the range of activities that are shared with children, or fail to include them in relatively mundane or informal activities, because they do not look like conventional forms. In a world that is saturated in print, and where the means to create narratives through a range of media are commonplace, the notion of 'basic literacy skills' strips culture, colour and confidence from our children's earliest experiences of 'text'.

Re-defining literacy

What is my definition of literacy? It is this:

> Knowledge and understanding of the literal and intended meanings of cultural symbols and tools which convey meaning, and the ability to make practical and creative use of these symbolic forms to communicate effectively in the widest range of settings and contexts: both synchronous and asynchronous, face-to-face and virtual.

This is broad, but is open to thoughtful practical operationalization. It encompasses letter-sound knowledge and print-based engagement without privileging that form of communication over the other options. It flags the application and purpose of literacy as well as its processes. In many ways, this definition is not a radical departure from those that have been expressed before. The challenge, however, is to keep the spirit of this definition central to the way in which assessment frameworks for early years practitioners, and developmental milestones for parents, are articulated.

References

Cole, D. R. and Masny, D. (2012) Introduction to mapping multiple literacies. In D. Masny and D. R. Cole (eds), *Mapping Multiple Literacies: An Introduction to Deleuzian Literacy Studies* (pp. 1–14). London: Continuum.

Early Education (2012). *Development Matters in the Early Years Foundation Stage (EYFS)*. London: Early Education.

Formby, S. (2014). Children's early literacy practices at home and in early years settings: Second annual survey of parents and practitioners. National Literacy Trust. Available from: www.literacytrust.org. uk/research/nlt_research/filter/our%20surveys.

Gee, J. P. (1990). *Social Linguistics and Literacies: Ideology in Discourses.* New York: Falmer Press.

Hsin, C.-T., Li, M.-C. and Tsai, C.-C. (2014). The influence of young children's use of technology on their learning: A review. *Educational Technology & Society, 17*(4), 85–99.

Humphries, J. (2007). I h8 txt msgs: How texting is wrecking our language. *Mail Online,* 24 September 2007. Available from: www.dailymail.co.uk/news/article-483511/I-h8-txt-msgs-How-texting-wrecking-language.html.

Kurcirkova, N., Messer, D., Sheehy, K. and Panadero, C. F. (2014) Children's engagement with educational iPad apps: Insights from a Spanish classroom. *Computers & Education, 71,* 175–184.

Lankshear, C. and Knobel, M. (eds) (2003). *New Literacies: Changing Knowledge and Classroom Learning.* Buckingham: Open University Press.

Levy, R. (2009). 'You have to understand words . . . but not read them': Young children becoming readers in a digital age. *Journal of Research in Reading, 32*(1), 75–91. doi:10.1111/j.1467-9817.2008. 01382.x.

Marsh, J. and Hallet, E. (2008). Introduction. In J. Marsh and E. Hallet (eds), *Desirable Literacies: Approaches to Language and Literacy in the Early Years,* second edition (pp. xiii–xvii). London: Sage.

Masny, D. (2012). What is reading? A cartography of reading. In D. Masny and D. R. Cole (eds), *Mapping Multiple Literacies: An Introduction to Deleuzian Literacy Studies* (pp. 69–92). London: Continuum.

Maybin, J. (2007). Literacy under and over the desk: Oppositions and heterogeneity. *Language and Education, 21*(6), 515–530.

Maybin, J. (2013). What counts as reading? PIRLS, EastEnders and The Man on the Flying Trapeze. *Literacy, 47*(2), 59–66.

McFarlane, A. (2014). *Authentic Learning for the Digital Generation: Realising the Potential of Technology in the Classroom.* London: Routledge.

Merchant, G. (2009). Web 2.0, new literacies, and the idea of learning through participation. *English Teaching-Practice and Critique, 8*(3), 107–122.

Mullis, I. V. S., Martin, M. O. and Sainsbury, M. (2015) PIRLS 2016 Reading Framework. In Mullis, I. V. S. and Martin, M. O. (eds), PIRLS 2016 Assessment Framework, 2nd Edition (pp. 11–29). Chestnut Hill, MA: TIMSS & PIRLS International Study Center, Boston College.

Ofcom. (2012). *Children and Parents: Media Use and Attitudes Report.* Available from: http://stakeholders. ofcom.org.uk/binaries/research/media-literacy/oct2012/main.pdf.

Ofcom. (2015). Adult's media use and attitudes. Available from: http://stakeholders.ofcom.org. uk/binaries/research/media-literacy/media-lit-10years/2015_Adults_media_use_and_attitudes_ report.pdf.

Ohler, J. B. (2013). *Digital Storytelling in the Classroom,* second edition. Thousand Oaks, CA: Corwin/ Sage.

Pahl, K. (2005). Narrative spaces and multiple identities: Children's textual explorations of console games in home settings. In J. Marsh (ed.), *Popular Culture, New Media and Digital Literacy in Early Childhood* (pp. 126–145). Abingdon: Routledge.

Palmer, S. (2006). *Toxic Childhood: How the Modern World is Damaging Our Children and What We Can Do About It.* London: Orion.

Plester, B., Wood, C. and Joshi, P. (2009) Exploring the relationship between children's knowledge of text message abbreviations and school literacy outcomes. *British Journal of Developmental Psychology, 27,* 145–161.

Wells, A. (2012). *The Literate Mind.* Basingstoke: Palgrave Macmillan.

Wood, C. (2005). Beginning readers' use of 'talking books' software can affect their reading strategies. *Journal of Research in Reading, 28,* 170–182.

Wood, C., Jackson, E., Hart, L., Plester, B. and Wilde, L. (2011) The effect of text messaging on 9–10 year old children's reading, spelling and phonological awareness. *Journal of Computer Assisted Learning, 27,* 28–36.

Wood, C., Kemp, N. and Waldron, S. (2014) Exploring the longitudinal relationships between the use of grammar in text messaging and performance on grammatical tasks. *British Journal of Developmental Psychology, 32*(4), 415–429.

Wood, C., Littleton, K. and Chera, P. D. K. (2005). Beginning readers' use of talking books: Styles of working. *Literacy*, *39*, 135–141.

Wood, C., Meacham, S. Bowyer, S., Jackson, E. Tarczynski-Bowles, M. L. and Plester, B., (2011). A longitudinal study of the relationship between children's text messaging and literacy development. *British Journal of Psychology*, 102, 431–442.

Woronoff, P. (2007). Cell phone texting can endanger spelling. Available from: www.streetdirectory. com/travel_guide/158484/cell_phones/cell_phone_texting_can_endanger_spelling.html.

PART II

Early literacy around the world

This editorial summarizes the key issues discussed in the 14 region portraits included in this section. The authors contributing to this section were given the brief to cover the early literacy situation within some society or language community according to seven dimensions: phonological/lexical features of the language and orthographic representations; early literacy, including educational policies in relation to multilingual issues; policy implementation in practice; principal methods and content areas of literacy instruction; provision for children with special educational needs; variety of literacy resources available; and the major challenges for current and future early literacy provision.

Together, the chapters display a remarkable degree of variation across countries/societies on several dimensions. In some places, policies and practices for early literacy instruction are highly centralized, whereas in other places local educational authorities have considerable autonomy to select approaches, materials and curricula. Some language communities confront enormous regional or sociolinguistic variations of the national language, creating instructional challenges not present for countries where the variation in pronunciation, vocabulary and grammar is less salient. Some countries insist that young children should be protected from any formal instruction, whereas others start literacy training with children as young as three. In some places, play- and narrative-based approaches to early literacy dominate, whereas in others the focus is more on mastering the code rather than the meaning. All these dimensions of variation offer the researcher and the theorist rich fodder for considering the conditions that make literacy development easy or hard, universal or elitist, and enjoyable or laborious.

All chapters cover the fundamental principles of orthographic and associated phonological representation of the languages in their countries and the implications of these variations for literacy instruction. It is striking to see the varied definition of early literacy success in the individual countries' early years policies. While in some countries the focus is on code-based skills, in others it is more of a balance with meaning-construction skills. These policies are directly reflected in the documentation of early learning outcomes used, assessment and evaluation frameworks available; provision of professional training, funding and allocation of early years professionals.

Despite the many global factors contributing to the need to support multilingual literacy and language learning, educational policies concerning early literacy for diverse groups vary enormously. Traditionally monolingual societies, which during the last few decades have experienced large-scale immigration, have developed very different language and literacy policies to meet the learning needs of children who do not speak the language of instruction at home, varying from reception classes for children who have newly arrived to (transitional) mother-tongue education or bilingual programmes. To add to the variation, these policies may be designed differently in early education and in schools within the same country, as well as inside or outside of the public educational system. The process of learning to read and write may be different depending on the country region a child lives in and whether it is a region where one or several languages are spoken and historically recognized. Several chapters also address the language and literacy education (or lack thereof) offered to the country's aboriginal groups.

It is also striking to note the different levels of provision of early literacy resources for children from special populations in the individual countries, including the ways in which children with special needs are identified, and the interventions that are available for children who are failing. All authors stress that the issues for current and future early literacy provision in the countries are influenced by the shifting literacy practices within young children's lives, shaped by the presence of new technologies at home and at school.

The selection of the individual countries reflects our focus on interesting contrasts and countries with successful literacy instruction. The editorial selection was, of course, also influenced by the availability of literacy researchers and high-quality research concerning development and instruction of language and literacy in the respective countries. We were also mindful of the fact that additional content about well-studied contexts would not be as illuminating as covering new orthographies or different educational settings.

The editors found it very difficult to order the chapters according to any single principle. Some of the chapters deal with shallow and others with deep orthographies, but in some cases within a language/country the young children confront a shallow orthography that turns deep only after a few years of schooling, when diacritics signalling pronunciation details are deleted (Arabic, Hebrew). Some describe systems that have been successful in generating universally high levels of literacy, whereas others show high failure rates even in the first years of schooling. Some rely heavily on local and international research to guide their instructional decisions, whereas others follow traditional methods. In short, we ultimately decided simply to put the chapters in an arbitrary order, recognizing that readers are very likely to pick and choose those most relevant to their own educational contexts and concerns. There is, thus, no implicit expectation that these chapters will be read in order or in their entirety by any particular reader. Nonetheless, we urge everyone to sample the range of challenges and supports associated with different languages, orthographies, schooling systems, assessment approaches and ministries of education, in thinking about ensuring universal success in literacy for young children across the globe.

These chapters reflect something important about the state of knowledge about literacy development in each of these regions. However, the reader might also note that some chapters are focused on smaller and much more homogeneous groups than others. For example, Korean and Japanese readers are relatively small in number as compared with all Arabic or Chinese speakers. India and Africa both have very large populations but a great diversity in languages and scripts, both traditional and adapted. A homogeneous population, language and script as found in Korea, which uses Hangul, has afforded researchers the opportunity to focus more on cognitive and social aspects of literacy development in Korea in a more carefully controlled way. Many more questions remain about the situations involving literacy development in Africa or India simply because the populations, and their corresponding languages, beliefs and scripts, are complex in their heterogeneity. There is much research that remains to be done in such areas, which represent among the most populous in the world. We hope that these chapters collectively highlight the many factors that must be integrated in order to have a clear picture of early literacy development around the world.

6

THE PROVISION, PRACTICE AND POLICIES OF EARLY LITERACY IN NEW ZEALAND

Stuart McNaughton and Rebecca Jesson

New Zealand has a history of high engagement in literacy practices. Historical record shows very early adoption of literacy by Māori (the indigenous population), and an enthusiastic tribally based teaching programme, which meant that by the later 1800s over half of adult Māori could read in their own language (Simon, 1998). By the 1990s when the first of the international comparisons of literacy achievement across countries took place, New Zealand 9-year-olds and 14-year-olds were ranked highly (Elley, 1992), and this has been attributed to the presence of widespread literacy practices and high volumes of reading among both adults and students (Guthrie, 1981).

The societal and literacy context

New Zealand shares features of its traditional success in literacy with other small developed countries. But there are also unique features and specific challenges facing the population of 4.5 million in its provisions, practices and policies. These reflect a particular context created by its colonial and social context. For example, there is legislative and institutional recognition of the special status of the indigenous population and their language, so that there are three official languages (Te Reo Māori, English and Sign Language). Currently, 21 per cent of the population are Māori speakers (Statistics New Zealand, 2014). However, despite this history and recognition, what the international comparisons and national data have revealed are ongoing persistent disparities in literacy achievement for Māori and now also for the newer immigrant groups from Pacific Islands (Pasifika communities) and children from low socioeconomic status (SES) communities. Children from diverse Anglo/European backgrounds make up 53 per cent of the current school student population of 767,258 students, and a further 23.3 per cent are Māori students (Education Counts, 2014a). In addition, 9.8 per cent of students are from the growing Pasifika student populations and 10.2 per cent from Asian communities. There are both Māori/English bilingual and full Māori immersion schools and classrooms. Children in these classrooms receive systematic literacy instruction in Māori, but represent a small group of students (2.5 per cent). However, 19.2 per cent of the total school population currently are involved in some Māori language in English-medium classrooms, which provides limited instruction in reading and writing in Māori. The exposure to both languages and any associated bilingual literacy experiences is wider in early childhood: 11.5 per cent of all services provide the majority of their instruction and care through the Māori language, and 5 per cent of enrolled children are in full immersion Kohanga Reo (Māori early childhood language nests) (www.educationcounts.govt.nz/ statistics). The smaller numbers receiving systematic literacy instruction in Māori in schools represent ongoing concerns by parents about the quality of schooling choices and how best to promote the language through literacy provisions.

The educational system context

The education system contains a diverse, non-mandatory early childhood sector catering for children from birth through five; children can and mostly do enter the primary school on their fifth birthday. Over 95 per cent of new entrants to schools have participated in an early childhood educational centre within the six months prior to starting school (www. educationcounts.govt.nz/statistics).

The early childhood and school sectors are both administered under a centralized Ministry of Education, but each has its own national curriculum, and there is a parallel curriculum statement for Māori-medium schooling. These are broadly specified and open frameworks; teachers have considerable autonomy and are expected to be flexible problem solvers engaging in teaching as inquiry (Ministry of Education, 2007: 35). This autonomy is reflected in a history of innovation and initiatives in language and literacy practices arising from local problem solving (McNaughton, 2002).

The valued autonomy is present also at a school level in that each is managed by a locally elected board of trustees. Within this high-autonomy environment, quality is assessed by an Education Review Office which provides publically available reports (see www.ero. govt.nz/). This autonomy at teacher and school levels has produced a tension with the need to take effective interventions to scale, or to mandate practices in ways that reduce contextual variability between teachers and schools (Robinson et al., 2011).

Policy, curriculum models and assessments

National Standards introduced in 2010 define success in reading and writing in English-medium and Māori-medium schools at the end of each school year and on which schools are required to report (Ministry of Education, 2009, 2010). The standards were designed to increase accountability to parents, and through greater shared goals and consistency of practices to raise achievement and address disparities of outcomes between groups.

The National Standards require school teachers (but not teachers in early childhood settings) from the first year to make a formal judgement using a four-part scale called an Overall Teacher Judgement (OTJ) and to report twice a year on how each child is meeting the standard. The judgement is based on multiple and ongoing sources of information from daily activities including formal assessments. There are detailed resources with exemplars of the standards, and some professional development to support schools in implementing the standards. However, the dependability of the OTJs has been criticized as having inadequate school-to-school consistency and too much variability across time and year levels (Ward and Thomas, 2014). In response, an online tool with anchoring exemplars is being developed by the Ministry of Education to support teachers' judgements, thereby improving the reliability and consistency of judgements over time (see http://assessment.tki.org.nz/Assessment-tools-resources/Progress-and-Consistency-Tool).

Definitions of early literacy success

Before school

The early childhood curriculum reflects an explicitly constructivist view of learning that emphasizes child agency. There are no formal definitions or criteria for literacy success; rather an expectation of increasing 'competence' in dispositions such as curiosity (Ministry of Education, 1996).

The prescribed orientation to literacy practices and development is 'meaning construction'. For example, 'adults should read and tell stories, provide books, and use story times to allow children to exchange and extend ideas, reinforcing developing concepts of, and language for, shape, space, size, and colour as well as imaginative responses' (Ministry of Education, 1996: 73). The curriculum employs descriptors of children moving to school as 'likely to' have developed features such as enjoyment of books and concepts about print and knowledge of relationships (unspecified) between written and spoken words.

Research-based descriptions of practices support the intent of the documents. For example, observational data describe the nature of teaching as creating 'possibilities' within which teachers follow the lead of children as initiators of their learning, based on their interests and experiences (Dalli, 2011). Similarly, qualitative descriptions of children's learning highlight the development of their 'working theories', which researchers argue are indicative of what can more widely be recognized as knowledge, skills, attitudes and expectations (Hedges and Cooper, 2014).

Early years at school

The school curriculum has a view of development that assumes the need for more deliberate and direct instruction from school entry than that described in early childhood curriculum statements. The deliberateness is embodied in, and made accountable to, a government goal of 85 per cent of the national cohort of students achieving the expected standards at each year level (up to year 8 of schooling when students are approximately 13 years old).

The standards explicitly adopt a 'balanced text-based' framework, which incorporates both code-based and meaning construction foci, with success defined by specifying the level of texts able to be read and written across curriculum areas. For example, the national standard for reading at the end of the first year, when children are six years old, states: 'students will read, respond to, and think critically about fiction and non-fiction texts at the green level of Ready to Read (the core instructional series that supports reading in The New Zealand Curriculum)' (Ministry of Education, 2009: 19). Features of texts at this level are described. They have a single storyline or topic, with content mostly explicitly stated but with opportunities to make simple inferences. They contain high-frequency topic and interest words likely to be in a reader's oral vocabulary, strongly supported by the context or illustrations. The text sentences run over more than one line but do not split phrases, with a range of punctuation.

The standards after two years at school (seven-year-olds) continue the 'balanced text-based' approach. Now texts have settings and contexts that go beyond immediate prior knowledge and incorporate visual language features such as labelled diagrams, inset photographs and bold text for topic words that are linked to a glossary. They can contain more varied sentence structures, with frequent use of dialogue where multiple characters speak.

The Ready to Read series of texts are professionally graded (rather than using formulae such as lexiles) initially taking into account the range of text features, including length, incidence of high-frequency words, sentence complexity and length, familiarity of themes and support for meaning-making offered by illustrations. Texts are trialled by teachers and students, based on which final levels are assigned (Literacy Online, n.d.).

More detailed breakdown of the knowledge and skills that students are expected to draw from to meet the standard is provided in a set of *Literacy Learning Progressions* (Ministry of Education, 2010). This professional resource describes the code-based learning expected, such as phonemic awareness sufficient to identify and distinguish individual phonemes within words, and to segment phonemes; and knowledge of graphemes and phonemes and morphology to write and to solve unfamiliar words while reading.

Like the reading standards, writing standards also incorporate both code-based and meaning-based criteria for judging texts, to engage with curriculum content. The standard for writing emphasizes the expectation that students after one year will:

> create texts as they learn in a range of contexts across the New Zealand Curriculum within level 1 . . . use their writing to think about, record, and communicate experiences, ideas, and information to meet specific learning purposes across the curriculum.
>
> *(Ministry of Education, 2010: 20)*

In the professional resources there are descriptions of the expected code-based skills needed: for example by the end of the first year being able to segment words into syllables, and one-syllable words into phonemes, to write all consonants, accurately spell some key personal and high frequency words, and use capital letters and full stops. There are also descriptions of the process as well as the texts. After one year, students can be expected to plan for writing, using talk or pictures, as well as independently write simple texts to achieve their purposes. Texts will contain several sentences (some compound sentences with simple conjunctions) and will be based on transfer from their oral language and from their reading.

After two years, the writing standard specifies increasing ability to engage with curriculum content, with a continued emphasis on understanding purposes and audience as well as on the basis for writing in oral language and reading. There is more focus on linguistic, particularly grammatical, features.

These definitions formally establish what have been common beliefs and practices in reading and writing (McNaughton et al., 2000), but especially in the explicit emphasis on code-based details also reflect a response to debates and evidence-based recommendations from the mid-1990s. In 1997, a national Literacy Task Force supported by an expert group of literacy academics provided recommendations for change which included more focused instruction on component skills and knowledge such as alphabetic and phonemic awareness (Literacy Task Force, 1999). Researchers in the experts group provided evidence that beginning readers were taught strategies that relied too much on the semantic and syntactic context for identifying words and for decoding in general. While categorizing the New Zealand system as having a 'whole-language' approach to instruction was rejected by the full group as overly simplistic and unhelpful, specific evidence-based concerns, such as the over-reliance on context in word reading, were acknowledged and addressed.

Following a National Literacy Strategy in 1999, new guidelines for and descriptions of effective early literacy teaching were introduced (Ministry of Education, 2003). The identified practices included deliberate teaching of component skills and knowledge through guided and shared reading and writing.

Developmental patterns

Before school

Studies that have assessed children on entry to mainstream (English-speaking) schools indicate that, on average, children can identify (through naming, sounding or mentioning a word starting with) almost half of the letters in English; they know 10 of the 24 tested concepts about print (such as knowing the front of the book and the back of the book, and left to right directionality); and are able to write a word, usually their name (Gilmore, 1998; McNaughton et al., 2003).

As in other countries, there is wide variability in these general measures of early literacy on entry to school. This variability is associated with both SES and ethnicity (Tunmer et al., 2006). The results from mainstream school entry measures suggest an overall effect size difference of $d = 0.64$ on measures of concepts about print between Māori and Anglo/European five-year-olds. There are similarly sized disparities in achievement at school entry based on SES (Gilmore, 1998).

This variation can be attributed to unequal access to at least three sources of literacy practices and literacy resources that relate to school readiness. One is the styles and frequencies of family practices, such as reading to children and talking with children with more literate and school language, which are known to vary both between and within SES and cultural groups (McNaughton, 1996). A second is variations in access to and quality of early childhood provisions. A third is access to and use of resources such as books and writing materials, including new digital technologies.

Recent longitudinal research provides more detail about differences in frequency of literacy practices in the home (Morton et al., 2012). At nine months of age half of a cohort of 6,500 mothers reported reading once or several times a day, and only 16 per cent reported seldom or never reading to children, although higher percentages of Māori (22.3 per cent) and Pasifika mothers (18.8 per cent) reported infrequent reading. These differences were not apparent in singing or telling stories. Rates of 'reading seldom' were noticeably higher at two years (34.6 per cent), and both ethnicity and SES were independently related to reported rates.

The New Zealand research is consistent with international research in showing significant associations between high-quality ECE and school readiness as well as progress over the first years at school; and that high-quality ECE can mitigate the effect of low SES on school readiness and subsequent achievement at school (Dearing et al., 2009; Mitchell et al., 2008). Participation rates vary by ethnicity and SES, although importantly the differences are shrinking (www.educationcounts.govt.nz/statistics), and the issue now is one of equal access to quality and impact on literacy.

There is considerable variation in both structured activities and informal opportunities for literacy development in early childhood settings, and overall there is limited deliberate or direct fostering of specific literacy knowledge and skills (Education Review Office, 2011). While shared reading is common with a focus on concepts about print, observations show participation in structured literacy activities is for the children often voluntary. Some commercial phonics programmes are used and writing activities are often focused on letter formation. The limited deliberate promotion observed is consistent with the theoretical position and direction afforded by the curriculum. In addition, it is also attributed to teachers not having a well-articulated understanding of progressions in literacy and not being aware of how their programmes and practices support ongoing development.

There is little research into the development of literacy in Māori educational contexts, either before school or over the early years. The research that exists is consistent with international developmental research, that more advanced Māori oral language on entry to school is associated with early higher rates of progress in Māori across reading text levels and writing (McNaughton et al., 2006). Children with Māori immersion early childhood experience and advanced language also typically score more highly in word recognition and letter and sound identification, likely attributable to Māori having a very regular phonological system.

Early years of school

The 2013 national standards data (www.educationcounts.govt.nz) show that two-thirds of students could read texts at the expected level required after one year, and eight out of ten attained the required standard at the end of the second year. In writing, eight out of ten children could write texts at the required level. But disparities continue to present. Children in high SES schools had a 4.3 times greater probability of achieving the standard at the end of the first year than children in schools serving the lowest SES group. In writing, the odds were even higher (4.7 times). The figures for children in the Māori medium as judged against the Māori-medium standards are lower in both reading and writing, around six out of ten children achieving the standard.

After one year at school (when students are six years old) an early intervention literacy programme supplementary to classroom instruction is available funded by the New Zealand Ministry of Education (Ministry of Education, 2014). Reading Recovery (Clay, 2001) was designed to accelerate the reading and writing achievement of six-year-old children who are identified as having made less-than-expected progress after one year of classroom-based literacy teaching and also through a Response-to-Intervention process to identify the students who will need continued additional specialist literacy support. It provides daily one-to-one teaching which continues for about 12 to 20 weeks with a specially trained teacher.

Schools decide whether to implement Reading Recovery, and in 2013 the programme was provided by two-thirds of state schools (for 76 per cent of the total six-year-old population). In a Reading Recovery school, the lowest progress students from that school are selected based on a suite of assessments given at the end of the first year (Clay, 2005), and 10,933 of the six-year-old cohort in 2013 received the programme (around 20 per cent of the students in those schools).

Annually, around 80 per cent of Reading Recovery students make accelerated progress and are successfully 'discontinued' having reached the National Standard text level expected after two years at school. These rates reflect the international evidence base that Reading Recovery is highly effective in the short term (Jesson and Limbrick, 2014). What the most recent large-scale evaluation reveals in addition to confirming large positive effect sizes on a range of literacy measures, however, is the considerable site by site variability, indicating that contextual influences such as school and district leadership and resourcing influence effectiveness (Consortium for Policy Research in Education, 2014).

Issues facing New Zealand

Three major issues are pressing for New Zealand's literacy policy and practices:

1 Achieving more equitable outcomes

The issue of more equitable outcomes is longstanding and, although achieved in specific intervention programmes, has proven to be largely intractable at a national level. In upper levels of primary and in the middle secondary school years the international comparisons have consistently shown large SES and ethnicity differences (www.educationcounts.govt.nz/statistics).

There are two developmental explanations. One focuses on differential access to literacy practices before school and outside of school that contribute to development in school forms of literacy. Trajectories of development reflect the ongoing impact of this differential exposure and schools have been unable to make up the difference. A recent addition to the focus is the cumulative effect of the summer break on the disparities which are as apparent in New Zealand studies of reading (McNaughton et al., 2012) as they are elsewhere (Allington et al., 2010).

The second explanation focuses on mismatches between the teaching practices and curriculum in schools and the learning needs of underserved groups. This explanation takes several forms which hold differing implications for policy and practices. One assumes that the text-based framework does not provide the detailed code knowledge that Māori, Pasifika and children from poor communities need exposure to (Tunmer et al., 2006). An alternative position is that more direct teaching of the text-based approaches which capitalizes on children's incipient knowledge of texts and builds the language base necessary for school practices is needed (Phillips et al., 2004). A third position argues for the widespread expansion of Māori immersion schooling and bilingual teaching for Pasifika students (May, 2011; McCaffery and McFall-McCaffery, 2010). The latter would require a change in New Zealand's current languages policy and major changes to schooling provisions.

Evidence in support of these explanations draw on studies demonstrating the effects of developing and using texts that are more closely matched with the language and event knowledge of Māori and Pasifika students (McDowall and Parr, 2012); of changes in the core instructional designs of guided reading and shared reading to become more deliberate and explicit in how children are taught strategies (Phillips et al., 2004); of more deliberate and direct teaching which builds phonemic awareness (Tunmer et al., 2006); and of shifts to a more contextualized approach to designing literacy instruction (Jesson et al., 2011; Si'ilata et al., 2012).

To some extent schools have received support to use this range of evidence through professional learning and development, and the provision of new resources, and the national evidence indicates that gains in early accuracy and fluency of reading have eventuated. But more generalized changes in literacy achievement have not occurred (detailed further below). What now is needed is more deliberate scaling up of what the various studies have shown. To counter the existing constraints associated with autonomy at school and teacher levels, a new national policy is developing communities of up to ten schools to solve their achievement problems through the identification and sharing of effective practices (Ministry of Education, 2015).

Another area of development in policy and practice is about the transition between early childhood education and school. The design and implementation of measures of development through the early childhood years is needed (McLachlan and Arrow, 2011). Additionally, greater articulation between the curriculum statements should be created. Few studies have examined possible teaching approaches which could add value to the strengths of the meaning-construction approach before school. Nor has there been widespread testing, use and scaling of early childhood practices such as oral language exchanges which develop school-related vocabulary, well-planned reading with children and guidance in creating texts for different purposes to examine their impact on school success. As an initial step, more design-based research (Anderson and Shattuck, 2012) that systematically examines variability to identify sites of effectiveness, tests the design and redesign of instruction, and takes evidence-based designs to scale is needed.

The third area of policy development is the provision of guidance and access to resources for families. As in other countries there are programmes to increase access to resources, which in the case of literacy has mostly meant access to books (National Library of New Zealand, 2014). Like the international studies (Neuman and Celano, 2006), some of these have used libraries, with mixed success (Allpress and Gilbertson, 2014). Others use a 'book flood' approach, in which books are given to families or children and these have had some important effects (Tran et al., 2011). As noted earlier, the activity of reading to preschoolers is relatively widespread so a shift in focus from access to effective interactional styles and equitable patterns of usage is needed.

2 Comprehension and content literacy

The second general issue is a concern for how to build complex language uses with texts through early literacy practices that have significance for continued development through school. The developmental issue concerns how early literacy learning provides a basis for the literacy capabilities needed in the middle school years, including reading informational texts and critical literacy across content areas.

There are several sources of evidence for this concern. One is low achievement patterns in comprehension relative to increasingly higher achievement levels in fluency and accuracy of reading. A National Education Mentoring programme which examines the perform-ance of nine-year-olds across the curriculum areas showed that the percentages of nine-year-olds not able to read with fluency and accuracy at expected grade level dropped from a high in 1996 of 19 per cent (fiction) and 27 per cent (non-fiction) to 7 per cent and 15 per cent in 2004, and remained at these levels in 2008. By contrast, the levels of comprehension at nine years have if anything declined. While gaps between ethnic and SES groups have dropped in the overall reading assessments at nine years (they are still above effect sizes of 0.4 on various comparisons), this is largely due to substantial changes in accuracy and fluency and the national data support the research evidence that while these are necessary for increased comprehension, they are not sufficient. The contrast between fiction and non-fiction reading signals a concern for wider reading too (Crooks et al., 2009). The picture for writing achievement is similar. At nine years children are significantly better in surface versus deep features of their writing and there has been little change in overall achievement or reduction in the large differences between groups (National Education Monitoring Project, 2010).

These data signal a need to change the balance of the instructional design foci in the early years of school and in the articulation between curricula. The instructional design in the early years needs to have a stronger component focus on language acquisition at the word and supra-word levels through the reading and writing instructional approaches.

3 Digital access to and guidance for literacy

There are two sides to the third issue. On the one hand, there have been repeated reports claiming that students need to learn new skills and digital competencies to participate in and contribute to a rapidly changing twenty-first-century economy and society (21st Century

Learning Reference Group, 2014). On the other hand, there is little developmental evidence for just what the new literacy skills and competencies are, and what the new effective pedagogies might entail. The issue is a need for better research evidence and tested designs for literacy development in digital environments.

Currently, there is only limited use of digital technologies in early childhood services (Education Review Office, 2011). Thus impacts on literacy through early childhood settings are likely limited. But the most recent survey of the school sector shows that almost all schools report high levels of engagement with e-learning activities. Despite this widespread adoption there are challenging patterns. The ratio of students to school-owned computers has remained, since 2011, one computer per three students, and fewer than a quarter of schools report all their students have access to a personal digital device. Cost and network infrastructure issues mean there have been SES disparities in this picture (Research New Zealand, 2014), although these are rapidly reducing. Increasingly, the challenge for low-SES schools developing new forms of teaching and learning with 1:1 devices is to overcome the risk of a second digital divide in which the cognitive challenge of digital activities and what they might afford for literacy development is limited.

There are mixed predictions in the research literature about early literacy development in digital environments and the effects of digital teaching and learning platforms on early literacy development. The evidence to date shows that digital environments vary greatly in the depth of learning afforded, and that e-learning is often used as a powerful motivator for teaching traditional skills (Wright, 2010). However, as Attewell (2001) cautions, there is the danger that differential digital usage might exacerbate existing divides if low-SES students received a diet of lower order digital practice. In line with the history of local innovation, digital programmes are currently being developed by schools and groups of schools (see, for example, www.manaiakalani.org). Such local innovations are supported nationally by the development and sharing of digital resources to support Māori language (see http://elearning.tki.org.nz/ Teaching/Resources2/Maori-resources) as well as Pacific languages (see http://elearning.tki. org.nz/Teaching/Resources2/Pasifika-resources).

Conclusions

The historical context in New Zealand has meant that New Zealand has many unique features that influence the nature and outcomes of literacy instruction. Historically high levels of ambient literacy with widespread literacy practices, a relatively open curriculum, a traditionally meaning-based approach to literacy instruction and a history of teacher-led innovation combine to result in context specific approaches that work well for many students. But ongoing evidence of educational disparities has resulted in an increased policy focus on reducing achievement gaps, and explicit inclusion of code-based criteria in policy documents. In parallel, schools and researchers have continued to seek approaches that meet the needs of target groups. While some reduction of inequities is noted in the areas of accuracy and fluency, disparities continue in the reading comprehension which is required if students are to use their literacy skill to access the curriculum. The increasingly digital environment has added an additional literacy challenge for low-SES schools. In line with the historical New Zealand approach, school-led innovations seek solutions for addressing equity challenges using digital learning approaches.

References

21st Century Learning Reference Group. (2014). *Future focused learning in connected communities.* Retrieved from www.education.govt.nz/assets/Documents/Ministry/Initiatives/FutureFocused Learning30May2014.pdf.

Allington, R. L., McGill-Franzen, A., Camilli, G., Williams, L., Graff, J., Zeig, J. et al. (2010). Addressing summer reading setback among economically disadvantaged elementary students. *Reading Psychology, 31*(5), 411–427.

Allpress, J. A. and Gilbertson, A. K. (2014). *Dare to Explore III: Auckland Libraries' Summer Reading Adventure Evaluation.* Retrieved from www.aucklandlibraries.govt.nz/SiteCollectionDocuments/dare_to_explore_III_evaluation.pdf.

Anderson, T. and Shattuck, J. (2012). Design-based research: A decade of progress in education research? *Educational Researcher, 41*(1), 16–25. doi:10.3102/0013189x11428813.

Attewell, P. (2001). The first and second digital divides. *Sociology of Education, 74*(3), 252–259. doi:10.1080/02702711.2010.505165.

Clay, M. M. (2001). *Change Over Time in Children's Literacy Development.* Auckland: Heinemann.

Clay, M. M. (2005). *An Observation Survey of Early Literacy Achievement* (2nd edn). Auckland: Heinemann.

Consortium for Policy Research in Education. (2014). *Evaluation of the i3 scale-up of Reading Recovery year two report, 2012–13.* Retrieved from http://repository.upenn.edu/cpre_research reports/2.

Crooks, T., Smith, J. K., Flockton, L. and Allan, R. (2009). *Reading and Speaking: Assessment Results 2008.* Wellington: Ministry of Education.

Dalli, C. (2011). A curriculum of open possibilities: A New Zealand kindergarten teacher's view of professional practice. *Early Years, 31*(3), 229–243. doi:10.1080/09575146.2011.604841.

Dearing, E., McCartney, K. and Taylor, B. A. (2009). Does higher quality early child care promote low-income children's math and reading achievement in middle childhood? *Child Development, 80*(5), 1329–1349. doi:10.1111/j.1467-8624.2009.01336.x.

Education Review Office. (2011). *Literacy in Early Childhood Services: Teaching and Learning.* Retrieved from www.ero.govt.nz/National-Reports/Literacy-in-Early-Childhood-Services-Teaching-and-Learning-February-2011.

Elley, W. B. (1992). *How in the World Do Students Read? IEA Study of Reading Literacy.* Hague: International Association for the Evaluation of Educational Achievement.

Gilmore A. (1998). *School Entry Assessment: The First National Picture.* Wellington: Learning Media.

Guthrie, J. T. (1981). Reading in New Zealand: Achievement and volume. *Reading Research Quarterly, 17*(1), 6–27. doi:10.2307/747246.

Hedges, H. and Cooper, M. (2014). *Inquiring Minds, Meaningful Responses: Children's Interests, Inquiries and Working Theories.* Retrieved from www.tlri.org.nz/sites/default/files/projects/TLRI_Hedges %20Summary(final%20for%20website)2.pdf.

Jesson, R. and Limbrick, L. (2014). Can gains from early literacy interventions be sustained? The case of Reading Recovery. *Journal of Research in Reading, 37*(1), 102–117.

Jesson, R., McNaughton, S. and Parr, J. M. (2011). Drawing on intertextuality in culturally diverse classrooms: Implications for transfer of literacy knowledge. *English Teaching: Practice and Critique, 10*(2), 65–77.

Literacy Online (n.d.). *The History of Ready to Read.* Retrieved from http://literacyonline.tki.org.nz/Literacy-Online/Teacher-needs/Instructional-Series/Ready-to-Read/The-theory-behind-Ready-to-Read/The-history-of-Ready-to-Read.

Literacy Task Force. (1999). *Report of the Literacy Task Force.* Wellington: Ministry of Education.

May, S. (2011). *Language and Minority Rights: Ethnicity, Nationalism and the Politics of Language.* New York: Routledge.

McCaffery, J. J. and McFall-McCaffery, J. T. (2010). O tatou ō aga'i i fea? 'Oku tau ō ki fe? Where are we heading? Pasifika languages in Aotearoa/New Zealand. *AlterNative: An International Journal of Indigenous Scholarship, 6*(2): Special Supplement Issue Ngaahi Lea 'a e Kakai Pasifiki: Endangered Pacific Languages and Cultures), 86–121.

McDowall, S. and Parr, J. M. (2012). *Deliberate Design: An Analysis of the 2010–11 School Journals and Teacher Support Materials (A Summary Report).* Wellington: Learning Media.

McLachlan, C. and Arrow, A. (2011). Literacy in the early years in New Zealand: Policies, politics and pressing reasons for change. *Literacy, 45*(3), 126–133. doi:10.1111/j.1741-4369.2011.00598.x.

McNaughton, S. (1996). Ways of parenting and cultural identity. *Culture & Psychology*, 2(2), 173–201. doi:10.1177/1354067x9600200203.

McNaughton, S. (2002). *Meeting of Minds*. Wellington: Learning Media.

McNaughton, S., MacDonald, S., Barber, J., Farry, S. and Woodard, H. (2006). *Ngā Taumatua Research on Literacy Practices and Language Development (Te Reo) in Years 0–1 in Māori Medium Classrooms*. Wellington: Ministry of Education.

McNaughton, S., Lai, M. and Hsaio, S. (2012). Testing the effectiveness of an intervention model based on data use: A replication series across clusters of schools. *School Effectiveness and School Improvement*, 23(2), 203–228. doi:10.1080/09243453.2011.652126.

McNaughton, S., Phillips, G. and MacDonald, S. (2000). Curriculum channels and literacy development over the first year of instruction. *New Zealand Journal of Educational Studies*, 35(1), 49–59.

McNaughton, S., Phillips, G. and MacDonald, S. (2003). Profiling teaching and learning needs in beginning literacy instruction: The case of children in 'low decile' schools in New Zealand. *Journal of Literacy Research*, 35(2), 703–730.

Ministry of Education. (1996). *Te whāriki: He whāriki mātauranga mō ngā mokopuna o Aotearoa early childhood curriculum*. Wellington: Learning Media.

Ministry of Education. (2003). *Effective Literacy Practice in Years 1 to 4*. Wellington: Learning Media.

Ministry of Education. (2007). The *New Zealand Curriculum for English-Medium Teaching and Learning in Years 1–13*. Wellington: Learning Media.

Ministry of Education. (2009). *The New Zealand Curriculum Reading and Writing Standards*. Wellington: Learning Media.

Ministry of Education. (2010). *The Literacy Learning Progressions: Meeting the Reading and Writing Demands of the Curriculum*. Wellington: Learning Media.

Ministry of Education (2014). *Annual Monitoring of Reading Recovery: The Data for 2013*. Retrieved from www.educationcounts.govt.nz/publications/series/1547.

Ministry of Education. (2015). *Investing in Educational Success*. Wellington. Retrieved from www.education.govt.nz/ministry-of-education/specific-initiatives/investing-in-educational-success/.

Mitchell, L., Wylie, C. and Carr, M. (2008). *Outcomes of Early Childhood Education: Literature Review*. Wellington: Ministry of Education.

Morton, S. M. B., Atatoa Carr, P. E., Bandara, D. K., Grant, C. C., Ivory, V. C., Kingi, T. R. et al. (2012). *Growing Up in New Zealand: A Longitudinal Study of New Zealand Children and Their Families*. Auckland: Growing Up in New Zealand.

National Education Monitoring Project. (2010). *Writing, Reading and Mathematics Report*. Retrieved from http://nemp.otago.ac.nz/report/2010/index.htm.

National Library of New Zealand. (2014). *Sail into Summer Reading Programme*. Retrieved from: http://schools.natlib.govt.nz/creating-readers/summer-reading/sail-summer-reading-programme.

National Monitoring Study of Student Achievement (2012). *National Monitoring Study of Student Achievement*. Retrieved from http://nmssa.otago.ac.nz/reports/index.htm.

Neuman S.B. and Celano, D. (2006). The knowledge gap: Implications of levelling the playing field for low-income and middle-income children. *Reading Research Quarterly*, 41(2): 176–201.

Phillips, G., McNaughton, S. and MacDonald, S. (2004). Managing the mismatch: Enhancing early literacy progress for children with diverse language and cultural identities in mainstream urban schools in New Zealand. *Journal of Educational Psychology*, 96(2), 309–323.

Research New Zealand. (2014). *Digital Technologies in New Zealand Schools 2014 Report*. Retrieved from http://2020.org.nz/wp-content/uploads/2014/07/Digital-Technologies-in-School-2014-FINAL.pdf.

Robinson, V. M. J., McNaughton, S. and Timperley, H. (2011). Building capacity in a self-managing schooling system: The New Zealand experience. *Journal of Educational Administration*, 49(6), 720–738.

Si'ilata, R., Dreaver, K., Parr, J., Timperley, H. and Meissel, K. (2012). *Tula'i Mai! Making a Difference to Pasifika Student Achievement in Literacy*. Auckland. Retrieved from www.educationcounts.govt.nz/publications/pasifika/literacy-professional-development-project-2009-2010.

Simon, J. (ed.). (1998). *Nga kura Maori: The Native Schools System 1867–1969*. Auckland: Auckland University Press.

Statistics New Zealand. (2014). *Speakers of Te Reo Maori*. Retrieved from www.stats.govt.nz/browse_for_stats/snapshots-of-nz/nz-progress-indicators/home/social/speakers-of-te-reo-maori.aspx.

Tran, T.-B., McNaughton, S. and Jesson, R. (2011). *Books in Homes Research and Evaluation*. Auckland: Auckland UniServices.

Tunmer, W. E., Chapman, J. W. and Prochnow, J. E. (2006). Literate cultural capital at school entry predicts later school achievement: A seven year longitudinal study. *New Zealand Journal of Educational Studies, 41*(2), 183–204.

Ward, J. and Thomas, G. (2014). *National Standards: School Sample Monitoring and Evaluation Project 2010–2013*. Wellington: Ministry of Education.

Wright, N. (2010). *E-Learning and Implications for New Zealand Schools: A Literature Review*. Wellington: Ministry of Education.

7

GERMANIC-SPEAKING COUNTRIES

Germany and Austria as examples

Margit Böck

A general overview: the German-speaking area

The geographical/political area in which German has historically been the first language (*die Muttersprache*/the mother tongue) encompasses the Federal Republic of Germany (Germany hereafter) with its 16 states (*Laender*); the Republic of Austria (Austria) with its nine states; and 17 cantons of the Swiss Federation in which German is the only official language, as well as three cantons where German and French are co-official languages. For reasons of brevity, Switzerland, as well as some other areas with small numbers of German speakers, such as the (Italian) region of Südtirol, the Grand Duchy of Liechtenstein, the Grand Duchy of Luxembourg and a small area of Belgium, are not included in this chapter. The chapter will focus on administrative, social, cultural and linguistic factors that have significant effects on early literacy.

Consequences of state responsibility for early literacy in Germany and Austria

The 16 'states' of Germany have primary responsibility in the areas of education, science and *Kultur* ('cultural sovereignty'). On the higher political level, there is considerable consensus about foundational cultural assumptions in education. These have significant consequences for early childhood education in reading and writing, as will be discussed further. These cultural commonalities are shared, to a large extent, by Austria, which also has a federal structure. Broadly speaking, the school systems in Germany and Austria are comparable, particularly so in curricula and aims for early childhood provision.

The effect of dialects

The range of dialects across and within Germany and Austria pose significant difficulties for speakers of many dialects when they become readers and writers of standard German. For example, speakers of dialects from the far south of Germany and those from its northern seaboards are not readily understood by each other. There is a phonological, lexical, idiomatic and morphological and syntactic 'distance' between many dialects and standard German, which creates problems for many children coming to school learning to read, and more so learning to write, the standard language.

In addition, Germany and Austria have large populations of a non-German-language background. This includes children born in Germany or Austria to parents who have come from Turkey or South-Eastern Europe, as well as more recently large numbers of arrivals from various parts of the Middle East and North and Eastern Africa. Children (of all ages) come to school speaking neither the local dialect nor the standard language.

A cultural influence: the term 'literacy'

The word and the concept 'literacy' have no cognate in German. Over the last three decades or so, the term has gradually come into use as a *loanword*, in academic discussions. Translations into German have been attempted (e.g. *Literalität*) and with the German terms *Sprechsprache* (speech) and *Schriftsprache* (writing). Compared to 'literacy', they orient intellectual, academic, cultural and above all *pedagogic* attention in quite different ways.

A second issue among German speakers concerns the still dominant ideas in education circles around 'Bildung', with its overtones of cultivation and improvement. *Bildung* differs in its deeper meaning from the goal-oriented training and even more from instruction. Over the last two decades – with the participation of Germany and Austria in the PISA surveys – the Humboldtian conception of education as a humanistic enterprise has been joined by the much more pragmatic notions of education as preparation for the needs of an economy. The two exist in a not fully reconciled or integrated relationship.

The 'PISA-Schock' and 'literacy'

One factor directly plays into the tension between *Bildung* and training: the 'PISA-*Schock*', the metaphor describing the effects of the PISA results in 2000. The test showed unexpectedly low scores for reading among 15–16-year-old pupils. In particular, the test showed that children with a 'migration background' had worryingly low results, as did many children whose first language was German (Baumert et al., 2001; Haider and Reiter, 2001).

The results suggested the need for significant active intervention in the teaching and learning of reading and writing. This seemed particularly urgent for early childhood education (e.g. Roux, 2005; Stanzel-Tischler and Breit, 2009). In German-speaking cultures, the early childhood sector was traditionally identified with care rather than with education. The *Schock* and access to international research (e.g. EPPE: Sylva et al., 2004) brought early years' education into focus. It became recognized that socialization into reading (and writing) was not a matter that should be left to the start of formal schooling.

The *Kindergarten* (directly translated as *children's garden*, itself a potent and telling metaphor) has since been nudged to become a site of education with targeted support (*Förderung*). It is currently recognized as the site where first steps in reading and writing and in the direction of formal, standard (and ultimately academic) language can be taken (e.g. Charlotte-Bühler-Institut, 2009, 2010; Kieferle et al., 2013; Tietze and Viernickel, 2016; Viernickel et al., 2015).

At the same time, the aftermath of the PISA-*Schock* raised questions about early childhood educators (e.g. Fröhlich-Gildhoff et al., 2014). How are *they* educated? What training have they had? Does their professional preparation enable them to work systematically, to plan, to be aware of and sensitive to the needs of the children they educate? Do they have knowledge about support structures and possibilities? Do they have the skills and competences for analysis, for diagnosis and, where necessary, for designed and targeted support in practices and structures? And, importantly, what are their own practices and competences in relation to the language forms required for building knowledge and understanding?

Questions were asked about the extent to which the development of language in general could be seen as separate from the learning of reading and writing (e.g. Charlotte-Bühler-Institut, 2009, 2010; Jugendministerkonferenz and Kultusministerkonferenz, 2004). A whole set of issues needed new terms to replace what had previously been called 'pre-cursor capacities' (e.g. Österreichischer Buchklub der Jugend, 2007). General capacities that could act as a solid base for the learning of reading and writing were identified as targets of early years education (e.g. Tietze and Viernickel, 2016).

The German language: orthographic, semiotic and phonological matters and practices in reading (and writing)

English orthography is notoriously complex, given its history of successive waves of Germanic and Romance languages, overlaid by histories of layered borrowings and further complicated by the practices of distinct scribal traditions. That legacy – except for scribal traditions – does not apply to German writing and orthography. It has loanwords though these have not had an impact on the phonological ground rules and have not affected the orthography of German. As with English, however, the traditions of scribal schools have left confusing traces.

As a consequence, German orthography is relatively transparent (e.g. Nerius, 2007; Schründer-Lenzen, 2013). That is a great advantage to the German-speaking learner of writing and reading, whether native speakers or those coming from different language backgrounds and script systems.

Given the high number of immigrants who are native speakers of Arabic, it is important to mention *writing direction*. It affects not just written sequences but also how a page is to be read, even when it is largely covered by images. However, *writing direction* is becoming a matter of central importance for all children, as the reading practices associated with digital devices become increasingly normalized. Touchscreen devices, such as smartphones and tablets, provide access to text, which is not necessarily arranged in traditional lines nor necessarily read top to bottom. 'Linearity' is giving way to 'modularity' with its quite different *spatial arrangements* of elements, themselves largely modular in form (e.g. Kress, 2010). On these screens the left to right reading path is no longer the norm, whether in ordering and arrangement of elements or in engagement with them. This has effects on very young people currently emerging into early reading in all settings and in all reading formats (traditional pages or new screens).

Children who are used to digital devices, whether at home or in early childhood institutions, are developing a whole new set of practices and a lexicon to go with these – clicking, tapping, scrolling, sliding, touching, pressing – as means for activating the resources built into the device (e.g. Flewitt et al., 2015). The effects of such changes are difficult to assess; they may lead to an upheaval of conventional practices of writing and reading.

The relation between letters and sounds in German is not as predictable as in, for example, Spanish or Italian, but much more than in English. This means that a pedagogy (or, using the German term, *didactics*) using *prediction* as a hypothetical principle might be helpful, as a useful first try at word reading. It has a large effect on teaching reading – somewhat less so on writing – in German. A cautionary note: despite this relative transparency, orthography is an enormously contentious matter in German academic – and popular – debates.

The German version of the Roman alphabet has 30 letters, used to represent approximately 40 phonemes. The terms *phoneme* and *grapheme* (are intended to) indicate discrete and distinct entities in speech and in writing respectively. Some phonemes are represented by single-letter graphemes, others by graphemes that include several letters; similarly, some letters are used to represent different phonemes, in different grapheme contexts. Both are used to describe sounds for which there is no letter correspondence or vice-versa, representing combinations of either sounds or letters. For example, in the German word '*Schock*' – the English 'shock' – the word-initial fricative consonant, a *single sound*, is represented by *three letters/graphemes*: s, c, h. The word-final plosive consonant is represented by two letters/graphemes: c, k.

The *Umlaut*, as in ä, ö, ü, is also an effect of scribal conventions: in this case a 'shorthand' form of writing /ae/, /oe/ and /ue/, in which the letter /e/, in medieval script, looked like and could be readily reduced to two vertical lines, which in turn could become two small vertical lines – and then dots – above the vowel.

We cannot expect children learning the German script to know this orthographic history. Whatever their background, learners need to be given a helping didactic hand to make sense of these conventions. Nevertheless, it is the case that some script systems prove easier to deal with and learn than others.

Other issues produce difficulties, usually more for writing than for reading. German nouns should be written beginning with a capital letter, but not every five- or six-year-old will know what a noun is. This does not pose an immediate problem for reading. Dialect differences matter in different ways and to different degrees – and differently for writing and for reading. In some north German dialects /st/ is pronounced as in /stein/; in the South it is pronounced as /schtein/. Again, this produces no problem for beginning readers, but it does for beginning writers.

By far the largest amount of evidence available to any learner of a language is everyday speech. It is the stuff children constantly attend to in order to form hypotheses about the language they are learning. Little or no attention is paid by speakers to segmenting their stream of speech into words. In fact, to do so would result in odd ways of speaking. Yet, it produces real problems for learners of writing. Readers, on the other hand, deal with materials where words are presented as discrete elements. This is the case in German as it is in all cultures using an alphabetic script – though differently in each case.

All this impacts on the pedagogic approaches to be taken: the demands of policy, as well as the degree of power exerted towards conformity. Teachers need to consider the guidelines and emphases developed from policies; they need to factor in the implied cultural and social expectations about young children as learners in these policies. This is further influenced by the degree of diversity that early years teachers of reading (and writing) face in their groups. Their didactic/pedagogic decisions depend on careful assessment of all these factors.

In Germany in 2015, the proportion of children speaking a language other than German at home was 17.5 per cent (in Berlin 29.6 per cent, in Bavaria 15.6 per cent, in Thuringia 3.0 per cent) in *Kitas* (*Kita* is the commonly used abbreviation for *Kindertagesstätte* or day-care centre in Germany) (Bertelsmann Stiftung, 2015a). In Austrian kindergartens, in 2014, 26.4 per cent of children had not German as their mother tongue. With 61.7 per cent this proportion in Vienna is by far the largest (Statistik Austria, 2016).

Early childhood education, and success in early literacy learning

This chapter focuses on children aged 3–6, i.e. children who attend the *Kindergarten*.[1] In Austria, children's attendance during the last year of kindergarten has been compulsory since 2008. In Germany, there is no obligation to attend kindergarten, but children reaching the age of 3 have been entitled to go to the kindergarten since 1996. In 2014, 93 per cent of 3–6-year-olds attended a kindergarten in Germany (Bertelsmann Stiftung, 2015b).

A somewhat indirect indication of the link *and* the significance of early literacy institutions and their work comes from the PIRLS (in Germany called IGLU) study: 'Even though German Primary School students perform better in international comparisons than our 15 year-old students, *the qualifications and capacities of the pre-school period* and the work of the Primary School remain an educational policy of central importance – in particular with the aim of an "levelling-out" of social disparities' (Bos et al., 2007: 46, emphasis added).

Two points are relevant here. First, there are clear even if somewhat implicit aims and criteria evident in the work of early childhood institutions. The capacities fostered and the work done in sites of early childhood education are recognized as of central importance by both policy-makers and teachers in secondary schools. Second, a constant concern in the work of the institutions of early childhood language teaching is the goal of a *successful transition* to the next stage of the educational structure, the primary school: 'it has a function which is of outstanding relevance, particularly in *the frame of the present overall architecture* of the German school-system' (ibid., emphasis added). The transition from kindergarten to primary school has been, and remains, a topic for discussion, given the relative instability in schooling in general, and the relation between preschool and primary school.

Some German states, for instance, have *Bildungspläne* ('learning plans') for children that cover the age span from nought until ten or even 15 years, to support children's continuous learning and development (OECD, 2013: 123–125).

There are some key quantitatively based research studies that have evaluated the work concerning language education, including literacy, in early childhood institutions, the development of reading literacy, the implementation of educational programmes and related topics (see, for example, Pfost et al., 2013; Tietze et al., 2013; Viernickel et al., 2013). Children's language levels are tested in most of the German and Austrian states (e.g. Berlin about 1.5, Bavaria about two years before starting school)[2] to find out which children need specific support. However, there is a seemingly minimal emphasis in the policy-oriented documents on quantitatively based *metrics* for evaluation of work done in early childhood institutions. There are firm expectations about levels of competences in the work of early literacy learning and teaching, which are expected to be met at the point of transition to the first stage of formal schooling. These expectations are held by authorities in primary schools – with different measures applied in different states, all grappling with the issues.

In 2004, the State Ministers of Culture and Youth (Jugendministerkonferenz & Kultusministerkonferenz) in Germany devised a *Joint Frame Agreed by the States for Early Years Education in Day-Centres*.[3] A similar document was issued in Austria in 2009, with the *Cross-Federal Frame for Institutions of Early Years Education Educational Planning*[4] (Charlotte-Bühler-Institut, 2009), followed by *An Outline for the Final Year in Elementary Educational Institutions. Detailed Explanations Concerning the Cross-Federal Frame*[5] (Charlotte-Bühler-Institut, 2010). The former was 'An avowal [*Bekenntnis*/'commitment'] agreed by the governments of all the Federal States, for an educational mission for this type of institution and for the educational career for all children' (Charlotte-Bühler-Institut 2009: 1). The documents set out general expectations and guidelines for all early childhood settings in Germany and Austria.

So although the power for setting policy, curricula and other aspects resides with the states in both Germany[6] and Austria, there has been a preference on the part of the states to share aims, at a relatively high level of generality. The congruence rests on deeper principles: broadly, the Humboldtian (humanistic) legacy.

Clearly, the decision to issue standardized early childhood guidelines has had effects in terms of recognizably shared goals, aims and policies, even though it does not reach down as far as the development and contents of specific curricula. This leaves differences in implementation at the classroom level. Above all, the 'avowal' was bound to have effects on the *kind* of metrics that might or could be employed in documenting success. Metrics exist, though they are based on distinct conceptions about education.

These policy documents provide the core of early years education in reading and writing – as well as some measures and metrics. The term *Bildung* strongly plays into this, in its aims, conceptions and effects. It offers a generous, holistic conception of humans that affects early years education, and shapes the understandings of what may be involved in early stages in the learning of reading and writing.

Over the last two decades – with the crucial participation by Germany and Austria in the PISA surveys – and given support by large scale surveys from Anglo-Saxon societies, e.g. EPPE 'Effective Provision of Preschool Education' (Sylva et al., 2004) – the underlying perspective is changing. A significant change in thinking and practice is taking place, as illustrated by this quote from the policy document *An Outline for the Final Year in Elementary Educational Institutions* (Charlotte-Bühler-Institut, 2010), issued by the Austrian Federal Ministry for Economy, Family and Youth. The document sets out language competences that are assumed to have been acquired by children at the point of their transition from early childhood education to primary school, broadly at the age of six. The document provides

> the basis for guidance, support and *the documentation of the individual child's processes* of learning. . . . The first years of life have enormous significance for the learning processes of children . . . In a spirit of individual development, we can draw conclusions from this which are conducive to holistic learning across the various areas of education. The impulses . . . as well as longer-term interventions, *take as their starting point the ideas and interests of the children themselves* . . . considering their developmental steps, their abilities, and prepare for their future educational trajectory/career (Bildungslaufbahn) *without assuming or specifying developmental norms or any 'judgements'/'assessments' of competences.*
>
> *(p. 7,* emphasis added*)*

The document makes it clear that the module is not intended to be interpreted as a 'pre-determined catalogue of goals to be achieved or met. Nor does it constitute a compulsory requirement for a "syllabus" to be achieved, and to be met by each child at the same pace' (ibid.).

At the same time, there is continuing pressure towards more specific guidelines. The policy statements from all the states in Germany and Austria make it clear what assumptions exist about capacities and competences of children at the end of the period they have spent in institutions of early literacy learning and link these to their transition to the primary school. These policy documents provide useful indicators both about the *kinds* of learning experiences during the period in early education and about the *core expectations about children's capacities* at the end, as illustrated in this extract:

> At the age of five most children have far-reaching and differentiated linguistic competences in their first language; in relation to the general outlines of the system of sounds of their language (phonology), grammar (syntax and morphology); lexis (both the range of their 'lexicon' and its meanings); as well as speech performance

(pragmatics). In German the knowledge of grammar and syntax manifests itself in a largely correct positioning of verbs; in the ability to construct and use embedded sentences; in the use of the perfect tense; in the use of the 'perfect form' in telling a story, that is, in 'narrating'; and in the use of 'rich' vocabulary.

(Charlotte-Bühler-Institut, 2010: 28)

As far as phonological awareness is concerned, for children at this stage (5- or 6-year-olds), the document places emphasis on a differentiated understanding of the language phonology. Phonological awareness is perceived as closely connected to later competence in reading and orthography and at this point refers to 'care with formal aspects of sound as well as the capacity to make differentiations of phonological factors independently of the "content"/"meaning" of these units' (ibid.: 27). This degree of children's phonological awareness is made manifest in their 'ability to recognize rhymes; the ability to segment words into syllables; and the ability to segment syllables into their constituent letters' (ibid.).

The authors of the policy document assume that these abilities will be developed for most children in the *literacy* components in the final year of their early childhood education. This understanding draws on everyday linguistic experiences – it constitutes phonological awareness 'in an extended sense' (ibid.). By contrast, phonological awareness in a more narrow sense, such as the identification and comparison of single sounds, presupposes a conscious capacity for operations using formal linguistic categories (ibid.: 28).

Early literacy: 'documentation' and related issues

Currently, touchscreens are the most readily available way for documenting the everyday practice in early literacy education. In Germany, as in many other places, there is, however, a major issue of privacy, and the actual or latent fear of abusive intrusion, for lack of a better word, into the private domains and lives of those whose activities are documented. That itself is surrounded by often dauntingly demanding ethical requirements of obtaining permission for videoing or photographing children. In multicultural settings this is complicated by culturally differing attitudes to visual means of recording. This has led, so far, to a reluctance to use touchscreens for documenting early childhood practice (e.g. Senatsverwaltung für Bildung, Jugend und Wissenschaft, 2014).

In the absence of these means, more traditional and less intrusive methods continue: observations recorded in writing, by sketches or through interviews. In this context, the publication of a 115-page long *Mein Sprachlerntagebuch* ('My language learning diary'; see Senatsverwaltung für Bildung, Jugend und Wissenschaft, 2012) represents an example of how educators document the educational development of children in a *Kita*. At the same time, the book can be taken as evidence for *methods* and *content areas of literacy* instruction in early childhood. It is accompanied by an extensive guide of 30 pages, with detailed information about materials to use for early childhood teachers (Senatsverwaltung für Bildung, Jugend und Wissenschaft, 2008).

In Berlin, for each child at the kindergarten this learning diary has to be filled in by the educational staff together with the child. Topics regarding literacy are phonological awareness, interaction with language, linguistic structures and first experiences with visual and verbal language (Senatsverwaltung für Bildung, Jugend und Wissenschaft, 2012). The latter comprises 22 indicators; for example, you like to select picture-books on your own; you know which stories you like; you ask questions in relation to a story; you retell a story, even without pictures; you understand symbols and pictograms; you recognize your written name;

you ask adults to write something down; you write letters; you dictate words or sentences for a picture you have drawn (ibid.: 9).

In the *Sprachlerntagebuch*, the section on linguistic structures begins with a brief account of language development, from single-word utterances to very complex sentence structures. It goes into quite extraordinary detail, which could be considered as important information for teachers, but also as a challenge for the children. Consider this one example: 'in German sentences, the order of subject and predicate is changed in specific sentence types. The subject then follows the predicate. In formal terms this is called "inversion"' (ibid.: 93). The explanation is followed by a very helpful hint to the teacher on how and why this is difficult for German learners whose first languages contain different grammatical structures. It also gives examples of the likely sentence constructions by such speakers. Such accounts provide insight into other languages and can – when shared with the children – become very insightful for all the children, including those of different (linguistic) backgrounds. As for assessment, the document states that 'the differentiated observation of a child and the continuous use of the language learning diary enables the teacher to answer questions which arise about the child, without needing to subject the child to a "test situation", to an examination' (ibid.: 11).

The so far unresolved tensions in the overall vision of education within the German-speaking area is, by and large, reflected in the current policies and practices. The statement of aims and goals in terms of general capacities avoids a narrow conceptualization of success in relation to reading and writing. At the same time, the emphasis, for instance, on phonological awareness in analytic capacities – both in speech and writing – point to an unease about ignoring the seemingly more empirically objective and quantitatively graspable OECD view.

In a brief introduction for parents to the *Berlin Educational Programme*[7] (the *Sprachlerntagebuch* is part of this programme) the authors write: 'Adults make their experiences, knowledge, skills and abilities available to their children. They are curious to see what their children will do with them. They realize that *children are capable of creating something new out of something old* during this process' (Senatsverwaltung für Bildung, Jugend und Wissenschaft, 2004: 11, emphasis added). This formulation bestows agency and creativity to children's regular everyday actions: very much a Humboldian rather than an OECD position.

What is the country's educational policy in relation to multilingual literacy and language learning? Is there provision for children with special educational needs?

In all the political entities of the German-speaking area, there is a strong emphasis on the value of knowing several languages (if not necessarily the 'literacy' aspect of these languages). There is equally a strong emphasis on the children who are in the process of learning German as their second language, and the need to support these children.

As the document of the Austrian ministry of education states (a comment repeated in much the same form in documents from states in Germany):

> The process of acquisition of German as a second language has high priority and is seen as of fundamental significance. There is an attempt on the part of all responsible partners to provide favourable conditions. Given these . . . many children are able – after about one year learning the second language – to begin to cope in relatively complex situations.

> *(See Charlotte-Bühler-Institut, 2010: 28)*

For all young people in early childhood education settings it is assumed that they engage actively and continuously with several languages, which includes 'regional dialects, languages of linguistic minorities, and foreign languages' (ibid.). This concept suggests an interest in children's metalinguistic competences.

Provision for children with special educational needs

The document about *Bildungsprozesse* ('educational processes'; Charlotte-Bühler-Institut 2010: 6) pays attention to matters related to children with special educational needs. The question of 'failing' is here not such an issue as it is in educational systems and settings focused on explicitly stated goals. Matched with the resources of the *Sprachlerntagebuch*, and other means and the possibilities for recognition, including close attention paid to 'care', the *Bildungsprozesse* document is very much in alignment with the policy statements.

In Germany, there is, for instance, a programme with a 'federal reach' (2016–2019): the project *Sprach-Kitas* ('Language Kitas'), which offers opportunities for assistance in kindergartens with a high proportion of children who need support for their language development. The three main topics of this programme are language learning integrated in 'the everyday',[8] inclusive education and cooperation with the children's families.[9]

Characteristics of early childhood education in German-speaking areas

It is clear that the close control and narrow focus on highly specific/prescriptive goals and outcomes of some Anglophone curricula are not a feature of the educational thinking in Austria and Germany. It is essential to stress that teachers in German-speaking areas retain a high degree of professional autonomy and the philosophical/pedagogic orientation of some key policy documents encourages teachers' autonomy in implementing it at the classroom level (e.g. Charlotte-Bühler-Institut 2010; Tietze and Viernickel, 2016). Such an orientation is further reflected in methods, materials, timings and pace of work. In the German-speaking areas, the legacy of attentiveness and 'care', and of the metaphor of the 'children's garden' (the Kindergarten) are influential. By and large, funding is such that a relative wealth of materials are available, from the entirely traditional to the increasing presence of digital devices.

Major challenges for current and future early literacy provision

Funding is, without doubt, a key major issue, linked to other 'deeper' issues, including political, ideological and economic developments, which early childhood education is part of.

Political, ideological and economic developments

Education is a political matter par excellence. It deals quite directly with the matter of the immediate future, namely that of the next generation(s). Education policies reflect the aims of a society, and of the state that it supports. The current situation is that of uncertainty and insecurity. If there is no longer a strong sense of the need for a coherent society, then that will become evident in less attention paid to the importance of the school. This depends only in part on economic development, as explained next.

The cultural factor of the tussle between Humboldt and Neo-liberalism

The social, cultural and economic contestations that mark the present period in Western and Central Europe (and of course beyond) appear at the educational level in the German-speaking areas in terms of the opposing conceptions between the humanistic Humboldtian vision, and the economic and ideological vision of, say, the Organisation for Economic Co-operation and Development (OECD). What appears as a pedagogic issue in classrooms has its origins and causes in the world in which classrooms exist.

Those who work in and are committed to early childhood education are not usually engaged in and with the world of 'Politics'. Nevertheless, the values, the ways of being together, the respect shown and received, act as potent forces on those who are in these sites. They experience a way of being that might act as a model for them when they enter adulthood and can engage in the social world in ways that might bring those values into that world as an unremarkable model.

Development and funding of teachers' education, resources for working with children, recognition of the teachers' work

It is essential to attempt to produce the political – and with that the economic – climate to ensure that whatever vision we have of education, it is given conditions to succeed. Those who see the form of sociality that characterizes the sites and institutions of early childhood education and literacy as a vision that they fully endorse need to ensure that these institutions are fully integrated into their social environments; that those who work in them are recognized and properly rewarded financially for doing highly significant work for the society. That would demand education not just for the children, but for those who ensure the children's education. This would happen through funding for (initial and further) education, for research into the work done in these sites, to produce useable knowledge, which can be transmitted to children, as well as to their parents and to the community more widely. An important issue where funding is concerned is that children need time for learning, and teachers need time for supporting children in their learning, for being able to design situations and processes of learning. For that, it would be necessary that teachers can work with small groups of children, which, in turn, implies the need for well-educated and highly motivated staff for sites of early childhood education: for real kindergardens.

Acknowledgments

The author would like to thank the following practitioners and academics for their helpful suggestions and information on the topic: Elisabeth Eibl, Elfriede Kobler, Birgit Krainz, Dr Christa Preising and Professor Dr Renate Valtin.

Notes

1 Abbreviation used in Germany: *Kita* (*Kindertagesstätte*).
2 More information for Germany: www.bildungsserver.de/Sprachstandserhebungen-und-Sprachfoerderkonzepte-der-Bundeslaender-vorschulisch-und-im-Uebergang-zur-Grundschule--2308.html.
3 '*Gemeinsamer Rahmen der Länder für die frühe Bildung in Kindertageseinrichtungen.*'
4 *Bundesländerübergreifender BildungsRahmenPlan für elementare Bildungseinrichtungen in Österreich.*'
5 '*Modul für das letzte Jahr in elementaren Bildungseinrichtungen. Vertiefende Ausführungen zum bundesländerübergreifenden BildungsRahmenPlan.*'

6 Frames/programmes/guidelines of early education of the German states can be found at www.bildungs server.de/Bildungsplaene-der-Bundeslaender-fuer-die-fruehe-Bildung-in-Kindertageseinrichtungen-2027.html.
7 'Berliner Bildungsprogramm für Kitas und Kindertagespflege' (Senatsverwaltung für Bildung, Jugend und Wissenschaft, 2014).
8 Combined, if necessary, with specific programmes of language development.
9 Further information: http://sprach-kitas.fruehe-chancen.de/programm/ueber-das-programm/.

References

Baumert, J., Klieme, E., Neubrand, M., Prenzel, M., Schiefele, U., Schneider, W., Stanat, P., Tillmann, K.-J. and Weiß, M. (eds) (2001). PISA 2000. Basiskompetenzen von Schülerinnen und Schülern im internationalen Vergleich. Opladen: Leske + Budrich.

Bertelsmann Stiftung (2015a). Ländermonitor frühkindlicher Bildungssysteme. Ländermonitor – Übersicht. Tabellen 2015. Accessed online on 12 June 2016: www.laendermonitor.de/downloads-presse/index.nc.html.

Bertelsmann Stiftung (2015b). Ländermonitor frühkindlicher Bildungssysteme. Ländermonitor – Übersicht. Trends 2015. Accessed online on 12 June 2016: www.laendermonitor.de/downloads-presse/index.nc.html.

Bos, W., Lankes, E.-M., Prenzel, M., Schwippert, K., Valtin, R. and Walther, G. (2007). Erste Ergebnisse aus IGLU: Schülerleistungen am Ende der vierten Jahrgangsstufe im internationalen Vergleich. Sozialwissenschaftlicher Fachinformationsdienst soFid, Bildungsforschung 2007/1, 9–46. Accessed online on 12 June 2106: http://nbn-resolving.de/urn:nbn:de:0168-ssoar-201711.

Charlotte-Bühler-Institut (2009). Bundesländerübergreifender BildungsRahmenPlan für elementare Bildungseinrichtungen in Österreich. Issued by the Governments of the States of Austria, Municipal Administration of Vienna, Ministry of Education, Arts and Culture. Accessed online on 12 June 2016: www.bmb.gv.at/ministerium/vp/2009/bildungsrahmenplan_18698.pdf?4dtiae.

Charlotte-Bühler-Institut (2010). Modul für das letzte Jahr in elementaren Bildungseinrichtungen. Vertiefende Ausführungen zum bundesländerübergreifenden BildungsRahmenPlan. Issued by the Austrian Ministry of Economy, Family and Youth. Vienna. Accessed online on 12 June 2016: www.bmfj.gv.at/familie/kinderbetreuung/gratiskindergarten-verpflichtender-besuch/modul-letztes-jahr-elementare-bildungseinrichtung.html.

Flewitt, R., Messer, D. and Kucirkova, N. (2015). New directions for early literacy in a digital age: The iPad. Journal of Early Childhood Literacy, 15(3), 289–310.

Fröhlich-Gildhoff, K., Weltzien, D., Kirstein, N., Pietsch, S. and Rauh, K. (2014). Expertise: Kompetenzen früh-/kindheitspädagogischer Fachkräfte im Spannungsfeld von normativen Vorgaben und Praxis. Accessed online on 12 June 2016: www.bmfsfj.de/RedaktionBMFSFJ/Abteilung5/Pdf-Anlagen/14-expertise-kind heitspaedagogische-fachkraefte,property=pdf,bereich=bmfsfj,sprache=de,rwb=true.pdf.

Haider, G. and Reiter, C. (eds) (2001). PISA 2000. Nationaler Bericht. Innsbruck: StudienVerlag.

Jugendministerkonferenz & Kultusministerkonferenz (2004). Gemeinsamer Rahmen der Länder für die frühe Bildung in Kindertageseinrichtungen. Accessed online on 12 June 2016: www.kmk.org/fileadmin/Dateien/veroeffentlichungen_beschluesse/2004/2004_06_03-Fruehe-Bildung-Kinder tageseinrichtungen.pdf.

Kieferle, C., Reichert-Garschhammer, E. and Becker-Stoll, F. (eds) (2013). Sprachliche Bildung von Anfang an. Strategien, Konzepte und Erfahrungen. Göttingen: Vandenhoeck & Ruprecht.

Kress, G. (2010). Multimodality: A Social Semiotic Approach to Contemporary Communication. London: Routledge.

Nerius, D. (ed.) (2007). Deutsche Orthographie (4th edition). Darmstadt: Wissenschaftliche Buchgesellschaft.

OECD (2013). Starting Strong III. Eine Qualitäts-Toolbox für die frühkindliche Bildung, Betreuung und Erziehung. Deutsches Jugendinstitut (German edition of OECD (2012). Starting Strong III: A Quality Toolbox for Early Childhood Education and Care). Accessed online on 12 June 2016: www.fruehe-chancen.de/fileadmin/PDF/Archiv/starting_strong.pdf.

Österreichischer Buchklub der Jugend (2007). Leseförderung im Kindergarten. Praxismappe. Accessed online on 12 June 2016: www.family-literacy.at/static/media/familyliteracy/material/lesefoerde rung_im_kindergarten.pdf.

Pfost, M., Artelt, C. and Weinert, S. (eds) (2013). *The Development of Reading Literacy from Early Childhood to Adolescence Empirical Findings from the Bamberg BiKS Longitudinal Studies*. Bamberg: University of Bamberg Press.

Roux, S. (ed.) (2005). *PISA und die Folgen: Sprache und Sprachförderung im Kindergarten*. Landau: Verlag Empirische Pädagogik.

Schründer-Lenzen, A. (2013). *Schriftspracherwerb* (4th edition). Wiesbaden: Springer.

Senatsverwaltung für Bildung, Jugend und Wissenschaft (2004). *A Brief Overview of the Berlin Educational Program for the Education and Care of Children in Pre-School Prior to Starting Elementary School*. Weimar, Berlin: verlag das netz. Accessed online on 12 June 2016: www.kita-rominterallee.de/uploads/media/Berliner_Bildungsprogramm_elternfassung_englisch.pdf.

Senatsverwaltung für Bildung, Jugend und Wissenschaft, Berlin (2008). *Sprachlerntagebuch für Kindertagesstätten und Kindertagespflege. Handreichung für Erzieherinnen und Erzieher sowie Tagespflegepersonen*. Accessed online on 12 June 2016: www.berlin.de/imperia/md/content/sen-bildung/bildungswege/vorschulische_bildung/sprachlerntagebuch_handreichung_erzieher.pdf.

Senatsverwaltung für Bildung, Jugend und Wissenschaft, Berlin (2012). *Mein Sprachlerntagebuch*. Accessed online on 12 June 2016: www.berlin.de/imperia/md/content/sen-bildung/bildungswege/vorschulische_bildung/meinsprachlerntagebuch.pdf?start&ts=1460720337&file=meinsprachlerntagebuch.pdf.

Senatsverwaltung für Bildung, Jugend und Wissenschaft, Berlin (2014). *Berliner Bildungsprogramm für Kitas und Kindertagespflege*. Updated edition. Weimar, Berlin: verlag das netz. Accessed online on 12 June 2016: www.gew-berlin.de/public/media/berliner_bildungsprogramm_2014.pdf.

Stanzel-Tischler, E. and Breit, S. (2009). Frühkindliche Bildung, Betreuung und Erziehung und die Phase des Schuleintritts. In W. Specht (ed.), *Nationaler Bildungsbericht Österreich*. Graz: Leykam (pp. 15–32).

Statistik Austria (2016). Kindertagesheime, Kinderbetreuung. Accessed online on 12 June 2016: www.statistik.at/web_de/statistiken/menschen_und_gesellschaft/bildung_und_kultur/formales_bildungswesen/kindertagesheime_kinderbetreuung/index.html.

Sylva, K., Melhuish, E.C., Sammons, P., Siraj, I. and Taggart, B. (2004). *The Effective Provision of Pre-School Education (EPPE) Project: Technical Paper 12 – The Final Report*: Effective Pre-School Education. London: DfES/Institute of Education, University of London.

Tietze, W. and Viernickel, S. (eds) (2016). *Pädagogische Qualität in Tageseinrichtungen für Kinder: Ein Nationaler Kriterienkatalog* (revised edition). Weimar, Berlin: verlag das netz.

Tietze, W., Becker-Stoll, F., Bensel, J., Eckhardt, A. G., Haug-Schnabel, G., Kalicki, B., Keller, H. and Leydendecker, B. (eds) (2013). *NUBBEK. Nationale Untersuchung zur Bildung, Betreuung und Erziehung in der frühen Kindheit*. Weimar, Berlin: verlag das netz.

Viernickel, S., Fuchs-Rechlin, K., Strehmel, P., Preissing, C., Bensel, J. and Haug-Schnabel, G. (2015). *Qualität für alle: Wissenschaftlich begründete Standards für die Kindertagesbetreuung*. Freiburg: Herder.

Viernickel, S., Nentwig-Gesemann, I., Nicolai, K., Schwarz, S. and Zenker, L. (2013). Schlüssel zu guter Bildung, Erziehung und Betreuung. Bildungsaufgaben, Zeitkontingente und strukturelle Rahmenbedingungen in Kindertageseinrichtungen. Forschungsbericht. Alice Salomon Hochschule Berlin. Accessed online on 12 June 2016: www.gew.de/tarif/tvoed/sue/hintergrund/studien-schluessel-guter-bildung-anforderungen-und-rahmenbedingungen-der-bildungsarbeit-in-tageseinrichtungen-fuer-kinder/.

8

THE NORDIC COUNTRIES

Bente E. Hagtvet

The 'Nordic countries' are often perceived as a homogeneous unit of geographically close and politically and economically stable countries that share social democratic values rooted in a shared history and culture. While this is not wrong, it ignores significant political, economic and geographical differences that make it misleading. This chapter discusses some of their qualities and how they relate to early literacy education. These countries' policies and practices are then addressed, with a contrastive view on Norway and Finland. Finally, I will raise some concerns about future resources in the increasingly complex and multicultural learning communities of the Nordic preschools and schools.

The context of early literacy education in the Nordic countries

Geography, history and culture

Geographically, the Nordic countries constitute a Northern European and North Atlantic region consisting of five countries with 26 million inhabitants: Denmark (5.7 million), Finland (5.5 million), Iceland (325,700), Norway (5.1 million) and Sweden (9.6 million). In addition, there are three autonomous regions, the Åland Islands (28,700), associated with Finland, and the two Danish associates, the Faroe Islands (48,200) and Greenland (56,300) (Haagensen, 2014). Located between the Arctic and Atlantic Oceans, east of the Canadian Arctic Archipelago, Greenland is in the westernmost part of the Nordic region. In all of the north-ernmost parts of the Nordic region live the Sami population, an indigenous people who live in traditional settlement areas in northern Norway, Sweden, Finland and Russia. Though the majority lives in Norway, a precise population estimate is not available, as there is no official record of citizens with Sami identity.

These countries have much in common in terms of social structure and lifestyle, but governmentally and politically their only official inter-parliamentary body is the Nordic Council. Their differences in terms of systems of government, military alliances and foreign policy are quite profound. Norway, Denmark and Sweden are monarchies, while Iceland and Finland are republics. Denmark, Iceland and Norway are members of NATO, but Sweden and Finland are neutral. Finally, Finland, Sweden and Denmark are members of the EU; however, Iceland and Norway are members of the European Economic Area, but not the EU.

All of the Nordic countries are currently experiencing a period of population growth and complex demographic changes due to waves of immigration from Africa, Asia and the Middle East. Since 1990, the Nordic population has increased by more than three million (13 per cent), particularly in Iceland (28 per cent) and Norway (21 per cent) (Haagensen, 2014). In 2014, Norway and Denmark had the largest proportions of non-nationals, relatively speaking (11.1 per cent and 9.5 per cent, respectively), while Finland had the smallest (3.8 per cent). Sweden experienced the largest net population increase, with 115,845 new citizens. These trends have a clear impact on the Nordic educational systems.

Historically, two factors have impacted on Nordic identity and values, and more indirectly early literacy education. The first is related to the common linguistic heritage shared by Denmark, Iceland, Norway, Sweden and parts of Finland, and the second is socioeconomic in origin, often referred to as the 'Nordic (Welfare) Model' (Barth et al., 2014; Kvist et al., 2012).

The Nordic languages

The Nordic languages represent three language families: the *North Germanic languages* (Danish, Faroese, Icelandic, Norwegian and Swedish), the Finnish-Sami branch of the *Finno-Ugric languages* (Finnish and the Sami languages in Finland, Norway and Sweden), and the Eskimo-Aleut languages (spoken in Greenland, related to languages spoken in northern Canada and Alaska). Nearly 80 per cent of the Nordic population speak Danish, Norwegian or Swedish, which are mutually intelligible; another 20 per cent speak Finnish (6 per cent of the Finnish population speaks Swedish as their mother tongue). There are also a number of minority languages in the region, such as Kven in Norway, Karelian in southern Finland, Romani, spoken by the Romani people in all of the countries, and Sign Language for deaf or hard-of-hearing individuals.

The Nordic scripts are alphabetic, but they vary considerably in sound–letter correspondence. Finnish is regular, with a transparent, almost perfect, match between the phonological and orthographic structures (Lyytinen et al., 2006). The Icelandic, Norwegian and Swedish systems are semi-regular (Hagtvet et al., 2006; Pind, 2006), while Danish is irregular and non-transparent (Elbro, 2006). Also, the distinctiveness of phonological cues, such as their salience, strength or length, varies among the languages, and again it is Danish that has the least transparent and least distinct phonology. Bleses et al. (2011) showed that Danish children understand and use inflectional past-tense morphology later than Icelandic children, who learn a more distinct phonological structure. This difference is arguably due to phonetic differences in the strength and salience of the cues critical to past-tense suffix identification. By analogy, one would expect that these differences in orthographic and phonological transparency would make it harder to segment words' phonemic structure, and hence to learn to read in Danish, though to my knowledge this hypothesis has not been systematically tested (but see Aro and Wimmer, 2003; Furnes and Samuelsson, 2010; Lundberg, 1999).

The Nordic model

The 'Nordic (welfare) model' refers to the economic and social platform to which all Nordic countries adhere. The model was conceived in the 1930s as a means of stabilizing the economy by combining a free-market economy with a welfare state funded collectively by high taxes. Welfare in the 'Nordic model' is not only about helping those in special need of help; it is built into citizens' lives, with low-cost healthcare, free education from age six through university, highly subsidized preschools, free library services, and so on. One main reason that the Nordic countries receive top rankings in international evaluations of the structural quality of early childhood education and care (ECEC) (e.g. The Economist Intelligence Unit, 2012) may be the welfare model, which offers universal availability and subsidies to ensure access for underprivileged families and children in need.

Education is crucial to the sustainability of a model of society that depends on citizens' contribution and collaboration to survive, and the Nordic countries share the same general view on educational issues, not *only* on macro issues, such as equal access to ECEC, but also on curricular issues, such as the importance of teaching the principles of democracy, social responsibility and critical awareness, which, some would argue, are often taught at the cost of 'foundational skills', such as literacy. However, within the context of the Nordic welfare model, early literacy education may itself be seen as a democratization project and a gateway to universal participation in education and the workforce.

Although both citizens and political parties vary in their dedication to some of the ideas of the Nordic welfare model, egalitarian values permeate many segments of society, including the educational system and family life – even the way parents communicate with their children. This was illustrated in a study comparing mealtime conversations in 22 Norwegian and 22 US homes (Aukrust and Snow, 1998). Among other things, the Norwegian families produced more narrative talk, in particular stories about deviations from social scripts, while the American parents more often explained events and individual behaviours to their children. More specifically, the Norwegian parents tended to invite their children to talk about events, while the American parents quite regularly taught their children facts about the world and about social skills. The authors argued that these differences reflected Norwegian values of collectivism, egalitarianism and implicit social rules, in contrast to values of individualism and diversity, and the more explicit transmission of civic values in the USA.

A comprehensive education system

The Nordic model of education is a comprehensive, inclusive system with modest streaming of pupils, relatively few private schools and limited use of special institutions for children with special needs. In general, the Nordic countries share common views on basic educational issues, and all have gone far in founding educational priorities in human rights ideas such as 'inclusion' and 'equity'. An average government expenditure of 7.1 per cent of their GDP on educational institutions, from 6.2 per cent in Sweden to 8 per cent in Denmark, places the Nordic countries at the top among the OECD countries (OECD, 2014). When the welfare model was crafted some 80 years ago, the Nordic societies were ethnically homogeneous, and most children with special needs either got no education or were educated in state institutions of special education, often boarding schools. The inclusion of children with special needs and an increasing number of children with multicultural backgrounds in comprehensive educational systems is an educational, social, cultural and financial challenge. Although this has been carried out with much political and public support, it has also brought disagreements, and some special schools still exist. Also, with the possible exception of Finland (see below), the Nordic countries are challenged by some ugly facts regarding the power of the educational systems to reduce social differences. For example, children's social background is still a predictor of academic outcome (Bakken and Elstad, 2012; Jobér, 2012), and language skills at three to four years predict later language skills (Klem et al., in press). This has led some to wonder why welfare states do not raise welfare(d) kids (Ringmose et al., 2014).

Early literacy education in the Nordic countries

'Early literacy education' is an ambiguous notion. It commonly covers from birth to eight years of age (e.g. Gjems and Sheridan, 2015), which is also the convention used here. Covering this rather large age span means that the issues surrounding 'early literacy' touch upon at least two educational systems and two sets of jurisdiction rooted in the different educational philosophies and ethos of preschool and school. Over the last decade, Nordic early literacy *policy* has been, and still is, an area of increasing attention and change. Moreover, knowledge about early literacy *practices* is limited. Systematic observational studies are scarce, and those that do exist are mainly small-scale qualitative studies from which generalizations must be drawn with great care. Knowledge about literacy practices is mainly based on teacher reports. As there is often a discrepancy between what people say they do and what they actually do, this methodological limitation should not be underestimated.

Historically, 'early literacy education' has been synonymous with 'learning to read and write'. In all Nordic countries, formal introduction to the written language has been the responsibility of schools starting in a child's seventh year. The purpose of preschools (day-care centres) was originally to offer care to children whose parents (often single mothers) worked outside the home. The idea that preschools served an *educational* purpose was introduced in the nineteenth century, mainly by a middle-class demand for increased focus on children's *learning*. In the 1970s, Nordic women's increasing participation in the labour force demanded the provision of *both* safe and high-quality childcare (Karila, 2012; Korsvold, 2011). However, this did not necessarily include 'literacy'; on the contrary, teaching children to read and write was, and still is, the task of *early schooling*.

Early literacy education at school

In each Nordic country, the teachers' mandate is regulated by a national curriculum common to all schools and with no prescription of teaching method. However, the level of detail regarding pupils' learning goals varies across the countries, and both content and methods for teaching reading and writing vary across countries and classrooms. More generally, early schooling traditionally involves the systematic teaching of the alphabet, with an emphasis on a phonics instruction that integrates reading and writing of words and simple texts, in combination with an ABC book (Kristmundsson, 2007; Lundberg, 1999). The didactics of such teaching went through a period of controversies around 1980 to 1990, with disagreements between the proponents of 'whole language' and 'phonics' approaches, most predominantly in Sweden and Denmark (e.g. Frost, 1998; Hjälme, 1999). However, teachers in general continued to act independently and used 'a mix of both'; that is, they chose approaches that 'worked in practice'.

Informed by international research (e.g. Snow et al., 1998), the general trend today is to adhere to balanced methods, combining code-oriented ('phonics') and meaning-oriented ('whole-language') approaches (Frost, 2000). A 'writing to reading' approach may also be used (Hagtvet et al., 2012; Korsgaard et al., 2010; Trageton, 2003). On the whole, the teaching of reading and spelling in Nordic schools stands out as rather 'instruction driven' and 'material driven', but less so in Finland, where it is more teacher driven (Linnakylä et al., 1997).

Early literacy education at preschool

As a competence area, 'early literacy' is less focused in Nordic preschools than in schools. This is only natural, given its central position in schools and the rather strict division of labour between preschools and schools. Also, adhering to an ethos of holistic, child-centred, play-oriented and experiential approaches, and with a content focus on oral language, social and motor skills (Bennett, 2010; Einarsdottir and Wagner, 2006; OECD, 2006), many Nordic preschool teachers probably feel that the 'early literacy' they know of is rather alien to them (Broström et al., 2010; Einarsdottir, 2006). However, inter-country variations are noticeable; for example, the importance of *actively encouraging* children's early literacy is emphasized in Swedish guidelines for teacher training, but is barely mentioned in the Norwegian guidelines (Gjems and Sheridan, 2015); the Swedish plans also accentuate topics like 'teaching', 'learning' and 'knowledge' more than 'play' and 'care', while the latter are more highlighted in the plans of the other countries (Roth, 2014).

The idea that literacy practices may be carried out holistically in play, and that writing and reading skills may be acquired through guided, yet child-driven explorations, has traditionally received limited attention in the Nordic national guidelines for ECEC. However, more recent policy documents indicate that this situation is changing (e.g. the ongoing reform of the Finnish National Curriculum Framework (Explanations for the Core Curriculum, 2014; Sahlberg, 2015: Meld.St.19, 2015–2016 (Norway)). Three factors appear to drive this process: *societal changes*, new *research-based knowledge* about the importance of early education and *international and national education* policies. I will argue that these factors contribute to a growing awareness among preschool teachers and their educators of the relevance of 'early literacy' to ECEC.

Early literacy education in a process of change

Societal changes are presumably decisively affecting the ongoing change. Today's young Nordic mothers and fathers often work full-time once their child has turned one, which implies a great demand for ECEC. This need is reinforced by the rapidly growing multicultural population, who are encouraged by the national authorities to send their young children to ECEC to learn the language and be included in their new culture. In all of the Nordic countries, ECEC is increasingly seen as an active tool for integrating minority groups, supporting social mobility and preventing difficulties for children from less fortunate backgrounds. Therefore, affordable ECEC is offered to all children from the age of one year, and children from families with a multicultural background or who are in special need of care for other reasons are often offered subsidized education; if necessary, ECEC is offered free of charge (OECD, 2015). In all Nordic countries but Finland, more than 97 per cent of children between the ages of three and five were in ECEC services in 2011 (76 per cent in Finland); a reduced average of 50 per cent of one- to two-year-olds also attended (from 30 per cent in Finland to 70 per cent in Norway) (Eurydice, 2014). The participation of one-year-olds in ECEC provision has increased since 2011. ECEC provision, in other words, has replaced parents in the daily care of their children in significant ways. Therefore, it plays a vital role in supporting each child's development and potentially also in contributing to the reduction of social differences, including differences in access to literacy.

The second proposed driver of this process of change, *research-based knowledge about the importance of the early education*, has considerably influenced policy-makers and thereby national investments in ECEC. Findings have included, for example, the young developing brain's advanced ability to learn new words and new languages (Hart and Risley, 1995), the young child's great receptivity to word stimulation (Borgström et al., 2015), high-quality preschools' positive long-term effects on academic achievement (Barnett and Nores, 2015; Chambers et al., 2015; Gorey, 2001; Jensen et al., 2011; Pianta et al., 2009; Sylva et al., 2010) and the encouraging results of early intensive intervention for children with language and cognitive delays (Camilli et al., 2010; Ramey and Ramey, 2006).

Another line of influential research concerns studies of early literacy itself. Reading and writing skills are rooted in early oral and script-related 'precursor skills' that develop during the preschool years. An increased awareness of the importance of these 'emergent literacy skills' (Clay, 1995; Storch and Whitehurst, 2002; Sulzby, 1986; Whitehurst and Lonigan, 1998) has contributed to an expansion of 'literacy' as a phenomenon and construct. As an expanded notion, 'literacy' includes the comprehension and use of the language of books, for example decontextualized language, extended discourse, identification of rhymes and phonemes, recognition of letters and logos, pretend reading and invented/explorative writing. A further expansion of the literacy concept is implied in terms like 'multi-literacies' and 'digital literacy', referring to the combined texts, pictures and signs presented on digital screens. The digital revolution, which in less than two decades has changed the infrastructure of society, the way we communicate and even our notion of literacy itself, is thus another aspect of the ongoing societal changes, with potentially huge impacts on early literacy education. (For Nordic studies of emergent literacy skills, see, among others: Arnqvist, 2014; Aukrust, 2001; Dahlgren et al., 2013; Fast, 2007; Hagtvet, 1988; Heilä Ylikallio, 1994; Hofslundsengen et al., 2016; Jensen et al., 2010; Kjertmann, 2002; Korsgaard et al., 2010; Liberg, 2006; Lundberg et al., 1988; Magnusson and Pramling, 2011; Sheridan and Pramling Samuelsson, 2003; Skantz Åberg et al., 2015; Söderbergh, 2011; Svensson, 1998/2009.)

This process of reconceptualizing 'early literacy' by emphasizing its preschool emergent qualities and digital references may contribute to an increased appropriation of 'early literacy' among preschool teachers as a knowledge area of great relevance to their practice. The third driver of changes in early literacy education concerns an *active international and national educational policy* guiding the preschool sector towards increased structure and process quality in ECEC. The ongoing move towards multicultural and increasingly inclusive practices has been monitored by policy documents promoting ideas such as tolerance of individual differences, social responsibility and empathy from an early age (e.g. OECD, 2006, 2015). ECEC has become a political focus and a 'human rights' issue. The purpose of '*education* and care' (educare) in preschool is not, first and foremost, to prepare children for school or to provide care, but to educate the young child '*in its own right*', cognitively, socially, emotionally, linguistically – and literacy-wise.

The transition from preschool to school

A much-debated issue is the bridge between preschool and school. Reconciling preschools' conception of 'emergent literacy' as a developmental process with the curricular goals of schooling in ways that are not alien to either tradition is a vital challenge (Sandvik et al., 2014). Over the last 20 years, all Nordic countries have taken steps to link preschool to school via a transitional year with more academic content during children's sixth year (Broström et al., 2010). The most radical actions have been taken in Norway and Iceland, where school-entry age has been lowered from seven to six years, although it is still referred to as 'play school' in Iceland. In Denmark, Sweden and Finland, the transitional year has retained its preschool status, but its name has changed to 'school year zero' (Denmark), 'preschool class' (Sweden) and 'pre-primary education' (Finland). Below I discuss some of the intercountry differences in policies and practices of early literacy by comparing specific solutions chosen in Finland and Norway.

Nordic policies and practices as reflected in a comparison between Finland and Norway

Being similar in basic values and approaches to education, but different in many practical solutions, Finland and Norway constitute an interesting comparative case. They are similar in socioeconomic platform, population size, expenditure on education (Finland: 6.5 per cent; Norway; 7.4 per cent of GDP in 2011) (OECD, 2014) and pupils with special education needs (7 per cent of the total school population in both countries, Eurydice, 2014) and an estimated 5 per cent of the children in ECEC. They also have similar orthographies (Norway: semi-regular; Finland: regular) and basic educational priorities (both have received top rankings in international evaluations of the structural quality of ECEC provisions (Finland: 1; Norway: 3) (The Economist Intelligence Unit, 2012). However, in terms of pupil outcome, there are conspicuous differences in favour of Finnish pupils, who for over 20 years have topped the lists of international comparative studies, such as PISA, in all academic areas, including reading. Norwegian pupils have typically scored below, or around, the OECD average.

The reduction to two Nordic countries in comparison allows for more in-depth analyses in attempting to identify potential early literacy-related causal factors in the observed differences in reading level outcomes. The Finnish system is discussed in greater detail than the Norwegian because it is often seen as an educational success story – a miracle (Simola, 2005). It should be noted that the comparison is complicated by ongoing changes in the core curricula involving early literacy in both countries.

The case of Norway

Some national characteristics

Like other Nordic countries, Norway is highly industrialized. Women are a natural part of the labour market, and young families' dependence on ECEC services is considerable. Over the past decade, a politically driven expansion of ECEC provisions has covered the need for such services, and few, if any, countries allocate more resources to ECEC services than Norway (OECD, 2006). However, the scarcity of educated employees in the sector is a problem, and the general public feels that ECEC services' quality varies considerably (Meld. St.19, 2015–2016).

With the lowering of the school entrance age to six years in 1997, ten years of mandatory schooling was introduced (*School Reform 97*, 1997–1998). One important aim of the extra year was to facilitate children's transition to school by focusing on the learning areas of school, such as literacy, in the new Grade 1, via the child-centred, holistic and play-oriented didactics of preschool, and with no outcome goals for literacy skills prescribed until Grade 2. In 2006, a second reform, intended to strengthen children's basic skills, was introduced (*School Reform 06*, 2006–2008). Reading and writing instruction was now to begin in Grade 1, still without specific outcome goals until Grade 2. The principal national 'control mechanism' of reading and spelling instruction quality was – and still is – an external national test at the end of Grade 1 assessing alphabet knowledge, word reading and word spelling. One would suspect that this could have a washback effect on the teaching of literacy in Grade 1, but to my knowledge this has not been systematically evaluated.

Legislation and staffing of ECEC

The Ministry of Education is responsible for ECEC services, but their organization and quality assurance is largely decentralised. State regulations tend to be normative rather than absolute; for example, the staff–child ratio is normed to at least one trained adult for every seven to nine children under three years, and one for every 14–18 children above age three. Teachers should have at least three-year tertiary-level university college training, but due to the current shortage of qualified preschool teachers, about two-thirds of the workforce in ECEC provisions are assistants without sufficient qualifications (*Statistics Norway*, 2014). This lack of a formal qualification requirement for the many assistants in daily direct contact with children is seen as a serious threat to the quality of the Norwegian ECEC services (NOKUT, 2010; Meld.St.19, 2015–2016). Another concern is the shortage of qualified students applying for ECEC training; thus, all students with pre-qualifications above a normed minimum level are accepted (NOKUT, 2010). Nonetheless, approximately 90 per cent of educational leaders were trained preschool teachers in 2014, which is an improvement (*Statistics Norway*, 2015). The situation is less dramatic for school teachers, yet similar in terms of recruitment.

Educational goals and curriculum content for ECEC

The national curriculum plan (The Framework Plan, 2006) covers all ECEC age groups (1–5 years). It builds on a holistic pedagogical philosophy, with play and experiential learning as core didactic components. Seven 'learning areas' mirroring those pursued in school constitute the plan's key content components. One of these, 'communication, language and text', includes 'literacy', but topics such as 'digital literacy', 'emergent literacy' or 'links between oral and written language skills' are hardly mentioned. Given the open-endedness of this guidance, its implementation depends largely on individual teachers' initiative. The plan is under revision, and there are indications in existing process documents that 'early literacy' is an area undergoing change (Meld.St.19, 2015–2016).

Children in need of special services

Children who do not benefit from the ordinary educational programme (approximately 5 per cent) have the right to special needs support if their needs can be documented by relevant experts, most often the Municipal Pedagogical and Psychological Counselling Service (the PP-service), on referral by teachers or the local health nurse (who sees all children regularly). In addition, in 2015, another 15 per cent had a minority ethnic background and used Norwegian as a second language (versus 5 per cent in 2005) (*Statistics Norway*, 2015).

With ECEC being seen as preventive child welfare, day care may be fully funded for children considered at risk (OECD, 2006); also, centres that accept many migrant children may receive additional personnel and/or financial support. The PP-service is the expert and advisory authority in most of these matters and may, if needs be, refer a child further to special education resource centres that can help support the preschool or school. The referral processes vary somewhat across municipalities, and the impression created in the media and among parents is that the time from referral to when a child receives help is too often too long.

Teacher training

The Norwegian national guidelines for early childhood teacher education (2012) focus on six content areas, one of which is 'language, text and mathematics', covering topics such as 'knowledge about children's monolingual, multilingual and written language development' and 'the use of play in encouraging children's language learning'. These guidelines are implemented rather differently at the approximately 30 colleges training preschool teachers; therefore, both content and quality of training vary considerably (Meld.St.19, 2015–2016). Topics such as 'encouraging the children's emergent literacy' or 'prevention of reading problems' are not mentioned in the curricula of a fair number of colleges. The training of school teachers also varies across colleges, but the 'teaching of reading and writing' is in all cases highly prioritized.

The case of Finland

Some national characteristics

Finnish children start their nine years of compulsory education at the age of seven, preceded by a pre-primary compulsory programme from age six – either a half-day programme, free, as part of a full day of care, or at schools, organized by the schools. Before this age, municipal or private day-care institutions are available to all children from one year of age, with income-based financial assistance from the state.

The educational system is highly regarded by the Finnish public. This includes the ECEC services, which stand out in quality (Lindeboom and Buiskool, 2013). Literacy itself is likewise highly valued; most Finnish families read newspapers daily and are regular library users (Ahtola and Niemi, 2014; Korkeamäki and Dreher, 2011). Reading, therefore, naturally becomes a part of children's habitus; this is reinforced in schools, where pupils are not only encouraged to take a book home every day to read, but also taught *how to read*, such as strategies for word decoding and reading comprehension (Linnakylä et al., 1997).

Legislation and staffing of ECEC

The Ministry of Education is responsible for the total age group (nought to eight years), and the national legislation sets clear requirements regarding local services, such as the universal right to access, staff qualifications, staff–child ratios, curriculum guidelines and parental involvement in programmes. Yet in terms of regulation and power distribution, ECEC is a strongly decentralized system. Steered by some rather broad common national standards, the municipal authorities organize preschool, pre-primary and primary school education according to local needs. The level of detail at the local level varies across municipalities, but all services must submit a detailed curriculum plan with proposed goals to the municipal authority. These plans are used as an evaluation framework for the annual municipal inspection.

Parental involvement plays a crucial role in ensuring that quality preschool education is adapted to each child's needs, specifically in the development of an annual learning plan, which guides each child's learning progress. National initiatives to increase parental involvement are strictly implemented. In the past, for example, there was an initiative to strengthen the staff's ability to support parents and parenthood through 'educational partnerships'. Nevertheless, considerable local variation exists in parents' involvement in curricular activities (Lindeboom and Buiskool, 2013).

The staff–child ratios are presumably the best in the world, with one trained adult to four children under age three, and one to every seven above age three. The staff at Finnish ECEC centres are multidisciplinary and consist of the heads of centres and preschool teachers with a bachelor's or master's degree, children's nurses (with three years of secondary vocational training) and appropriately trained assistants. At least one-third of the staff must have a bachelor's degree or higher, and the rest upper secondary-level training. School teachers, including primary school, must have a master's degree.

Educational goals and curriculum content for ECEC

Educational activities in Finnish ECEC centres are guided by broad national 'goals for the child to reach', such as 'promotion of personal well-being', 'critical awareness' and 'social responsibility' (National Curriculum Guidelines on ECEC, 2004). Adult–child and child–child interaction is seen as essential; it strengthens children's self-esteem, stimulates their curiosity and promotes their language development and potential for learning. Content-wise, the vital role of language in children's development is highlighted, as is also the notion that preschool education should form a foundation for learning to read and write through, for example, literature, fairy tales and phonological awareness activities. The implementation of these regulations in practical activities is, however, entirely up to the teacher.

Pre-primary education should function as a bridge between preschool and school (National Core Curriculum for Pre-Primary Education, 2010). It comprises a set of 'subject areas', among which 'language and interaction' includes 'early literacy'. Teachers should initiate and support children's interest in observing, exploring and playing with spoken and written language via, for example, rhyming, phonological games, music and drama. The Explanations of the core curriculum (2014) further specify teachers' responsibilities. For example, children with a multicultural background should both receive qualified support in learning Finnish as a second language and experience their mother tongue as valuable and important. Also, children's emergent literacy should be supported through, for instance, play-oriented writing with digital tools. A recently highlighted knowledge area is 'multi-literacy'; that is skills for interpreting and producing verbal, visual, numerical and other messages. Digital competence is likewise seen as important. Taken together, a prominent quality of the Finnish curricula for ECEC and pre-primary education is their apparent rootedness in updated research on the development of early literacy.

As implied above, 'output targets', or goals of achievement, do not exist at this level. Nor does any external national assessment of individual children's performance. However, formative evaluations of children's progress relative to their individual learning plans are to be carried out regularly by the teachers (Lindeboom and Buiskool, 2013).

Children in need of special services

Within the Finnish ECEC system, children with special needs have the right to relevant special services. Special education is generally highly prioritized in teacher training education, and special education teachers are seen as valuable resources at schools and ECEC centres (Haussätter and Takala, 2008).

Children with a multicultural and multilingual background receive support in developing Finnish as a second language; some are also supported in developing their first language.

The national core curricula for basic education (2010) introduced a new plan for organizing educational support for children in need of extra attention following 'the prevention before cure principle'. Three levels of support are offered: *general* support (low-threshold support integrated into everyday learning), *intensified support* and *special support*. Intensified and special support are based on systematic assessments and planning in multi-professional teams and follow an individual learning and support plan.

A core element in the Finnish educational system is its built-in focus on pupil welfare, involving teams of special needs educators, school nurses, school social workers, school psychologists and school doctors (Ahtola and Niemi, 2013). The team, which meets regularly with relevant local staff members, is meant to initiate interventions at the individual, family and/or ECEC centre/classroom/school level.

According to Ahtola and Niemi (2013), the quality and organization of special education services largely explain why Finnish pupils with the lowest 20 per cent of scores on international literacy tests (e.g. PISA) strikingly outperform the corresponding subgroup in other countries. It might also explain the consistently small between-school variance. Ahtola and Niemi (2013) argue that the Finnish educational system appears to have an equalizing effect that begins in preschool and the early years of schooling. On this backdrop of academic success, it seems paradoxical that the psychological wellbeing of Finnish school children is a concern (Ahtola and Niemi, 2013). However, Finnish youngsters show more restless behaviour in class than pupils in comparable OECD countries and, when asked, they are more likely to state that they do not enjoy school (OECD, 2011). One possible interpretation of these findings is that the strong investment in the early years of schooling in Finland has not been followed up at the more advanced levels.

Teacher training

The teacher profession is an attractive career path for young people; only 10 per cent of applicants are admitted to teacher education for school teachers; for preschool teachers, it is 20 per cent (OECD, 2011; Sahlberg, 2010). Admission to teacher education is challenging, including an entrance exam with a written examination, an aptitude test and, finally, interviews. Teacher training programmes at universities or polytechnics are research based, with a strong focus on core topics of pedagogy, special needs education and didactics, as well as professionally oriented topics such as 'children's literature', 'music' and 'science'. 'Language and communication' plays a particularly dominant role. With the Finnish teacher seen as a key to quality, practising teachers have a high degree of autonomy, and no inspectorate agency checks teaching standards. Teachers' professional development is prioritized, and in-service training for educational personnel is funded (Eurydice, 2014).

Two similar Nordic educational systems with significant differences

This comparison of early literacy education in Norway and Finland aimed to elucidate some of the factors that may contribute to the advanced literacy skills of Finnish pupils, with a particular focus on early literacy education. Four factors have emerged as crucially important in understanding Finnish success: the *control mechanisms* built into the state–municipality relationship, *staff quality*, the *content* of the early literacy education services and the availability of *expertise resources*.

The control mechanisms of the state–municipality relationship are subtly different in the two countries, although the similarities at the system level are many. In terms of similarities, the educational systems for children from birth through age eight are organized under one ministry in both countries, with binding general national guidelines alongside decentralized curricula and service regulation and organization. However, the Finnish national requirements for local services seem more clearly formulated, and the control mechanisms seem more systematic. For example, Finnish municipal authorities have a clear mandate to follow up ('inspect') on the extent to which the goals formulated in a centre's curriculum plans have been reached. Norwegian municipalities have the same decentralized responsibility, but the follow-up appears less systematic, resulting in considerable variation across municipalities. Furthermore, the Finnish national requirements are specifically directed at key quality markers of ECEC, such as those used, for example, by the OECD and The Economist Intelligence Unit (2012): specific teacher–child ratios, staff qualifications and parental involvement in programmes. Equivalent requirements are more loosely formulated in Norwegian legislation. In summary, the Finnish control mechanisms appear more specific in kind, more precise in requirements and more strongly and systematically enforced.

The second factor, *staff quality*, is the area in which Norwegian and Finnish priorities and solutions are most noticeably different. While *many* Norwegian (preschool) teachers are highly qualified and motivated for their job, the Finnish are *typically* highly skilled and dedicated (Sahlberg, 2010). This has resulted in a general and noteworthy respect for Finnish teachers – among pupils, parents, politicians and bureaucrats. That neither politicians nor bureaucrats call for external evaluations of student outcomes, but instead prefer internal, teacher-driven formative evaluations, is a testimony to the Finnish trust in their teachers. It seems that this trust has replaced the accountability system that Norway and many other nations adhere to. Both politicians and bureaucrats have a share in this priority. The Finnish early literacy education benefits, for instance, from a solid teacher training education at the master's level (bachelor's level for preschools) and a research-based national core curriculum loyally implemented at the local level. Satisfying working conditions for teachers, with easy access to expertise, such as special education teachers, are also beneficial. Conversely, Norwegian teacher and preschool teacher training education is at the bachelor's level, and local curricula are rather diverse, while areas of great pedagogical importance ('core areas') may be missing or granted little attention. Local resource team availability may also be limited. A corollary of this is that Norwegian teachers' skills, knowledge and professional capacity tend to vary with training institution, local access to resource teams, in-service training and mentoring (Hausstätter and Takala, 2008; NOKUT, 2010). The relatively high percentage of unqualified assistants working in Norwegian ECEC services adds to these challenges.

In spite of a basic similarity in holistic and play-oriented didactic approaches in Finnish and Norwegian ECEC, *the content of early literacy education*, the third explanatory factor, varies noticeably. Finnish curricula for both ECEC and the pre-primary year highlight the early literacy skills that are *foundational* to reading and writing skills, and with a gradual and individually based increase in focus on letters and writing- and reading-related activities as the children get older. The Norwegian ECEC curriculum (The Framework Plan, 2006, currently under revision) also accentuates the importance of oral language skills, and to some extent also emergent literacy skills such as phonological language games, whereas script-related emergent literacy skills are mentioned only superficially. With the lowering of the school entrance age to six years, the stimulation of reading and writing skills in this age group has increased. Today most children are taught how to read and write. With a dearth of observation studies, knowledge about how children are taught is limited, but a qualified hypothesis is that the didactic approach is highly influenced by traditional basic reading and writing skills pedagogy as taught in the first grade of school (when the children were a year older). This gap in emphases and demands between the Norwegian ECEC and the new grade one may be challenging for some children. In the worst case, it may be an obstacle to positive literacy development. Such an abrupt transition from ECEC to school is not research based.

In sum, the Finnish curricula for 'early literacy' appear to be better founded in updated research than the Norwegian curricula; also preschool and school appear better bridged. This difference was highlighted by Afdal (2014) in a comparative study of the development of education policies and curricula in Norway and Finland. A main finding was that researchers and educators played a more active role in developing the curricula in Finland; in Norway, the important decisions seemed driven by ideology and politics.

The fourth and final factor presumably contributing to the Finnish success is *the availability of expertise resources*. Immediate access to expertise is crucial when a pupil's need for support exceeds the teacher's competence and professional insights. Recently, such expertise has become less available in many Norwegian municipalities. In Finland, it is easily available; 'the prevention before cure principle' is not an empty slogan, but an inherent part of the Finnish schools and work ethos (Ahtola and Niemi, 2014). The relatively high functioning of the pupils at the lower tail of the distribution of, for example, the PISA results (Ahtola and Niemi, 2014) indicates that particularly 'pupils at risk' profit from these resources.

Analysts of the systematically positive Finnish educational results underscore that they cannot be attributed to one factor alone; it is the totality of factors in combination that constitute the Finnish educational system (Simola, 2005). Other factors than those examined here, such as those related to national historical experiences and cultural traditions (Simola, 2005), may also play a role. However, those mentioned here are the ones that may be handled instrumentally at various institutional levels.

Future directions and challenges

A number of serious challenges face the Nordic countries as we approach the 2020s – challenges in the content, didactics and organization of early literacy education. The first concerns the *extensive immigration* to the Nordic countries. The inclusion of many new citizens demands a multicultural mindset that many Nordic preschool and school teachers are unfamiliar with. It may also challenge the Nordic model itself, with its associated premises of rights and duties, and the public acceptance of belonging to an egalitarian democratic society where basic values are shared. The Nordic educational systems will have to play a key role in passing on to all of their children not only the Nordic languages, but also the values and the duties associated with the Nordic model.

A second challenge concerns the needs of *young children to be guided toward digital competency* in age-appropriate ways, to take the best of the potentialities of the current digital revolution. Not only is this a demanding educational project for which teachers must be trained alongside the children, it is above all a project of democratization, where access to digital literacy is a tool to participation in the Nordic societies.

The third challenge follows from the other two and has to do with staff training: the success of future early literacy education will depend on the quality of teachers and other professional groups. Offering qualified early literacy education to all children within a complex inclusive system will only succeed if schools and preschools are well organized and teachers are well trained, highly dedicated and in regular collaboration with relevant and easily available expertise resources. Finland is an important reminder that this is not impossible.

References

Afdal, H. W. (2014). Fra politikk til praksis – konstruksjon av læreres profesjonelle kunnskap. [From politics to practice . . .] *Norsk Pedagogisk Tidsskrift, 6,* 469–468.

Ahtola, A. and Niemi, P. (2014). Does it work in Finland? School psychological services within a successful system of basic education. *School Psychology International, 35*(2), 136–151. doi:10.1177/0143034312469161.

Arnqvist, A. (2014). Forskning om de yngre barnens läs- och skrivlärande [Research on the literacy learning of the younger children in ECEC]. In M. Vinterek and A. Arnqvist (eds), *Pedagogiskt arbete: Enhet och mångfald* (pp. 21–37). Falun: Högskolan Dalarna.

Aro, M. and Wimmer, H. (2003). Learning to read: English in comparison to six more regular orthographies. *Applied Psycholinguistics, 24*, 621–635. doi:10.1017/S0142716403000316.

Aukrust, V. G. (2001). Talk focused talk in preschools – culturally formed socialization of talk. *First Language, 21*, 57–82. doi:10.1177/014272370102106103.

Aukrust, V. G. and Snow, C. (1998). Narratives and explanations during mealtime conversations in Norway and the US. *Language in Society, 27*(2), 221–246. doi:10.1017/S004740450019862.

Bakken, A. and Elstad, J. I. (2012). For store forventinger? Kunnskapsløftet og ulikheter i grunnskole-karakterer. [Too large expectations? Reform 2006 and differences in student outcome]. Norsk Institutt for forskning om oppvekst, velferd og aldring (NOVA). Report No. 7/2012.

Barnett, W. S. and Nores, M. (2015). Investment and productivity arguments for ECEC. In P. T. M. Marope and Y. Kaga (eds), *Investing Against Evidence: The Global State of Early Childhood Care and Education* (pp. 8–32). Paris: UNESCO Publishing.

Barth, E., Moene, K. O. and Willumsen, F. (2014). The Scandinavian model – An interpretation. *Journal of Public Economics, 117*, 60–72. http://dx.doi.org/10.1016/j.jpubeco.2014.04.001.

Bennett, J. (2010). Pedagogy in early childhood services with special reference to Nordic approaches. *Psychological Science and Education, 3*, 16–21.

Bleses, D., Basbøll, H. and Vach, W. (2011). Is Danish difficult to acquire? Evidence from Nordic past-tense studies. *Language and Cognitive Processes, 26*(8), 1193–1231. doi:10.1080/01690965.2010.515107.

Borgstrøm, K., Torkildsen, J.v.K. and Lindgren, M. (2015). Substantial gains in word learning ability between 20 and 24 months: A longitudinal ERP study. *Brain and Language, 149*, 33–45. doi:10.1016/j.bandl2015.07.002.

Broström, S., Einarsdottir, J. and Vrinioti, K. (2010). Transitions from preschool to primary school. In H. Müller (ed.), *Transition from Pre-School to School: Emphasizing Early Literacy – Comments and Reflections by Researchers from Eight European Countries* (pp. 16–20). Cologne: EU-Agency. Retrieved from www.ease-eu.com/documents/compendium/compendium.pdf.

Camilli, G., Vargas, S., Ryan, S. and Barnett, W. S. (2010). Meta-analysis of the effects of early education interventions on cognitive and social development. *The Teachers College Record, 112*(3), 579–620.

Chambers, B., Cheung, A. and Slavin, R. E. (2015). *Literacy and Language Outcomes of Balanced and Developmental Approaches to Early Childhood Education: A Systematic Review.* Baltimore, MD: Johns Hopkins University, Center for Research and Reform in Education.

Clay, M. (1995). *What Did I Write?Beginning Writing Behavior.* Auckland: Heinemann Education Books.

Dahlgren, G., Gustafsson, K., Mellgren, E. and Olsson, L. E. (2013). *Barn upptäcker skriftspråket* [*Children discovering the written language*]. 4th edition, Stockholm: Liber förlag.

The Economist Intelligence Unit. (2012). *Starting Well. Benchmarking Early Education Across the World (2012). A Report from the Economist Intelligence Unit.* Commissioned by LIEN Foundation.

Einarsdottir, J. (2006). From pre-school to primary school: When different contexts meet. *Scandinavian Journal of Educational Research, 50*(2), 165–184.

Einarsdottir, J. and Wagner, J. T. (eds). (2006). *Nordic Childhoods and Early Education: Philosophy, Research, Policy, and Practice in Denmark, Finland, Iceland, Norway, and Sweden.* Greenwich, CT: Information Age.

Elbro, C. (2006). Literacy acquisition in Danish: A deep orthography in cross-linguistic light. In R. Malatesha Joshi and P. G. Aaron (eds), *Handbook of Orthography and Literacy* (pp. 31–47). Mahwah, NJ: Lawrence Erlbaum.

Eurydice. (2014). *Key Data on Early Childhood Education and Care in Europe. Eurydice and Eurostat Report.* The EU Commission, Brussels. Luxembourg: Publications Office of the European Union. doi:10.2797/75270.

Explanations for the Core Curriculum of ECEC of 2014 [*Grunderna för förskoleundervisningens läroplan 2014*]. (2014). Föreskrifter och anvisningar 2014:94. Helsinki: The Finnish National Board of Education.

Fast, C. (2007). *Sju barn lär sig läsa och skriva* [*Seven children learn to read and write*] (doctoral dissertation). Stockholm: Elanders Gotab. Retrieved from www.diva-portal.org/smash/get/diva2:169656/FULLTEXT01.pdf.

Frost, J. (1998). *Læsepraksis – på teoretisk grundlag* [*The practice of reading – on theoretical foundations*]. København: Dansk psykologisk forlag.

Frost, J. (2000). From 'epi' through 'meta' to mastery: The balance of meaning and skill in early reading instruction. *Scandinavian Journal of Educational Research*, *44*(2), 125–144.

Furnes, B. and Samuelsson, S. (2010). Predicting reading and spelling difficulties in transparent and opaque orthographies: A comparison between Scandinavian and U.S./Australian children. *Dyslexia*, *16*(2), 119–142. doi:10.1002/dys.401.

Gjems, L. and Sheridan, S. (2015). Early literacy in Norwegian and Swedish preschool teacher education. *Psychology in Russia: State of the Art*, *8*(2), 4–17.

Gorey, K. M. (2001). Early childhood education: A meta-analytic affirmation of the short- and long-term benefits of educational opportunity. *School Psychology Quarterly*, *16*(1), 9–30.

Haagensen, K. M. (ed.). (2014). *Nordic Statistical Yearbook 2014*, Vol. 52. Copenhagen: Nordic Council of Ministers. Retrieved from http://dk.doi.org/10.6027/Nord2014-001.

Hagtvet, B. E. (1988). *Skriftspråkutvikling gjennom lek* [*Literacy development through play*]. Oslo: Oslo University Press.

Hagtvet, B., Flugstad, R. and Rygg, R. (2012). Oppdagende skriving i barnehage og skole et vindu til barns språklige kompetanse [Invented writing in preschool and school: A window to the child's language capabilities]. *Bedre Skole*, *2014*(2), 24–30.

Hagtvet, B., Helland, T. and Lyster, S. (2006). Literacy acquisition in Norwegian. In R. Malatesha Joshi and P. G. Aaron (eds), *Handbook of Orthography and Literacy* (pp. 15–30). Mahwah, NJ: Lawrence Erlbaum.

Hart, B. and Risley, R. T. (1995). *Meaningful Differences in the Everyday Experience of Young American Children*. Baltimore, MD: P.H. Brookes.

Hausstätter, R. S. and Takala, M. (2008). The core of special teacher education: A comparison of Finland and Norway. *European Journal of Special Needs Education*, *23*(2), 121–134. doi:10.1080/08856250801946251.

Heilä Ylikallio, R. (1994). *Mönster i förskolbarns möte med skriftspråket* [Patterns in preschool children's early encounters with the written language]. Åbo, Finland: Faculty of Education, Åbo Akademi.

Hjälme, A. (1999). *Kan man bli klok på läsdebatten? Analys av en pedagogisk kontrovers* [*Can you get any wiser from studying the reading debate? An analysis of an educational controversy*] (doctoral dissertation). Solna: Hjälme och Ekelund Publishers. Retrieved from www.johanita.se/anita/Kan%20man%20bli%20klok%20p%E5%20l%E4sdebatten.pdf.

Hofslundsengen, H. and Gustafsson, J.-E. (2016). Immediate and delayed effects of invented writing intervention in preschool. *Reading and Writing*, 1–23. Online 22 April 2016. doi:10.1007/s11145-016-9646-8.

Jensen, A. S., Broström, S. and Hansen, O.E. (2010). Critical perspectives on Danish early childhood education and care: Between the technical and the political. *Early Years*, *30*(3), 243–254, doi:10.1080/09575146.2010.506599.

Jensen, B., Holm, A. and Bremberg, S. (2011). *The effect of an inclusive ECEC-intervention program on child strengths and difficulties*. Working Paper Series, CSER WP No. 0009. Denmark: Center for Strategic Educational Research DPU, Aarhus University. Retrieved from http://edu.au.dk/fileadmin/www.dpu.dk/e-boeger/VIDA_rapporter/The_Effect_of_an_Inclusive_ECEC-intervention_Program_on_Child_Strengths_and_Difficulties.pdf.

Jobér, A. (2012). Social class in social science class. Doctoral Dissertation in Education. Malmö Studies in Educational Sciences, No 66. Faculty of Education and Society, Malmö University.

Karila, K. (2012). A Nordic perspective on early childhood education and care policy. *European Journal of Education*, *47*(4), 584–593.

Kjertmann, K. (2002). *Læsetilegnelse ikke kun en sag for skolen* [*Learning to read is not only a school matter*]. Copenhagen: Alinea.

Klem, M., Hagtvet, B. E., Hulme, C. and Gustafsson, J.-E. (in press). Screening for language delay: Growth trajectories of language ability in low- and high-performing children. *Journal of Speech, Language and Hearing Research*.

Korkeamäki, R.-L. and Dreher, M.J (2011). Early literacy practices and the Finnish national core curriculum. *Journal of Curriculum Studies*, *43*(1), 109–137.

Korsgaard, K., Vitger, M. and Hannibal, S. (2010). *Oppdagende skrivning: En vei inn i læsningen* [*Invented writing: A road to reading*]. Copenhagen: Dansklærerforeningen [The Danish Association for Teachers].

Korsvold, T. (2011). Dilemmas over childcare in Norway, Sweden and West Germany after 1945. In A. T. Kjørholt and J. Qvortrup (eds), *The Modern Child and the Flexible Labor Market: Child Care Policies and Practices at a Crossroad?* (pp. 19–37). Basingstoke: Palgrave Macmillan. doi:10.1080/00220271003801959.

Kristmundsson, G.B. (2007). *Læsning og skrivning i læreruddannelsen i Norden* [*Reading and writing in teacher training in the Nordic countries*]. Tema Nord 2007:559. København: Nordisk Ministerråd [Copenhagen; The Nordic Council].

Kvist, J., Fritzell, J. and Hvinden, B. and Kangas, O. (2012). *Changing Social Equality: The Nordic Welfare Model in the 21st Century*. Bristol: The Policy Press, University of Bristol.

Liberg, C. (2006). *Hur barn lär sig läsa och skriva* [*How children learn to read and write*]. 2nd edition. Lund: Studentlitteratur.

Lindeboom, G.-J. and Buiskool, B.-J. (2013). *Quality in early childhood education and care. Annex report country & case studies*. EU-Parliament, Directorate-General for Internal Policies. Brussels: The European Parliament.

Linnakylä, P., Törmäkangas, K. and Tønnessen, F. E. (1997). What is the difference between teaching reading in Finland and Norway? In J. Frost, A. Sletmo and F. E. Tønnessen (eds), *Skriften på veggen* [*The script on the wall*]. Copenhagen: Dansk Psykologisk Forlag.

Lundberg, I. (1999). Learning to read in Scandinavia. In M. Harris and G. Hatano (eds), *Learning to Read and Write: A Cross-Linguistic Perspective* (pp. 157–172). Cambridge: Cambridge University Press.

Lundberg, I., Frost, J. and Petersen, O.-P. (1988). Effects of an extensive program for stimulating phonological awareness in preschool children. *Reading Research Quarterly, 23*(3), 263–284.

Lyytinen, H., Aro, M., Holpainen, L., Leiwo, M., Lyytinen, P. and Tolvanen, A. (2006). Children's language and reading acquisition in a highly transparent orthography. In R. Malatesha Joshi and P. G. Aaron (eds), *Handbook of Orthography and Literacy* (pp. 47–64). Mahwah, NJ: Lawrence Erlbaum.

Magnusson, M. and Pramling, N. (2011). Signs of knowledge: The appropriation of a symbolic skill in a 5-year-old. *European Early Childhood Education Research Journal, 19*(3), 357–372.

Meld.St.19. (2015–2016). *Tid for lek og læring. Bedre innhold i barnehagen.* [*Time for play and learning. Improved content in the preschool*]. [White Paper 19, Report to the Parliament.] Oslo: Ministry of Education and Research.

National Core Curriculum for Pre-Primary Education. (2010). Helsinki: The Finnish National Board of Education.

National Curriculum Guidelines on Early Childhood Education and Care in Finland. (2004). Helsinki: The Ministry of Social Affairs and Health.

National Curriculum Plan of Early Childhood Education of Norway, The Framework Plan. (2006). Oslo: Ministry of Education and Research.

National Guidelines for Early Childhood Teacher Education of Norway. (2012). Oslo: Ministry of Education and Research.

NOKUT. (2010). *Evaluering av førskolelærerutdanning i Norge* [*The evaluation of preschool teacher training in Norway*]. Oslo: NOKUT [The Norwegian Agency for Quality Assurance in Education].

OECD. (2006). *Starting Strong II. Early Childhood Education and Care*. Paris: OECD.

OECD. (2011). *Education at a Glance 2011: OECD Indicators*. OECD Publishing. Retrieved from http://dx.doi.org/10.1787/eag-2011-en.

OECD. (2014). *Education at a Glance 2014: OECD Indicators*. OECD Publishing. Retrieved from http://dx.doi.org/10.1787/eag-2014-en.

OECD. (2015). *Education at a Glance 2015: OECD Indicators*. OECD Publishing. Retrieved from http://dx.doi.org/10.1787/eag-2015-en.

Pianta, R. C., Barnett, S. W., Burchinal, M. and Thornburg, K. R. (2009). The effects of preschool education: What we know, how public policy is or is not aligned with the evidence base, and what we need to know. *Psychological Science in the Public Interest, 10*(2), 49–88. Retrieved from http://dx.doi.org/10.1787/888933117174.

Pind, J. (2006). Evolution of an alphabetic writing system: The case of Icelandic. In R. Malatesha Joshi and P. G. Aaron (eds), *Handbook of Orthography and Literacy* (pp. 2–14). Mahwah, NJ: Lawrence Erlbaum.

Programme for International Student Assessment (PISA). (2012). *International Association for the Evaluation of Educational Achievement (IEA), Results in Focus: What 15 Year-Olds Know and What They Can Do with What They Know.* OECD, 2014.

Ramey, S. L. and Ramey, C. T. (2006). Early educational interventions: principles of effective and sustained benefits from targeted early education programs. In D. K. Dickinson and S. B. Neuman (eds), *Handbook of Early Literacy Research*, Vol. 2 (pp. 445–459). New York: Guilford Press.

Ringmose, C., Winther-Lindqvist, D. A. and Allerup, P. (2014). Do welfare states raise welfare(d) kids? Day-care institutions and inequality in the Danish welfare state. *Early Child Development and Care*, *184*(2), 177–193. http://dx.doi.org/10.1080/03004430.2013.775126.

Roth, A.-C. V. (2014). Nordic comparative analysis of guidelines for quality and content in early childhood education. *Tidsskrift for nordisk barnehageforskning* [*Nordic Early Childhood Education Research Journal*], *8*(1), 1–35.

Sahlberg, P. (2010). *The Secret to Finland's Success: Educating Teachers*. Stanford Center for Opportunity Policy in Education – Research Brief, September. Stanford, CA: School of Education, Stanford University.

Sahlberg, P. (2015). Finland's school reforms won't scrap subjects altogether. *The Conversation*, 25 March. Retrieved from http://theconversation.com/finlands-school-reforms-wont-scrap-subjects-altogether-39328.

Sandvik, J. M., van Daal, V. H. P and Adèr, H. J. (2014). Emergent literacy: Preschool teachers' beliefs and practices. *Journal of Early Childhood Literacy*, *14*(1), 28–52. doi:10.1177/1468798413478026.

School Reform. (2006–2008). Kunnskapsløftet L06. Oslo: Ministry of Education and Research.

School Reform 1997. (1997–1998). Reform 97. Oslo: Ministry of Church, Education and Research.

Sheridan, S. and Pramling Samuelsson, I. (2003). Learning through ICT in Swedish early childhood education from a pedagogical perspective of quality. *Childhood Education*, *79*(5), 276–282. doi:10.1080/00094056.2003.10521212.

Simola, H. (2005). The Finnish miracle of PISA: Historical and sociological remarks on teaching and teacher education. *Comparative Education*, *4*(94), 455–470.

Skantz Åberg, E., Lantz-Andersson, A. and Pramling, N. (2015). Children's digital storymaking: The negotiated nature of instructional literacy events. *Nordic Journal of Digital Literacy*, *10*(3), 170–189.

Snow, C.E., Burns, M. and Griffin, P. (1998), *Preventing Reading Difficulties in Young Children*. Washington, DC: Committee on the Prevention of Reading Difficulties in Young Children, National Research Council.

Söderbergh, R. (2011). Tal och skrift i samspel i den tidiga språkutvecklingen [Talk and script in interaction during early language development]. In R. Söderbergh (ed.), *Från joller till läsning och skrivning* (pp. 264–305). Malmö: Gleerups.

Statistics Norway. (2014). The Central Bureau of Statistics, Norway. Retrieved from www.ssb.no/utdanning/statistikker/barnehager/aar-endelige/2014-05-04.

Statistics Norway. (2015). The Central Bureau of Statistics, Norway. Retrieved from www.ssb.no/utdanning/statistikker/barnehager/aar-endelige/2015-05-04.

Storch, S.A. and Whitehurst, G.J. (2002). Oral language and code-related precursors to reading: Evidence from a longitudinal structural model. *Developmental Psychology*, *38*(6), 934–947. doi:10.1037//0012-1649.38.6.934.

Sulzby, E. (1986). Writing and reading: Signs of oral and written language organization in the young child. In W. H. Teale and E. Sulzby (eds), *Emergent Literacy, Writing and Reading* (pp. 50–89). Westport, CT: Ablex.

Svensson, A.-K. (1998/2009). *Barnet, språket och miljön. Från ord till mening. [The child, the language, and the environment. From word to meaning.]* Lund: Studentlitteratur.

Sylva, K., Melhuish, E., Sammons, P., Siraj-Blatchford, I and Taggart, B. (2010). *Early Childhood Matters: Evidence from the Effective Pre-School and Primary Education Project*. London: Routledge.

Trageton, A. (2003). Å skrive seg til lesing [From writing to reading]. Oslo: Universitetsforlaget.

Whitehurst, G. J. and Lonigan, C. J. (1998). Child development and emergent literacy. *Child Development*, *69*(3), 848–872. doi:10.1111/j.1467-8624.1998.tb06247.x.

9

LITERACY DEVELOPMENT IN ROMANCE LANGUAGES

Liliana Tolchinsky and Harriet Jisa

Romance languages are the group of modern languages that evolved from spoken Latin. While all the Romance languages are written with the Latin alphabet, the transparency of the orthographic systems vary considerably. In this chapter we will focus specifically on Spanish and French, two languages which can be placed at two extremes on a continuum of orthographic systems ranging from shallow (Spanish) to deep (French). These two languages provide a natural window into understanding how orthographic systems facilitate or impede early literacy.

Spanish is the most widely spoken of the modern Romance languages. According to Ethnologue it has the second largest number of native speakers after Chinese. About 6 per cent of the world's population, more than 400 million speakers, have Spanish as their first language. Most Spanish speakers are in Latin America; indeed of all the majority Spanish-speaking countries, only Equatorial Guinea and Spain are outside of America. Moreover, although Spanish is the official language of Spain it shares the linguistic space with several co-official languages that, depending on the Spanish region, are spoken at home and taught at school. Thus, learning reading and writing in Spain is rather different in monolingual communities such as Madrid compared to bilingual communities such as Galicia or Valencia.

According to Ethnologue, French holds the fourteenth place among the languages of the world for number of speakers. Currently it is estimated that there are 76 million speakers. Only English has more countries choosing it as an official language, however. Before 1930 in France, one person out of four spoke a regional language with their parents, this number dropping to 1 out of 10 in 1950 and 1 out of 20 in 1970 (Costa and Lambert, 2009). French became the language spoken by the entire population only in the middle of the twentieth century (Costa and Lambert, 2009). Today while some regional languages are taught in public school (Basque, Breton, Catalan, Occitan and Alsacien), the official language of instruction is French. In Switzerland, Belgium and Canada (Quebec) French is the language of schools in the French-speaking areas. In many former French colonies, French is also the language of schooling.

Language orthographic and phonological representations

Spanish is an inflectional language with rich morphology. Very few words consist of only one morpheme. Only interjections, conjunctions, prepositions and a subset of adverbs are immune to both inflection and derivation. Most nouns, adjectives and determinants are inflected for number and two grammatical genders corresponding to natural gender only for animate nouns. Spanish verbs can take about forty possible different verb affixes (Alcoba, 1999). Grammatical morphology is very regular in the spoken and written forms, and Spanish-speaking adults are able to generate and to write these forms even though they hear a word for the first time (Aguado, 2004). The only exception to this is the plural forms /s/ in Andalucian variety.

French is also relatively rich in morphology. The major contrast with Spanish, however, is that the majority of grammatical morphology is silent (Fayol, 2013). The plural provides an interesting example. Compare *les petits triangles rouges* ('the little red triangles') and *le petit triangle rouge* ('the little red triangle'). In written French the noun and the adjective are spelled with the plural −s. However, the only audible distinction is on the determiner, the other words being pronounced the same in the singular and the plural. Plural marking on verbs is also often not marked in spoken French, *il mange* ('he is eating') and *ils mangent* ('they are eating'). The plural is written with an −s on the pronoun and −*ent* on the verb, but neither of the plural markings are audible in spoken French.

Orthography

Spanish is written with a transparent orthography according to the two criteria proposed by Seymour et al. (2003): high spelling–sound predictability and a very simple syllabic structure. On top of these two features that were found to facilitate literacy learning, the names of most letters in Spanish are helpful to literacy learners, as most letter names contain the phoneme that the letter represents.

Spelling relations are highly predictable because there is a one-to-one correspondence from graphemes (letters and digraphs) to phonemes and from phonemes to graphemes in almost 75 per cent of cases. The pronunciation of graphemes has no variation across words except for three consonants (c, g and r), which are read in different rule-governed ways depending on the context (Cuetos and Suárez-Coalla, 2009).

The Romance languages have the syllable as their basic rhythmic unit. Newer and more refined analysis has shown, however, that there are subtle differences between Spanish and French, with French in an intermediate position between stress-timed English and syllable-timed Spanish (White and Mattys, 2007). Spanish has clear syllabic boundaries and a very simple syllabic structure, in which the most common types of syllable are consonant–vowel (CV) and consonant–vowel–consonant (CVC). There are few consonant clusters, all of which occur only at the beginning of the syllable, and only five simple vowels.

The French orthographic system presents one of the major challenges facing elementary school teachers. The French alphabet contains 26 letters (with four diacritics) to represent, depending on regional varieties, 32 to 36 phonemes. In contrast to Spanish, French orthography is not transparent. For example, the sound /o/ can be written in a variety of ways, including *o, au, aux, aut, aud, ot, eau*. However, these different written versions are always read /o/: phonemes can be represented with a variety of graphemes, but in general graphemes represent phonemes predictably. It has thus been argued that French is easier to read than to spell (Fayol, 2013). Many final letters in words are silent: /u/ can be written *oup*, as in *coup* (hit) or *oux* such as in *roux* (redhead). Although *goulot, bungalow, galop, beaux* all finish with the sound /o/, the orthographic representations differ.

The iconicity of both Spanish and French letter names help children grasp the fact that letters stand for sounds. The names of the vowels are completely iconic as they consist of the vowel sound (e.g. a for /a/), and the names of most consonants comprise two phonemes with the consonantal part of the letter name being the denoted phoneme (e.g. be for /b/).

As for many languages, knowing the names of letters is a good predictor for future reading and writing in French (Fayol, 2013). Children who know the names of letters learn the sound of letters more easily, especially when the word begins with the name of the letter (e.g. *vélo*, /velo/ 'bike') (Jaffré and Fayol, 1997). Upon entering primary school, however, knowing the sounds of letters is a better predictor of future reading and writing than knowing letter names, and serves as a bridge between writing and phonology (Foulin, 2005). There is significant variation among children in the first year of elementary school. Foulin (2007) asked children to identify the 26 letters. In general, 17 out of 26 were identified. However 20 per cent of low SES children could only identify 12 letters. The author shows that intervention, including drawing children's attention to the formal aspects of letters and to the direction of reading, improved children's recognition.

Phonological awareness has been found to predict successful literacy learning in different languages. However, the type of linguistic unit that best predicts successful reading depends on the language and on the characteristics of the orthography that children are learning (Goswami, 2002; Share, 2008). Awareness of phonemes is deemed to be crucial for reading acquisition in English (e.g. Muter et al., 1997). The association between phonemic awareness and reading is lower, however, in languages such as Spanish with a simple phonological structure and a consistent orthographic representation. The simplicity of the Spanish syllable structure and vowel system, reinforced by the consistency of Spanish orthography, may account for the role that syllables play in reading and for their predictive value for learning to read (Alvarez et al., 2001; Carreiras and Perea, 2002; Carrillo, 1994; Dominguez, 1996; Jiménez and Ortiz, 2000). Six- and seven-year-olds are significantly less proficient in phoneme isolation than in syllable deletion and attain conventional reading and writing in Spanish without being able to explicitly segment words into phonemes (Tolchinsky and Teberosky, 1998; but see Defior and Tudela, 1994).

Although sensitivity to morphology is very relevant for developing spelling abilities in French and other deep orthographies (e.g. Pacton and Fayol, 2003; Bryant et al., 2000) it is less crucial for shallow orthographies (Sanchez et al., 2012). The role of phonology is directly proportional to the shallowness of the orthography and inverse to the role of morphology; the deeper the orthography is, the more morphological information is needed to find the correct spelling. In languages with rich morphology and shallow orthography, words could, in principle, be (almost always) accurately spelled using nonlexical phoneme-to-grapheme conversion rules alone. In Spanish, dictation is a relatively easy task and even five-year-old children at the beginning of their school education are capable of writing unfamiliar words, including pseudowords, without difficulty (Cuetos, 1989). In general, spellers must resort to their morphological and lexical knowledge more frequently in French than in Spanish – or other transparent orthographies – in order to spell accurately (Defior et al., 2008). Studies have shown that there is a stronger reliance on sublexical procedures for shallow than for deep orthographies (Defior et al., 2008; Landerl et al., 1997; Notarnicola et al., 2012).

Morphological awareness has been shown to play an important role in learning to spell in French, as in English (Pacton et al., 2013; Rey et al., 2005: Pacton and Fayol, 2003; Pacton et al., 2005; Sénéchal, 2000). For example, children can use morphological information for the spelling of final silent consonants. For seven- and eight-year-olds, words such as *grand* ('big, tall') or *camp* ('camp') are correctly spelled earlier than words such as *jument* ('mare') or *tabac* ('tobacco') (Sénéchal, 2000). When the adjective *grand* is in feminine gender (*grande*), the final consonant is audible. The noun *camp* has a derived verb, *camper*, in which the consonant /p/ is pronounced. The phonological sequence /et/ can be written in four different ways (*ette*, *aite*, *ète* or *ête*). Pacton et al. (2005) dictated sentences with pseudowords containing /et/ in either diminutive or non-diminutive contexts. Children's spelling accuracy of −*ette*, the diminutive suffix, was facilitated when the pseudo words were used in the diminutive contexts.

In a longitudinal study of six-year-olds, Sprenger-Charolles and Siegel (1997) asked children to read and write regular words (*table*, 'table'), irregular words (*sept*, '7', *scie*, 'saw') and pseudowords with regular spelling (*sinope*, *turche*). Regular words and pseudowords were read and written before the irregular words. Irregular words were often regularized, *si* instead of *scie*. During the course of the study and with increasing exposure, the children's spelling improved and led the authors to propose that the children were constructing an orthographic lexicon in addition to a phonographic representation. The role of exposure to printed words as a basis for creating an orthographic lexicon is essential for French children (Martinet et al., 2004). The creation of an orthographic lexicon liberates the cognitive charge on young French word-writers.

Lété and Fayol (2013) measured reading times of third graders, fifth graders and adults in a priming task to investigate the features of the orthographic representation. The primes were either completely different (*poule*, 'chicken' – *jardin*, 'garden'), contained a substitution (*jartin* – *jardin*) or contained a permutation (*jadrin* – *jardin*), with the idea that reading times would be faster for substitutions and permutations. The third graders showed no difference between the conditions, suggesting that their reading is purely decoding. The fifth graders showed a priming effect for the substitution condition. For the adults, only the permutation condition showed faster reading times. The authors argue that the orthographic representation in the orthographic lexicon is flexible to a degree.

In principle Spanish children can read and spell words that they have never seen. However, Cuetos and Suárez-Coalla (2009) examined reading accuracy and speed of children five to ten years of age and found both an effect of lexicality and lexical frequency. Greater accuracy and speed were observed in the reading of words over pseudowords and of high-frequency over low-frequency words, especially as grade level increased. Therefore, the existence and use of orthographic representations probably begins to develop from very early on, alongside sublexical reading for unknown words and pseudowords.

Early literacy

In Spain preschool education (*Educación Infantil*) consists of six non-compulsory courses distributed into two cycles: first cycle (0–3) and second cycle (3–6). Primary school (ages 6–12) consists of six courses distributed into three cycles of two years each (initial, middle and high) and secondary education (ages 12–16). There are three types of school: public, subsidized and private. There are few public centres providing preschool education, and access is restricted to the less-favoured sector of society.

In 2000 most of Spain's autonomous communities (regional governments) gained full powers in the area of education and the current education law (*Ley Orgánica de Educación* 2/2006, 3 May) has defined a set of 'basic competencies' that are prescriptive for every community (2/2006: p. 17166). These indicate that, for preschool, code-centred abilities are secondary to the functional uses of literacy (pp. 480–482). A similar approach is proposed for the first cycle of primary school, although alongside this there is a growing concern for correct spelling and more emphasis on reading, including a recommendation that, at primary level, at least 30 minutes should be devoted to reading every day. Literacy is considered a competency that should 'cut across' the curriculum, and therefore much time is dedicated to reading and writing in the specific content areas (p. 43085).

Autonomous communities made their own directives in rather different ways. In Andalusia the local curriculum recommends 'To approach reading and writing through a diversity of texts related to daily life, and relating to written language as an instrument of communication, representation and pleasure' (428/2008, p. 8). The document contains clear methodological guidelines for relating reading and writing to different topics – from the most mundane (e.g. a shopping list) to the most literary, with a clear emphasis on exploiting every opportunity as a potential literacy event (p. 22). In first grade the approach remains highly functional but with a greater emphasis on orthographic knowledge. From preschool on, teachers are counselled to evaluate 'the advance of literacy, understood as the capacity to produce and interpret the texts used in our society' (428/2008, p. 22).

In contrast *Madrid* is a more code-oriented community. The preschool timetable needs to include a specific slot each day for reading and writing activities (22/2007, p. 7). There are clear directives as to the order in which linguistic units should be introduced both for reading and writing: letters, syllables, words and texts as well as activities for exercising precise reading. Additional importance is attached to reading aloud with adequate pronunciation, intonation and rhythm. Special mention is made of the instructional role played by 'the adult' (22/2007, p. 13) and not solely by pair interactions. For primary school the recommendations include both a concern for reading as an instrument for learning in every content area, for the correct use of Spanish language and the specific vocabulary of all content areas (p. 42). No specific consideration is given to autonomous writing. Rather, writing competence is evaluated through children's ability to copy and to take dictation. In primary schools, evaluation reflects text comprehension and production as well as spelling rules, tidiness of handwriting and correct use of language (p. 30).

In France, elementary education is divided into three cycles. The first cycle includes preschool (three- to five-year-olds). The second cycle includes the last year of nursery school and the first two years of elementary school (six- to eight-year-olds). The third cycle includes the last two years of elementary school. The cycle system is an attempt to break away from strict age-grading and to take into consideration individual variation in development.

Unlike Spain, the school system in France is highly centralized and administered under the Ministry of National Education (Ministère de l'Education Nationale). All programme and curriculum decisions are taken on a national level. Education is obligatory from the age of six years until the age of 16. Despite the fact that education is obligatory only at the age of six, 96 per cent of the population begins publicly financed preschools at three years of age.

During the first cycle emphasis is placed on communicative activities, such as show and tell. Nursery school classrooms have a book corner and reading stories to the children is an important activity, intended to make children sensitive to the differences between written and spoken French. Rhyming games, phoneme detection activities and games using minimal pairs are used to increase phonological awareness. A report edited by the Ministry of Education in 2013 (Le Cam et al., 2013) indicated that children entering first grade in 2011 showed significant improvement compared with children entering first grade in 1997, with phonology accounting for much of the improvement. The activities proposed in the first cycle aim to do three things: improve oral language skills, prepare for the acquisition of literacy skills and encourage the child to pay attention to formal aspects of language.

During the second cycle, the child continues to work on spoken language, improving pronunciation, articulation and control over intonation. In all classroom activities the teacher encourages children to exchange information, tell stories, describe situations, give a point of view and ask for further explanations. Written language is present in all aspects of classroom life. Children should write their lessons and they should begin to write original texts. The child should be able to coherently tell a story and recount a past event, to identify the essential parts of a short story, to summarize a story told or read, to comment on it and to supply other possible outcomes. By the end of the second cycle the child should be able to write a short text respecting the constraints appropriate to each type of writing task, including an introduction, appropriate vocabulary and complete syntax (the correct use of pronouns, connectors, tense and aspect).

During the third cycle, the teacher organizes activities in which the students practise recounting events, describing situations, giving explanations, formulating questions and justifications, arguing and expressing their opinions. This oral work is destined to improve the organization, coherence and clarity in the written expression of ideas. Different types of written texts are presented (narrative, descriptive and argumentative) and the child should be able to produce these different types of texts

While the official instructions that we have summarized very briefly are quite detailed concerning the achievements to be obtained for each cycle (cf. http://eduscol.education.fr), what actually goes on in the classroom to attain the goals set out in the official instructions is somewhat opaque. The 2013 report published by the Ministry of Education indicated that the level of performance in language of children leaving preschool and entering primary school was higher than the level of performance of children in 1997 and 2011. However, the same report indicated that in elementary school the level of performance of children born in 2005 had significantly decreased in reading comprehension, vocabulary and orthography.

Approaches to multilingualism

Spain offers a diversity of multilingual scenarios due to immigration processes and to historical characteristics of Spanish communities. After centuries of emigration Spain has recently experienced large-scale immigration. The percentage of foreign population in Spain increased steadily from 1981 (less than 1 per cent) to more than 12 per cent in 2011, but subsequently started to decrease for economic reasons. In contrast, the historical multilingualism of certain Spanish regions – Catalonia, Basque Country and Galicia – is strengthening, with the communities 'own languages' being attributed new status as co-official with Spanish, and as other communities (Balear Islands, Valencian Community, Navarra, Aragon y Asturias) increase the use of the local language in school.

Although the traditional view of France is that it is a monolingual country, over 70 languages are currently listed as languages of France (Cerquiglini, 1999), including regional languages and immigrant languages. The immigrant population increases constantly and in urban areas teachers are often in classrooms where French is not the first language of the majority of children. Special classes are provided for newly arriving immigrant children.

Influence of international assessments

International student assessment surveys are carried out under agreed conceptual and methodological frameworks. The relative position of countries' average test scores is the indicator that attracts most public attention and influences national education policies. Results of these assessments indicate that, at least since 2000, Spanish students' reading comprehension has not improved (Mullis et al., 2012; OECD, 2010). There is a lack (or poor dissemination) of effective strategies or programmes. Ripoll and Aguado (2014) showed that among the interventions that were applied to improve reading comprehension the best results are achieved by those interventions that are based on combining explicit teaching of reading and comprehension strategies. In contrast, few interventions based on improving decoding have been shown to significantly influence reading comprehension.

Since 2001 France has participated in the reading comprehension evaluation conducted within the PIRLS framework (Progress in International Reading Literacy Study). The aim of this evaluation is to assess reading comprehension in children who have completed their fourth year of primary school. The results for French children examined in 2001, 2006 and 2011 show a steady decrease in reading comprehension performance (Colmani and Le Cam, 2012). French children scored below the average of children in the European Union in 2011. The evaluation asks children to read texts and then to answer questions, either multiple choice or questions that require writing a short text. The French children show lower performance for the open-response questions, indicating that combining reading comprehension and written production is particularly challenging for French children. Interestingly, in the PIRLS 2011 evaluation of reading comprehension, the French and Spanish children perform very similarly. The two countries are below average both in literary and informational reading, and with similar scores in overall average reading achievements (Mullis et al., 2012).

Principal methods and content areas of literacy instruction

A comprehensive study (Tolchinsky et al., 2012) that comprises 13 per cent of the population of preschool and first-grade teachers from different geographical regions of Spain (Almeria, Asturias, Cantabria, Catalonia, Madrid, Valencia, Leon, the Basque Country and Valladolid) showed that more than 60 per cent of the teachers declared that they follow 'mixed' methods, 16 per cent a global method and the rest were distributed across phonic (8 per cent) syllabic (5 per cent) and constructivist (6 per cent).

In spite of the generalized use of these labels to denominate literacy teaching methods it is hard to know what kind of activities and content areas are implied by them. Therefore, the participants in the study were asked to respond to a more detailed questionnaire about the practices implemented in classroom in relation to *classroom dynamics, concern for situational learning, instructional activities* and *evaluation.* Results revealed three profiles of teaching practice that were termed *instructional, situational* and *multidimensional.*

Teachers who match the profile of *instructional practices* reported setting aside a specific amount of time in the school timetable for reading and writing activities. They rely heavily on knowledge of letters and sounds to teach reading and writing, work on phonological awareness and explicitly correct children's reading. Teachers in the *situational practices* group stated that they frequently organize reading and writing activities in small groups, make use of all kind of situations that arise in the classroom to teach vocabulary and assess children's progress by analysing production of short texts. They also reported using a wide range of printed materials in class, and encouraging children to write down the words they need even if they don't yet know the letters involved. Finally, teachers assigned to the profile of *multidimensional teaching* presented a mixed picture of practices. They also set aside specific time for reading and writing activities and rely heavily on knowledge of letters and phonological awareness to teach reading and writing but take advantage of situational learning, encourage independent writing and strategic reading.

Most teachers in preschool presented a *situational profile,* whereas the *instructional profile* was predominant among first-grade teachers, probably due to higher demands imposed by parents and policy-makers for systematic teaching of reading. A clear link emerged between self-declared teaching methods and practice profiles. *Instructionally oriented practices* were more frequent among teachers who claimed to follow syllabic or phonic methods, whereas *situation-oriented practices* were more common among followers of global or constructivist approaches.

Provision for children with special educational needs

Inclusive schooling is the prevalent ideology in Spain and France regarding children with special needs. Efforts are mobilized for children with special needs to remain in the same school context as typically developing children. Underlying this ideology is the conception of an interaction between students' characteristics and educational environment. The idea is that any student can experience learning difficulties at one time or another in their schooling. This approach has been particularly successful for early childhood education with very high enrolment rates and important learning achievements. However, in the transition from elementary to secondary education the 'dis-integration' of pupils with special needs affects 35 per cent of the students in Spain and is significantly more intense in public than in private schools (Alonso Parreño and Araoz Sánchez-Dopico, 2011; Echeita, 2011; Tobosc Martín et al., 2012).

There are no systematic screening procedures during preschool or first grades of primary school. The teacher is the main identifier of potential reading or writing difficulties. Once the teacher detects a potential problem, he/she can resort to specialized teachers, usually specialized in therapeutic pedagogy, or to centres for pedagogic orientation. Depending on the size and location of the school, these two resources are part of the school or are shared by groups of schools. In line with the inclusion principle, the goal is to find ways to attend to the child's needs within the same classroom by means of curricular adaptations or by separating the child for special attention for the shortest period of time possible. The main barrier to the fulfilment of these ideal aims lies in the lack of special preparation of the classroom teachers, who sometimes feel helpless when confronted with the needs of some children.

In 1981 Priority Education Zones (Zone d'Education Prioritaire, cf. www.education. gouv.fr#educationprioritaire) were created in the most impoverished areas, regrouping preschool, primary and middle school into zones that receive additional funding and support from the Ministry of Education. Teaching loads are adjusted so as to provide time for the teachers' participation in pedagogical teams. Supplementary personnel within these schools follow the children's progress and tutor children who are particularly challenged individually or in small groups. Parental cooperation is greatly encouraged, with the idea of firmly embedding the schools in the community. These priority zones were created with the aim of overcoming social class differences in school success.

Variety of literacy resources

Given the diversity of classroom settings and teaching practices it is difficult to provide a general view of available resources. In the official curricula one can find specific references to the need for creating distinct spaces in preschools for undertaking different activities (e.g. library, natural experiments). Emphasis is placed on the use of written messages in everyday life as well as the importance of relating to the children's life experiences for understanding and producing texts.

Both in Spain and France, preschool classrooms are organized by 'corners' – and the *library* or *reading corner* is obligatory in every preschool. However, some *library corners* display children's story books almost exclusively, while others contain a huge diversity of texts – recipes books, encyclopedias, music scores, gossip magazines, newspapers, calendars and so on. Moreover, while in some classrooms the printed materials are directly accessible to the child, in other classrooms they are kept in high and closed cupboards, only accessible to the teacher who brings them to the children for specific activities. The same diversity of availability applies to all kinds of materials. While in some classrooms erasers, tape and Tipp-Ex are available to the child when composing texts, because correcting is conceived as part of the writing process requiring that the writer have at his/her disposal all the necessary instruments, in other classrooms children must ask for permission to correct their texts. In the same line, while some kindergarteners are preparing the script of an oral exposition on Van Gogh paintings, in other kindergarten classrooms they use template-based materials of graded difficulty that emphasize exercising letter-recognition, letter-shape drawing and letter-to-sound mapping, moving systematically from one letter to the next.

Major challenges for current and future early literacy provision

Spanish children learn to decode isolated words very early. After a few months of formal instruction they are able to read accurately most words they are required to read, especially if they are frequent words. Children attain accurate decoding (and adequate levels of spelling) both in monolingual and multilingual environments in spite of being exposed to a diversity of teaching practices. Nevertheless, Spanish students have obtained one of the worst results in international evaluation (PISA, 2003; Mullis et al., 2012). Twice as many Spanish children score below level 1 of reading ability – the lowest level as measured by the PISA report – as at the highest level. Moreover, in the national evaluations the situation remains very similar: 30 per cent of students finish primary school without attaining the minimal level required for secondary school (Comunidad de Madrid, 2004). In spite of having learned to decode rather successfully and even given relatively favourable socioeconomic conditions, reading comprehension is still a major challenge for many Spanish-speaking children.

The situation is rather similar in France. A report published by the Haut Conseil de l'Education in 2007 (cf. www.hce.education.fr/gallery_files/site/21/40.pdf) indicated that 60 per cent of children leave elementary school with satisfactory results, 25 per cent show some weakness and 15 per cent show very severe weaknesses. One of the issues raised in that report concerns the necessity of continuing education for teachers, claiming that teachers are not sufficiently supported once they have finished their initial training. Another issue addressed in this report is the incapacity of the system to help children in difficulty. The majority of children who begin elementary school with weaknesses in reading readiness finish elementary school with severe weakness: primary education seems incapable of helping those children catch up.

Conclusion

We began this chapter by discussing the differences between Spanish and French orthographic systems and how they influence initial periods of acquiring literacy. Very young Spanish-speaking children are able to decode and transcribe unfamiliar words and pseudowords. Young French-speaking children are able to read and spell regular and frequent words, but irregular words and grammatical morphology remain a challenge throughout education.

We expected that these differences would be reflected in the challenges for literacy instruction and accomplishment that each country faces; and yet the challenges are similar in spite of the described differences. Neither Spanish nor French children after four years of elementary education appear prepared to fulfil the fundamental aim of literacy learning: to extract and use information from written language in reading comprehension. The goal for both countries is to find ways of overcoming this limitation.

References

Aguado-Orea, J. (2004). The acquisition of morphosyntax in Spanish: Implications for current theories of development. Doctoral thesis, Nottingham University.

Alcoba, S. (1999). Gramática y conducta en la elección del léxico. *Analecta Malacitana (AnMal electrónica)*, *3*, 51–84

Alonso Parreño, M. J. e I. de Araoz Sánchez-Dopico (2011). El impacto de la Convención Internacional sobre los Derechos de las Personas con Discapacidad en la legislación educativa española. Madrid. Cinca

Alvarez, C. J., Carreiras, M. and Taft, M. (2001). Syllables and morphemes: Contrasting frequency effects in Spanish. *Journal of Experimental Psychology. Learning, Memory, and Cognition*, *27*, 545–555.

Bryant, P., Nunes, T. and Bindman, M. (2000). The relations between children's linguistic awareness and spelling: The case of the apostrophe. *Reading and Writing*, *12*, 253–276.

Carreiras, M. and Perea, M. (2002). Masked priming effects with syllabic neighbors in the lexical decision task. *Journal of Experimental Psychology: Human Perception and Performance*, *28*, 1228–1242.

Carrillo, M. (1994). Development of phonological awareness and reading acquisition: A study in Spanish language. *Reading and Writing: An Interdisciplinary Journal*, *6*, 279–298.

Cerquiglini, B. (1999). *Les Langues de France*. Report delivered to the Ministre de l'éducation nationale, de la recherche et de la technologie et à la ministre de la culture et de la communication. Paris: Ministère de l'éducation nationale, de la recherche et de la technologie.

Colmani, M. and Le Cam, M. (2012). PIRLS 2011 – Etude international sur la lecture des élèves au CM1. Note d'information. Paris: Ministère de l'Education Nationale. http://cache.media.education.gouv.fr/file/2012/68/0/DEPP-NI-2012-21-PIRLS-2011-Etude-internationale-lecture-eleves-CM1_236680.pdf.

Comunidad de Madrid. (2004). Evaluación del Rendimiento Escolar: Lengua castellana y Literatura, 4° de Educación Primaria (2004) Inspección de Educación. Documento de Trabajo 17. Comunidad de Madrid.

Costa, J. and Lambert, P. (2009). France and language(s): Old policies and new challenges in education. Towards a renewed framework? In *CIDREE Yearbook: Language Policy and Practice in Europe – Emerging Challenges and Innovative Responses* (pp. 15–26). Brussels: CIDREE/DVO.

Cuetos, F. (1989). Word reading and spelling through the phonological route. *Journal for the Study of Education and Development*, *12*, 71–84. doi:10.1080/02103702.1989.10822228.

Cuetos, F. and Suárez-Coalla, P. (2009) From grapheme to word in reading acquisition in Spanish. *Applied Psycholinguistics*, *30*, 583–601

Decreto 22/2007, 10 May, BOCM 126, 29 May 2007.

Decreto 17/2008, 6 March, BOCM 61, March 2008.

Decreto 428/2008, 29 July, BOJA 164, 19 August 2008.

Defior, S., Alegría, J. and Titos, R. y Martos, F. (2008) Using morphology when spelling in a shallow orthographic system: The case of Spanish. *Cognitive Development*, *23*, 204–215. doi:10.1016/j.cogdev.2007.01.003.

Defior, S. and Tudela, P. (1994). Effect of phonological training on reading and writing acquisition. *Reading and Writing: An Interdisciplinary Journal*, *6*, 299–320.

Delpech D., George F. and Nok E. (ed.). (2001). *La conscience phonologique: Tests, éducation et rééducation.* Marseille: Solal.

Dominguez, A. (1996). Evaluación de los efectos a largo plazo de la enseñanza de habilidades de análisis fonológico en el aprendizaje de la lectura y de la escritura [The evaluation of long range effects of the teaching of phonological analysis abilities on learning to read and to write]. *Infancia y Aprendizaje*, *76*, 69–81.

Echeita, G. (2011) El proceso de inclusión educativa en España.¡Quien bien te quiere te hará llorar! *Participación Educativa, 18,* 121–132.

Fayol, M. (2013). *L'acquisition de l'écrit.* Paris: Presses Universitaires de France.

Foulin, J. A. (2005). Why is letter-name knowledge such a good predictor of learning to read? *Reading and Writing: An Interdisciplinary Journal, 18,* 129–155.

Foulin, J. N. (2007). La connaissance des lettres chez les pré-lecteurs: aspects pronostiques, fonctionnels et diagnostiques. *Psychologie Française, 52,* 431-444.

Goikoetxea, E. (2005). Levels of phonological awareness in preliterate and literate Spanish-speaking children. *Reading and Writing: An Interdisciplinary Journal, 18,* 51–79.

Goswami, U. (2002). In the beginning was the rhyme? A reflection on Hulme, Hatcher, Nation, Brown, Adams and Stuart. *Journal of Experimental Child Psychology, 82,* 47–57.

Jaffré, J.-P. and Fayol, M. (1997). *Orthographes, des systèmes aux usages.* Paris: Flamarion.

Jiménez, J. E. and Ortiz, M. R. (2000). Metalinguistic awareness and reading acquisition in the Spanish language. *The Spanish Journal of Psychology, 3,* 37–46.

Landerl, K. and Wimmer, H. y Frith, U. (1997) The impact of orthographic consistency on dyslexia: A German–English comparison. *Cognition, 63,* 315–334.

Le Cam, M., Rocher, T. and Verlet, I. (2013). Forte augmentation du niveau des acquis des élèves à l'entrée au CP entre 1997 et 2011. Paris: Ministère de l'éducation nationale. Note d'information. http://cache.media.education.gouv.fr/file/2013/11/2/DEPP_NI_2013_19_forte_augmentation_niveau_acquis_eleves_entree_CP_entre_1997_2011_269112.pdf.

Lété, B. and Fayol, M. (2013). Substituted-letter and transposed-letter effects in a masked priming paradigm with French developing readers and dyslexics. *Journal of Experimental Child Psychology, 114,* 47–62.

Ley Orgánica de Educación 2/2006. España: Madrid, BOE-A-200.

Martinet, C., Valdois, S. and Fayol, M. (2004). Lexical knowledge develops from the beginning of literacy acquisition. *Cognition, 91*(2), 11–22.

Mullis, I. V. S., Martin, M. O., Foy, P. and Drucker, K. T. (2012). *PIRLS 2011 International Results in Reading.* Chestnut Hill, MA: TIMSS & PIRLS International Study Center, Boston College.

Muter, V., Hulme, C., Snowling, M. and Taylor, S. (1997). Segmentation, not rhyming, predicts early progress in learning to read. *Journal of Experimental Child Psychology, 65,* 370–396.

Notarnicola A., Angelelli P., Judica A. and Zoccolotti P. (2012). The development of spelling skills in a shallow orthography: The case of the Italian language. *Reading and Writing International Journal, 25,* 1171–1194. doi:10.1007/s11145-011-9312-0.

Nunes, T., Bryant, P. and Bindman, M. (1997). Morphological spelling strategies: Developmental stages and processes. *Developmental Psychology, 33,* 637–649.

OECD (2010). *Education at a glance 2010: OECD Indicators.* OECD.

Pacton, S. and Fayol, M. (2003). How do French children use morphosyntactic information when they write? *Scientific Studies of Reading, 7,* 273–287.

Pacton, S., Fayol, M. and Perruchet, P. (2005). Children's implicit learning of graphotactic and morphological regularities. *Child Development, 76*(2), 324–339.

Pacton, S., Foulin, J. N., Casalis, S. and Treiman, R. (2013). Children benefit from morphological relatedness when they learn to spell new words. *Frontiers in Cognitive Science, 4,* 696. doi:10.3389/fpsyg.2013.00696.

PISA. (2003). *Informe Pisa 2003: Aprender para el mundo del mañana.* OECD.

Rey, A., Pacton, S. and Perruchet, P. (2005). L'erreur dans l'acqusition de l'orthographe. *Rééducation orthophonique, 222,* 101–119.

Ripoll J. C. and Aguado, G. (2014) La mejora de la comprensión lectora en español: un meta-análisis. *Revista de Psicodidáctica, 19*(1), 27–44. doi:10.1387/RevPsicodidact.9001.

Sanchez, M., Magnan, A. and Ecalle, J. (2012) Knowledge about word structure in beginning readers: What specific links are there with word reading and spelling? *European Journal of Psychology of Education, 27,* 299–317.

Sénéchal M. (2000). Morphological effects in children's spelling of French words. *Canadian Journal of Experimental Psychology, 54,* 76–86. doi:10.1037/h0087331.

Seymour, P. H. K., Aro, M., Erskine, J. M., Wimmer, H., Leybaert, J. Elbro, C. et al. (2003). Foundation literacy acquisition in European orthographies. *British Journal of Psychology, 94,* 143–174.

Share, D. L. (2008). On the anglocenticities of current reading research and practice: The perils of overreliance on an 'outlier' orthography. *Psychological Bulletin, 134,* 584–615.

Sprenger-Charolles, L. and Siegel, L. S. (1997). A longitudinal study of the effects of syllabic structure on the development of reading and spelling skills in French. *Applied Psycholinguistics, 18*, 485–505.

Tafa, E., 2008. Kindergarten reading and writing curricula in the European Union. *Literacy, 42*(3), 162–170.

Toboso Martín, M., Ferreira, M., Díaz Velázquez , E., Fernández-Cid, M., Enríquez Nuria Villa, E. and Fernández Concha Gómez de Esteban (2012) Sobre la educación inclusiva en España: políticas y prácticas. *Intersticios, 6*, 279–294

Tolchinsky, L. and Teberosky, A. (1998). The development of word segmentation and writing in two scripts. *Cognitive Development*, 13, 1–14.

Tolchinsky, L., Bigas, M. and Barragan, C. (2012) Pedagogical practices in the teaching of early literacy in Spain: Voices from the classroom and from the official curricula. *Research Papers in Education, 13*, 206–236. doi:10.1080/02671520903428580.

Tolchinsky, L., Levin, I., Aram, D. and McBride Chang, C. (2011). Building literacy in alphabetic, abjad and morphosyllabic systems. *Reading and Writing: An Interdisciplinary Journal, 25*, 1573–1598.

White, L. and Mattys, S. L. 2007. Calibrating rhythm: First language and second language studies. *Journal of Phonetics, 35*, 501–522.

10

LESSONS FROM COSTA RICA AND CHILE FOR EARLY LITERACY IN SPANISH-SPEAKING LATIN AMERICAN COUNTRIES

Alejandra Meneses, Ana María Rodino and Susana Mendive

Over the last decade, Latin American countries have made a good deal of economic progress; nevertheless, widespread social inequality persists in the region (UNESCO, 2013). Therefore, one of the greatest challenges facing the region today is how to advance in both equity and quality of education. In this sense, the development of literacy skills is crucial to improving opportunities to learn for all students. In this chapter, we understand *early literacy* as the 'set of skills, knowledge, and attitudes that are presumed to be developmental precursors to conventional forms of reading and writing' (Whitehurst and Lonigan, 1998: 849). This multidimensional notion combines processes related to *meaning*, which refers to the extraction, construction or production of meaning through oral or written language (e.g. vocabulary, concepts about print, oral and writing production, and oral comprehension); and *code*, which refers to mastering the alphabetic principle and reading words (e.g. alphabetic knowledge, phonological awareness, knowledge of sentence structure and phoneme-grapheme correspondence) (Connor, 2011).

This chapter offers an overview of early literacy provision in Costa Rica and Chile, two Spanish-speaking Latin American countries. Though they are in different phases of change, both countries are striving to improve the quality of early literacy. The analysis of these two cases may provide valuable insights for stakeholders and researchers in the 20 Spanish-speaking countries in the region, with an estimated 400 million speakers of Spanish as a first language.

The chapter addresses the following questions: How should early literacy be taught based on the nature of Spanish as a writing system and language in Latin America? How do Costa Rica and Chile define early literacy learning in their official curricula? Are the curricula more focused on *code-based* or *meaning-construction* skills? How wide is the gap between the intended curriculum, pre- and in-service teacher training, and the actual implementation of learning opportunities for early literacy in Chile? What are the main challenges for early literacy in countries like Costa Rica and Chile?

Similarities between early literacy provision in Costa Rica and Chile

There are some marked similarities between these two countries with regard to early literacy provision.

Early literacy with a semi-transparent orthography and a simple phonological system

Spanish has a simple phonological structure, with 24 phonemes (five vowels and 19 consonants), although pronunciation varies to some degree throughout Latin America (22 phonemes) and Spain (23 or 24 phonemes) (Ardila and Roselli, 2014; Defior and Serrano, 2014). The most common syllable structure is consonant–vowel (CV) (52.6 per cent) and consonant–vowel–consonant (CVC) (19 per cent) (Guerra, 1983) and the longest syllables are composed of five phonemes.

The Spanish writing system consists of 27 letters and five digraphs (*ch, ll, rr, gu, qu*) and is considered to be a semi-transparent orthographic system. Defior and Serrano (2014) pointed out that even though eight phonemes are represented by different graphemes, only four graphemes represent multiple phonemes.[1] Additionally, two graphemes pose a challenge for learning to decode (*h* and *x*).[2]

The highly consistent alphabetic principle in Spanish makes the decoding process easier to master for Spanish-speaking children than for those using opaque systems; even so, the main challenge for the former group is still learning to spell. The semi-transparency of the writing system and the simplicity of spoken Latin American Spanish have educational implications that should be taken into account, especially because many early literacy instructional proposals in Latin America have been drawn from French and English (Seymour, 2005; Bravo-Valdivieso and Escobar, 2014). These implications include the following:

- In Spanish, code-skills are rapidly acquired with systematic activities, and learning challenges are related to specific letters (*c, g, y, r, h*), syllabic composition (CVV,[3] CVVC, CCV, CCVC, CCVVC, CCVCC) and word length (three or more syllables).
- Unlike in English, effective instructional practices to develop phonological awareness focus on phonemes rather than onset-rime (Guardia, 2014).
- The development of code-skills at the word level through systematic and explicit phonics instruction can be consolidated between the first and second grade.

By contrast, the development of meaning-construction skills poses a major learning challenge; it is therefore necessary to invest more time and resources into developing comprehension through oral language.

Early literacy in the centralized educational policies of Costa Rica and Chile

In both Costa Rica and Chile, the Ministry of Education sets the educational policy for early childhood education, which includes students ranging in age from nought to six, while elementary school starts when children turn six years old. In both countries, the early literacy education policies are centralized to ensure the same learning objectives for all students; however, in both cases, the policies permit open and flexible curricula, allowing schools to determine how to achieve early literacy learning goals.

The Costa Rican education system is managed by the Ministry of Public Education (MEP). Early literacy instruction entails two levels: (a) *Preschool* (ages four to six) and (b) the content area *Spanish Language for Cycle I of Elementary School* (which includes the first, second and third grades, for children ages six to nine). Currently, the Costa Rican system is substantially revamping its understanding of two developmental processes previously ignored or misunderstood: *early childhood* is now seen as a particular stage of development to be taken into account alongside other considerations when defining educational goals and methods, and *early literacy* is viewed as a particular stage in children's language development that should be promoted separately from other goals (Programa Estado de la Nación, 2011). In the past, Costa Rica has had practically no coordination between the preschool and elementary education levels, as they have been perceived as strictly distinct from one another. Literacy acquisition has long been considered a concern solely for the elementary level, since it was expected to commence only when children reached the age of seven, during the first grade.

Costa Rica's National Reading and Writing Policy[4] has declared that literacy for children with disabilities and multilingual language learning is a national priority (MEP, 2013b). In Costa Rica, multilingual literacy involves fostering competencies in a foreign language (usually English or French), in Costa Rican Sign Language and in Spanish as a second language for the indigenous and deaf populations. This policy charges the MEP with certain duties, such as developing study programmes, reading materials, methodological guides, good practices and teacher-training courses.

The current Chilean national curriculum for children aged nought to six was enacted in 2001; it is organized around three pillars, one of which is *Communication* (including verbal and artistic language), and includes two stages: the first preschool cycle (ages nought to three) and the second preschool cycle (ages four to six) (MINEDUC, 2001). In 2008, the Ministry of Education published *Study Programs* for the second preschool cycle, which help guide teachers in attaining learning goals, but do not suggest learning goal sequences organized by educational domains or a minimum number of hours to devote to each learning goal. For the elementary school grades, the Ministry of Education has issued both *Study Programs* and *Educational Plans*, which establish a minimum number of hours per domain and educational level. From the first to the fourth grade, it is expected that 304 out of 1,140 hours a year be devoted to *Language and Communication*. In schools where *Indigenous Language* is offered as a course, it is expected that 152 hours more be allocated for this subject (MINEDUC, 2012). The current Chilean early literacy curriculum establishes common learning goals, but does not provide detailed guidelines about the teaching practices that should be used to attain such learning goals (OECD, 2012).

Early literacy curriculum: code-based or meaning-construction skills?

Both the Costa Rican and Chilean curricula lack a model specifying how to integrate and emphasize code-based and meaning-construction skills. To illustrate this issue in more detail, Mendive and Meneses (2017) analysed the Chilean curriculum (nought to 8 years old) for *opportunities to learn* (Meneses et al., 2014; Porter et al., 2007), defined as the presence of a skill in a literacy- or language-specific content. Based on Connor (2011), each learning goal (LG) was classified as either *meaning-focused* or *code-focused*.[5]

The analysis revealed that the official Chilean curriculum emphasizes meaning-construction over code-based skills in the teaching of language and early literacy to children between nought and eight years old. Across grades, over 80 per cent of LGs are meaning-focused, but the figure is even higher in the first cycle, where 100 per cent of LGs are devoted to that focus. This emphasis sits in stark contrast with the purported balanced-curriculum approach.

In the meaning-construction category, the main LG domain across all grades, except the first grade, concerns knowledge about how people communicate in a specific context, referred to as *pragmatic or social communication knowledge* (Figure 10.1). In the first and second cycles, *oral production* is the second most frequent domain, along with *print knowledge* in the

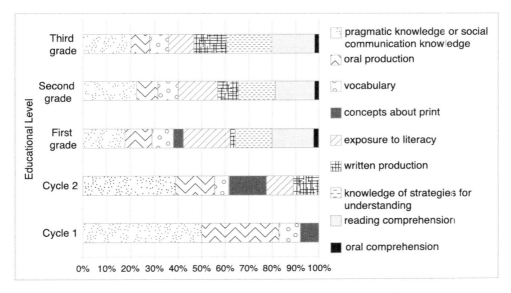

Figure 10.1 Percentages of meaning-focused learning goals by educational levels

second cycle. Even into the elementary grades, *pragmatic or social communication* still prevails. Finally, in the elementary school grades, there is a clear emphasis on LGs oriented towards developing *strategies for understanding* and *reading comprehension*.

In summary, although the curricula from both countries espouse a balanced model to develop literacy, in the Chilean list of LGs, meaning-construction skills are emphasized over code-based skills. A similar analysis of the curriculum in Costa Rica and other countries could help identify which early literacy approach is being conveyed to teachers.

Early literacy teacher preparation: space to improve

Although education reforms in Costa Rica and Chile have progressed to different stages, for these countries to successfully implement their goals, they both require coherent and profound teacher education to promote early literacy. As mentioned briefly above and further explicated later in this chapter, Costa Rica is in the midst of enacting reforms to improve early literacy provision. Teacher practices and attitudes towards the new content prescribed by the reforms will be crucial to their success. Costa Rican preschool, first- and second-grade teachers have to fully understand the rationale behind the reforms, commit to them and apply them consistently in their classrooms. They also need to be aware of the importance of explaining the curricular changes to families. To do so, the MEP is offering all in-service public teachers a short training, which is currently being implemented.

On the one hand, the situation in Costa Rica is favourable, as both educational authorities and technicians have demonstrated unanimous commitment to the reforms, backed by suitable academic and financial resources[6] and supported by the professional credentials of current teachers, which should facilitate understanding of the causes, goals and content of the curricular reforms.[7]

On the other hand, there is also uncertainty and a variety of restrictions. First, it's not clear whether there are enough instructional support resources available to teachers, students and families to assist them in implementing the reforms. Second, beyond official diplomas, do teachers have a sufficiently solid understanding of the principles of childhood, language and literacy development so as to implement the reforms in a reliable and effective way?[8] Third, how well can the MEP sustain these policy reforms in the long run if future teachers continue to enter the system poorly prepared and insufficiently aware of core elements of the reform, such as literacy development and early literacy? Should the MEP be permanently retraining teachers? Logic suggests that pre-service teacher education should be adapted to the new norms, but this is problematic for the MEP, because initial teacher training is in the hands of autonomous universities, both public and private.

In Chile, the teaching profession has undergone a series of changes and been subject to contradictory social pressures. On the one hand, enrolment at the 48 institutions that offer education majors for either the preschool or elementary school levels increased significantly between 2000 and 2008 (Cox et al., 2010). Private universities provide most of the majors, although they have newer programmes and adhere to lower-quality regulations than traditional universities. On the other hand, burgeoning social demand to improve the quality of pre-service and in-service training has highlighted the lack of teacher specialization in the disciplinary domains (Ávalos, 2010; Cox et al., 2010).

Consequently, the 2004 OECD report about education policy in Chile emphasized the gap between children's capacities – as expected in the official curriculum following the reform changes – and teacher knowledge and practices for promoting more complex opportunities to learn.

The Chilean Ministry of Education has developed pedagogical content knowledge standards for prospective teachers, which are also used to guide the National Certification System Evaluation (INICIA). Unfortunately, preschool teacher standards are too general to serve as guidelines for the literacy curricula of teacher training programmes. Our own analyses of INICIA results reveal that around 50 per cent of evaluated teachers demonstrate an unacceptable level of content and pedagogical knowledge in the language area.

The scarce up-to-date research regarding Chilean educators' knowledge about how to teach reading and writing in early childhood suggests that pre-service programmes offer few specific models for teaching early literacy, and few practical chances to rehearse and reflect on the knowledge acquired (Adlerstein et al., 2016; Cisternas et al., 2013; Facultad de Educación PUC/MINEDUC, 2011).

Although there are some parallels between Costa Rica and Chile in initial literacy provision, in the next section we will paint a more detailed portrait of the state of affairs in each country, looking at the major challenges for early literacy in Costa Rica and Chile.

Costa Rica's case: policy transition

Costa Rica's reforms are an attempt to correct the serious discontinuities between the preschool and early elementary school grades and the resulting weak performance in literacy. A very upsetting outcome was the high proportion of children forced to repeat first grade because they failed to achieve the goal of learning to read Spanish during the school year. Between 2006 and 2011, the percentage of students who had to repeat the first grade annually ranged from 10.8 per cent to 14.7 per cent, the highest of the six grades comprising the elementary level (Programa Estado de la Nación, 2011; Rodino, 2010). Besides, quite a few first-grade students who are promoted to the second grade are nonetheless placed into 'curricular adaptation', meaning that from that point forward, they will be taught and evaluated with a simplified study programme because they have learning difficulties.

No studies have been carried out to quantify the issue, but observations suggest that the assumed 'learning difficulties' are diagnosed based on the fact that these students finish first grade without being able to read (decode) at an acceptable level.

Evidence of insufficient literacy achievement persists. Costa Rican children who complete elementary school typically develop basic reading and writing competencies. However, not all reach a suitable level of proficiency enabling them to successfully meet later educational and employment demands. Periodic exams by the MEP in Spanish showed unsatisfactory achievement, while PISA 2010 reading results revealed that students were evenly distributed into thirds: one-third scored at the minimum acceptable level of achievement, one-third below that level and only another one-third above (Programa Estado de la Nación, 2013; Rodino, 2013). PISA 2012 replicated these results.

Thus, the former MEP administration set as a strategic priority for the 2011–2014 term the strengthening of literacy competencies, which it planned to achieve by transforming the teaching of Spanish across all educational levels. The MEP also devised a new national Reading and Writing Policy for the entire system. The MEP began to design study programmes in 2011 that were approved in 2013 (Spanish for cycle I) and 2014 (preschool). Implementation commenced one year later.

Curricular reform in preschool

The former preschool study programmes, eliminated in 2014, had been in effect since 1995 (for five- to six-year-olds) and 2000 (for four- to five-year-olds) (MEP, 1995, 2000). These study programmes were based on a very general and limited notion of human development, marked by the following flaws:

- an unbalanced view of child development with a focus on social and emotional, but not cognitive development;
- a restricted interpretation of language development with a strong focus on daily oral language – especially conversation – but little or no encouragement of pre-reading and writing skills;
- no notion of the literacy development continuum and its emergent literacy stage;
- weak assessment of early learning outcomes, particularly regarding cognitive and language development, due to the lack of a well-defined evaluation framework and instruments;
- extreme disparities between the class structure and environment at the preschool level and the next grade level (first grade), plus no actual preparation of children to transition smoothly between levels.

Further exacerbating these limitations, the former preschool authority held and enforced an even narrower interpretation of early literacy. An official statement was released against 'inducing conventional reading and writing processes in the preschool classroom' because doing so would allegedly encourage 'fictitious processes far away from the characteristics, needs, and interests of preschool children' and thus would support an 'academic practice' that 'distorts the goals of preschool education' (MEP, 2004). Teachers were dissuaded from displaying writing in the classroom – letters and common words, including children's names, simple everyday sentences, printed posters or big books, and the like were discouraged. Any pedagogical work on emergent literacy skills was considered inappropriate and even harmful for five- and six-year-olds.

However, the new policy and study programmes (MEP, 2014a) have ushered in significant and developmentally sound reforms, mainly because they:

- are structured as unified documents with a single conceptual and methodological framework that encompasses the study content and activities for the pre-kindergarten and kindergarten levels, lending it a sense of sequence and cohesion;
- provide teachers with an explicit and clear account of its developmental and pedagogic approach, making it a reference for daily consultation and further professional development;
- detail the general knowledge and skills students are expected to have acquired upon completing preschool and make strides towards defining learning outcomes and providing a framework for designing assessment instruments;
- address student diversity by defining three performance levels at which teachers can place students in order to assist in individual progress;
- favour a balanced view of child development with equal attention to all of its dimensions – in particular, cognitive and literacy development;
- take into account the literacy development continuum and foster emergent literacy skills (e.g. phonological awareness, word segmentation, vocabulary building, oral and written expression, oral and graphic text comprehension and creation, motivation towards reading as a source of enjoyment and learning, identifying written language in the environment and writing the student's name). They also stipulate daily reading periods, a literate environment and all kinds of communicative exchanges;
- require teachers to smooth the transition to the next school level and restore the valuable goal of preparing preschoolers for the challenges of elementary school with a dual purpose: to foster their later academic performance and to level the playing field for children from disadvantaged or culturally different families.

Curricular reform in Spanish language for cycle I of elementary school

In Costa Rica, the preschool and cycle I reforms were formulated simultaneously. However, the process for the latter set of reforms was quicker and less contentious than the former because the first grade and the subject of Spanish language have historically been the level and content area responsible for early literacy instruction. Moreover, there was a clear agreement among MEP authorities, elementary curriculum technicians and national experts concerning the deficiencies in this field and the changes that needed to be made.

The current study programme (MEP, 2013a) heralded substantial changes, including the following:

- The first and second grades are now viewed as a unit extending from six to eight years of age. Much attention is paid to their effective integration by strengthening the connection between study content and teaching practices, and reducing administrative stumbling blocks, such as the first-grade deadline previously imposed on children for learning to read and, specifically, decode. The intimidating and ineffectual practice of having poor readers repeat the first grade has been eliminated.
- Recommendations were issued to school principals to assign each group of students the same teacher for the first and second years.
- The adoption of a communicative-functional approach expands the focus of the definition of early literacy success. While the former programme fundamentally emphasized

code-based skills, the new one adds in meaning-construction skills, the result being a balanced-skills approach.

- Grammar is not ignored, but is rather explored using the children's own language products. The goal is to achieve autonomy of expression with grammatical correctness.
- Teachers are guided to create plenty of spaces for students' text production, both oral and written, using multiple mediation strategies, with an emphasis on dialogues, reading and writing workshops.
- Learning outcomes are regularly documented and evaluated by teachers using techniques they can select from a set of alternatives suggested by the study programme (e.g. daily work observation, checklists, performance records, numerical and descriptive scales, interviews, teacher diaries and student portfolios). Every three months, teachers prepare a qualitative performance report for each family including information about the child's progress. The MEP Evaluation Department has provided a model for this quarterly report, and annual reports have supplanted the former first-grade exams and passing/non-passing grades (MEP, 2013a).
- Special effort is being made to supply teachers with support resources, either by including them in the study programme (e.g. instructional activities and assessment instruments) or by appending them as additional materials (e.g. theoretical readings about neuroscience and cognitive and literacy development) (MEP, 2014b).

Costa Rica's policy has always been to let teachers select their own methods for literacy instruction. However, the study programme suggests several methods – typically the phonetic, syllabic, 'eclectic', and global or whole-language methods – and even proposes a preferred method. For instance, the current programme suggests the phonetic method, but not as a requirement. Anecdotal evidence suggests that teachers use a variety of methods, sometimes in combination.

Literacy education follows the national policy on the inclusion of children with special needs into mainstream classrooms (Law 7600, 1996). The cycle I Spanish programme starts by taking into account each student's ability level and works from there up through explicit instruction. The public school system also has some support teachers who assist the regular classroom teachers in handling children with learning difficulties, mainly in Spanish and Maths. They are assigned to one school and rotate across grades and classrooms; sometimes they assist several schools. However, their number is insufficient to meet the needs of the whole system.

One weak aspect of early literacy instruction is that reading and writing resources are not equally available to all children. One-quarter of the country's public schools (about 1,000 schools) have school libraries with a considerable number of books, including the official list of two hundred titles suggested for the elementary level. The rest of the schools have a monthly budget to buy materials, but principals have the discretion to allocate funds for other school demands and teachers must take initiative to request specific books. On average, preschool classrooms may have 30 books in the so-called 'reading area' for children to play with, while first-grade classrooms seldom have more than ten.

The challenges ahead for Costa Rica

The policies described in this chapter are certainly good news for early literacy education in Costa Rica. At present, hopes are high, but so too are the obstacles ahead. The first challenge will be to implement the new study programmes, which will be put into practice nationwide in 2015. This initial implementation will be a trial period for Costa Rica.

Thus, the main issues facing current and future literacy provision in the country are related to modifying current conditions. In brief, the main issues Costa Rica will need to address are as follows:

1 *Study the changes that are under way.* In order to avoid any conceptual or operational interference in the new study programmes, all of the factors that might impact their implementation ought to be studied and managed by the MEP.
2 *Improve initial teacher training, particularly in early childhood development and literacy development, emphasizing the literacy continuum and early literacy.* Initial teacher training is provided by universities, which are autonomous institutions. Hence, the MEP cannot directly compel them to teach specific content. However, the MEP can and should discuss with teacher training institutions the ways in which their teaching programmes can better adhere to national policies, supervise their academic quality and put in place strategies for hiring well-prepared new teachers.
3 *Develop a variety of teaching and learning resources for literacy development, particularly early literacy.* Resources must include theoretical and instructional materials, other classroom resources (such as age- and culture-appropriate children's books), teacher support groups (for exchanging good practices or advice on how to deal with particular difficulties) and, ideally, mentoring experiences.

It's important that Costa Rica build a rich assortment of resources for literacy and early literacy education in Spanish – resources that would address a variety of topics and real educational problems, and would be up-to-date, well-researched, well-designed and made available to all teachers. Other Latin American countries are facing a similar challenge.

The Chilean case: from curricular implementation to early literacy teacher preparation

Unlike in Costa Rica, where reforms are under way, Chile is in the midst of ongoing efforts to implement the curriculum modifications developed a decade ago.

Curricular domains and teacher implementation at the classroom level

Although the Chilean system emphasizes meaning-construction over code-based skills (Mendive and Meneses, 2017), there are differences between the official curriculum and the curriculum actually put into practice. In effect, oral language skills are underdeveloped in the early childhood years (Facultad de Educación PUC/MINEDUC, 2011), despite the fact that the national curriculum emphasizes these skills (e.g. *oral production* and *pragmatic or social communication knowledge*; see corresponding percentages in Figure 10.1).

Research suggests that the curriculum is not necessarily the primary factor guiding the content taught in preschool classrooms, because in the second cycle the most frequently implemented domains emphasized code and meaning – *exposure to literacy* and *phonological awareness* (Facultad de Educación PUC/MINEDUC, 2011) – while the least frequently implemented domain was *vocabulary*. Conversely, the national curriculum is more closely tied to what is taught in elementary classrooms (Facultad de Educación PUC/MINEDUC, 2011). The most frequently implemented domain observed was *reading comprehension* – which is consistent with the national curriculum's emphasis (Figure 10.1) – while the least frequently observed domains were *oral comprehension* and *vocabulary*, both of which are also underrepresented in the national curriculum (Figure 10.1).

Early literacy assessment: does it inform teaching?

Interviews reveal that the teachers plan and evaluate early literacy instruction without considering the diversity of student performance levels, despite the fact that the large-scale study with the students of same teachers identified three early literacy performance levels from the second cycle to second grade (Facultad de Educación PUC/MINEDUC, 2011).

Observational studies have revealed a trend towards implementing whole-group rather than small-group activities (Facultad de Educación PUC/MINEDUC, 2011), even after interventions that aimed to encourage individualized teaching (Strasser et al., 2016a). These results suggest that teachers have difficulties in dealing with differences in motivation, attention and levels of learning in their students, a finding that also has been self-reported by early childhood teachers (Facultad de Educación PUC/MINEDUC, 2011).

The challenges ahead for Chile

Three challenges for Chile are critical to improving the quality of early literacy provision: (a) a recalibrated early literacy curriculum, (b) a more supportive early literacy curriculum and (c) more specific early literacy training in teacher programmes, considering both pre- and in-service teachers.

A recalibrated early literacy curriculum

The frequency and distribution of LGs in the Chilean early literacy curriculum underrepresent some domains and overrepresent others. Because vocabulary plays a central role in language and literacy development (Dickinson, 2011; Strasser and del Río, 2013), it is remarkable that proportionally few LGs are targeted towards developing *vocabulary* (Figure 10.1). The lack of explicit vocabulary instruction in pre-service training helps explain the low level of explicit vocabulary instruction in Chilean classrooms. On the other hand, *pragmatic or social communication knowledge* is the most represented domain in the early literacy curriculum (Figure 10.1) – though apparently absent from daily lessons (Facultad de Educación PUC/MINEDUC, 2011). Nonetheless, the ability to understand the intentions of others is less a matter of instruction, and more the result of maturational processes which develop at similar ages cross-culturally (Trevarthen, 1988), and which grow incidentally from opportunities for joint attention and activities (Tomasello, 2011). A more strategic goal could be to teach students turn-taking skills and to consider other people's opinions and contributions (Resnick et al., 2009).

Oral production is a domain implemented at a rather low rate in Chilean classrooms; however, research shows that the ability to produce oral narratives is related to reading comprehension (Oakhill and Cain, 2012) and school success (O'Neill et al., 2004). More pre-service and in-service training is required for teachers to learn how to develop and assess oral language skills through practical pedagogical strategies (modelling and rehearsal) and thus facilitate implementation.

Two LG domains are missing from education for children aged nought to six: *exposure to literacy* in the first cycle (ages nought to four) and *oral comprehension* throughout the entire period. The absence of LGs oriented towards reading books aloud to children in the first cycle is especially noticeable, in light of its relevance for developing vocabulary (Strasser et al., 2016b), oral comprehension (Strasser et al., 2013) and Spanish syntactic knowledge (Pérez-Leroux et al., 2012).

Reading comprehension – present in elementary level LGs – might be better developed if the preschool curriculum included LGs about *oral comprehension* and *knowledge of strategies for reading understanding*. In addition, some LGs are needed to promote cognitively complex processes, such as inferences, self-monitoring and causality (Strasser and del Río, 2013). Finally, LGs should include not only narratives but also explanatory texts (Bridges et al., 2012).

Overall, it seems that teachers have grasped one portion of the national curriculum to a greater extent than the other. They are indeed implementing domains related to meaning-construction skills and the use of texts, such as exposure to literacy in the second cycle, text comprehension and strategies for reading understanding, while paying less attention to oral language domains, which include vocabulary and print, pragmatic or social communication knowledge.

A more supportive early literacy curriculum

The Chilean curriculum is still far from being a tool to help teachers develop meaning-construction skills in students. There is a dearth of specificity in the early literacy curriculum at different levels; in particular, there is scant instructional guidance on how to implement LGs, especially for the first and second cycles. For instance, there is a lack of specificity regarding the quantity and types of words that should be learned as vocabulary items, as well as the types of texts to which students should be exposed. Moreover, learning objectives are very general and there is a lack of complex progression in some domains across grades (i.e. some learning goals in the areas of *pragmatic and social communication skills, oral production* and *vocabulary* are redundant across grades), which makes it difficult for teachers to plan and evaluate their teaching. Desirable specifications would provide more guidance for instruction and assessment to adjust teaching to classroom diversity, with special study programmes for the first preschool cycle, and for all levels, defining LGs through observable behaviours and increasing the complexity of learning progressions.

More specific early literacy approaches for teacher training programmes

There is consensus that Chilean educational policy needs to shift its focus from school system coverage to boosting educational quality by basing teacher education on profound disciplinary and strong pedagogical content knowledge, and implementing a practice-based curriculum (Ávalos, 2010; Cox, 2007; Cox et al., 2010). Nevertheless, no specific research is yet available about the impact of the quality of teacher education programmes on teacher effectiveness in the language and literacy domain.

Early literacy instructional practices are complex and teachers need intensive opportunities to learn them. A recent study of the effectiveness of professional development programmes has shown how difficult it is for preschool teachers to devote less time to traditional practices (e.g. teaching letters and words) and spend more time implementing novel practices (e.g. teaching vocabulary) (Mendive et al., 2015). Therefore, future teacher-training programmes should consider:

- *How to improve the quality of language input* to build on and expand child talk and thinking (Hamre, et al., 2012). For example, systematically incorporating book reading would expose children to higher lexical diversity, more syntactic complexity and more talk about vocabulary, without having to displace or upgrade the teacher workforce (Dickinson et al., 2014).

- *How to develop practical knowledge about teaching in small groups*, including classroom management strategies and the use of formative feedback to build children's language skills, along with policies to reduce the teacher–child ratio. In Chile, the teacher–child ratio is 1:22 in classrooms for three- to six-year-olds. By contrast, in the US, this ratio is 1:13 (MINEDUC, 2014).
- *How to deal with student diversity.* Teachers must be familiar with tools to evaluate and detect both special needs and progress in specific early literacy domains; in addition, they must be aware of how to use strategies to plan their teaching according to different performance levels.

Besides improving the quality of teacher training, it would also be beneficial to promote the social value of teaching. In Chile, teachers currently earn less than other university graduates. Within the teaching profession, early childhood teachers are paid even less; on average, they earn 9 per cent less than elementary school teachers after ten years, and as compared to other related professionals, they earn between 95 per cent and 128 per cent less over the same time period (MINEDUC, 2014). On the other hand, more regulation is needed to prevent teachers who receive better pre-service training from systematically working with children from more affluent backgrounds, as is the case nowadays (Ortúzar et al., 2009).

Final considerations

Improving both pre- and in-service teacher training for early literacy is an urgent challenge, not only for the countries examined here, but also for the entire Latin American region. According to Fillmore and Snow (2002), teacher preparation poses a great challenge because prospective teachers must know how oral and written language is organized at different unit levels (graphemic, morphological, lexical, syntactic, textual, pragmatic and discourse levels) and used in everyday and academic contexts. Furthermore, teachers must be prepared to foster opportunities for early literacy learning as communicators capable of conveying language and literacy knowledge in their teaching and monitoring practices, thus effectively supporting language and literacy development across educational levels. More research about the effect of teaching practices on literacy learning in children, as well as the exchange of ideas and results in the region, will be necessary to inform the changes that should be made to teacher training, with a special focus on the challenges unique to the Spanish language, as we have suggested in this chapter.

In the realm of pre-service training, one challenge is that the governments in both Costa Rica and Chile have limited power to influence the curricula used by autonomous universities. Costa Rica and Chile should share their experiences with teacher certification systems and the implementation of standards for teacher preparation.

An expectation of this in-depth review of early literacy education in Chile and Costa Rica was to contribute to other countries in the region that are in the process of making crucial decisions in the early literacy domain. In a region of limited resources, the shared Spanish language might be an advantage when designing teacher resources, measurement instruments or curricular documents. For example, the Costa Rican set of resources to support teachers to document and assess child learning might be a good starting point that could be further adapted to cultural particularities.

Additionally, the fine-grained analysis of the learning goals of the Chilean curriculum presented here might serve as a useful guideline in analysing whether learning goals truly reflect the emphases of each country's approach to teaching early literacy.

For Latin American countries, it will be crucial to advance from coverage to education quality, especially in early literacy provision. Coherence among the declared, enacted and assessed curricula, teacher preparation for literacy and language, and effective evidence-based strategies and resources will contribute to improving opportunities to learn for all children in the region.

Notes

1 For example, *g* /g/ 'gato', /x/ 'gente'; *c* /k/ 'casa', /s/ 'cielo,' *y* /ʎ/ 'yeso', /i/ 'rey'; *r* /ɾ/ 'cara', /r/ 'rama'.
2 The *h* has no corresponding phoneme, and *x* can be pronounced not only as different phonemes (/s/ 'xilófono,' /j/ 'México'), but also as a sequence of phonemes (/ks/ 'examen').
3 C = consonant, V = vowel.
4 In Spanish: *Política nacional de lectura y escritura*.
5 If the LG was broadly classified into the *meaning-construction category*, the LG was in turn coded into one of the following options: *oral production, strategies for understanding, pragmatic or social communication knowledge, vocabulary, print knowledge, oral comprehension, genre knowledge, written production, exposure to literacy* and *reading understanding*. Instead, if the LG was classified into the *code-based skills* category, it could in turn be coded into: *phonological awareness, fluency, fine motor skills, knowledge of sentence structure, spelling, decoding words* and *alphabetic knowledge*.
6 The commitment was unaffected by the 2014 change in administration. Although this should be the norm, since educational policies are state policies, this is often not the case in Latin American nations.
7 A considerable portion of elementary school teachers and practically all preschool teachers hold teaching diplomas from public or private universities (bachelor, licentiate and, at the preschool level, even master's degrees).
8 Initial teacher training varies widely in breadth and depth depending on the quality of the university programme attended. At present, there are three public universities and over 20 private institutions that offer teaching programmes.

References

Adlerstein, C., Pardo, M., Díaz, C. and Villalón, M. (2016). Formación para la enseñanza del lenguaje oral y escrito en carreras de educación parvularia: Variedad de aproximaciones y similares dilemas. *Estudios Pedagógicos*, 42(1), 17–36. doi:10.4067/S0718-07052016000100002

Ardila, A. and Rosselli, M. (2014). Spanish and the characteristics of acquired disorders in reading and writing. *Estudios de Psicología*, 35(3), 502–518. doi:10.1080/02109395.2014.965453.

Ávalos, B. (2010). Formación inicial docente en Chile: calidad y políticas. In C. Bellei, D. Contreras and J. P. Valenzuela (eds), *Ecos de la revolución pingüina: Avances, debates y silencios en la reforma educacional* (pp. 257–284). Santiago: Universidad de Chile and UNICEF.

Bravo-Valdivieso, L. and Escobar, J. P. (2014). How transparent is Spanish orthography? *Estudios de Psicología*, 35(3), 442–449. doi:10.1080/02109395.2014.965455.

Bridges, M. S., Justice, J. M., Hogan, T. P. and Gray, S. (2012). Promoting lower- and higher level language skills in early education classrooms. In R. C. Pianta, W. S. Barnett, L. M. Justice and S. M. Sheridan (eds), *Handbook of Early Childhood Education* (pp. 177–193). New York: Guilford Press.

Cisternas, T., Latorre, M. and Alegría, M. (2013). *¿Cómo enseña usted este tema? Conocimientos didácticos que subyacen a las prácticas de profesores de educación básica. Un análisis a seis temas fundamentales en la enseñanza de la lectura, la escritura y las matemáticas*. Santiago de Chile: Universidad Alberto Hurtado, Centro de Investigación y Desarrollo en Educación (CIDE).

Connor, C. (2011). Child characteristics–instruction interactions: Implications for students' literacy skills development in the early grades. In S. Neuman and D. Dickinson (eds), *Handbook of Early Literacy Research: Volume 3* (pp. 256–278). New York: Guilford Press.

Cox, C. (2007). Educación en el bicentenario: Dos agendas y calidad de la política. *Pensamiento Educativo*, 40(1), 175–204.

Cox, C., Meckes, G. L. and Bascopé, J. M. (2010). La institucionalidad formadora de profesores en Chile en la década del 2000: Velocidad del mercado y parsimonia de las políticas. *Pensamiento Educativo*, *46*(1), 205–245.

Defior, S. and Serrano, F. (2014). Diachronic and synchronic aspects of Spanish: the relationship with literacy acquisition. *Estudios de Psicología*, *35*(3), 450–475. doi:10.1080/02109395.2014.974422.

Dickinson, D. K. (2011). Teachers' language practices and academic outcomes of preschool children. *Science*, *333*(6045), 964–967. doi:10.1126/science.1204526.

Dickinson, D. K., Hofer, K. G., Barnes E. M. and Grifenhagen, J. F. (2014). Examining teachers' language in Head Start classrooms from a Systemic Linguistics Approach. *Early Childhood Research Quarterly*, *29*(3) 231–244.

Facultad de Educación PUC/MINEDUC. (2011). *Alfabetización en establecimientos chilenos subvencionados* (Final Report). Santiago de Chile: Facultad de Educación, Pontificia Universidad Católica de Chile.

Fillmore, L. and Snow, C. (2002). What teachers need to know about language. In C. Temple, C. Snow and D. Christian (eds), *What Teachers Need to Know about Language* (pp. 7–54). McHenry, IL: Delta Systems.

Guardia, P. (2014). Is consonant rhyme important when learning to read in Spanish? *Estudios de Psicología*, *35*(3), 567–583. doi: 10.1080/02109395.2014.965459.

Guerra, R. (1983). Estudio estadístico de la sílaba en español. In M. Esgueva and M. Cantarero (eds). *Estudio de fonética I* (pp. 9–112). Madrid: CSIC.

Hamre, B. K., Downer, J. T., Jamil, F. M. and Pianta, R. C. (2012). Enhancing teachers' intentional use of effective interactions with children. In R. C. Pianta, W. S. Barnett, L. M. Justice and S. M. Sheridan (eds), *Handbook of Early Childhood Education* (pp. 507–532). New York: Guilford Press.

Mendive, S. and Meneses, A. (2017). *Differences between Declared and Enacted Chilean Curriculum in Language and Early Literacy Domains*. Manuscript in preparation.

Mendive, S., Weiland, C., Yoshikawa, H. and Snow, C. (2015). Opening the black box: Intervention fidelity in a randomized trial of a preschool teacher professional development program. *Journal of Educational Psychology*, *108*(1): 130–145. doi:10.1037/edu0000047.

Meneses, A., Montenegro, M. and Ruiz, M. (2014). Textos escolares para aprender ciencias: habilidades, contenidos y lenguaje académico. In M. De la Cerda (ed.), *Evidencias para políticas públicas en educación: Selección de investigaciones sexto Concurso FONIDE* (pp. 233–277). Santiago: MINEDUC.

MEP (1995). *Programa de estudio ciclo de transición. Educación preescolar*. San José de Costa Rica.

MEP (2000). *Programa de estudio ciclo materno infantil. Educación preescolar*. San José de Costa Rica.

MEP (2004). Documento *respecto a la escolarización de la educación preescolar*. San José de Costa Rica.

MEP (2013a). *Programa de estudio español - I ciclo de la educación general básica*. San José de Costa Rica.

MEP (2013b). *Política nacional de lectura y escritura*. San José de Costa Rica.

MEP (2014a). *Programa de estudio educación preescolar. Ciclo materno infantil (Grupo Interactivo II) – Ciclo de Transición*. San José de Costa Rica.

MEP (2014b). *Antología para docentes: Apoyo para la implementación del nuevo programa de español para 1er ciclo*. San José de Costa Rica.

MINEDUC (2001). *Bases curriculares de la educación parvularia*. Santiago de Chile.

MINEDUC (2012). *Bases curriculares educación básica*. Santiago de Chile.

MINEDUC (2014). *Estado del arte de educación parvularia en Chile*. Santiago de Chile.

Oakhill, J. V. and Cain, K. (2012). The precursors of reading ability in young readers: Evidence from a four-year longitudinal study. *Scientific Studies of Reading*, *16*(2), 91–121. doi:10.1080/10888438. 2010.529219.

O'Neill, D. K., Pearce, M. J. and Pick, J. L. (2004). Preschool children's narratives and performance on the Peabody Individualized Achievement Test Revised: Evidence of a relation between early narrative and later mathematical ability. *First Language*, *24*(2), 149–183. doi:10.1177/0142723704043529.

Organisation for Economic Co-operation and Development. (2012). *Starting Strong III: A Quality Toolbox for Early Childhood Education and Care*. Paris: OECD.

Ortúzar, M., Flores, C., Milesi, C. and Cox, C. (2009). Aspectos de la formación inicial docente y su influencia en el rendimiento académico de los alumnos. In *Camino al Bicentenario. Propuestas para Chile*. Santiago (pp. 155–186). Chile: Centro de Políticas Públicas UC.

Pérez-Leroux, A. T., Castilla-Earls, A. P. and Brunner, J. (2012). General and specific effects of lexicon in grammar: Determiner and object pronoun omissions in child Spanish. *Journal of Speech Language and Hearing Research*, *55*(2), 313–327. doi:10.1044/1092c4388.

Porter, A. C., Smithson, J., Blank, R. and Zeidner, T. (2007). Alignment as a teacher variable. *Applied Measurement in Education, 20*(1), 27–51.

Programa Estado de la Nación (2011). Capítulo 2: Educación Preescolar, Anexo 2. Procesos iniciales de lectoescritura en preescolar. In *Tercer Informe Estado de la Educación*. San José de Costa Rica.

Programa Estado de la Nación (2013). Capítulo 5: Sección Pruebas estandarizadas y PISA: una breve caracterización. In *Cuarto Informe Estado de la Educación*. San José de Costa Rica.

Resnick, L. B., Snow, C. E. and New Standards (Organization). (2009). *Speaking and Listening for Preschool through Third Grade*. Newark, DE: New Standards/International Reading Association.

Rodino, A. M. (2010). *Educación en la edad preescolar*. Investigación para el Informe Estado de la Educación III (2011).

Rodino, A. M. (2013). *La competencia lectora de los estudiantes costarricenses según la evaluación PISA 2009+*. Investigación para el Informe Estado de la Educación IV.

Seymour, P. H. K. (2005). Early reading development in European orthographies. In M. J. Snowling and C. Hulme (eds), *The Science of Reading: A Handbook* (pp. 296–315). Malden, MA: Blackwell.

Strasser, K., Larraín, A. y Lissi, M. R. (2013). Effects of storybook reading style on comprehension: The role of word elaboration and coherence questions. *Early Education and Development, 24*(5), 616–639. doi:10.1080/10409289.2012.715570.

Strasser, K., Mendive, S., Vergara, D. and Darricades, M. (2016a). Sobrecarga cognitiva en el aula preescolar: ¿Puede una lista de cotejo elevar la calidad del lenguaje dirigido a niños y niñas de nivel medio mayor? *Revista Estudios Política Educativa, 3*, 106–137.

Strasser, K. and del Río, F. (2013). The role of comprehension monitoring, theory of mind, and vocabulary depth in predicting story comprehension and recall of kindergarten children. *Reading Research Quarterly, 49*(2), 169–187. doi:10.1002/rrq.68.

Strasser, K., Vergara, D. and del Río, F. (2016b). Contributions of print exposure to first and second grade oral language and reading in Chile. *Journal of Research in Reading*. doi:10.1111/1467-9817.12086

Tomasello, M. (2011). Language development. In U. Goswami (ed.), *The Wiley-Blackwell Handbook of Childhood Cognitive Development* (pp. 239–257). Chichester: Wiley-Blackwell.

Trevarthen, C. (1988). Universal cooperative motives: How infants begin to know the language and culture of their parents. In G. Jahoda and I. M. Lewis (eds), *Acquiring Culture: Cross-Cultural Studies in Child Development* (pp. 37–90). Beckenham: Croom Helm.

UNESCO and Agencia Española de Cooperación Internacional para el Desarrollo (2013). *Situación educativa de América Latina: Hacia la educación de calidad para todos al 2015*. Santiago de Chile: UNESCO, Oficina Regional de Educación para América Latina y el Caribe.

Whitehurst, G. and Lonigan, C. (1998). Child development and emergent literacy. *Child Development, 69*(3), 848–872.

11

EARLY LITERACY POLICY AND PRACTICE IN POLAND

Elżbieta Awramiuk, Grażyna Krasowicz-Kupis
and Magdalena Smoczyńska

This chapter aims to review the policy and practice of early literacy education in Poland for native Polish-speaking children. It opens with a brief overview of the Polish language and Polish educational system, followed by a discussion of the structure of the Polish phonology and orthography and its impact on early literacy development. The focus is then shifted to the early Polish literacy policy and its implementation. The provision for children with special educational needs as well as variety of literacy materials are also reviewed. The chapter closes with a discussion of major challenges for the current and future early literacy provision.

Polish is an Indo-European language belonging to the Slavic group. It is the official language of Poland with its population of 38.5 million, as well as one of the official languages of the European Union. The actual size of the Polish population is difficult to estimate, given that many Poles have moved to Western Europe in the past decade and are still migrating and immigrating.

Contemporary Poland is a very ethnically and linguistically homogeneous country, with 97 per cent of its population speaking Polish as their mother tongue. Minorities, which account for the remaining 3 per cent of the population, are either national (Byelorussian, Lithuanian, German, Ukrainian) or ethnic (Karaim, Lemko, Romani and Tatar). Members of minorities who live in Poland are predominantly bilingual.

Another important fact is that the Polish language used in contemporary Poland shows relatively little variation. Standard literary language, which is the main variety taught in schools and used in the media, is uniform. In the north, there is a small community speaking a regional language called Kashubian. Additionally, in a few regions, there are larger groups of people who still speak dialects of Polish at home, such as the Podhale dialect used among inhabitants of the Tatra mountains in the south or the Silesian dialect in the south-western Poland. However, most of these people can also use the standard variety of Polish. Generally speaking, in most of the Poland's territory, regional variation within spoken Polish is limited to minor phonetic and lexical differences.

The national educational policy is developed and enforced centrally by the Ministry of National Education, while the administration of education is decentralized and delegated to local authorities (communes). Compulsory education lasts from the age of six to 16, and is free in public schools. Educational institutions include preschool facilities as well as schools of primary, lower secondary, upper secondary and post-secondary levels.

The optional preschool education, which is offered to children aged from three to five, is attended by 72 per cent of Polish children. The mandatory age of starting school is seven years old, but according to a recent regulation, parents may decide to send their children to school at the age of six, provided they have completed a preschool (kindergarten) preparation class one year earlier.

Primary school is divided into two cycles of three years. The first cycle (grade: one to three, age: seven to nine) offers integrated teaching: pupils are taught all subjects by one teacher specialized in early childhood education. In the second cycle (grade: four to six, age: ten to twelve), teaching is subject-based and provided by several teachers. All pupils who leave primary school have to continue their education at a general three-year lower secondary school, with a compulsory external examination taken at the end. Free public education offered at further levels is not compulsory.

The existing educational system was created in 1999, with numerous subsequent modifications introduced over the last 16 years. The recent political developments have brought significant changes to the educational policy, some of them reversing the status quo, such as the recent abolishing of a regulation lowering the school entry age from seven down to six years. These trends indicate that the information presented in this chapter may become outdated by the time the current government leaves office.

Typological characteristics of Polish and its impact on orthographic and phonological representations

In terms of comparative morphological typology, Polish is typically referred to as a fusional inflecting language, characterized by rich morphology, both inflectional and derivational. Nouns, adjectives and verbs are inflected according to complex declensional and conjugational paradigms, therefore each word appears in a range of varying forms. The use of inflectional endings and derivational suffixes is associated with numerous systemic morphological alternations of the word stem or root. Alternations concern stem vowels and/or consonants, for example:

/drog/   *drog-a* 'road' (Nom. Sg.)
/droʥ/   *drodz-e* 'road' (Dat. Sg.)
/druk/   *dróg-Ø* 'road' (Gen. Pl.)
/druʒ/   *po-dróż-n-y* 'traveller'
/druʃ/   *dróż-k-a* 'small road' (diminutive)

The phonological inventory consists of 37 phonemes, among them six vowels, three semivowels and 28 consonants (Ostaszewska and Tambor, 2004). The ratio of consonants to vowels is relatively high (as it is the case of most Slavic languages). Unlike in Czech or Slovak, vowel length is not distinctive in Polish. Contrary to Russian, where the word stress is distinctive and unstressed vowels undergo reduction, Polish has indistinctive penultimate stress, which does not influence the pronunciation of sounds (as it is the case, for instance, in English).

Among consonants there are characteristic three series of sibilants and affricates: dental /s/, /z/, /t͡s/, /d͡z/, palatal /ɕ/, /ʑ/, /t͡ɕ/, /d͡ʑ/ and alveolar /ʃ/, /ʒ/, /t͡ʃ/, /d͡ʒ/. Polish pronunciation involves systematic devoicing of voiced consonants, occurring either in final position or preceding an unvoiced consonant, with the voiced phoneme being preserved in writing (comparable with German). The prosodic structure of Polish words allows for open and closed syllables as well as for a number of consonant clusters to occur.

The Polish alphabet, created on the basis of the borrowed Latin alphabet, is composed of 23 basic letters and nine supplementary letters (with diacritics): A Ą B C Ć D E Ę F G H I J K L Ł M N Ń O Ó P R S Ś T U W Y Z Ź Ż. Additionally, 11 diagraphs (SI, CI, NI, ZI, DZ, RZ, CH, SZ, CZ, DŹ, DŻ) and one trigraph (DZI) are used to represent Polish phonemes. Altogether, the Polish alphabetical system uses 44 graphemes, i.e. letters and letter combinations referring to particular phonemes.

Only 14 letters of the Polish alphabet, namely A, Ć, E, F, H, J, L, Ł, M, Ń, O, Ó, P, T, are always read in the same way regardless of the graphic and phonological context. As for the remaining letters, their correct reading requires an analysis of the closest graphic context because some letters, namely C, D, G, I, K, N, R, S, Z, Ż and Ź, may appear not in their basic function of designating phonemes but as a part of complex graphemes referring to other phonemes, e.g. letter Z used to form digraphs such as DZ, SZ, CZ, RZ.

There are eight phonemes which have double graphemic designations. Five of them form a series referring to soft consonants: Ś = SI, Ź = ZI, Ć = CI, DŹ = DZI and Ń = NI. Depending on the phonetic/graphemic context, softness may be marked either by a diacritic or by the letter I. Children have to learn the rule governing their distribution, but it is not very difficult.

Most difficulties in the acquisition in Polish spelling are caused by the following three, historically motivated, doublets, namely:

U = Ó corresponding to /u/
Ż = RZ corresponding to /ʒ/
H = CH corresponding to /x/

Their distribution is much less systematic, as they are related to historical changes in Polish phonology and morphophonology, which may be quite obscure to contemporary speakers of Polish. In order to decide which grapheme has to be used in a given word form, one has to refer to a complex system of rules, many of them requiring the reference to the lexical meaning of the word as well as the related morphological units: other inflected forms of the word or other words derivationally related. In addition to this, there is a corpus of words containing phonemes /u/, /ʒ/ and /x/, whose spelling is not rule-governed at all and has to be memorized. Orthographic problems involving those three doublets significantly impair transparency of the Polish spelling and create difficulties, which can persist in the adult age with some people.

How transparent is the Polish orthography? Transparency refers mainly to the relationship between sound (Ph for Phoneme) and sign (G for Grapheme). In transparent (shallow) systems, there is a full correspondence between them: one phoneme is always represented by one grapheme and vice versa (Ph = G). However, such systems are very rare among natural languages.

Some Polish words, such as *chrzan* ('horseradish'), for example, may appear 'scary' to non-native speakers. However, the graphic system is not as complicated as it seems. In the case of *chrzan*, two out of five consonant letters are parts of digraphs, thus the word contains only three consonantal phonemes: /xʃan/. Overall, Polish spelling is moderately transparent (shallow) as compared with some other languages, such as English or French. However, it is not as shallow as that of Serbian or Croatian, which are known for having a very close match between graphemic and phonetic representation.

When evaluating the transparency of the graphic system, one should distinguish two directions of the G–Ph relationship. The transparency of mapping from graphemic to phonemic form (G → Ph) determines how easy it is to read words in a given language, i.e. to decode them into the strings of sounds. The transparency of mapping from phonemic to graphemic form (Ph → G) determines how easy it is to write words in a given language, i.e. to convert a string of sounds into a correct graphic form.

In general, the transparency of Polish writing system is much higher in the G → Ph than in the Ph → G direction, which means that it is much easier to read than to write in Polish. Unlike in English, one can decode a Polish written text and read it correctly without even knowing what it means. Of course, since the correspondence of letters and sounds is not perfect, readers have to first acquire some general rules about digraphs, alternative marking of soft consonants, devoicing and others, but they do not need morphological information in order to decode words correctly. However, in the Ph → G direction, the correspondence is not as transparent and proper spelling (orthography) is not that simple. One has to refer to morphology, both lexical and inflectional/derivational, in order to decide about the specific issues in the specific case: for example, whether an unvoiced consonant should be written as such or replaced by the original voiced counterpart (e.g. the string /kot/ may be written as *kot* 'cat' or *kod* 'code', depending on the meaning) or which one of the graphic doublets to choose for phonemes /u/, /x/ and /ʒ/. For instance, hearing the sequence of phonemes /druk/ one has to use the semantic and syntactic context in order to decide whether it refers to the lexeme *druk* 'print' or the Gen. Pl. form *dróg* of *droga* 'road'. When the latter is chosen, before writing correctly the form *dróg* one has to refer to the Nom. Sg. form *drog-a*, which contains the information that /k/ is in fact a devoiced /g/ and therefore should be written with G, whereas the phoneme /u/ should be written as Ó rather than U, because the regular morphonological alternation of /o/ vs. /u/ is rendered in writing as O vs. Ó.

Principal methods and content areas of literacy instruction

Acquisition of literacy may start with graphic signs and the sounds to which they refer (G → Ph, reading first) or with phonemes and the way in which they are designated in writing (Ph → G, writing first). Due to the properties of the Polish orthographic system, the first option seems to be more appropriate for Polish children. However, in order to prevent them from applying the phonological strategy in the other direction (i.e. when learning to write), it is highly recommended by Polish educational authorities that learning to read and write takes place in parallel (simultaneously). Common practice in Polish literacy education follows this recommendation.

On the other hand, due to the inflectional characteristics of the Polish language, the global method (the global recognition of words) seems ineffective, as words appear in many different forms. The characteristics of relatively shallow alphabetical writing suggest the coexistence of analytical (from large units like words to smaller units) and synthetic (from small units to larger units) processes throughout learning to read and write. Therefore, the optimal method of teaching literacy, which prevails in Poland, is the lexical variant of the analytical and synthetic method. It consists in performing a visual and auditory analysis of a word containing a letter or phoneme, and then synthesizing it back. The adequacy of this method is confirmed by research on how children acquire reading and writing in Polish language – beginning with the stage of analytical reading based on phonemic analysis (Krasowicz-Kupis, 2006; Awramiuk and Krasowicz-Kupis, 2014).

Learning to read and write focuses on common goals: mastering technical skills, development of the ability to understand/speak and to increase emotional involvement in the performance of both activities. Practical tasks in phonetic analysis involve auditory isolation of phones in a word. The most common type of such practice tasks involves pronunciation of a word and deciding on the location of a given phone. At the beginning, children search for initial and final phones, and with increasing hearing sensitivity in children, the level of difficulty increases, as a searched phone may occur anywhere in a word. Often, practice tasks in phonetic analysis are reinforced by visual stimuli in which the phonetic structure of analysed words is visualized.

In the teaching process, during the introduction of a new letter, many primers follow the principle: presentation of the entire word (*woda* 'water'), division into syllables (*wo-da*), division into phones (*w-o-d-a*) and re-presentation of the entire word (*woda*).

The core curriculum does not impose any single teaching method. A teacher has the right to choose his or her teaching method independently, taking into account the individual abilities of the children and bearing in mind that teaching of reading and writing should be combined. In addition to the analytical-synthetic method in its lexical variant, which is the most popular method of teaching literacy in Poland, other teaching methods are also applied. Among the abundance of teaching proposals, there are those in which a syllable is the basic unit of analysis and/or synthesis, and those that completely break with the traditional approach, proposing the global reading method. New teaching materials demonstrate a clear trend to introduce a variety of elements; for example elements of the global method are introduced in the analytic-synthetic method.

At the initial stage of learning, an important role is given to concepts used for distinguishing the elements of language such as sentence, word, syllable, phone and letter. They do not occur in isolation but form a template with some key concepts. This conceptual structure helps the children to organize their knowledge in a hierarchical order. Moreover, these concepts may serve as a consistent and logical basis for conscious learning at higher levels of education. Children learn concepts through observation and independent thinking (e.g. drawing conclusions, summarizing), rather than by learning their definitions.

Early literacy

Learning to read and write begins in Poland in grade 1. Kindergarten education aims to develop children's readiness to learn to read and write (e.g. manual skills and eye–hand coordination, phonological skills), as well as ignite children's interest in reading and writing.

At the preparatory stage, attention is given to both the technical aspect of the acquired skills (*code-based skills*) and reading comprehension (*meaning-construction skills*). Reading begins with monosyllabic words, thus children are in contact with the meaning of graphic strings that they learn from the very beginning. The inventory of letters used at first is limited to the most unproblematic ones. Gradually, digraphs and more difficult letters and letter combinations are introduced. After the first year at school, children would have eventually acquired all the letters of the alphabet. They can read and understand brief texts and write simple, short sentences, giving attention to the aesthetics and correctness of writing. Over time, the pragmatic aspect of reading and writing gains importance.

The core curriculum identifies final learning outcomes for the entire three-year cycle of early childhood education (CC, 2014: 11–12), not for particular grades. Distribution of material and decisions on how much time should be devoted to mastering knowledge and skills in specific areas are made solely by the teacher, who can adjust the teaching to individual pupils' needs.

According to the core curriculum, pupils who successfully complete grade three education should be able to read and make sense of texts written for their reading level. They should also be able to search for necessary information in a text, as well as use child-friendly dictionaries. They are supposed to read children's literature, both books of their choice and those indicated by the teacher, and to speak about them. They should also be able to produce oral and written communications composed of several sentences (short stories and descriptions, personal letters, greetings, invitations). They should have learned to write clearly and neatly, giving attention to correctness in terms of grammar, spelling and punctuation.

Minorities who live in Poland have the right to be taught the minority language and culture at school. The core curriculum for preschool education takes into account preparation for speaking the language of a national or ethnic minority, or a regional language (Kashubian). These guidelines are implemented by kindergartens. Children who belong to national and ethnic minorities and to communities speaking a regional language may continue learning their language at later stages of education or, if there is a school offering it, they can receive teaching in the minority language. Learning outcomes at the end of early childhood education in terms of the native language of a national or ethnic minority are consistent with the objectives defined for Polish language education.

There has been a recent increase in children for whom Polish is a foreign language. These children's parents are either refugees from other countries or people who settle in Poland for professional or personal reasons. For such children, additional Polish language classes, compensatory school subject classes and classes about the language and culture of their country of origin are organized. There is also a rising number of Polish citizens who attended schools operating in foreign education systems. With the support of the Ministry of National Education, several additional materials are being developed to support children from different backgrounds (Barzykowski et al., 2013).

The learning of a modern foreign language begins in kindergarten. Preparing children to speak a modern foreign language is included in various activities carried out under the preschool education programme and takes place mainly in a fun way. Within the early childhood education cycle, foreign language tuition is provided by a qualified teacher during separate classes. According to national curricula, pupils who complete grade three should be able to produce, understand, read and copy words and simple sentences in the foreign language they learn. Children should be supported in communicating with people who speak another language and motivated to learn foreign languages.

Throughout grades one to three, there is no quantitative grading: only descriptive assessment is used. It is based on careful systematic and multi-dimensional observation of the child by the teacher, who takes into account the child's performance and progress, as well as the results from tests, worksheets and workbooks.

A 'semester assessment' is the result of a six-month observation of a child, and is the basis for issuing report cards drawn up on the basis of the core curriculum. It also provides guidelines for further work. In addition to typical school skills, reading, writing and counting, other factors are taken into account, such as ability to cooperate with others, organization of one's own work, interests and abilities.

Policy implementation in practice

Legislation has introduced identical quality assurance approaches in early childhood and school education. These include three main elements, which aim to improve the quality of education, and are as follows:

- system of pedagogical supervision, including evaluating outcomes of educational, care-related and other statutory activities undertaken by schools and supporting schools in the performance of their tasks;
- internal teacher appraisal, including assessment of teachers' performance, carried out by the school head as part of internal pedagogical supervision;
- external pupil assessment, carried out by institutions which are external to the school, including the Regional and Central Examination Boards (Smoczyńska et al., 2012).

At the end of early childhood education stage in primary school, there are no mandatory state exams, as is the case at the end of the entire primary school education cycle.[1] Schools may participate in voluntary national or international tests that assess the achievements of pupils as well as the school's performance. The most common test is the National Study of Third Graders' Skills (OBUT), which has been in place since 2010. OBUT's primary objective is to provide schools with information on the level of knowledge and skills of individual pupils and classes that complete the first stage of education, and thus to determine at which level children are, in terms of their:

- basic skills (reading, mathematics, communication);
- Polish language and mathematics teaching content;
- use of background knowledge and skills for problem-solving (Pregler, 2014).

An important result of this study is to provide the schools with national comparative data in terms of individual students, classes and the entire school. After analysing such a report, teachers obtain additional information about each child's strengths and the difficulties that the child faces regarding the skills under examination. A summary of class and school results in different skill areas is most important for the improvement of the school's effectiveness. OBUT results are also one of the key elements for internal school review and identifying opportunities to improve teacher practice (Pregler, 2014).

In 2011, Polish third-graders took part in an international reading skill study – PIRLS (*Progress in International Reading Literacy Study*), the aim of which was to assess reading comprehension (Konarzewski, 2012). Tests used in PIRLS measure the four basic skills that make up the reading proficiency: (1) finding information that meets specified criteria in a text; (2) drawing conclusions from evidence contained in a text; (3) combining and interpreting the information contained in a text; (4) examining and evaluating the content, language and layout of a text.

In the PIRLS context, the OBUT study, which assessed a similar set of specific skills, allowed teachers to conduct an objective assessment of their pupils' reading skills, serving also as a valuable element of their teaching skills self-assessment. In PIRLS, Polish children were ranked 28th among children from the 45 countries participating in the study. If we take into account their age, Polish pupils were classified close to the middle of the scale, i.e. 11th among their peers from 22 countries who participated in the study (Konarzewski, 2012).

Future teachers may upgrade their qualifications at higher education and postgraduate courses. Training for teaching in kindergarten and in grades one to three of primary school is offered as part of education studies. Graduates have basic knowledge and skills in Polish language, mathematics and natural science (including the ability to create texts, make mathematical calculations and demonstrate natural phenomena with experiments). The acquisition of these competencies is a prerequisite to begin teacher training, which includes basics of psychology and pedagogy – at a general education level, as well as tailored to a particular educational stage.

Provision for children with special educational needs (SEN)

Adapting educational requirements to the individual psychophysical and educational needs of children with SEN refers primarily to the groups that have been referred to special education and to individual learning or have been issued with a statement by a psychological and pedagogical unit, for example concerning specific learning difficulties or language disorders. The Polish education system provides the possibility to organize early development support, which is carried out in order to stimulate the motor, cognitive, emotional and social development of a child from the diagnosis of a disability to the beginning of schooling. Early development support teams function under the regulation of the Ministry of National Education (Regulation, 2013), ensuring that every child and the child's family receive specialist support and development stimulation in accordance with the child's abilities.

In the case of children who are subject to compulsory schooling and who qualify for the SEN group due to disability, the education system provides the opportunity for them to receive education in all types of schools – public, integration and special schools in accordance with children's individual developmental and educational needs and abilities.

Special education for a child is based on a decision that such a need exists issued by a public psychological and pedagogical unit or other specialized entity. Special education covers pupils who require special organization of learning and working methods (deaf and hard of hearing children, children with visual impairment, physical disability, including aphasia, intellectual difficulties and autism, including Asperger's syndrome). Psychological and pedagogical assistance for all SEN children includes assessment, providing direct assistance to pupils and their parents, implementation of preventive tasks and supporting educational institutions.

Unfortunately, children with learning difficulties do not receive systemic support. In this area, diagnosis, which begins with school readiness screening and screening for risk of disorders such as dyslexia, is most efficient. It allows children 'at risk' to receive support measures and for them to be possibly referred for in-depth specialized diagnostic tests (Bogdanowicz, 2008).

A child with dyslexia or another learning disorder obtains a specialist opinion stating the diagnosis. On its basis, the child may participate in therapeutic classes (remedial, speech therapy, compensatory) at school. According to the statement issued by a psychological and pedagogical unit, a teacher is required to adapt educational requirements to the individual psychological and educational needs of the pupil taking into account his or her abilities/strengths and limitations/dysfunctions. In addition, a pupil with dyslexia has the right to have the conditions and forms of state examinations adjusted.

Early literacy resources

A primer is the basic teaching material for early literacy. For many years, commercialized and sponsored primers were available on the Polish education market. The choice of a primer was made by the teacher.

In most EU countries, providing free access to basic teaching aids to pupils at the compulsory education stage is a standard practice. In 2014, a decision was made that the state would bear the costs of providing pupils in primary and secondary schools with free access to textbooks, as well as practice materials intended for compulsory general education. Changes in this area are being implemented gradually. The first free textbook, *Nasz elementarz* (Our primer), was developed at the request of the Ministry of National Education in 2014 for first-grade pupils. Currently, the choice of appropriate teaching materials is still made by a teacher and approved by the school head.

A modern primer is not only a textbook intended for early literacy, but also a textbook that introduces knowledge in mathematics, natural science, art and social relations. The *new* textbook is accompanied by a rich teaching framework in the form of a curriculum, worksheets and letter albums for children, materials for teachers (teaching guides with class scenarios, a proposed distribution of material and artistic inspirations) and adaptation for children with special educational needs (visually impaired, hard-of-hearing or deaf children, children with learning difficulties and/or communication difficulties). The content of the textbook is to be interpreted as a suggestion, which may be used in different ways by each teacher. Its purpose is to provide inspiration to the teachers rather than to be followed to the letter.

Other publications also offer comprehensive educational packages. Typically, they contain additional practice materials for pupils, guides for teachers and kits for children with difficulties in learning to read and write. The basic textbook in the first grade is supplemented by textbooks and educational materials for learning modern foreign languages. There are also textbooks for minority pupils whose learning process is aimed at preserving a sense of national, ethnic and linguistic identity.

Learning to write at the initial stage during the first year involves familiarizing children with the shape and manner of writing of upper-case and lower-case letters, and writing the letters in words. Particular attention is given to proper copying of letter shapes, their appropriate merging, and linking the sound of words with their graphic image. Learning to write is supported with special sheets, which contain graphic practice tasks as well as sheets for learning to write letters and numbers in which children first write letter-like signs. Children then reproduce the shape of letters in their standard form and copy syllables, words and sentences. Graphomotoric practice tasks are usually boring and tedious, but they tend to be more attractive when they are carried out in a fun way (e.g. 'Connect the dots and see who has visited Kate's garden') and allow children to experiment with different kinds of graphic materials and surfaces.

There are workbooks for learning to write by right-handed and left-handed children, books for therapeutic work at school and at home for pupils with a risk of dyslexia or who experience difficulties in learning to read and write. Pupils with special educational needs have access to a variety of therapeutic materials at every learning stage.

According to national curricula, the selection of written material to read has to include the following genres of children's literature: fairy tales, fables, legends, short stories, poems, comics, while their selection should be guided by the real reading skills of children and their educational needs. Children should be taught to memorize poems, fragments of prose and lyrics. The National Study of Third Graders' Skills conducted in the years 2006–2011 and the OBUT study showed that pupils are better at reading literary texts and short texts rather than popular science texts, and prose rather than poetry (Murawska, 2011).

There is no set reading list for children in early childhood education programmes. Teachers are free to select children's literature, but despite the freedom of choice, many teachers resort to traditional publications, including worldwide literary masterpieces, such as fairy tales by Andersen and Perrault, Milne's *Winnie the Pooh* and Polish classical prose and poetry by Brzechwa, Tuwim, Chotomska and Makuszyński. Teachers use a variety of methods to encourage pupils to read: they read aloud excerpts of books in the classroom, organize contacts with the school or public library, encourage children to prepare a book presentation and organize reading and writing competitions.

Major challenges for current and future early literacy provision

In the PISA study of reading and interpretation skills (2012), Polish 15-year-olds were among the best in the EU, along with students from Finland and Ireland. During the last three years, the average reading result of Polish students has significantly improved, which is interpreted as a positive effect of curriculum modifications over the last decade. However, not all problems have been resolved. Despite the measures taken, there is certainly much to be done in terms of developing effective solutions to support the education of children with different linguistic and cultural experiences. Poland is a fairly uniform country in terms of culture and language, but taking into account the experiences of other democratic countries, we may expect this situation to change.

In reference to children with SEN, the Polish education system provides the opportunity to organize specialized teaching methods in different forms: it provides the right for parents to choose the form of education, an individualized learning process adapted to the psychophysical abilities of pupils, revalidation classes and psychological support. However, in the case of children with specific learning disabilities such as dyslexia and language impairment, that is children who are most exposed to failures in early literacy, there are no adequate system solutions, and the existing regulations are too universal. In the case of language disorders, there is little knowledge about the issue and practically no solutions at all.

A further challenge for the current system is the obligatory learning of a foreign language at the primary school level. There are many educated English philologists in Poland, but not all of them have the talent and qualifications to work with young children. Currently, not enough kindergarten teachers are qualified to teach a foreign language.

During preparation of this chapter, Poland's educational policy was undergoing changes. The country is facing different challenges, and the coming years will show how they will be handled.

Note

1 This exam will be abolished in the future, as announced recently by the Minister of National Education.

References

Awramiuk, E. and Krasowicz-Kupis, G. (2014). Reading and spelling acquisition in Polish: Educational and linguistic determinants. *L1-Educational Studies in Language and Literature, 13–14*, 1–24. Retrieved from http://dx.doi.org/10.17239/l1esll-2014.01.13.

Barzykowski, K., Grzymała-Moszczyńska, H., Dzida, D., Grzymała-Moszczyńska, J. and Kosno, M. (2013). *Wybrane zagadnienia diagnozy psychologicznej dzieci i młodzieży w kontekście wielokulturowości oraz wielojęzyczności*. Warszawa: ORE.

Bogdanowicz, M. (2008). Model diagnozowania dysleksji rozwojowej. *Dysleksja, 1*, 7–12.

CC (2014). *General education core curriculum for primary schools*, appendix No. 2 to the Regulation of the Ministry of Science and Higher Education of 30 May 2014 Amending Regulation on the core curriculum for pre-school education and general education in particular types of schools. *Journal of Laws of 2014*, No. 0, Item 803.

Konarzewski, K. (2012). *TIMSS i PIRLS 2011. Osiągnięcia szkolne polskich trzecioklasistów w perspektywie międzynarodowej*. Warszawa: CKE. Retrieved from www.wzzso.pl/osi.pdf.

Krasowicz-Kupis, G. (2006). *Rozwój i ocena umiejętności czytania dzieci sześcioletnich.* Warszawa: CMPPP.

Murawska, B. (2011). *Pozwólmy dzieciom czytać.* Warszawa: CKE.

Nasz elementarz (2014). MEN. Retrieved from http://naszelementarz.men.gov.pl.

Ostaszewska, D. and Tambor, J. (2004). *Fonetyka i fonologia współczesnego języka polskiego.* 2nd edition. Warszawa: Wydawnictwo Naukowe PWN.

PISA (2012). Programme for International Student Assessment OECD PISA. Polish 2012 result. Retrieved from www.ibe.edu.pl/images/prasa/PISA-2012-raport_krajowy.pdf.

Pregler, A. (ed.) (2014). *Ogólnopolskie Badanie Umiejętności Trzecioklasistów Raport OBUT 2013.* Warszawa: IBE. Retrieved from http://biblioteka-krk.ibe.edu.pl/opac_css/doc_num.php?explnum_id=785.

Regulation (2013). Regulation of the Ministry of National Education of 11 October 2013 on the organization of children's early development support. Journal of Laws of 2013, No. 0, item 1257.

Smoczyńska, A., Górowska-Fells, M., Maluchnik, B., Płatos, B., Chojnacki, M., and Smolik M. (eds) (2012). *The System of Education in Poland.* Warsaw: Foundation for the Development of the Education System. Retrieved from http://eurydice.org.pl/wp-content/uploads/2014/10/system2012.pdf.

12

EARLY EDUCATION IN LITERACY IN TURKEY IN COMPARISON TO THE BALKAN COUNTRIES

Ilgım Veryeri Alaca and Aylin C. Küntay

This chapter gives an overview of early literacy education, with a focus primarily on Turkey, but including the Balkan countries as well. The focus is on Turkey as a case study since it plays a critical role bridging Europe and the Middle East. A review of policy and practice in preschool education is provided, along with the key research concerned with early learning outcomes for Turkish children.

The dominant languages used in the Balkan Peninsula stem from three branches: (1) Indo European (including Greek and Albanian) and Slavic (including Bosnian, Croatian, Serbian, Bulgarian and Macedonian); (2) Romance (Romanian and Aromun); and (3) Ural Altaic (Turkish). Latin, Greek and Cyrillic alphabets are in common use. Use of particular languages in the Balkan countries has been influenced by politics, social change and conflicts, whereby related transformations are still ongoing in certain areas. Issues related to settling on language policies and standards, including in cases where Bosnian, Montenegrin, Croatian and Serbian are spoken nationally, has made it difficult to develop early literacy strategies (Greenberg, 2004).

Balkan languages, though coming from diverse language families, share certain typological similarities due to cultural correspondence. This was noted in Trubetzkoy (1928), who referred to relationships between different languages that show similarities in sentence structure and word-formation as constituting 'linguistic areas' (or '*sprachbund*' in German) (Friedman, 2011: 276). The Balkan Sprachbund – identified as those languages which have been spoken in the Ottoman Empire since the early Middle Ages – consist of common typological properties, created as a result of a multilingual setting and related contact among diverse languages (Friedman, 2011).

Early literacy

In this section, we review early literacy education in relation to each country's educational policies. We begin with a focus on Turkey. In the European Union (EU), research in literacy education initiated a shift from the school readiness approach to the adaptation of emergent literacy strategies, dropping the age for the beginning of compulsory education in certain countries. Earlier compulsory education has led to a further set of changes with the objective of creating play-based literacy environments for children to perceive literacy as an extension of their life and play (Tafa, 2008). Maximizing participation in early education has brought with it a set of challenges, including issues related to quality and equity, especially in the case of Turkey. The non-obligatory preschool age dropped to 36 months in 2006. In 2012, mandatory school entry age dropped to 66 months from 72 months. This change was sudden and it did not allow for a smooth transition in terms of curricular planning and adequate teacher training. In regards to literacy development, children without preschool experience had a harder time with certain issues related to literacy, for instance with phonemic awareness (Sert, 2014). The influence of recent research on curriculum required amendments not only for new and experienced teachers but also for education specialists, librarians, policy-makers and monitoring parties. Similar to Russia and India, public educational expenditure relative to gross domestic product (GDP) remained less than 5 per cent in Turkey, gaining the lowest ranks among G20 countries (Eurostat, 2014). While the average time spent in education did rise to 12 years in 2012, drop-out rates in compulsory education are approximately 15 per cent and the average length of schooling for girls is less than five years. According to the United Nations Educational, Scientific and Cultural Organization (UNESCO), the allocated funds to create the infrastructure to educate young children and meet the objectives for Education for All by 2015 have not been adequate (Cemalcilar and Göksen, 2014). A new system based on new educational insights has required the hiring of new teachers, building new classrooms, producing educational materials, as well as investing in school libraries and librarians, a set of objectives that was difficult to achieve in a short period of time.

The EU has been instrumental in setting standards among members and candidate states. One of its aims has been to improve the quality of early childhood education, as well as raise participation in early childhood education to 95 per cent by 2015 starting with children aged four. These efforts have been conducted in tandem with similar projects by global non-governmental organizations (NGOs) such as UNICEF and the World Bank, and have been undertaken with the acknowledgement that early childhood education plays a role in staving off risks of poverty in the future. EU member and candidate states in Eastern Europe including Turkey have been successful in raising the ratio of participation in preschool education since 2000. The gross enrolment ratio of preschool enrolment in the Balkans is highest in Bulgaria (80 per cent males, 79 per cent females) and lowest in Bosnia Herzegovina (18 per cent males, 17 per cent females) according to the 2008–2012 statistics (UNICEF, 2014). In Turkey, the gross enrolment rate for pre-primary education rose from 6.7 per cent in 2001 to 29.2 per cent in 2011 (Eurostat, 2014). Not surprisingly, recent research confirmed that 'Turkey has the lowest enrolment rate among the so-called newly industrialized countries' (Agirdag et al., 2015: 546). According to a recent report by Educational Reform Initiative and ACEV, participation in preschool education has not increased for five-year-olds in Turkey, and has been documented to be about 54 per cent in the 2014–15 academic year, down from 66 per cent in 2011 (Oral et al., 2016).

In early childhood education, especially in Turkey, equity and quality have been key issues of focus. The Tenth Development Plan (2014–18) introduced the Mobile Classroom (for children aged 36–66 months), the Summer Preschool programme (for children aged 60–66 months) and the Project for Increasing Enrolment Rates Especially for Girls (ISEG, 2011–13). The Turkey Country Programme (2006–07) and the Pre-School Education Project (2010–13) are supported by the United Nations Children's Fund (UNICEF). The Childhood Development and Education Project and the pilot Pre-primary Parent–Child Education Programme Project (1999–2012) were designed to encourage support for parents in education (OECD, 2013). The rigorous implementations in relation to early literacy education encouraged meaning-construction skills in Turkey. In transforming curricula, a reconsideration of the balance between code-based skills versus meaning-construction skills in early literacy instruction has been triggered with reference to the Programme for International Student Achievement (PISA). Studies associate skills tested in PISA with preschool exposure to books and shared reading (OECD, 2013). In the last decade, education as regards to reading has gone through a set of changes. Phonics, as well as meaning-construction strategies, have been introduced. Yet, Turkey's low scores in PISA in 2009 indicate that meaning-construction skills, which are an indicator of text comprehension, have room for improvement (Blanchy and Şaşmaz, 2011). Despite some improvements between 2003 and 2012, Turkey's performance in PISA remained one year behind the Organisation for Co-operation and Development (OECD) average with 25 per cent of 15-year-olds not being able to analyse and understand what they read, regarded as 'functionally illiterate' by the OECD (Aedo, 2013).

Having one of the top preschool enrolment ratios in Balkans, meaning-making skills could be developed further in Greece as well. In a study by Stellakis (2012) the Greek teachers emphasized the role of multimodal communication in literacy, putting the emphasis on understanding a 'letter' as a sound and as a symbol, but they also highlighted the importance of phonemic awareness and phoneme–grapheme correspondence. In other words, the previous approaches to literacy have highlighted phonics instruction as a priority while overlooking the impact of reading for meaning making. Similar to the situation in Turkey, teachers mentioned a lack of adequate knowledge of recent research in this field, noting that training sessions would be beneficial and that meaning-making processes in the classroom could be developed further (Stellakis, 2012).

Orthographic and phonological representations

Below we summarize the basic principles of orthographic and associated phonological representation of the key Balkan language(s), mentioning the effects of each in terms of literacy education. A comparative research in consistent and inconsistent orthographies aiming to identify the best predictors of literacy after measuring phoneme awareness, letter knowledge, RAN[1] (rapid automized naming) show individual differences are substantial and 'the same mechanisms are involved in learning to read in any alphabetic ortography' (Caravolas et al., 2013: 1406). A cross-linguistic study is necessary for understanding literacy growth comparatively, while also enhancing the sharing of language-specific tools, which are crucial in developing solutions that are adequate for all the diverse linguistic contexts of the Balkans and Turkey. Bulgarian, Serbian and Macedonian are all written in the Cyrillic alphabet (Serbian is also written using the Latin alphabet). Turkish, Croatian and Romanian are written in the Latin alphabet while Greek is written in the Greek alphabet. Turkish, Bulgarian, Romanian, Macedonian, Serbian, Croatian and Bosnian have phonemic orthography, where the spelling of the words corresponds transparently to the way they are pronounced which facilitates reading acquisition (Seymour et al., 2003).

Turkish is a verb final SOV (subject, object, verb) language, using a rich set of nominal and verbal inflections to indicate grammatical relations. The Turkish alphabet consists of 29 letters (21 consonants, 8 vowels). Capitalization is utilized at the beginning of sentences as well as for proper nouns. Consonants and vowels are often organized in a CVC (consonant, vowel, consonant) sequence. All syllables have a vowel and cannot start with two consonants, with the exception of certain loanwords (Göksel and Kerslake, 2005). With its transparent orthography, Turkish has a simple letter–sound relationship, which is supportive of early phonological awareness skills (Öney and Durgunoğlu, 1997). A study by Babayiğit and Stainthorp (2007) suggested that spelling was a more reliable index of phonological processing skills in Turkish since word-level reading skills develop fast. Follow-up research with children aged between 67.7 months and 90.6 months indicated that listening comprehension rather than simple word reading is more influential in predicting meaning-making outcomes in Turkish (Babayiğit and Stainthorp, 2013).

Greek is written in Greek script with 24 letters, using both capital and lower-case letters. Sigma is an exception – it appears as a third case – as it can take on an extra lower-case form. Greek does not have a phonemic orthography. Its word order is SVO, yet in comparison to English, word order can be flexible, and object pronouns tend to precede the verb (Adams, 1987). Investigating syllable and phoneme awareness's contribution to reading and spelling in Greek (via measures including syllable awareness, phoneme awareness, reading and spelling) showed that students have a tendency to dissect words into syllables (Aidinis and Nunes, 2001). A one-year-long study on Greek indicated that in line with transparent languages (as in the case of Turkish), speech rate was more predictive of reading and spelling skills than RAN (Nikolopoulos, 2006).

Educational policy in relation to multilingual literacy

In many of the countries reviewed in this chapter, there are large minorities who are caught between the aspiration of passing on their own ethnic linguistic capacities to new generations and the pragmatics of being able to speak the language of the majority population in the country. The situation has become more complex with the developments in the European Union with regulations about national minorities outlined in the European Charter for Regional and Minority Languages (Council of Europe, 2014). In this section, we summarize how this has worked out with regards to Turkey and the minority populations living there. We compare the Turkish case to those of Bulgaria and Macedonia, particularly with regards to efforts regarding the Romani, because the programme was effective and might be employed as a model for other cases.

Since the foundation of the Republic in 1923, Turkish has been the official language of education in Turkey. Educational policies have been mostly reticent in relation to multilingual literacy and language learning. The Kurdish population has, in particular, grappled with the lack of a policy concerning multilingual literacy since Kurdish learning children are exposed to Turkish mostly only after they start primary school (Ceyhan and Koçbaş, 2011). According to recent statistics, resources for children and adults are mostly in Turkish, with some materials available in English.[2] Bilingual books are uncommon, but one notable picture-book series has been created through the International Bilingual Children's Books Project carried out by Anadolu Kültür in 2011, which has introduced Turkish–Greek, Turkish–Armenian and Turkish–Kurdish bilingual books. There have been many attempts to call for mother-tongue-based education in Turkey (e.g. Derince, 2012), but there has been little progress on the policy level.

Similar to Turkey, there are minority populations living in the Balkan countries. Issues related to language and ethnicity have been debated for nearly two centuries, and the current expectation is to adjust to the globalization trends characterizing the twenty-first century. To give an idea of recent developments in the area, Bulgaria – a country that includes Jewish, Romanian, Turkish, Armenian, Russian and Aromanian minorities – did for a long time not provide support for minority languages. In fact, the Bulgarian state made attempts to change the names of Turkish minorities only in 1984–85. More recently, however, there have been attempts to draw attention to the need for a curriculum for Turkish children. In 1999, Bulgaria signed the Framework Convention for the Protection of National Minorities, in support of the country's accession to the EU (Angelov and Marshall, 2006). A pilot study successfully introduced Bulgarian to Roma children who were not attending kindergarten. During this intervention, experts worked with parents at home. They utilized bilingual methods where information was first introduced in Romani and then translated to Bulgarian. The project was supported by a book entitled *I Learn Bulgarian* (Kyuchukov, 2006).

Roma minorities have been a disadvantaged group in the Balkans and other parts of Europe. An absence of kindergartens has been a general problem for Roma communities. Similar to the Bulgarian case, in Macedonia the 'Education for Roma children in the year before starting school' project helped the children prepare for the primary school while learning Macedonian. Comprehensive community-based programmes have been emerging for these communities, for instance in Serbia since 2009 (Macura-Milovanović, 2013). Social inclusion in the Western Balkans has been an ongoing challenge in Albania, Bosnia and Herzegovina, Croatia, Kosovo and the Former Yugoslav Republic of Macedonia, Montenegro and Serbia. A lack of funds and infrastructure have played a critical role in terms of making it difficult for children to attend school. In Romania, summer kindergarten programmes were recently introduced to ensure that more children are able to gain a kindergarten experience before starting primary school. In Macedonia, there are numerous initiatives to help disadvantaged children and their families, starting from birth through to the age of six. Some are geared towards parents, and are aimed at building a more educational atmosphere at home. There are also attempts to include children with special needs in regular schools. The inclusion project works towards improving the attitudes of parents and people involved with children requiring special education (UNESCO, 2006).

Documentation of early learning outcomes

Policy implementation in practice

Levels of policy implementation vary in the Balkans and in Turkey. In this section, we analyse how national early years policy applies to the curriculum, and draw the lines between evaluation frameworks and the professional training of early years professionals. Among these endeavours, monitoring is a continuous work in progress. In general, curriculum assessment and monitoring school readiness have barely emerged in the region. In Turkey, there is no nationwide system that would monitor children's school readiness or keep track of children's language development. The Turkish Communicative Development Inventory (TCDI) has been recently developed to assess language competence of Turkish-speaking children between the ages of eight months and 36 months (Acarlar et al., 2011). The programme is for children younger than three years of age, and can be utilized on a more regular basis to track slow language development in very young children (Aktürk, 2012). In Albania, the Ministry of Education has approved a set of standards for child development, yet the extent of its implementation and of monitoring is uncertain. In Macedonia, there is not a standard test to measure school readiness, but an assessment is practised at age six and seven, before primary school enrolment. In Romania, by the 2004/2005 school year, 86 per cent of children would have started school with a preschool experience. Recent policies have targeted children with a focus on the disadvantaged, such as the Roma minority and children with special educational needs. Children's development in Romania is monitored mostly for health. In 2005, a draft early education programme was adapted by the Ministry of Education (UNESCO, 2006). In Greece, the adoption of a new curriculum in 1999 and an emergent literacy approach in 2003 implemented standards where preschool and first grade teachers evaluated the status of their students using a set of assessment tools. Translation and standardization of the CAP (Concept about Print) observational task, which has also been translated into French, Hebrew, Danish and Slovak, has been found to be useful to understand children's knowledge of print. CAP evaluates four- to seven-year-olds' print knowledge via items such as line sequence, letter and word concepts as well as meaning of punctuation (Tafa, 2009).

In terms of policy implementation, a review of the outcomes for the Basic Education Project supported by the World Bank in Turkey reveals that theory surpasses practice. While enrolment rates to pre-primary and primary school have increased, and while teachers with higher education degrees have been hired, and student-centred educational approaches have been adopted, the issues connected to inclusion, equity and participation, as well as critical thinking in the classroom, remain unresolved (McClure, 2014). Similarly, while Educational Childhood Development (ECD) programmes such as 'parent training' offered by the Mother and Child Foundation (AÇEV) exist in Turkey, in practice the programme reaches only a limited number of families. In 2009, for instance, it reached only 3 per cent of birth to six-year-old children and their parents. In terms of ECD policies, related legal frameworks and the implementation of programmes, ECD information and a policy focus do exist. However, the coordination and financing of the programmes, and monitoring the quality of this type of intervention, are still work in progress. UNICEF has advised a widespread ECD strategy, setting standards that would be necessary for reaching all children. Such a strategy would need to include the participation of both the private sector and the NGOs (Vegas et al., 2010).

Principal methods and content areas of literacy instruction

Against the backdrop of major curriculum changes, we analyse key classroom methods for literacy instruction in Turkey in comparison with the Balkans in this section. Supported by the EU and UNESCO, preschools in Turkey apply emergent literacy support programmes for children from 36 to 66 months of age. The programmes do not teach letters or how to write them; rather, children are encouraged to sing songs, recite rhymes and riddles, play games (e.g. finger games) and read poetry. Teachers are encouraged to carry on discussions with children about picture books that they read together (MoNE, 2013). This approach is continued in the first grade with the Sound Based Sentence Method (SBSM), which was adapted in Turkey between 2004 and 2005 by eliminating the Whole Language Method (which has been used since 1981 and can be linked with Gestalt psychology and the focus on the sentence, followed by words and then the syllable). Since the adaptation was fast, and teachers' instructional materials did not have adequate examples for each letter of the alphabet, the SBSM method turned out to be challenging for some teachers (Kartal, 2011; Kutluca Canbulat, 2013). The writing curriculum starts with phonemes in the first grade with cursive handwriting, which can be an obstacle for those first graders who did not go through a preschool experience (Babayiğit and Konedralı, 2009) but effective for other students who were exposed to emergent writing (Akyol, 2013). Rather than being narrowly focused on just reading and writing, literacy instruction is now linked to listening comprehension and coherent discourse formation in speech, in line with constructivist approaches in learning adapted in 2004.

In Greece, the concept of whole-day kindergartens emerged in 1997–98.[3] In 1999, Greece adapted an emergent literacy perspective rather than reading-readiness in preschools under the National Kindergarten Curriculum in relation to the Language Programme. Literacy activities have been categorized into two areas: teacher-initiated activities and children's free-choice activities, both of which have been implemented across the whole curriculum. Teacher-initiated activities are information about print (e.g. letter concept, word concept, line sequence, punctuation), phonological awareness (e.g. sentence, word, syllable, phoneme awareness and rhyming), writing activities (e.g. writing names, stories, messages, journal writing) and storybook activities (e.g. reading stories and visiting libraries). Children's activities on the other hand include playing with letters on a magnetic board, pretend reading to other children and writing during different activities such as music and art (Tafa, 2004). In Macedonia, preschool programmes are flexible, with the non-formal approach supporting the development of the child more holistically (UNESCO, 2006).

Provision of early literacy for children with special educational needs

While the question of how to cater for children with special education needs has been debated in the entire Balkan region, each country does not define and treat special populations in the same way. In Turkey, for example, the Special Education Services Regulations of Turkey (SESRT) set the standards in education for children with special educational needs such as visual and hearing impairment, orthopaedic impairment, intellectual disability, autism, emotional and behavioural impairment, as well as gifted and talented children. Speech or language impairments are not listed as disabilities by SESRT. Education has been offered in 122 kindergartens within special education schools and 52 primary schools, where children with mild intellectual disabilities have been placed. Besides these efforts, 66,941 students have been enrolled in primary schools as part of inclusive education, encouraging them to be integral parts of society (Meral and Turnbull, 2014).

Variety of literacy resources

Literacy resources are of key importance for nurturing early reading and writing skills. A recent study carried out in Turkey indicated that literacy materials can compensate for limited language skills for children at risk of developing language difficulties (Baydar et al., 2014). Quality literacy materials are accessed by the privileged middle class and rich families in Turkey, but not others, leading to gaps between children from high and low social economic groups (Alonso, 2010). The social infrastructure that could support children from low social economic backgrounds with literacy materials, and which should include children's libraries and the children's section of public libraries, is not currently sufficient. The population of Turkey as of 2013 is estimated to be 76,667,864. In Turkey there is one national library, 1,118 public libraries (1,367 in 2004 – the number is thus declining) and 533 university libraries (there were 242 in 2004, thus a marked increase). The number of registered members to the libraries is 1,025,846; the number of registered children members to libraries is 479,207. Approximately, 243 publishers are interested in publishing children's books (TÜİK, 2013).

In Turkey, the MoNE (Ministry of National Education) offers a centralized system that decides about education as well as about textbooks, including their printing and distribution. Some other institutions such as UNICEF Turkey and AÇEV are key players in the development of early literacy in Turkey. With the preschool act, there is an increasing effort to make a variety of literacy materials available. One of these efforts has been *Cotton Candy*, a workbook that teaches children about basic shapes, numbers and colours.[4] While education focuses on the student and encourages active engagement with literacy materials, and should be supportive of teachers to utilize libraries, the presence of libraries, especially rich ones with picture books, is scarce (MoNE, 2009). The Z-libraries (enriched libraries) project, run by MoNE, reorganized approximately 400 libraries, reflecting on the need for engaging spaces and resources in schools, including preschools. Z-libraries may be able to gain further momentum with the hiring of active school librarians and developing book collections based on contemporary titles.

There have been some attempts to integrate information and communication technologies (ICT) into the primary school system through the Basic Education Project (BEP) and the FATİH Project. Much of these funds, however, were spent on the hardware rather than effective teaching software programmes. The effective use of tablets in education, which would require the development of compatible interactive curriculum, adequate in-service training and the monitoring of ICT integration, has not been sufficiently realized. Lack of internet access accompanied with restrictions implemented on tablets has reduced their initial capacity as a new mode of instruction (Akcaoglu et al., 2014).

Major challenges for current and future early literacy provision

The rapid change in policies at the beginning of the twenty-first century in early literacy education has not been sufficient in terms of reaching all children, parents and teachers. Implementations in the education system, bridging research and practice, establishing effective teacher-training programmes, creating diverse literacy materials and introducing student-centred educational models, as well as making good use of technological innovations, would benefit from further improvement. In the case of Turkey, lack of awareness on the part of most parents about early literacy in connection with a lack of a literacy environment at home and in the social environment of the child is a major obstacle. Current mandates such as cursive writing in the first grade is often challenging for the children, and has the unintended side effect of decreasing children's interest in literacy activities (Akman and Aşkın, 2012; Babayiğit, 2013). An important question is how to create a vision for literacy teaching with an interdisciplinary group of scholars and teachers who can closely work with the decision-makers. While MoNE plays a centralized role in Turkey, input by other stakeholders (NGOs, the private sector) could be beneficial in terms of jumpstarting literacy and encouraging children to recognize the joy of reading. Recent research indicates key challenges for Turkey: monitoring by ECE experts, the cost of new teachers and developing literacy materials for an expanding curriculum (Vegas et al., 2010). The alarming gap that needs to be covered in relation to literacy calls for a considerable effort.

The obstacles for current and future early literacy provision in Turkey and the Balkans are extensive. In general, a sustainable system that introduces policy-makers as well as families and teachers to current international research, including literacy research methodologies and new multimodal literacies such as information literacy and visual literacy, would contribute to effective literacy education in the countries discussed in this chapter. An emerging sense of children's school readiness accompanied with longitudinal tests should be expanded to evaluate the efficiency of existing programmes. Research in relation to language development and literacy ought to be tied more strongly to literacy education. Tools to develop country-specific tests, standards and literacy materials are necessary, since the structure of each language system is unique. Comparative data from recent research can bridge knowledge and expertise in language learning and early literacy. The benefit of taking into account those most in need, such as children who require special education as well as refugee children, should be better understood by policy-makers and those who implement government guidelines. Failing to do so exacerbates the problem of policies not being implemented in practice and of running programmes that do not reach a broad spectrum of children. Lastly, inclusive education and minority issues are major challenges that require attention.

Notes

1 RAN is naming familiar symbols such as pictures, letters and numbers and it is a significant indicator of reading development (De Jong 2011).
2 8130 books: 7507 Turkish, 481 English, 32 Arabic, 15 German and 95 other (TÜİK, 2013).
3 The number of kindergartens in Greece rose from 160 in 1997–1998 to 1323 in 2001–2002 supported by Greek Law 2525, which promotes preschool education geared towards children aged four to six (Tafa, 2004).
4 Supported by EU and UNICEF, 1,131,082 copies of the *Cotton Candy* workbook have been printed and distributed nationally by MoNE as an education material under the project Supporting Preschool Education, 2014.

References

Acarlar, F., Aksu-Koç, A., Aktürk, B., Ates, B., Küntay, A.C., Maviş, İ., Sofu, H., Topbaş, S. and Turan, F. (2011). Early lexical and morphological development assessed by using the Turkish Communicative Development Inventory: A large sample stud. Poster presented at the 12th Congress of the International Association for the Study of Child Language, Montreal, Canada.

Adams, D. (1987). *Essential Modern Greek Grammar*. New York: Dover Publications.

Aedo, C., Naqvi, N. H. and Cahu, P. (2013). *Promoting Excellence in Turkey's Schools*. Washington, DC: World Bank.

Agirdag, O., Yazici, Z. and Sierens, S. (2015). Trends in pre-school enrolment in Turkey: Unequal access and differential consequences. *Comparative Education, 51* (4), 537–554. doi:10.1080/03050068.2015.1081796.

Aidinis, A. and Nunes, T. (2001). The role of different levels of phonological awareness in the development of reading and spelling in Greek. *Reading and Writing, 14*, 145–177.

Akcaoglu, M., Gumus, S., Bellibas, M. S. and Boyer, D. M. (2014). Policy, practice, and reality: Exploring a nation-wide technology implementation in Turkish schools. *Technology, Pedagogy and Education*, 1–15. doi:10.1080/1475939X.2014.899264.

Akman, E. and Aşkın, İ. (2012). Ses temelli cümle yöntemine eleştirel bir bakış (A critical view of phoneme based sentence method). *Gazi University Journal of Gazi Educational Faculty (GEFAD/GUJGEF), 32*(1), 1–18.

Aktürk, B. (2012). Understanding the gestural, lexical and grammatical development of Turkish speaking infants and toddlers: Validity study of the Turkish communicative development inventory (TIGE). Thesis, İstanbul: Koç University. Retrieved from http://digitalcollections.library.ku.edu.tr/cdm/ref/collection/TEZ/id/20518.

Akyol, H. (2013) *Türkçe İlk Okuma Yazma Öğretimi (Primary Literacy Education in Turkish)* (13th edn) Ankara: Pegem Publications.

Alonso, J. D., McLaughlin, M. and Oral, I. (2010). *Improving the Quality and Equity of Basic Education in Turkey: Challenges and Options*. Washington, DC: World Bank.

Angelov, A. G. and Marshall, D. F. (2006). Introduction: Ethnolinguistic minority language policies in Bulgaria and their Balkan context. *International Journal of the Sociology of Language, 179*, 1–28. doi:10.1515/IJSL.2006.022.

Babayiğit, S. (2013). Türkçe'de İlkokuma-yazma öğretiminde kullanılan yöntem tartışmalarına global bir bakış (The discussions on the methods of early reading instruction in Turkish: A global perspective). Paper presented at the 6th Turkish International Education, 4–6 July, University of Niğde, Niğde, Turkey.

Babayiğit, S. and Konedralı, G. (2009). *KKTC'deki ilk okuma-yazma öğretimi ile ilgili uygulamalar ve bunlara ilişkin öğretmen görüş ve değerlendirmeleri (Teacher views and evaluations related to the elementary reading instruction practices in the Turkish Republic of Northern Cyprus*). [Project Report]. University of the West of England.

Babayiğit, S. and Stainthorp, R. (2007). Preliterate phonological awareness and early literacy skills in Turkish. *Journal of Research in Reading, 30*(4), 394–413. doi:10.1111/j.1467-9817.2007.00350.x.

Babayiğit, S. and Stainthorp, R. (2013). Correlates of early reading comprehension skills: A componential analysis. *Educational Psychology 34*(2), 185–207. doi:10.1080/01443410.2013.785045.

Baydar, N., Küntay, A. C., Yağmurlu, B., Aydemir, N., Çankaya, D., Gökşen, F. and Cemalcilar, Z. (2014). 'It takes a village' to support the vocabulary development of children with multiple risk factors. *Developmental Psychology, 50*(4), 1014–1025. doi:http://dx.doi.org/10.1037/a0034785.

Blanchy, N. K. and Şaşmaz, A. (2011). PISA 2009: Where does Turkey stand? *Turkish Policy Quarterly, 10*(2), 125–134.

Caravolas M., Lervåg, A., Defior, S., Málková, G. S. and Hulme, C. (2013). Different patterns, but equivalent predictors, of growth in reading in consistent and inconsistent orthographies. *Psychological Science, 24*(8), 1398–1407.

Cemalcilar, Z. and Gökşen, F. (2014). Inequality in social capital: Social capital, social risk and drop-out in the Turkish education system. *British Journal of Sociology of Education, 35*(1), 94–114. dci:10.1080/01425692.2012.740807.

Ceyhan, M. A. and Koçbaş, D. (2011). *Literacy Acquisition in Schools in the Context of Migration and Multilinguilism* [LAS Project Turkey Report]. İstanbul: İstanbul Bilgi University.

Council of Europe (2014). *European Charter for Regional and Minority Languages*. Retrieved from www.coe.int/t/dg4/education/minlang/Default_en.asp.

De Jong, P. F. (2011). What discrete and serial rapid automatized naming can reveal about reading. *Scientific Studies of Reading, 15*(4), 314–337. doi:10.1080/10888438.2010.485624.

Derince, M. Ş. (2012). *Mother-Tongue Based Multilingual and Multidialectal Dynamic Education: Models for the Schooling of Kurdish Students*. [Report prepared by Diyarbakır Institute for Political and Social Research]. Diyarbakır/İstanbul: Disa Publications.

Eurostat (2014). *Eurostat: The EU in the World 2014: A Statistical Portrait*. Luxembourg: Publications Office of the European Union.

Friedman, V. A. (2011). The Balkan languages and Balkan linguistics. *Annual Review of Anthropology, 40*, 275–291. doi:10.1146/annurev-anthro-081309-145932.

Göksel, A. and Kerslake, C. (2005). *Turkish: A Comprehensive Grammar*. New York: Routledge.

Greenberg, R. D. (2004). *Language and Identity in the Balkans: Serbo-Croatian and Its Disintegration*. Oxford: Oxford University Press.

Kartal, H. (2011). Ses Temelli Cümle Yönteminde Sesi Hissetme ve Tanımaya Yönelik Türkçe Dersi Öğretim Programı ve Kılavuzu'nda Yer Alan Uygulamaların Değerlendirilmesi. *Türkçe Eğitimi ve Öğretimi Araştırmaları Dergisi* (*Journal of Turkish Language Education and Teaching Researches*), *1*(2). Retrieved from www.ted.gazi.edu.tr/index.php/files/article/download/12/15.

Kutluca Canbulat, A. N. (2013). Ses temelli cümle yöntemi ile ilk okuma yazma öğretiminde anlamlı okumayı etkileyen unsurlar (The factors affecting meaningful reading through phonetic based method). *Mediterranean Journal of Humanities, 3*(2), 173–191. doi:10.13114/MJH/201322478.

Kyuchukov, H. (2006). Early home literacy of Roma children in Bulgaria. *Education et sociétés plurilingues, 20*, June, 51–62.

Macura-Milovanović, S. (2013). Pre-primary education of Roma children in Serbia: Barriers and possibilities. *CEPS Journal: Center for Educational Policy Studies Journal, 3* (2), 9–28.

McClure, K. R. (2014). Education for economic growth or human development? The capabilities approach and the World Bank's Basic Education Project in Turkey. *Compare: A Journal of Comparative and International Education, 44*(3), 472–492. doi:10.1080/03057925.2012.750498.

Meral, B. F. and Turnbull, H. R. (2014). Analysis of special education policy in Turkey and United States: Improving Turkey's policy for students with intellectual disability. *Journal of Policy and Practice in Intellectual Disabilities, 11*(3), 165–175. doi:10.1111/jppi.12083.

MoNE (Ministry of National Education) (2009). Talim ve Terbiye Kurulu Başkanlığı, İlköğretim Türkçe Dersi Öğretim Programı ve Kılavuzu, 1. ve 5. Ankara: Sınıflar.

MoNE (Ministry of National Education) (2013). Temel Eğitim Genel Müdürlüğü Okul Öncesi Eğitim Programı (Basic Education Coordination Preschool Programme). Ankara.

Nikolopoulos, D., Goulandris, N., Hulme, C. and Snowling, M. (2006). The cognitive bases of learning to read and spell in Greek: Evidence from a longitudinal study. *Journal of Experimental Child Psychology, 94*, 1–17. doi:10.1016/j.jecp.2005.11.006.

Organisation for Economic Co-operation and Development (OECD) (2013). *Education Policy Outlook: Turkey*. Retrieved from http://abdigm.meb.gov.tr/meb_iys_dosyalar/2013_11/15024437_educationpolicyoutlookturkey.pdf.

Öney, B. and Durgunoğlu, A. Y. (1997). Beginning to read in Turkish: A phonologically transparent orthography. *Applied Psycholinguistic, 18*, 1–15.

Oral, I., Yaşar, D. and Tüzün, I. (2016) *Her Çocuğa Eşit Fırsat: Türkiye'de Erken Çocukluk Eğitiminin Durumu ve Öneriler (An Equal Opportunity for Every Child: The Status of Early Childhood Education in Turkey and Propositions)*. Retrieved from http://erg.sabanciuniv.edu/tr/node/1585.

Sert, N. (2014). School entry age: 66 months of age for literacy skills. *Procedia-Social and Behavioural Sciences, 141*, 25–29. doi:10.1016/j.sbspro.2014.05.007.

Seymour, P. H. K., Aro, M. and Erskine, J. M. (2003). Foundation literacy acquisition in European orthographies. *British Journal of Psychology, 94*, 143–174.

Stellakis, N. (2012). Greek kindergarten teachers' beliefs and practices in early literacy. *Literacy, 46*(2), 67–72. doi:10.1111/j.1741-4369.2011.00573.x.

Tafa, E. (2004). Literacy activities in half- and whole-day Greek kindergarten classrooms. *Journal of Early Childhood Research, 2*(1), 85–102.

Tafa, E. (2008). Kindergarten reading and writing curricula in the European Union. *Literacy, 42*(3), 162–170.

Tafa, E. (2009). The standardization of the concepts about print into Greek. *Literacy Teaching and Learning, 13*(1 & 2.), 1–24.

TÜİK (Turkish Statistical Institute) (2013). Culture statistics. Retrieved from www.tuik .gov.tr/UstMenu.do?metod=temelist.

TÜİK (Turkish Statistical Institute) (2014). *Statistics on Child*. Ankara: Turkish Statistical Institute, Printing Division.

UNESCO (2006). *Global Education Monitoring Report*. Retrieved from www.unesco.org/new/en/education/themes/leading-the-international-agenda/efareport/reports/. Retrieved 10.April.2015.

UNICEF (2014). *The State of the World's Children 2014 in Numbers: Every Child Counts. Revealing Disparities, Advancing Children's Rights*. New York: United Nations Children's Fund.

Vegas, E., Aran, M. and Jelamschi, L. (2010). A policy framework for early childhood development and its applications to Turkey. *Conference on Early Childhood Development*. UNICEF.

13

AFRICAN COUNTRIES

Sylvia Chanda Kalindi and Bestern Kaani

Literacy is generally considered to be an inevitable aspect of social and economic development at both the individual and society levels. Recent advancements in technology demand that people are able to navigate the world around them independently by invoking their reading and writing skills. Perceptions of what constitute early childhood literacy and literacy practices vary significantly across both cultural and socioeconomical divides. The foci of teaching–learning goals and related objectives are usually defined by the available resources and future prospects. Some dominant Western societies are purely monolingual, implying that literacy practices espoused evolve around a single language used at home, school and play. Literacy practices in multilingual societies vary significantly from one-language societies. They may require more than one medium of transmission because students use more than two languages. The African continent has more than 2000 languages and dialects spoken by more than one billion inhabitants. Until very recently, African literacies were based predominantly on oral traditions passed on from generation to generation. However, the advent of colonialism in the early twentieth century brought about new literacy practices with foreign languages and instructional practices.

This chapter explores early childhood literacy practices that African countries use to transmit literacy skills in schools. Despite the multiplicity of languages within and across national boundaries, educational practices in Africa are in some ways comparable because of the homogeneous nature of socioeconomic challenges facing the continent. The chapter begins with a general overview of language policies particularly vis-à-vis the dichotomy between students' mother tongue and school language. Variations in orthography are also discussed to determine how they influence literacy policy and its implementation. To provide a clear picture of the early childhood literacy practices in Africa in general and sub-Saharan Africa in particular, Zambia has been used as an illustration because not only does it provide a good example of multilingualism, but multiple language policy shifts over the years are noteworthy and well documented (Matafwali, 2005; Tambulukani and Bus, 2011; Williams, 1998).

The question of school language and ethnicity in Africa

Africans, especially in countries south of the Sahara desert, are generally multilingual. Languages are also very closely defined by both ethnicity and tribal affiliation (Marten and

Kula, 2008). These ethnic groupings are differentiated mainly by subtle variations in the languages spoken. Languages spoken within close proximity are widely intelligible across tribes. However, the capacity to understand other tribes' languages fades as the geographical distances get wider between languages or dialects. This situation poses significant challenges for school instructions, especially regarding the choice of languages to adopt for literacy instruction. For instance, due to challenges involved in using all languages for literacy instructions, only seven languages of the 70 languages and dialects spoken across the Zambian landscape are used.

Language policies across the African continent

Most African educational systems are bilingual as learners are taught initial literacy skills in their first language along with a foreign *official* language. With the exception of Ghana and Nigeria where the English language is exclusively used, in the rest of the continent students are now taught in their mother tongue or predominant local language at the beginning of literacy instruction. Foreign languages are only used in higher-grade levels. Almost all African countries have adopted their colonizing power's language as de facto or official languages after attaining political independence (Plonski et al., 2013). Due to a wide linguistic diversity across the continent, first languages vary considerably both within and across national boundaries. The main languages used as official languages in sub-Saharan African countries are English and French, with Portuguese spoken in Angola, Mozambique and Equatorial Guinea. Tanzania, for reasons of political ideology and expediency, is the only sub-Saharan African country that never adopted a foreign language in the sub-Saharan region. Instead Kiswahili is the official language (McGregor, 1971). The strip of African countries bordering the Mediterranean Sea is entirely Arabic speaking.

There has also been a lot of debate regarding the merits and demerits of adopting foreign or second languages for school instruction. One school of thought argues that learning to read in a foreign language is detrimental to students' cognitive development (Serpell, 1978; Williams, 1998), while Senapati et al. (2012) counter-argue that teaching children – particularly in the English language – fosters their cognitive processing. Johnson (1970) stated that using foreign languages as a medium of school instruction, especially in developing countries, was problematic because it was 'educationally undesirable specifically in that it limited what content could be taught, the methods by which it could be taught and the whole nature of what might be experienced as part of the educational process' (p. 203). In relation to the Zambian situation, Chikalanga (1990), Serpell (1978) and Sharma (1973) have noted that the *straight-for-English* language policy, which the country adopted immediately after political independence, led to gross retardation in literacy development. This is mainly because, apart from students possessing limited second-language oral proficiency, teaching–learning materials used fail to account for students' everyday experiences (Mhaka-Mutepfa and Seabi, 2011). Moreover, learning one's own culture, indigenous knowledge systems and local technologies is, in the broader sense, what is considered as literacy.

On the other hand, Sa (2007) argues that for stakeholders such as politicians, educationists, economists and parents in the developing Anglophone countries,

> Competence in English can be regarded as a form of human capital useful to them in seeking employment, where the return on investment in English is a wage premium (or perhaps, access to higher-paying job categories that require knowledge of English).
>
> *(p. 10)*

For this school of thought, learning the English language is deliberately encouraged to take advantage of opportunities provided by the ability to read, write and communicate. Consequently, reading, writing and speaking in English is a means to an end, not an end in and of itself. Therefore, it does not matter how or how many students learn to read; what matters is that those who become proficient make the transition from poverty to a better life by accessing better paying job opportunities. Serpell (1989), cited in Williams (2014), noted that in some countries, being literate in English is equal to being educated. For instance, education stakeholders in Tanzania have been questioning the country's Kiswahili language policy because the majority of the high paying job opportunities requiring communication in a widely spoken language are being taken up by English-speaking professionals from neighbouring countries. Mazrui (1997) noted that many wealthier parents send their children to English-teaching private schools or government schools in neighbouring countries to make them more competitive on the job market.

However, due to persistent poor reading outcomes, low progression rates and high school drop-out rates in second language speaking education systems in Africa (Chikalanga, 1990; Nkamba and Kanyika, 1998; Sharma, 1973; Williams, 1998), most countries are re-introducing mother–tongue-based early literacy programmes. Many recent studies have shown strong support for the efficacy of familiar language instruction (Ouane and Glanz, 2010; Sampa, 2005; Tambulukani et al., 1999). Learning basic literacy in familiar languages facilitates smooth transition to unfamiliar language literacy (Durgunoğlu, 2000; Pillunat and Adone, 2009). Consequently, some countries have been prompt to adopt mother-tongue literacy in the early stages of instruction.

Fundamental principles of the orthographic and phonological representation of Zambian languages

The development of most African orthographies used in literacy instructions was informed by the official writing systems of the colonizing powers (Chimuka, 1977). All orthographies in sub-Saharan Africa are based on the alphabetic notation of the Latin writing system in which a graphemic symbol represents a single phonological segment (Kemp, 2006). However, unlike relatively opaque English writing systems, African orthographies exhibit highly transparent associations between phonology and orthography (Schroeder, 2010). Therefore, whereas readers of the orthographically opaque English language rely primarily on prior lexical knowledge to aid the decoding process, African orthographies are largely phonetically decoded.

With the exception of Ethiopian Amharic and Arabic orthographies, most African writing systems are based on the orthographic and phonological structure of the Latin alphabet. Consequently, the orthographic transcriptions of orthographies of most former English colonies are modelled on the English writing system. Zambian orthographies exhibit significant similarities (Chimuka, 1977; Kaani and Joshi, 2013). For instance, the five vowels (*a, e, i, o* and *u*) map directly on to English vowels as follows: /a/ as in *at*, /e/ as in *head*, /i/ in *hit*, /o/ in *hot* and /u/ in *book* in almost all Zambian languages. The same applies to consonants, although some vary depending on whether they are stressed or hit softly. In Chitonga, letters *b* and *k* and digraph *ch* are either stressed or hit softly. For example, the sound *k* can either be stressed using digraphs *kk* as in *kkala* (*sit*) or hit softly as in *kala* (*finger nail*). According to Schroeder (2010: 31), 'The double consonant in a word is used to indicate a single strong emphasis on the consonant'. In comparison to the English orthography, all seven school languages in Zambia exhibit very low phonetic density – 'the ratio between the number of vowels and consonants in a word' (Alcock, 2005: 416). African orthographies only have open syllables typically exhibiting CV, CVV (for long vowel sounds) or CCV (for digraphs) characteristics, with syllables *always* ending in vowels. The English orthography, on the other hand, has six different types of syllables (open, closed, r-controlled, the vowel pair, silent *e* and consonant −*le* syllables).

African orthographies are generally very transparent − the number of graphemes is almost always equal to the number of its phonemes and consistently pronounced. For instance, the Nyanja orthography has 29 phonemes, which map perfectly into the 29 graphemes (Kaani and Joshi, 2013). In addition to the traditional single letter graphemes, the Nyanja orthography also has the following common digraphs; *ts* as in *tsiku*, *dz* in *umodzi* and *ph* in *phiri*, which are written and pronounced consistently the same way. Therefore, the phonetic density ratio for Nyanja is a perfect one (29/29 = 1) compared to the English orthography with 44 phonemes written in more than 250 different ways (Joshi et al., 2008/9). This high consistency in grapheme–phoneme correspondences among African languages facilitates both reading and spelling because basic knowledge of letter-sound relationships enables novices to read any words (Aro and Wimmer, 2003; Landerl and Wimmer, 2008).

However, there are some noticeable variations in grapheme to phoneme correspondences in African orthographies. The major source of orthographic variations is lack of cross-language harmonization and coordination in the development process. This is mainly because initially the development of orthographies was exclusively done by missionaries, who restricted their exercise to specific dialects, ethnic communities and mission stations (Mwanakatwe, 1974; Snelson, 1974). As a result, their perspectives and scope did not extend beyond dialects or languages in the mission stations' immediate hinterland. The scopes of the orthographies developed were unique and in language-specific ways. Kashoki (1978) described the process of orthography development in Africa as being sporadic, haphazard, official, semi-official and non-official.

Failure to harmonize orthographies affects efficient cross-linguistic transfer of basic literacy skills between languages. For example, graphemes representing stressed and soft *b* phonemes in Nyanja and Tonga orthographies are different. In Nyanja, the softly hit *b* sound is denoted by *ŵ* as in *Malaŵi*, while the stressed *b* sound is a single *b* as in *bala*, whereas in Tonga stressed and soft *b* are depicted by single and double *b*'s digraphs respectively. The Bemba orthography does not have a hard /b/ sound, but soft /b/ is analogous to the Tonga single *b*. Logically, students initially taught literacy in Tonga and later transitioned to Nyanja will be confused by such inconsistences. This lack of orthographic equivalence has significant implications for literacy instruction across the continent, specifically because teacher education programmes are generally unresponsive to these linguistic variations. Additionally, teachers whose native language and educational background is in one orthography are often indiscriminately posted to teach in regions where there is a different school language.

Orthographic depth has a strong influence on early literacy development (Aro and Wimmer, 2003; Kaani and Joshi, 2013; Landerl and Wimmer, 2008; Seymour et al., 2003). Seymour and colleagues found that novice readers immersed in transparent Finnish and Spanish orthographies had an unassailable advantage over their counterparts taught in orthographically opaque languages such as English. It is, therefore, logical to argue that poor literacy proficiency demonstrated by Zambian students, when taught in English, may in part be explained by the idiosyncrasies of its orthography (Serpell, 1978; Williams, 1998). Williams compared literacy skills of Malawian and Zambian fourth graders and reported substantial variations in favour of the former, who are initially taught in their mother tongue Chewa. It appears Malawians benefited strongly from both orthographic transparency and language familiarity.

The definition of early literacy success according to Zambian literacy policy

The country's national education agenda is to produce 'full and well-rounded . . . pupils, so that each can develop into a complete person, for his or her own personal fulfilment and the good of society' (Ministry of Education, 1996: 29). Hence, in the early stages, literacy education is fundamentally aimed at enabling 'pupils to read and write clearly, correctly and confidently, in a Zambian language and in English, and to acquire basic numeracy and problem-solving skills' (p. 34), to enable them to participate in civil, social and economic programmes to foster development.

Following the persistent failures of the Straight-for-English language policy (Chikalanga, 1990; Sharma, 1973; Williams, 1998) and the subsequent introduction of the mother-tongue-based literacy policy (Sampa, 2005; Tambulukani and Bus, 2011; Tambulukani et al., 1999), the focus has also shifted from meaning-based (whole-word) to code-based approaches. Currently, Zambia's literacy programme was developed to take advantage of not only the orthographic transparency of the local language (Seymour et al., 2003), but also language familiarity (Tambulukani et al., 1999). The early literacy curriculum is mainly designed to foster the development and consolidation of reading and writing skills in Zambian languages before introducing English-based instructions (Ministry of Education, 2012). The Zambian literacy curriculum was developed based on prevailing best practices in reading research. Curriculum developers considered the importance of five building blocks – phonemic awareness, phonics, fluency, vocabulary and reading comprehension – essential to the reading process. They acknowledge that 'Effective reading instruction is based on both macro and micro approaches' (Ministry of Education, 2012: 5). Teachers are, therefore, expected to be explicit and systematic in teaching, as well as to provide opportunities for reading practice.

In preschool, literacy instructions revolve around oral language activities, with a focus predominantly on students' phonemic awareness development. Success is, therefore, defined by the ability to orally discriminate various sounds. Early instructional activities include reciting nursery rhymes, before introducing students to meaning-focused activities based on everyday play concrete objects. For instance, a teacher may present an apple, that is the actual fruit, with a view to introducing the initial short *a* sound in the word *apple* later. When students get to grade school, the focus of literacy activities shifts from phonemic awareness to phonics – letter–sound correspondences – whilst gradually introducing simple words. At this stage, the initial sound in the word *apple* is also presented in its written words. Due to the local language's orthographic transparency and students' good oral/listening comprehension, decoding abilities are relatively easy to develop through self-teaching mechanisms (Share, 2008).

Although many students transition from mother-tongue-based literacy to English with fairly well-developed phonemic awareness and phonics skills, teachers fail to take advantage of this basic knowledge. This is because teaching literacy in the opaque English orthography varies considerably from transparent local languages; knowing the alphabetic principle, although a necessary prerequisite, is not sufficient for mastery reading in English (Seymour et al., 2003; Ziegler and Goswami, 2005). Literacy teachers, unfortunately, tend to rely heavily on meaning-based whole-word approaches. Williams (1996) provided an example of a typical literacy lesson in English-speaking countries in southern African.

Teacher: We are going to read the story that is *Chuma and the Rhino*. That is paragraph three and four, which has been written on the board. Who can read the first sentence in paragraph three? Yes?

Pupil: Look at that hippo's mouth father.

Teacher:	Read aloud.
Pupil:	Look at that hippo's mouth father.
Teacher:	Once more.
Pupil:	Look at that hippo's mouth father.
Teacher:	Yes. The sentence is 'Look at that hippo's mouth father'.
Class:	Look at that hippo's mouth father.
Teacher:	Look at that hippo's mouth father.
Class:	Look at that hippo's mouth father.

(Williams, 1996: 199–200)

This example illustrates how teachers' instruction focuses on sentence-level meaning in English literacy lessons, with rote-repetition as the most prominent feature. The teacher fails to engage students at the micro level to emphasis phonological processing. Typically, these reading-like activities may only better qualify as literacy practice rather than literacy instruction or reading comprehension training.

At preschool and first-grade levels, students' literacy proficiency is typically measured using orally presented phonemic awareness assessments in addition to visual discrimination of alphabet letters and the alphabetical principle skills. By second grade, literacy assessments involve decoding by sounding out initial consonant sounds, word attack and related phonics knowledge. Higher-order skills such as locating and identifying syllables, proficiency in silent reading of short grade-appropriate passages and answering of comprehension questions are also evaluated at this level. Writing proficiency measures focus on copying and completion of sentences on work-cards (Ministry of Education, 2003). Sadly, the Zambian Basic Education Syllabus does not provide specific guidelines regarding how these skills can be assessed; nor does it offer alternative remedial strategies in case of failure to meet expected literacy goals.

How closely are the major foci of the national early years policy translated into curriculum models?

In Zambia, as noted earlier, the early literacy curriculum has solid research-based theoretical underpinnings (McCardle et al., 2008). There is, however, a considerable gap between curricular provisions and their implementation. Translating national early literacy policies into actionable objectives has been challenging for most African countries. Both national and international surveys monitoring literacy achievement across education systems show lower than expected literacy achievement in Africa (Chinapah, 2003). Zambia was among the lowest achieving countries on both the Monitoring Learning Achievement (MLA) and Southern and East Africa Consortium for Monitoring Educational Quality (SACMEQ) surveys (Chinapah, 2003; Nkamba and Kanyika, 1998; Spaull, 2011). Only a small number of students participating in these evaluation studies met expected levels of performance. The main conclusion from these research findings is that generally literacy levels are better in students' mother tongue than in the second language.

Factors influencing the variation in reading achievement

Several factors have been attributed to the existing gap between expected early literacy achievement and actual outcomes. Inadequate teacher preparation and poor literacy policy implementation are the main culprits (Kelly and Kanyika, 2000; Williams, 2014). Moats

(1994) found a strong correlation between teacher preparedness and student achievement. In addition, 'Poor instruction due to poor teacher knowledge due to poor teacher preparation has been suggested as one of the major causes of reading failure' (Cantrell et al., 2012: 528). The recent introduction of mother tongue literacy instruction was not accompanied by professional development efforts to improve skills of both pre- and in-service teachers. According to Cantrell et al. (2012), successful teachers have a good understanding of basic language constructs in reading. Therefore, teachers must receive appropriate training accompanied by constant professional development; otherwise, teachers 'cannot pass on understanding of the basic language constructs considered essential for early reading success when they do not possess that understanding' (Cantrell et al., 2012: 527).

Principal methods and content areas of literacy instruction: notable classroom methods of literacy instruction

As earlier indicated, early literacy instruction in most sub-Saharan countries are in the mother tongue or the familiar language in line with research indicating that literacy is learnt best when the language of instruction is familiar (Williams, 1998). For example, in Kenya, the language policy specifies the use of the mother tongue in the first three primary grades, while English becomes the language of instruction from the fourth grade (Commeyras and Inyega, 2007). Most countries in Southern Africa have adopted the South African Breakthrough-To-Literacy (BTL) programme aimed at teaching initial literacy in native languages. The Zambian version of the BTL, New Breakthrough to Literacy (NBTL), was translated into seven major local languages and officially launched nationwide in 2003 (Sampa, 2005). Students transition to English at second grade using the Step Into English (SITE) component, and between grades 3 and 7, the Read On course continues with dual language instruction in English and a native language (Ministry of Education, 1996). In addition to employing the language experience approach, the NBTL also incorporates approaches like Phonics, Look and Say and 'Real Books' (Ministry of Education, 2002). The New Breakthrough To Literacy (NBTL) course has three stages. The first stage involved introducing learners to the class routine, pre-reading activities and a set of core vocabulary items. In stage two, learners worked on sets of core vocabulary. After acquiring basic literacy, tasks on more challenging work was introduced. It is important to note here that, currently, Zambia is in the process of changing the literacy programme to extend the period of literacy instruction in the mother tongue to three years (Luffman, 2014).

The most common approach across sub-Saharan Africa in native language literacy instruction is the syllabic method – 'division of words into syllables'. In reading, 'words are broken down into syllables phonemically, according to their sound' (Thomas, 2003: 198) – thus, teachers create syllable charts based on vowels *a e i o u* to form syllables such as *sa se si so su, fa fe fi fo fu* using consonants. The syllable chart is mainly used for making up different words and also alerts learners to the different sound components in a word (Commeyras and Inyega, 2007; Tambulukani and Bus, 2011). In view of the orthographic transparency of Bantu languages in sub-Saharan Africa, the syllabic 'consonant–vowel' approach is suitable. It is, however, important to note here that the effectiveness of any literacy instruction method adopted depends, in part, on the teacher's content and pedagogical knowledge. In a study aimed at improving the teaching and learning of basic literacy in Africa, Akyeampong and colleagues (2013) observed that training in reading instruction is focused mostly on content rather than teaching methods. For instance, only one single semester or term is allocated to teaching methods in Ghana and Mali. In Senegal and

Tanzania, the study found that 'teaching reading does not even merit a topic on its own' (Akyeampong et al., 2013: 275).

Although there is very little information regarding how literacy instruction/related activities is generally done in preschools from the sub-Saharan region in Africa (as will be highlighted later in this chapter), Zimba's (2011) study highlighted some salient emergent literacy support practices in preschools. Working among various early learning centres in the North-Western province of Zambia, Zimba observed that reading was mainly done using charts or flashcards while reading from books was reserved for first graders. Furthermore it was rare in most schools to find children actively involved in shared book reading or to find students being supported to read, although teachers were seen reading to the children. According to Zimba, preschools in Zambia tend to have a more formal approach to learning as opposed to the play-oriented style of learning typical of early learning centres in developed countries (2011).

Provision of early literacy for special needs children

Several African countries have made positive strides towards meeting the second Millennium Development Goal (MDG) of achieving universal primary education. The introduction of free compulsory primary education has tremendously increased enrolment rates, including compulsory education for students with special education needs (SEN). For instance, Zambia has adopted a policy ensuring that children are assessed to determine their specific needs before school placement (Paananen et al., 2011). However, although access is almost guaranteed, the quality of education provided, especially among SEN pupils, has not improved. Most African countries lack qualified personnel to carry out the assessments. In Zambia, for example, there are very few psychologists and the available few are mainly found in the big cities. Inadequate funding to special needs centres and scarcity of spaces in local schools also make it difficult to adequately attend to the literacy needs of children with learning disabilities. Depending on the economic status of the area where a child is located, identification and placement of SEN may be made by the class teacher, parent or even a medical doctor. However, as Paananen, February, Kalima et al. (2011) noted, ideal assessment and intervention involving multidisciplinary teams, as is the case in countries like Finland, is still a pipe dream in many African countries.

Various non-governmental organizations have partnered with African governments to improve identification and remediation skills of primary sector educationists such as classroom teachers, special education teachers and psychologists. For example, the Niilo Maki Institute (MNI), a Finnish non-governmental organization, has had projects in Kenya, Namibia and Zambia for close to two decades (NMI, 2011). Although some countries like Kenya now have special education assessment centres in every district, for most other countries, these centres are only found in national capitals or major cities and have generally not trickled down to schools in the rural regions of the countries. Furthermore, the major problem in most African countries is that the means of diagnosing learning disabilities such as dyslexia is based on Western norms because there are no empirically established norms for locally available assessment tools.

Interventions for children lagging behind

Although most governments through policy documents and implemented literacy programmes do recognize the need for intervention or remedial work for pupils lagging behind in literacy tasks, the situation at the school level is not encouraging. For instance, in Namibia, although the law requires that students who lag behind receive additional learning support, its implementation is being hindered by insufficient human and material resources. According to Paananen, February, Hihambo et al. (2011), where additional remedial services are available, they may not always be monitored or adequately evaluated to determine their effectiveness.

Availability of literacy resources to foster reading and writing skills at various ability levels

Since the introduction of free education, most public schools in sub-Saharan Africa have had to cope with increasingly large class sizes. This has resulted in various difficulties such as having inadequate literacy resources to foster reading and writing skills. In countries like Zimbabwe where Early Childhood Development (ECD) programmes enrolment is mandatory, Moyo et al. (2012) observed that even at this very early stage, the teacher–pupil ratio is very high, typically above 20. In Zambia, ECD class sizes ranged from 45 to 80 young children (Iruka et al., 2012). The unprecedented high demand for education has negatively impacted the government's efforts to effectively source and disburse literacy resources to all schools. Lack of teaching resources including picture books or toys for the ECD programmes is more acute in rural than urban areas. In cases where the ECD is run by communities, peasant parents fail to financially sustain viable programmes. In an evaluation of early childhood education programmes in Zambia, Matafwali and Munsaka (2011) highlighted the fact that these programmes are still in their infancy. They found that in most centres, teaching and learning materials were not adequate, and in most cases no efforts were made by the teachers to employ locally available materials. Although in countries like Namibia and South Africa, governments are the most actively involved in providing and monitoring the ECD programmes, for most other countries it is the private sector that is more actively involved in early childhood education (Kalindi, 2015). The absence of government efforts in monitoring literacy education in early childhood centres frequently leads to adoption of poorly designed curricula unsuitable for the needs of early learners (for more details see Matafwali and Munsaka, 2011; Moyo et al., 2012). On a positive note, however, most governments are slowly incorporating early childhood education into the formal structures of their education systems. For example, in Zambia, a few identified pilot schools have now incorporated early childhood centres as well alongside conventional primary education. Similar ECD efforts in Zimbabwe and Mozambique are, however, compounded by financial constraints.

An Early Grade Reading and Mathematics Assessment in Zambia also indicated that the availability of resources for teachers and pupils in the early grades is low, with only 8 per cent of schools receiving the appropriate number of textbooks for the population of pupils at the beginning of the school year. This study further showed that on average 20 per cent of the pupils had a language textbook, while the majority of classrooms had textbooks for 10 per cent or fewer of their pupils (Collins et al., 2012). Although this scenario only highlights the Zambian situation, the situation is typical of most countries in sub-Saharan Africa; they are all faced with challenges of big class sizes and constrained funding. Spaull's (2011) review of school performance in Botswana, Namibia, Mozambique and South Africa pointed out that the problem of 'lack of textbook-access is now commonly accepted in the South African research' (p. 50). This review further found that sixth graders in Botswana and Mozambique had the highest proportion of pupils–textbook ratio. However, concerning a review of classroom based literature in southern Africa, the situation in countries like Namibia, Botswana and South Africa could be completely different.

Since early literacy instruction in most of sub-Saharan Africa now starts with the familiar native language, most of the recent published children's books are also beginning to reflect original African settings and are mostly based on typical African folklore – oral stories designed to express 'societal expectations, values and morals' (Peek and Yankah, 2004: 418) – depicting animal characters such as hares, lions, elephants, hyenas and other common fauna and flora. It is assumed that the familiarity of this literature would encourage students to read and get help from parents, most of whom are semi-literate, to assist in their children's education.

Three major concerns for current and future literacy provision in Africa

Despite concerted efforts to improve early literacy prospects of children, Africa is still facing and may continue to face three major challenges (Marope, 2005). The first concern relates to students' school readiness and responsiveness to early literacy acquisition. The majority of new entrants to either preschool or grade school come from poorly educated households lacking in basic understanding of the essence of ECDDE (Zuilkowski et al., 2012). Without an appropriate home background to necessitate the smooth acquisition of literacy skills, students are bound to fail. The second concern, in line with school readiness, is related to language policies adopted by sub-Saharan African countries. Due to linguistic variations across the continent, there are usually mismatches between students' mother tongue and the official school language, and new learners are not orally competent in school languages. Oral proficiency significantly affects literacy outcomes (Williams, 1998). More research to understand the interplay between languages of instruction and literacy is required as this area is significantly under-researched.

Thirdly, despite low literacy proficiency among novice learners in Africa, especially in the sub-Saharan region, there have been no deliberate efforts on the part of education authorities to ameliorate the problems through early identification, assessment and remediation programmes (Aro and Ahonen, 2013). There is a general lack of assessment, intervention and remediation programmes mainly due to lack of empirical evidence to guide policy development – the little available research on early literacy is based on instruments that are not culturally appropriate because no local interpretation norms are available. Extensive research on these three issues is required to strengthen early literacy programmes in Africa.

Conclusion

In this chapter, we explored early literacy practices across Africa, with particular emphasis on the sub-Saharan region, where literacy skills are acquired in a language other than the learners' mother tongue. Acquiring oral language competence in one's mother tongue before the school language raises pertinent issues. With the exception of Tanzania, all sub-Saharan countries have adopted a respective colonializing country's language as their official languages upon acquiring political independence as local languages were not transcribed into written forms at the time. Examples from countries like Zambia show that reading proficiency in especially English speaking was significantly poor and studies demonstrated that poor instructions – including under-qualified teachers and a dearth of teaching–learning material, in addition to the orthographic depth of the English language – were responsible for the status. Consequently, there is an emerging trend of adopting mother-tongue instruction before introducing foreign and more challenging orthographies in later grades, and using more effective phonics-based approaches in early literacy teaching in Africa. The good news is that reading outcomes are on the upward swing since the change in policy was implemented, but more research is needed to determine what works and what needs to be changed.

References

Akyeampong, K., Lussier, K., Pryor, J. and Westbrook, J. (2013). Improving teaching and learning of basic maths and reading in Africa: Does teacher preparation count? *International Journal of Educational Development*, *33*(3), 272–282.

Alcock, K. J. (2005). Literacy in Kiswahili. In R. M. Joshi and P. G. Aaron (eds), *Handbook of Orthography and Literacy*. Mahwah, NJ: Erlbaum.

Aro, M. and Wimmer, H. (2003). Learning to read: English in comparison to six more regular orthographies. *Applied Psycholinguistics*, *24*, 621–635.

Aro, T. and Ahonen, T. (2013). *Assessment of Learning Disabilities: Cooperation between Teachers, Psychologists and Parents: African Edition*. Jyvaskyla: NMI.

Cantrell, E., Washburn, E. K., Joshi, R. M. and Hougen, M. (2012). Peter effect in the preparation of reading teachers. *Scientific Studies of Reading*. Advance online publication. doi:10.1080/10888438.2011.601434.

Chikalanga, W. I. (1990). *Inferencing in the Reading Process*. Unpublished PhD thesis, University of Reading.

Chinapah, V. (2003). *Monitoring Learning Achievement (MLA) Project in Africa*. Paris: Association for the Development of Education in Africa (ADEA).

Chimuka, S. S. (1977). *Zambian Languages: Orthography Approved by the Ministry of Education*. Lusaka: NECZAM.

Collins, P., De Galbert, P., Hartwell, A., Kochetkova, E., Mulcahy-Dunn, A., Nimbalkar, A. and Ralaingita, W. (2012). Pupil performance, pedagogic practice, and school management: An SSME pilot in Zambia. EdData II Technical and Managerial Assistance, Task Number 7. Research Triangle Park, NC: Research Triangle Institute.

Commeyras, M. and Inyega, H. N. (2007). An integrative review of teaching reading in Kenyan primary schools. *Reading Research Quarterly*, *42*(2), 258–281.

Durgunoğlu, A. Y. (2000). Cross-linguistic transfer in literacy development and implications for language learners. *Annals of Dyslexia*, *52*, 189–204.

Iruka, I. U., Mount-Cors, M. F., Odom, S. L., Naoom, S. and Van Dyke, M. (2012). Development and sustainability of high-quality early childhood education programs in Zambia. In J. A. Sutterby (ed.), *Early Education in a Global Context: Advances in Early Education and Day Care* (pp. 127–158). Bingley: Emerald Group Publishing Limited.

Johnson, K. (1970). Problems resulting from the use of English as a second language medium of instruction. *Kivung*, *3*, 203–201.

Joshi, R. M., Treiman, R., Carreker, S. and Moats, L. C. (2008/9). How words cast their spell: Spelling instruction focused on language, not memory, improves reading and writing. *American Educator*, *32*(4), 6–43.

Kaani, B. and Joshi, R. M. (2013). Effects of orthographic opacity on spelling proficiency: A cross-linguistic comparison of Nyanja and English orthographies. *Insights on Learning Disabilities*, *10*, 45–66.

Kalindi, S. C. (2015). Education in sub-Saharan Africa. In D. James (ed.), *The International Encyclopaedia of Social and Behavioural Sciences*, vol. 7 (pp. 198–209). Oxford: Elsevier.

Kashoki, M. E. (1978). *Harmonization of African Languages: Standardization of Orthography in Zambia*. Experts' meeting on the 'The transcription and harmonization of African languages', Niamey, Niger.

Kelly. M. J. (1999). *The Origins and Development of Education in Zambia: From Pre-Colonial Times to 1996: A Book of Notes and Readings*. Lusaka: Image Publishers.

Kelly, M. J. and Kanyika, J. (2000). *Learning Achievement at the Middle Basic Level: Zambia's National Assessment Project*. Lusaka: Ministry of Education-Zambia.

Kemp, J. A. (2006). Phonetic transcription: History. In K. Brown (ed.), *Encyclopaedia of Language and Linguistics* (pp. 396–410). London: Elsevier.

Landerl, K. and Wimmer, H. (2008). Development of word reading fluency and spelling in a consistent orthography: An 8-year follow-up. *Journal of Educational Psychology, 100,* 150–161.

Luffman, L. (2014). Are African languages important for education? Retrieved on 29 June 2015 from www.soschildrensvillages.org.uk/news/blog.

Marope, M. T. (2005). *Namibia Human Capital and Knowledge Development for Economic Growth with Equity.* Washington, DC: Africa Region Human Development Working Paper Series – No. 84, The World Bank.

Marten, L. and Kula, N. (2008). Zambia: One Zambia, one nation, many languages. In A. Simpson (ed.), *Language and National Identity in Africa* (pp. 291–313). Oxford: Oxford University Press.

Matafwali, B. (2005). *Nature and Prevalence of Reading Difficulties in Grade Three: The Case of Lusaka Province.* Unpublished M. Ed. Dissertation. Lusaka: University of Zambia.

Matafwali, B. and Munsaka, E. (2011). An evaluation of community based early childhood education programmes in Zambia: A case of four selected districts. *Journal of Early Childhood Education, 5,* 109–140.

Mazrui, A. (1997). The World Bank, the language question and the future of African Education. *Race and Class, 38*(3), 35–48.

McCardle, P., Chhabra, V. and Kapinus, B. (eds) (2008). *Reading Research in Action.* Baltimore, MA: Paul H. Brookes Publishing Co.

McGregor, G. P. (1971). *English in Africa: A Guide to the Teaching of English as a Second Language with Particular Reference to the Post-Primary School Stages.* London: Heinemann Educational Books Ltd and UNESCO.

Mhaka-Mutepfa, M. and Seabi, J. M. (2011). Developmental assessment of African school children in Zimbabwe. In A. B. Nsamenang and T. M. S. Tshombe (eds), *Handbook of African Educational Theories and Practices: A Generative Teacher Education Curriculum.* Bamenda: Presses Universitaires d'Afrique.

Ministry of Education. (1996). *Educating Our Future: National Policy on Education.* Lusaka: Zambia Education Publishing House.

Ministry of Education. (2003). *Zambia Basic Education Syllabi: Grades 1–7.* Lusaka: Curriculum Development Centre.

Ministry of Education. (2012). *The Basic School Curriculum Framework.* Lusaka: Ministry of Education.

Moats, L. C. (1994). The missing foundation in teacher education: Knowledge of the structure of spoken and written language. *Annals of Dyslexia, 44,* 81–102.

Moyo, J., Wadesango, N. and Murebwa, M. (2012). Factors that affect the implementation of early childhood development programmes in Zimbabwe. *Stud Tribes Tribals, 10*(2), 141–149.

Mwanakatwe, J. (1974). *The Growth of Education in Zambia since Independence.* Nairobi: Oxford University Press.

Niilo Maki Institute (NMI) (2011). Evaluation report of education for children with learning disabilities: African–European Co-operation for Promoting Higher Education and Research Project – Kenya, Namibia Zambia and Finland. Jyvaskyla, NMI.

Nkamba, M. and Kanyika, J. (1998). The quality of education: Some policy suggestions based on a survey of schools. *SACMEQ Policy Research Report No. 5.* Paris: International Institute for Educational Planning.

Ouane, A. and Glanz, C. (2010). *Why and How Africa Should Invest in African Languages and Multilingual Education: An Evidence- and Practice-Based Policy Advocacy Brief.* Hamburg: ADEA/UNESCO.

Paananen, M., February, P., Hihambo, C., Hengari, J., Mowes, A., Muindi, D., Kwena, J. and Adhiambo-Oteino, C. (2011). Making conclusions and planning support. In T. Aro and T. Ahonen (eds), *Assessment of Learning Disabilities: Cooperation between Teachers, Psychologists and Parents.* African Edition. Jyvaskyla: NMI.

Paananen, M., February, P., Kalima, K., Mowes, A. and Kariuki, D. (2011). Learning disability assessment. In T. Aro and T. Ahonen (eds), *Assessment of Learning Disabilities: Cooperation between Teachers, Psychologists and Parents.* African Edition. Jyvaskyla: NMI.

Peek, P. K. and Yankah, K. (2004). *African Folklore: An Encyclopaedia.* New York: Routledge.

Pillunat, A. and Adone, D. (2009). Word recognition in German primary children with English as a second language: Evidence for positive transfer. Paper presented at the 33rd Boston University Conference on Language Development in Boston, MA.

Plonski, P., Teferra, A. and Brady, R. (2013). Why are more African countries adopting English as an official language? Presented at African Studies Association Annual Conference in Baltimore, MD.

Sa, E. (2007). Language policy for education and development in Tanzania. Retrieved from: www.swarthmore.edu/SocSci/Linguistics/Papers/2007/ sa_eleuthera.pdf on 14 December 2014.

Sampa, F. (2005). Country case study: Primary Reading Programme, improving access and quality education in basic schools. A paper commissioned by ADEA for its Biennial Meeting, December 2003.

Schroeder, L. (2010). *Bantu Orthography Manual* (rev. edn). SIL e-Books, 9. [Dallas]: SIL International. www.sil.org/silepubs/abstract.asp?id=52716.

Senapati, P., Patnaik, N. and Dash, M. (2012). Role of medium of instruction on the development of cognitive processes. *Journal of Education and Practice, 3*, 58–66.

Serpell, R. (1978). Some developments in Zambia since 1971. In S. I. Ohannessian and M .E. Kashoki (eds), *Language in Zambia* (pp. 424–447). London: International African Institute.

Seymour, P. H. K., Aro, M. and Erskine, J. M. (2003). Foundation literacy acquisition in European orthographies. *British Journal of Psychology, 94*, 143–174.

Share, D. L. (2008). On the Anglocentricities of current reading research and practice: The perils of overreliance on an 'outlier' orthography. *Psychological Bulletin, 134*(4), 584–615.

Sharma R. (1973). *The Reading Skills of Grade 3 Children* (mimeo). Psychological Service Report 2/1973, Ministry of Education and Culture, Lusaka.

Snelson, P. D. (1974). *Educational Development in Northern Rhodesia, 1883–1845*. Lusaka: National Educational Company of Zambia.

Spaull, N. (2011). SACMEQ working paper: Primary school performance in Botswana, Namibia, Mozambique and South Africa. South and Eastern Africa Consortium for Monitoring Educational Quality SACMEQ.

Tambulukani, G. and Bus, Y. G. (2011). Linguistic diversity: A contributory factor to reading problems in Zambian schools. *Applied Linguistics, 32*, 1–21.

Tambulukani, G., Sampa, F., Musuku, R. and Linehan, S. (1999). Reading in Zambia: A quiet revolution through the primary reading programme. In S. Manaka (ed.), *Proceedings of the 1st Pan-African Conference on Reading for All* (pp. 170–175). Pretoria: International Reading Association, READ & UNESCO/DANIDA.

Thomas, G. G. (2003). *Creating Literacy Instruction for All Children*. Boston, MA: Allyn & Bacon.

Williams, E. (1996) Reading in two languages at year five in African primary schools. *Applied Linguistics, 17*, 182–209.

Williams, E. (1998). Report on reading in English in primary schools in Zambia. *Education Research Report, Serial # 5*. London: Overseas Development Administration.

Williams, E. (2014). *Bridges and Barriers: Language in African Education and Development*. New York: Routledge.

Zambia Ministry of Education. (2002). *New Breakthrough to Literacy Grades 1: Teacher's Guide*. Lusaka: Longman, Zambia Limited.

Ziegler, J. C. and Goswami, U. (2005). Reading acquisition, developmental dyslexia, and skilled reading across languages: A psycholinguistic grain size theory. *Psychological Bulletin, 131*, 3–29.

Zimba, T. M. (2011). *Emergent Literacy Support in Early Childhood Education in Selected Preschools of Kasempa and Solwezi Districts of Zambia*. Unpublished M. Ed. Dissertation. Lusaka: University of Zambia.

Zuilkowski, S. S., Fink, G., Moucheraud, C. and Matafwali, B. (2012). Early childhood education, child development and school readiness: Evidence from Zambia. *South African Journal of Childhood Education, 2*(2), 117–136.

14

EARLY LITERACY POLICY AND PRACTICE IN ISRAEL

Dorit Aram and Aviva Sverdlov

In this chapter we review the early literacy policy and practice in Israeli preschool education. First, we describe the early education structure. Second, we refer to the major characteristics of Hebrew that affect early literacy development and its promotion (for elaboration on the Arabic language, see Saiegh-Haddad and Everatt's chapter in this book). Then, we overview the history of literacy promotion in Israel and focus on the New National Early Literacy Curriculum and its implementation. Finally, we discuss future challenges in the arena of early literacy.

The early education system

Israel's early education system reveals a cultural and social diversity. About 75 per cent of the students are Jewish and attend Hebrew-speaking educational institutions and 25 per cent are Arab, Druze and Bedouin, who attend Arabic-speaking institutions. All the state preschools[1] (Jewish and Arab) share the same curriculum, with adjustments to fit the different languages, cultures and religions. In this chapter we focus on Hebrew. In Israel, education is free and compulsory from age three. All the four- and five-year-olds and more than 90 per cent of three-year-olds study in pedagogically supervised educational settings and children go to first grade when they are six. Preschool classes contain up to 35 children (average 28). In each class the staff includes a certified early education teacher, usually holding a degree equivalent to a minimum bachelor's degree, and a paraprofessional assistant. The vast majority of the state preschools operate as autonomous administrative units in a one-floor building with an attached playground. The teachers in each class are the pedagogical and administrative directors of their classes. Preschools operate from 8.00–14.00, six days a week.

Hebrew language characteristics: effects on early literacy development and promotion

Letters and letter knowledge

Hebrew is an abjad writing system, written from right to left. The alphabet comprises 22 square letters that represent consonants. Four of the letters serve the dual function of representing consonants and vowels. Five of the letters have different forms when they appear at the end of a word. The letter names are acrophonic (e.g. letter SHIN begins with the phonemic sound that the letter represents – /sh/). Therefore, the letter names are powerful cues, highly effective in facilitating letter naming and spelling in preschools (Levin, 2007).

The unvowelled orthography is the default in Hebrew. The vowel indication can be added by means of diacritics and vowel letters. The diacritics provide a vowel for the preceding consonant and are marked mainly below the letter. The vowelled Hebrew (with the diacritics) has almost perfect grapheme-to-phoneme correspondence. Diacritics are used mainly in the Bible, poetry and children's books. Children in preschool are exposed to scripts with and without diacritics. They learn to read in first grade using diacritics but they stop using them by the beginning of third grade. Young Hebrew speaking children represent consonants significantly more than vowels in their early writing and reading (Levin et al., 2013).

Phonology

Hebrew syllables' structure is mainly CV and CVC. Hebrew does not include single phoneme words. This sound structure, along with the Hebrew orthography, explains children's difficulty in isolating phonemic sounds (Share and Blum, 2005). When asked to report the sounds of printed letters or instructed to provide a phoneme, they often respond with a CV sound (Levin et al., 2006).

Morphology

Hebrew is characterized by derivational morphology, based on the 'root-plus-pattern' system. Typically, the root consists of three consonants and represents the base morpheme that carries the semantic core meaning of words. Appending prefixes or suffixes to the 'root' forms typical patterns for grammatical inflections such as gender, person, number and tense. Moreover, many function words (*to*, *from*, *the*, etc.) and possessives (*my*, *his*) are frequently affixed to both nouns and pronouns (Ravid, 2011). As a result of the morphemic density, a single word in Hebrew may be the equivalent of a full sentence. For example: AHAVTIA – *I loved her*. Studies have reported the significant and unique contribution of morphological awareness in preschool to children's reading and spelling acquisition (Levin et al., 2001). Preschoolers are familiar with a large number of root-related word families, and make productive and mostly correct use of basic morphological forms.

The history of early literacy promotion in Israel

The early education system in Israel has always paid great attention to language but the content, extent and methods to promote language have been an ongoing debate. With the establishment of the State of Israel (1948), teaching Hebrew to young children was a part of the vision of reviving Hebrew as a 'shared language' that would unify Israel's population of immigrants from more than 80 different countries. At this stage, preschool teachers had a unique role of imparting Hebrew language to children and through the children to their families. Emphasis was placed on enriching children's oral language through conversations, songs, stories and rhymes in everyday activities.

In the late 1950s, Israel was a country of 650,000 citizens. Israel then absorbed nearly one million immigrants from Europe and Islamic countries (Central Bureau of Immigration to Israel 1948–1972, Jerusalem). Many of these immigrating children suffered from environmental deprivation. In this context, the education system highlighted the importance of early language development as the foundation for the conceptualization skills that are critical for school learning (Michalowitz, 1999). Consequently, the system switched from a naturalistic approach to the systematic fostering of oral language through structured, small group activities. Preschool teachers were required to systematically teach oral language skills such as receptive and expressive vocabulary, pronunciations, fluency, listening and conversation skills.

In the 1970s, aiming to close achievements gaps related to socioeconomic status (SES) and cultural differences, early education policy-makers debated intensely the pros and cons of teaching reading in preschool. Results of experimental programmes indicated that teaching reading in preschool contributed to children's reading in first grade. In spite of this, policy-makers decided not to implement this approach. They concluded that oral language is the most important literacy component and that teaching reading will put an unnecessary stress on preschoolers at the expense of other age-appropriate activities (e.g. free play, creativity) (Yanay, 1992).

In the 1990s, the Israeli education system adopted the 'whole-language' approach to early literacy and reading acquisition (Brosh-Vaitz, 2006). The claim that literacy is acquired 'naturally' shifted the focus from structured, language-promoting activities to creating a literacy-rich environment providing opportunities to practise interrelated language skills (speaking, comprehending, reading and writing) (Ministry of Education (MoE), 1995). Preschool teachers were instructed to avoid dealing intentionally with 'alphabetical skills' (e.g. letter knowledge, letter–sound correspondence) and to focus on providing children with opportunities to participate in authentic literacy activities.

At the beginning of the twenty-first century, the 'Reading Committee' released worrisome official data regarding the poor reading achievement in Israel (Shapira, 2001). This committee stressed that the early education system is responsible for initiating the process of literacy acquisition by intentionally promoting early literacy skills. Following these recommendations, the Ministry of Education (MoE) established a committee of experts whose aim was to offer practical ways to promote early literacy as a foundation for learning to read and write (Levin, 2001). The committee stated that nurturing early literacy has to become an essential component of the early education curriculum and determined the competencies that should be achieved prior to entering school. Based on these recommendations, the MoE established a curriculum committee which developed the current national early literacy curriculum for Hebrew speaking children (MoE, 2006) and Arabic speaking children (MoE, 2008). This curriculum defines the required goals, expected competencies and teaching methods. It refers in a balanced manner to five major early literacy domains: alphabetic skills, emergent writing and reading, oral language, communication skills and book immersion.

The publication of the curriculum raised a concern among some professionals, who argued that teaching alphabetic skills and early reading and writing in preschool is useless and 'robs children of their childhood'. Others thought that promoting letter knowledge in the early education system is developmentally too early and expressed their concern regarding the tendency to focus on measurable alphabetic skills at the expense of wider linguistic enrichment (e.g. Shimron, 2006).

Keeping in mind that for many years preschool teachers' perceptions were shaped by the prevailing approach that early literacy has to be acquired mainly through everyday activities, the curriculum requirements constituted a major change. To ensure proper implementation of the reform, the MoE invested significant resources in the training of professional staff (educational counsellors, pedagogical supervisors and teachers). Training programmes were developed and carried out in close collaboration with academic experts. In a study that took place in 2010–2011, nearly all of a quasi-random sample of preschool teachers (119 out of 120) reported that they had attended in-service training in literacy, with most of them (106 out of 120) reporting learning about the programme across more than 56 hours. Most of the teachers obtained ongoing professional guidance from counsellors who specialized in the field of early literacy (Sverdlov et al., 2014).

The National Literacy Curriculum: foundations for reading and writing

Goals

According to the curriculum, the main expected early literacy competencies for children prior to entering school are as follows:

1   *Alphabetic knowledge and early reading and writing* – familiarity with the alphabet, phono-logical awareness, understanding the alphabetic principle (letter–sound correspondence), understanding the functions of written texts, being motivated to engage in reading and writing activities;
2   *Linguistic efficiency* – possessing a rich vocabulary, using morphologically sophisticated and syntactically correct spoken language at an age-appropriate level, using efficient listening and oral skills to manage conversations;
3   *Book immersion* – being acquainted with literature and motivated to listen to books, familiarity with the books' vocabulary and expressions, and understanding of concepts of print.

Setting national goals was intended to develop indicators and to create a unified commitment to promote children's literacy upon their first steps into the early education system. Children's early entrance into the education system – and the systematic early literacy intervention accompanying the three years of preschool – helps to promote children from lower socioeconomic backgrounds and give all children a solid starting point in terms of literacy, prior to their initiation into grade school.

The expected competencies in each domain were broken down into three separate age groups – three to four years old; four to five years old; five to six years old – that would take into account developmental differences. The following are examples of the expected competencies for each age groups in three sub-domains:

Phonological awareness: three to four years old: identifies rhymes and enjoys rhyming, produces rhymes, identifies repetitive patterns in children's stories, recites short songs and rhymes; four to five years old: produces rhymes with meaningful words, breaks words into syllables, merges syllables into words, identifies, isolates and compare syllables; five to six years old: breaks words into sub-syllables units (CV) and phonemes, merges sub-syllables and syllables into words, compares sub-syllables and syllables.
Emergent writing: three to four years old: uses pseudo letters; four to five years old: uses random letters, writes his/her own name, integrates writing into play and everyday activities; five to six years old: includes some grapho-phonemic representations in writing.
Book immersion: three to four years old: shows an interest in books and a willingness to participate in shared reading, recognizes few books by name/cover, recognizes phrases from familiar books and recites them, chooses books based on his/her preferences; four to

five years old: recognizes a variety of books by name, initiates re-reading of books, relates to books by various criteria such as themes or genres; five to six years old: chooses books based on his/her preference of authors, specific subjects or genres, uses books as a source of information on a variety of issues.

Didactic guidelines

Alongside the detailed sub-goals in each domain, the curriculum provides teachers with didactic guidelines detailing how to integrate literacy in everyday activities while keeping the 'preschool spirit'. In addition to these general guidelines, the curriculum offers proposals for specific activities to promote each sub-goal by age-group. For example, in the early writing domain, for the three- to four-year-old children, the curriculum suggests writing the child's name on his/her art projects and talking about the characteristics of written language when sharing books with the children. For the four- to five-year-old children, teachers are guided to encourage children to use writing in their play and to write their names, support children's writing on the computer, initiate creative activities that include writing (e.g. spelling words using letters cut from newspapers) and initiate functional writing activities (e.g. birthday greetings, writing lists, recipes). When children are at their last year in the early education system (five to six years old) the curriculum guides the teacher to encourage children to write frequently and to support their understanding of letter–sound correspondences during writing.

Assessment

The curriculum emphasizes teachers' autonomy in selecting the instruction methods and the specific goals that they want to emphasize in their classes, based on ongoing assessment of children's needs. According to the Curriculum and the Preschool Education Practice Guidelines (2010) the assessment should be based on information gathered during routine preschool activities through observations. In their assessment of children's literacy, teachers have to refer to the expected competencies defined in the National Curriculum. For each competency according to the age group, the curriculum describes specific behaviours indicating that goals have been reached. For example, in the writing domain, when a three-year-old child points to a written text and asks 'What does this say', it is an indication that he/she achieved the age-appropriate expected competency. The curriculum also offers tools for ongoing documentation of children's performance.

The curriculum implementation: an assessment study

Sverdlov et al. (2014) studied the implementation of the early literacy curriculum six years after its introduction. Teachers (N = 120) responded to questionnaires and twelve teachers also participated in an interview. Teachers reported that they are intensively promoting all areas of literacy. The most frequently reported activity that takes place in preschools on a daily basis is 'reading books to children'. Teachers reported that following the new curriculum, there has been an increase in literacy activities across all the domains. The biggest change relates to activities relating to advancing children's alphabet skills. Interestingly, when asked about their preferences, teachers regard the advancement of oral language, communication skills and book immersion as more important than the advancement of alphabet skills and emergent writing and reading.

Current practices

Today, great attention is given to designing a literacy-rich environment that encourages literacy activities and facilitates independent learning. Preschools are filled with print, books, literacy games, letters and writing materials. This rich environment 'invites' children to engage in literacy activities, both individually and in groups, during most of the school day. Each preschool has a library containing books from various genres (usually more than 150 books). Further, the reading area in each preschool is equipped with furniture that allows children to read and to enjoy follow-up reading activities (e.g. retell or dramatize a story) comfortably.

Fostering literacy is integrated in everyday activities. Teachers relate to literacy in all the preschool's themes (e.g. holidays, seasons, weather) throughout the year, and through the research projects that they run. Additionally, they work daily with small groups (four to six children) in accordance with a defined plan based on teachers' assessments of children's differing needs (MoE, 2010). Some of these activities are aimed at directly promoting literacy skills, (e.g. telling a story while following pictures and writing it down), while others promote literacy indirectly, while addressing other issues, (e.g. telling and documenting the process of projects accomplished by children).

Children are encouraged to borrow books from the preschool library weekly to read at home. Technology and interactive media are integrated into most of the early education classrooms, with the degree of implementation depending upon the teacher's beliefs and technological skills. Typically, there is at least one computer and printer in a class. With the guidance of adults, children are encouraged to use office tools such as Paint, Word and PowerPoint. They are also engaged, either individually or with friends, with interactive computer games focusing on literacy and mathematics skills. In the last ten years, the use of the internet has become more common in the preschools, mainly for gathering information and for creating communication networks of the children and their families. The use of electronic books is rare in Israeli preschools, even though studies performed in Israel revealed that reading e-books to young children promotes their literacy development (Korat et al., 2014; Korat and Shamir, 2012).

Encouraging shared book-reading

Acknowledging the importance of shared book reading, the Ministry of Education (MoE) in collaboration with co-founding partners invested in programmes for encouraging reading. The main programme is the PJ Library, initiated by the Harold Grinspoon Foundation. Founded in 2009, the programme offers young children and their families an opportunity to create a tradition of reading stories together at home. The preschools receive one book monthly for each child and a copy for the class library. The teachers introduce the book, engaging children in fun and educational activities surrounding the books' stories. Then, children receive a copy for their home libraries. Books for the programme are selected by a pedagogical committee, with reference to the children's ages. In addition to their high literary quality, the books are chosen to invite discussion on universal values or ideas and their reflection in the Jewish heritage. Overall, during their three years in the early education system, children are given a gift of 24 books (eight books each school year). This programme benefits 96 per cent of the children in the public Hebrew-speaking preschools, including special education classes.

Matkabat al-Fanoos (Lantary Library) is the PJ Library's 'sister programme', operating in accordance with similar principles in Arabic-speaking preschools (supported also by the Price

Family Charitable Fund). The programme has been in place since 2014, and benefits nearly 100 per cent of children in public Arab preschools. In both programmes (PJ Library and Matkabat al-Fanoos), the last pages of each book include suggestions to parents for joint activities and discussions. Moreover, in the Arab families it encourages practice of Standard Arabic.

Over 900 (11 per cent) preschools in Israel take part in a 'Book Parade' programme initiated by the MoE to encourage shared book reading. Preschools that join the programme receive books for their library selected by a committee of professionals (15 books for five- to six-year-olds and ten books for four- to five-year-olds). The teachers are encouraged to integrate repeated reading of these books in their classes followed by related activities. At the end of the school year, children are invited to vote for their favourite book among the books being offered.

Early literacy responses to particular needs

Ultra-orthodox children

About 25 per cent of the Jewish children in Israel come from ultra-Orthodox families and attend independent educational institutions that are not fully committed to the state curriculum. The methods used in the ultra-Orthodox preschools for boys (girls do not study in these classes) differ from the centralized policy. In these preschools, emphasis is placed on religious study, with children as young as three years old learning to read using the traditional 'Cheder' code-based method. The method is based on rote learning of letters and their combination with diacritics (e.g. the letter BEIT /b/ in combination with the diacritic for /aa/ − /ba/, then in combination with the diacritic /ee/ − /be/, etc.) and then teaching the reading of words and sentences phonetically by repetition. The unique importance of early reading in the ultra-Orthodox community derives from the lengthy Jewish tradition according to which one learns to read in order to study the Old Testament from a very young age (Brosh-Vaitz, 2006). Girls study in separate preschools that generally follow the MoE curriculum.

Children with special needs

Special education programmes are provided for children with special needs from three years of age. The special education preschool teachers are committed to the general literacy curriculum, ensuring children's progress by providing specific support according to the children's needs. Teachers are obligated to assess children's general development. For this assessment they use a systematic observation tool called 'Mabatim', developed by the Department for Preschool Education in the Ministry of Education. Using this tool, teachers describe the children's functioning in all areas of development, including language and literacy. Based on teachers' assessments, children who experience difficulties are diagnosed by the school psychologist and, in coordination with parents, are presented to a local professional placement committee. The committee then decides upon the child's eligibility for special education services.

Most of the children in the early education system who have been assigned to special education services are integrated in preschools (full or part time) with appropriate assistance on the basis of need and availability (e.g. part-time special education personal preschool teachers, language clinicians). Additionally, there are special education preschools, where small groups of children who are lacking in language, communication or speech skills are taught by special education preschool teachers and get support from multi-professional staff, such as language clinicians, occupational therapists or physical therapists, according to their needs.

Children from multilingual families

Israel is a country with a population of about eight million. From 1948 until today, more than three million people have immigrated to Israel. As of 2015, approximately 10 per cent of Israeli children are from families who have immigrated to Israel in the last decade (mainly from the former Soviet Union countries, France and Ethiopia). To date, however, there have been no specific literacy curricula or guidelines for the early education system (unlike the primary schools) regarding the children for whom Hebrew is their second language.

From the establishment of Israel, immigrants were encouraged to speak only Hebrew with their children. Since the early 1990s, Israeli language policy has changed and immigrants are encouraged to maintain their original language and culture.

One of the high points of immigration to Israel was between 1990 and 2001 when about 1,000,000 immigrants arrived, most of them from the former Soviet Union. Many of them retain their language from the country of origin as the primary language at home and are interested in maintaining the heritage language in the generation born in Israel. In response to this need, an organization of Russian-speaking immigrant teachers and private entrepreneurs are offering programmes, such as bilingual preschools, outside the official state institutions.

Challenges to be addressed in the coming years

In this chapter we have discussed early literacy within the early education system in Israel, highlighting the features of the Hebrew language and the Israeli society. We have reviewed the changes that occurred in early literacy policy in Israel and focused on current practices. The first findings regarding the outcomes of the new curriculum are encouraging. Recently, the National Authority for Measurement and Evaluation in Education at the Ministry of Education (RAMA) assessed the alphabet and phonological skills of a representative sample of more than 500 children upon entering the first grade. The results showed that 80 per cent of the children correctly named 18–22 letters (out of 22), 96 per cent identified initial syllables and 91 per cent identified the initial phoneme.

Still, we see important challenges to be addressed in the coming years.

Promoting emergent writing

Studies have pointed to the benefit of writing activities on young children's literacy achievements in preschool and to children's reading achievements in first grade (Levin and Aram, 2013; Ouellette and Sénéchal, 2008). Research in Israel showed that parents' supporting early writing, communicating the steps in the word encoding process and encouraging their children to carry out these steps relates to children's early literacy (Aram and Levin, 2001, 2011) and predicts children's reading and writing achievements in second grade beyond the child's early literacy and the family's SES (Aram and Levin, 2004). However, research on preschool teachers' beliefs on the importance of literacy goals revealed that promoting emergent writing is perceived to be the least important literacy goal: less than promoting oral language, communication skills, book immersion or alphabetic skills. Further, the average frequency of activities promoting emergent writing-reading consistently appeared to be lowest (Sverdlov et al., 2014). Teachers and even their mentors and supervisors may not yet be sufficiently familiar with the evidence-based conclusions regarding the benefit of invented spelling activities on children's literacy achievements. A collaboration between researchers and early-education professionals is needed to raise the awareness of preschool teachers as to the importance of promoting emergent writing and developing methods to practise writing in preschools while keeping the 'preschool spirit'.

The use of digital, interactive media

There is a growing understanding that technology and interactive media are tools that can promote effective learning when they are used intentionally by early childhood educators. The use of digital media supports various learning goals, such as literacy goals, and at the same time helps to build digital literacy skills, such as using technology to access information, to communicate with others, for independent learning (NAEYC and the Fred Rogers Center, 2012)

In Israeli preschools, the use of digital media is very limited. For instance, reading books is reported as the most frequent activity in the preschool, but the use of electronic books (e-books) is rare. In light of research that indicates that children benefit from activities with e-books to the same extent that they benefit from reading printed books, it is important to raise teachers' awareness of their existence and help them learn how to select and use them (Korat et al., 2014; Korat and Shamir, 2012).

The integration of digital technologies can be expected to take time due to objective constraints including limited software, few high-quality, Hebrew e-books, high cost of digital devices and low level of teachers' digital literacy. Given the increasing reliance on technology and interactive media, however, it is important to find ways to incorporate them into early literacy instruction.

Coordinating expectations between parents and teachers

It is important to acknowledge the need for close relationships between parents and preschool teachers (Powell et al., 2012). Research has found incongruences between teachers' own beliefs and their perceptions of parents' beliefs regarding early literacy goals (Sverdlov et al., 2014). Teachers expressed the belief that oral language and communication skills are considerably more important than alphabetic skills or emergent writing–reading. At the same time, they think that parents consider the promotion of alphabetic skills and emergent writing–reading as the most important goals. According to teachers, parents are driven by the ambition to procure the best academic 'starting point' for their children as they enter school and they assume that knowing how to read upon entering first grade will guarantee their children's success. In contrast, preschool teachers think that communication and social skills are the key factors for later success. This perceived incongruence between teachers' beliefs and their perceptions about parents' beliefs has to be acknowledged and discussed. It is important to open a dialogue between teachers and parents regarding early literacy development and promotion in the preschool and at home.

In conclusion, the early literacy policy in Israel is based on major findings from international research and on local studies that focus on Hebrew characteristics and the specific ways to promote them. Beyond the language specifics, the early literacy policy and practices are influenced by the challenges of the political situation, the diverse population and the education system. Israeli researchers continue to work with their colleagues around the world hoping to contribute new knowledge to improve the future of early literacy education.

Note

1 Preschools in this chapter refer to educational institutes for children aged three to six.

References

Aram, D. and Levin, I. (2001). Mother–child joint writing in low SES: Socio-cultural factors, maternal mediation and emergent literacy. *Cognitive Development*, *16*(3), 831–852.

Aram, D. and Levin, I. (2004). The role of maternal mediation of writing to kindergartners in promoting literacy in school: A longitudinal perspective. *Reading and Writing: An Interdisciplinary Journal*, *17*(4), 387–409.

Aram, D. and Levin, I. (2011). Home support of children in the writing process: Contributions to early literacy. In S. Neuman and D. Dickinson (eds), *Handbook of Early Literacy* (Vol. 3) (pp. 189–199). New York: Guilford.

Brosh-Vaitz, S. (2006). On the state of literacy in Israel. *Education for All Global Monitoring Report*, UNESCO Online. Retrieved on 12 January 2015 from http://unesdoc.unesco.org/images/0014/001459/145954e.pdf.

Korat, O., Levin, I., Atishkin, S. and Turgeman, M. (2014) E-book as facilitator of vocabulary acquisition: Support of adults, dynamic dictionary and static dictionary. *Reading and Writing*, 27, 613–629.

Korat, O. and Shamir, A. (2012). Direct and indirect teaching: Using e-books for supporting vocabulary, word reading, and story comprehension for young children. *Journal of Educational Computing Research*, *46*(2), 135–152.

Levin, I. (2007). The role of Hebrew letter names in early literacy: The case of multi-phonemic acrophonic names. *Journal of Experimental Child Psychology*, *98*, 193–216.

Levin, I. (and committee) (2001). Promoting written and oral language in preschool: Towards emergent reading and writing. A report invited by the Israeli Ministry of Education. (Hebrew).

Levin, I. and Aram, D. (2012). Mother–child joint writing and storybook reading and their effects on kindergartners' literacy: An intervention study. *Reading and Writing: An Interdisciplinary Journal*, *25*(1), 217–249.

Levin, I. and Aram, D. (2013). Promoting early literacy via practicing invented spelling: A comparison of different mediation routines. *Reading Research Quarterly*, *48*(3), 1–16.

Levin, I., Aram, D., Tolchinsky, L. and McBride, C. (2013). Maternal mediation of writing and children's early spelling and reading: The Semitic abjad versus the European alphabet. *Writing Systems Research*, *2*, 134–155.

Levin, I., Ravid, D. and Rapaport, S. (2001). Morphology and spelling among Hebrew-speaking children: From preschool to first grade. *Journal of Child Language*, *28*(3), 741–772.

Levin, I., Shatil-Carmon, S. and Asif-Rave, O. (2006). Learning of letter names and sounds and contribution to word reading. *Journal of Experimental Child Psychology*, *93*(2), 139–165.

Michalowitz, R. (1999). Hinuch kdam yesidi be-Yiśra'el (Preschool education in Israel). In E. Peled (ed.), *Youvel le-maarechet ha-hinuch be-Yiśra'el* (pp. 859–879). Jerusalem: Misrad ha-hinuch. [Hebrew]

Ministry of Education. (2010). *Preschool Education Practice Guidelines*. Jerusalem: Ministry of Education.

Ministry of Education, Sport and Culture. (1995). *A Comprehensive for Curriculum in Israeli Preschools*. Jerusalem: Ministry of Education.

Ministry of Education, Sport and Culture. (2006). *Tochnit limudim 'Tashtih likrat kria ve-ktiva ba-gan'* (National Curriculum: A Foundation Towards Reading and Writing in the Kindergarten). Jerusalem: Ministry of Education, Sport and Culture. [Hebrew]

Ministry of Education, Sport and Culture. (2008). *Tochnit limudim 'Tashtih likrat kria ve-ktiva ba-gan k-sfat ha-em'* (National Curriculum: A Foundation Towards Reading and Writing for Native Arabic speakers in the Kindergarten). Jerusalem: Ministry of Education, Sport and Culture. [Arabic]

National Association for the Education of Young Children & the Fred Rogers Center for Early Learning and Children's Media at Saint Vincent College. (2012). *Technology and Interactive Media as Tools in Early Childhood Programs Serving Children from Birth through Age 8*. Joint position statement. Reston, VA.

Ouellette, G. and Sénéchal, M. (2008). Pathways to literacy: A study of invented spelling and its role in learning to read. *Child Development*, *79*, 899–913.

Powell, D. R., Son, S.-H., File, N. and Froiland, J. M. (2012). Changes in parent involvement across the transition from public school prekindergarten to first grade and children's academic outcomes. *The Elementary School Journal, 113*(2), 276–300. www.jstor.org/stable/10.1086/667726.

Ravid, D. (2003). A developmental perspective on root perception in Hebrew and Palestinian Arabic. In Y. Shimron (ed.), *Language Processing and Acquisition in Languages of Semitic, Root-Based Morphology* (pp. 293–319). Amsterdam: Benjamins.

Ravid, D. (2011). *Spelling Morphology: The Psycholinguistics of Hebrew Spelling* (Vol. 3). New York: Springer.

Shapira, A. (2001). *Reading Committee Report*. Submitted to the Israeli Ministry of Education. [Hebrew]

Share, D. L. and Blum, P. (2005). Hebrew speakers: Onsets and rimes or bodies and codas? *Journal of Experimental Child Psychology, 9*, 182–202.

Shimron, J. (2006). Ha-nezek ole al ha-toelet (The damage exceeds the benefit). *Hed ha- hinuch*, July–August, 28–33. [Hebrew]

Sverdlov, A., Aram, D. and Levin, I. (2014). Kindergarten teachers' literacy beliefs and self-reported practices: On the heels of a new national literacy curriculum. *Teaching and Teacher Education, 39*, 44–55.

Yanay, I. (1992). *Sidrat teuda ha-gil ha-rach*. (Preschool documentary series). Jerusalem: Misrad ha-hinuch. [Hebrew]

15

EARLY LITERACY EDUCATION IN ARABIC

Elinor Saiegh-Haddad and John Everatt

The chapter discusses early literacy education in Arabic for native Arabic-speaking children in four Arabic-speaking groups: the Palestinian Arab citizens in Israel, the Palestinians in the occupied Palestinian territories and native Arabic-speaking children in two Gulf countries: Kuwait and Saudi Arabia. The chapter aims to provide a representative portrayal of the theory and practice of early literacy education in these regions. It reveals potential shared conceptions regarding the basic components of early reading development, but also some different challenges. A main challenge that all groups face, however, is the translation of such concepts into teacher training and appropriate materials for the teaching of literacy in Standard Arabic, especially in the light of diglossia. The chapter opens with a brief overview of the structure of the Arabic phonology and orthography based on a comprehensive chapter authored by Saiegh-Haddad and Henkin-Roitfarb and published in the *Handbook of Arabic Literacy: Insights and Perspectives* (Saiegh-Haddad and Joshi, 2014). Then, issues in early Arabic literacy education in each of the country contexts are discussed. The chapter closes with a discussion of major challenges for current and future early literacy provision in Arabic.

The structure of Arabic phonology and orthography[1]

The most conspicuous feature of the Arabic language is diglossia (Ferguson, 1959; Maamouri, 1998; Saiegh-Haddad, 2012) which has a direct impact on language and literacy acquisition in Arabic (Khamis-Dakwar, 2012; Laks and Berman, 2014; Myhill, 2014; Saiegh-Haddad, 2003, 2004, 2005, 2007, 2012, in press; Saiegh-Haddad et al., 2011; Saiegh-Haddad and Spolsky, 2014). According to Ferguson, a diglossic context is characterized by a stable co-existence of two linguistically related language varieties: a *High*, primarily written, variety and a *Low* spoken variety. These are used for distinct sets of complementary functions and in different spheres of social interaction. The spoken variety, the naturally acquired mother tongue, is used in everyday interpersonal communication whereas the standard variety is acquired mainly formally and is the language of reading and writing. Modern Standard Arabic (MSA or Standard Arabic), a modern descendant of Classical Arabic and Literary Arabic, is to a high degree uniform across the Arabic-speaking world and is the only language variety that has a conventional written form. Therefore, Standard Arabic is the language in which the classically defined literacy functions are executed and it is the only variety through which reading and writing is taught at school. Hence, once children enter school, they are formally and extensively exposed to Modern Standard Arabic as the language of reading and writing. Spoken interactions, even inside the classroom, may be conducted in Spoken Arabic or in a semi-standard variety known as 'Educated Spoken Arabic' (Badawi, 1973), except probably during Arabic lessons, where Standard Arabic is more dominant, at least in aspiration (Amara, 1995).

Despite such deceivingly dichotomous context, and while Spoken Arabic is undoubtedly the primary spoken language, native speakers of Arabic, including young children, are actively and constantly engaged with Standard Arabic as well; they pray, do their homework and study for their exams in Standard Arabic, and they also watch many TV programmes and dubbed series in this variety. Thus, besides proficiency in using Spoken Arabic, linguistic proficiency in Arabic involves, from an early age, concurrent proficiency in Standard Arabic. It is noteworthy that modern functions of literacy, including electronic writing in the social media, such as Facebook and SMS, are often conducted in the local spoken dialects using either the Roman alphabet along with a few numerals representing some of the unique Arabic sounds, or a modified version of the Arabic alphabet. The use of this variety for reading and writing in the electronic media emerges naturally among users and no formal instruction in using it is provided.

The phonemic inventory of Standard Arabic comprises 28 consonantal phonemes and six vowel phonemes, and all syllables in Standard Arabic begin with a single consonant (C) serving as the syllable onset and necessarily followed by a vowel (V), as the syllable nucleus/peak. The syllabic structure of Arabic is relatively simple with CV and CVC types the most predominant. The phonological structure of Standard Arabic is usually at variance with that of Spoken Arabic, which typically comprises a smaller set of consonants and a larger number of vowels.

It is not possible to describe the phonological and orthographic structure of Arabic without a description of its morphology. This is because morphology is central to both the orthographic and the phonological structure of Arabic words. Arabic is a highly agglutinated language. A predominant inflectional system common to both nouns and verbs in Standard Arabic involves primarily stem-final vowels which denote the syntactic categories of case for nouns and adjectives and mood for verbs (Saiegh-Haddad and Henkin-Roitfarb, 2014). These inflectional categories have disappeared from all dialects of Spoken Arabic. Agglutination in Arabic extends to a set of clitics, including direct objects, possessives, prepositions and other grammatical markers that attach to the word as unstressed prefixes or suffixes resulting in one-word phrases and clauses.

Another compelling feature of the morphology of Semitic Arabic is its non-linear or non-concatenative structure (Larcher, 2006; McCarthy, 1981). Words in Arabic are minimally bi-morphemic comprising two independently unpronounceable bound morphemes: a root and a word-pattern. The tri-consonantal root (e.g. XBZ 'bake', DHN 'paint', ḤLQ 'shave' or 'have a hair-cut', ṬBB 'medicate') provides the core semantic meaning shared by all words within a root-related family of lexical items whereas the word-pattern (e.g. agentive CaCCa:C /xabba:z/ 'baker', /dahhan/ 'painter' /ħallaq/ 'barber' and CaCi:C /ṭabi:b/ 'doctor') links all word-pattern-related lexical items as having the same prosodic structure (e.g. stress, vowels) and a similar categorical meaning and part of speech.

Arabic is written from right to left in a cursive script, in which all but six letters, 'kicking letters', may ligate forward to a following letter. Arabic orthography is primarily a representation of Standard Arabic. It consists of 28 letters that represent the consonants of the language (three of them ا و ي act as *matres lectionis* 'mothers of reading' and are also used to represent the three Standard Arabic long vowels) and an optional system of diacritics that map mainly the phonemic short vowels and the morpho-syntactic stem-final endings. Diacritics are also used to represent other minor phonological features such as null vowellization and consonant doubling (for more, see Saiegh-Haddad and Henkin-Roitfarb, 2014). The fact that the Arabic orthography is corroborated by a system of diacritics results in two orthographies: a vowelled grapho-phonologically shallow orthography and an unvowelled grapho-phonologically deep yet morpho-orthographically transparent orthography. The bulk of Arabic texts are unvowelled while vowellization is commonly used in the teaching of reading, as well as in religious and literary texts and in children's literature.

Implications for literacy instruction in Arabic

A defining feature of diglossia is paired lexical items (Ferguson, 1959). Paired lexical items (or cognates) make about 40 per cent of the lexicon of young children (Saiegh-Haddad and Spolsky, 2014) – though the exact percentage might vary in different spoken Arabic dialects. Paired lexical items are a manifestation of the phonological distance between Standard and Spoken Arabic. In Arabic some phonemes are present only in the standard variety and may therefore not be familiar to children when they embark upon the acquisition of reading in the first grade. Research has shown that these phonemes are a particular stumbling block for children's acquisition of phonological awareness and word decoding in Arabic (Saiegh-Haddad, 2003, 2004, 2005, 2007; Saiegh-Haddad et al., 2011). In light of that, initial reading acquisition in Arabic requires both the acquisition of the phonological representation of the basic phonemic units as well as their orthographic representation. This task is compounded by the fact that some letters are used to represent the phonemes that are shared by Spoken and Standard Arabic and this might result in children confusing Standard phonemes with Spoken phonemes, and in difficulty linking the different phonemes with the specific letters that represent them in the Arabic orthography.

Given the phonological distance between Spoken and Standard Arabic, when a child is not familiar with a word, s/he might not be familiar with the concept of the word or with its phonological form, or with both phonological form and meaning (Saiegh-Haddad, 2004). This implies that even when the phonological form of the word is regularly represented, as in shallow vowelled Arabic, phonological recoding might not automatically lead to lexical access because the concept encoded has a different phonological representation in the lexicon of speakers. This has important implications for orthographic depth and reading development in Arabic (Saiegh-Haddad and Henkin-Roitfarb, 2014; Saiegh-Haddad and Schiff, 2016).

Leaving aside diglossia and the psycholinguistic reality of orthographic depth in Arabic, vowelled Arabic orthography maps Standard Arabic consonants and long vowels in a rather regular way. This implies that, in keeping with other shallow orthographies, word decoding in Arabic should be easy to master (Seymour et al., 2003). Yet, research has shown that this is not the case (Saiegh-Haddad, in press) and reasons proposed have included diglossia, use of diacritics, letter complexity and reading instructional methods (for more, see *Handbook of Arabic Literacy: Insights and Perspectives*, 2014). Unvowelled Arabic is grapho-phonologically deep due to the absence of the optional diacritics mapping the short vowels, rather than to equivocal graphemes as is the case in English. This orthography, though grapho-phonologically underspecified, is a fully specified and morpho-orthographically consistent *abjad* (Daniels, 1992) with a regular relationship between the consonantal material of words mapping its morphological structure (root consonants in particular) and their orthographic representation.

This, together with the centrality of morphology in the lexicon of Arabic native speakers, appears to enhance morphological processing in reading and spelling, even among very young learners (Abu-Rabia et al., 2003; Saiegh-Haddad, 2013; Taha and Saiegh-Haddad, 2016a, 2016b) and even in Arabic L2 (Farran et al., 2011; Saiegh-Haddad and Geva, 2008). This implies the importance of developing morphological awareness in Arabic as a way of leveraging morphological processing in reading and spelling (Saiegh-Haddad, in press).

Early literacy education in Arabic

In this section, we will discuss early literacy education in Arabic in four native Arabic-speaking groups: the Palestinian Arab citizens in Israel, the Palestinians in the occupied Palestinian territories and Arabic-speaking children in two Gulf countries: Kuwait and Saudi Arabia.

The case of Israel and the occupied Palestinian territories[2]

Arabic literacy policy and practice in Israel

Arabic is the mother tongue of approximately one and a half million Palestinian Arab citizens of Israel, native speakers of the Palestinian Arabic vernacular, all of whom acquire Arabic as L1. Moreover, the great majority attend Arabic-medium schools and study *all* school subjects in Arabic, with Hebrew introduced only in the third grade (age eight to nine years) and taught as a foreign language. English is introduced as a third written language in the fourth grade, a second foreign language after Hebrew and a fourth oral language after Spoken Arabic, Standard Arabic, Hebrew and English. Education in Israel is centralized. Therefore, one ministry and one pedagogical secretariat is in charge of education in all pre-college/university institutions, Jewish and Arab. However, under the auspices of the Ministry of Education, an Arabic language division is responsible for the specific curricula (content and method) followed in Arab schools. All of the Arab schools in Israel are non-boarding coeducational public schools. There are a few private Christian schools (serving 33,000 students) and they all comply generally with the regulations of the Ministry of Education and its nationally endorsed curriculum. All primary education in Israel is free from age three and compulsory from age five, one year before grade 1, through to ten. Grade retaking is not common. The general policy is for students failing nationally administered exams and/or in-school exams to be identified and given suitable intervention and support. Students with learning/reading disabilities are integrated within the regular classrooms but are drawn from their classrooms for intervention and extra help by special education teachers.

The concept of early literacy as adopted by the division of Arabic in the Israeli Ministry of Education has undergone a remarkable makeover in recent years and following the publication, in 2009, of the *Curriculum for Arabic Language Education: Language, Literature and Culture, for the elementary school: Grades: 1–6* (Ministry of Education, 2009). The New Curriculum conceives early literacy within the framework of current theories, underscoring the central role of word-level reading (Perfetti, 1985, 2007) and underlying metalinguistic insights, while accommodating the linguistic and orthographic characteristics of Arabic (Saiegh-Haddad and Henkin-Roitfarb, 2014). Three characteristics define the concept of early literacy as depicted by the New Curriculum. First, it focuses on the teaching of basic decoding skills in the early grades following a synthetic phonics approach. Second, given the shallow orthography of vowellized Arabic, it projects a fast, successful transition from basic decoding of words and simple sentences to reading simple texts; extended simple texts are used in the early grades to provide practice in decoding and in order to enhance the development of fluency and orthographic self-teaching (Share, 1995). Third, given the diglossic nature of Arabic, the new curriculum mandates capitalization on the spoken vernacular of the learners in leveraging literacy education in Standard Arabic. This latter feature is reflected in the following assumption:

> The child comes to school having developed a very rich and varied linguistic knowledge especially in Spoken Arabic, and to some extent also in Standard Arabic . . . The acquisition and the development of Spoken and Standard Arabic start in early childhood and continue throughout the elementary school grades.
>
> *(p. 12)*

The New Curriculum book devotes a special section (Chapter 3, p. 18) to a theoretical discussion of literacy acquisition in the first grade, as well as a discussion of the impact of diglossia (Saiegh-Haddad, 2003, 3004, 2005, 2007, 2012; Saiegh-Haddad et al., 2011) and concludes with the argument that proper, direct instruction and sufficient practice in word decoding should generate high levels of decoding accuracy by the end of the first grade. At the same time, it concedes that the linguistic distance between Standard Arabic and Spoken Arabic might make simple decoding more challenging, especially when letters encode phonemes absent from the spoken variety of children. These aspects of the linguistic distance between the two languages should be taken into account when teaching basic decoding skills, and in phonological awareness instruction in Arabic. The chapter reminds the reader of the importance of developing rapid and accurate decoding skills for decontextualized words, especially given old practices of training children to guess the meanings of words out of context as a literacy education goal. According to the New Curriculum, children are expected, by the end of the first grade, to have mastered all the letters of the Arabic alphabet in their different shapes, as well as all the diacritics denoting short vowels, consonant doubling and null vowellization. They are also expected to read simple texts accurately and to spell with accuracy orthographically shallow content words as well as opaque, yet high-frequency function words such as pronouns and prepositions.

The New Curriculum comprises a separate curriculum for literacy preparation in preschool (three- to five-year-olds) – *Foundation of Reading and Writing in Arabic as a Mother Tongue: A Preschool Curriculum* (Ministry of Education, 2008). The objective of this curriculum is

> to enhance the development of early literacy with special focus on the basic components that pave the way for reading and writing at school . . . The aim is not to teach children the decoding of words and texts or the writing of texts using conventional spelling.
>
> *(p. 10)*

Novel facets of the Arabic language and literacy curriculum for preschool in Arabic-speaking schools in Israel include acknowledging, for the first time, the importance of the spoken vernacular of children in leveraging literacy acquisition in Standard Arabic. This is reflected in the following assumption:

> The starting point in the development of basic literacy skills in Arabic is the spoken language, and this is for the following reasons: a) Standard Arabic and Spoken Arabic share many structural linguistic features; b) the linguistic knowledge and

representations that the child brings to the literacy learning task are almost wholly in Spoken Arabic; c) some aspects of the linguistic reservoir that the child has in Spoken Arabic can be used to leverage Standard Arabic literacy acquisition; and d) some basic literacy skills in Spoken Arabic may be conducive to the acquisition of literacy in Standard Arabic.

(p. 9)

Second, the new preschool curriculum acknowledges the intimate relationship between preschool language and literacy skills and literacy acquisition and academic achievement in higher grades. Third, it assumes that literacy acquisition is grafted on acquisition of a number of language and literacy components including phonological awareness, morphological awareness, letter knowledge, print concepts and lexical knowledge. Fourth, it stresses that oral language comprehension skills in Standard Arabic contribute to literacy acquisition in Standard Arabic. Fifth, it concedes that literacy does not develop spontaneously and it requires explicit mediation and instruction. (For more details, see Aram and Sverdlov, this volume.)

The conceptualization and benchmarks of early Arabic literacy success in Israel are reflected in the content of a regionally administered Arabic literacy diagnostic test administered in phases throughout the first grade. This is the فحص القراءة والكتابة للصف الاول 'Test of Reading and Writing in Arabic in the 1st Grade', an individually administered diagnostic assessment battery intended to identify children with reading delay and to specify the basic literacy components that they might have failed to develop so that suitable intervention may be designed. The battery includes the following sub-tests: letter knowledge (name and sound), phonological awareness, syllable decoding, word reading (familiar and unfamiliar), oral reading fluency (short-text reading), reading comprehension (sentence–picture matching, sentence completion and text comprehension), listening comprehension (sentence–picture matching) and word spelling. In addition to the sub-tests delineated above, care has been taken within each sub-test to address the characteristics of the Arabic language and orthography. In the letter–sound knowledge sub-test, the letters are broken down into categories according to the potential difficulties they may present, for example letters mapping diglossic phonemes absent from the spoken vernacular of the learner, such as the phonemes /θ/ and /ð/ (spelled ث and ذ, respectively), which are absent from most northern Palestinian dialects. (While the identity of the absent phonemes might vary from one learner to another, depending on their spoken vernacular backgrounds, the category of diglossic phonemes occurs in all dialects, restricted to a small subset of marked phonemes.) Another category consists of letters mapping velarized (or emphatic) phonemes, such as /ṣ/ or /ḍ/ (spelled ص and ض, respectively) which are difficult for children to discriminate from their non-velarized counterparts /s/ and /d/ (س and د, respectively). Another consideration is variations in letter shape (allography), hence the use of two letter–sound knowledge tasks, testing both the default shape of the letter and the various ligated shapes. Finally, as speed may be a more sensitive indicator of mastery than accuracy, especially in Arabic shallow orthography, some tasks (e.g. letter–sound knowledge and reading) measure speed in addition to accuracy. The diagnostic battery is administered in three phases and is distributed free to all teachers across the country together with a CD depicting a three-hour lecture presenting the theoretical framework for the test, as well as the structure, administration and scoring of the tests delivered by the coordinator of the committee and the head of the Arabic language division at the National Authority for Testing and Evaluation at the Ministry of Education. The lecture is delivered in Arabic and it may be accessed through the website of the Ministry of Education.

Another assessment tool is known as امتحان النجاعة والنماء للقراءة باللغة الام للصف الثاني or the *Mizav Test*, which is an achievement test administered at the end of the second grade. The content specifications for this test reflect the benchmarks of literacy education at the end of the second grade: (i) word decoding tested using word–picture matching tasks or sentence completion; (ii) reading comprehension tested at the sentence level, the paragraph level and at the text level; (iii) spelling; (iv) writing ability; and (v) familiarity with basic grammatical constructions of Arabic, such as subject–verb and noun–adjective agreement, using functional tasks that are authentic and communicative in nature.

The benchmarks of Arabic literacy education in Israel are also reflected in the content and format of a new series of reading primers (grades 1–6) entitled العربية لغتنا 'Arabic is our language'. This book series includes reading primers for the first to the sixth grade developed by the Centre of Educational Technology over the last six years or so, and immediately after the new curriculum appeared in 2009.

Arabic literacy policy and practice in the Palestinian territories

The 'Palestinian territories' include the West Bank (including East Jerusalem) and the Gaza Strip. The Palestinian Central Bureau of Statistics estimated that the Palestinian population of the West Bank and the Gaza Strip amounted to 3.94 million in 2009 and approximately 4.3 million in 2014. Education in the Palestinian territories is centralized in regard to its curriculum, textbooks, instructions and regulations, with the Ministry of Education and Higher Education responsible for the whole education sector from pre-primary to higher education and for recruiting and training teachers. In the Palestinian territories education system, compulsory basic education includes grades one to ten. Repetition of years does not occur in grades one to three; however, the ministry policy is for students in grades four to twelve to repeat a grade where they do not perform well.

Like in Israel, the objectives of the new curriculum in the Palestinian territories reflect the cultural, linguistic and national values of Palestinians and they include the general aim of fostering in young students (grades one to four) pride in their religion, language, Arabism and homeland (Country of Palestine, The Ministry of Education and Higher Education, Teacher's Guide 2010–2011). At a more linguistic level, the new curriculum states the following general objectives:

> Training in the listening skill and in listening comprehension, proper articulation of the sounds of letters, reading vowelized texts aloud accurately and with expression, reading written texts silently with proper speed, clear and errorless (hand) writing (meaning with no spelling mistakes), acquiring a large enough lexicon that would enable students to express themselves, acquiring the ability to express themselves using a simple yet correct form of Standard Arabic, learning by-heart verses from the Quran as well as from other religious and literary sources, imitating linguistic patterns presented to them.
>
> *(p. 3)*

With respect to basic literacy education, the objectives of Arabic language education also include the following: listening carefully to the teacher's oral reading, discriminating between the different forms of letters according to their position in the word, recognizing short and long vowels, as well as other diacritics, reading words and sentences accurately, understanding words and sentences, discriminating between the standard phonemes that are represented by some letters and their spoken equivalents, discriminating between letters whose phonemes are phonetically similar or those whose shapes are visually similar, and segmenting words into syllables and phonemes (p. 4).

In the Palestinian territories, the nationally used textbook لغتنا الجميلة 'Our Beautiful Language' (Muslim et al., 2012) developed by the Department of Curriculum Development of the Palestine Ministry of Education is, as stated by the authors, 'a translation of the general guidelines of the curriculum of the Arabic language and literature' (Preface). In this book, the authors argue that, in accordance with the research literature, they have followed a synthetic/analytic (phonetic) approach to the teaching of reading. They also claim that, in the presentation of the different letters, they have taken into consideration their phonetic and visual properties as well as their relative frequency in the language. Finally, it is stated that the book follows a systematic structure with each section starting with a speaking activity, followed by reading exercises, letter extraction and finally by a writing activity (not spelling).

The books that had been in use in schools in the Palestinian territories prior to the development of this new curriculum were mainly Jordanian and Egyptian, and were conceived by experts as not suitable either in form (orthographic representation) or in content for the Palestinian student. For instance, Barhuum (1997) argued that the Egyptian books created difficulties in word decoding for beginning readers because some of the orthographic conventions used were different from those followed in Palestine, such as the deletion of the dots from the letter ya? ي or the inconsistent use of short vowel diacritics. Additionally, Kurdi (1997) argued that the preponderance of old (literary and religious) over modern texts in these books was not conducive to enhancing literacy that would relate to the language use experienced by children in present day Palestine. In light of such criticism, the new book series developed by the Palestinian Ministry of Education (Muslim et al., 2012) aims 'for the content of the texts to be extracted from the local environment of the students and from what they hear and see, so that they do not feel linguistically alienated' (Preface).

Early literacy education in Arabic: the case of Gulf-Arabic countries

The Arabic-speaking countries in the Gulf region are a good contrast with Arabic-speaking populations in Israel and Palestine. Most of the societies within the Gulf region are based on strongly held traditions and tribal affiliations, as well as government structures based around deeply embedded monarchical and religious leadership/values. However, the oil-based wealth and the aim to modernize education has led to a conflict between the need for rapid change and a commitment to traditional values and concepts. For education, this can mean a struggle between learning traditional content stated explicitly by text or tutor, and hence acquired by rote and with deference to the teacher, versus developing creative and entrepreneurial citizens who can change with variations in circumstances, based on their own initiative. Although education systems vary across the region, the two examples in this subsection (Saudi Arabia and Kuwait) exemplify many of these features and should provide the reader with an overview of some of the educational issues that concern many.

Education systems and policies

The Kingdom of Saudi Arabia is the largest country within the Middle East area with a total population of nearly 30 million (Saudi Arabian Government Central Department of Statistics and Information www.cdsi.gov.sa/english/ based on 2010 census). Eight Arab countries border Saudi Arabia (Jordan, Iraq, Kuwait, Qatar, the United Arab Emirates, Oman, Yemen and Bahrain) and there are economic, cultural and educational links among all. Kuwait has about 1.5 million Kuwaiti citizens, but also a large number of itinerant workers, many from elsewhere in the Arab and Muslim world. Kuwait has many similarities to Saudi Arabia in education provisions. Most government schools in the region (and all government mainstream schools in Saudi Arabia and Kuwait) offer single-sex education. Many private schools, often developed to cater for the itinerant workforce, are also used by citizens. Both public and private schools are supervised by divisions of the Ministry of Education.

The organization of education is also similar. Children may attend kindergarten, which is normally not compulsory, for one or two years. Primary school lasts for about five to six years, and is followed by secondary/high school and then college/university. Primary school is compulsory and typically starts at age six (though the age ranges of children in classes suggests that this is not rigorously enforced). Many students complete high school, and there is a growing population of college/university students, with university entry typically dependent on level of attainment in high school examinations. (For further information on early education structures, see UNESCO International Bureau of Education, 2006, and UNESCO International Bureau of Education, 2011.)

Ministries of Education are primarily responsible for planning and strategic issues, as well as monitoring the development of policies. They set the curriculum to be taught in schools and the areas covered, which typically include the Holy Quran, the Arabic language, mathematics and science, arts and citizenship, and the English language: in Kuwait, English language and literacy lessons start in the initial years of schooling, but later in the primary years in other countries in the region. Committees appointed through a ministry write and revise the textbooks used to teach subjects around the country. Ministries also oversee assessments of student achievement that occur during and/or at the end of each education level. In many cases there are compulsory examinations leading to progression to the next level, particularly at the end of the primary school stage. Ministry administrators determine learning levels and progression criteria, which allow the child to be assessed against prescribed subject knowledge and skills. Consistent with ministry (and hence the teacher's) focus, examinations typically assess the student's mastery of the contents of ministry-produced textbooks.

The education system in Saudi Arabia has been a main target for national investment and development. For example, the Ministry of Education's ten-year plan from 2004 to 2014 (Ministry of Education General Directorate for Planning, 2005) for the development of education includes statements about the importance of an integrated and comprehensive education system as part of a long-term commitment to improvement (Ministry of Economy and Planning, 2010). (See discussions on the evidence of change in Alhamed et al., 2007, and Alsunbl et al., 2008.) In addition, the government-backed Tatweer (Development) project aims to take education into the modern era to cope with the global scientific and economic revolution (Ministry of Education, 2009; see also discussions in Al-Mikaimzi, 2008). It identified curriculum and learning materials, the learning environment, teacher training and professional development, and the promotion of extra-curricular activities, as areas in need of development and enhancement in Saudi Arabia.

Similar investment has been evident in Kuwait. Increases in compulsory education over the years have led the State of Kuwait General Secretary of the Supreme Council for Planning and Development (2010) to report that basic literacy grew to nearly 100 per cent of 15–25-year-olds in 2008. However, basic literacy here seems to refer to a relatively low level and there are still many children and adults with poor reading and writing skills: the 2011 Progress in International Reading and Literacy Study placed Kuwait near the bottom of countries assessed. Therefore, despite progress in participation, there are still discussions (both in the popular press and academic publications) about major limitations in the education system (see Ayoub, 2012; see also Almoosa et al., 2012; Burnery and Mohammed, 2002). Critiques target the highly theoretical nature of the curriculum, and its focus on memorization rather than under-standing, as well as concerns about teacher training standards. Often, teaching in primary schools is more about finishing the curriculum than delivering the lesson or involving students. Kuwaiti youth, particularly males, do not seem to value teaching as a profession: Kuwaitis make up only about 20–25 per cent of teachers in Kuwait (see discussions in Al-Sharaf, 2006, and Ayoub, 2012). This leads to a dependence on teachers from other countries, mostly from other Arabic-speaking countries (Egypt, Lebanon, Jordan, Syria). However, there is little evidence that these teachers are chosen carefully; and differences in background can lead to disruption problems in classrooms.

The ethos of teacher training courses is also transmitting information from tutor to student teacher, not the best way to develop or assess competencies in the student teachers. Most courses are theoretical in focus, with field-based training being a relatively minor part of preparation prior to taking charge of classrooms. As such, many teachers have little or no understanding of special needs, and little experience of varying teaching to accommodate different needs (although there are attempts to improve such teacher practical experience: see Al-Manabri et al., 2013). If learning difficulties are discussed in teacher-training courses, coverage is almost entirely theoretical in nature (Elbeheri and Everatt, 2011).

Kuwait and Saudi Arabia have both ratified the United Nations Convention on the Rights of Persons with Disabilities (www.un.org/disabilities/countries.asp?id=166). However, inclusion can be viewed as a major challenge for education systems (see discussions in Mitchell, 2010), and mainstream specialist support for students with special needs is sparse in the region (see also Almoosa et al., 2012). Although Saudi Arabia has been doing relatively well in terms of including children with disabilities (Al-Mousa, 2010), the numbers of children identified as experiencing special support (UNESCO International Bureau of Education, 2011) is lower than might be expected given the size of the population and may reflect an under-identification of children with special educational needs. There is still evidence of a shortage of appropriately trained professionals in the field of special education (Alquraini, 2011), a problem faced by many Arab world countries (e.g. Gaad, 2011).

Literacy teaching and learning

The teaching of reading and writing may also suffer from the emphasis on teaching a curriculum that is prevalent in many Gulf Arab countries. Often, teachers feel that they have to follow strictly the content of, and the sequence provided within, ministry-produced curriculum textbooks, the principal objectives being little more than to complete the content within the prescribed period and to prepare the students to pass examinations. As such, reading is seen as a product of classroom routine, involving little enjoyment and relentless practice. In many curricula early teaching of reading involves statements about rules or the use of word cards and similar materials, so the teacher's focus is on enhancing sight vocabulary. Whole-word and look-and-say-type teaching strategies are used to enable children to memorize the visual forms of words that are selected from vocabularies that a ministry would expect the child to acquire. Reading materials typically include pictures/drawings next to a word in order to teach children to link written words with their meaning. However, the pronun-ciations of sounds within words are considered in early teaching, and there seems to be a growing recognition of the importance of phonological processing skills in the region. Typically, in primary school, there is more of an emphasis on phonological features related to written words by the end of first grade and into following grades. Here letter–sound combinations may be presented with a whole word that contains the letter, and with a picture for context/meaning. The focus is to develop children's ability to identify letter sounds and letter names in context (i.e. in words and related to meaning). Although sounding-out strategies will be taught, with the aim to facilitate word decoding, many teachers focus on words and their meanings as much as sounds within words – potentially because the teachers themselves may not have a good grasp of phonics. Furthermore, the rote learning of links between sounds and written forms leads to teaching decoding as another set of materials to learn rather than providing strategies to support learning. In many curricular materials, letters are presented individually to the child as well as in words (letters change shape depending on their position within Arabic words), with children being taught to write letters with and without vowel diacritics.

By the end of grade three and into grade four, the emphasis is on reading comprehension skills and related grammatical knowledge, as formal school assessments become increasingly important so that teachers focus on test success. The curriculum progressions and assessment policies lead to teachers emphasizing the rules (typically grammatical) of the orthography and acquiring vocabulary, rather than linking written to spoken forms. Given the teacher's own experience of learning to read (which may explain their poor awareness of sounds within words), the traditional emphasis on morphological aspects of the language in teaching the orthography, and the use of non-vowellized text in materials read by adults (in addition to the language/orthography features described in the first part of this chapter, such as diglossia), it is hardly surprising that many children in the Gulf-Arab countries have difficulty with decoding and learning new written words. This is despite evidence that in Arabic, those with better phonological awareness and decoding skills are typically the better readers (Abu-Rabia et al., 2003; Al-Mannai and Everatt, 2005; Elbeheri and Everatt, 2007; Saiegh-Haddad, in press; Taibah and Haynes, 2011).

Major challenges for current and future early literacy provision in Arabic

Diglossia

Diglossia has been empirically shown to impact on literacy development in Arabic (e.g. Saiegh-Haddad, 2003, 2004, 2007; Saiegh-Haddad and Schiff, 2016). Therefore, it has to be incorporated into the teaching of Standard Arabic. As explicitly noted in the curriculum used in Israel (and to a somewhat lesser degree in the one used in the Palestinian territories, as well as in teaching materials in the Gulf countries), the phonological distance between Standard Arabic and the spoken vernacular used and naturally acquired by children can create problems for the application of a successful phonetic-based approach and should, therefore, be given sufficient attention and proper treatment. The impact of the phonological distance is not limited to some phonemes represented by a few of the Arabic letters, but extends to the phonological representations of words stored in the lexicon of children. The quality of these representations impacts on word-level reading and spelling development as well as reading comprehension (Saiegh-Haddad, in press; Saiegh-Haddad et al., 2011; Saiegh-Haddad and Haj, submitted; Saiegh-Haddad and Schiff, 2016).

The status of spoken Arabic

The new curriculum used in Israel clearly states that a starting point in the development of literacy in Standard Arabic is the language that the child brings to the literacy learning task, the spoken language. It also states that the spoken language can be capitalized upon in order to leverage Standard Arabic literacy acquisition. For instance, high phonemic awareness for spoken Arabic phonological forms is key to developing awareness of Standard phonological structures (Saiegh-Haddad, 2003). Similarly, a large lexicon in Spoken Arabic and good language comprehension and expression skills facilitate further vocabulary learning, comprehension and expression in Standard Arabic. In contrast with this positive and valuable attitude to the spoken language of children, according to the authors of the Arabic language primer لغتنا الجميلة 'Our Beautiful Language' used in Palestine, the goal of the book is 'to help students relinquish spoken Arabic forms and use Standard Arabic forms instead' (Muslim et al., 2012, Preface). Indeed, while some aspect of Spoken Arabic may interfere with performance in Standard Arabic and should be relinquished in favour of more standard forms, others should be capitalized upon to enhance language and literacy development in Standard Arabic. Moreover, even when some Spoken Arabic structures must be relinquished and inhibited, such inhibition, especially in the early grades, should be mediated and hence consciously executed. In other words, the potential interference from Spoken Arabic should be explicitly explained to children leading to proper management and control of language processing. This may be particularly challenging in some countries in the Arab world, for example Kuwait, where the majority of teachers grew up using a different form of spoken Arabic to that used by the Kuwaiti children in their classrooms, but explicit reference in course materials of such linguistic links may support teachers' understanding of the sound structures in Arabic, as well as promoting better learning in their students.

Knowledge versus skill

Language and literacy education has for over five decades now realized the importance of teaching communicative and functional language skill development, in contrast to a focus on knowledge about language. This perspective has to be more strongly stressed in the teaching of Standard Arabic language and literacy. It will certainly require the development of proper materials that are more functional and communicative in nature and that contribute to practice in fluency and skill building and teacher training in how to better implement such approaches (Saiegh-Haddad and Spolsky, 2014).

Teacher training

As mentioned above, there is a need to implement a system of learning and teaching across the education system that recognizes the key elements of language and literacy, and the primary aim (based on a clear educational philosophy) of developing skills. This needs to be started in student–teacher training colleges, and should include elements that consider the potential for diversity of learning, which will help inform a better understanding of learning and how to implement a curriculum for learning, as well as explaining links between language and literacy for better teacher competence in reading and writing tuition. Training within schools should also be emphasized, particularly in contexts where teaching is undergoing major change and development. This student–teacher training should be followed up with good supervision practices and continuing professional development practices.

Conclusion

In this chapter, we have attempted a portrayal of the philosophy and practice in early literacy education in four Arabic-speaking groups: the Palestinian Arab citizens in Israel and the

Palestinians in the occupied Palestinian territories (covered by the first author), as well as Arabic speaking in two Gulf countries: Kuwait and Saudi Arabia (covered by the second author). We have revealed some commonalities and differences in the concept of early literacy education in the different states and have pinpointed some of the challenges that these communities face. We found that, in general, early literacy education in Arabic is grounded in shared conceptions regarding the basic components of early reading development even if those conceptions are yet to be implemented fully in schools.

Acknowledgement

We would like to thank our colleagues, friends and students in the various Arabic-speaking countries for sharing curricula, book copies and other documents with us and for helping us make sense of literacy policy and practice in the various regions.

Notes

1 This section of the chapter is based on Saiegh-Haddad and Henkin-Roitfarb (2014). For a detailed discussion see this reference.
2 This section is based on our understanding of the educational theory and practice followed in occupied Palestine as represented in the materials that our Palestinian friends and colleagues have kindly shared with us.

References

Abu-Rabia, S., Share, D. and Mansour, M. S. (2003). Word recognition and basic cognitive processes among reading-disabled and normal readers in Arabic. *Reading and Writing: An Interdisciplinary Journal*, *16*(5), 423–442.

Alhamed, M., Zeyadah, M., Alotaibi, B. and Motawli, N. (2007). *Education in Saudi Arabia: Vision to Present and Predicting Future* (fourth edition). Ryiadh: Alrushd Library.

Al-Manabri, M., Al-Sharhan, A., Elbeheri, G., Jasem, I. M. and Everatt, J. (2013). Supporting teachers in inclusive practices: Collaboration between special and mainstream schools in Kuwait. *Preventing School Failure*, *57*(3), 130–134.

Al-Mannai, H. A. and Everatt, J. (2005). Phonological processing skills as predictors of literacy amongst Arabic speaking Bahraini school children. *Dyslexia*, *11*(4), 269–291.

Al-Mikaimzi, A. (2008). *Tatweer Project Set to Transform Education*. Retrieved from www.moe.gov.sa/openshare/englishcon/e27_10_2008_094255.html.

Almoosa, A. S., Storey, V. and Keller, C. (2012). Meeting the needs of all: Why schools in Kuwait are failing to meet their moral obligation and what can be learned from the U.S. education system. *Journal of Alternative Perspectives in the Social Sciences*, *3*(4), 997–1018.

Al-Mousa, N. A. (2010). *The Experience of the Kingdom of Saudi Arabia in Mainstreaming Students with Special Educational Needs in Public Schools (A Success Story)*. Riyadh: Arab Bureau of Education for the Gulf States.

Alquraini, T. (2011). Special education in Saudi Arabia: Challenges, perspectives, future possibilities. *International Journal of Special Education*, *26*(2), 149–159.

Al-Sharaf, A. (2006). New perspectives on teacher education in Kuwait. *Journal of Education for Teaching: International Research and Pedagogy*, *32*(1), 105–109.

Alsunbl, A., Alkhateb, M., Motoaly, M. and Abduljawad, N. (2008). *Education System in Saudi Arabia* (eighth edition). Riyadh: Alkhrije.

Amara, M. H. (1995). Arabic diglossia in the classroom: Assumptions and reality. In S. Izrae'el and R. Drory (eds), *Israel Oriental Studies*, vol. 15, *Language and Culture in the Near East* (pp. 131–142). Leiden: E.J. Brill.

Amara, M. H. (2007). Teaching Hebrew to Palestinian pupils in Israel. *Current Issues in Language Planning*, *8*, 243–257.

Ayoub, R. (2012). Educational crisis in Kuwait: Reasons & solution. *Alqabas Newspaper*, 31 March. Retrieved from www.alqabas.com.kw/.

Badawi, E. (1973). *Levels of Modern Arabic in Egypt.* Cairo: dar al-ma'arif. [In Arabic]

Barhuum, M. (1997). Evaluating the curriculum for teaching the Arabic Language in the six primary grades in the West Bank and the Gaza Strip. In Abu Laghad, I., Nakhli, H., Barakat, Y., Nashwas, Y., Kurdi, W., Gerbawi, A., Abu Daqa, S., Deeb, W. and Shaqlia, J. (eds), *The First Palestinian Curriculum of General Education: A Comprehensive Plan: Palestinian Curriculum Development Centre* (pp. 337–350). Alwan Press. Bet Hanina, Alquds. [In Arabic]

Burney, N. A. and Mohammed, O. E. (2002). The efficiency of the public education system in Kuwait. *The Social Science Journal*, *39*(2), 277–286.

Daniels, P. T. (1992). The syllabic origin of writing and the segmental origin of the alphabet. In P. Downing, S. D. Lima and M. Noonan (eds), *The Linguistics of Literacy* (pp. 83–110). Amsterdam: John Benjamins.

Elbeheri, G. and Everatt, J. (2007). Literacy ability and phonological processing skills amongst dyslexic and non-dyslexic speakers of Arabic. *Reading and Writing: An Interdisciplinary Journal, 20*(3), 273–294.

Elbeheri, E. and Everatt, J. (2011). Dyslexia support in higher education in the Arab world. *Journal of Inclusive Practice in Further and Higher Education, 3(1)*, 43–49.

Farran, L., Bingham, G. and Mathews, M. (2011). The relationship between language and reading in bilingual English–Arabic children. *Reading & Writing: An Interdisciplinary Journal, 25*, 2153–2181.

Ferguson, C. (1959). Diglossia. *Word*, 15, 325–340.

Gaad, E. (2011). *Inclusive Education in the Middle East.* New York: Routledge.

Khamis-Dakwar, R., Froud, K. and Gordon, P. (2012). Acquiring diglossia: Mutual influences of formal and colloquial Arabic on children's grammaticality judgments. *Journal of Child Language, 39*, 1–29.

Kurdi, W. (1997). A critique of the Arabic Language books from the seventh to the twelfth grades used in the West Bank and the Gaza Strip. In I. Abu Laghad, H. Nakhli, Y. Barakat, Y. Nashwas, W. Kurdi, A. Gerbawi, S. Abu Daqa, W. Deeb and J. Shaqlia (eds.), *The First Palestinian Curriculum of General Education: A Comprehensive Plan: Palestinian Curriculum Development Centre* (pp. 351–402). Alwan Press. Bet Hanina, Alquds.

Laks, L. and R. A. Berman. (2014). A new look at diglossia: Modality-driven distinctions between spoken and written narratives in Jordanian Arabic. In E. Saiegh-Haddad and M. Joshi (eds), *Handbook of Arabic Literacy* (pp. 241–254). Dordrecht: Springer.

Larcher, P. (2006). Derivation. In K. Versteegh (ed.), *The Encyclopedia of Arabic Language and Linguistics* (Vol. I, pp. 573–579). Leiden: E. J. Brill.

Maamouri, M. (1998). *Language Education and Human Development: Arabic Diglossia and Its Impact on the Quality of Education in the Arab Region.* World Bank, Mediterranean Development Forum.

McCarthy, J. (1981). A prosodic theory of non-concatenative morphology. *Linguistic Inquiry, 12*, 373–418.

Ministry of Economy and Planning (2010). *Kingdom of Saudi Arabia Millennium Development Goals Report 2010.* Riyadh: United Nations Development Programme.

Ministry of Education (2009). *Curriculum for Arabic Language Education: Language, Literature and Culture for the Elementary School (Grades: 1–6).* Centre for Curriculum Planning and Development. Ministry of Education, Israel. Secretariat of Pedagogy.

Ministry of Education (2008). *Foundation of Reading and Writing in Arabic as a Mother Tongue: A Preschool Curriculum.* Centre for Curriculum Planning and Development. Secretariat of Pedagogy. Ministry of Education. Israel.

Ministry of Education (2009). *Tatweer: A Confident Jump Towards Excellence.* Ryiadh: Ministry of Education.

Ministry of Education General Directorate for Planning (2005). *Executive Summary of the Ministry of Education Ten-Year Plan, 2004-2014.* Ryiadh: Ministry of Education. www.moe.gov.sa/.

Mitchell, D. (2010). *Education that Fits: Review of International Trends in the Education of Students with Special Educational Needs*: Final report. Christchurch: University of Canterbury.

Muslim, A., Ghawadri, F., Hasan, H. and Halas, M. (2012). *Our Beautiful Language.* Centre of Curriculum Development, Ministry of Education, Country of Palestine. www.shobiddak.com/grades/1.

Myhill, J. (2014). The effect of diglossia on literacy in Arabic and other languages. In E. Saiegh-Haddad and M. Joshi (eds), *Handbook of Arabic Literacy* (pp. 197–223). Dordrecht: Springer.

Perfetti, C. A. (1985). *Reading Ability*. New York: Oxford University Press.

Perfetti, C. (2007). Reading ability: Lexical quality to comprehension. *Scientific Studies of Reading, 11*, 1–27.

PIRLS (2011). *PIRLS 2011 International Results in Reading*. http://timssandpirls.bc.edu/pirls2011/international-results-pirls.html.

Saiegh-Haddad, E. (2003). Linguistic distance and initial reading acquisition: The case of Arabic diglossia. *Applied Psycholinguistics, 24*, 431–451.

Saiegh-Haddad, E. (2004). The impact of phonemic and lexical distance on the phonological analysis of words and pseudowords in a diglossic context. *Applied Psycholinguistics, 25*, 495–512.

Saiegh-Haddad, E. (2005). Correlates of reading fluency in Arabic: Diglossic and orthographic factors. *Reading and Writing: An Interdisciplinary Journal, 18*, 559–582.

Saiegh-Haddad, E. (2007). Linguistic constraints on children's ability to isolate phonemes in Arabic. *Applied Psycholinguistics, 28*, 605–625.

Saiegh-Haddad, E. (2012). Literacy reflexes of Arabic diglossia. In M. Leikin, M. Schwartz and Y. Tobin (eds), *Current Issues in Bilingualism: Cognitive and Sociolinguistic Perspectives* (pp. 43–55). Dordrecht: Springer.

Saiegh-Haddad, E. (2013). A tale of one letter: Morphological processing in early Arabic spelling. *Writing Systems Research*, 5, 169–188.

Saiegh-Haddad, E. (in press). Learning to read in Arabic. In L. Verhoeven, L. and C. A. Perfetti (eds), *Reading Acquisition Across Languages and Writing Systems: An International Handbook*. Cambridge: Cambridge University Press.

Saiegh-Haddad, E. and Geva, E. (2008). Morphological awareness, phonological awareness, and reading in English–Arabic bilingual children. *Reading and Writing: An Interdisciplinary Journal, 21*, 481–504.

Saiegh-Haddad, E. and Haj, L. *The Impact of Diglossia on Phonological Representation in the Arabic Mental Lexicon*. Manuscript submitted for publication.

Saiegh-Haddad, E. and Henkin-Roitfarb, R. (2014). The structure of Arabic language and orthography. In E. Saiegh-Haddad and M. Joshi (eds), *Handbook of Arabic Literacy: Insights and Perspectives* (pp. 3–28). Dordrecht: Springer.

Saiegh-Haddad, E. and Joshi, M. (eds) *Handbook of Arabic Literacy: Insights and Perspectives* (pp. 3–28). Dordrecht: Springer.

Saiegh-Haddad, E., Levin, I., Hende, N. and Ziv, M. (2011). The linguistic affiliation constraint and phoneme recognition in diglossic Arabic. *Journal of Child Language, 38*, 297–315.

Saiegh-Haddad, E. and Schiff, R. (2016). The impact of diglossia on voweled and unvoweled word reading in Arabic: A developmental study from childhood to adolescence. *Scientific Studies of Reading, 20*, 311–324.

Saiegh-Haddad, E. and Spolsky, B. (2014). Acquiring literacy in a diglossic context: Problems and prospects. In E. Saiegh-Haddad and M. Joshi (eds), *Handbook of Arabic Literacy: Insights and Perspectives* (pp. 225–240). Dordrecht: Springer.

Seymour, P. H. K., Aro, M. and Erskine, J. M. (2003). Foundation literacy skills in European orthographies. *British Journal of Psychology, 94*, 143–174.

Share, D. (1995). Phonological recoding and self-teaching: *Sine qua non* of reading acquisition. *Cognition, 55*, 151–218.

State of Kuwait General Secretary of the Supreme Council for Planning and Development (2010). *Kuwait Country Report on the Millennium Development Goals: Achievements and Challenges*. Kuwait: United Nations Development Programme.

Taha, H. and Saiegh-Haddad, E. (2016a). The role of phonological versus morphological skills in the development of Arabic spelling: An intervention study. *Journal of Psycholinguistic Research, 45*, 507–535.

Taha, H. and Saiegh-Haddad, E. (2016b). Morphology and spelling in Arabic: Development and interface. *Journal of Psycholinguistic Research*. Online copy available.

Taibah, N. and Haynes, C. (2011). Contributions of phonological processing skills to reading skills in Arabic speaking children. *Reading and Writing: An Interdisciplinary Journal, 24*(9), 1019–1042.

UNESCO International Bureau of Education (2006). *Kuwait: Early Childhood Care and Education (ECCE) Programmes*. www.ibe.unesco.org/.

UNESCO International Bureau of Education (2011). *World Data on Education: Saudi Arabia*. www.ibe.unesco.org/

16

EARLY LITERACY POLICY AND PRACTICE IN KOREA

Jeung-Ryeul Cho

Korean students rank top in the international comparisons of students' performance in reading, maths and science (PISA, 2012). In Korea, as in other Asian countries, this accomplishment might be related to early literacy education as well as parents' high expectations for their children's educational attainment from a young age (e.g. Lee et al., 2000). This chapter begins with a description of the key characteristics of the Korean language and writing, followed by a description of early literacy provision, policy and practice. Note that Korea is divided into two: South and North. Both Koreas use the same language and script 'Hangul' although their usage has been changed since they were separated after the Korean War (1950–1953). Only the literacy education and policy of South Korea is reviewed in this chapter.

Early literacy education system

Korea has two types of early education institutions: kindergarten and 'Children's House'. Kindergartens are under the supervision of the Ministry of Education whereas Children's House is a day-care centre under the supervision of the Ministry of Health and Welfare. Korean children start attending kindergarten between the ages of three to five. Kindergartens are independent of primary schools. In general, kindergartens are for children from middle-income families, whereas Children's House is for welfare and childcare facilities especially for working mothers and lower-income families. Children's House takes care of children from ages nought to five. Most kindergartens operate from 9 a.m. to 2 p.m. for five days a week, whereas Children's House is open from 8 a.m. to 7 p.m. for six days a week. About 47 per cent and 43 per cent of three- to five-year-old Korean children attend kindergarten and Children's House, respectively (Kim et al., 2014). The average student number in a preschool class is 30 or fewer. Children enter primary school at the age of six. Elementary school education is compulsory but preschool is not. The preschool education fee depends on parents' family income.

Preschool teachers

There are two groups of kindergartens: public kindergartens (53 per cent) and private kindergartens (47 per cent) (Kim et al., 2014). Kindergarten teachers should have a certificate after graduation of an early education major from a four-year university or a two-year college. Public kindergarten teachers should get a teacher's licence after passing a teacher's licence examination that is administered by the Ministry of Education. Teachers in Children's House should have a nursery school teaching certificate issued from the Ministry of Health and Welfare after taking classes and engaging in teaching practice for three or four semesters from an open university, a digital university, a life-long education centre, a two-year college or a four-year university.

Characteristics of Korean language and early literacy development

Korean alphabet and syllable blocks

A new phonetic script, Hangul, was invented in the fifteenth century to facilitate the literacy of the Korean people. Before the creation of Hangul, Chinese characters called Hanja had been used to write for more than ten centuries. Through an almost 500-year revision since its creation, contemporary Hangul has alphabetic letters of 21 vowels and 19 consonant letters. Each Hangul letter makes a sound, representing transparent letter–sound correspondences. Each Korean consonant has a name and represents one sound, but each vowel has the same name as the sound it represents. The names of Korean basic consonants consist of two syllables in a CV (consonant + vowel) VC (vowel + consonant) or CVC (consonant + vowel + consonant) form. In general, each consonant name starts with its own sound and ends with the sound value of the letter made at the syllable-final position. For instance, the letter 'ㄱ' has the name 기역 /gi. jəg/ and represents the sound /g/ or /k/.

Hangul letters are written in a square block, called Gulja, to depict each Korean syllable, which includes letters systematically from top to bottom and from left to right. The Korean Gulja structure is simple, having mostly CV (e.g. 나 /na/ 'I', 코 /ko/ 'nose'), CVC (e.g., 별 /bjəl/ 'star', 곰 /gom/ 'bear'), and CVCC (닭 /dak/ 'chicken') structures. Hangul Gulja shows a clear syllable boundary within a Korean Hangul word, which is similar to Chinese characters. Gulja is visually salient and it is considered to be the basic unit of Korean written word recognition (Simpson and Kang, 2004). For these reasons, Hangul is called an alphabetic syllabary. That is, Hangul is considered as an alphabet and/or a syllabary (Taylor and Taylor, 2014). Phonological alternations occur in reading multi-syllable words, although they are often predictable from sound context due to the phenomena of simple coda, resyllabification and consonant assimilation.

Morphology

The Korean language has a rich morphology that has the three major types of morphological structures of compounding, inflection and derivation. Korean has many compounds and homophones as in Chinese. More than half of Korean vocabulary words consist of Sino-Korean words that originated from the Chinese language and have been used in Korea from ancient times. Sino-Korean words can be written in both Hangul and Hanja (Chinese characters) such as 학교 and 學校 /hak.gjo/ 'school'. Multisyllable Sino-Korean words as well as many native Korean words are compounds. Homophones are prevalent in Korea as well. Korean Hangul also has a rich morphology of derivational complex word formation, just as in English. Most derivations are generated through affixation. Korean suffixation in verbs and adjectives is the most productive and complex formation of inflectional words.

Emergent literacy

Korean children learn to read with the CV Gulja in their names and high frequency words at the ages of four or so. Only later do children learn to divide these Gulja into component letters. Korean children learn CV Gulja earlier than alphabet letter names and sounds. For example, in one study, four- and five-year-old Korean children identified 78 per cent and 96 per cent of CV Gulja, respectively, 54 per cent and 76 per cent for consonant letter names; 29 per cent and 68 per cent of consonant sounds (J.-R. Cho, 2009). Later, Korean children learned to add a consonant letter at a coda position to CV Gulja to make CVC Gulja. In addition, CV Gulja reading at Time 1 contributed longitudinally to Time 2 Hangul word reading six months later even with Time 1 letter knowledge and reading were controlled (J.-R. Cho, 2009). When they enter a primary school, most children master reading regular and irregular words.

Interestingly, Korean people tend to divide syllables into CV body and coda rather than onset-rime phonological units (Yi, 1998; Yoon et al., 2002). Korean children develop coda awareness earlier than onset awareness (Cho and McBride-Chang, 2005). This coda sensitivity is facilitative of regular and irregular Hangul word recognition among kindergartners (Cho et al., 2008). On the other hand, letter name and sound knowledge have moderate relations with Hangul word reading, which may be related to the syllable block printing of Hangul and long names of Korean consonant letters (J.-R. Cho, 2009).

Traditional Hangul instruction

From the mid-fifteenth to the mid-twentieth century before the influence of Western methods, the CV Gulja chart had been used typically for teaching Hangul (Taylor and Taylor, 2014). A typical CV Gulja chart contains 14 basic consonant letters in rows and ten basic vowel letters in columns to form 140 CV Gulja. Children learn to read and memorize CV Gulja in order and later learn to add a coda to the CV Gulja. However, the use of this chart has been reduced since the 1980s partly because of the strong influence of foreign literacy instructional methods of whole word and phonics methods. Although a CV Gulja chart is not popularly used these days, it was favoured as an effective method for less educated people before the twentieth century. Using the CV chart, children are often taught to read all of the syllable blocks in the order of the vowels or consonants. CV Gulja are almost always regular in their pronunciation, following the grapheme-to-phoneme correspondence rules of the Korean language, whereas the reading of multi-syllable words is often subject to phonological changes due to the morphophonemic writing and assimilation phenomena of the Korean language.

Early literacy education policy and private education

Literacy policies and curriculums

The first kindergarten curriculum was started in 1969 in Korea and revised seven times between then and 2007. The first curriculum included listening and speaking as language skills, whereas reading and spelling was included from the third curriculum (Lee, 2004). In 2012, a new curriculum called Nuri (meaning 'the world' in Korean) was implemented to combine the curriculums of kindergarten and Children's House in order to attempt to realize childcare as welfare (Ministry of Education, Science, and Technology and Ministry of Health and Welfare, 2013). As in the previous kindergarten curricula, the Nuri curriculum focuses on language and communication skills and includes reading and writing, as well as listening and speaking. Nuri and the previous curricula emphasize the need for children to have an interest in reading and books. The teachers' manuals of the seventh and Nuri curricula explicitly specify that alphabet letters and decoding skills are not taught to children. Instead, it is suggested that kindergartens use whole-word methods and informal play-oriented methods to encourage children's motivation to read and write. The teachers' manual of the Nuri curriculum specifies not to teach children to read Gulja but to help them find familiar Gulja in daily lives. According to the manual, teachers are supposed to expose children to many reading materials to provide a readable environment for them, to encourage children to read and to read out picture books to children.

Specifically, the reading curriculum includes the educational purposes of 'having an interest in the contents of the text', 'identifying familiar Gulja around you', 'enjoying reading books and taking good care of books' and 'consulting books about what children are curious about'. As for popular activities, teachers help children to find familiar Gulja around them from cookie boxes, cartoon characters, lunch boxes, friends' names and magazines. Teachers encourage children to read friends' names from the day's menu, find important information from books, introduce their favourite books to friends, borrow books from the library and repair damaged books.

The writing curriculum aims to encourage children to 'understand that speech can be written', 'try to write their own name and familiar Gulja', 'try to write Gulja or similar forms to express their own feelings, thinking and experience' and 'have an interest to learn about writing tools'. As for writing activities, teachers are to encourage children to scribble, draw or write anything, teach them how to hold a pencil and write strokes, give ideas about relations of speech and print, make story books and book covers, write records after observation and learn to use writing utensils such as chalk, a marker pen and the computer.

A national survey showed that Korean teachers and parents strongly supported whole-language approaches in literacy education. Cho (2003) reported that 70 per cent of kindergarten teachers believed that children automatically learn reading and writing in daily lives; 27 per cent of teachers believed that children learn by themselves by playing with reading materials and texts. Similarly, 52 per cent of parents believed that automatic literacy learning takes place in daily lives and 20 per cent believed children learn on their own. However, only 2 per cent of teachers and 15 per cent of parents believed that children learn literacy via adults' supervision and intervention.

Private education

About 90 per cent of children attend kindergartens and Children's House (Kim et al., 2014). Meanwhile, about 85 per cent of children have had additional learning opportunities at home, such as studying commercially available workbooks as part of home education or through enrolment in private institutions (e.g. Korean Association of Child Studies and Hangul Education Research Center, 2002). Specifically, about 76 per cent and 85 per cent of children aged three to five received private education respectively in 2006 and 2009 for Hangul reading from commercial worksheets (S.-S. Cho, 2009; Lee, 2006). Therefore, 70 per cent of children master Hangul reading before entering elementary school although kindergartens do not teach decoding skills, and official literacy education is supposed to begin in primary school. The high rate of private education might be related to Korean parents' high expectations for children's educational attainment from a young age (e.g.

Lee et al., 2000). The high proportion of private education is considered as the highest in OECD countries and it costs more than 10 per cent of family income on average (Statistics Korea, 2015).

Since the start of the commercial worksheet business in 1976, its popularity has dramatically increased so that eight million Korean children and students were enrolled in commercial worksheet companies in 2008 (S.-S. Cho, 2009). In this worksheet business, teachers visit once a week each child's house for ten to fifteen minutes and check children's performance. The price is not very expensive compared with private tutors and private institutions. Children study 20 and 30 pages of worksheets that consist simply of drill and practice. Private education teachers employ a focused and directed teaching method rather than informal play-oriented methods (S.-S. Cho, 2009). The major purpose of Hangul worksheets is to help children to master Hangul decoding. The curriculum focuses on decoding and encoding skills including alphabet names and sounds, and letter–sound correspondences.

Private education teachers at commercial markets are hired from private education companies. A survey (S.-S. Cho, 2009) reported that 30 per cent of private education teachers graduated from two-year college; 70 per cent graduated from four-year universities or above. About 36 per cent of private education teachers had a kindergarten teachers' certificate or nursery school teaching certificate; 11 per cent had an elementary and secondary school teachers' certificate. About 78 per cent of them reported that they regularly attend workshops for children's reading and writing. On the other hand, 26 per cent of kindergarten teachers had training and workshops about literacy teaching methods (Cho, 2003). This difference shows that private education teachers are more trained and updated on children's literacy acquisition of Hangul.

Current practices

Hangul literacy instructions

Different institutions use different instructional methods for early Hangul acquisition. Korean kindergartens employ a whole-word method, based on the Korean governmental kindergarten curriculum, whereas a phonics method is used by most private learning places and private tutors who visit homes with commercial worksheets (e.g. Lee and Lee, 2007; Lee et al., 2000). The whole-word method emphasizes having an interest in books and reading books rather than decoding skills. In contrast, the phonics method emphasizes learning of letter names and sound–letter correspondences. Both methods of whole word and phonics were first introduced from Western countries after the Independence of Korea from Japan in 1945 and have been implemented for early literacy education since then.

Practices of Hangul education

A survey (Cho, 2003) investigated Hangul teaching methods with which kindergarten teachers taught children to read. The result showed that 70 per cent of teachers taught children with familiar words; 19 per cent taught words in sentences and context; 8 per cent taught alphabet letters and combination of letters; 3 per cent taught the basic CV Gulja chart. In a recent survey (J.-R. Cho, 2009) of kindergarten teachers, 100 per cent of the teachers presented their children with stories to read, 81 per cent taught the children to read and spell words, 48 per cent taught reading and spelling of Gulja, 44 per cent taught alphabet letters and 31 per cent used the CV Gulja chart.

Effective Hangul literacy instructions from Korean mothers

Cho et al. (forthcoming) examined literate mediation strategies that Korean mothers use when individually coaching their four- and five-year-old children about writing Hangul words, and they investigated effective maternal strategies that facilitate children's Hangul reading. The whole episode of mother–child joint writing was videotaped, and eight strategies of maternal literate mediation were identified. These eight strategies focused on Gulja matching, meaning, visual strokes, holistic visualization, Gulja structure, alphabet letters, CV Gulja and coda. Among the strategies, there were developmental differences in the use of the coda strategy, which was mentioned more often by the mothers of five-year-old children. The maternal CV and coda strategies in particular were highly associated with CV Gulja reading and word reading in children, respectively. However, other strategies were not associated with Hangul reading. This study further demonstrated the unique contribution of the maternal CV strategy to children's independent CV Gulja reading and the unique contribution of the maternal coda strategy to children's word reading after controlling for children's writing skill, vocabulary and demographics such as children's age and mother's education.

Home literacy environment

A Korean study (Lee, 2006) analysed parental questionnaires reporting on 152 children aged four and five from middle socioeconomic status (SES) regarding home literacy environment. The survey reported that 13.2 per cent of Korean families had fewer than 40 children's books, 26.3 per cent had 41–80 books; 21.7 per cent had 81–120 books; 38.8 per cent owned more than 212 books. The frequency of monthly visits to the library was none for 42.1 per cent of parents, one to two visits for 50 per cent of parents, and more than three to four times for 7.9 per cent of parents. Korean children read books for 25 minutes a day on average. By way of comparison, Foy and Mann (2003) reported on a survey of American parents from middle SES and of children aged four. The average number of children's books in American homes was 81.30 books (range: 0–250) and the frequency of visiting the library was 1.10 visit (range: 0–4) per month.

Digital devices

Today, young children grow up in very different social conditions from previous generations, mainly through the ubiquity of digital technologies. Digital devices are diverse and include computers, game players, DVD players, mobile phones, smartphones, tablets and digital cameras (see Chapters 2 and 3 in this volume). The use of digital devices is popular in Korea, and young children use them from an early age. In particular, the use of smart devices (tablet and smartphone) has increased among children as well as adults in Korea. Kim (2014) reported that 69.4 per cent of children under age six used a computer, 45.9 per cent used mobile phones, 90.3 per cent used a smart phone, 21.9 per cent used a tablet and 17.9 per cent used a game player. Children first used mobile phones on average from the ages of two to three, smart phones from the ages of three to five, computers from age three and the tablet from age five. Kim (2014) reported that children used computers and smart devices most often when their parents did housekeeping. Children used many different types of computer programs for a range of activities, including social networking, language learning and entertainment.

Library

Most classrooms have a library and a separate place for reading and writing in preschools. The average number of children's books in kindergartens is 25 books (range: 12–36) in and near Seoul (Cho, 2001). The average number is 23 books in kindergartens and Children's House in a local province where most children are from multicultural families in which mothers have come to Korea for marriage (Lee, 2013). In addition, most preschool classrooms have a computer, a TV, a video player, video tapes, a calendar, word and picture cards, and other devices for literacy education.

Practising early writing

Before 1990, in Korea, young children learnt to draw lines and copy Gulja with drill and practice (Lee, 2004). Their writing was based on directive instruction methods and activities including copying Gulja, consonant and vowel letters and words with repetition. In the era, kindergarten teachers used worksheets to teach Hangul and gave homework to children with worksheets. Children learned Gulja and consonant and vowel names from worksheets.

Writing activities, however, have decreased after the whole language perspective became popular in Korea. Cho (2001) surveyed 110 kindergarten teachers regarding their beliefs about writing education for four- and five-year-old children. The study also observed writing activities of 26 teachers and rated the literacy environment of kindergartens. The results showed that 63 per cent of teachers reported having a whole language perspective whereas 37 per cent reported having a traditional view of drill and practice. Various writing activities of children were observed in the classrooms such as writing simple words and sentences, copying Gulja after the teacher, writing and making a story after reading a picture book or a picture, writing the child's name, writing consonant and vowel letters, writing a friend's name, and writing numbers in the activities of birthday card making and others. Choi (2009) conducted a survey with 190 teachers of kindergarten and Children's House in a southwest province of Korea regarding writing education. Although about 85 per cent of teachers believed that writing education is not necessary for the kindergarten level, 79 per cent of teachers taught writing to their children due to parents' demand. Many teachers reported that they know little about a specific curriculum for writing, they got information about writing education from other teachers and workshops. Thus, preschool teachers need to be informed about effective literacy instructions about Hangul reading and writing.

Early literacy responses to particular needs

Children with special needs

Special education programmes are provided for children with special needs from the age of three to promote appropriate education opportunities and high-quality education services from an early age in Korea. Three stages have been suggested to classify children with special needs. First, local schools or parents refer children who may need special education to a Special Education Supporting Centre (SESC) with the consent of parents and the inclusion of a child's screening test. Second, the SESC conducts IQ testing and other diagnostic tests for suspected disorders in children. Finally, a Special Education Management Committee is appointed to select children with special needs and assign them to schools based on parents' request. The number of preschool children with special needs increased from 3,303 in 2010 to 3,367 in 2011 (Ministry of Education, Science, & Technology, 2011). About 76 per cent of preschool children with special needs receive inclusive education and the rest of 24 per cent attend special education preschools. Among the children receiving inclusive education, 60 per cent of them study in inclusive classes and 40 per cent in special education classes. Kindergartens that are subject to inclusive education have to make a classroom of special education for every four children with special needs. The Korean government supports preschool children with special needs with free preschool education, free after-school activities and vouchers for free therapy and counselling according to their needs.

Children from multilingual families

Korea has been known as a racially homogeneous country until the late twentieth century. However, people from other countries have moved to Korea to work, study and get married since 1980. In 2010, about 2 per cent of the Korean people (about 1.2 million people) were from foreign countries (Statistics Korea, 2010). About 10 per cent of them came to Korea for marriage. Most of the multicultural families live in underprivileged environments such as remote rural areas and urban slums. Children from multicultural families tend to have low levels of Korean language skills, literacy and school achievement (Park et al., 2014). Recently, the Korean government has attempted to provide academic and social support to the children from multicultural families in order to improve their school adjustment through educational intervention, consulting and counselling. However, there have been no special curricula for the early literacy education regarding the acquisition of Korean language and literacy among young children.

Major concerns for current and future literacy provision in Korea

Teaching Hangul in formal education

Basic skills for Hangul decoding have to be taught in formal education such as in kindergarten and grade 1 rather than in private education. Note that about 80 per cent of children aged four and five receive a private education in Hangul reading and over 70 per cent of children master Hangul decoding before they enter primary school (e.g. Cho and McBride-Chang, 2005). Although Hangul decoding is supposed to be taught in grade 1, grade 1 actually does not focus on Hangul reading because over 70 per cent children already know how to read Hangul. In other words, 30 per cent of children are not taught Hangul adequately either at kindergarten and grade 1 or in private education and this is partly due to living in under-privileged environments that typically are families that are poor, rural, multicultural or a combination of these factors. Those children may be at high risk of developing reading difficulties and learning underachievement. A recent study (Cho, 2015) reported that 28 per cent, 20 per cent, 6 per cent and 8 per cent of children, respectively, had not yet mastered reading of CVC Gulja with transparent letter–sound correspondences at the end of kindergarten, in the middle of grade 1, at the end of grade 1 and in the middle of grade 2. The data show that children are not taught to read CVC Gulja in the first semester of grade 1 and about 8 per cent of Korean second graders still had not yet mastered reading of CVC Gulja. Kindergartens need to teach children basic Hangul Gulja such as CV Gulja. In addition, children who have not yet mastered Hangul decoding at the start of grade 1 should be extensively trained with extra literacy reading programmes in grade 1; otherwise they face long-term literacy failure.

In addition, private education for literacy education should be decreased in Korea. The high dependency of private education prevents public education from working normally and making progress. Eventually, it polarizes further differences between students: that is rich versus poor.

Teacher education

School teachers in kindergarten and elementary school need to be educated about the processes of Hangul acquisition and specific reading and writing learning difficulties in Korea. Many Korean people including teachers and parents believe that Hangul can be learned easily, that Korean children learn Hangul by themselves without any help of adults (e.g. Cho, 2003) and that Korean children do not have reading difficulties. This is partly why Korean literacy development and impairment were not the focus of many scholarly investigations in the past. More research about acquisition of Korean language and literacy should be conducted and the findings should inform the practices of teachers and parents of young children.

Effective teaching instructions of Hangul

Effective teaching methods of Korean literacy should be studied in depth. Early Hangul education in kindergartens and private education favour whole-word and phonics methods that were imported from Western societies. But Korean language and script have a specific characteristic as an alphasyllabary (Taylor and Taylor, 2014). A recent study on effective maternal strategies to teach Hangul reported that instructions focused on CV and coda were associated with children's Hangul reading in young Korean children (Cho et al., forthcoming). Specifically, it would be ideal to teach CV Gulja within a CV chart first and then coda information for optimally teaching how to read and write Hangul words. CV charts could be particularly useful to teach Hangul to young children with poor emergent literacy skills and in poorer environments.

In conclusion, Hangul has some specifics as an alphasyllabary. More Korean researchers continue to study specific methods of promoting literacy based on the characteristics of Hangul and Korean language, as well as general methods from abroad. Major findings from research can and should now be better reflected in early literacy policy and practices to advance early literacy education in Korea. Ultimately, researchers, educational administrators, preschool teachers and parents should collaborate to increase early literacy development and to reduce literacy impairment among young Korean children.

Acknowledgement

This paper was supported by the National Research Foundation of Korea Grant funded by the Korean Government (NRF-2016S1A2A2912359).

References

Cho, H. S. (2003). *Perception of Kindergarten Teachers and Parents about Reading and Writing Education for Early Childhood.* Unpublished master's thesis, Ewha Womans University, Seoul.

Cho, I. S. (2001). *Study on the Kindergarten Teachers' Belief and Practice in Writing Education.* Unpublished master's thesis, Yonsei University, Seoul.

Cho, J. R. (2009). Syllable and letter knowledge in early Korean Hangul reading. *Journal of Educational Psychology, 101,* 938–947.

Cho, J.-R. (2015). Students with reading and writing learning disabilities in Korea. Presented at the 6th International Conference on School and Teaching at Chungju National University of Education, Chungju.

Cho, J. R. and McBride-Chang, C. (2005). Correlates of Korean Hangul acquisition among kinder-gartners and second graders. *Scientific Studies of Reading*, *9*(1), 3–16.

Cho, J. R., McBride, C. and Lin, D. (forthcoming). The relation of maternal literate mediation strategies and socio-emotional comments to Korean children's Hangul reading. *Applied Psycholinguistics*.

Cho, J. R., McBride-Chang, C. and Park, S. G. (2008). Phonological awareness and morphological awareness: Differential associations to regular and irregular word recognition in early Korean Hangul readers. *Reading and Writing: An Interdisciplinary Journal*, *21*, 255–274.

Cho, S.-S. (2009). *Perception of Hangeul Studying Paper Teachers on Literacy Education for Early Childhood*. Unpublished master's thesis, Kyunghui University, Seoul.

Choi, S.-S. (2009). *The Actual Conditions and the Cognition of Teachers about Childhood Writing Education*. Unpublished master's thesis, Gwangju University, Gwangju.

Foy, J.G. and Mann, V. (2003). Home literacy environment and phonological awareness in preschool children: Differential effects for rhyme and phoneme awareness. *Applied Psycholinguistics*, *24*, 59–88.

Kim, E.-S., Lee, J.-W., Kim, H.-J. and Bae J.-A. (2014). *Comparison of Operation Conditions and Needs Analyses in Korean Kindergartens and Children's House*. Seoul: Korea Institute of Child Care and Education.

Kim, Y. A. (2014). Young children's digital-media use and parents and teachers' perspectives. *Korean Journal of Children's Media*, *13*(1), 95–115.

Korean Association of Child Studies & Hansol Education Research Center. (2002). *Child Development Report 2001*. Seoul: Hansol Educaion.

Lee, C.-S, (2004). *Language arts for young children*. Seoul: Hanjisa.

Lee. J.A. (2013). Picture-book reading interaction of multiculture young children and its effect on receptive language and expressive language. *Korean Journal of Child Care and Education*, *77*, 101–122.

Lee, J., Park, E. and Kim, H. (2000). Literacy education in Korea: A sociocultural perspective. *Childhood Education*, *76*, 347–351.

Lee, K. and Lee, S. (2007). A study on the beginning literacy instruction's actual state through the commercial Korean language textbooks' analysis. *New Korean Education*, *75*, 215–248.

Lee, S. I. (2006). *The Relationship between Home Literacy Environment and Children's Language Ability*. Unpublished master's thesis, Chungang University, Seoul.

Ministry of Education, Science, and Technology. (2011). Statistics for special education of 2011. Seoul: Ministry of Education, Science, and Technology.

Ministry of Education, Science, and Technology & Ministry of Health and Welfare. (2013). Nuri curriculum: Teachers' manual. Seoul: Ministry of Education, Science, and Technology & Ministry of Health and Welfare.

Park, S.-G., Cho, J.-R. and Park, S. (2014). Comparisons of Korean literacy and cognitive-linguistic skills among preschool children from rural and urban communities and multicultural families. *Korean Journal of Speech-Language & Hearing Disorders*, *23*, 33–46.

PISA (2012). *PISA 2012 Results in Focus: What 15-Years-Olds Know and What They Can Do with They Know*. Retrieved from www, oecd. org/pisa,/keyfindings,/pisa-2012-results-overview.

Simpson, G. B. and Kang, H. (2004). Syllable processing in alphabet Korean. *Reading and Writing*, *17*, 137–151.

Statistics Korea. (2015). Korean social index of 2014. Retrieved from http://kostat.go.kr/portal/korea/kor_nw/2/1/index.board?bmode=read&aSeq=334501.

Taylor, I. and Taylor, M. M. (2014). *Writing and Literacy in Chinese, Korean and Japanese: Revised edition*. Amsterdam: John Benjamins Publishing Co.

Yi, K. (1998). The internal structure of Korean syllables: Rhyme or body? *Korean Journal of Experimental and Cognitive Psychology*, *10*, 67–83.

Yoon, H. K., Bolger, D. J., Kwon, O. S. and Perfetti, C. A. (2002). Syllable units in reading: A difference between Korean and English. In L. Berhoeven, C. Elbo and P. Reitsma (eds), *Precursors of Functional Literacy* (pp. 139–164). Amsterdam/Philadelphia: John Benjamins Publishing Company.

17

EARLY LITERACY POLICY AND PRACTICE IN JAPAN

Eiko Kato-Otani

There are things taken for granted in one's native language and culture. The Japanese orthographic system is such an example. It is natural for Japanese people to use four different orthographic systems: *Hiragana* (Japanese syllabary), *Katakana* (used for foreign or borrowed words), *Kanji* (Chinese characters) and *Romaji* (romanized Japanese). In this respect, Japanese is a unique language because it has four different modes of written expressions. A sentence can be written in *Hiragana*, *Katakana*, *Kanji* and *Romaji*. In addition, Japanese script can be written horizontally from left to right, or vertically from top to bottom. Having four different writing systems seems to be complicated to people who need to learn only one. Japanese children, however, grow up in such a literacy world and acquire necessary literacy skills. When formal schooling begins in the first grade, elementary school teachers teach their students step by step how to read and write these four different scripts according to the policies established by the Ministry of Education, Culture, Sports, Science and Technology (MEXT).

Although the Japanese writing system looks complex, the literacy rate in Japan is high (Literacy, n.d.). The government measures the literacy rate using the school attendance rate (*Shikijiritsu*, n.d.). Nine years of compulsory education begins in the first grade, and the non-compulsory senior high school attendance rate is over 97 per cent (*Kotogakko*, n.d.). About 50 per cent of senior high school students enter university (*Heisei*, 2014). If junior college and technical college are included, 80 per cent of students receive education after senior high school. According to the survey about compulsory education conducted by the MEXT in 2003, 90 per cent of elementary school students and 78 per cent of junior high school students are satisfied with their schooling (*Kotogakko*, n.d.). The MEXT also surveyed how students think about each subject. About 10 per cent of elementary school students said that they liked language arts very much and about 40 per cent of them said that they like it (*Kyokano*, n.d.). For arithmetic, 26.7 per cent of students said that they like it very much and 31.6 per cent of them like it. For science, 29 per cent of students said that they like it very much and 33.9 per cent of them like it. It is clear that students show less favourable attitudes towards language arts than arithmetic and science.

Language orthographic and phonological representations

Japanese children first learn to read and write *Hiragana*. *Katakana* is taught in the second semester of the first grade and is completed by the end of the first semester of the second grade.

Children need to understand what kinds of words (loan and foreign words) should be written in *Katakana*. *Kanji* instruction starts from the second semester of the first grade and continues to the end of high school. Simple *Kanji* characters are first introduced, and both the writing and reading of the *Kanji* are practised. Students are expected to master 1,006 characters by the end of the sixth grade. In each grade, there is a list of *Kanji* characters students need to master. By the end of high school, students have acquired about 2,000 *Kanji* characters. There are two different readings of *Kanji*: *on* and *kun*. For example, the *Kanji* for a tree is 木 and is read as [moku] (Type *on*) or [ki] (Type *kun*). Sixty per cent of *Kanji* have two types of reading, and some *Kanji* have multiple readings. In Japanese writing, a word is written by using *Kanji* and *Hiragana*. For example, 'go' is written as '行く'. This *Hiragana* following the *Kanji* is called *okurigana*.

Romaji (romanized Japanese) is introduced to students in the third grade of elementary school. Instruction of *Romaji* is different from learning the English alphabet. Students need to learn how Japanese words can be written in *Romaji* used in street and station names, direction boards, etc. There are two types of *Romaji*: *Kunreisiki*, the official *kana* romanization system, and the Hepburn system, developed by an American missionary of the same name, to transcribe the sounds of Japanese for Westerners. Students learn *Kunreisiki* first and then learn the Hepburn system.

All the sounds are independent vowels, or a consonant followed by vowel. As both *Hiragana* and *Katakana* are syllabic, they are relatively easy to read because there is an almost one-to-one correspondence between symbol and pronounceable sounds. Omniglot provides a detailed explanation of *Hiragana*, *Katakana*, *Kanji* and *Romaji* (Ager, 1998–2015a, 1998–2015b, 1998–2015c, 1998–2015d).

Early literacy

Preschool

Formal schooling begins in the first grade, and kindergarten is not compulsory. However, parents place children in preschool for reasons ranging from childcare to early education. It is important to note that there are three different types of preschools for young children, each type overseen by a different ministry. Thus, there are some differences and similarities among these schools' policies and structures.

A day-care centre, *hoikuen*, is under the administration of the Ministry of Health, Labor and Welfare (MOHLW). Kindergarten, *youchien*, are under the administration of the MEXT. As there is a greater need for childcare for working parents today, the lack of daycare centres is a serious issue. Therefore, the government has tried to combine these two facilities and established *nintei kodomo en* in 2006, to meet the increasing demands for childcare. This centre is certified by each prefecture's regulations based on the guidelines which the MEXT and the MOHLW decide (*Nintei*, n.d.).

Although each type of school is administered by a different group, the aims of the language section stated in the courses of study and the guide to childcare are almost the same (Course of study for kindergarten, 2008; *Hoikusho*, 2008; *Hoikusho*, 2011). Children need to express themselves in their own spoken words and to develop listening skills to understand others. They should become familiar with picture books and stories. Although teaching *Hiragana* is not mentioned in the guidelines, having children become interested in characters and experience the joy of communication using characters in their daily life is included.

Elementary school

Although public schools are administered by the municipal boards of education, personnel administration and curriculum are managed by the MEXT and the prefectural boards of education. The revision of the course of study primarily grants leeway for educational content based on each school's discretion. However, the MEXT determines the criteria, the character of the course of study and the administrative framework for textbook selection. The municipal boards of education organize a 'standard curriculum' and supervise small municipalities.

The course of study for elementary school (see the policy section below for details) defines early literacy success based on code learning in Grades 1 and 2 (Course of study for elementary, 2008; *Shogakko*, 2008). As Japanese children need to learn different writing systems, it is important for them to master *Hiragana*, *Katakana* and the required *Kanji* of the first two years. However, this code-focused instruction does not occur independent of meaning. Along with the form and pronunciation of each character, children are taught how it is used in a word, phrase or sentence (see Figure 17.1). They read stories, which get longer in Grade 2 textbooks (Miyaji et al., 2014b; Miyaji et al., 2014c). After they master *Hiragana*, they can express their thoughts in writing. For example, there is a letter-writing project in Grade 1, encouraging children to send a postcard to their grandparents or relatives. Through such activities, they come to know what kind of role written language plays. In addition to these projects, students are given written homework, quizzes and tests to measure their mastery. How well they understand what they read is measured by reading aloud.

By examining the courses of study, textbooks and workbooks, the definition of literacy success in Grade 1 and 2 is both code based as well as meaning-construction based. In order to read and write, students need to learn the code. They also need to learn the role of written language in their life. In PISA, students are tested on how they use different kinds of written text they face in their lives. Students are required not only to decode information and understand the literal interpretation, but they also must get information, interpret the text and examine what they read. Those who are placed in Level 5 are 'capable of sophisticated critical thinking and may contribute to a world-class knowledge workers in tomorrow's economy' (OECD, n.d.: 34).

Policy implementation in practice

The revision of the courses of study generally occurs every ten years. The latest revision in 2008 continues to aim to nurture a 'Zest for Life' in students who live in a rapidly changing society (Improvement, n.d.). The 2008 courses of study enriched the content of education and increased the number of class periods. It emphasizes the balance between acquiring 'basic and fundamental knowledge and knowledge and skills' and fostering 'the ability to think, make decisions, and express oneself' (Improvement, n.d.; *Gengo*, 2011).

The MEXT employed a more relaxed education policy, called *yutori kyoiku*, in 2002 (*Atarashii*, n.d.) to reform the so-called 'education hell' (Nagano, 2009) Japanese students had faced for a long time. However, the low performance of Japanese students in the results of the 2003 PISA shocked the MEXT. Japanese students went down on the list in every area tested. In the reading section, Japanese students were placed 14th out of the 41 countries that participated. They were placed 8th of the 32 countries in 2000 (PISA, n.d.). They were placed 15th out of the 57 countries in 2006. This is believed to have affected the 2008

Figure 17.1 Example of a *Hiragana* writing practice in a Grade 1 textbook

Source: Miyaji et al., 2014a

courses of study. The overall goal of Japanese language study is stated in the courses of study 2008 as follows (Course of study for elementary, 2008: 1):

> To develop in pupils the ability to properly express and accurately comprehend the Japanese language, to increase the ability to communicate, to develop the ability to think and imagine and sense of language, to deepen interest in the Japanese language, and to develop an attitude of respect for the Japanese language.

The National Assessment of Academic Ability in mathematics and Japanese have been given to Grade 6 students since 2007 (*Zenkokutekina*, n.d.). The results have shown that there are some challenges in the utilization of knowledge and skills. They affect the improvement in policies and teaching. Students performed better in the 2009 and 2012 PISA results. Japanese students were placed 8th out of the 65 countries in Reading in 2009 and 4th in 2012 (OECD, 2010, 2014). This shows that 'courses of study' affect students' learning.

Principal methods and content areas of literacy instruction

Preschool

Although *Hiragana* instruction begins in the first grade, young children first begin to recognize *Hiragana* when they start preschool. Children's belongings are all labelled in *Hiragana* and they begin to recognize how their name and their friends' names are written in *Hiragana*. There are signs and written information in schools. By making children aware of these things, adults expect them to learn that there is a written language.

Having children become interested in and aware of a written language is a goal included in both the course of study (Course of study for kindergarten, 2008) and the guide to childcare (*Hoikusho*, 2008). There are activities by which children become interested in characters such as picture books, *karuta*, Japanese card games and a pretend post office or store role play. In the *karuta* game, a teacher reads the word of a card, children find the matching picture card by listening. The first letter of the script is written on the picture card (see Figure 17.2). Even if children cannot recognize the *Hiragana* letter, it is possible to find the correct card by looking at the picture. Through the game, children are expected to become familiar with *Hiragana*. In post-office role play, children pretend to write a letter and use fake money to buy stamps. Through pretend play like this, children come to understand written materials such as symbols, signs and money.

Elementary school

Literacy instruction begins from *Hiragana*, moving on to *Katakana* and *Kanji* in a step-by-step manner in elementary school. The first grade Japanese language book has a chart of *Hiragana* with a picture (see Figure 17.3) (Miyaji et al., 2014a). For example, あ [a] is written with a picture of あり [ant]. Students chant the syllables across a row, [a] [i] [u] [e] [o] as a group, [ka] [ki] [ku] [ke] [ko] and so on following their teacher's model reading. They also chant reading down the columns, e.g., [a] [ka] [sa] [ta] [na] [ha] [ma] [ya] [ra] [wa] [-n]. By learning how *Hiragana* is placed in order, they learn how to read each character. Students are instructed to pay attention to the shape of each character. Students are also instructed to pay attention to a voice consonant mark ' ゛ ', a semi-voiced sound mark ' ゜ ', small *kana*, and how long vowels and geminate consonants are treated in written language. After they are able to read *Hiragana* characters, they practise reading words in the textbook.

Figure 17.2   Karuta, Japanese card game

Source: *Hiragana dobutsu*, n.d.

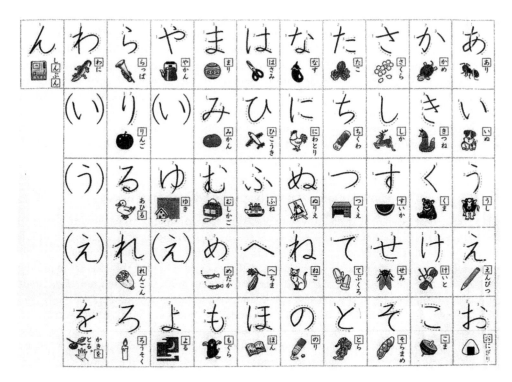

Figure 17.3   Hiragana chart in the Grade 1 textbook

Source: Miyaji et al., 2014a

Reading aloud is often practised with children. Students repeat after their teacher's reading or read with their teacher. Although there is no space between words in Japanese writing, these reading materials have spaces between words to help students notice the ending of each word. Reading aloud is done in classes and given as homework. By listening to students' reading aloud, teachers or parents can see whether or not they segment words properly. In addition, the same word has a different meaning depending on its intonation. For example, '*hashi*' is 'chopsticks' if a higher pitch is given to the first syllable and it is a 'bridge' if a higher pitch is given to the second syllable. As *Hiragana* is phonogramic, reading aloud is considered to be important because teachers can see how children treat words.

An important part of *Katakana* instruction is learning when *Katakana* should be used. Students need to understand that *Katakana* is used for loanwords such as computer and chocolate.

Kanji instruction begins in the second semester of the first grade. Students need to master 80 *Kanji* characters that are allocated to Grade 1, 160 in Grade 2, 200 in Grade 3, 200 in Grade 4, 185 in Grade 5 and 181 in Grade 6. They start to learn simple characters – those with few strokes. In total, they learn 1006 *Kanji* characters in elementary school.

In order to have students understand how *Kanji* are created, there is a story about *Kanji* in the Grade 1 textbook (Miyaji et al., 2014a). In this story, a rabbit and a raccoon were taking cover from a sudden shower under the tree. The tree illustration looks like a *Kanji* character 木 (see Figures 17.4 and 17.5). In this way, teachers have students understand that *Kanji* developed from pictures of things. By understanding that *Kanji* are an ideograms, students are helped to comprehend what each character means.

To teach how to write *Hiragana*, *Katakana* and *Kanji*, a penmanship workbook or drills are used (see Figure 17.6) (*Kurikaeshi*, n.d.). Teaching a proper sitting posture is included in the courses of study (Course of study for elementary, 2008; *Shogakko*, 2008) as well as in the Grade 1 textbook (see Figure 17.7). How to hold a pencil correctly is also taught. Items included in the penmanship workbook are to practise characters correctly, pay attention to length and direction, border and intersection of strokes, and the orthodox order of writing. As shown in the penmanship workbook in Figure 17.6, the strokes are numbered to show the correct order for writing them. Students practise writing *Kanji* used in a word, phrase and sentence, as shown in Figure 17.6. Therefore, children learn to understand how independent *Kanji* can be used in context.

Provision for children with special educational needs

After a classroom teacher first identifies students who have trouble learning how to read and write, they need to examine whether it is caused by lack of practice or learning disorders (Hirose, personal communication, 18 December 2014). The normal procedure is that a developmental test or a medical exam is administered. Based on the results, the internal schooling guidance committee (*Tokubetsu*, n.d.) and/or the schooling guidance committee of the educational board in the city or town decides how students should be treated. Various approaches such as providing an additional teacher in the student's classroom, small group instruction, team teaching or instruction in homogeneous groups are instituted. Small classes may be established for children with comparatively mild disabilities. Children with disabilities who are enrolled in regular classes may visit resource rooms to receive special instruction.

Figure 17.4 Story illustration in the Grade 1 textbook

Source: Miyaji et al., 2014a

Figure 17.5 *Kanji* are ideograms illustrated in the Grade 1 textbook

Source: Miyaji et al., 2014a

Figure 17.6   Penmanship workbook

Source: *Kurikaeshi*, n.d.

Figure 17.7   Proper sitting posture and pencil holding in the Grade 1 textbook

Source: Miyaji et al., 2014a

Variety of literacy materials available

For preschool children, both the course of study (Course of study for kindergarten, 2008) and the guide to childcare (*Hoikusho*, 2008) suggest the use of picture books to develop children's early literacy. For elementary school children, picture book stories are used in textbooks (Miyaji et al., 2014a). For learning how to write *Hiragana*, *Katakana* and *Kanji*, template-based workbooks (*Kurikaeshi*, n.d.) are provided in addition to the textbooks in Grade 1. For writing development, teachers provide project type worksheets that require one of the scripts in Grade 2. Upper-grade students work on projects like making a newspaper (*Kokugoryoku*, 2008).

In order to promote reading, the MEXT created a reading programme plan in 2002 (*Kodomo*, 2002), involving family, community and school. The municipal governments as well as public libraries provide picture-book-reading workshops for parents. The course of study states that children should be educated to learn the joy of reading (Course of study for elementary, 2008). Therefore, 'morning reading time' is exercised in over 8,000 schools. In 1993, the MEXT established a guideline for the number of books each school should have based on the number of classes it has (*Gakko*, 2011). The average number of books elementary schools had was 9,601 and the average annual expenditure for an elementary school library was $4,500 in 2014 (*2014 Nendo*, n.d.). The Grade 1 textbook (Miyaji et al., 2014a) has a list of recommended books that includes various types of books.

Major challenges for current and future early literacy provision

As kindergarten is not compulsory in Japan, the early literacy instruction children receive depends on their parents and preschool. Although the course of study and the guide to child-care state that preschool teachers should read picture books to children, how adults and children should interact with picture books is not prescribed, despite the widespread evidence that interactions during book reading are important for children's language and cognitive development (Bus et al., 1995; Dickinson and Snow, 1987; Goldfield and Snow, 1984; Ninio, 1980; Scarborough et al., 1991; Snow, 1983; Snow and Ninio, 1986; Sorsby and Martlew, 1991; Teale, 1986). In the book-reading research in Japan, Japanese mothers did not use challenging talk, such as 'why' questions during book reading (Kato-Otani, 2003) to develop cognitive skills. As found in Minami's study, Japanese children learn how to tell a story from their mothers' narrative styles (1996). These studies show that adults are a model of language skills for children.

Children should also become familiar with written language and teachers provide necessary early instruction. However, education-focused private preschools and educational service companies attract parents who want their children to receive early education. Thus, when children enter elementary school, there are students who have different literacy skills. This is a challenge for elementary school teachers who teach Grade 1. Some children are fully capable of reading and writing *Hiragana* and others need to learn how to write it. As mentioned in the early childhood education section, different ministries supervise different types of preschools. The purpose of each school was originally different as they served different populations. The teacher qualifications are also different. Thus, more precise and universal guidelines for early literacy instruction at the preschool level should be established by the government. According to the Action Program for Pre-School Education (*Yoji*, n.d.), the MEXT will continue to promote a unified centre for early childhood education and care, *nintei kodomo en*. One of the policies of the Action Program for Pre-School Education includes cooperation between preschool and elementary school education (*Nintei*, n.d.). This may connect preschool and elementary education.

The first two years of elementary school education focuses on how to read and write *Hiragana, Katakana* and *Kanji*. However, to avoid the Chinese saying 'A mere scholar, unable to practically use what he has learned', the course of study suggests various projects in which to use the literacy skills students have acquired, such as collecting information on events, analysing them, writing a report and giving a presentation. In order to do so, students need to cultivate introspection, develop the desire to learn and think, learn to be independent to make decisions, take actions or deal with problems. There are classroom activities proposed by various scholars to promote student development in these areas (Ando, 2008; Uematsu and Kenmochi, 2014; Saigo, 2012; *Kokugoryoku*, 2008). It will take more time to examine how the current course of study is working for such purposes. Teacher training is also important and necessary to shift from knowledge-based instruction to more student-centred, active learning instruction.

Japan is, by and large, a homogeneous and monolingual society. However, the number of foreign children whose parents come to Japan for job opportunities is increasing. Japanese as a Second Language instruction is established in schools in which there are a number of foreign students. However, developing the multilingual literacy or language skills of these children is not discussed much. Raising these children in a bilingual environment is not easy because of the lack of resources, teachers and funding. The number of foreign children is expected to grow because Japan needs workers due to the decreased birth rate. If Japan continues to have these students in schools, serious examinations and discussion about multilingual literacy and language skills should begin.

References

2014 nendo gakko toshokan chosa no kekka [Results of 2014 school library survey]. (n.d.). Retrieved 1 December 2014, from School Library Association website: www.j-sla.or.jp/material/research/2008-2.html.

Ager, S. (1998–2015a). Japanese *Hiragana. Omniglot: The Online Encyclopedia of Writing Systems and Languages.* Retrieved 27 December 2015 from www.omniglot.com/writing/japanese_hiragana.htm.

Ager, S. (1998–2015b). Japanese *Katakana. Omniglot: The Online Encyclopedia of Writing Systems and Languages.* Retrieved 27 December 2015 from www.omniglot.com/writing/japanese_katakana.htm.

Ager, S. (1998–2015c). Japanese *Kanji. Omniglot: The Online Encyclopedia of Writing Systems and Languages.* Retrieved 27 December 2015 from www.omniglot.com/writing/japanese_kanji.htm

Ager, S. (1998–2015d). Japanese *Kanji. Omniglot: The Online Encyclopedia of Writing Systems and Languages.* Retrieved 27 December 2015 from www.omniglot.com/writing/japanese_romaji.htm.

Ando, T. (ed.). (2008). *Shogakko gakushu shido yoryo no kaisetsu to tenkai kokugohen* [Practical guide and development of the course of study for elementary school Japanese language arts]. Tokyo: Kyoiku Shuppan.

Atarashii gakushu shido yoryo no shuna pointo heisei 14nendo kara jisshi [Main points of the new course of study enacted from 2002]. (n.d.). Retrieved 1 December 2014, from Government of Japan, Ministry of Education, Culture, Sports, Science and Technology [MEXT] website: www.mext.go.jp/a_menu/shotou/cs/1320944.htm.

Bus, A. G., van IJzendoorn, M. H. and Pellegrini, A. D. (1995). Joint book reading makes for success in learning to read: A meta-analysis on intergenerational transmission of literacy. *Review of Educational Research, 65* (1), 1–21.

Course of study for elementary school: Japanese Language. (2008). Retrieved 15 November 2014, from Government of Japan, Ministry of Education, Culture, Sports, Science and Technology [MEXT] website: www.mext.go.jp/component/english/__icsFiles/afieldfile/2011/03/17/1303755_003.pdf.

Course of study for kindergarten. (2008). Retrieved 1 November 2014, from Government of Japan, Ministry of Education, Culture, Sports, Science and Technology [MEXT] website: www.mext.go.jp/component/english/__icsFiles/afieldfile/2011/04/07/1303755_002.pdf.

Dickinson, D. K. and Snow, C. E. (1987). Interrelationships among prereading and oral language skills in kindergartners from two social classes. *Early Childhood Research Quarterly, 2*, 1–25.

Gakko toshokan hyojun [Standards for school libraries]. (n.d.). Retrieved 1 December 2014, from Government of Japan, Ministry of Education, Culture, Sports, Science and Technology [MEXT] website: www.mext.go.jp/a_menu/sports/dokusyo/hourei/cont_001/016.htm.

Gengo katsudo no jujitsu ni kansuru shido jireishu: Shikoryoku, handanryoku, hyogenryokuno ikuseini mukete shogakkoban [Collection of lessons for developing students' cognitive, judgment, expressive ability in language arts of elementary school]. (2011). Ministry of Education, Culture, Sports, Science and Technology. Tokyo: Tokyo Shoseki.

Goldfield, B. A. and Snow, C. E. (1984). Reading books with children: The mechanics of parental influence on children's reading achievement. In J. Flood (ed.), *Promoting Reading Comprehension* (pp. 204–215). Newark, DE: International Reading Association.

Heisei 26nendo gakko kihonchosa (sokuhochi) no kohyoni tsuite [About the 2014 School Survey]. (2014). Retrieved 31 August 2015, from Government of Japan, Ministry of Education, Culture, Sports, Science and Technology [MEXT] website: www.mext.go.jp/component/b_menu/houdou/__icsFiles/afieldfile/2014/08/07/1350732_01.pdf.

Hiragana dobutsu eawase karuta [*Hiragana* animal card game]. (n.d.). Tokyo: Gakken Kyoiku, Shuppan.

Hoikusho hoiku shishin [Child care guidelines]. (2011). Retrieved 1 November 2014, from Government of Japan, Ministry of Health, Labor and Welfare [MOHLW] website: www.mhlw.go.jp/bunya/kodomo/hoiku04/pdf/hoiku04a.pdf.

Hoikusho hoiku shishin kaisetusho [Revised child care guidelines]. (2008). Retrieved 1 November 2014, from Government of Japan, Ministry of Health, Labor and Welfare [MOHLW] website: www.mhlw.go.jp/bunya/kodomo/hoiku04/pdf/hoiku04b_0001.pdf.

Improvement of academic abilities: Courses of Study. (n.d.). Retrieved 1 December 2014, from Government of Japan, Ministry of Education, Culture, Sports, Science and Technology [MEXT] website: www.mext.go.jp/a_menu/shotou/gaikokugo/ and www.mext.go.jp/english/elsec/1303755.htm.

Kato-Otani, E. (2003). *Mother–Child Interactions during Book Reading and Maternal Beliefs about Book Reading*. Unpublished doctoral dissertation, Harvard University, Cambridge, MA.

Kodomo no dokusho katsudo no suishin ni kansuru kihontekina keikaku [Basic plan for promotion of children's book reading]. (2002). Retrieved 1 December 2014, from Government of Japan, Ministry of Education, Culture, Sports, Science and Technology [MEXT] website: www.mext.go.jp/a_menu/sports/dokusyo/hourei/cont_001/003.pdf.

Kokugoryoku Kojo Moderu Kenkyukai. (2008). *Shogakko shingakushu shidoyoryo pointo to jugyo zukuri* [New Course of Study for elementary school: Points and lesson plans]. Tokyo: Toyokan Shuppan.

Kotogakko kyoiku [High school education]. (n.d.). Retrieved 31 August 2015, from Government of Japan, Ministry of Education, Culture, Sports, Science and Technology [MEXT] website: www.mext.go.jp/component/a_menu/education/detail/__icsFiles/afieldfile/2011/09/27/1299178_01.pdf.

Kurikaeshi Kanji doriru 1nen Ge [Grade 1 repeated *Kanji* drill]. (n.d.), Tokyo: Benesse cooperation.

Kyoka no sukikirai, gakko seikatsu no manzokudo, gakko kyoikuni motomerumono [Likes and dislikes of school subjects, school satisfaction, and what was demanded in schooling]. (n.d.). Retrieved 31 August 2015, from Government of Japan, Ministry of Education, Culture, Sports, Science and Technology [MEXT] website: www.mext.go.jp/b_menu/shingi/chukyo/chukyo3/siryo/07070908/007/003.pdf.

Literacy and language classes in community centres. (n.d.). Retrieved 31 August 2015, from UNESCO Institute for Lifelong Learning website: www.unesco.org/uil/litbase/?menu=14&country=JP&programme=131.

Minami, M. (1996). Japanese preschool children's narrative development. *First Language, 16*(48), 339–363.

Miyaji, Y. et al. (2014a). *Kokugo 1 jo kazaguruma* [Japanese language arts textbook grade 1A pinwheel]. Tokyo: Mitsumura Tosho.

Miyaji, Y. et al. (2014b). *Kokugo 2 jo tampopo* [Japanese language arts textbook grade 2A dandelions]. Tokyo: Mitsumura Tosho.

Miyaji, Y. et al. (2014c). *Kokugo 2 ge akatombo* [Japanese language arts textbook grade 2B red dragonfly]. Tokyo: Mitsumura Tosho.

Nagano, Y. (2009, April). Japan's 'exam hell' now reaches into preschool. *Christian Science Monitor.* Retrieved 1 Novemeber 2014, www.csmonitor.com/World/Asia-Pacific/2009/0423/p06s01-woap.html.

Ninio, A. (1980). Picture-book in mother–infant dyads belonging to two subgroups in Israel. *Child Development, 51,* 587–589.

Nintei kodomo en [Centre for early childhood education and care]. (n.d.). Retrieved 1 November 2014, from Government of Japan, Ministry of Education, Culture, Sports, Science and Technology & Ministry of Health, Labor and Welfare [MOHLW], *Yoho renkei suishinshitsu* [Office for the Advancement of Kindergarten and Day-care Centre] website: www.youho.go.jp/gaiyo.html.

OECD (2010). PISA 2009 results: Executive summary. Retrieved 1 December 2014, from OECD website: www.oecd.org/pisa/pisaproducts/46619703.pdf.

OECD (2014). PISA 2012 results in focus: What 15-year-olds know and what they can do with what they know. Retrieved 1 December 2014, from OECD website: www.oecd.org/pisa/keyfindings/pisa-2012-results-overview.pdf.

OECD (n.d.). First results from PISA 2003: Executive Summary. Retrieved 1 December 2014, from OECD website: www.oecd.org/edu/school/programmeforinternationalstudentassessmentpisa/34002454.pdf.

PISA OECD seito no gakushu totatsudo chosa 2003nen chosa [PISA 2003 assessment]. (n.d.). Retrieved 1 December 2014, from Government of Japan, Ministry of Education, Culture, Sports, Science and Technology [MEXT] website: www.mext.go.jp/b_menu/toukei/001/04120101.htm.

Saigo, T. (ed.) (2012). *Mono no mikata, kangaekata o sodateru shogakko ichigakunen kokugo no jugyo* [Elementary school Japanese language arts grade 1 lessons for developing students' view points and ways of thinking]. Tokyo: Shin Dokushosha.

Scarborough, H. S., Dobrich, W. and Hager, M. (1991). Preschool literacy experience and later reading achievement. *Journal of Learning Disabilities, 24,* 508–511.

Shikijiritsu no shirabekata [Literacy rate research methods]. (n.d.). Retrieved 31 August 2015, from National Diet Library website: https://rnavi.ndl.go.jp/research_guide/entry/post-397.php.

Shogakko gakushu shido yoryo [Course of study for elementary school]. (2008). Ministry of Education, Culture, Sports, Science and Technology. Tokyo: Tokyo Shoseki.

Snow, C. E. (1983). Literacy and language: Relationships during the preschool years. *Harvard Educational Review, 53,* 165–189.

Snow, C. E. and Ninio, A. (1986). The contracts of literacy: What children learn from learning to read books. In W. H. Teale and E. Sulzby (eds), *Emergent Literacy: Writing and Reading* (pp. 116–138). Norwood, NJ: Ablex.

Sorsby, A., J. and Martlew , M. (1991). Representational demands in mothers' talk to preschool children in two contexts: Picture book reading and a modeling task. *Journal of Child Language, 18*(2), 373–395.

Teale, W. H. (1986). Home background and young children's literacy development. In W. H. Teale and E. Sulzby (eds), *Emergent Literacy: Writing and Reading* (pp. 173–206). Norwood, NJ: Ablex.

Tokubetsu shien kyoiku ni tsuite [About special needs education]. (n.d.). Retrieved 1 December 2014, from Government of Japan, Ministry of Education, Culture, Sports, Science and Technology [MEXT] website: www.mext.go.jp/a_menu/shotou/tokubetu/material/1298167.htm.

Uematsu, M. and Kenmochi, T. (eds). (2014). *Shogakko kokugo bansho de miru zentangenno jugyono subete ichinen jo* [The A to Z of elementary school Japanese language arts grade 1A]. Tokyo: Toyokan Shuppansha.

Yoji kyoiku shinko akushon puroguramu hombun [Early childhood education action program editorial content]. (n.d.). Retrieved 1 December 2014, from Government of Japan, Ministry of Education, Culture, Sports, Science and Technology [MEXT] website: www.mext.go.jp/a_menu/shotou/youchien/07121721/001.htm.

Zenkokutekina gakuryoku chosa: Zenkoku gakuryoku and gakushu jokyo chosa nado [Survey on academic performance nationwide: Academic performance and learning situations, etc]. (n.d.). Retrieved 1 December 2014, from Government of Japan, Ministry of Education, Culture, Sports, Science and Technology [MEXT] website: www.mext.go.jp/a_menu/shotou/gakuryoku-chousa/zenkoku/1344101.htm.

18

CHINESE-SPEAKING SOCIETIES

Li Yin and Yuting Sun

Chinese is one of the oldest writing systems in the world. The earliest extant writing examples of Chinese date back to 3,500 years ago. The Chinese language is the most spoken language. Over 1.3 billion people in the world speak Chinese as a first language, mostly in the People's Republic of China (mainland China), Hong Kong and Taiwan.

These three societies differ in a number of ways that may influence children's literacy development. Mandarin (Putonghua), the standard spoken Chinese, is the official language in mainland China and Taiwan, whereas Cantonese, a Chinese language spoken in Canton province and its neighbouring areas in Southern China, is mostly used in Hong Kong. Simplified script (e.g. '妈'/mom) is used in mainland China, whereas traditional script (e.g. '媽'/mom) is used in Hong Kong and Taiwan. Children in mainland China receive formal literacy instruction from age six in primary school, whereas children in Hong Kong start formal literacy learning from age three in kindergarten. In mainland China, pinyin, an alphabetic coding system using 26 Roman letters and four tone marks representing the pronunciation of Chinese characters, is taught in the first grade of primary school to help children learn to read new characters. In Taiwan, Zhuyin Fuhao, a phonetic script used to show the pronunciation of Chinese characters, is used to help children learn to read new characters; in Hong Kong, no phonological coding system is available; visual–verbal memorization ('look and say method') is the principal method of teaching and learning new characters.

Orthographic and phonological representations in Chinese fundamental principles

The basic units of written Chinese are characters. One character usually represents a morpheme. There are about 7,000 morphemes in Mandarin but only about 1,200 syllables, so that more than five morphemes share one spoken syllable on average (Shu, 2003). The large number of single-syllable homophones is a salient feature in Chinese.

The basic units of spoken Chinese are syllables. Chinese syllables can be subdivided into an onset and a rime. A further subdivision into phonemes is possible, but not necessary for learning to read Chinese (Anderson and Li, 2005). Chinese is a tonal language, having four lexical tones (in Mandarin Chinese) that differentiate the meanings of morphemes that otherwise have the same syllable forms.

The Chinese writing system is known for its visual complexity. The smallest unit of the Chinese writing system is the stroke. A stroke is a dot or a line written in one continuous movement. Among the 3,500 common characters listed in the Dictionary of Chinese Character Information (1988), the majority have 6–13 strokes. The complex characters have as many as 20 strokes and over (e.g. '獾') and the simplest ones have only one stroke (e.g. '一').

More than 80 per cent of Chinese characters are compound characters. A compound character (e.g. '瞪'/deng4/stare) consists of two parts: a semantic radical (e.g. '目'/eye) which provides some information about meaning, and a phonetic radical (e.g. '登'/deng1) which provides some information about pronunciation (Hoosain, 1991). Compound characters have a spatial structure. Left–right and top–down structures are the two major types of character structures. About 59 per cent of characters in primary school textbooks in Hong Kong have left–right structures and 25 per cent of characters have top–bottom structures (Tong and McBride, 2014). A radical usually appears in a specific position in a character. In a left–right structure character, the semantic radical usually appears on the left and the phonetic radical falls on the right, whereas in a top–bottom structure character, the semantic radical usually appears at the top and the phonetic radical usually appears at the bottom. Some radicals or subcomponents appear only in fixed positions. For example, the radical '讠' appears only on the left and '刂' appears only on the right of characters.

It should be noted that neither the semantic radical nor the phonetic radical always provide reliable clues of a character's meaning or sound, respectively. However, the semantic radical is more reliable in providing a meaning cue than is the phonetic radical in providing a sound cue, due to the higher frequencies of semantic radicals than those of phonetic radicals in Chinese. The predictive accuracy of the phonetic radical for communicating sound information is 40 per cent if the lexical tone information is excluded and 25 per cent if it is included (Shu et al., 2003).

Phonological sensitivity is an excellent marker of reading variability in Chinese, as universally found across writing systems (Ziegler et al., 2010). Pinyin knowledge, which reflects both segmental awareness (e.g. syllable, onset-rime) and suprasegmental awareness (lexical tone), was uniquely concurrently associated with Chinese word reading in one study (Siok and Fletcher, 2001) and uniquely predictive of Chinese reading in kindergarteners (Lin et al., 2010) and school-age children (Pan et al., 2011).

Morphological awareness, including sensitivity to homophones/homographs and lexical compounding in Chinese, is particularly important in learning to read Chinese, given that many syllables and words in Chinese are pronounced similarly and learners must be sensitive to differences in meanings. Chinese children's ability to create new compound words from known morphemes was significantly associated with word reading (McBride-Chang et al., 2011; Wagner, 2003) in one early study and longitudinally predicts word reading (Tong et al., 2009). Children with difficulties in learning to read Chinese often have difficulties in morphological awareness (e.g. Lei et al., 2011; McBride-Chang et al., 2011)

Visual-orthographic knowledge and copying skills are also important for Chinese reading and writing acquisition (Anderson et al., 2013; Tan et al., 2005; Wang et al., 2013; Wang et al., 2015) and impairment (Ho et al., 2004), given the high visual complexity and fairly predictable internal structure of Chinese characters, as described earlier.

Implications for literacy instruction

Generally, in Chinese classrooms children are not explicitly taught the formation rules of Chinese characters. Rote memorization and copying practice predominate in the teaching of characters (Wu et al., 1999). Findings of recent research on Chinese literacy provide two major implications for early literacy education in Chinese.

First, young children develop implicit knowledge about the internal structure of Chinese despite lack of direct instruction, which suggests the importance of informal literacy experience in the early years. Children live in worlds surrounded by print; they acquire an understanding of the regularities of the printed world and its relationship with the spoken language before explicit instruction is available (Miller, 2002). Chinese kindergarteners develop knowledge about the formal characteristics of writing quite early. From the age of two, Chinese children can produce distinctions between writing and drawing in conventional ways appreciated by adults, reflecting their cross-domain knowledge about writing (Treiman and Yin, 2011). From the age of three, they can produce important visual distinctions between name writing and non-name single-character writing, indicating their within-domain knowledge about different types of writing (Yin and Treiman, 2013). From the age of four, they typically show sensitivity to the structural, phonetic and positional regularities of Chinese radicals and such sensitivity explained unique variance in Chinese reading and writing one year later after statistically controlling for age and IQ in one study (Yin and McBride, 2015). Five-year-old children enter an important stage of orthographic knowledge development (Zhao and Li, 2014): five-year-olds were found to pay more attention than younger children to the visual form information of Chinese within the print environment (Zhao et al., 2014), and their reading experience was significantly related to the neural specialization of word processing above and beyond the effect of maturation (Li et al., 2013). These findings provide evidence for implicit learning of Chinese in informal settings.

Second, explicit instruction of Chinese literacy skills is significantly related to later literacy outcomes, which suggests the positive contribution of formal literacy instruction after the age of five. Li et al. (2008) followed 88 kindergarteners (mean age five years) in Hong Kong, where formal literacy instruction is commonly provided, and Beijing, where formal literacy instruction is prohibited. They found that Hong Kong children surpassed Beijing children in literacy attainments concurrently and three years later. After controlling for age, site, maternal education and teacher qualification, formal literacy activities significantly contributed to literacy attainment at primary school. Chow et al. (2008) found that an integration of metalinguistic training and parent–child dialogic reading better prepared kindergartners (mean age 5.2 years) in Hong Kong for learning to read than did conducting parent–child dialogic reading alone. Packard et al. (2006) found that first graders in Beijing who received explicit orthographic and morphological instruction performed significantly better after two semesters in their ability to copy characters and to write them from memory than did the control groups. These findings point to the potential positive contribution of direct literacy skill training after the age of five.

Early literacy

Definition of early literacy success

In mainland China, preschool education is not part of the nine-year compulsory education. There are 198,553 kindergartens in mainland China, of which 30 per cent are public and 70 per cent are private (National Educational Development Statistics Bulletin, 2013). In Taiwan, preschool education is provided by both public and private kindergartens or childcare centres. In Hong Kong, all kindergartens and nursery schools are private. In 2007, 1,001 kindergartens were registered at the Education Bureau of Hong Kong.

The three Chinese-speaking societies all advocate age-appropriate, child-centred, whole-person development in early education, with the goal of achieving balanced development in domains of physical health, language, society, science and arts/aesthetics (Curriculum Development Council of Hong Kong, 2006; Ministry of Education of the People's Republic of China, 2012; Ministry of Education of Taiwan, 2012).

Early literacy education aims to prepare children to read and write, with an emphasis on fostering children's ability to construct meaning and express ideas, rather than training decoding skills. For example, in mainland China, the *Guidelines for Preschool and Kindergarten Education (Trial Version, 2001)* states that the goal of early literacy education is to 'develop children's pre-reading and pre-writing skills'. The *Guide to 3-to-6-year-old Children's Learning and Development (2012)* provides detailed expectations for children at each developmental stage and offers educational suggestions and strategies for teachers and parents.

Three objectives are outlined for early literacy education: 1) to help children develop interest in reading and form positive reading habits; 2) to enable children to master basic reading comprehension skills; and 3) to foster children's interest and ability in expressing ideas through pictures or words.

In terms of reading, two- to -three-year-olds are expected to develop interest in exploring picture books and writings in their daily environment, recognize the writing of the group they belong to and describe key people or objects in the pictures. Three-to-four-year-olds are expected to understand short stories, describe details in pictures, differentiate between writing and drawing, and know that writings can express a meaning. They are also expected to know the position of books' names and recognize their own names. Four-to-five-year-olds are expected to know that signs and symbols express certain meanings and serve certain functions and to appreciate the emotions and feelings expressed in stories. Five-to-six-year-olds are expected to be able to tell the major content, plot and theme of the stories they read, appreciate the beauty of language in the stories and create different endings for the stories.

In terms of writing, children are expected to use graphic symbols to express emotion and feeling at age four, use self-invented graphic symbols to indicate space, object or record action at age five and create picture books at age six. Taking correct body gestures when drawing and writing is emphasized from age four.

Policy for multilingual literacy and language learning

Mainland China and Taiwan are monolingual societies. In mainland China, although English is introduced in some kindergartens, there is no mention of English or other foreign language in official policies. In Taiwan, children are directed to 'know that different cultures have different languages', but no official policy is available for second or foreign languages.

Hong Kong is a bilingual society where English is spoken as a second language. Cantonese is the mother tongue of most Hong Kong children and is used in preschools. *Guide to the Pre-primary Curriculum* (2006) states that developing proficiency in the mother tongue is of primary importance; and the goal of learning English is to ensure that children 1) develop interest in English; 2) understand simple everyday conversations; and 3) can sing and recite nursery rhymes in English.

Policy implementation in practice

Current situation

Gaps exist between policy and practice in all three societies. In mainland China, the level of policy implementation differs greatly between developed and underdeveloped regions, and between urban and rural areas. For example, in Beijing, 83 per cent of the 152 kindergartens in Haidian district are public kindergartens administered by the government. Of these, 79 per cent are first-class kindergartens where state policies are observed (*Haidian District Preschool Education Three-year Action Plan*, 2011–2013). Contrastingly, in rural areas of mainland China, 75 per cent of early childhood institutions are 'pre-primary classes' where teachers give long and direct teaching of Chinese characters taken from the Grade 1 syllabus (Zhang and Zhou, 2005). In Hong Kong, explicit teaching of reading and writing is common practice in kindergartens (Li et al., 2012).

Factors influencing the implementation of early literacy policy

Traditional Chinese culture

Confucianism has been deeply rooted in China since 2000 years ago when Emperor Wu Di declared it the official state philosophy. Receiving education was considered a way to master knowledge and moral integrity, both of which are needed for passing imperial exams to gain a government position and uphold family honour. In modern Chinese societies, the examination-oriented educational system and parents' high expectations for children's mastery of knowledge and skills are deeply influenced by this tradition. Chinese parents wish their children to receive formal literacy instruction as early as possible in order to gain an advantage in examinations in the primary school.

In addition, traditional Chinese literacy instruction features repeated reading, reciting and copying. Teachers are the authority in the classroom and students obey and follow. For centuries, Chinese children have been learning Chinese through repeatedly reading and reciting classics and copying characters from books using a brush. In the process of copying, children were expected to learn the various components of characters, the correct steps of strokes and the balance of a character within a square space. This long-standing tradition of literacy instruction contradicts the expectation of modern early literacy policies, which advocate child-centredness, fostering interest and not just skill drills and tests. Teachers struggle between requirements of government policies and expectations of exam-oriented parents.

Practical constraints

Two practical constraints impede early literacy policy implementation in China: regional development disparity and insufficient professional training.

Gaps exist between developed and underdeveloped regions in mainland China. According to the *Educational Statistics Yearbook of China* (2005), the average early childhood education expenditure per child in the rural area was 247 RMB in Fujian province, a coastal developed province, but was only 107 RMB in Shaanxi province, a less developed inland province. In 2005, 48 per cent of early childhood workers had no professional qualifications in urban areas, but the number was 72 per cent in rural areas. In practice, early literacy policies are better implemented in developed regions than in less developed regions.

Insufficient teacher training is a common problem in mainland China, Hong Kong and Taiwan. Lee and Tseng (2008) reported that in Taiwan some preschool teachers felt cultural tensions and conflicts in implementing developmentally and individually appropriate education. In mainland China and Hong Kong, many kindergarten teachers lack the motivation to make changes because they have little confidence in their ability to implement reform in their classrooms. At the same time, teachers struggle to meet the demands of highly expectant parents (Li et al., 2011; Liu and Feng, 2005).

Professional training of early years professionals

Continuous efforts are made in the three societies to improve professional training for kindergarten professionals.

In mainland China, in-service professional training for kindergarten teachers is provided at three levels. At the national level, a nationwide early education professional training programme called 'China National Training Program for Kindergarten Teachers' was launched in 2011. The programme consists of three-year training sessions. In each session, 10,000 kindergarten principals and backbone teachers are selected nationwide and trained intensively. At the province level, local education administrations organize continuing education programmes in which local kindergarten teachers can complete a certain number of required courses in a flexible manner within a certain period. At the kindergarten level, the *Kindergarten Feature Training Program* (KFTP) is developed by each kindergarten. KFTP is aimed at improving kindergarten teachers' professional skills, strengthening each kindergarten's unique features and building shared identity among kindergarten teachers (Yan, 2015).

In Hong Kong, the Special Education and Kindergarten Education Division of the Education Bureau organizes a wide range of in-service training events such as workshops, seminars and school-based programmes for kindergarten teachers and staff. These training events help teachers improve professional knowledge and skills and keep them updated about the latest developments in education and reform.

In Taiwan, preschool teachers receive professional training from three channels: evening classes at the universities, seminars or workshops organized by private educational institutions and non-profit organizations, and kindergarten exchange programmes between Taiwan and foreign countries (Qin, 2012).

Principal methods and content areas of literacy instruction

There is a common trend of incorporating Western pedagogies into Chinese kindergarten practice in the three societies (Lee and Tseng, 2008; Li et al., 2012). Emphasis on integrated teaching and learning is reflected in the official guidelines for early literacy instruction. In mainland China, formal literacy instruction featuring rote memorization and repeated drilling is prohibited in kindergartens (Li and Rao, 2005; Li et al., 2012). Teachers are encouraged to develop children's pre-reading and pre-writing skills through shared reading and integrated literacy activities. When reading, teachers should draw children's attention to the conventions of book reading, facilitate children's comprehension through questions and answers about story plots and relevant pictures, and guide children to appreciate the rhythms and rhymes of the language (Dang, 2011; Zhou, 2009). After reading, children are encouraged to share their thoughts, collaboratively recall the plots of stories with the aid of pictures and re-create endings imaginatively (Zhou, 2009). Writing is integrated into drawing activities and plays. Instead of character copying, games, such as connecting dots contouring an object, are recommended to foster children's eye–hand coordination and fine motor skills.

Due to traditional cultural influence and practical constraints discussed earlier, Western pedagogies are adapted in Chinese societies to accommodate local needs. Formal literacy instruction is provided to varying degrees. For example, in Hong Kong, formal literacy instruction is still prevailing in kindergartens (Li et al., 2012). The teacher reads aloud a new character to the whole class, directs children's attention to the spatial organization and order of its strokes, and asks the class to repeat the pronunciation (Chan et al., 2008; Li and Rao, 2005).

Provision for children with special educational needs

In mainland China, an early literacy provision for children with special educational needs is insufficient. Support for three-to-six-year-olds with disabilities and developmental delays is mostly provided by local Associations of Persons with Disabilities (LAPDs) and independent NGOs (Hu and Yang, 2013). Some social education agencies provide kindergarten classes in special education schools. Efforts are being made to provide integrated preschool education for children with special educational needs. For example, 18 kindergartens in Beijing set up inclusive classes in 2007, but the scope of efforts is far from enough to meet the demand of the whole population of children with special educational needs (Hu and Yang, 2013). To date, no standard identification and intervention systems are available in mainland China for kindergarten children with special educational needs. Experienced teachers may detect children with learning problems, but due to lack of knowledge and systematic assessment tools, a large number of at-risk children are being overlooked in mainland China (Liu and Lin, 2009). Moreover, some Chinese parents are reluctant to accept that their children have learning difficulties and miss the optimal time for early intervention.

In Hong Kong, a more mature government-supported system is available to serve young children with special educational needs. In 2005, the Hong Kong government launched the Comprehensive Child Development Service, which integrates resources of the medical and healthcare sectors, educational agencies and social welfare systems to provide early identification and intervention services for children in need of special support in kindergartens. Kindergarten teachers detect children with potential learning needs with the help of *Pre-Primary Children's Development and Behaviour Management – Teacher Resource Kit* issued by the Hong Kong government. After detection, teachers refer children to local maternal and child health centres for assessment. Children receive further assessment at Child Assessment Services if needed, and may also be referred to medical facilities for specialized consultation or receive pre-primary training services provided by special childcare centres (Education Bureau, 2008, 2014). In addition to providing identification tips, the *Teacher Resource Kit* also supplies teachers with various strategies to cope with children's problems such as word learning difficulties and poor language abilities.

Variety of literacy materials available

Across the three societies, children have plenty of opportunities to interact with literacy materials, such as children's literature, everyday character cards and written works constructed by teachers and children, and they have various types of writing equipment with which to draw, scribble and experiment.

Picture-book reading is a major type of literacy activity in all three places. The picture books typically feature a simple plot, vivid characterization and attractive illustrations. The language and vocabulary are relevant to children's daily life experience. Kindergartens usually have book corners where children can easily access a wide variety of picture books. In Li and Rao's (2005) survey with teachers from four kindergartens in Beijing, 53 per cent of the teachers reported having over 50 books for children in their classrooms and 88 per cent of the teachers reported updating the bookshelves once a month.

The books selected for children represent diverse contents, values and aesthetic features in order to provide children with rich and diversified reading experience (Zhou, 2009). Four genres are typically selected in mainland China: poem/nursery rhyme, narrative, prose and science (Zhou, 2009). The traditional Chinese poems are considered as particularly appropriate for Chinese young children. The reading materials usually have the content of Chinese traditional nursery songs, folklore and traditional Chinese festivals. In Taiwan, similarly, reading materials selected for young children are often related to traditional Chinese culture and Taiwanese conventions. Children also have opportunities to read about foreign mythologies, nursery rhymes and fairy tales (Zhou, 2009).

Children have easy access to writing equipment such as pencils, crayons and paper in the classrooms. In Hong Kong, for example, there are writing areas where children can practise drawing and writing with various writing materials (Chan et al., 2008). Across the three societies, children are encouraged to express ideas and feelings through pictures, symbols and writings.

Major challenges for current and future early literacy provision

There are three major challenges for early literacy provision in China.

First, gaps between policy and practice may exist for a long time. Chinese traditional views on education and practical constraints may continue to influence the implementation of modern early literacy policies. However, narrowing the gap is both possible and promising, for example through promoting professional training for kindergarten teachers, especially those in rural areas and economically disadvantaged regions.

Second, more basic research is needed to understand how young Chinese children develop pre-reading and pre-writing skills. Due to the unique characteristics of the Chinese orthography, findings from research on alphabetic writing systems may not be directly generalizable to Chinese children. As Pine and Yu (2012) pointed out, Chinese literacy experts should spend time in kindergarten classrooms, conduct action research in collaboration with kindergarten teachers and translate theories into strategies that are feasible in practice.

Third, more work is needed to support young children with special educational needs in China. As described earlier, Hong Kong does a better job than mainland China in this regard. In mainland China, the population of children aged between nought and six is 100 million, whereas in Hong Kong, the number is 0.4 million. Take dyslexia, for example: the prevalence rate of this learning disability is 9.7 per cent in Hong Kong (Chan et al., 2007) and 8 per cent in mainland China (Wu et al., 2004). This means that 38,800 young children at risk for dyslexia in Hong Kong can be detected early in kindergarten and provided with timely intervention, but the 8,000,000 at-risk children in mainland China are, regrettably, largely unidentified and unaided.

References

Anderson, R. C., Ku, Y.-M., Li, W., Chen, X., Wu, X. and Shu. H. (2013). Learning to see the patterns in Chinese characters. *Scientific Studies of Reading, 17,* 41–56.

Anderson, R. C. and Li, W. (2005). A cross-language perspective on learning to read. In A. Mckeough, J. L. Lupart, L. Philips and V. Timmons (eds), *Understanding Literacy Development: A Global View* (pp. 65–91). Hillsdale, NJ: Erlbaum.

Chan, L., Juan, C. Z. and Foon, C. L. (2008). Chinese preschool children's literacy development: From emergent to conventional writing. *Early Years, 28*(2), 135–148.

Chow, B. W., McBride-Chang, C., Cheung, H. and Chow, C. S. (2008). Dialogic reading and morphology training in Chinese children: Effects on language and literacy. *Developmental Psychology, 44*(1), 233–244.

Curriculum Development Council (2006). *Guide to the Pre-primary Curriculum.* Hong Kong Special Administrative Region.

Dang, A. (2011). Exploration of reading characteristics of first-year kindergarteners and teaching strategies. *Journal of Changchun Educational Institute, 27*(10), 160–161 (in Chinese).

Dictionary of Chinese Character Information (1988). Beijing: Science Publishers (in Chinese).

Education Bureau (2014). *Comprehensive Child Development Service.* The Hong Kong Special Administrative Region.

Education Bureau (2008). Operation guide on the whole school approach to integrated education. The Hong Kong Special Administrative Region.

Ho, C. S.-H., Chan, D. W.-O., Lee, S.-H., Tsang, S.-M. and Luan, V. H. (2004). Cognitive profiling and preliminary suibtyping in Chinese developmental dyslexia. *Cognition, 91*(1), 173–186.

Hoosain, R. (1991). *Psycholinguistic Implications for Linguistic Relativity: A Case Study of Chinese.* Hillsdale, NJ: Lawrence Erlbaum Associates.

Hu, X. and Yang, X. (2013). Early intervention practices in China: Present situation and future directions. *Infants & Young Children, 26*(1), 4–16.

Lee, I. F. and Tseng, C. L. (2008). Cultural conflicts of the child-centered approach to early childhood education in Taiwan. *Early Years, 28*(2), 183–196.

Lei, L., Pan, J., Liu, H., McBride-Chang, C., Li, H., Zhang, Y. and Shu, H. (2011). Developmental trajectories of reading development and impairment from ages 3 to 8 years in Chinese children. *Journal of Child Psychology and Psychiatry, 52*, 212–220.

Li, H. and Rao, N. (2005). Curricular and instructional influences on early literacy attainment: Evidence from Beijing, Hong Kong and Singapore. *International Journal of Early Years Education, 13*(3), 235–253.

Li, H., Rao, N. and Tse, S. K. (2012). Adapting western pedagogies for Chinese literacy instruction: Case studies of Hong Kong, Shenzhen, and Singapore preschools. *Early Education and Development, 23*, 603–621.

Li, H., Wang, X. C. and Wong, J. M. S. (2011). Early childhood curriculum reform in China: Perspectives from examining teachers' beliefs and practices in Chinese literacy teaching. *Chinese Education and Society, 44*(6), 5–23.

Li, S., Lee, K., Zhao, J., Yang, Z., He, S. and Weng, X. (2013). Neural competition as a developmental process: Early hemispheric specialization for word processing delays specialization for face processing. *Neuropsychologia, 51*, 950–959.

Liu, Y. and Feng, X. (2005). Kindergarten educational reform during the past two decades in mainland China: Achievements and problems. *International Journal of Early Years Education, 13*(2), 93–99.

Liu, X. and Lin, M. (2009). The diagnosis and intervention for Chinese development dyslexia. *Journal of Youth Studies, 12*(2), 101–107.

McBride-Chang, C., Lam, F., Lam, C., Chan, B., Fong, C. Y. C., Wong, T. T. Y. and Wong, S. W. L. (2011). Early predictors of dyslexia in Chinese children: Familial history of dyslexia, language delay, and cognitive profiles. *Journal of Child Psychology and Psychiatry, 52*, 204–211.

McBride-Chang, C., Shu, H., Zhou, A., Wat, C.-P. and Wagner, R. K. (2003). Morphological awareness uniquely predicts young children's Chinese character recognition. *Journal of Educational Psychology, 95*, 743–751.

Miller, F. C. (2002). Children's early understanding of writing and language: The impact of characters and alphabetic orthographies. In W. Li, J. S. Gaffney and J. L. Packard (eds), *Chinese Language Acquisition: Theoretical and Pedagogical Issues* (pp. 17–29). The Netherlands: Kluwer.

Ministry of Education (2001). *Guidelines for Preschool and Kindergarten Education (Trial Version).* People's Republic of China.

Ministry of Education (2012). *Guide to 3-to-6-year-old Children's Learning and Development.* People's Republic of China.

Ministry of Education (2012). *Kindergarten Education and Care Curriculum Outlines (Trial Version)*. Taiwan.

Packard, J. L., Chen, X., Li, L., Wu, X., Gaffney, J. S., Li, H. and Anderson, R. C. (2006). Explicit instruction in orthographic structure and word morphology helps Chinese children learn to write characters. *Reading and Writing: An Interdisciplinary Journal, 19*, 457–487.

Pan, J., McBride-Chang, C., Shu, H., Lin, H., Zhang, Y. and Li, H. (2011). What is in the naming? A 5-year longitudinal study of early rapid naming and phonological sensitivity in relation to subsequent reading skills in both native Chinese and English as a second language. *Journal of Educational Psychology, 103*(4), 897–908.

Pine, N. and Yu, Z. (2012). Early literacy education in China: A historical overview. In C. B. Leung and J. Ruan (eds), *Perspectives on Teaching and Learning Chinese Literacy in China* (pp. 81–105). Multilingual Education.

Qin, F. (2012). Reflections on the modern preschool teacher management reform in Taiwan. *Journal of Guangzhou Institute of Socialism, 3*, 68–71 (in Chinese).

Shu, H. (2003). Chinese writing system and learning to read. *International Journal of Psychology, 38*(5), 274–285.

Shu, H., Chen, X., Anderson, R. C., Wu, N. and Xuan, Y. (2003). Properties of school Chinese: Implications for learning to read. *Child Development, 74*, 27–47.

Siok, W. T. and Fletcher, P. (2001). The role of phonological awareness and visual–orthographic skills in Chinese reading acquisition. *Development Psychology, 37*(6), 886–899.

Tan, L. H., Spinks, J. A., Eden, G. F., Perfetti, C. A. and Siok, W. T. (2005). Reading depends on writing, in Chinese. *Proceedings of the National Academy of Sciences of the United States of America, 102*, 8781–8785.

Tong, X. & McBride, C. (2014). Chinese children's statistical learning of orthographic regularities: Positional constraints and character structure, *Scientific Studies of Reading, 18*(4), 291–308.

Tong, X., McBride-Chang, C., Shu, H. and Wong, A. M. (2009). Morphological awareness, orthographic knowledge, and spelling errors: Keys to understanding early Chinese literacy acquisition. *Scientific Studies of Reading, 13*, 426–452.

Treiman, R. and Yin, L. (2011). Early differentiation between drawing and writing in Chinese children. *Journal of Experimental Child Psychology, 108*, 786–801.

Wang, Y., McBride-Chang, C. and Chan, S. F. (2013). Correlates of Chinese kindergartners' word reading and writing: The unique role of copying skills. *Reading and Writing*, 1–22.

Wang, Y., Yin, L. and McBride, C. (2015). Unique predictors of early reading and writing: A one-year longitudinal study of Chinese kindergarteners. *Early Childhood Research Quarterly, 32*(3), 51–59.

Wu, X., Li, W. and Anderson, R. C. (1999). Reading instruction in China. *Journal of Curriculum Studies, 31*, 571–586.

Yan, H. (2015). *Promoting Kindergarten Teacher's Professional Development*. Beijing: China Light Industry Press (in Chinese).

Yin, L. and McBride, C. (2015). Chinese kindergarteners learn to read characters analytically. *Psychological Science, 26*(4), 424–432.

Yin, L. and Treiman, R. (2013). Name writing in Mandarin-speaking children. *Journal of Experimental Child Psychology, 116*, 199–215.

Zhao, J. and Li, S. (2014). Development of form recognition of visual word in Chinese children of 3 to 6 years. *Journal of Psychological Science, 37*(2), 357–362 (in Chinese).

Zhao, J., Zhao, P., Weng, X. and Li, S. (2014). Do preschool children learn to read words from environmental print? *PLoS ONE, 9*(1). e85745. doi:10.1371/journal. pone.0085745.

Zhou, J. (2009). Reflections on early reading instruction activities in the kindergarten. *Early Childhood Education, 12*, 15–17 (in Chinese).

Ziegler, J.C., Bertrand, D., Tóth, D., Csépe, V., Reis, A., Faísca, L. et al. (2010). Orthographic depth and its impact on universal predictors of reading: A cross-language investigation. *Psychological Science, 21*, 551–559.

19

INDIA

The policy and practice of early literacy acquisition in the akshara languages

Shaher Banu Vagh, Sonali Nag and Rukmini Banerji

India is a country of many pluralities as reflected in its linguistic, geographic, religious, cultural and socioeconomic diversity. All of this poses significant challenges for its education system, which spans the spectrum from high-fee-charging privately managed schools to publicly funded government schools. Some schools along this spectrum are partially aided and some are not recognized by education authorities. Typically, the high-cost private schools provide English as the primary language of instruction, while government schools are more varied, offering instruction in one of the Indian languages and English. Even though in recent years there has been an increase in 'affordable' low-cost private schools, government schools continue to provide schooling to the majority of India's children (ASER Centre, 2014). These schools, catering to the most disadvantaged amongst the urban and rural poor, are bogged down with systemic issues of poor infrastructure, inadequate teaching–learning resources and prevalence of multi-grade classrooms run by teachers only trained for mono-grade services.[1] It is therefore noteworthy that by focusing on the pedagogy of reading and writing in the akshara languages in the Indian government schools, our discussion inevitably becomes linked to issues of socioeconomic 'disadvantage'.

The Indian constitution legislates the provision of free and compulsory education for all children aged six to 14 years and places the primary responsibility of ensuring access to school, enrolment, attendance and completion on the government (Right to Education Act, 2009). Preschool education is not mandatory. Yet, there are several opportunities for preschool participation through programmes managed by the government, non-government organizations and the private sector. The first two are the largest providers of these services through Anganwadi and Balwadi programmes that tend to serve as feeder preschools for government and low-cost private schools. Anganwadis, as part of the Integrated Child Development Services (ICDS), provide basic health services, nutrition and preschool education for children from birth to six years. As such, the preschool component in these programmes is diluted, because one Anganwadi worker functions as the teacher, basic healthcare provider and liaison between the community and government. Balwadi programmes offered by the government and non-governmental organizations for children aged three to six are more focused on preparing children for the demands of formal schooling. National rural estimates indicate that about 63 per cent of three-year-olds and 77 per cent of four-year-olds are enrolled in a preschool programme (ASER Centre, 2014). National urban estimates are not available, but small-scale surveys indicate that preschool participation rates for children in urban centres are similar to rural estimates except that children in urban areas are more likely to attend a private preschool instead of government centres (ASER Centre, 2014). By five years of age the majority of the children in rural and urban areas tend to be enrolled in first grade.

What gets taught and how it is taught? Policy guidelines

The National Curriculum Framework (NCF, 2005) tends to be the steering document providing guidelines for curricular focus and pedagogical approaches at the primary grades and beyond. The most recent iteration of NCF and the ensuing National Curriculum Framework for Teacher Education (NCFTE, 2009) stresses a 'constructivist' and 'participatory' approach to learning as a means to redress the mechanistic instructional approaches of rote memorization, drill-based pedagogy and decontextualized, didactic and textbook-centric teaching approaches reminiscent of the behaviourist paradigm. Some of its guidelines specific to oral language and literacy development are the importance of: a) instruction in a child's native language particularly in the primary years; b) multilingual classrooms;[2] c) an integrated approach to learning to read and write; d) the use of diverse and authentic print-rich materials that value children's cultures and experiences, promote language learning and facilitate children in abstracting rules of grammar; e) children as active participants; f) 'expressiveness' rather than just 'correctness' in oral and written language use; and g) linking language assessments to proficiency rather than the mandated syllabus. On teacher education, NCF and NCFTE mandate ongoing and onsite professional development as a means to prepare and support teachers to implement strategies in consonance with the 'constructivist' approach. Although states exercise autonomy in the development and implementation of the curriculum, the NCF tends to be the overarching guiding document.

Policy recommendations for the preschool stage emphasize the development of oral language skills in the child's native language and on utilizing developmentally appropriate, flexible and individualized teaching practices to ensure holistic development and to prepare the child for schooling (National Focus Group on Early Childhood Education, NCERT, 2006). Some suggested activities for three- to five-year-olds are dramatic play, play with manipulative objects, talking and listening to stories, exposure to print in a print-rich but meaningful context and encouraging children's interest in the functional aspects of written language such as the writing of their own names. The guidelines discourage activities that are designed 'solely to teach the alphabet, phonics, and penmanship' (NCERT, 2006).

English in the primary school years

Government schools provide instruction in any one of the 46 Indian languages and English, an associate official language (Dutta and Bala, 2012). Children attending non-English medium schools also learn English as a second language. The grade at which English teaching commences varies depending on the state or union territory (UT) policy.[3] In a majority of the states and UTs (21 states and five UTs) English is introduced in the first grade. Despite English being an aspirational language, the quality of English language instruction in government schools and overall level of learning is less than desirable (Dutta and Bala, 2012; Nag et al., 2014). A recent national rural survey indicates that about 30 per cent of children in grade 3 are unable to correctly identify four out of five upper-case letters and just 47 per cent of children in grade 8 are able to read a simple sentence such as 'I like to read' or 'What is the time?' and of these only 63 per cent can define the meaning of words read (ASER Centre, 2014).

A thorough discussion of these issues merits its own chapter. In this chapter, we focus on literacy acquisition in the akshara languages. In the following sections we offer a brief overview of the phonology and orthography of the akshara languages using examples from a northern Indo-Aryan language, Hindi and a southern Dravidian language, Kannada. We discuss the insights about literacy development provided by reading acquisition research in the akshara languages and describe typical instructional practices in mainstream government schools. Of particular interest are the links between policy, research and practice, and the implications of these findings for literacy development in India.

The akshara languages

Phonological and orthographic representations

India's linguistic landscape is marked by 22 official languages but an overall count of close to 780 languages (Devy, 2014). The Indo-Aryan and the Dravidian language families, which we focus upon in this chapter, have distinct orthographies but are derived from the ancient writing system of Brahmi and thus share many common features.

In the Indic orthographies, the basic orthographic unit (the akshara) represents sounds at the level of the syllable with constituent parts of the akshara encoding phonemic information. Hence, these writing systems have most commonly been referred to as an *alphasyllabary* (Salomon, 2000). Akshara can be vowels (/V/), consonants with an inherent (unmarked) vowel (/Ca/), consonants with other vowel markers (/CV/) or with the vowel suppressed (/C/), consonant clusters (or conjoint consonants) appearing with an inherent or marked vowel (e.g. /CCa/, /CCV/, /CCCV/). Examples of the different types of akshara are presented in Table 19.1. Although the akshara systems make provision for a phonemic consonant (e.g. in Hindi, the use of the '*halant*', a marker placed beneath the consonant to mark vowel suppression as in क् /k/), in practice it is not uniformly used and is rarely introduced in early literacy instruction. A basic symbol set, referred to by different names such as the *varnamala/varnamale* of Hindi/Kannada, comprises the primary forms of vowels (/V/), consonant–vowel pairs (/Ca/, /CV/) and a handful of conjoint consonants with the inherent vowel (/CCa/), which visually may or may not be decomposable into constituent phonemic units (e.g. the Hindi /ksha/ in Table 19.1).

Vowels in an akshara orthography have two representations, a primary and a secondary form. Vowels appear in their primary form in syllable initial positions (with some exceptions), and in their secondary form as diacritics called *matra/gunita* (Hindi/Kannada). Hence, a second symbol set is a well-structured consonant–vowel matrix referred to as the *barakhadi/kagunita* (Hindi/Kannada) comprising consonants with the full complement of vowel ligatures (/CV/). A phonemic marker such as the vowel ligature can appear on the top, bottom, left or right of the consonantal base, thus resulting in non-linear visual representations of the orthographic units (see the vowel ligatures with the consonant base /k/ in Table 19.1 for Hindi and Kannada). Additionally, consonants within consonant clusters are also represented in their secondary forms, which typically involve halving the consonant when it is placed linearly or stacking consonants (see the CCV and CCCV akshara in Table 19.1). Both arrangements index vowel suppression in one of the consonants in the cluster. Thus a single symbol block (the singleton akshara) may represent two or more phonemic markers. The number of distinct singleton akshara runs to several hundred, given the highly productive

Table 19.1 Orthographic examples of different types of akshara

	Hindi	Kannada
Primary forms of vowels	अ /a/, आ /aa/, इ /i/, ई /ii/, उ /u/, ऊ /uu/	ಅ /a/, ಆ /aa/, ಇ /i/, ಈ /ii/, ಉ /u/, ಊ /uu/
Primary forms of consonants with the inherent vowel (CV)	क /ka/, ख /kha/, त /ta/, र /ra/, ध /dha/	ಕ /ka/, ಖ /kha/, ತ /ta/, ರ /ra/, ಧ /dha/
Consonant with ligature vowel (CV)	का /kaa/, कि /ki/, की /kii/, कु /ku/, कू /kuu/	ಕಾ /kaa/, ಕಿ /ki/, ಕೀ /kii/, ಕು /ku/, ಕೂ /kuu/
Consonants with inherent vowel (CCa, CCCa)	स्प्र /spra/, क्ष /ksha/, स्थ /stha/, त्य /tya/	ಸ್ಪ್ರ /spra/, ಕ್ಷ /ksha/, ಸ್ಥ /stha/, ತ್ಯ /tya/
Consonants with ligature vowel (CCV, CCCV)	क्कु /kku/, ख्या /khyaa/, स्त्री /strii/, ड्ढा /ddhaa/	ಕ್ಕು /kku/, ಖ್ಯಾ /khyaa/, ಸ್ತ್ರೀ /strii/, ಡ್ಢಾ /ddhaa/

Table 19.2 Illustrative examples of matched and mismatched orthography to phonology mappings

Hindi	Kannada	Akshara mappings Hindi; Kannada	Akshara to phonology mappings Hindi; Kannada
लता	ಲತಾ	<la.taa> <CV.CV>	/la.taa/ /open syllable.open syllable/
लक्ष्मी	ಲಕ್ಷ್ಮೀ	<la.kshmii> <CV.CCCV>	/la.ksh.mii/ /body.coda.open syllable)/
लक्ष्मण	ಲಕ್ಷ್ಮಣ	<la.kshma.N>; <la.kshma.Na> <CV.CCCV.C>; <CV/CCCV.CV>	/la.ksh.ma.N/; /la.ksh.ma.Na/ /body.coda.body.coda/; /body.coda. open syllable. open syllable /

nature of consonant clusters, rendering the orthographies as 'extensive' (Nag, 2007, 2013). However, an important feature of the akshara orthography is that, except for the inherent vowel and a few conjoint consonants (such as the Hindi /ksha/ in Table 19.1), all akshara units can be deconstructed into their constituent phonemic units. The non-linear alignment of the phonemic markers and the presence of multiple phonemes within a single akshara unit tend to increase the visual and phonological complexity of akshara (Nag et al., 2014).

Akshara in words encode phonological information in several ways. Table 19.2 gives examples of phonology–orthography mappings for Hindi and Kannada. Another example is the open and closed syllable word pair, /maa.taa/ (mother) and /maal/ (goods). Both are two-akshara Hindi words (<CV.CV> and <CV.C>), the latter distinguished as a body and coda encoding. In multisyllabic words, the mapping of akshara to phonology is determined by the process of re-syllabification whereby the post-vocalic consonant of an initial closed syllable initiates the next akshara, forming a coda-open syllable unit, e.g. /laksh.mii/ (good fortune, <CV.CCCV>) or a coda-body unit, e.g. /laksh.maN/ (a name, <CV.CCCV.C>; also see Table 19.2). The process of re-syllabification results in the formation of a wide range of consonant clusters as well as mismatched phonology–orthography mappings.

Literacy acquisition research in the akshara languages: challenges and implications for learning to read

Literacy acquisition research with fluent and beginning readers offers insights on the cognitive-linguistic underpinning of reading development in the akshara languages. The evidence suggests that although the mapping of phonology to orthography is near perfect, mastering an akshara system presents several orthography-specific learning demands.

Young learners have to master an extensive set of orthographic units that tend to extend the 'learning to read' phase (Nag, 2007; Sircar and Nag, 2013; Tiwari et al., 2011). While the acquisition of the simple akshara (V, Ca) is rapid over Grades 1 and 2, the acquisition of more complex akshara, that is akshara with ligatures (CV, CCV, CCCV), seems to extend well into Grade 4 (Nag, 2007; see Table 19.1). The pace of acquisition is, however, confounded by socioeconomic disadvantage and poor school quality and nature of instruction (Nag, 2007). Further factors in mastering the complex akshara are related to: (a) visual complexity driven by the use of ligatures that are non-linearly aligned in individual akshara, (b) phonological complexity encoded in multiple phonemic markers, (c) frequency of akshara in children's literature and d) the lack of explicit instruction on many of these akshara that are left to incidental learning from encounters in print (Nag, 2013; Nag, et al., 2014; Sircar and Nag, 2013).

The late acquisition of complex akshara parallels the slower emergence of phonemic awareness (Nag, 2007; Patel, 2004; Sircar and Nag, 2013). Fluent readers tend to demonstrate greater phonemic processing skills, suggesting that analytical skills that help readers deconstruct an akshara into its phonemic constituents accompany the greatest gains for accurately and efficiently decoding the complex akshara (Nag, 2007; Nag and Snowling, 2012). The shift to an analytic strategy is important given the high variety of complex akshara and the fact that the complex akshara (with a few exceptions) are not individually taught. It is, then, not surprising that the ability to read complex akshara tends to set the pace for reading development and failure to do so is indicative of struggling readers (Nag and Snowling, 2011). Importantly, in keeping with the alphasyllabic nature of the orthography, both syllabic processing skills and phonemic processing skills continue to be significant predictors of reading accuracy through the middle school years (Nag and Snowling, 2012).

Spelling development research provides additional insights into the orthographic effects of the Indic alphasyllabaries. The simple akshara are the easiest to spell and to read. Complex akshara pose a challenge and their position in a word has implications for spelling accuracy (Bengali: Sircar and Nag, 2013; Kannada: Nag et al., 2010; Hindi: Vaid and Gupta, 2002). Re-syllabification, which results in mismatched phonology-orthography mapping (as illustrated in Table 19.2), imposes additional processing demands that are greater for spelling than reading (Nag, 2013). Spelling errors are also commonly noted for vowels, which may be due to overlooking its phonemic marker or confusion in the phonemic markers representing short and long vowel pairs, some of which differ only in visuo-spatial orientation (e.g. see the representations in Hindi for /ki/ and /kii/ in Table 19.1). Analyses of errors for vowels and the complex akshara also further implicate the role of phonology and the use of analytic strategies rather than mere global akshara recall. Further, diglossia, a phenomenon ubiquitous across India, also influences spelling accuracy and adds another dimension to the debate about phonological versus orthographic influences on spelling ability. For instance, in Bihar speakers of regional dialects tend to not distinguish between the phonemes 'sh' and 's' or between 'dh' and 'r'. As a consequence, the Hindi words written as *shaadi* (marriage) and *padha* (read) are articulated as 'saadi' and 'para'.

Reading comprehension has been much less explored relative to the acquisition of akshara knowledge and decoding. Evidence from Kannada and Gujarati indicates that even prior to gaining complete mastery of the akshara, young learners do read with comprehension (i.e. are able to retrieve factual information) underscoring the importance of a strong lexical repertoire (Nag and Snowling, 2012; Patel, 2004). However, substantial contributions of decoding ability and phonological processing skills are noted even in the middle school years, given the extended phase of akshara learning (Nag and Snowling, 2012).

What, then, does the learning to read process in the akshara languages entail? The research by Nag and colleagues suggests that instruction in the primary grades, beginning first grade onwards, necessitates the acquisition of symbol–sound mappings for the singleton akshara; that is the primary forms of vowels and the consonants with the inherent vowel and subsequently the matrix of consonant-ligatured vowel units. Key learning demands at this stage are the ability to discriminate between phonetically similar symbols (e.g. /s/, /sh/; /n/, /N/ in Hindi and Kannada) and the learning of the wide array of CV units represented in the *barakhadi/ kagunita* matrix. The later emergence of phonemic processing skills suggests that children initially view these singleton akshara as global rather than de-constructable units, most likely because (a) the vowels and the consonants with the inherent vowel cannot be visually deconstructed and (b) instruction for those consonant and vowel units which can be deconstructed tends to centre on the global symbol. However, with increasing exposure to and acquisition of akshara children begin to abstract the embedded phonemic information, and move from being global to analytic users of the akshara. The nature of instruction also facilitates the shift from global to analytic strategies. The evidence suggests that despite the early prominence of the syllable, a phonemic level of abstraction is essential if mastery of the akshara, an extensive set, is to be complete and efficient. Such phonemic abstraction of the complex akshara is especially useful when mismatched phonology-orthography mappings have to be decoded and encoded. Thus, successful reading in the akshara languages entails the use of both large and small grain size units of phonology with the more easily accessible large units, the syllables, being the starting point for the understanding of symbol–sound mapping principles. This suggests that the quality of early orthographic representations is likely to be different from the later orthographic representations; these, in turn, have differing implications for reading and spelling. Lexical bootstrapping ensures, for example, that the task of reading is relatively easier than spelling the same word. Moreover, the ability of young learners to read with comprehension despite the extended period of akshara acquisition suggests the vital role of lexical bootstrapping in scaffolding comprehension. Better comprehenders tend to demonstrate not just better reading accuracy and phonological skills but also higher lexical awareness, vocabulary depth and inflection knowledge. These several lines of research then underscore the importance of language proficiency from the early stages for successful decoding and reading comprehension.

Policy implementation in practice

Literacy instruction: policy, practice and research

The policy mandate for native language instruction is complicated to implement given India's linguistic diversity. Several languages tend to be grouped under a single 'mother tongue'. For instance, for speakers of Rajasthani, Bhojpuri, Maithili and several other languages, Hindi is designated as their 'mother tongue' for schooling (see Figure 19.1). However, children who speak these diverse languages struggle to interact in the Hindi language classroom. A related issue is the presence of regional variations that amounts to a diglossic situation when children have to converse in the standard varieties taught in schools. The complexity of the learning situation is further compounded by the lack of pedagogical strategies to deal with the diverse linguistic profiles in the early years language classroom even though the NCF (2005) states that multilingualism 'must be used as a resource, classroom strategy and a goal by a creative language teacher' (p. 36).

A common refrain noted in policy, practice and research circles for the primary school years is the reliance on prescribed textbooks in mainstream classrooms. Surely, there is nothing wrong with teachers following the mandated curriculum. However, concerns have to do with the sole reliance on a single print resource. Added to this is the use of decontextualized instructional strategies and pace of instruction that is dictated by the curriculum rather than by the diverse learning needs of the children in the classrooms. In the absence of formal assessments in the primary school years textbooks also tend to be used as a metric for progress and as a means to judge teacher performance.

Reading instruction typically begins in the first grade with the learning of symbol–sound mapping for the primary forms of vowels and consonants with the inherent vowel. These

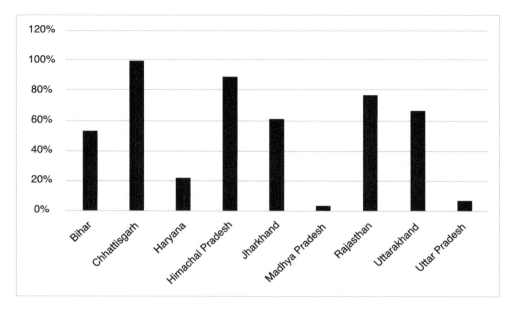

Figure 19.1 Percentage of children from nine Hindi-speaking states whose home language is different from the school language based on rural state-representative samples

Source: ASER, 2011

mappings may also be reinforced via the word association method where children memorize the singleton akshara along with a word that starts with the target akshara, e.g. 'ka' for *kamal/ kamala* (lotus, Hindi/Kannada). Following closely, the consonant with the ligature vowels are taught as syllable strings with a common consonant base and changes in the paired vowel marker, e.g. '*ka, kaa, ki, kii*' (see Table 19.1). Instruction of the phonemic markers may vary with customary practice tending towards global more than analytic strategies; this is an approach evident in the currently prescribed textbooks for the Hindi- and Kannada-speaking states of Bihar and Karnataka as well. Young learners may extract insights about the phonemic markers from visual and aural comparisons of the consonant with vowel ligature units when engaging in rhythmic choral recitations and copy-writing activities. Word formation involves focus on the constituent akshara by de-constructing and re-constructing words. There is consensus that learning to read in traditional mainstream classrooms is a decontextualized, sequential and stage-like process (Bhattacharjea et al., 2011; Dyer, 2008; Jayaram, 2008a, 2008b; Nag, 2007; Patel, 2004). Little or no effort is devoted to ensuring that children can generalize beyond the akshara-word associations or use the symbol–sound mappings in a generative manner. Put differently, although policy mandates (e.g. NCF, 2006) recommend a 'constructivist' approach, in practice teachers tend to employ a transmission model of teaching where students are passive recipients rather than active meaning-makers.

Writing is an important component of the language classroom and is greatly valued by parents and teachers right from the preschool years (Vagh, 2009), perhaps because it is a tangible aspect of literacy acquisition. Some first-grade state textbooks incorporate 'pre-writing' skills such as drawing lines and circles and colouring, but this tends to be a token practice. Writing, in the preschool and primary grade years, mostly occurs in conjunction with learning the symbol–sound mappings and spellings via copy-writing tasks focusing on mechanistic aspects of accurate formation of the akshara and neat handwriting. Homework in the preschool and primary school years also mainly entails copy writing. Moreover, when children engage in expressive writing, the focus is on correct spelling and syntax and less on writing as a mode to express, create and communicate.

Teachers' central role is to oversee the recitation and writing work and the focus in these activities is on correct enunciation, accurate symbol–sound mappings and neat handwriting. Errors in akshara identification or in copy writing or the inability to keep pace with the instruction are addressed through additional practice and at times through peer tutoring. Lesson plans are not the norm and sole reliance on textbooks is ubiquitous (also see Bhattacharjea et al., 2011; Dyer, 2008; Patel, 2004; Saigal, 2012).

Although whole-class instruction is typical, teachers may at times assign copy-writing work differentiated by ability levels. Differentiated teaching is uncommon and individualized instruction is difficult given the large class sizes. The Right to Education Act (2009) mandates one teacher for every 30 children in the primary grade classrooms; however, multi-grade teaching is prevalent. For instance, in 63 per cent of rural schools, grade 2 children were observed sitting with one or more other grades (ASER Centre, 2014). Much variation is noted at the preschool level as well; in a study of 40 preschools for example, class sizes varied from ten to 40 with an average class size of 21 (Vagh, 2009).

In the mainstream primary grade classrooms, few opportunities are provided for oral language development, storytelling, children re-constructing stories, the functional uses of literacy and meaning-making. There is little use of open-ended questions to stimulate expressive language ability or to draw upon children's experiences as a learning resource. It is not at all uncommon to observe children reciting and memorizing standard responses to questions based on reading materials. Comprehension demands also tend to be limited to factual retrieval, and inferential reasoning is not actively encouraged. Despite textbook reforms to incorporate more engaging, contextualized activities centred on meaning-making and requiring the active engagement of learners, instructional practice remains unchanged most likely because teachers fail to transact the essence of these activities in the absence of training that imparts its pedagogical intent (also see Bhattacharjea et al., 2011; Clarke, 2001; Jayaram 2008a).

At the preschool stage as well, despite the policy guidelines, most programmes tend to replicate teaching practices prevalent in primary grade classrooms such as the explicit teaching of the akshara using mechanistic drill work and rote memorization. The reliance on such activities is in part due to absence of adequate professional development for new teachers, a trickledown of primary grade classroom practices and in part due to parental pressure to provide 'school-like' instruction (Muralidharan and Kaul, 1999; Prochner, 2002; Vagh, 2009).

However, within this milieu of traditional practices, some teachers at both the preschool and primary school level have made the shift towards relatively more engaging, contextualized and differentiated instructional strategies, primarily through participation in in-service professional development programmes. Innovations in instructional approaches have mostly been driven by non-government organizations such as Organization for Early Literacy Promotion, Pratham, The Promise Foundation and Vikramshila, often in collaboration with state governments. It is, however, beyond the scope of this chapter to describe and discuss these initiatives.

Assessments

Formal assessments are not the norm in the early years. Policy mandates formative assessments and a no-detention policy up until grade 8. However, in the absence of measurable grade-appropriate competencies, teachers are challenged to make productive use of informal assessments. State-mandated systems like the Continuous and Comprehensive Evaluation (CCE) are seen by teachers as bureaucratic formalities rather than a means to review and revise lesson plans. The reality, then, is that teachers consider the completion of the prescribed syllabus to be the goal irrespective of children's ability to keep pace with the curriculum. Recent national rural assessments indicate dismally low levels of reading, with fewer than 50 per cent of fifth-graders able to accurately decode a second-grade text (ASER, 2014). Such low levels of accomplishment merely exacerbate the learning problem, especially when teachers maintain instructional pace with the curriculum rather than student attainment levels.

Teacher education and professional development

Teacher education for the primary school years is typically a two-year post-higher secondary education certificate course. Although educational reform in the past decade has steered pedagogical practices towards a constructivist approach (NCF, 2005; NCFTE, 2009), and there is a growing body of work about the theory and instruction of literacy acquisition (e.g. Nag, in press), the transfer into practice is minimal and not well formulated. Typically, the prescribed curriculum or textbooks form the basis of training, and emphasis is on the standard language variety. Professional development programmes also follow the transmission model where teacher trainers are seen as the 'experts' and teacher trainees as the 'recipients'. Current pre-service programmes also do not adequately prepare teachers for the contextual realities of mainstream government schools such as low learning-teaching resources, age variation within grades, low preschool participation, multi-grade classrooms, wide heterogeneity in learning levels, diversity in children's linguistic profiles and home supports for learning.

Educational qualifications required for the preschool stage is lower. Typically, for Anganwadi and Balwadi programmes, teachers need to have completed at a minimum between eight to ten years of formal schooling. Recruited teachers then receive pre-service training that varies in duration depending on the organization offering these services as does the opportunity to participate in ongoing professional development programmes.

Literacy resources: home and school

A specific requirement for teachers is to work with children who have little or no exposure to print resources and literacy practices at home even though schooling is highly valued by the family. Some barriers to print access and parent involvement (see Figure 19.2) relate to the low- or no-schooling status of most parents, non-native school instruction, the disconnect between decontextualized school activities and the everyday uses of literacy, and parents' low purchasing power.

Mirroring the situation in the classroom, textbooks are potentially the only child-directed print encountered by children at home. The absence of rich-print resources when learning to read an extensive set of orthographic units doubly contributes to a protracted learning process. This is because it denies children exposure to print materials that can facilitate stable phonology–orthography linkages, provide exposure to diverse akshara and help generate insight into the context-dependent rules of akshara formation. In addition, it denies children the additional benefits of enhanced vocabulary, comprehension and world knowledge. All of this in turn have significant negative consequences for children's ability to keep pace with the curriculum and results in a slowing down of reading attainments.

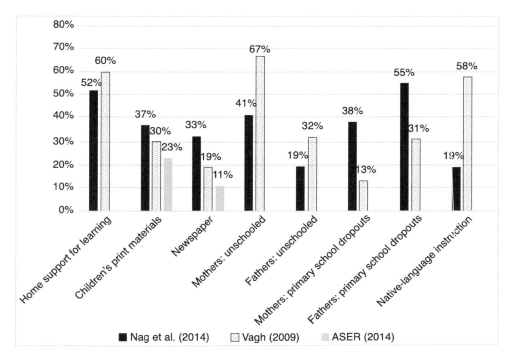

Figure 19.2   Home profiles of children from low-income communities

Sources: Nag et al. (2014) attending public-funded Kannada nursery and primary schools (n = 163);
Vagh (2009) attending Hindi preschools (n = 160); ASER (2014) national rural survey of children
aged 3–16 (no. of households = 341070)

A substantial impediment to the access to authentic and meaningful text has been the
absence of a robust body of accessible children's literature in many Indian languages, despite
the rich literary tradition for adult literature. The past two decades, though, have witnessed
an exponential increase in the availability of low-cost children's literature in Indian languages
by several indigenous and not-for-profit publishing houses. The NCERT publishes some
graded reading materials as well, for example the Barkha series. In recent years, efforts by
non-governmental organizations, in many cases in collaboration with state governments,
have infused the early language classroom with reading materials of many genres and formats
such as story cards, autobiographies, world knowledge books and big and small books, for
example *Bodhi Vriksh Karyakram* (2008) in Bihar and *Chili Pili Cheela* (2007) in Karnataka.

Major challenges for current and future early literacy provisions

The descriptions above of mainstream instructional practices suggest an obvious mismatch
between policy frameworks for early literacy instruction and its implementation. Policy
mandates focusing on oral language proficiency in the early years and a whole language
approach to literacy instruction. However, classroom practices primarily rely on mechanistic
reading and writing activities. Despite textbook reforms being aligned to policy recommendations, there is ineffective inclusion of creative and developmentally appropriate pedagogic
intent into the practice of emerging or established teachers. The ensuing dilution in

curricular transaction is perhaps the most obvious dissonance between policy and classroom practices. While the importance of oral language development is widely acknowledged, its neglect in practice has adverse implications for literacy acquisition. A well-formulated teacher training programme about the pedagogy for reading and writing instruction is also sorely lacking, resulting in an over-reliance on the prescribed curriculum and fall-back on the deeply entrenched mechanistic strategies for the teaching of reading and writing.

A missing link in shaping the policy and practice of literacy development is the evidence generated from robust reading acquisition research in the akshara languages, which can alert practitioners to the distinct learning demands associated with akshara literacy development and set a realistic pace for its acquisition. The evidence calls for a focus on oral language proficiency, access to varied and extensive reading materials, and contextualized teaching strategies. Importantly, the evidence questions the absence of explicit analytic reading instruction strategies and a potential mismatch between intended and actual pace of akshara acquisition. The first major challenge for early literacy provision is in ensuring that oral language proficiency occupies a central role in the early grades, especially given the diversity in children's linguistic profiles. Second, given the poor-print home environments of children attending government schools, it is imperative to increase access and exposure to a variety of reading materials. Third, teachers need to be trained to offer balanced and contextualized literacy instruction. Analytic decoding instruction will make explicit the strategies needed for encoding and decoding complex akshara, thus ensuring that these useful insights are not left to mere incidental learning. Such explicit instruction (not to be confused with the mechanistic approaches of rote learning) have to complement opportunities that value meaning-making and oral and written expression through the reading of diverse texts and creative writing activities. Contextualized instruction would draw upon children's own languages, world knowledge and home culture to enhance oral language proficiency, text comprehension and make explicit the link between formal school activities and literacy use in everyday life. Fourth, given the high prevalence of multi-grade classrooms and wide heterogeneity in student learning levels, teachers have to be effectively trained to capitalize on the opportunity for differentiated teaching via multi-ability lesson planning.

The most recent government initiative 'Padhe Bharat, Badhe Bharat' (MHRD, 2014) aims to address some of these issues by putting the spotlight on the early years. Similar to the national curriculum frameworks it is aligned to a 'constructivist' pedagogy, although it is perhaps the first policy document that formally acknowledges the importance of phonological awareness. However, given the recency of this initiative it remains to be seen how the suggested instructional focus translates into formulating a pedagogy of reading and writing instruction to train teachers and inform classroom practice.

Notes

1 These issues are also applicable to the low-cost private schooling system.
2 Indian schools follow the three-language formula whereby children in non-Hindi-speaking states learn the regional language, Hindi and English, and children in Hindi-speaking states learn Hindi, an Indian language not spoken in their area and English. In practice, however, some states follow a two-language formula, and for some children none of the school languages are their home language.
3 India is a union of 29 states and seven union territories.

References

Annual Status of Education Report (ASER). (2014). New Delhi: ASER Centre.

Annual Status of Education Report (ASER). (2011). New Delhi: ASER Centre.

ASER Centre (2014). Urban ward survey 2014. Retrieved from www.asercentre.org/p/64.html.

Bhattacharjea, S., Wadhwa, S. and Banerji, R. (2011). *Inside Primary Schools: A Study of Teaching and Learning in Rural India*. Mumbai: Pratham Mumbai Education Initiative.

Bodhi Vriksh Karyakram. (2008). *Reading and Books for Young Children in Bihar. Bihar*: Pratham and Bihar Government.

Chili Pili Cheela. (2007). *Kannada Reading Cards*. Bangalore: The Promise Foundation. National Institute of Advanced Studies and Sarva Shiksha Abhiyan (Karnataka).

Clarke, P. (2001). *Teaching and Learning: The Culture of Pedagogy*. New Delhi: Sage Publications.

Devy, G. N. (2014). *People's Survey of India Vol 1: The Being of Bhasha: A General Introduction*. New Delhi: Orient Blackswan.

Dutta, U. and Bala, N. (2012). Teaching of English at primary levels in government schools. New Delhi: National Council of Educational Research and Training and EdCIL (India) Ltd. Retrieved from www.ncert.nic.in/departments/nie/del/publication/pdf/english_primary_level.pdf.

Dyer, C. (2008). Early years literacy in Indian urban schools: Structural, social and pedagogical issues. *Language in Education*, *22*(5), 237–253.

Jayaram, K. (2008a). Early literacy project: Explorations and reflections. Part 1: Theoretical perspectives. *Contemporary Education Dialogue*, *5*(2), 133–174.

Jayaram, K. (2008b). Early literacy project: Explorations and reflections. Part 2: Interventions in Hindi classrooms. *Contemporary Education Dialogue*, *5*(2), 175–211.

Ministry of Human Resource Development: Department of School Education & Literacy (MHRD). (2014). *Padhe Bharat Badhe Bharat: Early Reading and Writing with Comprehension & Early Mathematics Programme*. Government of India: MHRD.

Muralidharan, R. and Kaul, V. (1999). Integrated early childhood development: The Indian experience. In L.E.Eldering and P. P. M.Leseman (eds), *Effective Early Education: Cross-Cultural Perspectives*. New York: Falmer Press.

Nag, S. (2007). Early reading in Kannada: The pace of acquisition of orthographic knowledge and phonemic awareness. *Journal of Research in Reading*, *30*(1), 7–22.

Nag, S. (2013). Akshara-phonology mappings: The common yet uncommon case of the consonant cluster. *Writing Systems Research*, *6*, 105–119.

Nag, S. (in press). Learning to read Kannada and other languages of South Asia. In C. Perfetti and L. Verhoeven (eds), *Reading Acquisition Across Languages and Writing Systems*. Cambridge: Cambridge University Press.

Nag, S., Ramkumar, S., Miranda, R., Sutar, L., Krishna, M., Aravind, S., Kala, B. and Arulmani, G. (2014). Home and school learning environment: Field notes from eight urban, public-funded nursery and primary schools. Working Paper. Bangalore: The Promise Foundation.

Nag, S. and Snowling, M. J. (2011). Cognitive profiles of poor readers of Kannada. *Reading & Writing: An Interdisciplinary Journal*, *24*(6), 657–676.

Nag, S. and Snowling, M. J. (2012). Reading in an alphasyllabary: Implications for a language-universal theory of learning to read. *Scientific Studies of Reading*, *16*(5), 404–423.

Nag, S., Snowling, M. J., Quinlan, P. and Hulme, C. (2014). Child and symbol factors in learning to read a visually complex writing system. *Scientific Studies of Reading*, *18*(5), 309–324.

Nag, S., Treiman, R. and Snowling, M. J. (2010). Learning to spell in an alphasyllabary: The case of Kannada. *Writing Systems Research*, *1*(2), 1–12.

National Council for Educational Research and Training (NCERT). (2006). The National Focus Group on Teaching of Indian Languages: Position paper. New Delhi: NCERT.

National Council of Educational Research and Training (2006). National focus group on early childhood education. National Council of Educational Research and Training, New Delhi. Retrieved from www.ncert.nic.in/html/pdf/schoolcurriculum/position_papers/early_childhood_education.pdf.

National Curriculum Framework (NCF). (2005). New Delhi: National Council for Educational Research and Training.

National Curriculum Framework for Teacher Education (NCFTE). (2009). *Towards Preparing Professional and Humane Teacher*. New Delhi: National Council for Teacher Education.

Patel, P. G. (2004). *Reading Acquisition in India: Models of Learning and Dyslexia*. New Delhi: Sage Publishers.

Prochner, L. (2002). Preschool and playway in India. *Childhood*, 9(4), 435–453.

Saigal, A. (2012). Demonstrating a situated learning approach for in-service teacher education in rural India: The Quality Education Programme in Rajasthan. *Teaching and Teacher Education, 28*, 1009–1017.

Salomon, R. (2000). Typological observations on the Indic Script Group and its relationship to other alphasyllabaries. *Studies on the Linguistic Sciences, 30*(1), 87–103.

Sircar, S. and Nag, S. (2013). Akshara-syllable mappings in Bengali: A language-specific skill for reading. In H. Winskell and P. Padakanayya (eds), *South and South-East Asian Psycholinguistics* (pp. 202–211). Cambridge: Cambridge University Press.

Tiwari, S., Nair, R. and Krishnan, G. (2011). A preliminary investigation of akshara knowledge in the Malayalam alphasyllabary: Extension of Nag's (2007) study. *Writing Systems Research, 3*(2), 145–151.

Vagh, S. B. (2009). *Learning at Home and at School: A Longitudinal Study of Hindi Language and Emergent Literacy Skills of Young Children from Low-Income Families in India*. Unpublished doctoral dissertation, Harvard Graduate School of Education, Massachusetts.

Vaid, J. and Gupta, A. (2002).Exploring word recognition in a semi-alphabetic script: The case of Devanagari. *Brain and Language, 81*, 679–690.

PART III

Research findings and future directions

The final third of this volume focuses on various aspects of literacy scaffolding that can enrich young children's learning. There is a long and exciting tradition of literacy researchers adapting traditional reading and writing activities in ways that optimize them. Results of typical storybook reading, word recognition and writing activities have all been refined in ways informed by past research interventions. This collection of chapters highlights such traditions, bringing in examples from different cultures to emphasize the variability of such approaches and their appropriateness to many places around the world.

In parallel to theoretical models of literacy learning and debates about the extent to which such models are universal or specific to a particular activity, context, script or region, consumers of research and reviews of literacy studies also seek practical ideas about how to improve children's literacy learning. What can parents do? What can teachers do? How can adults help children to learn to read and write efficiently, both for typically developing children and also for those who might have a particular learning difficulty that makes literacy learning more arduous?

The thematically defined chapters in Part III address critical issues in current research, many of which have already been touched upon in Parts I and II. These chapters outline research-endorsed practices designed to support early reading and writing skills, with examples drawn from home, school and community contexts. A number of the chapters offer evidence of literacy-focused interventions targeting the specific skills required to become a proficient reader and writer, such as phonological sensitivity, vocabulary and narrative skills. Other chapters consider how specific language practices might foster the development of such skills in children. More specifically, there is an interest in how vocabulary skills are supported in shared book reading and narrative skills in drama-based interventions or in discussions with parents and teachers. The common perspective underlying all this research is that the quality of the verbal interaction children participate in impacts their reading and writing by supporting their oral language learning. Although schools constitute an important context for learning to read and write in most countries around the world, the chapters in this section remind us that children's literacy skills are also fostered by the informal learning opportunities offered in everyday encounters in non-school settings. Finally, several chapters examine interventions that target specific populations, such as children with language learning difficulties, thus extending the information available in Part II about early literacy provision for children in need of special care and research attention in various regions around the world.

Deborah Wells Rowe begins this section by focusing on writing, including invented spelling, name writing and broader writing of connected text. Rowe highlights the value of collaborative writing between adults and children and shows how, when caregivers scaffold the writing of children, children's writing and sometimes their reading skills tend to improve. From the sociocultural perspective, fostering an ethos of writing in the classroom and at home, with an understanding that writing is a communicative activity, is beneficial for children. At the same time, a focus on individual word writing can sometimes be useful as well. When children make use of their phonological skills to analyse the sequence of sounds in words, they make an important transition in the writing process over time.

Ulla Richardson and Lea Nieminen highlight the importance of phonological sensitivity for alphabetic language word recognition in their chapter. When children are able to break words down into smaller segments, including syllables, rimes and phonemes, this facilitates their word reading. Mapping speech sounds on to individual letters or other segments (sometimes called grain sizes, Ziegler and Goswami, 2005) such as rimes (ough, eigh, ign) is a key task in learning to read in many alphabetic languages. The authors highlight cross-cultural evidence for this and then introduce GraphoGame, an important tool accessible via cell phone (mobile technology) or computer, which has been used across several languages to teach and reinforce understanding of the connection between speech sounds and graphemes in children.

Monique Sénéchal highlights all the ways in which shared book reading is helpful for children, and one way in which it is not (facilitating word recognition in text). Sénéchal specifies the conditions under which shared book reading is most effective and explains why. The review shows that, for example, there are more studies demonstrating that shared book reading improves breadth of vocabulary knowledge than depth of vocabulary knowledge, though results are promising in both aspects. It is also interesting to note that shared book reading has been demonstrated to be effective in stimulating children's vocabulary development in a range of linguistic and social environments worldwide.

The theme of vocabulary development is further pursued in Vibeke Grøver's chapter, with a detailed examination of the optimal conditions for children's vocabulary learning. Though children may learn new words from mere exposure inside or outside of book reading, vocabulary instruction is most efficient if words are embedded in a meaningful and engaging discourse, in which children are invited to participate to identify their meaning and use them for the purpose of communication.

The chapter by Wendy Mages considers how to support narrative skills through drama-based interventions. The author focuses on four different ways to encourage children's story-telling and other narrative skills. Such skills can be either in oral or written form and are often facilitated in the context of formal educational settings. Wages' summary of literature shows that while some interventions can be used effectively with children aged three to six years, many more, particularly those focused on writing skills, extend to primary/elementary school-aged children.

Allyssa McCabe's chapter explores narratives in younger children, with a particular focus on how children reflect on and represent their own personal stories. Children's narratives appear to be enhanced by the input that parents and sometimes teachers give via in-depth discussions about their lives. Narrative practice facilitates a progressive development of children's own story-telling skills. Such patterns are similar across cultures, though the styles of narratives can differ substantially. For example, Japanese children show a preference producing their narratives in sets of three stanzas and Chinese and Taiwanese children downplay evaluation when they tell stories – patterns that are different from European and US children.

The importance of narratives is further highlighted in the next chapter by Kathy Short, Maria Acevedo, Dorea Kleker and Lauren Pangle. These authors put forward the concept of 'storying' and specify the many ways in which it is beneficial for children's learning. For instance, through storying, children can make sense of their own lives, introduce their own experiences and vocabulary, and learn from one another. Drawing on the funds of knowledge perspective (Gonzalez et al., 2005) and using the narrative inquiry methodology, Short and colleagues outline how children's engagement in storying in the classroom can provide authentic opportunities for communicating their ideas to peers and adults.

In the following chapter, K. S. Richard Wong presents an overview of various types of literacy-related interventions that are helpful for stimulating early oral language skills. The focus in this chapter is on different possible sources of intervention for young children. Dialogic reading, one type of shared book reading, is highlighted, as are some effective classroom-based programmes (e.g. Opening the World of Learning). Some of these interventions can work well with children with language difficulties, either when such children are supported individually or in classroom settings. Many variables can, of course, influence how the interventions are related to child outcomes, including the nature of such difficulties (particularly receptive vs. expressive vocabulary), children's motivation and previous experiences of success or failure, and techniques used for interventions by parents, teachers and clinicians. Overall, the data show that there is reason for considerable optimism about the effectiveness of classroom interventions for children's oral language skills.

While most of the chapters in this section deal with literacy in the child's first language, the chapter by Jim Anderson, Ann Anderson and Harini Rajagopal brings to the fore the need for programmes that would acknowledge and promote bilingual family literacy. Many of the ideas discussed in previous chapters, including scaffolding of writing, phonological awareness and oral language skills development through shared book reading, are revisited in this chapter, with a focus on the ways in which families can support their children with literacy skills in both a first and a second language (where the second language is English). Results of such programmes have been relatively promising. Interestingly, in some studies, a stronger focus on first language skills also seems to transfer to English as a second language.

Victoria Purcell-Gates extends the Anderson et al. chapter by highlighting more precisely the role of parents in promoting literacy at home. While acknowledging big differences in cultural perspectives around the world, Purcell-Gates focuses on how various kinds of shared reading materials can stimulate children to understand the role of literacy in their world. Beyond this, parents lay the foundation for children's broad learning, word recognition and narrative skills with many varied interactions with their children. All together, these resources and practices contribute, as Purcell-Gates writes in her chapter, to the 'patterned ways that reading and writing are used within the home as a type of culture'.

Taken together, this section of the handbook broadens and deepens our view of literacy development, with a rich collection of strongly argued and evidence-based research papers. Literacy learning means many things to many people, and these chapters reflect the various ways in which literacy is researched and conceptualized by leading researchers in the field. We are fortunate to have these complementary summaries as frameworks for both the theoretical and practical aspects of literacy learning around the world. Cultural and linguistic factors may influence the precise ways in which these are implemented (for example, invented spelling is likely not as useful or fruitful in young Chinese children as in children learning an alphabetic orthography), but overall these reviews are applicable globally. This collection of chapters thus highlights the importance of learning and teaching both for oral and printed word recognition and for broader comprehension and composition skills in language and in print.

References

González, N., Moll, L. and Amanti, C. (2005). *Funds of Knowledge: Theorizing Practices in Households, Communities, and Classrooms*. New York: Erlbaum.

Ziegler, J. C. and Goswami, U. (2005). Reading acquisition, developmental dyslexia, and skilled reading across languages: a psycholinguistic grain size theory. *Psychological Bulletin, 131*(1), 3–29.

20

THE VALUE OF WRITING IN EARLY CHILDHOOD

Deborah Wells Rowe

This chapter reviews research describing what children learn through early writing experiences from birth to age six. Component skills studies show that writing words using invented spelling is positively related to reading sub-skills (e.g. phonological awareness and alphabet knowledge), and to later independent reading, writing and spelling. Writing longer texts requires children to orchestrate transcription skills such as handwriting and invented spelling, and is also related to children's developing oral language skills. Sociocultural research shows that children begin building foundational understandings about writing by age two. Play provides important opportunities, motivation and shared contexts for writing. Across the preschool years, children form and test progressively more sophisticated hypotheses about writing processes and genre features. Through emergent writing, children form identities as writers, metacognitively reflect on writing processes and text features, and learn about the social uses of print. Although empirical research builds a strong case for the importance of writing in early childhood, many preschoolers have few opportunities to compose their own texts using emergent writing. I argue that the dissemination of research-based information on early writing development and supportive preschool writing contexts should be given high priority in educational efforts directed at parents, caregivers and teachers of young children.

The value of writing in early childhood

Today, researchers and educators have access to almost a half century of research describing young children's explorations of writing in alphabetic languages. Beginning in the 1970s, seminal work conducted from an emergent literacy perspective (e.g. Harste et al., 1984; Teale and Sulzby, 1986) established that, very early in life, children in literate societies begin to learn about writing through informal observation and playful participation in writing events with caregivers and peers. An extensive body of research supports the notion that preschoolers' unconventional 'scribbles' are not random, but, instead, are organized by the child's developing hypotheses about print. Further, research supports the contention that early writing experiences are an important venue for children's construction of understandings about print uses in social situations.

My goal in this chapter is to review contemporary research for evidence describing what children learn through early writing experiences from birth to age six. While acknowledging foundational twentieth-century research, I primarily focus on studies of young children's writing in alphabetic languages published between 2000 and the present. Given space limitations, I have further narrowed my focus to studies of children learning to write in one language. Readers are directed to other sources (e.g. Reyes, 2012) for reviews of research on emergent bi-literacy. First, I review research exploring the component skills making up young children's early writing performances and their concurrent and longitudinal relationships to reading and writing. Then, I follow the sociocultural turn to review studies exploring what young children learn as they compose their own messages in home, community and classroom events, and how their writing is shaped by the sociocultural practices in which writing is embedded.

The state of early writing instruction in the United States

Despite researchers' almost universal agreement that young children build foundational understandings about print through their early explorations of writing, this research has had less impact than might be expected in the USA. Several recent studies (Gerde et al., 2015; Zhang et al., 2015) conducted in US preschools have shown that while children have access to writing materials, relatively little time is devoted to writing. Teacher scaffolding of children's writing occurs infrequently and typically involves low-level supports such as reminding children to put their names on their papers or writing letters for children to copy. Teacher modelling most often occurs without explicit explanations of writing processes.

Researchers have hypothesized several possible causes for this research–practice disconnect. One possibility is that the emphasis on beginning reading in curricular materials and US education policy may have pushed writing to the margins of curricular priorities. Another possibility is that some early childhood teachers may lack knowledge about emergent literacy processes and the kinds of teaching strategies that support early writing (Gerde et al., 2015). Whatever the reason for past practice, US policy-makers have recently foregrounded writing as central to college and career readiness (National Governors Association Center for Best Practices and the Council of Chief State School Officers, 2010). However, despite this new attention to writing in elementary and secondary classrooms, preschool writing remains largely unaddressed.

Writing development in early childhood

What does writing look like in early childhood? Which kinds of unconventional marks count as writing? Answers to these questions are foundational to any appraisal of the importance of writing experiences in early childhood. Contemporary researchers have suggested that emergent literacy 'involves the skills, knowledge, and attitudes that are developmental precursors to conventional forms of reading and writing' (Connor et al., 2006: 689). Collectively, emergent literacy research has challenged the notion that conventional handwriting and spelling are the watershed criteria for identifying the beginnings of writing. Instead, Goodman (1986) has defined reading and writing as 'human interaction with print when the reader and writer believe that they are making sense of and through written language' (p. 6). From this perspective, researchers view young children's unconventional scribbles as the beginnings of writing as well as windows on children's current understandings of print.

Contemporary research has documented both developmental progressions and variation in children's writing and the understandings it reveals. Puranik and Lonigan's (2011) study of three- to five-year-olds' writing supported the contention that children first learn universal features of writing characteristic of all alphabetic languages such as linearity and segmentation and then later construct understandings of language-specific features such as directional patterns and the shapes of symbols. Many studies of writing in alphabetic languages have described a general progression in the forms children use for writing, moving from undifferentiated scribbles toward more conventional forms that approximate alphabet letters (e.g. Sulzby, 1985). In a recent study, Rowe and Wilson (2015) confirmed earlier work showing that children move from global to more specific and conventional understandings of writing forms, directional patterns, message content and speech–print matching. Findings also confirmed previous work showing age-related variability as well as differences in trajectories that included temporary 'regressions' from more to less sophisticated writing forms.

Contemporary studies of early childhood writing build on an extensive research base describing the major waypoints, patterns of variability and expected directions of travel along some common developmental paths for writing forms, directionality, intentionality and message content. This research is important because it establishes that, during the preschool years, writing serves as a venue for children's construction and testing of hypotheses about print processes and social uses.

Component skills research

Researchers working from psychological perspectives have often adopted a simple view of writing (Juel, 2006) that holds that written language involves transcribing spoken language into print, and that writing development occurs in a bottom-up fashion with transcription skills such as handwriting and spelling supporting later development of ideational and discourse processes. Since, in this model, low-level transcription skills are assumed to precede and free up attentional resources for high-level processes such as planning content (Berninger et al., 2002), considerable attention has been devoted to understanding the skills young children need to spell and write words. An important line of early writing research has used a component skills approach to study the contributions of cognitive and linguistic skills (e.g. phonological awareness, letter identification, receptive or expressive vocabulary) and foundational literacy knowledge (e.g. concepts about print, letter names) to children's early writing and reading. This research has most often measured children's language and literacy skills outside the writing act and then studied their concurrent or longitudinal relationship to a carefully controlled writing or reading performance, usually name writing, writing letters, spelling dictated words, or standard decoding and comprehension tasks. Only a few studies have examined the predictive relations between component skills and children's writing of longer texts. This research has modelled hypothesized relationships between component sub-skills and young children's writing (as indexed by word writing). Below, I review contemporary studies from this line of work, focusing on the value of engaging children in writing experiences in the years between birth and age seven.

Home-based writing

Contemporary research has confirmed and extended our understanding of the importance of writing in early childhood by exploring the predictive relations between children's home writing experiences and literacy outcomes. For example, working in the United Kingdom,

Dunsmuir and Blatchford (2004) found that the amount of home writing at age five was one of several home background variables correlated with writing at school entry and remained the only home background variable with a statistically significant relationship to writing at age seven.

Component skills studies have also explored the nature and longitudinal effects of parental support for writing in early childhood. Two kinds of parental support during writing were positively related to later measures of children's spelling, comprehension, decoding and phonological awareness: grapho-phonemic supports (inventing spellings by segmenting words and applying letter–sound correspondence) and print supports (handwriting support for forming letters) (Aram and Levin, 2004; Skibbe et al., 2013).

Overall, contemporary research shows children, whose parents engaged them in rich writing events (i.e. events where parents helped children invent spellings by explaining orthographic principles as they segmented words into sounds, used letter–sound correspondence to select letters and then helped children gain independence in necessary handwriting skills), had better skills in segmenting and blending sounds, reading words, comprehending what they read and inventing spellings for words when measured one to two years later. These relationships appear to hold for both younger and older preschoolers in the three- to five-year-old age range, and across several different alphabetic languages.

Name writing

Puranik and Lonigan (2011) have pointed out that a large proportion of existing work on early writing has focused on children's name writing. Name writing is of great personal importance to children. The given name is often the first word a child learns to write. Name writing provides initial opportunities for print learning, as evidenced by research showing that children's pre-phonological spellings often rely heavily on name letters to spell other words (Treiman et al., 2001). Additionally, name writing is significantly related to letter knowledge (e.g. Bloodgood, 1999). However, contemporary research also shows that children may approach name writing differently from other words (e.g. Puranik and Lonigan, 2012). Children may learn their names as a well-practised string, while using strategies such as letter–sound correspondence to spell other words (Levin and Ehri, 2009). As a result, name writing is frequently more conventional than the child's writing of other words and messages (Levin et al., 2005). Overall, contemporary research suggests that while name writing is associated with emergent literacy skills and can provide authentic opportunities for print learning, children may approach the task of writing their names differently than writing other words and messages.

Word writing and invented spelling

Researchers have also conducted studies of the predictive relationships between young children's word writing (using invented spelling) and literacy sub-skills including phonological awareness, letter knowledge, handwriting, word reading and oral language skills. Most research studying connections between word writing and invented spelling has been conducted with four- and five-year-olds who have initial levels of conventional alphabet knowledge and are beginning to explore letter–sound relationships.

Results are consistent in finding a bidirectional, predictive relationship between children's phonological awareness and their ability to invent spellings for words dictated to them by researchers. Phonological awareness has been found to make a unique and significant contribution to children's ability to invent spellings for words (e.g. Puranik et al., 2011) and children's level of writing predicts their phonological awareness scores (Vernon et al., 2004). Letter writing and alphabet knowledge also have been shown to make unique and significant contributions to children's word-writing scores (Puranik et al., 2011)

To further explore the causal relations between these component skills and word writing, and to test scaffolding approaches that might have practical significance for instruction, researchers have conducted experimental studies comparing different ways of engaging children in writing words using inventing spelling. Recent studies found that the most effective manner of supporting invented spelling included: adult scaffolding of phoneme segmentation, use of letter–sound knowledge and letter writing along with additional context-specific explanations of the alphabetic principle (Levin and Aram, 2013) or feedback on the target words' conventional spellings (Ouellette and Sénéchal, 2008).

These findings are consistent with outcomes of the US National Early Literacy Panel's (NELP) (National Early Literacy Panel, 2008) meta-analysis aimed at determining which preschool skills and abilities predict later reading, writing and spelling in grade one and beyond. Results showed that writing/name writing was one of six variables consistently identified as a moderate predictor of children's later decoding, reading comprehension and spelling. As in the studies reviewed here, phonological awareness and alphabet knowledge were also shown to be moderate predicators of later spelling (word writing). Finally, measures of spelling and invented spelling in kindergarten or earlier were strong predictors of both decoding and spelling measured in grade one and beyond.

Overall, both contemporary studies and the NELP meta-analysis support the conclusion that writing experiences that support four- and five-year-olds in inventing spellings for words and draw children's attention to the ways letters represent sounds lead to better performance on code-focused writing/reading measures. Children who have opportunities to explore how the print system works in the context of writing appear to be connecting key literacy sub-skills related to beginning reading.

Text writing

Though research framed by the simple view of writing (Juel, 2006) acknowledges that writing involves both generating and encoding messages, only a few studies conducted from a component skills perspective have required young children to generate their own messages or to compose texts longer than a word. Two related studies (Kim et al., 2011; Puranik and AlOtaiba, 2012) have examined the component skills that contribute to kindergarteners' ability to write longer texts – in this case, a personal narrative about children's kindergarten experiences. Consistent with findings for older students (Graham et al., 2000), these studies found that mastery of transcription skills was an important ingredient in writing development. At the end of kindergarten, the number of words and ideas children included in their texts was related to their ability to write letters fluently and to spell words. Kim and colleagues (2011) found that oral language measures were also uniquely related to end-of-kindergarten writing of personal narratives. This finding suggests that oral language skills are foundational for writing connected texts because children must generate ideas and express them with language, as well as focus on encoding messages in print.

Comparing contributions of early writing and storybook reading

Given these findings, researchers have been interested in comparing the outcomes of preschoolers' joint writing experiences with those provided by adult–child storybook reading

– the preschool literacy activity most frequently recommended to caregivers and early childhood teachers (e.g. US Department of Education, 2003) and discussed in more detail in this volume by Monique Sénéchal.

Aram and Biron (2004) directly compared literacy outcomes of preschool instruction focused on either joint reading or joint writing, with a control group receiving the usual preschool instruction. Both the reading and writing intervention groups made significant progress on receptive vocabulary and listening comprehension, with no significant differences between groups. However, the joint writing group outperformed the reading and control groups on word reading, word writing, letter knowledge, phonological awareness and orthographic awareness.

Overall, research suggests that early childhood experiences focusing on the grapho-phonemic code in the context of writing meaningful words can have beneficial effects on both writing and vocabulary knowledge. Writing is a multidimensional activity that includes both meaning- and code-focused processes that require children to consider the context of writing, the meaning to be represented and how to encode the message with print. Contemporary research suggests that when children engage with adults in joint writing for meaningful purposes, their learning opportunities are extended beyond those available in shared book reading.

Conclusions: component skills and early childhood writing

Contemporary studies conducted from a component skills perspective have focused on identifying the skills young children use as they write, and on predictive relationships between preschool writing experiences and later reading and writing. The research reviewed above supports the following conclusions about the importance of writing in early childhood:

1   Writing at home with parental support for invented spelling and letter writing is related to positive reading and writing outcomes when children enter school.
2   Name writing, one of the most common early childhood writing activities, is related to key literacy sub-skills, but also appears to be learned differently from children's composing of other messages. Name writing may not be a good indicator of children's strategies for composing their own messages.
3   Writing words using invented spelling is an opportunity to connect key literacy sub-skills (e.g. phonological awareness, alphabet knowledge) that are positively related to later writing, and to beginning reading.
4   Writing longer spans of connected text (phrases, sentences and paragraphs) requires children to orchestrate transcription skills such as letter writing and invented spelling, but is also related to children's developing oral language skills such as vocabulary.
5   Shared writing with adults presents opportunities for learning that complement and extend other early literacy activities, such as shared book reading.

Sociocultural studies

In the sections that follow, I review contemporary research conducted from sociocultural perspectives to further address the question of what children can learn through early explorations of writing. Researchers studying the beginnings of writing from sociocultural perspectives (e.g. Dyson, 2003; Gee, 2003) have assumed that learning to write not only involves encoding print on the page, but also learning how to participate with others in local literacy events. Participation in writing events requires young children to take up writing roles and employ socio-cognitive writing processes (e.g. idea generation, encoding, revision) appropriate for accomplishing local literacy practices. Learning to write is shaped by the social interactions, linguistic resources, cultural materials, roles and identities available in the everyday events in which children participate as writers.

Studies conducted from these perspectives have often used qualitative methods to record early writing interactions in authentic contexts where children interact with others as they write their own messages. Rather than keeping the context for writing in the background, researchers have examined the ways that children's writing is shaped by the wide variety of local literacy practices in which children participate. Themes emerging from this research are described next.

Foundational understandings about writing

While most studies of early writing have been conducted with older preschoolers, a few researchers have focused on describing foundational understanding that one- to three-year-olds form in their initial explorations of writing. These studies (Lancaster, 2007; Rowe, 2008a) have shown that beginning writers learn intentionality (i.e. understanding that marks represent linguistic messages) over time as adults draw their attention to their marks and negotiate how they can be read. Children in this age group also learn other foundational 'social contracts', about the material features of texts and expected relations between people and texts (Rowe, 2008b).

Summing up, contemporary research suggests that children begin to learn foundational ideas about writing as they interact with adults around their texts. Adults demonstrate socially valued message types and ways of using texts in these interactions, and guide children's participation as writers. In the contexts observed to date, most of this teaching occurred implicitly as part of ongoing interaction and many of the foundational principles were so taken for granted by adults that they were not conscious targets for instruction (Rowe, 2008a). In these early writing interactions, children learn social contracts for participating as writers that are not taught as part of formal instruction.

Writing forms and processes

Contemporary studies confirm earlier work showing that, as children write their own messages, they construct personal hypotheses about print forms and conventions (Whitmore et al., 2004). Rowe and Wilson's (2015) cross-sectional and longitudinal analyses have shown that two- to five-year-olds' writing forms, directional patterns, message content and speech/print matching become progressively more conventional over time.

Researchers have also observed the beginnings of important writing processes such as idea generation, genre organization and revision in preschoolers' writing. Ray and Glover (2008) report that three- and four-year-olds displayed emergent forms of these key writing processes as they chose topics, developed their messages, used narrative or information genre features, and revised their texts by adding, moving or removing information. Similarly, Kissel and colleagues (2011) found that four-year-olds revised their work to respond to audience interests.

Overall, contemporary research confirms that when children have opportunities to compose their own texts and to use them for social purposes, they form and test progressively more sophisticated hypotheses about print forms and conventions. They also begin to learn about key writing processes including topic selection, idea generation, genre-specific text organization and revision.

Metacognitive awareness

Research suggests that children become consciously aware of both writing processes and meanings as they engage in writing (Dyson, 2003). Jacobs (2004) found that kindergarteners' metacognition about writing grew with more experience. Ghiso (2010) reported that children's writing provided teachers and children with a meaningful context for explicit discussion of writing features such as genre, structure, revision, grammar and conventions. Overall, research suggests that as children talk about their writing, they have meaningful opportunities to metacognitively reflect on the writing processes, genre structures and language used in their texts.

Writing purposes and associated genres

When young children write in their classrooms and homes, they participate in literacy events that are as diverse as those settings. Through participation in local writing events, young children begin to construct knowledge of the social uses and textual genres associated with home and school literacy practices. Developmental research on children's writing of information reports and stories (Donovan and Smolkin, 2002) has shown that children construct emergent understandings of expository and narrative text structures. Children's stories and information reports become more developed and conventional with experience and instruction. Recent work by Ghiso (2013) has shown that the genre-related structure of children's texts also depends on the degree to which adults encourage young writers to structure their texts around conventional frames. Overall, contemporary research extends and confirms seminal work (e.g. Harste et al., 1984) showing that, through writing, young children construct knowledge about the organizational structures, lexical choices and social purposes associated with different genres.

Writing and play

For many contemporary researchers, play is no longer seen as a context for writing, but instead as a part of the process of 'doing' writing. Wohlwend (2008), for example, has argued that play is a powerful form of multimodal meaning making – a form of literacy in its own right. Lysaker et al. (2010) found that five- and six-year-olds spontaneously used playful ways of participating in writing activities including singing and chanting, expressions of strong emotion, pretend play and fantasy. They concluded that connecting school writing with play created an energized and personally meaningful environment that sustained children's writing, provided authentic reasons for revision, and valued imagination and pretending as ways of learning and knowing.

Overall, contemporary research suggests that playful approaches to writing may be especially important for preschoolers. For this age group, play can provide opportunities, motivation and a shared context for writing. Children appear to use play as means of linking school writing activities to their personal experiences, and as an arena for trying out ways of using writing to accomplish social goals.

Culturally and personally relevant writing

A number of researchers have studied writing activities designed to publicly value the out-of-school experiences of children from culturally and linguistically diverse backgrounds and encourage them to use their cultural knowledge and heritage languages as resources for school writing. For example, Rowe and Miller (2016) invited four-year-olds to use digital cameras to take their own photos in home and community spaces, and then to use touchscreen tablets to write texts to accompany the photos. Results showed that children were able to use emergent writing on the tablet's touchscreen to create captions for their photos, and then to use the tablet's audio-recording tool to record dual-language narrations for their e-books. Children's use of both their languages increased when family and community members helped record multilingual demonstration books including all the children's languages.

In another study, Martínez-Álvarez and her colleagues (2012) invited six-year-old Spanish–English emergent bilinguals to take cameras home and then to write stories and comics based on the photos using both page-based and digital tools. Results showed that children who participated in composing activities grounded in their own experiences outperformed a control group on end-of-year measures of text length, text complexity and richness of imagery. Student interviews indicated that children valued opportunities to include their family and community experiences in their school writing, and analysis of their texts showed that they portrayed aspects of their personal and cultural identities.

Though these studies explicitly invited children to create texts that foregrounded their home and community experiences, Dyson (2003) has shown that six-year-olds draw on home and community funds of knowledge regardless of the writing topic. Dyson's research shows that young writers use recontextualization processes to select and remix textual material from both inside and outside school.

Overall, contemporary research has shown that young children from culturally and linguistically diverse backgrounds showed high levels of engagement, improved language and writing, and increased self-esteem when they had opportunities to integrate family stories and community experiences into their schoolwork (Bernhard et al., 2006). Researchers have concluded that activities that explicitly valued children's cultural experiences supported their participation as writers. However, research has also shown that children necessarily draw on and recontextualize cultural resources during writing, even when the writing activity does not overtly foreground home and community experiences.

Identity

For young children, participating in writing also involves important identity work. Adults play an important role in fostering children's literate identities when they talk to them as if they were writers and name their unconventional marks as writing (Rowe, 2008a). Kissel and colleagues (2011) found that when four-year-olds were recognized for specific writing skills such as map-making, the children adjusted their writing practices to maintain and further develop their identities as writers.

Writing is also an arena where children develop their personal identities. Like older authors, children construct a composing voice (Dyson, 2010) that reflects their cultural experiences and personal interests. Compton-Lilly (2006) found that children's literate identities were intimately connected to race, culture and gender. Children used writing as a means of constructing their affiliations with peers around popular culture and media interests that reflected their gendered and cultural identities.

Overall, contemporary research shows that, as children write, they have opportunities to form identities as the kinds of persons who can use writing for academic and social purposes. Children develop a writing voice that reflects their cultural, racial and gendered experiences, and use their literate identities to mediate their interactions with others.

Conclusions: sociocultural studies

Contemporary studies conducted from sociocultural perspectives have focused on describing what young children are learning about writing through social participation in local literacy events. Research supports the following conclusions about the importance of writing in early childhood:

1   As early as age two, children construct understandings about writing that are rarely taught directly, but are foundational for their participation as writers.
2   Through participation in writing events, children form and test progressively more sophisticated hypotheses about writing processes such as idea generation, encoding processes and revision.
3   Writing can encourage metacognitive reflection on writing processes and text features.
4   Children learn about social purposes for writing and construct emergent understandings of the genre features.
5   Play provides opportunities, motivation and shared contexts for writing. In play, children link school writing to personal and peer culture experiences, and try out writing roles and processes in a low-risk environment.
6   Children do important identity work as they engage as writers.
7   Children learn to re-contextualize culturally and personally meaningful content in their writing. Culturally relevant writing experiences foster high levels of engagement and motivation, as well as positive self-esteem.

Making the case for writing in early childhood

My goal in this chapter has been to provide empirical answers to basic questions about the value of engaging preschoolers in writing. Despite differences in research focus, theoretical framing, methodology, writing measures and writing activities, contemporary research converges on one conclusion: writing can provide powerful opportunities for literacy learning in early childhood. When children have opportunities to compose their own messages and when their emergent writing attempts are valued and supported, they begin forming foundational knowledge about writing processes and the use of writing as a mode of social discourse (Tolchinksy, 2015).

Research shows that children are careful observers of the world around them, and for many, print is a visible and important part of the environment. When they have access to writing tools, and are invited to participate as writers, they put their considerable skills as learners to work in noticing what writing looks like, how it is used to get things done in the world and what kinds of written messages they are likely to encounter in different places and social situations. In other words, 'scribbling' is important. It serves as a test bench for literacy learning. Emergent writing is the way children test out their current ideas about writing.

Writing provides an authentic opportunity for preschoolers to integrate what they are being taught about print (e.g. letter names and shapes, how to write their name) with their own observations. Through writing, preschoolers begin to construct their own understandings of print processes such as speech–print match, phoneme segmentation and letter–sound correspondence. Research shows that such early experiences with writing build a strong foundation for success in learning to read.

When children write as participants in authentic, meaningful activities, they not only learn about the technical aspects of encoding spoken words in print, but also how writing is used in social situations. As children begin to playfully take up their roles as writers in everyday experiences at home and school, they come to see themselves as writers. Both seminal and contemporary research show that, for young children, writing and play are linked. Children experiment with writing as part of dramatic play and participate in writing events playfully. In early childhood, play provides a meaningful context for children's explorations of writing.

Though these empirical findings build a strong case for the importance of early childhood writing experiences, many preschoolers have few opportunities to compose their own texts using emergent forms of writing. It is not uncommon for US preschools (Gerde et al., 2015; Pelatti et al., 2014; Zhang et al., 2015) to limit young children's writing to copying alphabet letters and writing their names. This disconnect between research and educational practice is a practical problem that deserves attention from researchers, curriculum developers and policy-makers. The dissemination of research-based information on early writing development and supportive preschool writing contexts should be given high priority in educational efforts directed at parents, caregivers and teachers of young children.

References

Aram, D. and Biron, S. (2004). Joint storybook reading and joint writing interventions among low SES preschoolers: Differential contributions to early literacy. *Early Childhood Research Quarterly*, *19*, 588–610.

Aram, D. and Levin, I. (2004). The role of maternal mediation of writing to kindergarteners in promoting literacy in school: A longitudinal perspective. *Reading & Writing: An Interdisciplinary Journal*, *17*(4), 387–409.

Bernhard, J. K., Cummins, J., Campoy, F. I., Ada, A. F., Winsler, A. and Bleiker, C. (2006). Identity texts and literacy development among preschool English language learners: Enhancing learning opportunities for children at risk for learning disabilities. *Teachers College Record*, *108*(11), 2280–2405.

Berninger, V. W., Vaughn, K., Abbott, R. D., Begay, K., Coleman, K. B., Curtin, G. and Graham, S. (2002). Teaching spelling and composition alone and together: Implications for the simple view of writing. *Journal of Educational Psychology*, *94*(2), 291–304.

Bloodgood, J. (1999). What's in a name? Children's name writing and name acquisition. *Reading Research Quarterly*, *34*, 342–367.

Compton-Lilly, C. (2006). Identity, childhood culture, and literacy learning: A case study. *Journal of Early Childhood Literacy*, *6*(1), 57–76.

Connor, C. M., Morrison, F. J. and Slominski, L. (2006). Preschool instruction and children's emergent literacy growth. *Journal of Educational Psychology*, *98*(4), 665–689.

Donovan, C. A. and Smolkin, L. B. (2002). Children's genre knowledge: An examination of K-5 students' performance on multiple tasks providing different levels of scaffolding. *Reading Research Quarterly*, *37*(4), 428–465.

Dunsmuir, S. and Blatchford, P. (2004). Predictors of writing competence in 4- to 7-year-old children. *British Journal of Educational Psychology*, *74*, 461–483.

Dyson, A. (2003). *The Brothers and Sisters Learn to Write. Popular Literacies and School Cultures*. New York: Teachers College Press.

Dyson, A. (2010). Writing childhoods under construction: Re-visioning 'copying' in early childhood. *Journal of Early Childhood Literacy, 10*(1), 7–31.

Gee, J. P. (2003). A sociocultural perspective on early literacy development. In S. B. Neuman and D. Dickinson (eds), *Handbook of Early Literacy Research* (pp. 30–42). New York: Guilford Press.

Gerde, H. K., Bingham, G. E. and Pendergast, M. L. (2015). Reliability and validity of the Writing Resources and Interactions in Teaching Environments (WRITE) for preschool classrooms. *Early Childhood Research Quarterly, 31*, 34–46.

Ghiso, M. P. (2010). Peer and teacher talk in a first-grade writing community: Constructing multiple possibilities for authorship. In R. T. Jiménez, V. J. Risko, M. K. Hundley and D. W. Rowe (eds), *59th Yearbook of the National Reading Conference* (pp. 382–394). Oak Creek, WI: National Reading Conference.

Ghiso, M. P. (2013). Playing with/through non-fiction texts: Young children authoring their relationships with history. *Journal of Early Childhood Literacy, 13*(1), 26–51. doi:10.1177/1468798411430093.

Graham, S., Harris, K. R. and Fink, B. (2000). Is handwriting causally related to learning to write? Treatment of handwriting problems in beginning writers. *Journal of Educational Psychology, 92*(4), 620–633.

Harste, J. C., Woodward, V. A. and Burke, C. L. (1984). *Language Stories and Literacy Lessons.* Portsmouth, NH: Heinemann.

Jacobs, G. M. (2004). A classroom investigation of the growth of metacognitie awareness in kindergarten children through the writing process. *Early Childhood Education Journal, 32*(1), 17–23.

Juel, C. (2006). The impact of early school experiences on initial reading. In D. K. Dickinson and S. B. Neuman (eds), *Handbook of Early Literacy Research* (pp. 410–426). New York: Guilford Press.

Kim, Y.-S., AlOtaiba, S., Puranik, C. S., Folsom, J. S., Greulich, L. and Wagner, R. K. (2011). Componential skills of beginning writing: An exploratory study. *Learning and Individual Differences, 21*, 517–525.

Kissel, B., Hansen, J., Tower, H. and Lawrence, J. (2011). The influential interactions of pre-kindergarten writers. *Journal of Early Childhood Literacy, 11*(4), 425–452. doi:10.1177/1468798411416580.

Lancaster, L. (2007). Representing the ways of the world: How children under three start to use syntax in graphic signs. *Journal of Early Childhood Literacy, 7*(3), 123–154.

Levin, I. and Aram, D. (2013). Promoting early literacy via practicing invented spelling: A comparison of different mediation routines. *Reading Research Quarterly, 48*(3), 221–236.

Levin, I., Both-DeVries, A., Aram, D. and Bus, A. G. (2005). Writing starts with own name writing: From scribbling to conventional spelling in Israeli and Dutch children. *Applied Psycholinguistics, 26*, 463–477.

Levin, I. and Ehri, L. C. (2009). Young children's ability to read and spell their own and classmates' names: The role of letter knowledge. *Scientific Studies of Reading, 13*(3), 249–273.

Lysaker, J., Wheat, J. and Benson, E. (2010). Children's spontaneous play in writer's workshop. *Journal of Early Childhood Literacy, 10*(2), 209–229.

Martínez-Álvarez, P., Ghiso, M. P. and Martínez, I. (2012). Creative literacies and learning with Latino emergent bilinguals. *LEARNing Landscapes, 6*(1), 273–298.

National Early Literacy Panel. (2008). *Developing Early Literacy. Report of the National Early Literacy Panel. A Scientific Synthesis of Early Literacy Development and Implications for Intervention.* Jessup, MD: National Institute for Literacy.

National Governors Association Center for Best Practices and the Council of Chief State School Officers. (2010). *Common Core State Standards for English Language Arts & Literacy in History/Social Studies, Science, and Technical Subjects.* Washington, DC: National Governors Association Center for Best Practices and the Council of Chief State School Officers.

Ouellette, G. and Sénéchal, M. (2008). Pathways to literacy: A study of invented spelling and its role in learning to read. *Child Development, 79*(4), 899–913.

Pelatti, C. Y., Piasta, S. B., Justice, L. M. and O'Connell, A. (2014). Language and literacy learning opportunities in early childhood classrooms: Children's typical experiences and within-classroom variability. *Early Childhood Research Quarterly, 29*(4), 445–456. doi:http://dx.doi.org/10.1016/j.ecresq.2014.05.004.

Puranik, C. S. and AlOtaiba, S. (2012). Examining the contribution of handwriting and spelling to written expression in kindergarten children. *Reading & Writing: An International Journal, 25*, 1523–1546.

Puranik, C. S. and Lonigan, C. J. (2011). From scribbles to scrabble: Preschool children's developing knowledge of written language. *Reading and Writing: An Interdisciplinary Journal, 24*(5), 567–589.

Puranik, C. S. and Lonigan, C. J. (2012). Name-writing proficiency, not name length is associated with preschool children's emergent literacy skills. *Early Childhood Research Quarterly, 27*, 284–294.

Puranik, C. S., Lonigan, C. J. and Kim, Y.-S. (2011). Contributions of emergent literacy skills to name writing, letter writing, and spelling in preschool children. *Early Childhood Research Quarterly, 26*, 465–474.

Ray, K. W. and Glover, M. (2008). *Already Ready: Nurturing Writers in Preschool and Kindergarten.* Portsmouth, NH: Heinemann.

Reyes, I. (2012). Biliteracy among children and youths. *Reading Research Quarterly, 47*(3), 307–327.

Rowe, D. W. (2008a). The social construction of intentionality: Two-year-olds' and adults' participation at a preschool writing center. *Research in the Teaching of English, 42*(4), 387–434.

Rowe, D. W. (2008b). Social contracts for writing: Negotiating shared understandings about text in the preschool years. *Reading Research Quarterly, 43*(1), 66–95.

Rowe, D. W. and Miller, M. E. (2016). Designing for diverse classrooms: Using iPads and digital cameras to compose eBooks with emergent bilingual/biliterate four year olds. *Journal of Early Childhood Literacy, 16*(4), 425–472. doi:10.1177/1468798415593622.

Rowe, D. W. and Wilson, S. (2015). The development of a descriptive measure of early childhood writing: Results from the Write Start! Writing Assessment. *Journal of Literacy Research, 47*(2), 245–292.

Skibbe, L. E., Bindman, S. W., Hindman, A. H., Aram, D. and Morrison, F. J. (2013). Longitudinal relations between parental writing support and preschoolers' language and literacy skills. *Reading Research Quarterly, 48*(4), 387–401.

Sulzby, E. (1985). Kindergarteners as writers and readers. In M. Farr (ed.), *Advances in Writing Research: Children's Early Writing* (Vol. 1, pp. 127–200). Norwood, NJ: Ablex.

Teale, W. and Sulzby, E. (1986). Introduction. Emergent literacy as a perspective for examining how young children become writers and readers. In W. Teale and E. Sulzby (eds), *Emergent Literacy* (pp. vii–xxv). Norwood, NJ: Ablex.

Tolchinksy, L. (2015). From text to language and back: The emergence of written language. In C. A. MacArthur, S. Graham and J. Fitzgerald (eds), *Handbook of Writing Research* (2nd edn). New York: Guilford.

Treiman, R., Kessler, B. and Bourassa, D. (2001). Children's own names influence their spelling. *Applied Psycholinguistics, 22*, 555–570.

U.S. Department of Education. (2003). *Reading Tips for Parents.* Washington, DC: U.S. Department of Education.

Vernon, S., Calderón, G. and Castro, L. (2004). The relationship between phonological awareness and writing in Spanish-speaking kindergarteners. *Written Language and Literacy, 7*(1), 101–118.

Whitmore, K. F., Martens, P., Goodman, Y. and Owocki, G. (2004). Critical lessons from the transactional perspective on early literacy research. *Journal of Early Childhood Literacy, 4*(3), 291–325.

Wohlwend, K. (2008). Play as a literacy of possibilities: Expanding meanings in practices, materials, and spaces. *Language Arts, 86*(2), 127–136.

Zhang, C., Hur, J., Diamond, K. E. and Powell, D. (2015). Classroom writing environments and children's early writing skills: An observational study in Head Start classrooms. *Early Childhood Education Journal, 43*(4), 307–315. doi:10.1007/s10643-014-0655-4.

21

THE CONTRIBUTIONS
AND LIMITS OF PHONOLOGICAL
AWARENESS IN LEARNING
TO READ

Ulla Richardson and Lea Nieminen

In this chapter, we describe the role of phonological awareness in learning to read and how it varies in different alphabetic orthographies. We provide an overview of the concept of phonological awareness and how it is typically assessed while pointing out the contributions as well as the limitations connected to phonological awareness in learning to read. In addition, we provide a practical example in which phonological awareness plays a role by presenting evidence of the effectiveness of an instructional method in which the relationship between the phonology and orthography of a particular target language is taken into account in designing an instructional digital training tool for learners of varying skill levels. Taken together, the evidence points towards a significant predictive power of phonological awareness in reading skills in alphabetic orthographies. This facilitates important early identification of children at risk for reading difficulties and thus provides the basis for targeted treatment in which phonological awareness plays a role. However, the degree of importance of phonological awareness seems to be highly dependent on the type of connection spoken language has to its written language form.

At the time children start to learn to read, they already have effortlessly become masters in using spoken language for communication. However, to master written language as well, a conscious effort is needed when trying to understand what written symbols stand for and how a written system relates to familiar, naturally acquired spoken language. In practice, this means that a child needs someone to show that written strings of symbols can be meaningful. Typically, attention is also paid to smaller meaningless units such as single letters in alphabetic orthographies. Working from meaningless units toward meaningful expressions is a new type of exercise altogether in learners' communication. When doing this, learners start attending to phonology, the underlying abstract sound system of their spoken language in order to learn how this system on the one hand relates to phonetics, the actual produced spoken language sounds, and, on the other hand, to the symbols used in writing. This process takes time and effort but typically children learn the basics of decoding within only a few months or sometimes up to several years depending on the nature of the target language and its relationship to its orthography.

The role of phonological processing, including phonological awareness in learning to read, has been shown to play a critical part in the process (e.g., Brady & Shankweiler, 2013). Poor phonological awareness detectable for example in an inability to segment words into smaller units is reflected in poor reading and writing skills. This finding particularly at the early stages of learning to read and write has been shown in many studies although mainly in connection with the English language and orthography. In this chapter, we describe the role of phonological awareness in learning to read in different alphabetic orthographies. At first, as an essential background, we will look into the nature and development of phonological awareness.

Phonological awareness

According to Gombért (e.g. 1992), metaphonological development (phonological awareness) can be considered to be a part of both metalinguistic and metacognitive development. The first signs of the ability to discriminate sounds are present already very early in a child's life. However, only discrimination of linguistic sounds is the first step of metaphonological development and this comes only with the experience with linguistic elements in the child's environment. If the child is able to distinguish between two linguistic sounds, for example *jail* vs. *whale*, it does not yet mean that the phonological difference between the initial sounds has been consciously identified by the child. However, this unconscious behaviour is a prerequisite for developing a conscious skill of identifying sounds.

Gombért (1992) describes how metaphonological identification occurs in several different phonological units. Syllabic identification refers to the ability, for example, to tap according to syllables within words. To do this a child needs to be able to break down a meaningful word into meaningless but natural, relatively easily distinguishable linguistic units, which are syllables. Another easily distinguishable and large meaningless phonological unit is a rhyme unit. Rhyme identification entails understanding that the ends of the words sound the same as for example in the words *l-ight* and *k-ite*.

In learning to identify smaller phonological units, single speech sounds, a child needs to learn to further analyse spoken words to perceive the smallest meaningless parts they are made of. Speech sounds are very short, and, partly due to coarticulation, difficult to perceive and segment. On top of that they are difficult to pronounce on their own in comparison to larger units such as syllables and rhymes, which provide even fewer possibilities to make these sounds less abstract and more explicit. Thus, cognitively, individual speech sounds' phonological identification is a demanding task. Apart from basic sensory abilities such as hearing, a child needs to be able to retrieve from his or her lexicon[1] items that both resemble and differ slightly, and start inferring what parts and properties could be considered as integral parts of spoken language that are associated with meaning in a way that by using these particular units they can affect the meaning of a word. However, it should be noted here that even very young infants can detect small differences between speech sounds while around six to nine months of age infants start to pay attention only to those features that are linguistically relevant for their native language environment (e.g., Kuhl et al., 1992; Richardson et al., 2003; Werker and Tees, 1984) and this ability is reflected in their speech production as well. This type of natural phonological development does not necessarily imply, however, that children would be able to consciously identify small speech elements without specific cognitive effort.

After distinguishing speech sounds from other sounds, and distinguishing speech sounds from one another and developing the ability to count and identify them, the third step in the development of phonological awareness is to gain control over the phonological information of the language. This metaphonological control includes, for example, the ability to intentionally manipulate syllables and sounds. In practice this means that a child is able to change the order of sounds or syllables in a word, or delete and add them. The easiest task is to delete the final or initial syllable or sound, whereas manipulating the medial units is much more demanding and requires a high degree of conscious control (Gombért, 1992). It should be noted that the development of phonological awareness to different sizes of perceptual segments of speech is the same in different types of languages with first the bigger units such as syllables and rhymes being more salient and readily available to children before they start to be aware of single phonemes (Ziegler and Goswami, 2005). Also being able to perceive bigger units in words facilitates access to smaller units when noticing similarities and differences (*s-ack tr-ack b-ack*).

The abilities to discriminate, identify and manipulate phonological information correspond to what is generally called phonological awareness or sometimes phonological sensitivity. It is this awareness that has been said to be one of the most important prerequisites of learning to read and the main difficulty associated with dyslexia, a specific developmental difficulty in learning to read. However, there is not a clear consensus on whether phonological awareness is really a prerequisite or a by-product or a consequence of learning to read. For example, it has been shown that reading improves phonological awareness greatly and that this relationship is at least reciprocal instead of uni-directional (e.g., Perfetti et al., 1987).

It is not possible to get direct information on children's phonological awareness skills, and therefore researchers have designed several types of tasks in an effort to find out what children are able to understand of the phonological form of their native language. Phonological awareness has typically been assessed with tasks in which children need to either auditorily perceive, deduce and decide on the similarity or difference of speech units or to identify stimuli. Moreover, different manipulation skills are required in order to perform successfully in the tasks designed to measure phonological awareness. Sound deletion or replacements of single sounds, syllables or rhymes are typically included in the tasks. The tasks require children to remember the single items or sometimes a string of words, and thus, they also place demands on both short-term and working memory capacity. Typically the focus in the tasks is most often limited to the quality of different size speech segments per se rather than suprasegmental features such as linguistic stress, pitch or phonotactics.

The kind of demanding cognitive exercise that is needed in phonological awareness tasks is not necessary at all for using spoken language and probably does not interest children before they start to learn to read. It is likely that only after being explicitly instructed that, for example, a particular letter is associated most often with a particular sound, children start more or less consciously analysing where this sound occurs in their spoken language. To facilitate the discovery of the connection between written and spoken language, teachers often use both visual and auditory examples to demonstrate the connection such as 'This is the letter *d* and it stands for the sound [d] as in the word *dog*'. This kind of an explicit demonstration works well if the name of the letter and the sound associated with the letter are consistently used and represented, as is the case in more transparent orthographies.

With more opaque orthographies the task is much more complex if only phoneme and grapheme size units are used at the beginning of instruction. Phonemes are not represented consistently at all by single letters and vice versa but more often a more consistently represented connection is between larger units such as is the case with rime[2] units in the English language. Next we will look in more detail at the role of phonological awareness in different alphabetic orthographies.

The role of phonological awareness in learning to read languages with an alphabetic orthography

The modern writing systems can be divided into three basic categories according to what kind of a linguistic unit each written symbol represents. Two of the systems, alphabetical and syllabary, are based on phonemes and syllables respectively, which are phonological and meaningless speech units, but the third one, the logographic system, has its correspondents in morphemes or whole words which both convey meanings. The alphabetical writing system is the most common system in the Western world. It is a system where a relatively small set of written symbols, that is letters of an alphabet, in principle represent individual sounds of the target language. Not all alphabetic orthographies use the same script, the system of written symbols. For example this text, just like texts in the majority of European languages, is written in Latin script, but if this was translated into Russian or Greek the script would change to Cyrillic or Greek script respectively.

The number of phonemes in different languages varies a lot and so does the number of letters used in writing the languages. For example, Rotokas, one of the languages spoken in Papua New Guinea, has only 11 different phonemes and it is written with a set of 12 letters: A E G I K O P R S T U V, with both S and T referring to the phoneme /t/ but in different word positions. In contrast, in English, there is a set of 26 letters corresponding to as many as 44 different phonemes. If Rotokas or English had adopted a syllabic writing system, the number of symbols used in writing would be remarkably larger because there are always many more different syllables than different sounds in languages. When comparing Rotokas with 12 letters and English with 26 letters to the logographic writing system of Chinese with 60,000 characters, we can see that there are 5000 times more symbols to memorize in Chinese than in Rotokas and approximately 2300 times more symbols than in English.

Generally speaking, the fewer symbols there are, the easier they are to learn and remember. However, having fewer symbols is not just an advantage: it also means that the system is more abstract. Namely, in logographic systems the counterpart of a symbol is a meaningful unit but in alphabetic systems the counterparts are meaningless sounds or sound combinations. In addition, classification of sounds is not necessarily easy because in a spoken language, sounds are always co-articulated with other sounds. This creates small differences that the writer must recognize and know precisely where the boundary of two different sounds is and which letter to use accordingly (Treiman and Kessler, 2005).

Each language applying an alphabetic writing system does it differently; in other words they have different orthography, spelling rules. Seymour et al. (2003) have investigated how different European orthographies can be placed on a continuum from transparent (shallow) to opaque (deep) orthography. A simple and ideal transparent orthography has a consistent one-to-one relationship between sounds and letters: the same letter always in all word contexts corresponds to the same sound and vice versa. The description almost perfectly suits the Finnish orthography which is said to be one of the most transparent orthographies in the world. The consistent correspondence from spelling to reading and vice versa makes the connection highly explicit, thus facilitating learners' understanding of the phonemic structure of the language.

On the other end of the continuum there are languages in which the relationship between sounds and written symbols is inconsistent and not straightforward. English is a good example of this since the same sound may be written in several different ways (e.g. phoneme *f* in the words *fish*, *enough* and ***philosophy***) and the same letter may refer to different sounds (e.g. the letter *a* in the words *man*, *make*, *car* and *walk*). Thus, English learners need more exposure to different words, their morphology as well as phonology, to learn how the small set of letters or letter strings represents a much larger number of sounds. Most alphabetic orthographies fall somewhere between these two extremes. The rule of thumb is that the more opaque the orthography is, the longer it takes to learn to read it because of all the inconsistencies and irregularities it has.

In alphabetic orthographies the role of phonological awareness in reading development has been at the centre of investigations for over 30 years now. Many investigations have reported a close connection between phonological awareness and reading skills especially around the time when children learn to read (e.g. Adams, 1990; Goswami and Bryant, 1990; Griffin et al., 1998). Similar findings have also been shown even several years before children start to learn to read (Puolakanaho et al., 2007). A majority of these investigations have been conducted in learners of English. Regardless of the types of assessment tasks, the evidence shows that phonological awareness skills predict reading skills in English and have a significant impact on reading and writing accuracy during the first years of school. Apart from the language limitation, these studies typically focus on phoneme awareness (phonemic awareness) possibly partly due to the rather simplistic idea that just understanding that letters represent speech sounds is sufficient in learning to read for all learners in different types of languages.

Learning the alphabet in English either with the letter names or corresponding letter sounds is not enough to be able to read and write in English. This is due to the non-transparent orthography of English on a grapheme–phoneme level. The fact that virtually none of the English phonemes are represented consistently in all word contexts with the very same letter(s) or vice versa shatters the illusion that just by mastering letter–sound connections, learners would know how to decode or spell all words in English. Due to this inconsistent nature of phoneme–grapheme connections, it takes rather a long time and experience with written English to discover the most frequently and consistently behaving letter strings to learn to read and write accurately. Investigations by Seymour and his colleagues (2003) showed that in highly irregular orthographies such as English it takes up to two years to reach the same decoding level that can be reached in only one or two months in a highly consistent orthographies such as Finnish. In written English, especially vowel sounds are represented in a way that makes it absolutely necessary to look at the larger contexts such as the rime unit in which the letter exists. The connection between rime units to speech sounds is more consistent than that of single letters (see, e.g., Goswami, 2002). Also syllable structures in English are complex which adds to the challenges of auditorily detecting different elements within the complex structures. Therefore, learners need to pay attention to longer letter strings, but importantly also to the morphological, sometimes also syntactic and semantic context in order to accurately realize connections between written and spoken language units in English.

The inconsistencies between spoken and written English are due to the discrepancy of the forms of modern spoken English with the forms and rules of the English orthography that have remained static over hundreds of years while spoken language has been influenced by French and other languages and gone through sound changes (see, e.g., Crystal, 2012). Thus, written English does not comply with the simple alphabetic principle. English learners who have poor phonological sensitivity to start with are guided to written language with the help of the letter–sound connections to crack the alphabetic code but these basic tools do not reveal the connection between written and spoken languages in most cases. This means that at first struggling learners in effect need to learn that spoken language has small units such as phonemes and these can be represented by written letters. After this, by trying to apply these tools they need to discover that they actually must learn how to disregard them in many aspects in order to learn to decode English words. Therefore, learning to read in English for struggling learners is doubly difficult.

In more transparent alphabetic orthographies, by learning the alphabetic principle with a relatively small set of letters, children can quickly learn to decode and spell any words in their language without previously being exposed to them. However, the predictive value of phonological awareness tasks is high regarding early reading skills even in languages with transparent orthographies. In a cross-linguistic study by Ziegler et al. (2010) the specific question regarding the importance of phonological awareness in different types of orthographies was investigated. They found that in both the more transparent and less transparent alphabetic orthographies included in the study (Finnish, Hungarian, Dutch, Portuguese and French) phonological awareness had a significant impact on developing reading skills (Ziegler et al., 2010). There are also studies that do not support this finding. For example Georgiou et al. (2008) showed that children's performance in phonological awareness tasks did not correlate with their reading skills in Greek.

In languages with transparent alphabetic orthographies the straightforward system where learning what speech sound each letter stands for seems to be enough to guide even the most struggling learners to decode words accurately, although the decoding process might be painstakingly slow. This implies that already at the time children have learned the letter sounds, they will be able to perform accurately in tasks that measure phonological awareness. Therefore, the correlation and prediction power of phonological awareness tasks diminish in these types of languages after children have learned the connections of the letters to speech sounds used in the language. If a child already knows the alphabetic principle this may help her/him to count and identify sounds, especially in transparent orthographies where counting and identifying sounds is closely related to the task of counting and identifying the letters in a word. In fact, the effect of reading skills on performance in phonological awareness tasks has been shown in several studies. Ziegler et al. (2004) showed that adult readers are significantly slower to decide whether words such as *pain* and *lane* rhyme due to the knowledge that they are spelled differently whereas preliterate children do not have such problems. Similarly, Goswami et al. (2005) showed that preliterate German and English speaking children are as good at rhyme judgements with phonologically similar word structures since their performance relies solely on auditory perception, but once they start to learn to read, German children's performance surpasses that of English at rhyme judgements due to the consistent spelling patterns of German. Therefore, when children have learnt the basics of reading skills in transparent orthographies, other types of skill assessment tasks, such as rapid automatized naming tasks, become more powerful in predicting reading skills' level. Also the level of decoding skill is measured more meaningfully with the time spent in a reading task rather than accuracy.

Utilizing phonological awareness skills and the role of orthography in an effective reading method: the case of GraphoGame

As phonological awareness skills seem to have an impact on early stages of reading either directly or indirectly, reading instructions and programmes typically include some level of training with phonological aspects of the target language. One such programme is the digital learning environment, GraphoGame, developed within a multidisciplinary research and development team in Finland at the University of Jyväskylä and the local non-governmental organization the Niilo Mäki Institute, specializing in learning disabilities (see more on

GraphoGame, e.g. Heikkilä et al., 2013; Lyytinen et al., 2007; Richardson and Lyytinen, 2014; Saine et al., 2011).

The GraphoGame training method provides training with the basic building blocks of the target language in a game like environment in which learners' task is to connect spoken language units to the corresponding written language units. Importantly, the nature of the target language and its orthography is taken into account in the design of the method. Since the method aims to help specifically struggling learners, specific attention is paid to the quality of spoken language units presented in the game. The idea is that since learners need to listen to the speech sounds (single sounds to words and sentences) many times during gaming, this provides an opportunity to improve their phonological representations, since one of the prevailing theories is that poor readers have poor or fuzzy phonological representations (e.g. Elbro et al., 1998). In addition, by constantly having learners connect speech sounds with their corresponding written units (i.e. auditory–visual stimuli paring), the method makes the connection concrete and explicit, and therefore it facilitates the understanding of the phonological system and how the system is represented in written language. Another central feature of the method is that with each target language, the specific connection of written language units to spoken language units is utilized so that the most consistent and frequently occurring written units are presented with their corresponding spoken language units. For example, in English, the most consistently used written units in terms of the corresponding speech sounds are not single letters as is the case with transparent orthographies, but instead longer letter strings. For example, rime units are used, and the rime units are presented first to facilitate learning of the connection between written and spoken language units (Kyle et al., 2013). The game environment provides a good platform for intensive training, since it provides plenty of repetition in short time periods especially for those who need more training. The game adjusts its level of difficulty according to each player's skills so that it is sufficiently challenging without being too difficult or easy (see Richardson and Lyytinen, 2014).

The GraphoGame method has been developed for several different languages. Since the method is evidence based, the impact of each language version is investigated in controlled intervention studies. The evidence on the positive effects of training with the method is encouraging. So far, the game has been developed already for over 20 languages, including languages such as Finnish, Greek, Spanish, German, French, English, Kiswahili and Chinese using both Pinyin (Mainland China) and Zhu-Yin-Fu-Hao (Taiwan). A short version of the character game for Mandarin Chinese has also been developed. In all of the game versions, the effect of training is evident even after very short intervention periods of approximately 5–11 hours within 6–12 weeks. For instance, the results of the intervention study conducted with the English GraphoGame based on rime units showed that after only a 12-week intervention period with a total of 11 hours[3] of training with GraphoGame, children's word-reading skills improved by 0.69 standard scores per hour (Kyle et al., 2013), a clear indication of effective reading intervention (cf. Torgersen et al., 2001). Brain studies conducted in Switzerland with six- to seven-year-old kindergarten children playing German GraphoGame revealed significant changes in brain activation showing emerging print sensitivity after training merely three to four hours within six weeks (Brem et al., 2010). Thus, this method in which specific features of each spoken language and its orthography are carefully taken into consideration in an individually adaptive training environment seems to be an efficient way to enhance learning even for struggling learners. This can be taken as proof that it is essential to focus on both learners' spoken language skills, particular the phonology, as well as on the relationship of orthography to spoken language, in order to support children's reading development efficiently.

Summary

In sum, it seems that phonological awareness has a significant impact on developing reading skills especially in alphabetic writing systems. The impact merely diminishes or strengthens due to the specific characteristics of the language and orthography children are learning. The limitations of phonological awareness and its power for explaining learning or struggling in learning, however, might emerge particularly when logographic orthographies are concerned. However, regardless of the writing system, it is quite clear that teaching methods should take into account the important role of spoken language in learning to read together with the relationship it has with its orthography. The numerous studies on phonological awareness in developing reading skills clearly show the importance of assessing phonological awareness skills early in development since the predictive power of phonological awareness for detecting reading difficulties is significant in most orthographies. In turn, information on poor phonological awareness skills enables targeted early treatment that will help both in improving phonological awareness and reading skills at the same time, at least in alphabetic languages.

Notes

1 A lexicon refers here to the knowledge or mental database that a native speaker has about his or her own native language in terms of words and phrases, including meaning and usage but also form.
2 The term rime refers to a spelling pattern rather than just the phonological segments within a syllable from the vowel sound onwards to the end of the syllable (vowel sounds constitute the nucleus of a rhyme unit and the following consonants at the end of the syllable constitute the coda part of the rhyme unit).
3 GraphoGame training was done in short periods (10–15 minutes) at a time, typically once a day per school day.

References

Adams, M. J. (1990). Beginning to read: Learning and thinking about print. Cambridge, MA: MIT Press.

Brady, S. A. and Shankweiler, D. P. (2013). *Phonological Processes in Literacy: A Tribute to Isabelle Y. Liberman*. New York: Routledge.

Brem, S., Bach, S., Kucian, K., Kujala, J. V., Guttorm, T. K., Martin, E. et al. (2010). Brain sensitivity to print emerges when children learn letter–speech sound correspondences. *Proceedings of the National Academy of Sciences*, 107(17), 7939–7944.

Crystal, D. (2012). *Spell It Out: The Singular Story of English Spelling*. London: Profile Books.

Elbro, C., Borstrøm, I. and Petersen, D. K. (1998). Predicting dyslexia from kindergarten: The importance of distinctness of phonological representations of lexical items. *Reading Research Quarterly*, 33(1), 36–60.

Georgiou, G. K., Parrila, R. and Papadopoulos, T. C. (2008). Predictors of word decoding and reading fluency across languages varying in orthographic consistency. *Journal of Educational Psychology*, 100(3), 566–580.

Gombért, J. É. (1992). *Metalinguistic Development*. Translated by Tim Pownall. Hemel Hempstead: Harvester Wheatsheaf.

Goswami, U. (2002). In the beginning was the rhyme? A reflection on Hulme, Hatcher, Nation, Brown, Adams, and Stuart. *Journal of Experimental Child Psychology*, 82(1), 47–57.

Goswami, U. C. and Bryant, P. (1990). *Phonological Skills and Learning to Read*. Hove: Psychology Press.

Goswami, U., Ziegler, J. C. and Richardson, U. (2005). The effects of spelling consistency on phonological awareness: A comparison of English and German. *Journal of Experimental Child Psychology*, 92(4), 345–365.

Griffin, P., Burns, M. S. and Snow, C. E. (eds). (1998). *Preventing Reading Difficulties in Young Children*. Washington, DC: National Academies Press.

Heikkilä, R., Aro, M., Närhi, V., Westerholm, J. and Ahonen, T. (2013). Does training in syllable recognition improve reading speed? A computer-based trial with poor readers from second and third grade. *Scientific Studies of Reading*, *17*(6), 398–414.

Kuhl, P. K., Williams, K. A., Lacerda, F., Stevens, K. N. and Lindblom, B. (1992). Linguistic experience alters phonetic perception in infants by 6 months of age. *Science*, *255*(5044), 606–608.

Kyle, F., Kujala, J., Richardson, U., Lyytinen, H. and Goswami, U. (2013). Assessing the effectiveness of two theoretically motivated computer-assisted reading interventions in the United Kingdom: GG Rime and GG Phoneme. *Reading Research Quarterly*, *48*(1), 61–76.

Lyytinen, H., Ronimus, M., Alanko, A., Poikkeus, A. M. and Taanila, M. (2007). Early identification of dyslexia and the use of computer game-based practice to support reading acquisition. *Nordic Psychology*, *59*(2), 109–126.

Perfetti, C. A., Beck, I., Bell, L. and Hughes, C. (1987). Phonemic knowledge and learning to read are reciprocal: A longitudinal study. *Merrill-Palmer Quarterly*, *33*, 283–319.

Puolakanaho, A., Ahonen, T., Aro, M., Eklund, K., Leppänen, P. H., Poikkeus, A. M. et al. (2007). Very early phonological and language skills: estimating individual risk of reading disability. *Journal of Child Psychology and Psychiatry*, *48*(9), 923–931.

Richardson, U., Leppänen, P. H., Leiwo, M. and Lyytinen, H. (2003). Speech perception of infants with high familial risk for dyslexia differ at the age of 6 months. *Developmental Neuropsychology*, *23*(3), 385–397.

Richardson, U. and Lyytinen, H. (2014). The GraphoGame method: the theoretical and methodological background of the technology-enhanced learning environment for learning to read. *Human Technology: An Interdisciplinary Journal on Humans in ICT Environments*, *10*(1), 39–60.

Saine, N. L., Lerkkanen, M. K., Ahonen, T., Tolvanen, A. and Lyytinen, H. (2011). Computer-assisted remedial reading intervention for school beginners at risk for reading disability. *Child Development*, *82*(3), 1013–1028.

Seymour, P. H. K., Aro, M. and Erskine, J. (2003). Foundation literacy acquisition in European orthographies. *British Journal of Psychology*, *94*, 143–174.

Torgesen, J. K., Alexander, A. W., Wagner, R. K., Rashotte, C. A., Voeller, K. K. and Conway, T. (2001). Intensive remedial instruction for children with severe reading disabilities immediate and long-term outcomes from two instructional approaches. *Journal of Learning Disabilities*, *34*(1), 33–58.

Treiman, R. and Kessler, B. (2005). Writing systems and spelling development. In M. J. Snowling and C. Hulme (eds), *The Science of Reading: A Handbook* (pp. 120–134). Malden, MA: Blackwell.

Werker, J. F. and Tees, R. C. (1984). Cross-language speech perception: Evidence for perceptual reorganization during the first year of life. *Infant Behavior and Development*, *7*(1), 49–63.

Ziegler, J. C., Bertrand, D., Tóth, D., Csépe, V., Reis, A., Faísca, L. et al. (2010). Orthographic depth and its impact on universal predictors of reading a cross-language investigation. *Psychological Science*, *21*(4), 551–559.

Ziegler, J. C., Ferrand, L. and Montant, M. (2004). Visual phonology: The effects of orthographic consistency on different auditory word recognition tasks. *Memory and Cognition*, *32*(5), 732–741.

Ziegler, J. C. and Goswami, U. (2005). Reading acquisition, developmental dyslexia, and skilled reading across languages: A psycholinguistic grain size theory. *Psychological Bulletin*, *131*(1), 3–29.

22

SHARED BOOK READING

An informal literacy activity par excellence

Monique Sénéchal

Parents read books to their young children for the enjoyment and quality time it provides. During storybook reading, however, young children can also learn. In this chapter, the research reviewed showed that young children's oral language is enhanced: (1) when they participate in multiple readings of books rather than a single reading; (2) when they are actively involved rather than listening passively to the book rendition; (3) and that different types of active involvement affect differently how children learn to comprehend, to produce and to describe novel words. In contrast to these positive effects of book reading on young children's oral language, a synthesis of nine studies showed that shared reading was not a source of early literacy learning (e.g. alphabet knowledge) for young children. Rather than improving early literacy per se, perhaps shared reading increases children's motivation to read for pleasure. Hints of this were found in two longitudinal studies where parent reports of the frequency of shared reading or the amount of time spent reading during the preschool years predicted four years later the frequency with which their children reported reading for pleasure as well as children's intrinsic motivation to read.

Shared book reading: an informal literacy activity par excellence

During shared reading, adult and child can enjoy the language, stories and illustrations in children's books. When asked why they read books to their four- and five-year-old children, parents endorsed most strongly statements that they read for enjoyment and sharing quality time with their child (Audet et al., 2008). During shared reading, however, children can also learn. There are three characteristics of shared book reading that can foster learning about the world and about language (Sénéchal et al., 1996). First, the language used in children's books is more complex than that typically used during conversation (Hayes and Ahrens, 1988). Also, the language used by mothers is more complex during shared reading than during free play or when remembering events (Crain-Thoreson et al., 2001). As such, children may be exposed to new lexical, grammatical and syntactic forms during shared reading episodes. Second, children, during shared reading, have the undivided attention of an adult who can define, explain and question to facilitate children's understanding or impart new knowledge. Third, books can be read repeatedly, thus providing multiple exposures to new knowledge. Because of these features, shared book reading is the single most studied aspect of children's home literacy environment.

In this chapter, the research reviewed examined the benefits of shared reading in its various forms. Shared reading is a generic term that includes all forms of book reading to a young child, and as such it does not presuppose that the reader will interact with the child during the book rendition. In some studies, it is the frequency of shared reading events that is measured without consideration to the quality of the reading episodes. In other studies, it is the effect of adult–child interactions during the reading episodes that is examined. The chapter consists of three sections: first, a description of the benefits on oral language of shared reading in general, and dialogic reading in particular; second, a consideration of how specific aspects of shared reading enhance vocabulary acquisition; and third, an examination of whether shared reading promotes early literacy. In each section, only studies that included an alternative treatment and/or control conditions were reviewed because such research designs are necessary to evaluate the effects of shared reading.

How shared reading can enhance child oral language

Shared reading can be a dialogic environment that contains many opportunities for adults to scaffold learning. Observations of parents reading to 9-, 18- and 27-month-old children show the emergence of that dialogue (Sénéchal et al., 1995). Investigation of the natural reading behaviours of parents with their young children, however, finds that parents do not typically engage in interactive reading with their children (Whitehurst et al., 1988). Parents' reading style include few dialogic reading behaviours, mainly involving yes/no questions or directives, and most often consists of reading the text directly without engaging the child in the story (Huebner and Meltzoff, 2005).

Recognizing that a more active role in storybook reading may be beneficial to children's language development, Whitehurst et al. (1988) designed a method, called *dialogic reading*, meant to encourage adults to create dialogues during story time. During dialogic reading, the adult reader encourages children's oral contributions using open-ended questions, repetition of good responses, expansion of incomplete responses to illustrate the difference between what was said and what could have been said, as well as the use of praise. In a series of studies, Whitehurst and colleagues clearly showed that three- to five-year-old children learned new vocabulary when adults used dialogic reading (e.g. Arnold et al., 1994; Lonigan and Whitehurst, 1998; Whitehurst et al., 1994). This seminal research led other researchers to assess the benefits of dialogic reading.

Recent meta-analytic reviews continue to show that dialogic reading has a positive effect on young children's vocabulary (Marulis and Neuman, 2010; Mol et al., 2009; Mol et al., 2008; National Early Literacy Panel, 2008; van Steensel et al., 2011). Considering only the 13 non-overlapping studies across these meta-analyses showed that dialogic reading has a moderate positive effect on children's vocabulary ($ES = .42$ on standardized tests). These meta-analyses also included 39 studies on other forms of interactive reading, studies that included specific types of interactions such as asking questions or giving explanations of novel words. This set of studies also had a moderate positive effect on children's vocabulary ($ES = .80$, experimenter designed tests). Taken together, the combined findings of five meta-analyses show clearly that dialogic reading and other forms of interactive reading can be beneficial to young children's vocabulary. In the studies included in the meta-analyses, readers could be parents, educators or experimenters. In most of these studies, however, children were typically developing. A detailed description of a study on reading to children with language delays is presented next.

Early differences in vocabulary knowledge have long-term effects: children with stronger vocabularies in kindergarten have stronger phonemic awareness one year later as well as better reading comprehension skills four years later (Sénéchal et al., 2006). Moreover, four-year-old children with larger vocabularies learn novel words more easily during shared reading than do children with smaller vocabularies (Sénéchal et al., 1995). Given these findings, it is important to intervene early in the lives of young children whose vocabulary development shows signs of delay.

Hargrave and Sénéchal (2000) conducted a dialogic-reading intervention study with four-year-old children ($N = 36$), who had poor expressive (spoken) vocabulary. The children were at risk for long-term deficits in language development because the children's expressive vocabularies were, on average, 13 months behind on a standardized expressive vocabulary test and their parents had an education level below the national average. The children attended one of two day-care centres associated with high-school programmes for adults. Both day-care centres had circle times in which book reading occurred occasionally. As part of the intervention, the educators were asked to read every day during circle times. They were to read a set of books at least twice during a four-week period. Educators at one centre were asked to read in their customary or regular fashion and educators at the other centre were trained to read in a dialogic manner.

Observations of educators reading at the beginning of the intervention showed no difference across conditions – in fact, educators asked few questions, seldom expanded or praised the children, and did not model or repeat child utterances. During the intervention, however, educators trained in dialogic reading asked 13 times more *wh*-questions, repeated, modelled and expanded the children's utterances, and gave more praise than did the untrained educators. At the end of four weeks, children who experienced dialogic reading made expressive vocabulary gains that were equivalent to those that would normally occur over four months. In contrast, the children who experienced regular reading did not make significant gains on the standardized expressive vocabulary test. Thus, increasing the active participation of children during reading may be a useful way to facilitate the vocabulary development of children at risk for delays.

Hargrave and Sénéchal were also interested in the vocabulary development occurring in the centre where educators read in their regular fashion. Hence, they included a test of expressive vocabulary that measured how many novel words children learned from the set of storybooks read to them. The use of this sensitive measure revealed that children at the regular-reading centre also made statistically significant expressive vocabulary gains, albeit more modest than did the children in the dialogic-reading centre. Thus, although the impact of reading varies considerably depending upon the level of interaction between the adult and the children, any reading is presumably better than none.

Hargrave and Sénéchal provided another important extension to the literature on reading interventions. In contrast to some other studies, dialogic reading was incorporated into the existing structure of the day-cares. One consequence of this procedure was that each educator at both centres was responsible for eight children during circle time whereas the ratio used by Whitehurst and colleagues typically did not exceed five children per educator. Therefore, Hargrave and Sénéchal's findings indicate that dialogic reading is effective with the larger groups of children that are typical of many day-care centres. This result suggests that the effectiveness of active reading is not limited by factors that might lead busy educators to dispense with it. The research reviewed so far has been limited to vocabulary acquisition. The study presented next extends the research on dialogic reading to children's narrative skills.

A young child's language development includes the ability to tell stories. Constructing oral stories allows young children to verbalize real or imagined events in ways that not only communicate social messages to others but that help them derive meaning from experiences (Nelson, 2007). To be understood by naïve conversational partners, however, children's stories should be structured chronologically, include causal links to the goals and motivations of characters, and provide sufficient background information (Peterson, 1994). This story-construction knowledge is assumed to develop through parent–child routines such as shared reading. The limited correlational evidence on the frequency of shared reading, however, has not supported the idea that children gain knowledge about narratives from the context of storybooks alone (e.g. Sénéchal et al., 2008). Rather than the frequency of shared reading, perhaps it is the case that shared reading enhances children's narrative skills only when adults adopt a dialogic interaction style.

Although the dialogic reading literature focuses on improving vocabulary skills, the types of *wh*-questions used to create dialogues during shared reading could also be beneficial to children's narrative skills. A search of the published literature yielded only two studies that assessed the impact of dialogic reading on narrative knowledge. Zevenbergen et al. (2003) determined that a dialogic reading intervention enhanced children's inclusion of some important aspects of narratives within their stories, such as more detail about characters' mental states and motivation, as well as the use of dialogue. Children in this study retold a story they had just heard. In contrast, Lever and Sénéchal (2011) showed that dialogic reading could enhance a wider range of narrative components in children's telling and retelling of stories. In their study, five-year-old children listened, over eight weeks, to biweekly dialogic readings conducted in small groups. During the readings, the dialogic-reading questions focused on the story plot. In this study, the control-group children participated in an alternative activity. The findings supported the notion that some, but not all dimensions of narrative skills are sensitive to dialogic discourse during shared reading. After the intervention, children in the dialogic-reading group told stories that were better structured and more easily understood than did children who were in the alternative-treatment group. Also, the dialogic-reading children's retelling of a story included more references to characters' mental states and emotions than the retelling of the alternative-treatment children. Contrary to expectation, however, dialogic reading did not affect the complexity of the language children used in their stories or their inclusion of cohesive ties (e.g. words like *because, so, since*). Finally, and replicating well-established findings, expressive vocabulary gains were found for the dialogic-reading children as compared to the alternative-treatment children.

In sum, there is considerable evidence supporting the notion that dialogic reading can enhance children's receptive and expressive vocabulary. There is more limited evidence that it can also improve specific aspects of children's narrative abilities. The body of research reviewed provides sound evidence for parents and educators to read to young children in a dialogic manner. Because dialogic reading is so multi-faceted, one cannot ascertain whether all facets are necessary for improvements to occur. In the second section of this chapter, experimental studies that tested the effects of specific aspects of shared reading are reviewed.

How specific aspects of shared reading enhance child vocabulary

In a series of older studies, Sénéchal and colleagues examined factors that might influence how much new vocabulary children learn from shared reading. In this section, the Sénéchal studies are revisited, followed by more recent research. As will be seen, researchers continue to examine how three- to five-year-old children might learn from shared reading.

In the experimental work on shared reading conducted in Sénéchal's lab, the studies use a common method that consisted of reading to children unfamiliar books containing novel words. The novel words were unfamiliar to young children, but were synonyms of concepts that were presumably familiar. For example, young children may not know the words *infant*, *angling* and *elderly* but they are likely to be familiar with the words *baby*, *fishing* and *old*. The novel words were introduced in the text and illustrated in the book. Children's knowledge of the novel words was tested before and after reading the books to assess learning. Two types of word knowledge were of interest, namely children's comprehension of novel words or receptive vocabulary and their production of novel words or expressive vocabulary. Children's comprehension was measured by testing whether the children could select an unfamiliar illustration of the novel words from an array of four pictures. In contrast, children's production was measured by children's capacity to recall novel words using the book pictures as retrieval cues.

Sénéchal and Cornell (1993) found that four- and five-year-old children could comprehend novel words after a single exposure to a book and tended to remember the novel words one week after the reading episodes. Children, on average, learned two novel words from a single storybook session. It is important to put this number in context: researchers have estimated that young children learn approximately five novel words a day (Read, 1980; Templin, 1957). The results of Sénéchal and Cornell showed that some novel word learning can come from listening to adults reading storybooks.

Sénéchal and Cornell, however, did not find differences in how much children learned when they were actively responding to questions during book reading versus passively listening. It is possible that a single reading of the book was not sufficient to allow the emergence of potential differences in vocabulary acquisition as a function of child active involvement. To address the issue of whether the number of reading episodes would interact with the activities occurring during reading, Sénéchal et al. (1995) examined whether the differences between active and passive reading would appear when the books were read twice. They found that after two readings, four-year-old children who actively participated during book reading both comprehended and produced more novel words than children who passively listened to the story. Active participation could take two forms: pointing to the illustrations or labelling the novel words. Although both forms of participation helped children to recognize novel words, answering labelling questions helped children to produce more novel words than did pointing. Furthermore, children who had larger vocabularies, as measured with a standardized receptive vocabulary test, learned more words than did children who had smaller vocabularies. This finding indicated that children who initially had greater knowledge or abilities benefited more from shared reading.

Sénéchal (1997) replicated and extended these findings by showing that three- and four-year-olds could comprehend and produce more novel words when they labelled the novel words during book reading than when they listened passively to the story. In this study, the books were read three times. The requirement for children to label the pictures had a powerful effect on children's production of novel words. Children who listened to one reading of the book could not produce any novel words and children who listened passively to three readings of the book could produce one novel word. In contrast, children who were asked for labels of novel words during the three book readings were able to produce three novel words. Sénéchal argued that label requests are effective because they provide children with practice at retrieving the novel words.

Sénéchal's work on shared reading has shown that features of shared reading as well as child factors affect vocabulary learning. Whether the effects of these features and factors have been replicated is examined next in a series of studies conducted with three- to five-year-old children. The first finding is that books need to be read more than once in order to produce differential effects of adult–child interactions. In recent research, repeating the reading of the same books is an integral part of studies on shared reading (e.g. Kucirkova et al., 2014; Loftus et al., 2010; Reese and Cox, 1999; Walsh and Blewitt, 2006; Walsh and Rose, 2013).

The second finding is that child active participation produces greater learning than simply listening to the book rendition. To date, most of the research on shared reading investigated some form of child active participation (e.g. Blewitt et al., 2009; Coyne et al., 2009). Moreover, the type of active participation seems to differentially affect learning. For example, Blewitt et al. (2009; Study 2) found that pairing where- and why-questions during shared reading was just as effective for receptive vocabulary growth than asking the questions separately. However, children learned more expressive knowledge about the words when the questions were paired.

The third finding is that the amount of learning varies as a function of children's known vocabulary. Young children with larger vocabularies learned more words than do children with smaller vocabularies. This latter finding was also found in Robbins and Ehri (1994) and has been replicated in a number of shared reading studies (e.g. Blewitt et al., 2009; Coyne et al., 2004; Silverman et al., 2013).

Recent research on interactive shared reading has also advanced our understanding of other dimensions of child vocabulary learning. Recall that most often, children are introduced to novel (rare) synonyms for known concepts. Recent research has extended the research to learning novel concepts. For instance, Horst et al. (2011) showed that children who were read the same book three times gained more robust knowledge about novel words for novel concepts than children who were exposed to the same novel words in three different books. In addition, Ard and Beverly (2004) showed that actively involving children during shared reading is also beneficial to learning novel concepts.

The research reviewed so far focused on vocabulary breadth, that is, the number of words learned. There is a limited set of studies, however, that focused on children's ability to define each novel word, that is the depth of their learning (e.g. Blewitt et al., 2009; Justice et al., 2005). Coyne et al. (2009) showed that during readings of the book: (1) providing additional information and interactions about the novel words facilitated learning more than incidental exposure in the book context alone; (2) providing additional questions and interactions after the book reading enhanced learning more than limiting the interactions to before and during the reading; and (3) after eight weeks, children's performance on receptive vocabulary had not changed, whereas there was evidence of forgetting on the measure of children's definitions.

In sum, certain factors influence young children's learning during shared reading, these are: (1) multiple readings of books; (2) children's active involvement; (3) different types of interactions affect differently how children learn to comprehend, to produce and to describe novel words; and (4) more opportunities to learn vocabulary might be required for children with more limited vocabularies. The studies described so far in this chapter focused on child oral language. In the next section, the issue of whether shared reading can enhance children's literacy is examined.

Does shared reading promote early literacy?

During shared reading, parents and children could also discuss the printed text. Observations of parent–child interactions, however, revealed that parents seldom comment on print during these interactions. For example, in a study by Hindman et al. (2008), the majority of remarks (85 per cent) made by American parents during shared reading with their four-year-olds were meaning-related (e.g. labelling, summarizing, discussing novel words), whereas only 15 per cent were code-related (e.g. teaching names or sounds of letters, decoding words). In addition, Hindman et al. (2013) showed that only 1 per cent of mothers pointed out letters or sounds during shared reading. Similar findings had been reported in other observational research (Audet et al., 2008; Deckner et al., 2006; Stadler and McEvoy, 2003).

Observational research has also shown that four- and five-year-olds tend to look at the illustrations, not the written words, during shared reading (Evans and Saint-Aubin, 2005), unless their attention is drawn to the print (Justice et al., 2008). Moreover, intervention research in which parents are asked to focus on letters during shared reading did not yield statistically significant improvements in letter knowledge in samples of young children (Justice and Ezell, 2000; Justice et al., 2011). A recent study conducted with at-risk children also did not show a statistically significant effect size (ES = .21) in print knowledge for children whose parents had been trained in shared reading versus children in the control group (Anthony et al., 2014). If shared reading is not used frequently to stimulate early literacy, if young children do not look at print readily, and if young children do not learn more when parents highlight letters during shared reading, then how do parents stimulate their child's early literacy knowledge? A recent study by Martini and Sénéchal (2012) might help answer this question.

Martini and Sénéchal (2012) documented the activities and contexts that parents used to help their child learn about literacy. Examples of learning contexts include using familiar household items, street signs, games, the mail, newspapers, as well as children's books. They found that parents generally reported using a wide variety of learning contexts: of the 18 presented, parents selected on average 14 different contexts that they used at least some of the time. Moreover, Martini and Sénéchal found that parents who reported teaching about literacy more frequently tended to use a greater number of learning contexts. Martini and Sénéchal concluded that parents focus on naturally occurring activities to impart knowledge about the alphabet, printing and reading words. The reported frequency of teaching along with the numerous contexts used might also suggest that these teaching moments are not very long in duration. Importantly, frequent teaching moments that are varied and short in duration might indicate parents' sensitivity to the attention span and interest of their young child as well as the difficulty of the task at hand. Learning the alphabet, for example, requires learning to discriminate the different forms of letters, learning that letters are symbols that represent individual speech sounds and learning that letters have names and sounds that may or may not be the same (for an excellent description of the complexity of learning to write words, see Treiman and Kessler, 2014). Additional support for the view that parents stimulate literacy knowledge in a variety of contexts comes from analyses of everyday parent–child conversations demonstrating that parents sometimes talked to their children about letters, asking questions about letter shapes and letter–word associations (e.g. Robins et al., 2013).

In their synthesis of shared-reading intervention studies, the National Early Literacy Panel (2008) found that shared reading enhanced children's conceptual knowledge about print (*ES* = .51, 4 studies), but not alphabet knowledge (*ES* = -.06, 2 studies) or phoneme awareness (*ES* = .11, 2 studies). Second, the powerful role of parent tutoring was evident when focussing on early literacy. Sénéchal (2014) updated a synthesis of intervention studies on early literacy (Sénéchal and Young, 2008) and found that parent tutoring (*ES* = .94, 4 studies, 282 families) enhanced early literacy (e.g. alphabet knowledge, reading readiness, beginning reading or invented spelling) and reading skills. A smaller, but still statistically significant effect was found when parents were trained to tutor their children during specific literacy activities as well as trained in shared reading (*ES* = .33, 6 studies, 551 families). In contrast, shared reading alone did not produce statistically significant effects on these early literacy outcomes (*ES* = .09, 9 studies, 509 families). Thus, the benefits of shared reading are limited to children's oral language development, which will eventually be important for reading comprehension.

Conclusion

The findings on shared reading discussed in the first two sections of this chapter provide some valuable information for parents and educators. Adults can enhance children's learning during storybook reading by actively encouraging them to participate. For example, encouraging children to label the pictures can enhance their ability to use these words at some other time. Children at risk for language delays are likely to greatly benefit from active reading, however, any reading is better than none. Furthermore, reading a book two or more times increases the likelihood that children learn novel words. These evidence-based practices are in accord with the view that young children's vocabulary development can be enhanced by their participation in shared storybook reading.

In contrast to these positive effects of shared reading on oral language, the third section showed that shared reading was not a source of early literacy learning for children. Hence, it seems that parents of young children got it right in limiting the number of print-focused interactions during shared reading. This is food for thought for researchers and educators who might be tempted to transform shared reading into a source of early literacy learning. Numerous questions still need to be addressed about shared reading. For example, rather than improving early literacy per se, perhaps shared reading increases children's motivation to read for pleasure. Hints of this were found in two longitudinal studies where parent reports of the frequency of shared reading or amount of time spent reading during the preschool years predicted four years later the frequency with which their children reported reading for pleasure (Sénéchal, 2006) as well as children's intrinsic motivation to read (Gottfried et al., 2015).

References

Anthony, J. L., Williams, J. M., Zhang, Z., Landry, S. H. and Dunkelberger, M. J. (2014). Experimental evaluation of the value added by raising a reader and supplemental parent training in shared reading. *Early Education and Development*, 25, 493–514. doi:10.1080/10409289.2013.812484.

Ard, L. M. and Beverly, B. L. (2004). Preschool word learning during joint book reading effect of adult questions and comments. *Communication Disorders Quarterly*, 26, 17–28.

Arnold, D. H., Lonigan, C. J., Whitehurst, G. L. and Epstein, J. N. (1994). Accelerating language development through picture-book reading: Replication and extension to a videotape training format. *Journal of Educational Psychology*, 86, 235–243.

Audet, D., Evans, M. A., Mitchell, K and Reynolds, K. (2008). Shared book reading: parental goals across the primary grades and goal–behavior relationships in junior kindergarten. *Early Education and Development*, 19, 113–138.

Blewitt, P., Rump, K. M., Shealy, S. E. and Cook, S. A. (2009). Shared book reading: When and how questions affect young children's word learning. *Journal of Educational Psychology*, 101, 294–304. doi:10.1037/a0013844

Coyne, M. D., McCoach, D. B., Loftus, S., Zipoli, R., Jr. and Kapp, S. (2009). Direct vocabulary instruction in kindergarten: Teaching for breadth versus depth. *The Elementary School Journal*, 110, 1–18. doi:http://dx.doi.org/10.1086/598840.

Coyne, M. D., Simmons, D. C., Kame'enui, E. J. and Stoolmiller, M. (2004). Teaching vocabulary during shared storybook readings: An examination of differential effects. *Exceptionality*, 12, 145–162.

Crain-Thoreson, C., Dhalin, M. P. and Powell, T. A. (2001). Parent–child interaction in three conversational contexts: Variations in style and strategy. In J. Brooks-Gunn and P. Rebello (eds), *Sourcebook on Emergent Literacy* (pp. 23–37). San Francisco: Jossey-Bass.

Deckner, D. F., Adamnson, L. B. and Bakeman, R. (2006). Child and maternal contributions to shared reading: Effects on language and literacy development. *Applied Developmental Psychology, 27*, 31–41.

Evans, M. A. and Saint-Aubin, J. (2005). What children are looking at during shared storybook reading: Evidence from eye movements. *Psychological Science, 16*, 913–920.

Gottfried, A. W., Schlackman, J., Gottfried, A. E. and Boutin-Martinez, A. S. (2015) Parental provision of early literacy environment as related to reading and educational outcomes across the academic lifespan. *Parenting: Science and Practice, 15*, 24–38, doi:10.1080/15295192.2015.992736.

Hargrave, A. C. and Sénéchal, M. (2000). A book reading intervention with preschool children who have limited vocabularies: The benefits of regular reading and dialogic reading. *Early Childhood Research Quarterly, 15*, 75–90.

Hayes, D. P. and Ahrens, M. G. (1988). Vocabulary simplification for children: a special case of 'motherese'? *Journal of Child Language, 15*, 395–410. doi:10.1017/S0305000900012411.

Hindman, A. H., Connor, C. M., Jewkes, A. M. and Morrison, F. J. (2008). Untangling the effects of shared book reading: Multiple factors and their associations with preschool literacy outcomes. *Early Childhood Research Quarterly, 23*, 330–350.

Hindman, A. H., Skibbe, L. E. and Foster, T. D. (2013). Exploring the variety of parental talk during shared book reading and its contributions to preschool language and literacy: Evidence from the Early Childhood Longitudinal Study-Birth Cohort. *Reading and Writing: An Interdisciplinary Journal, 27*, 287–313.

Horst, J. S., Parsons, K. L. and Bryan, N. M. (2011). Get the story straight: Contextual repetition promotes word learning from storybooks. *Frontiers in Psychology, 2*, 17. doi:10.3389/fpsyg.2011.00017.

Huebner, C. E. and Meltzoff, A. N. (2005). Intervention to change parent–child reading style: A comparison of instructional methods. *Applied Developmental Psychology, 26*, 296–313.

Justice, L. M. and Ezell, H. K. (2000). Enhancing children's print and word awareness through home-based parent intervention. *American Journal of Speech-Language Pathology, 9*, 257–269.

Justice, L. M., Meier, J. and Walpole, S. (2005). Learning novel words from storybooks: An efficacy study with at-risk kindergartners. *Language, Speech, and Hearing Services in Schools, 36*, 17–32. doi:http://dx.doi.org/10.1044/0161-1461(2005/003.

Justice, L. M., Pullen, P. C. and Pence, K. (2008). Influence of verbal and nonverbal references to print on preschoolers' visual attention to print during storybook reading. *Developmental Psychology, 44*, 855.

Justice, L. M., Skibbe, L. E., McGinty, A. S., Piasta, S. B. and Petrill, S. A. (2011). Feasibility, efficacy, and social validity of home-based storybook reading intervention for children with language impairment. *Journal of Speech, Language, and Hearing Research, 54*, 523–538. doi:10.1044/1092-4388 (2010/09-0151).

Kucirkova, N., Messer, D. and Sheehy, K. (2014). Reading personalized books with preschool children enhances their word acquisition. *First Language, 34*, 227–243.

Lever, R. and Sénéchal, M. (2011). Discussing stories: How a dialogic reading intervention improves kindergarteners' oral narrative construction. *Journal of Experimental Child Psychology, 108*, 1–24. doi:10.1016/j.jecp.2010.07.002.

Loftus, S. M., Coyne, M. D., McCoach, D. B., Zipoli, R. and Pullen, P. C. (2010). Effects of a supplemental vocabulary intervention on the word knowledge of kindergarten students at risk for language and literacy difficulties. *Learning Disabilities Research and Practice, 25*, 124–136. doi:http://dx.doi.org/10.1111/j.1540-5826.2010.00310.x.

Lonigan, C. J. and Whitehurst, G. J. (1998). Examination of the relative efficacy of parent and teacher involvement in a shared-reading intervention for preschool children from low-income backgrounds. *Early Childhood Research Quarterly, 13*, 263–290.

Martini, F. and Sénéchal, M. (2012). Learning literacy skills at home: Parent teaching, expectations, and child interest. *Canadian Journal of Behavioural Science, 44*, 210–221.

Marulis, L. M. and Neuman, S. B. (2010). The effects of vocabulary intervention on young children's word learning: A meta-analysis. *Review of Educational Research, 80*, 300–335. doi:10.3102/0034654310377087.

Mol, S. E., Bus, A. G. and de Jong, M. T. (2009). Interactive book reading in early education: a tool to stimulate print knowledge as well as oral language. *Review of Educational Research, 79*, 979–1007. doi:10.3102/0034654309332561.

Mol, S. E., Bus, A. G., de Jong, M. T. and Smeets, D. J. H. (2008). Added value of dialogic parent–child book readings: A meta-analysis. *Early Education and Development*, *19*, 7–26. doi:10.1080/10409280701838603.

National Early Literacy Panel. (2008). *Developing Early Literacy: Report of the National Early Literacy Panel*. Washington, DC: National Institute for Literacy.

Nelson, K. (2007). *Young Minds in Social Worlds: Experience, Meaning and Memory*. Cambridge, MA: Harvard University Press.

Peterson, C. (1994). Narrative skills and social class. *Canadian Journal of Education*, *19*, 251–269.

Read, C. (1980). What children know about language: Three examples. *Language Arts*, 57, 144–148.

Reese, E. and Cox, A. (1999). Quality of adult book reading affects children's emergent literacy. *Developmental Psychology*, *35*, 20–28.

Robbins, C. and Ehri, L.C. (1994). Reading storybooks to kindergartners helps them learn new vocabulary words. *Journal of Educational Psychology*, *86*, 54–64.

Robins, S., Treiman, R. and Rosales, N. (2013). Letter knowledge in parent–child conversation. *Reading and Writing: An Interdisciplinary Journal*, *27*, 407–429. doi:10.1007/s11145-013-9450-7.

Sénéchal, M. (1997). The differential effect of storybook reading on preschoolers' acquisition of expressive and receptive vocabulary. *Journal of Child Language*, *24*, 123–138.

Sénéchal, M. (2006). Testing the home literacy model: Parent involvement in kindergarten is differentially related to grade 4 reading comprehension, fluency, spelling, and reading for pleasure. *Scientific Studies of Reading*, *10*, 59–87.

Sénéchal, M. (2014). Young children's home literacy experiences. In A. Pollatsek and R. Treiman (eds), *The Oxford Handbook of Reading* (pp. 397–414). New York: Oxford University Press.

Sénéchal, M. and Cornell, E. H. (1993). Vocabulary acquisition through shared reading experiences. *Reading Research Quarterly*, *28*, 360–374.

Sénéchal, M., Cornell, E. H. and Broda, L. S. (1995). Age-related changes in the organization of parent-infant interactions during picture-book reading. *Early Childhood Research Quarterly*, *10*, 317–337.

Sénéchal, M., LeFevre, J.-A, Hudson, E. and Lawson, P. (1996). Knowledge of picture-books as a predictor of young children's vocabulary development. *Journal of Educational Psychology*, 88, 520–536.

Sénéchal, M., Ouellette, G. and Rodney, D. (2006). The misunderstood giant: On the predictive role of vocabulary to reading. In S. B. Neuman and D. Dickinson (eds), *Handbook of Early Literacy* (Vol. 2, pp. 173–182). New York: Guilford Press.

Sénéchal, M., Pagan, S., Lever, R. and Ouellette, G. P. (2008). Relations among the frequency of shared reading and 4-year-old children's vocabulary, morphological and syntax comprehension, and narrative skills. *Early Education and Development*, *19*, 27–44.

Sénéchal, M., Thomas, E. and Monker, J.-A. (1995). Individual differences in 4-year-olds' ability to learn new vocabulary. *Journal of Educational Psychology*, *87*, 218–229.

Sénéchal, M. and Young, L. (2008). The effect of family literacy interventions on children's acquisition of reading from kindergarten to grade 3: A meta-analytic review. *Review of Educational Research*, *78*, 880–907. doi:10.3102/0034654308320319.

Silverman, R., Crandell, J. D. and Carlis, L. (2013). Read alouds and beyond: The effects of read aloud extension activities on vocabulary in head start classrooms. *Early Education and Development*, *24*, 98–122. doi:10.1080/10409289.2011.649679

Stadler, M. A. and McEvoy, M. A. (2003). The effect of text genre on parent use of joint book reading strategies to promote phonological awareness. *Early Childhood Research Quarterly*, *18*(4), 502–512.

Templin, M. (1957). *Certain Language Skills in Children*. Minneapolis, MN: University of Minnesota Press.

Treiman, R. and Kessler, B. (2014). *How Children Learn to Write Words*. New York: Oxford University Press.

van Steensel, R., McElvany, N., Kurvers, J. and Herppich, S. (2011). How effective are family literacy programs? Results of a meta-analysis. *Review of Educational Research*, *81*, 69–96.

Walsh, B. A. and Blewitt, P. (2006). The effect of questioning style during storybook reading on novel vocabulary acquisition of preschoolers. *Early Childhood Education Journal*, *33*, 273–278. doi:10.1007/s10643-005-0052-0.

Walsh, B. A. and Rose, K. K. (2013). Impact of adult vocabulary noneliciting and eliciting questions on the novel vocabulary acquisition of preschoolers enrolled in Head Start. *Journal of Research in Childhood Education*, *27*, 31–45. doi:10.1080/02568543.2012.712085.

Whitehurst, G. L., Arnold, D. S., Epstein, J. N., Angell, A. L., Smith, M., and Fischel, J. E. (1994). A picture book reading intervention in day-care and home for children from low-income families. *Developmental Psychology*, *30*(5), 679–689.

Whitehurst, G. J., Falco, F. L., Lonigan, J. E., Fischel, J. E., DeBaryshe, M. C., Valdez-Menchaca, M. C. and Caulfield, M. (1988). Accelerating language development through picture book reading. *Developmental Psychology*, *24*, 552–559.

Zevenbergen, A., Whitehurst, G. and Zevenebergen, J. (2003). Effects of a shared-reading intervention on the inclusion of evaluative devices in narratives of children from low-income families. *Applied Development Psychology*, *24*, 1–15.

23

FOSTERING VOCABULARY IN EARLY CHILDHOOD EDUCATION

Vibeke Grøver

Children's vocabulary skills when they enter school are powerful predictors of their reading comprehension years later. This chapter reviews vocabulary instruction and its impact on children's word learning in early education. Though children also learn from mere exposure to words, rich word meaning explanations support word learning. Vocabulary instruction is most efficient if new words are embedded in meaningful and engaging discourse in which children are invited to participate in identifying word meaning and actively applying the new words. When exposed to new words children have a better chance of arriving successfully at an understanding if they make use of their pragmatic skills. There is some evidence that rich vocabulary instruction such as embedding new words in extended discussions may be more beneficial to children with more developed vocabulary skills. From a practitioner perspective, adapting and fine-tuning the vocabulary instruction to the learner's needs seems crucial.

The power of words in building narrative and knowledge

Two preschool examples of shared book-reading will introduce this chapter. In the first, teacher Anne and a small group of second-language speakers of Norwegian were reading a wordless picture book about preparing pancakes, the protagonists being an elderly woman and her cat and dog. Turning to the page where the dog and cat are waiting to be served pancakes, the teacher introduced what she expected to be a new word for these young second-language speakers: to 'anticipate' something (in italics below). She explained the meaning of 'anticipating' by using more common words such as 'think', 'hope', 'look forward' – trying to add a new layer to the story that was not captured by the words she expected the children would know already (for the ease of reading examples are offered in English translation only):

Example 1

Anne: the dog and cat are sitting there and *anticipating* something.
Anne: why are they *anticipating* something?
Child 1:   because they wait until it will taste good – they are wondering if it will taste good.
Anne: okay – nn – that is why they are *anticipating* – they are thinking about something – maybe hoping for something – they are looking forward to something.

Child 2:	they are excited about the pancakes because they love pancakes very much.
Anne:	yes they are excited about the pancakes – they are *anticipating* – they are sitting there waiting – they look forward – they love pancakes.
Child 1:	Anne?
Anne:	yes?
Child 1:	I don't think the dog and cat will get anything.
Anne:	I think they will – because they have waited for so long – they have been anticipating so much and now they are sitting there and looking forward – they have collected all the *ingredients* – the things we mix – and now they are sitting there and *fantasizing* about the delicious pancakes – they are making an image in their heads about the pancakes that are so nice.

Previously the group had worked with the words 'ingredients' and 'fantasize' and the example illustrates how the teacher revisited these words in the narrative she co-constructed with the children, re-exposing them to words she wanted them to learn while introducing new ones.

The second example is sampled from another preschool in which the teacher Liv read an expository book about animals on the African savannah. In the text the word 'herd' was essential in portraying the zebras' way of living. While the teacher pointed to the illustration of a group of zebras in the book, she reviewed the word 'herd' that she had previously taught the children and checked whether they understood the word before she continued teaching them:

Example 2

Liv:	the zebras live in herds – can you remember what a *herd* is?
Child 1:	that is when many animals are together.
Liv:	yes the zebras live in *herds* because then it is easier for them to defend themselves against enemies.

The purpose of this chapter is to review vocabulary instruction and its impact on children's vocabulary learning in early education. The examples above serve to illustrate word instruction embedded in creating an engaging narrative or building knowledge; word instruction with a purpose outside of word learning per se. The chapter will first address instructional strategies that have proved to be efficient with young children, asking what these strategies are like and for whom they work. Next, the chapter will discuss whether children acquire word-learning strategies in vocabulary programmes that may support their general word learning, beyond the words targeted in instruction. Finally, directions for future research will be identified. But first – what is the research rationale for studying children's knowledge of the particular language component that words represent?

Why vocabulary?

Children's vocabularies – their knowledge of word meanings – have for many years received interest in research addressing early literacy. This is not without reason. There is robust evidence suggesting that children's vocabulary skills when they enter school are powerful predictors of their reading comprehension years later (Cunningham and Stanovich, 1997; Elleman et al., 2009; Snow et al., 2007; Song et al., 2015; Storch and Whitehurst, 2002).

Differences in vocabulary skills among children emerge in early childhood, reflecting the number of words and different words they are exposed to in their home settings (Hart and Risley, 1995; Hurtado et al., 2008; Pan et al., 2005; Rowe, 2012) and in preschool (Bowers and Vasilyeva, 2011; Grøver Aukrust, 2007; Rydland et al., 2014). By the time children enter elementary school, there is already considerable variability in the breadth and depth of their vocabularies. For example, Biemiller (2005) estimated that lower-quartile English-speaking children begin kindergarten with a thousand fewer root word meanings than average children and continue to acquire fewer words during the first years of schooling, resulting in 2000 fewer root words by the end of second grade.

The number of words children know is associated with socioeconomic differences in speech directed to young children. Children from low-income families acquire their vocabularies at slower rates than children from more privileged backgrounds (Farkas and Beron, 2004; Hoff, 2003). Hart and Risley (1995) observed children in their homes during the first years of their lives and estimated that a child from a professional family on average was exposed to three times as many words as a child from a poor family (42 million words as opposed to 13 million words). Moreover, children's relative vocabulary sizes from preschool to the elementary and middle school years demonstrate a remarkable stability (Snow et al., 2007). In a recent study Rydland et al. (2014) found that vocabulary differences among second-language learners at the age of school entry remained until fifth grade, pointing to the importance of promoting vocabulary in the early years. Some studies (e.g. Penno et al., 2002; Sénéchal et al., 1995) have even demonstrated a widening of vocabulary discrepancies across children after the early years, often talked about as the Matthew effect (Stanovich, 1986), referring to the 'rich getting richer and the poor poorer' over the course of development; or, those who have more, get more. The stability in children's vocabulary sizes relative to each other suggests that vocabulary skill trajectories are not easily affected. Still, identifying ways of overcoming the Matthew effect has been a major motivation behind studies asking whether children's vocabularies can be instructionally supported in early childhood education.

What is efficient vocabulary instruction?

Word-meaning explanations are more efficient than mere exposure to words

A substantial body of literature suggests that structured and supported oral activities are a promising way to foster vocabulary development in children. Shared book reading, such as demonstrated by teachers Anne and Liv in the examples above, has been a primary base for vocabulary interventions with young children (for review, see Sénéchal this volume). In experimental studies that have examined the effects of vocabulary instruction on young children's word learning, a simple research design is characterized by assigning children randomly to an intervention or control group and analysing whether children who receive the vocabulary intervention learn more words than children who do not receive the intervention. In research designs with more experimental groups involved, studies have in addition compared types of vocabulary instruction and identified those that appear most beneficial to children's word learning.

Penno et al. (2002) examined the potential additive effects of explaining word meaning on children's vocabulary growth. They compared children's word learning resulting from mere word exposure with word learning resulting from explicit word-meaning explanations, in both cases when children listened to stories. Although vocabulary learning occurred incidentally through mere exposure, children made greater vocabulary gains when teachers in addition offered word explanations. A similar conclusion was drawn by Beck and McKeown (2007) in two studies of kindergartners and first-grade children. Children who were taught the targeted words learned more words than children who received no instruction, and the vocabulary gains were larger for words that received more instruction. The findings indicate that word learning does not occur easily and that it requires multiple exposures. Nielsen and Friesen (2012) investigated the effect of a storybook-based intervention on kindergarten students' vocabulary development. The intervention group received vocabulary instruction (preplanned definitions explicitly taught and reviewed) and made greater gains on both standardized and non-standardized measures of vocabulary than did the control-group children. Similarly, Justice et al. (2005) examined the effect of small-group storybook reading with adult elaboration of words in context on the acquisition of vocabulary words for at-risk kindergartners. Though word-learning results were modest, children in the treatment group acquired more instructed words than the comparison group. They found no effect of storybook reading on non-instructed words. Likewise, Pollard-Durodola et al. (2011) in a study of preschool children at risk for vocabulary delay found significant intervention effects on researcher-developed measures. The intervention supported vocabulary development by using conceptually related books and explicitly teaching word meaning during shared book reading.

Extended and rich word-meaning explanations are more efficient than simple word explanations

While the studies reviewed so far compared word-meaning instruction to mere exposure, other studies have compared different types of vocabulary instruction to young children. Coyne et al. (2007) compared extended instruction of target words (teaching word meaning in a way that included both contextual and definitional information, multiple exposures to target words, and experiences that promoted deep processing of word meanings) to incidental exposure (words appeared in the story, but were not taught or discussed explicitly), and also compared extended instruction to embedded instruction (providing simple definitions within the context of the story). They found that extended discussion resulted in greater word learning than either incidental exposure or embedded instruction. In a follow-up study Coyne et al. (2009) compared embedded and extended word instructional approaches with kindergarten students. Extended word instruction resulted in deeper word knowledge while embedded instruction resulted in more partial knowledge of the target words. Likewise Silverman (2007) found that kindergarten children whose teachers offered semantic instruction (comparing words) or anchored instruction (paying attention to spoken or written forms of the word) learned more words than children whose teachers restricted their word instruction to defining words.

Zucker et al. (2013) examined longitudinal relations between at-risk preschool children's reading experiences and their language and literacy in kindergarten and first grade. Teachers' use of extra-textual talk during shared reading in preschool was significantly related to children's vocabulary development in kindergarten. Their findings converge with other studies regarding the importance of teachers' extra-textual talk for word learning. A study by Dickinson and Smith (1994) revealed a strong association between teachers' analytical talk when reading books with children and the children's receptive vocabulary skills. Dickinson and Porche (2011) showed that children's fourth-grade receptive vocabulary was related to their exposure to challenging, inferential talk during preschool book reading, with kindergarten vocabulary mediating these effects. Furthermore, Hindman et al. (2008) found that exposure to talk about inferential topics (predicting, inferencing) rather than literal topics (labelling, describing) predicted children's short-term vocabulary skills.

Chlapana and Tafa (2014) examined the effects of different instructional strategies on second-language learners' vocabulary acquisition during storybook reading. Children aged four to six years, learning Greek as their second language, were randomly assigned to two different treatment conditions and one control condition. In the first experimental group, the children were provided brief explanations of target words, in the second group, children were actively involved in discussing target words, while the control group read the stories without any explanation of target words. The researchers found that the impact was larger for instructed than non-instructed words and that children in the interactive instruction setting learned more words than children who only received a brief explanation. Their results converge with findings from other studies of young second-language learners' response to vocabulary instruction, concluding that children benefit from rich explanations and from being actively invited in the word meaning defining process (Collins, 2010; Lugo-Neris et al., 2010).

Summing up, when comparing instruction-based word learning to word learning resulting from mere word exposure, instruction results in more words being learned. Effective vocabulary instruction offers multiple exposures to the target words, invites the child to participate in discussions of word meaning (rather than solely presenting a definition) and allows rich opportunities to use the word in meaningful contexts.

Who benefits the most from vocabulary instruction?

According to the Matthew effect, privileged children will to a larger extent than their less-privileged peers benefit from good instruction. However, the motivation behind vocabulary instruction is often compensatory: to enhance word learning in children who are demographically at risk and/or are second-language learners, and thus expected to lag behind their peers in vocabulary acquisition. A crucial question therefore is: to what extent do vocabulary interventions support the children who need it most?

Investigations addressing this question have reached contradictory conclusions. Justice et al. (2005) examined the effect of small-group storybook reading on the acquisition of vocabulary words and hypothesized that adult elaboration of words in context accelerated vocabulary growth. Children with low vocabulary scores made greater gains on elaborated words (though results were modest for all children). Other studies have found no differential effects. Zucker et al. (2013) in their study of teachers' extra-textual talk and its impact on children's vocabulary did not find that children's initial vocabulary skills moderated the effects of book reading on vocabulary learning. Similarly, Pollard-Durodola et al. (2011) found effects of vocabulary instruction, but no differential effects as a result of whether children had high versus low entry-level vocabulary knowledge. Thus, the gap between children with high and low vocabulary scores was not reduced in this study. In their review of 19 studies, NELP (2008) concluded that language-enhancing interventions supported a broad range of children, with no differences in intervention effectiveness for children based on socioeconomic or language status.

Conversely, some studies found that children with low vocabulary skills benefitted less from vocabulary instruction than their peers with more word knowledge. Students with higher initial vocabulary scores were more likely to learn word meanings through extended discussion than students with lower initial vocabulary scores (see Chlapana and Tafa, 2014 on bilingual learners; see Cabell et al., 2011; Coyne et al., 2007, Loftus et al., 2010; Penno et al., 2002 on monolingual learners). Sénéchal et al. (1995) found that children's entry-level vocabulary knowledge was an important predictor of vocabulary gains from listening to stories. According to these studies, extended vocabulary instruction is differentially effective, favouring students with more developed vocabularies. Likewise, Marulis and Neuman (2010) found in their meta-analysis that socioeconomically advantaged children were significantly more likely to benefit from vocabulary intervention. They concluded that vocabulary interventions are not sufficiently powerful to close the word gap – even in the preschool and kindergarten years. Though their results indicated an overall effect size of .88 when treatment children in vocabulary intervention studies were compared to non-treatment children, the effect sizes were significant lower for economically disadvantaged children. Moreover, some studies have suggested that children with low vocabulary skills tend to be less able to make use of incidental vocabulary learning opportunities; that is, to learn from mere exposure (Justice et al., 2005; Sénéchal et al., 1995), possibly because they know fewer of the other words and thus have less basis for inferring meanings of unknown words.

Few studies have investigated treatment effects by language status, comparing language majority with language minority speakers. Two studies of middle-school students concluded that language-minority students (ELLs) benefitted as much, but not more than children who were monolingual English speakers, hence they remained below their majority-language peers at posttest (Carlo et al., 2012). On the other hand, Han et al. (2014) studied dual-language learners and monolingual English learners from low-income families who received an intervention programme addressing oral language skills over several years. They concluded that although the gap between dual-language learners and monolingual learners developed early, with strong early intervention the gap seemed to be closed. The two groups participating in the study showed similar vocabulary developmental trajectories from kindergarten to second grade and both groups demonstrated age-appropriate achievements on an increasing number of oral language measures over time.

Vocabulary learning as an interaction effect of vocabulary skills and vocabulary instruction

Some studies have investigated treatment effects as a result of interaction between vocabulary skills and specific vocabulary instructional strategies. Coyne et al. 2009 compared vocabulary learning in two treatment conditions, embedded and extended instruction. Children learned more words in the extended condition, but this applied particularly to students with more advanced vocabulary prior to the intervention. Likewise, Reese and Cox (1999) found that pre-kindergartners with higher initial vocabulary skills made greater gains when instruction included extended talk before and after read-alouds. Children with lower initial vocabulary skills benefitted, however, more from instruction that focused on description of pictures during read-alouds. Silverman and Crandell (2010) compared differential effects of various word instruction strategies. They found that acting-out and illustrating words using pictures was positively related to vocabulary learning for children with low pre-intervention vocabulary scores, while this type of intervention correlated negatively with post-intervention results for children with high vocabulary scores before the intervention. Defining words in non-read-aloud settings seemed on the other hand to have a greater effect for children with higher pre-intervention vocabulary scores than for children with lower scores, though the relationship was positive for both groups of children. Consequently, the authors concluded that children with high versus low vocabulary scores before the intervention responded differently to interventions.

Though findings are somewhat contradictory, most studies suggest that vocabulary interventions do not close the gap between children who are disadvantaged due to socioeconomic factors or to being language minority learners and more advantaged learners. There is some evidence, though more would be needed to arrive at a solid conclusion, that advanced vocabulary instruction such as embedding new words in extended discussions may not be equally beneficial to all children irrespective of their initial vocabulary skills. From a practitioner perspective, adapting and fine-tuning the vocabulary instruction to the learner's needs seems crucial.

Limited evidence that vocabulary knowledge transfers beyond the targeted words

Several decades ago Stahl and Fairbanks (1986) concluded in a meta-analysis that vocabulary instruction transferred to global vocabulary measures not containing the target words of instruction. However, later studies have suggested that word learning as an effect of instruction does not easily transfer to non-instructed words in a way that can be assessed by distant, standardized measures (Apthorp et al., 2012; Biemiller and Boote, 2006; Elleman et al., 2009; Pearson et al., 2007). Of the studies reviewed above, only Silverman (2007) and Nielsen and Friesen (2012) concluded with gains in general vocabulary.

Recently, Apthorp et al. (2012) in a cluster-randomized study found a positive effect on students' vocabulary skills in kindergarten and elementary school after one year of explicit rich vocabulary teaching. The intervention included structured, weekly lesson plans for the teaching of new words and structured language activities to engage children in deep and active processing, providing multiple exposures and opportunities for use. The intervention had positive proximal effects on vocabulary (on measures closely aligned with the content and procedures of the instructional programme). They concluded that the intervention improved targeted vocabulary while 'expecting global effects may be overly optimistic' (p. 160). Likewise, Neuman et al. (2011) in another cluster-randomized study investigated the effects of a vocabulary intervention programme for three- and four-year-old preschoolers. The intervention was designed to teach word knowledge and conceptual development. The treatment classrooms outperformed control classrooms on all researcher-created outcome measures (curriculum-related word knowledge), but with no significant differences on standardized vocabulary measurements.

These findings concur with the conclusion drawn by Marulis and Neuman (2010) who in their meta-analysis of the effects of vocabulary interventions on young children's word learning reported greater effects for researcher-created measures compared to standardized measures. If vocabulary instruction were to result in increased word learning skills (not only increased understanding of the words taught), we would expect such gains to appear in standardized assessment only some time after the intervention, when the child has had a chance to apply the new word-learning skills. As yet, there appears to be some, but limited, evidence of word instruction being generalized to new words above the words instructed.

Future directions for vocabulary instruction research

Supporting teacher capacity to enhance children's vocabulary skills

In a study of word exposure in Norwegian preschools Grøver Aukrust (2007) found large differences in the total number of words, total number of different words and the discourse complexity that bilingual children were exposed to in preschool, with implications for their long-term second-language vocabulary development. The huge variability in teacher talk was surprising as Norwegian early education commonly is expected to be of fairly homogeneous quality across institutions (Lekhal et al., 2012). Similarly, in a study in US preschools, Dickinson et al. (2008) demonstrated that preschool teachers rarely engaged children in extended discourse and rarely used sophisticated strategies to support language learning. Scheiner and Gorsetmen (2009) also reported that many preschool teachers had difficulties in identifying places in stories where an inference had to be discussed for children to comprehend the text. The findings point to the need for enhancing the capacity of teachers to engage children in vocabulary-supporting talk.

Reviews of vocabulary intervention effects on children's word learning conclude that effect sizes improve when the intervention is highly controlled and conducted by the experimenter (Elleman et al., 2009; Marulis and Neuman, 2010). When classroom teachers implement the intervention, a larger variability in the outcomes for children is reported, again suggesting variability in the uptake of the intervention by teachers (for discussion, see Vuattoux et al., 2014). Milburn et al. (2014) investigated in a short-term study whether professional development increased preschool teachers' use of conversational strategies during book reading. They found that teachers in the experimental group used more open questions, were more responsive and used more different words, indicating that professional development can yield promising outcomes and enhance teachers' abilities to support children's language. We need more research into professional development that would build on and extend teachers' instructional repertoire in work with learners with diverse vocabulary skills.

Is vocabulary enough?

Thirty years ago Stahl and Fairbanks (1986) formulated three principles for effective vocabulary instruction: teaching both definitional and contextual information, promoting depth of processing and providing multiple encounters of words. These principles still have some validity. More recent research has additionally taught us that embedding word definitions in extended discussions in which children are invited to participate in identifying word meaning and actively applying the new words supports children's word knowledge.

When teacher Anne (Example 1 above) revisited words such as 'ingredients' and 'fantasize' while she developed the pancake narrative with the children, she exposed them to words previously used in another context. Similarly, when teacher Liv checked the children's understanding of the word 'herd' it was because she needed the word to build knowledge about the zebras' way of defending themselves. The teachers used the targeted words as tools in developing a more complex narrative and in building knowledge with an expository children's book as a starting point. The examples illustrate word learning embedded in discourse forms that young children are commonly exposed to in preschool. Good text comprehenders tend to have a more sophisticated understanding of discourse types such as narrative discourse, reasoning and arguments which may help them in successfully interpreting word meaning. Studies reviewed above concluded that word instruction embedded in analytic or inferential talk is more efficient. Future research should further examine potential relationships between children's mastering of basic discourse structures and their word comprehension.

In Example 1 teacher Anne introduced the perspectives of the story protagonists when she taught the children the meaning of the word 'anticipate'. To fully understand the word the children had to take the perspective of the protagonists in the story – what made the dog and cat think, hope, look forward to the pancakes? Certainly, comprehending and using words in a sophisticated way presupposes a capacity to take different perspectives: as listeners we apply the perspective of the speaker, inferring what he or she intends to express by using the word, and as speakers, we take into consideration the perspectives of the listener/the audience, how the word will be understood. The teacher in Example 1 was not referring to something that could be pointed out in a picture; to comprehend the specific meaning of the word 'anticipate', the children had to take her perspective as narrator – to try to identify which dimensions of the narrative she paid distinct attention to.

Relationships between word learning and perspective-taking are a fairly unexplored area. The two examples introducing this chapter were sampled from conversations between teachers and bilingual learners. Particularly for this group of learners, who might have a less developed vocabulary in either of their languages, considering instructional strategies that invite them to use their discourse knowledge (potentially transferrable across languages) and their perspective-taking skills in interpreting word meaning might be instructionally relevant.

Conclusion

Even an efficient vocabulary instruction programme will only be able to teach children a small percentage of the words they acquire; most words are learned incidentally in everyday settings – and moreover most words are not easily learned. Intervention studies and observational studies of relations between word exposure and vocabulary learning concur in their conclusions: words are learned most efficiently if they are embedded in meaningful, engaging and extended discourse. To get a deeper grasp of word meaning children need multiple exposures in a variety of talk contexts. Finally, when exposed to new words children might have a better chance of arriving successfully at an understanding if they make use of their pragmatic skills such as identifying the type of discourse the word appears within and applying their perspective-taking skills. The ways in which vocabulary programmes might include pragmatic instruction in supporting even young children's word learning is an area in need of further investigation.

References

Apthorp, H., Randel, B., Cherasaro, T., Clark, T., McKeown, M. and Beck, I. (2012). Effects of a supplemental vocabulary program on word knowledge and passage comprehension. *Journal of Research on Educational Effectiveness*, *5*(2), 160–188. doi:10.1080/19345747.2012.660240.

Beck, I. and McKeown, M. G. (2007). Increasing young low-income children's oral vocabulary repertoires through rich and focused instruction. *The Elementary School Journal*, *107*(3), 251–271. doi:10.1086/511706.

Biemiller, A. (2005). Size and sequence in vocabulary development: Implications for schooling words for primary grade vocabulary instruction. In I. E. H. Hiebert and M. L. Kamil (eds), *Teaching and Learning Vocabulary: Bringing Research to Practice* (pp. 223–235). New York: Routledge.

Biemiller, A. and Boote, C. (2006). An effective method for building meaning vocabulary in primary grades. *Journal of Educational Psychology*, *98* (1), 44–62. doi:10.1037/0022-0663.98.1.44.

Bowers, E. P. and Vasilyeva, M. (2011). The relation between teacher input and lexical growth of preschoolers. *Applied Psycholinguistics*, *32*(1), 221–241. doi:10.1017/S0142716410000354.

Cabell, S. Q., Justice, L. M., Piasta, S. B., Curenton, S. M., Wiggins, A., Turnbull, K. P. and Petscher, Y. (2011). The impact of teacher responsivity education on preschoolers' language and literacy skills. *American Journal of Speech-Language Pathology*, *20*(4), 315–330. doi:10.1044/1058-0360(2011/10-0104.

Carlo, M. S., August, D., McLaughlin, B., Snow, C., Dressler, C., Lippman, D. et al. (2004). Closing the gap: Addressing the vocabulary needs of English-language learners in bilingual and mainstream classrooms. *Reading Research Quarterly, 39*(2), 188–215. doi:10.1598/RRQ.39.2.3.

Chlapana, E. and Tafa, E. (2014). Effective practices to enhance immigrant kindergartners' second language vocabulary learning through storybook reading. *Reading and Writing, 27*(9), 1619–1640. doi:10.1007/s11145-014-9510-7.

Collins, M. F. (2010). ELL preschoolers' English vocabulary acquisition from storybook reading. *Early Childhood Research Quarterly, 25*(1), 84–97. doi:10.1016/j.ecresq.2009.07.009.

Coyne, M. D., McCoach, B. and Kapp, S. (2007). Vocabulary intervention for kindergarten students: Comparing extended instruction to embedded instruction and incidental exposure. *Learning Disability Quarterly, 30*(2), 74–88.

Coyne, M. D., McCoach, D. B., Loftus, S., Zipoli Jr., R. and Kapp, S. (2009). Direct vocabulary instruction in kindergarten: Teaching for breadth versus depth. *Elementary School Journal, 110*(1), 1–18. doi:10.1086/598840.

Cunningham, A. E. and Stanovich, K. E. (1997). Early reading acquisition and its relation to reading experience and ability 10 years later. *Developmental Psychology, 33*(6), 934–945. doi:10.1037/0012-1649.33.6.934.

Dickinson, D. and Smith, M. W. (1994). Long-term effects of preschool teachers' book reading on low-income children's vocabulary and story comprehension. *Reading Research Quarterly, 29*, 104–122.

Dickinson, D. K., Darrow, C. L. and Tinubu, T. A. (2008). Patterns of teacher–child conversations in head start classrooms: Implications for an empirically grounded approach to professional development. *Early Education and Development, 19*(3), 396–429. doi:10.1080/10409280802065403.

Dickinson, D. K. and Porche, M. V. (2011). Relation between language experiences in preschool classrooms and children's kindergarten and fourth-grade language and reading abilities. *Child Development, 82*(3), 870–886. doi:10.1111/j.1467-8624.2011.01576.x.

Elleman, A., Lindo, E., Morphy, P. and Compton, D. (2009). The impact of vocabulary instruction on passage-level comprehension of school-aged children: A meta-analysis. *Journal of Research on Educational Effectiveness, 2*(1), 1–44. doi:10.1080/19345740802539200.

Farkas, G. and Beron, K. (2004). The detailed age trajectory of oral vocabulary knowledge: Differences by class and race. *Social Science Research, 33*(3), 464–497. doi:10.1016/j.ssresearch.2003.08.001.

Grøver Aukrust, V. (2007). Young children acquiring second language vocabulary in preschool group-time: Does amount, diversity, and discourse complexity of teacher talk matter? *Journal of Research in Childhood Education, 22*(1), 17–37.

Han, M., Vukelich, C., Buell, M. and Meacham, S. (2014). Beating the odds: A longitudinal investigation of low-income dual-language and monolingual children's English language and literacy performance. *Early Education and Development, 25*(6), 841–858. doi:10.1080/10409289.2014.866920.

Hart, B. and Risley, T. (1995). *Meaningful Differences in the Everyday Experiences of Young American Children*. Baltimore, MD: Brookes Publishing.

Hindman, A. H., Connor, C. M., Jewkes, A. M. and Morrison, F. J. (2008). Untangling the effects of shared book reading: Multiple factors and their associations with preschool literacy outcomes. *Early Childhood Research Quarterly, 23*(3), 330–350. doi:10.1016/j.ecresq.2008.01.005.

Hoff, E. (2003). The specificity of environmental influence: Socioeconomic status affects early vocabulary development via maternal speech. *Child Development, 74*(5), 1368–1378.

Hurtado, N., Markman, V. and Fernald, A. (2008). Does input influence uptake? Links between maternal talk, processing speed, and vocabulary size in Spanish-learning children. *Developmental Science, 11*(6), F31–F39. doi:10.1111/j.1467-7687.2008.00768.x.

Justice, L. M., Meier, J. and Walpole, S. (2005). Learning new words from storybooks: An efficacy study within at-risk kindergartners. *Language, Speech and Hearing Services in Schools, 36*(1), 17–32. doi:10.1044/0161-1461(2005/003).

Lekhal, R., von Soest, T., Wang, M., Grøver Aukrust, V. and Schjølberg, S. (2012). Norway's high-quality center care reduces late talking in high- and low-risk groups. *Journal of Developmental and Behavioral Pediatrics, 33*(7), 562–569. doi:10.1097/DBP.0b013e3182648727.

Loftus, S. M., Coyne, M., McCoach, B., Ziploi, R. and Pullen, P. (2010). Effects of a supplemental vocabulary intervention on the word knowledge of kindergarten students at risk for language and literacy difficulties. *Learning Disabilities Research and Practice, 25*(3), 124–136. doi:10.1111/j.1540-5826.2010.00310.x.

Lugo-Neris, M., Wood Jackson, C. and Goldstein, H. (2010). Facilitating vocabulary acquisition of young English language learners. *Language, Speech and Hearing Services in Schools, 41*, 314–327.

Marulis, L. M. and Neuman, S. B. (2010). The effects of vocabulary intervention on young children's word learning: A meta-analysis. *Review of Educational Research, 80*(3), 300–335. doi:10.3102/0034654310377087.

Milburn, T. F., Girolametto, L., Weitzman, E. and Greenberg, J. (2014). Enhancing preschool educators' ability to facilitate conversations during shared book reading. *Journal of Early Childhood Literacy, 14*, 105–140. doi:10.1177/1468798413478261.

National Early Literacy Panel (NELP) (2008). *Developing Early Literacy: A Scientific Synthesis of Early Literacy Development and Implications for Intervention.* National Institute for Literacy.

Neuman, S., Newman, E. and Dwyer, J. (2011). Educational effects of a vocabulary intervention on preschollers' word knowledge and conceptual development: A cluster-randomozed trial. *Reading Research Quarterly, 46*(3), 249–272. doi:10.1598/RRQ.46.3.3.

Nielsen, D. C. and Friesen, L. D. (2012). A study of the effectiveness of a small-group intervention on the vocabulary and narrative development of at-risk kindergarten children. *Reading Psychology, 33* (3), 269–299. doi:10.1080/02702711.2010.508671.

Pan, B. A., Rowe, M. L., Singer, J. D. and Snow, C. E. (2005). Maternal correlates of growth in toddler vocabulary production in low-income families. *Child Development, 76*(4), 763–782. doi:10.1111/j.1467-8624.2005.00876.x.

Pearson, P. D., Hiebert, E. and Kamil, M. (2007). Vocabulary assessment: What do we know and what do we need to learn. *Reading Research Quarterly, 42*(2), 282–296. doi:10.1598/RRQ.42.2.4.

Penno, J., Wilkinson, I. and Moore, D. (2002). Vocabulary acquisition from teacher explanation and repeated listening to stories: Do they overcome the Matthew effect? *Journal of Educational Psychology, 94*(1), 23–33. doi:10.1037//0022-0663.94.1.23.

Pollard-Durodola, S., Gonzalez, J., Simmons, D., Kwok, O., Taylor, A., Davis, M., Kim, M. and Simmons, L. (2011). The effects of an intensive shared book-reading intervention for preschool children at risk for vocabulary delay. *Exceptional Children, 77*(2), 161–183.

Reese, E. and Cox, A. (1999). Quality of adult book reading affects children's emergent literacy. *Developmental Psychology, 35*(1), 20–28.

Rowe, M. L. (2012). A longitudinal investigation of the role of quantity and quality of child-directed speech vocabulary development. *Child Development, 83*(5), 1762–1774. doi:10.1111/j.1467-8624.2012.01805.x.

Rydland, V., Grøver, V. and Lawrence, J. (2014). The second-language vocabulary trajectories of Turkish immigrant children in Norway from ages five to ten: The role of preschool talk exposure, maternal education, and co-ethnic concentration in the neighborhood. *Journal of Child Language, 41*(2), 352–381. doi:10.1017/S0305000912000712.

Scheiner, E. and Gorsetman, C. (2009). Do preschool teachers consider inferences for book discussions? *Early Child Development and Care, 179*(5), 595–608. doi:10.1080/03004430701425851.

Sénéchal, M., Thomas, E. and Monker, J. (1995). Individual differences in 4-year-old children's acquisition of vocabulary during storybook reading. *Journal of Educational Psychology, 87*(2), 218–229.

Silverman, R. (2007). Vocabulary development of English-Language and English-Only learners in kindergarten. *The Elementary School Journal, 107*, 365–383.

Silverman, R. and Crandell, J. D. (2010). Vocabulary practices in prekindergarten and kindergarten classrooms. *Reading Research Quarterly, 45* (3), 318–340. doi:10.1598/RRQ.45.3.3.

Snow, C. E., Porche, M. V., Tabors, P. O. and Harris, S. R. (2007). *Is Literacy Enough? Pathways to Academic Success for Adolescents.* Baltimore, MD: Paul H. Brookes.

Song, S., Su, M., Kang, C., Liu, H., Zhang, Y., McBride-Chang, C. Tardif, T., Li, H., Zhang, Z. and Shu, H. (2015). Tracing children's vocabulary development from preschool through the school-age years: An 8-year longitudinal study. *Developmental Science, 18*(1), 119–131. doi:10.1111/desc.12190.

Stahl, S. A. and Fairbanks, M. M. (1986). The effects of vocabulary instruction: A model-based meta-analysis. *Review of Educational Research, 56* (1), 72–110.

Stanovich, K. E. (1986). Matthew effects in reading: Some consequences of individual differences in the acquisition of literacy. *Reading Research Quarterly, 21*(4), 360–407.

Storch, S. and Whitehurst, G.J. (2002). Oral language and code-related precursors to reading: Evidence from a longitudinal structural model. *Developmental Psychology, 38*(6), 934–947. doi:10.1037//0012-1649.38.6.934.

Vuattoux, D., Japel, C., Dion, E. and Dupéré, V. (2014). Targeting the specific vocabulary needs of at-risk preschoolers: A randomized study of the effectiveness of an educator-implemented intervention. *Prevention Science*, *15*(2), 156–164. doi:10.1007/s11121-013-0379-5.

Zucker, T., Cabell, S., Justice, L., Pentimonti, J. and Kaderavek, J. (2013). The role of frequent, interactive prekindergarten shared reading in the longitudinal development of language and literacy skills. *Developmental Psychology*, *49*(8), 1425–1439. doi:10.1037/a0030347.

24

DRAMA-BASED INTERVENTIONS AND NARRATIVE

Wendy K. Mages

This chapter identifies four general types of drama-based interventions designed to promote young children's narrative development: play-training interventions, writing-improvement interventions, Paley-paradigm interventions and readers-theatre interventions. These diverse interdisciplinary interventions were designed to foster a variety of narrative outcomes, such as the production, comprehension and/or recall of either oral or written narratives. The merits and challenges of the research on drama-based narrative interventions, and the potential these interventions hold for supporting young children's acquisition of narrative skills and influencing early childhood education curricula, are discussed.

This chapter focuses on drama-based interventions designed to promote narrative development in young children.[1] Although *narratives* can be defined in many ways (McCabe, 1991), an investigation of drama-based interventions requires a broad definition, such as Hicks's (1991) definition of narrative discourse as 'the linguistic means through which speakers represent both real-life and fictional events' (p. 55). To represent the diversity in the literature, an effort was made to discuss all interventions that employed adult-facilitated drama or theatre activities to foster young children's narrative skills. The drama interventions described in this chapter focus on a variety of narrative outcomes, such as the production, comprehension and/or recall of either oral or written narratives. In addition, there is diversity in the types of drama interventions designed to foster narrative development in young learners. These interventions can be categorized under four general headings: play-training interventions, writing-improvement interventions, Paley-paradigm interventions and readers-theatre interventions.

Children's language development (Snow et al., 1998) and narrative skills (DeTemple and Tabors, 1996), such as storytelling and story comprehension, have been linked to scholastic success. Peterson and McCabe (1994) noted 'the ability to produce decontextualized language is a crucial skill underlying literacy acquisition' (p. 937). The research suggests that for children to succeed in school, they must learn to tell a story, or relate a series of events, that can be understood by listeners who were not present when the events took place. Yet, Paris and Paris (2003) found children often begin school unable to create a sufficiently informative and well-structured narrative. Therefore, it is important to find engaging ways to foster young children's narrative development.

It is worth noting that children from different cultures or ethnic groups acquire different narrative styles (Blum-Kulka and Snow, 1992; Heath, 1982; Westby, 1985) and a child's home culture affects his or her familiarity with narrative conventions and forms (Michaels, 1981). When a child's narrative conventions are similar to those used in school, classroom activities, such as 'show-and-tell,' can serve as 'oral preparation for literacy' (Michaels, 1981: 423). However, when a child's narrative style and classroom discourse conventions differ, it can impede a child's ability to succeed in school (Westby, 1985). Drama curricula may provide an engaging and effective method for educators to support children's acquisition and development of narrative understanding and production and, specifically, to help children, whose narrative discourse is not typical of academic discourse, add school-style narratives to their repertoire of narrative genres.

Drama practitioners and classroom teachers have developed a variety of drama and theatre forms, including improvisation, theatre games, and other performance activities and conventions (Cooper, 1993, 2009; Heinig, 1992; McCaslin, 1996; Paley, 1981, 1990; Spolin, 1963, 1986; Young and Vardell, 1993). Many of the techniques used in educational drama immerse participants in language-rich environments and many drama strategies incorporate the use of literature, including stories, plays and poems. Although some of the techniques described in the literature involve non-verbal activities, such as pantomime or tableaux, these silent activities are often used to embody ideas and images from literary sources. Thus, drama and theatre participation is often used as a way to enhance and improve literacy learning.

Drama practitioners maintain that drama participation fosters language development (Fox, 1987; Heinig, 1992; McCaslin, 1996; Paley, 1981, 1990). For example, Heinig (1992) contends enacting a story mandates a close examination of the story and its content, which she believes fosters story comprehension skills. Wagner (1988) highlights the similarities between the mental processes used for dramatic play and literacy: both require decontextualized language and narrative sequencing. Similarly, Brown and Pleydell (1999) note language arts and drama use many of the same speaking and listening skills. They also emphasize that children learn language through 'practice, and drama can create a strong stimulus for the use and practice of language in a natural and spontaneous environment' (p. 6). Cooper (1993) concurs, noting the dramatization of adult-authored stories 'provides children with a model of "book language" and story form' (p. 56). In sum, educators and researchers believe drama participation provides a language-rich environment and enacting stories can help children develop an understanding of story structure and content. Moreover, they believe drama participation offers an introduction to forms and functions of narrative discourse, while it motivates and engages children in language and literacy-related behaviours (Cooper, 2005; Cremin et al., n.d.; Martinez et al., 1998/1999; McCaslin, 1996; Nicolopoulou, 2002).

'Educational systems concerned with accountability need research to validate the claims of the beneficial effects of creative drama' (Vitz, 1983: 17). Although scholars have noted flaws in some of the drama research, findings from the extant research suggest that early childhood drama participation promotes language development (Conard, 1998; Kardash and Wright, 1987; Mages, 2008; Miller and Mason, 1983; Nicolopoulou, 2002; Podlozny, 2000; Vitz, 1983; Wagner, 1998). Specifically, the literature provides evidence that drama participation positively affects children's language acquisition, story comprehension, story production, story recall, story retelling and story writing, as well as the listening and speaking skills of English-language learners (Brady and Millard, 2012; Greenfader and Brouillette, 2013; Keehn, 2003; Mages, 2008; Moore and Caldwell, 1990, 1993; Nicolopoulou et al., 2006).

Meta-analyses have confirmed drama's positive effect on children's language development. In a meta-analysis investigating the link between drama participation and language development, Podlozny (2000) found evidence to suggest drama facilitates story understanding, story recall, oral language development and writing achievement. A more recent meta-analysis (Lee et al., 2015), investigating the effect of 'drama-based pedagogy' (DBP) on a variety of outcomes, found DBP had a positive effect on English language arts. Earlier meta-analyses (Conard, 1992; Kardash and Wright, 1987) also indicated drama had a positive effect on children's language development. If, as the research literature suggests, drama can improve children's language skills, then it seems to follow that drama participation could be an effective strategy to promote children's narrative development.

Play-training interventions

Many of the early studies of the effect of drama on language development were designed to investigate whether engaging in the language-rich environment and linguistic interactions of dramatic play could increase the sophistication of young children's language skills. Some of these studies invited children to enact a theme, such as a trip to a fast-food restaurant (Dansky, 1980) or animals in the jungle (Shmukler and Naveh, 1984–1985), and some invited children to re-enact a structured story or folk tale (Pellegrini and Galda, 1982; Saltz et al., 1977; Shmukler and Naveh, 1984–1985; Silvern, 1980). Using various measures to evaluate aspects of narrative skill, including criterion referenced tests, open-ended questions, Cloze tests, picture sequencing tasks and retell tasks, this body of research, as a whole, indicates drama participation is an effective way to foster narrative development for some or all of the participants (Mages, 2008). For example, Saltz and Johnson (1974) found drama afffected preschoolers' story-sequencing and storytelling skills and Pellegrini and Galda (1982) found drama positively affected the story-comprehension skils of kindergarteners and first graders, but did not make a statistically significant difference for second graders. Although, Pellegrini and Galda's quantiative analyses did not provide evidence that drama significantly improved the narratives of second graders, Galda (1982) noticed qualitative differences; second graders in the drama treatment 'used a more dramatic tone, included more details, and recreated the conversation between characters' (Galda, 1982: 54). Play-training studies once constituted an active and productive line of research. Yet, in recent years, few if any studies have focused on this type of drama intervention.

Although not designed as a play-training study, Nielson (1993) conducted a study using similar methods. Nielson investigated children's understanding of stories when a read-aloud was accompanied by one of four activities: drawing, discussion, drama (retelling the story with puppets and reenacting the story) or identification of print features. Nielson found low-achieving kindergarteners in the drama group did significantly better than low-achieving children in the other groups; she found no effect of condition for middle- or high-achieving children.

Writing-improvement interventions

Although similar to play-training studies, writing-improvement studies are concerned with promoting narrative writing and tend to focus on children in the primary grades. Moore and Caldwell (1990, 1993) studied the effect of drama on the writing skills of second and third graders. Their research, which compared the effects of three pre-writing activities – drama, drawing or discussion – on students' writing, found no significant difference between the drama and drawing conditions, but found these conditions each provided significantly better support for writing than traditional discussions (Moore and Caldwell, 1993). Moore and Caldwell (1990, 1993) concluded that different media or modes of preparation differently affected children's narrative performance.

A more recent study by Brady and Millard (2012) combined technology with drama to improve children's story writing skills. This intervention included a DVD of videos featuring a male storyteller narrating stories. According to Brady and Millard (2012), the limited view of the storyteller in the videos, framed to include only the storyteller's head and shoulders, helped focus children's attention on the teller's voice and facial expressions and on the language of the narratives. Video viewing was combined with drama, role-play and oral storytelling workshops designed to engage seven- to nine-year-olds in key aspects of narrative. Comparing samples of children's pre-intervention writing to their post-intervention writing, the researchers found 'a marked change', noting improvement in the children's narrative skills, including their ability to use temporal connections, complex sentences, literary language and story sequencing. They found the combination of the storytelling videos, drama strategies, role-play workshops and oral storytelling sessions had a positive impact on children's story writing. Brady and Millard (2012) noted that 'different modes of telling provide different affordances for meaning making and knowledge of this is important in supporting children's use of narrative elements such as action or character' (p. 23). Thus, to effectively nurture young learners' narrative capacities, it would be worthwhile for educators to consider employing multiple modes of representation and engagement.

Paley-paradigm interventions

Paley-paradigm interventions combine storytelling with story enactment. Paley (1981), an early childhood educator, developed a curriculum that, in addition to offering children opportunities to dramatize adult-authored stories, encouraged children to dictate their own stories and then enact the stories they created. McNamee and her colleagues (McNamee, 1987; McNamee et al., 1985, 1986) were the first to research the effect of a Paley-style storytelling/story-acting intervention, comparing it to an intervention that only included storytelling. Their study, which included children from three to six years old, found drama positively affected the complexity and coherence of narratives told by the older children (four to six years old), but that drama did not have an effect on the narratives of the youngest group of children. Warash and Workman (1993) also investigated the use of the Paley paradigm with preschoolers and found the children's stories improved over the course of the intervention.

Fein Ardila-Rey and Groth (2000) conducted a study comparing the effects of the Paley paradigm to the effects of the 'author's chair' on the narrative free-play activities of kindergarteners. All of the children in the study dictated stories; half of the children enacted the stories they wrote and half did not. The ones who did not dramatize the stories participated in the 'author's chair', in which the teacher read a child-authored story to the class, after which the child-author, sitting in the designated author's chair, responded to classmates' questions and comments. These researchers found children in the author's-chair condition gravitated to book-making activities and became interested in book features, such as indices and illustrations. In contrast, children in the drama condition were less interested in making books and focused more on integrating characters and action into their stories. Analyses of the children's free-play activities revealed narrative and literacy-related activities increased for children in the drama condition, but these activities decreased for children in the author's-chair condition. Although the intervention lasted only 12 weeks, the researchers found that after three months the interventions continued to differently affect children's free play.

Nicolopoulou and her colleagues (Nicolopoulou, 1996, 1997, 2002, 2006; Nicolopoulou et al., 1994; Richner and Nicolopoulou, 2001) have also researched the effect of the Paley paradigm on children's narrative development. Looking across her studies, which included preschoolers from low-income, middle-income and upper-middle-income families, Nicolopoulou (2002) found participation in a storytelling/story-acting intervention positively affected children's narrative competence; children who participated in Paley-style drama activities showed improvement in the complexity and sophistication in their narratives. Nicolopoulou attributed the children's improvement to the dramatization of the stories, which intrinsically provided a multisensory experience that afforded opportunities for children to evaluate the stories they wrote. This opportunity for self-evaluation helped children better understand and produce the features and characteristics of well-written narratives. Nicolopoulou also emphasized that Paley-style dramas, which feature the classroom presentation of enacted child-authored stories, have the potential to harnesses the positive influences of children's peer-culture; participation fosters a sense of belonging and inclusion in a community of storytellers and good stories garner peer appreciation. Hence, the classroom culture and children's desire to participate with others in a story-dramatization motivated and encouraged the creation of interesting well-developed narratives to enact with and for classmates.

In one iteration of Nicolopoulou's (2006) research, the Paley-style drama curriculum affected the genre of children's journal entries. Inspired by the storytelling/story-acting paradigm, children began to create story narratives about the pictures they had drawn in their journals. Thus, it seemed children were able to transfer their newly acquired narrative understanding from the storytelling/story-acting context to a new literacy context.

MakeBelieve Arts (2015c), a London-based theatre and education company that provides intervention implementation workshops and teacher professional development, developed 'Helicopter Stories' (MakeBelieve Arts, 2015), an intervention that uses techniques based on Paley's storytelling/story-acting paradigm, and the 'Helicopter Technique' (Cremin et al., n.d.: 13), an in-service teacher-training programme designed to help teachers lead the storytelling/story-acting curriculum. In contrast to previous research on Paley-paradigm drama interventions, an evaluation study (Cremin et al., n.d.) of MakeBelieve Arts' Helicopter Technique could not substantiate claims that participating in an eight-week implementation of Helicopter Stories fostered children's narrative development. They did find, however, that Helicopter Stories motivated children's engagement in literacy-related activities. The lack of evidence to support children's narrative development in this study may be attributable to a relatively short-term intervention.

Until recently, the use of the Paley paradigm had been limited to particular classrooms, particular schools or particularly interested practitioners. In response to the Boston Public Schools' adoption of the Common Core Standards (2010), the Boston student-outcome data and the desire to help students meet the standards, the Boston Public Schools Department of Early Childhood (n.d.; Mardell, 2013; Sachs et al., 2014) launched The Boston Listens Project, which provides teacher professional development and supports for the implementation of a Paley-paradigm curriculum. Mardell (Sachs et al., 2014) explained that 'storytelling and story acting provide a rich context for vocabulary development as children listen to and use words in authentic ways' and dramatizing stories 'brings words to life' (p. 176). He elaborated, 'storytelling and story acting also develop essential narrative abilities; they provide a bridge between the contextualized speech of young children and the decontextualized language of books and writing' (p. 176). In the pilot season of Boston Listens, approximately half of the 165 early childhood educators who had participated in the professional develop-ment training programme on the storytelling/story-acting technique attempted to facilitate the Paley paradigm in their classrooms (Sachs et al., 2014). The programme goal was to build on this initial implementation until all 165 teachers incorporated the Paley paradigm into their classroom praxis.

This systematic large-scale implementation of a Paley-paradigm drama intervention is important for a number of reasons. First, it affords a large group of public-school children an opportunity to engage in a curriculum that has often been shown to positively influence language and literacy development. Second, a district-supported programme has the potential to foster teacher collaboratives and learning communities, in which teachers can share suc-cessful implementation practices and work together to identify productive ways to address paradigmatic challenges. Nicolopoulou and Cole (2010) found involvement in a learning community can be beneficial for teachers and for the successful implementation and refine-ment of a storytelling/story-acting curriculum. Finally, the implementation of the Boston Listens Project could provide a rich research opportunity to investigate the effects of a Paley-paradigm drama intervention on children's language and literacy development within a large urban public school system. It would be particularly valuable if a longitudinal evaluation study, using both quantitative and qualitative measures, could assess child learning outcomes, as well as identify factors that promote or inhibit successful programme implementation.

Readers-theatre interventions

Most drama interventions are designed to engage participants in a multisensory embodied experience. In other words, children are encouraged to use both their voices and their bodies to portray a character in a drama. Readers-theatre interventions differ from the other drama interventions in that the actors rely less on physical gestures and the full embodiment of a character and rely more on using their voices to express the characters' emotions and intentions and to communicate the message of the story. Worthy and Prater (2002) explained that in readers theatre 'the focus is on how the participants convey meaning through their interpretive reading' (p. 294). Similarly, Martinez et al. (1998/1999) noted, 'The per-former's goal is to read a script aloud effectively, enabling the audience to visualize the action' (p. 326).

Many proponents of readers theatre relate it to a practice known as 'repeated reading' (Martinez et al., 1998/1999; Tsou, 2011; Worthy and Broaddus, 2002; Worthy and Prater, 2002; Young and Rasinski, 2009). The National Reading Panel (2000) found repeated reading to be beneficial for a number of reading outcomes including comprehension. Readers-theatre proponents also maintain that readers theatre provides 'an authentic com-munication event' (Millin and Rinehart, 1999: 72) that motivates readers to want engage in the repeated reading of a text (Keehn, 2003; Martinez et al., 1998/1999; Millin and Rinehart, 1999; Vasinda and McLeod, 2011; Worthy and Prater, 2002; Young and Rasinski, 2009). Although readers theatre is not a new technique, it is often implemented with older students (Griffith and Rasinski, 2004; Tsou, 2011; Young and Vardell, 1993). A number of studies, however, investigated the effect of readers theatre on the narrative comprehension skills of children in the second and third grades.

Martinez et al. (1998/1999) studied the effect of a ten-week readers-theatre intervention on second graders' reading and found students made measureable gains in reading speed. They also attributed students' motivation to engage in reading and writing activities to the students' participation in readers theatre.

Millin and Rinehart (1999) conducted a study of second-grade students from low-income families. Students who participated in the readers-theatre intervention made significantly greater gains in reading comprehension than those who did not participate in readers theatre. Similarly, Keehn (2003) found that readers theatre fostered second graders' reading fluency and comprehension and was particularly beneficial for students who began the intervention with less proficient reading skills. Interestingly, she found no significant benefits to children's fluency or comprehension when explicit fluency instruction was added to the readers-theatre curriculum.

Vasinda and McLeod (2011), who modelled their intervention on traditional readers-theatre interventions (Griffith and Rasinski, 2004; Martinez et al., 1998/1999), added a technological component – podcasting – to their readers-theatre intervention with second and third graders. As part of this intervention, students made audio recordings of their readers-theatre performances. These recordings were then uploaded to an internet platform that allowed the performances to be shared with the children's families. Vasinda and McLeod (2011) found that a ten-week readers-theatre intervention with podcasting helped struggling readers, defined as 'students who scored a year below their current grade level' (p. 489), gain an average of 1.13 years on their grade-equivalency scores. Vasinda and McLeod (2011) contended that the 'permanency' of the podcasts and an audience that included class-mates and family members contributed to the children's success. Specifically, they asserted the podcasts allowed children to listen to their own reading performances and this self-evaluation component contributed to reading development and improvement. In addition, they discussed 'audio as a visualizing medium' (p. 494) and thought the podcasts supported students' ability to visualize what they read.

Discussion

The drama interventions designed to promote children's narrative competence suggest there are a variety of ways to use drama to help children acquire skills necessary for understanding and creating well-crafted oral and written narratives. Of the interventions, play-training inter-ventions are the most researched. This line of research has a number of strengths, including the number of different researchers who investigated this topic, the types of standardized measures that were employed, the use of multiple conditions and a control group, the methods used to test alternate hypotheses and variables, such as interactions between age and con-dition, and the fairly broad age-range of the participants. The quantity of play-training interventions and the diversity of researchers involved allowed later studies to build upon earlier research in order to challenge assumptions, correct weaknesses, refine the research model and attempt to discover the factors that made a particular intervention effective.

In contrast, early childhood studies of readers-theatre and writing interventions are fewer in number and, due to the level of reading and writing proficiency required to participate, have been limited to use with second and third graders. Although it may be possible to extend the scope of the readers-theatre or writing interventions by adapting them for use with first graders, the requisite literacy skills needed for these interventions make them less suitable for very younger children. Nonetheless, these paradigms provide useful insights and methods for fostering narrative competence in the early primary grades and provide fertile grounds for continued research.

The Paley paradigm is particularly notable, because, unlike other interventions used with preschoolers and kindergarteners, this is the only model that integrates narrative construction into the intervention curriculum; play-training studies used narrative assessments, but did not give participants multiple opportunities to practise creating narrative discourse within the intervention itself. Although the number of studies and researchers investigating this paradigm are limited, there is evidence to suggest that this method is often used in early childhood education (Cooper, 1993; MakeBelieve Arts, 2015b; Paley, 1999). In addition, professional development programmes have been designed to teach educators to implement this technique (MakeBelieve Arts, 2015a; Rice University, 2011), suggesting there is a population of early childhood teachers interested in learning to integrate this method into their praxis. Although this method is most often championed for use with preschools and kindergartens, there is evidence this paradigm can easily be adapted for use with older children (Cooper, 1993). Finally, the Boston Listens project demonstrates the Paley paradigm can be brought to scale (Mardell, 2013; Sachs et al., 2014).

Research has identified multiple drama strategies that promote the development of children's oral and written narrative competence. However, as Wagner (1998) discussed, it is important that research studies on the educational efficacy of drama build upon and extend the extant research. Similarly, Shavelson and Towne (2002) averred, 'Rarely does one study produce unequivocal and durable results; multiple methods, applied over time and tied to evidentiary standards, are essential to establishing a base of scientific knowledge' (p. 2). Although drama interventions focused on narrative development are promising, replication studies and studies that demonstrate drama interventions can successfully be brought to scale are needed to substantiate the utility of drama as an educational initiative to foster narrative competence. Without such evidence, it is hard to make a case for investing limited funds and allocating limited class time to these endeavours.

It is noteworthy that research on the efficacy of drama in education is an interdisciplinary enterprise. The interdisciplinary nature of this research adds to its richness, as it adds a level of complexity to the methods, measures and theories employed (see Mages, 2008, for a discussion of the methods and measures used in drama research). The multitude of measures, the variety of disciplinary-specific notions of what constitutes rigorous research and valid evidence, and the diversity of theoretical perspectives often make it difficult to compare results across studies.

Interestingly, much of the research on the effect of drama on narrative is conducted by scholars whose expertise is in a field other than educational drama, such as psychology, language and literacy, and early childhood education. This may be due, in part, to differences in the value disciplines place on quantitative research methods. Flemming et al. (2010) observed that qualitative research has 'become the dominant orthodoxy in arts and drama' and hypothesize this is because researchers in the arts 'are more at home with narratives than numbers', as narratives better reflect the 'ambiguities and complexities' of artistic processes (p. 178).

Yet, in the age of accountability, it is often necessary to provide quantitative evidence to demonstrate efficacy or to compare a new method or strategy to the status quo. Scientific methods allow researchers to systematically manipulate variables to determine the factor or factors that can cause similar-seeming interventions to obtain diverse or contradictory results. For example, it would be useful to determine why the evaluation study of MakeBelieve Arts (Cremin et al., n.d.) was unable to demonstrate an effect of a Paley-paradigm intervention on narrative, yet other studies (Fein et al., 2000; McNamee, 1987; McNamee et al., 1985, 1986; Nicolopoulou, 1996, 1997, 2002, 2006; Nicolopoulou et al., 1994; Richner and Nicolopoulou, 2001; Warash and Workman, 1993) were able to demonstrate this association.

As educators and administrators consider ways to engage young learners, support their acquisition of literacy skills and enable them to meet rigorous standards of competence, the inclusion of drama interventions in the curriculum will depend, to a great extent, on the quality of research demonstrating its efficacy. It will, thus, be necessary for researchers using a variety of research theories, methods and measures to be cognizant of the extant drama research across disciplines and to conscientiously build on and extend what is known about the relation of drama participation to narrative development. Although quantitative research may not be as prevalent among researchers with expertise in educational drama, it will be important that scholars and practitioners who specialize in educational drama share their knowledge and expertise in ways that contribute to and strengthen the research valued by educators and administrators who determine what is included in school curricula. Accomplishing these objectives may require scholars to form interdisciplinary research consortiums that are able to integrate and communicate discipline-specific and multidisciplinary research. A concerted effort to advance the utility and rigour of research investigating the effect of drama interventions on narrative acquisition and development may elucidate particularly effective drama strategies, as well as factors that inhibit the implementation or utility of a particular approach. In an era that venerates research-based practices in education, the role of drama in early childhood education may very well depend on the strength and rigour of research that can clearly demonstrate drama is a valuable technique that engages leaners, as it fosters language and literacy development.

Note

1 Following age guidelines set by National Association for the Education of Young Children (n.d.), this discussion focuses on interventions designed for children from birth to eight years old.

References

Blum-Kulka, S. and Snow, C. E. (1992). Developing autonomy for tellers, tales, and telling in family narrative events. *Journal of Narrative & Life History*, 2(3), 187–217.

Boston Public Schools Department of Early Childhood. (n.d.). *Storytelling: The Boston Listens Project*. Retrieved 15 February 2015, from http://bpsearlychildhood.weebly.com/storytelling. html.

Brady, J. and Millard, E. (2012). Weaving new meanings: Evaluating children's written responses to a story telling resource package. *Literacy*, 46(1), 17–24. doi:10.1111/j.1741-4369.2011.00582.x.

Brown, V. and Pleydell, S. (1999). *The Dramatic Difference: Drama in the Preschool and Kindergarten Classroom*. Portsmouth, NH: Heinemann.

Common Core State Standards Initiative. (2010). *Common Core State Standards for English Language Arts and Literacy in History/Social Studies, Science, and Technical Subjects*. Available from www.corestandards. org/wp-content/uploads/ELA_Standards.pdf.

Conard, F. (1992). *The Arts in Education and a Meta-Analysis*. Unpublished Doctoral Dissertation, Purdue University.

Conard, F. (1998). Meta-analysis of the effectiveness of creative drama. In B. J. Wagner (ed.), *Educational Drama and Language Arts: What Research Shows* (pp. 199–211). Portsmouth, NH: Heinemann.

Cooper, P. (1993). *When Stories Come to School: Telling, Writing, and Performing Stories in the Early Childhood Classroom*. New York: Teachers & Writers Collaborative.

Cooper, P. M. (2005). Literacy learning and pedagogical purpose in Vivian Paley's 'storytelling curriculum'. *Journal of Early Childhood Literacy*, 5(3), 229–251.

Cooper, P. M. (2009). *The Classrooms All Young Children Need: Lessons in Teaching from Vivian Paley*. Chicago: University of Chicago Press.

Cremin, T., Swann, J., Flewitt, R., Faulkner, D. and Kucirkova, N. (n.d.). Evaluation report of MakeBelieve Arts helicopter technique of storytelling and story acting. Retrieved from http://static1. squarespace.com/static/53ad7934e4b0a25fee7c47b2/t/53baab80e4b0afc035d389fb/1404742528104/ Helicopter+Technique+Evaluation.pdf.

Dansky, J. L. (1980). Cognitive consequences of sociodramatic play and exploration training for economically disadvantaged preschoolers. *Journal of Child Psychology & Psychiatry & Allied Disciplines*, *21*(1), 47–58.

DeTemple, J. M. and Tabors, P. O. (1996). Children's story retelling as a predictor of early reading achievement. Quebec City, Quebec: Biennial Meeting of the International Society for the Study of Behavioral Development. Retrieved from www.eric.ed.gov/ERICWebPortal/detail?accno= ED403543.

Fein, G. G., Ardila-Rey, A. E. and Groth, L. A. (2000). The narrative connection: Stories and literacy. In K. A. Roskos and J. F. Christie (eds), *Play and Literacy in Early Childhood: Research from Multiple Perspectives* (pp. 27–43). Mahwah, NJ: Lawrence Erlbaum Associates.

Flemming, M., Merrell, C. and Tymms, P. (2010). The impact of drama in pupils' language, mathematics, and attitude in two primary schols. *Research in Drama Education*, *9*(2), 177–197. doi:10.1080/ 1356978042000255067.

Fox, M. (1987). *Teaching Drama to Young Children*. Portsmouth, NH: Heinemann.

Galda, L. (1982). Playing about a story: Its impact on comprehension. *Reading Teacher*, *36*(1), 52–55.

Greenfader, C. M. and Brouillette, L. (2013). Boosting language skills of English learners though dramatization and movement. *The Reading Teacher*, *67*(3), 171–180. doi:10.1002/TRTR.1192.

Griffith, L. W. and Rasinski, T. V. (2004). A focus on fluency: How one teacher incorporated fluency with her reading curriculum. *The Reading Teacher*, *58*(2), 126–137. doi:10.1598/RT.58.2.1.

Heath, S. B. (1982). What no bedtime story means: Narrative skills at home and school. *Language in Society*, *11*(1), 49–76. Retrieved from www.jstor.org/stable/4167291.

Heinig, R. B. (1992). *Improvisation with Favorite Tales: Integrating Drama into the Reading/Writing Classroom*. Portsmouth, NH: Heinemann.

Hicks, D. (1991). Kinds of narrtive: Genre skills among first graders from two communities. In A. McCabe and C. Peterson (eds), *Developing Narrative Structure* (pp. 55–87). Hillsdale, NJ: Lawrence Erlbaum Associates.

Kardash, C. A. M. and Wright, L. (1987). Does creative drama benefit elementary school srudents: A meta-analysis. *Youth Theatre Journal*, *1*(3), 11–18.

Keehn, S. (2003). The effect of instruction and practice through readers theatre on young readers' oral reading fluency. *Reading Research and Instruction*, *42*(4), 40–61. doi:10.1080/19388070309558395.

Lee, B. K., Patall, E. A., Cawthon, S. W. and Steingut, R. R. (2015). The effect of drama-based pedagogy on PreK-16 outcomes: A meta-analysis of resaerch from 1985–2012. *Review of Educational Research*, *85*(1), 3–49. doi:10.3102/0034654314540477.

Mages, W. K. (2008). Does creative drama promote language development in early childhood? A review of the methods and measures employed in the empirical literature. *Review of Educational Research*, *78*(1), 124–152. doi:10.3102/0034654307313401.

MakeBelieve Arts. (2015a). *Helicopter Starter Training*. Retrieved 20 February 2015, from www. makebelievearts.co.uk/helicopter-training.

MakeBelieve Arts. (2015b). *Helicopter Stories Centres of Excellence*, Retrieved 20 February 2015, from www.makebelievearts.co.uk/centres-of-excellence.

MakeBelieve Arts. (2015c). *Welcome to MakeBelieve Arts!* Retrieved 15 February 2015, from www. makebelievearts.co.uk/.

Mardell, B. (2013). Boston listens: Vivian Paley's storytelling/story acting in an urban school district. *New England Reading Association Journal*, *49*(1), 58–67.

Martinez, M., Roser, N. L. and Strecker, S. (1998/1999). 'I never though I could be a star': A readers theatre ticket to fluency. *The Reading Teacher*, *52*(4), 326–334.

McCabe, A. (1991). Preface: Sturcture as a way of understsanding narrative. In A. McCabe and C. Peterson (eds), *Developing Narrative Structure* (pp. ix–xvii). Hillsdale, NJ: Lawrence Erlbaum Associates.

McCaslin, N. (1996). *Creative Drama in the Classroom and Beyond* (6th edn). White Plains, NY: Longman Publishers.

McNamee, G. D. (1987). The social origins of narrative skills. In M. Hickman (ed.), *Social and Functional Approaches to Language and Thought* (pp. 287–304). New York: Academic Press, Inc.

McNamee, G. D., McLane, J. B., Cooper, P. M. and Kerwin, S. M. (1985). Cognition and affect in early literacy development. *Early Child Development & Care*, *20*(4), 229–244.

McNamee, G. D., McLane, J. B., Cooper, P. M. and Kerwin, S. M. (1986). Cognition and affect in early literacy development. In S. Burroughs and R. Evans (eds), *Play, Language, and*

Socialisation: Perspectives on Adult Roles (pp. 209–224). New York: Gordon and Breach Science Publishers.

Michaels, S. (1981). 'Sharing time': Children's narrative styles and differential access to literacy. *Language in Society*, *10*(3), 423–442.

Miller, G. and Mason, G. E. (1983). Dramatic improvisation: Risk-free role playing for improving reading performance. *Reading Teacher*, *37*(2), 128–131.

Millin, S. K. and Rinehart, S. D. (1999). Some of the benefits of readers theater participation for second grade Title I students. *Reading Research and Instruction*, *39*(1), 71–88.

Moore, B. H. and Caldwell, H. (1990). The art of planning: Drama as rehearsal for writing in the primary grades. *Youth Theatre Journal*, *4*(3), 13–20.

Moore, B. H. and Caldwell, H. (1993). Drama and drawing for narrative writing in primary grades. *Journal of Educational Research*, *87*(2), 100–110.

National Association for the Education of Young Children. (n.d.). *Our Mission and Strategic Direction*. Retrieved from www.naeyc.org/about/mission.

National Reading Panel. (2000). Teaching children to read: An evidence-based assessment of the scientific research literature on reading and its implications for reading instruction. Retrieved from www.nichd.nih.gov/publications/pubs/nrp/Documents/report.pdf.

Nicolopoulou, A. (1996). Narrative development in social context. In D. I. Slobin, J. Gerhardt, A. Kyratzis and J. Guo (eds), *Social Interaction, Social Context, and Language: Essays in Honor of Susan Ervin-Tipp* (pp. 369–390). Mahwah, NJ: Lawrence Erlbaum Associates.

Nicolopoulou, A. (1997). Worldmaking and identity formation in children's narrative play-acting. In B. D. Cox and C. Lightfoot (eds), *Sociogenetic Perspectives on Internalization* (pp. 157–187). Mahwah, NJ: Lawrence Erlbaum Associates.

Nicolopoulou, A. (2002). Peer-group culture and narrative development. In S. Blum-Kulka and C. E. Snow (eds), *Talking to Adults: The Contribution of Multiparty Discourse to Language Acquisition* (pp. 117–152). Mahwah, NJ: Lawrence Erlbaum Associates.

Nicolopoulou, A. (2006). The interplay of play and narrative in children's development: Theoretical reflections and concrete examples. In A. Göncü and S. Gaskins (eds), *Play and Development: Evolutionary, Sociocultural, and Functional Perspectives* (pp. 247–273). Mahwah, NJ: Lawrence Erlbaum Associates.

Nicolopoulou, A. and Cole, M. (2010). Design experimentation as a theoretical and empirical tool for developmental pedagogical research. *Pedagogies: An International Journal*, *5*(1), 61–71. doi:10.1080/15544800903406316.

Nicolopoulou, A., McDowell, J. and Brockmeyer, C. (2006). Narrtive play and emergent literacy: Storytelling and story-acting meet journal writing. In D. G. Singer, R. M. Golinkoff and K. Hirsh-Pasek (eds), *Play = Learning: How Play Motivates and Enhances Children's Cognitive and Social-Emotional Growth* (pp. 124–144). Oxford: Oxford University Press.

Nicolopoulou, A., Scales, B. and Weintraub, J. (1994). Gender differences and symbolic imagination in the stories of four-year-olds. In A. H. Dyson and C. Genishi (eds), *The Need for Story: Cultural Diversity in Classroom and Community* (pp. 102–123). Urbana, IL: National Council of Teachers of English.

Nielsen, D. C. (1993). The effects of four models of group interaction with storybooks on the literacy growth of low-achieving kindergarten children. In D. J. Leu and C. K. Kinzer (eds), *Examining Central Issues in Literacy Research, Theory, and Practice: Forty-Second Yearbook of the National Reading Conference* (Vol. 42, pp. 279–287). Chicago: National Reading Conference.

Paley, V. G. (1981). *Wally's Stories: Conversations in the Kindergarten*. Cambridge, MA: Harvard University Press.

Paley, V. G. (1990). *The Boy Who Would Be a Helicopter: The Uses of Storytelling in the Classroom*. Cambridge, MA: Harvard University Press.

Paley, V. G. (1999). *The Kindness of Children*. Cambridge, MA: Harvard University Press.

Paris, A. H. and Paris, S. G. (2003). Assessing narrative comprehension in young children. *Reading Research Quarterly*, *38*(1), 36–76.

Pellegrini, A. D. and Galda, L. (1982). The effects of thematic-fantasy play training on the development of children's story comprehension. *American Educational Research Journal*, *19*(3), 443–452.

Peterson, C. and McCabe, A. (1994). A social interactionist account of developing decontextualized narrative skill. *Developmental Psychology*, *30*(6), 937–948.

Podlozny, A. (2000). Strengthening verbal skills through the use of classroom drama: A clear link. *Journal of Aesthetic Education*, *34*(3–4), 239–275.

Rice University. (2011). *School Literacy and Culture: Classroom Storytelling Project*. Retrieved 20 February 2015, from http://centerforeducation.rice.edu/slc/csp.html.

Richner, E. S. and Nicolopoulou, A. (2001). The narrative construction of differing conceptions of the person in the development of young children's social understanding. *Early Education & Development*, *12*(3), 393–432.

Sachs, J., Mardell, B. and Boni, M. (2014). Storytelling, sory acting, and literacy in Boston Public Schools: An interview with Jason Sachs, Ben Mardell, and Marina Boni. *American Journal of Play*, *6*(2), 173–189.

Saltz, E., Dixon, D. and Johnson, J. (1977). Training disadvantaged preschoolers on various fantasy activities: Effects on cognitive functioning and impulse control. *Child Development*, *48*(2), 367–380.

Saltz, E. and Johnson, J. (1974). Training for thematic-fantasy play in culturally disadvantaged children: Preliminary results. *Journal of Educational Psychology*, *66*(4), 623–630.

Shavelson, R. J. and Towne, L. (eds). (2002). *Scientific Research in Education*. Washington, DC: National Academy Press.

Shmukler, D. and Naveh, I. (1984–1985). Structured vs. unstructured play training with economically disadvantaged preschoolers. *Imagination, Cognition & Personality*, *4*(3), 293–304.

Silvern, S. B. (1980). Play, pictures, and repetition: Mediators in aural prose learning. *Educational Communication & Technology*, *28*(2), 134–139.

Snow, C. E., Burns, M. S. and Griffin, P. (eds). (1998). *Preventing Reading Difficulties in Young Children*. Washington, DC: National Academy Press.

Spolin, V. (1963). *Improvisation for the Theater: A Handbook of Teaching and Directing Techniques*. Evanston, IL: Northwestern University Press.

Spolin, V. (1986). *Theater Games for the Classroom: A Teacher's Handbook*. Evanston, IL: Northwestern University Press.

Tsou, W. (2011). The application of readers theater to FLES (foreign language in the elementary schools) reading and writing. *Foreign Language Annals*, *44*(4), 727–748.

Vasinda, S. and McLeod, J. (2011). Extending readers theatre: A powerful and purposeful match with podcasting. *The Reading Teacher*, *64*(7), 486–497. doi:10.1598/RT.64.7.2.

Vitz, K. (1983). A review of empirical research in drama and language. *Children's Theatre Review*, *32*(4), 17–25.

Wagner, B. J. (1988). Research currents: Does classroom drama affect the arts of language? *Language Arts*, *65*(1), 46–55.

Wagner, B. J. (1998). *Educational Drama and Language Arts: What Research Shows*. Portsmouth, NH: Heinemann.

Warash, B. G. and Workman, M. (1993). All life's a stage: Children dictate and reenact personal experiences. *Dimensions of Early Childhood*, *21*(4), 9–12.

Westby, C. E. (1985). Learning to talk-talking to learn: Oral-literate language differences. In C. S. Simon (ed.), *Communication Skills and Classroom Success: Therapy Methodologies for Language-Learning Disabled Students* (pp. 181–213). San Diego, CA: College-Hill.

Worthy, J. and Broaddus, K. (2002). Fluency beyond the primary grades: From group performance to silent, independent reading. *The Reading Teacher*, *55*(4), 334–343.

Worthy, J. and Prater, K. (2002). 'I thought about it all night': Readers theatre for reading fluency and motivation. *The Reading Teacher*, *56*(3), 294–297.

Young, C. and Rasinski, T. (2009). Implementing readers theatre as an approach to classroom fluency instruction. *The Reading Teacher*, *63*(1), 4–13.

Young, T. A. and Vardell, S. (1993). Weaving readers theatre and nonfiction into the curricla. *The Reading Teacher*, *46*(5), 396–406.

25

CHILDREN'S PERSONAL NARRATIVES REFLECT WHERE THEY COME FROM, REVEAL WHO THEY ARE AND PREDICT WHERE THEY ARE GOING

Allyssa McCabe

Narration is the linguistic meeting ground of culture, cognition and emotion. Children develop the ability to narrate between the ages of two and six years. Parents who talk extensively with their children about past experiences make their children strong story-tellers by the age of five, which predicts literacy skill ten years later. Parents differ individually and culturally in the aspects of the past they choose to emphasize with children, resulting in narratives that are structured in a variety of ways, which require numerous analyses to delineate. Traumatic brain injury, specific language impairment and autism compromise narration. Cultural differences should never be mistaken for deficits and vice versa.

In this chapter, I consider narratives that convey real or pretend memories of something that happened, usually told verbally and usually told in the past tense (McCabe, 1991a), often as a sequence of events. The present chapter will summarize my programme of research on the development of personal narration, a programme begun in 1974 and guided by a social interactionist approach to language acquisition.

Children typically develop the ability to narrate past personal experiences sometime around their second birthdays (Nelson, 1989). We have learned much about this ability, its causes and its consequences in the past 40 years. Narration reflects and affects a child's cultural, linguistic, cognitive and emotional resources. Only when we are well informed about how narrative develops with age, in particular families, various cultures and children with devel-opmental challenges, will we be able to provide the information families and practitioners need to help all children achieve academic success.

Why narrative?

Scholars have identified many precursors to literacy, especially phonological awareness and letter-level skills (Scarborough, 2001), but have largely neglected narration. However, recent research increasingly demonstrates the importance of narration to literacy acquisition and to other life skills. Children's ability to narrate at the beginning of kindergarten predicts their first-grade reading comprehension, vocabulary, global language and narrative ability (Dickinson and Kaiser, in progress). The ability of children to produce a narrative at the end of preschool also predicts fourth, seventh and tenth grade reading comprehension (Snow et al., 2007). Moreover, children's narrative conversations with parents predict their future social problem-solving skills (Leyva et al., 2012); in particular, parental resolution of negative experiences predicts better problem-solving skills at the end of pre-kindergarten.

Narrative is the primary means of making sense of our experiences, a key way in which we form intimacy with others, how we report to medical personnel what happened to us and how much pain we are in, and how we testify to officers, lawyers, judges and juries about what we experienced or witnessed and what role we played in such events (McCabe, 1996). To tell a coherent narrative is to have come to terms with what an experience was and meant to one and is the raw material of therapy.

About narrative

There are numerous types of narrative, although the most commonly collected narratives in the field of child development are stories told in response to story stems or wordless picture books, story retellings and personal narratives. One's choice of narrative genre should be determined by one's research goals. My own goals as a psychologist have led me to prefer personal narration. First, personal narratives are used in diverse cultures, whereas fictional narratives are not universal (e.g. Janes and Karmani, 2001). Second, I am interested in studying cultural differences in narration, which are obscured in retelling wordless picture books; wordless picture books obviate the narrator's choice of story and flowers, animals and other aspects of illustrations have meanings that differ by culture (Slobin, 2011). Third, children with developmental challenges perform better on personal narratives than on narrations of wordless picture books (McCabe et al., 2008); even when the length of what such children say in response to picture books exceeds that of personal narratives, it often consists of present-tense picture description rather than genuine past-tense narration of events (Berman, 1995; McCabe et al., 2008).

About narrative analyses

There are many ways of analysing narrative, and each provides a distinct picture. Just as narratives themselves are our way of understanding experience, narrative analyses are our way of understanding narratives (McCabe, 1991b). To fully appreciate the richness and diversity of children's narratives requires numerous analyses. In this chapter we present analyses in the context of the narratives they illuminate rather than on their own terms. The most illuminating analyses of children's narratives include: High Point Analysis (Peterson and McCabe, 1983, adapted from Labov and Waletsky, 1967), Stanza analysis (Hymes, 1982), Narrative Assessment Profile (McCabe and Bliss, 2003) and Africanist analysis (Champion et al., 2003, adapted from Okpewho, 1992).

Development of narration

At approximately two years, children begin to narrate past events, often those just past. For example, a 23-month-old boy's first narrative was, 'Hug bow-wow. An'ya hug bow-wow.'

This was a reference to playing with his babysitter and her dog. At 30.5 months, that same boy told the following two-event narrative in conversation:

Mother: Did you like the puppy?'
Child: He taste my knee.
Mother: He tasted your knee?
Child: Theth. And puppy chase me.

The subsequent development of narration by children aged four through nine has been documented (Peterson and McCabe, 1983). By four years of age, children string more events together, but they jump around chronologically and leave things out, producing leapfrog narratives, as in the following narrative by a 28-month-old boy:

Child: Fall down.
Mother: What happened?
Child: Hurt face. An'ya wipe it like dat (gestures).
Mother: What happened then?
Child: Uh. Rocks.
Mother: No rocks?

The child's mother never discovers what the rocks were about. Did the child trip over rocks and hurt his face?

By five years of age, children have straightened out event sequencing, though they tend to end their narratives prematurely at the emotional climax, eschewing resolution, as did the following five-year-old boy.

Child: Do you know what? Every single tree fell down on our house. Cause there's a snowstorm. I picked them up with one, with my pinky. All of them with my pinky. Do you believe that?
Interviewer: No.
Child: I did.

While this narrative began in fact with the snowstorm, it ended in fantastic evaluation. We never know how the fallen trees were actually dispatched.

At six years of age, European North American (ENA) children produce a classic narrative, in High Point Analysis terminology (High Point categories in bold), as did the six-year-old boy below:

Abstract
Hi, Sally, I broke my arm.

Orientation
Well . . . the day, two days ago, I was climbing the the tree.

Complicating Actions
and I . . . Well see, I went towards the LOW branch and . . . I got caught with my baving suit? I dangled my hands down and they got bent.

310

Evaluated High Point

Because it was like this hard surface under it. Then they bent like in two triangles. But luckily it was my left arm that broke . . .

Resolving Action

My mom was in the shower, so I SCREAMED for Jessica, and Jessica goed, told my mom . . . I had to go to the hospital and get . . . It was much more worser than you think because I had to . . . go into the operation room . . . and I had to take anesthesia and I had to fall, fall, fall asleep, and they bended my arm back. And I have my cast on.

Coda

Do you want to sign my cast?

In this classic narrative, the child begins with a headlining abstract, narrates a series of complicating actions that culminate in a highly evaluated climax, proceeds to narrate actions that resolve the issue and returns the narrative to the present conversation in which it was embedded – a classic narrative.

Although the narratives in this chapter so far have been produced by ENA children, the developmental sequence just described is not limited to that group. A similar pattern has been found for low-income Chilean children (Barra and McCabe, 2013), low-income Californians from Spanish-speaking Mexican heritage backgrounds (Guerra, 2008), Chinese (Zhang, 2013) and Taiwanese children from varied socioeconomic backgrounds (Lai, 2013).

Individual differences in narration: family and culture

Once we notice age differences in the quality of narration, individual differences at each age also stand out. That is, some narrators are vastly better than their peers. Parallel and independent efforts to tie such individual differences to differences in parental input previously documented for non-narrative language production began in the 1980s with two groups: (1) Fivush and colleagues and (2) McCabe and Peterson. Fivush and Fromhoff (1988) recorded conversation about the past from ten white, middle-class mothers of 2½-year-olds and discerned that some were talkative and elaborative, whereas others were less talkative and repetitive. McCabe and Peterson (1991) collected recordings from ten white, middle-class Canadian children and parents every month for 18 months beginning when the children were approximately 25–27 months old. Those authors found what they termed a topic-extending style of conversation (similar to the elaborative style), as well as topic-switching, repetitive and confrontational input about the past. McCabe and Peterson (1991) found that more topic extension provided by parents predicted longer child narratives over time. Since the publication of these studies, many additional studies have reported congruent results; reviewing these studies, Fivush et al. (2006) found that elaborative (topic-extending) reminiscing consistently predicts optimal child narration.

Furthermore, what parents focus on in talk about the past differs in ways that predict children's future focus. For example, parents who focus questions on orientation (setting information about where and when something occurred) at the expense of plot have children who subsequently do the same in their own narration (Peterson and McCabe, 1992, 1996). Children whose parents ask many questions regarding causation eventually talk more than peers about causality (McCabe and Peterson, 1996). Parents tend to emphasize what was said (versus done) in the past with their daughters, and girls end up more likely than boys to report talk (Ely and McCabe, 1993, 1996; Ely et al., 1996; Ely et al., 1995).

As noted, the majority of the work in this section showing how parental input predicts children's narrative productions involved ENA children. In addition to individual differences in narration within a particular age group in a particular culture, pronounced cultural differences in the ways parents talk to children about the past have been reported. Japanese mothers (Minami and McCabe, 1995), for example, value brief turns by their children and succinct narratives that consist of several similar experiences instead of lengthy accounts of one experience; they do not wish their children to embarrass themselves by telling listeners things that those listeners could be expected to figure out for themselves. Spanish mothers, in contrast to both ENA and Japanese mothers, employ what Melzi (2000) calls a 'conversation-focused' rather than a story-focused strategy, a strategy to avoid silences. Latino parents also emphasize the importance of family, including extended family (Cristofaro and Tamis-LeMonda, 2008). Emotion words and, especially for girls, diminutives figure prominently in Latino mother–child narrative conversations (King and Gallagher, 2008).

Chinese immigrant parents more often mention where events were held and the people involved, actions involving others and negative behaviours performed by their children compared to ENA parents during mealtime conversations (Koh and Wang, 2013). Unfortunately, we have little information regarding parent narrative input in many cultures.

Cultural differences in narration

As a result of differential parental interest in various aspects of the past, children develop discourse styles valued by their culture of origin, and, in the case of bilingual children, regardless of which language(s) they speak.

Minami and McCabe (1991) employed a stanza analysis based on Hymes (1982) to analyse personal narratives of five- to nine-year-old Japanese children that revealed a pattern in which such children regularly combine two or three similar experiences in one coherent narrative, and each narrative comprises sets of three verses; almost 60 per cent of the stanzas produced by the children showed this pattern of three verses per stanza – a numerical regularity not found to be as pronounced in narratives from other cultures so far. The narratives are quite succinct, in keeping with cultural values to avoid verbosity, which is considered insulting to listeners, a sign of poor manners and stupidity. Note that the stanzas below are groups of sentences more tightly related to each other than to other sentences in the same narrative.

This is an example by an eight-year-old Japanese boy:

1   As for the first shot,
2   (I) got (it) at Ehime.
3   (It) hurt a lot

4   As for the second shot,
5   (I) knew (it) would hurt.
6   (It) didn't hurt so much.

7   The next one didn't hurt so much either.
8   As for the last shot, you know.
9   (It) didn't hurt at all.

Chang and McCabe (2013) analysed personal narratives of Taiwanese children focusing on the evaluative component of High Point Analysis and compared them to those in the Peterson and McCabe (1983) ENA corpus. Whereas 50 per cent of the ENA children's narrative comments were at least partially evaluative and there was no significant age difference between four and nine years, only 25 per cent of the oldest Taiwanese children's comments (nine-year-olds) were evaluative and this represented a significant increase from the age of three. Wang (2013) has also demonstrated many ways in which Chinese narrators downplay evaluation in comparison to ENAs. In fact, Wang (2013: 52) speaks of an 'emotional muteness' to be found in Chinese autobiography. A key result of such a contrast is that native and overseas Asians, compared with European and ENAs, have later onset of autobiographical memory, remember fewer childhood memories and report fewer specific details about those memories (Wang, 2013). Evaluation evidently functions as a mnemonic device in autobiographical narration (McCabe and Chang, 2013). Consider the following narrative (translated from Taiwanese; evaluation underlined) from a girl, aged six years four months:

Interviewer:	Yesterday when I cleaned my room, a cockroach crawled up my leg. I was frightened . . . Have you ever been frightened by anything?
Child:	I was <u>frightened</u> (by a cockroach) before too but I forgot. Once when I already was having a bath . . . My older saw . . . My older saw . . . Saw a caterpillar on me.
Interviewer:	(laughs) Then what?
Child:	(laughs) When I took a bath last time. Then washed then touched a . . . When my older sister saw the caterpillar on me, I did not know I did not know what that was.
Interviewer:	Then what?
Child:	And my older sister saw (that). then <u>she was frightened</u>.
Experimenter:	(laughs) Your sister was frightened.
Child:	Then my mom took a piece of toilet paper. Then she caught the caterpillar (and) threw (it) away. Then there were a bunch of ants in my house. <u>I was frightened one time</u>.
Interviewer:	What happened?
Child:	I was frightened . . . there were a bunch of, a bunch of, <u>super many</u> ants in my house . . . Then (she) took a that . . . A tape . . . Then took a tape when (she) took a tape to stick, then (my) mom took my tapes.
Interviewer:	Oh.
Child:	(She took a tape) to stick (the ants) and then (she) took another tape again. Older sister did not help at all because she was drawing.

First of all, there was relatively minimal evaluation in this narrative, and what there was was repetitive ('frightened'). Also, similar to their Japanese peers, about one-third to half of Taiwanese six- to eight-year-olds narrated at least one story that consisted of a collection of experiences. In contrast, of the 1124 personal narratives in the original Peterson and McCabe (1983) ENA corpus, only 33 (2.93 per cent) were narratives that included mention of more than one experience, whereas 54 of 596 (9.1 per cent) narratives in the Taiwanese corpus related collections of experiences, a significant difference.

Labov and Waletsky (1997/1967) required one sequence of two specific past-tense events in order for any discourse to be called a narrative, a definition I strictly adhered to at first (Peterson and McCabe, 1983). However, when we began studying Latino children's narration, we were forced to re-examine this definition. Fully 49 per cent of one sample of Latino narratives (Silva and McCabe, 1996) contained only one event and would not have qualified as worthy of further study. In a sample of Dominican American seven- to eight-year-old children and Costa Rican six- to nine-year-old children approximately 20 per cent of the narratives also consisted of minimal events (Cuneo et al., 2008). Fewer than 10 per cent of the Dominican American and Costa Rican sample narratives were complete episodes in Story Grammar (i.e. goals, plans to meet those goals, consequences) revolving around planning (Stein and Glenn, 1979). In fact, in some samples of Latino narration, a key feature of the narration is a relative de-emphasis on linearity or temporal sequence, especially in comparison to ENAs (Sparks, 2008; Uccelli, 2008). Also, Latino children incorporate their parents' emphasis on including extended family members in their narratives (Silva and McCabe, 1996). Both an abundance of family members and a lack of linear sequencing (leading to low High Point and Story Grammar structure codes) are obvious in the example below:

> Yes, to grandma (to visit in hospital). My mother wanted to take her to the hospital, but grandma didn't wanted to go, but we took her. They didn't do anything to her. And another old lady was there. We looked at her but she was not grandma. The old lady was just talking and talking with my mom and with my sister A. Big sister who lives in Riverside (. . .) And we took her home. But she wanted to go to another house, which was my aunt's house, but that house was very ugly, and my aunt had too many dogs and the house was dirty. And then we took her . . . to my aunt's. And now grandma says that my sister and my aunt keep the house clean and that it has a new roof. And today we are going to visit her. At her school.
>
> *(Mexican American girl, seven years)*

There is only one event here – so a strict Labovian High point analysis would not classify it as a narrative; modified High Point Analysis would classify it as a minimal, one-event narrative (McCabe and Rollins, 1994): 'Then we took her to . . . my aunt's.' Yet clearly this was an important experience to the child, and she gives many descriptive details that figured in the planning regarding placement of the grandmother (Story Grammar Analysis would classify this as a Descriptive Sequence – the most primitive kind of narrative). The story is all about four members of her family and herself. No regular stanza pattern has been discerned for any Latino group examined so far. But rather than seeing such narratives as lacking desired characteristics, Uccelli (2008: 201) suggests that in much Latino narration 'temporal organization [is] subordinated to . . . evaluative purposes'. In contrast, other groups of children subordinate evaluation within the limits of linear sequencing.

African American children tell diverse forms of narratives (Champion, 2003), but two kinds predominate: (1) They often produce a classic, topic-centred narrative of the sort ENAs age six years and up produce at their most sophisticated. In fact, African American children produce classic narratives at a higher rate than their ENA peers (Champion et al., 1995). (2) Alternatively, African American children sometimes produce a performative narrative (Champion and McCabe, in press) that consists of multiple related events (like Japanese and Taiwanese children's narratives). Below is an example of both:

Classic Narrative produced by a ten-year-old African American:

Orientation

No but my little brother, He . . . was real young. I think he was two years old. An' my mother was drivin'. An' my uncle was in fron' seat. An' me an' my younger cousin dat

lives in Baltimore – she's eight years old. Her name is Whitney. An' my little brother
was sittin' next to us. An' we was lookin' aroun'.
An' he started playin' with da door. An' the door was unlocked.

Complicating Action

An' he opened the door an' fell out the car. An' he was flippin' back. An' he his head
was busted open an' he had to get stitches.

Evaluative High Point

An' me an my cousin Whitney was sittin' in the back o' the car cryin'. Because he fell
out the car. My mother kep' goin.' An' he did

Resolving Action

Then my uncle Al said, 'Rhonda stop the car because he fell out the car.' An' she got
out the car. An' she was actin' crazy. An' she got out the car. An' she was actin' crazy.
An' she got 'im, like she like OH MY GOD she like MY BABY! And he got a cast
around his head, An' he got stitches an' we brought him home

Here is a Performative Narrative (displayed below in stanzas of approximately four lines
each) produced by an eight-year-old African American girl called Vivian:

We went to the dentist before
and I was g'tting' my tooth pulled
and . . . the dentist said, 'Oh, it's not gonna hurt.'
and he was lying to me.

It hurt.
It hurted so bad I coulda gone on screamin' even though I think some.
(I don't know what it was like.)
I was, in my mouth like, I was like, 'Oh that hurt!'
He said no, it wouldn't hurt . . .

The narrator describes in vivid detail several more dental experiences, concluding:

And so my cousin, he wanted to take out his tooth,
and he didn't know what to do,
so I told him.
'I'm a Pullin' Teeth Expert.

Pull out your own tooth,
but if you need somebody to do it,
Call me,
and I'll be over.'

Such performative narratives are more frequently told to audiences of peers than to adults.

The narratives of Haitian American children (Champion et al., 2003), like those of Haitian
American adults (Champion et al., in press), require yet another analysis, as there is no
apparent patterning in stanzas of specific line-length, nor forms adequately described by
either Story Grammar or High Point Analysis. The following narrative would be classified
as a two-event (minimal) narrative in High Point Analysis (and a primitive descriptive

sequence in Story Grammar (Stein and Glenn, 1979, after Propp, 1968/1928)). To depict the strength of such a narrative requires an Africanist analysis derived from the work of Okpewho (1992) in analysing African oral literature. In particular, note the singing and gesturing and poetic use of repetition (rep), parallelism (par: i.e. contrasts within similar grammatical structures) and detailing (det: piling up descriptive detail) in the following narrative told by a seven-year-old Haitian American girl (in English):

And once when I was in this wedding,	
I was a flower girl.	
And my friend Isadora too was a flower girl.	rep, par
And I was wearing this dress.	
Can I show the dress?	rep
It was a long dress with a ribbon around it.	rep, det
It was a blue dress.	rep, par, det
It was a long dress.	rep, par, det
And they stuck something on it.	det
I think it's still there.	
And it was a pretty dress.	rep, par, det
And I was sooo lucky	
Because there was a flower girl with curly hair	
—the same thing as me—	
at this other wedding.	
This flower girl—they wore ugly dresses.	
They was green.	det
And my friend said it was ugly dress.	rep, det
And my friend said it was ugly dress.	rep, det
Their hair was ugly.	rep, det
This girl had, her hair was like this, like that	
(demonstrates).	det
And it was up	det
And curled up	rep, par, det
And curled.	rep, par, det
I I was like ewww!	
I was glad I wasn't that flower girl!	
Because, and her hair was like, did she wake up in the morning?	
And these other flower girls—their hair was different from my hair.	rep, par
Cause theirs was curly too,	rep, det
But it was different.	rep, par, det
It was skinny curly.	rep, par, det
But I don't like the dress	
And I don't like their hairs,	rep, par
But they had this same flower girl from at the wedding.	
It wasn't different.	rep, par, det
And the reception: Ghetto superstar.	
And I like 'Ghetto Superstar'	rep
It goes (singing), 'Ghetto superstar, that is what you are.'	rep
Yeah, Maya sings it.	det
Maya and Pras from the Fugees.	det
Can I show you the dress now?	rep

Differences in narration due to disorders

Narration is a complex process neurologically, and thus it is affected in different systematic ways by different disorders.

Biddle et al. (1996) interviewed children and adults with Traumatic Brain Injury (TBI) and compared them to age- and ethnicity-matched individuals without such injury. The narratives were analysed using what is now known as the Narrative Assessment Profile (McCabe and Bliss, 2003). Narratives of individuals with TBI were significantly more dysfluent (more false starts, internal corrections, filled and unfilled pauses), more redundant and placed a strikingly greater burden on listeners to make sense of what was told. Note the repetitiousness (e.g. finding the pig, getting lost, thinking they would not make it) and the many key omissions (e.g. what happened to the pig, why they got lost, how they found their way home) in the following narrative by a ENA adult male with TBI, aged 31 years:

> (Long pause). About the only really good time I can remember getting lost was in West Virginia. Me and my brother had been walking into the woods one day and we found a pig in the woods. A pig. Pig got out of my uncle's . . . pig, uh . . . So we found a pig around. And then we found out that we did get lost. So we went walking through the woods for about two hours, until it got really dark. Then we found a house and went back home. But during the time that we were lost, we were really scared cause we didn't think we were going to make it back. And I got all upset and started crying like a little wimp. And I didn't think we were goin make it back. But we did. It was a little traumatic for me . . . cause I didn't think we were going to make it.

Specific Language Impairment (SLI) affects narrative profoundly. ENA eight- to ten-year-old boys with SLI narratives were compared to both an age-matched and a language-matched sample (Miranda et al., 1998). All six dimensions of the Narrative Assessment Profile (McCabe and Bliss, 2003) were impaired in these children. Specifically, Topic Maintenance, Event Sequencing, Explicitness and Referencing were severely impaired, while conjunctive cohesion and fluency were somewhat impaired. The following narrative by an eight-year-old ENA boy with SLI exemplifies these issues:

> I had a X-ray because they're checking on my leg. And I was scared that I was goin' up there and they gave me a balloon. And I went to, um, Toys-R-Us and gave me a toy. But I never, I, uh, I just broke my leg and I just fall down on my bike because I got hurt and my Band-Aids on me, put their off. And I jumped out of my bike and I . . . I flied and then I jumped down. And I um um our grandma, um she died. She was getting older, our grandma. And she died and the, uh, our grandma.
>
> And she died and the, uh funeral, my ma and dad went to the funeral. And the, Aunt Cindy was there too. And we, uh, they, um, uh, everybody was sad that um, a that died and on my birthday I went on my bike . . . And I jum . . . I just jump on my bike and I just balance on my, and I did it with a, I did do it with only my hands . . .

Individuals with High Functioning Autism Spectrum (HFASD) Disorder also show impaired narration. McCabe et al. (2013) interviewed ENA young men with and without HFASD and found that the narratives of men with HFASD were greatly impaired in one of two ways. Many were quite minimal – the sort of narrative produced by two- to three-year-olds with typical development, such as the following – the longest narrative produced by an ENA man, 19 years old, with HFASD:

Participant: I got stung on a trampoline.
Interviewer: Oh wow, on your foot
Participant: Not on my foot
Interviewer: Where was it? (this specific question is a departure from protocol by a graduate student in trying very hard to get the man to talk)
Participant: Right here

The other way in which men with HFASD displayed impaired narration was by producing rambling narratives that left things out and jumped around in time – the kind of narrative produced by four-year-olds with typical development:

Participant: Ummm, let's see ahhh, well it started off. I went up to Vermont. I was supposed to go to Vermont like um, on Friday evening. But then my mom decided to go so, we ended up going on Saturday morning. And then we um, well the whole reason we were going to Vermont was so I could go up to one of the Vermont places because I have a couple friends who play airsoft up there.
Interviewer: Oh cool.
Participant: Yeah. And um, we were gonna meet up because we have a group that does Vietnam reenactments kinda thing.
Interviewer: Oh cool.
Participant: And so like we do military shows and dress up in like the Vietnam gear and do all the like reenactment kind of thing with the airsoft guns. And the airsoft guns are like little 6mm plastic pellet guns, but not really like a pellet. It is more like a paintball gun, but looks like more realism . . .

The participant talks on and on for half an hour on the same general subject until the tape runs out. Unfortunately, he leaves listeners with no understanding of why he told the story. In both these cases, the men with HFASD showed poor awareness of social cues, avoidance of processing emotional information and general pragmatic problems typical of individuals with ASD. Although High Point analysis was sufficient to distinguish narratives of individuals with HFASD from those with typical development, the various dimensions of Narrative Assessment Profile (McCabe and Bliss, 2003) were also examined; conjunctive cohesion of individuals with HFASD was the key dimension that was significantly impaired.

Difference versus deficit

Once we are familiar with cultural differences in narration as well as differences due to individual challenges, we are in a position to discern difference and deficit. Identifying cultural difference as deficits involves falsely assigning labels to children that may in fact become self-fulfilling prophecies of failure, while mistaking individual deficits for cultural differences involves denying children who deserve them services that could be beneficial – neither one an acceptable mistake. For example, Champion and McCabe (in press) present examples of the two kinds of African American children's narratives – classical and performative – that show impairment.

Classic narrative with impairment

My daddy. Him, my, our car. And <u>him got it back. Him car got stolen and him got it back. Him got it back.</u> It, it was a hole. When <u>him got it back</u>, there was a hole. <u>When him got it back</u>, there was a hole. <u>Him got it back.</u> He took the speakers in their hole. There was a hole for the speakers. Bigger. It was . . . it was a speaker right here and a speaker right there. And when it got stolen now, <u>him got speakers back</u>. Go through here.

(4;8 African American boy with SLI)

Performative narrative with impairment

When I get some pets, they be, they be using it in our house. Because we be taking them outside and they don't be move because they don't need to move. Ain't no need to use the bathroom though. When they come in there, they use it. We be going outside quickest. We be running outs . . . out the door. <u>We be on the door</u>, and we run out through it.

And our pappy in the back, uh, and she, uh, he use it. He got a big cage for all of them. We got lots of dogs. Once when we have five dogs and none ran away . . .

(4;7 African American boy with SLI)

In the first narrative, we see underlined constructions that are not acceptable in African American English, as well as considerable repetitiousness. In the second, we see an underlined construction also not typical of African American English, along with the general appropriate performative characteristics of talking about multiple experiences pertaining to pets.

While bilingualism may confer benefits and need not result in problems acquiring language (McCabe et al., 2013), some children who are bilingual nonetheless do also suffer language impairment, and narrative is one facet of language that is often impaired. Bilingual eight- to eleven-year-olds, half with SLI, half Typically Developing (TD), produced a personal narrative in both English and Spanish (McCabe and Bliss, 2005). Children classified as TD produced longer narratives in both languages. For both groups, there were also significant correlations between English and Spanish narratives in utterances, orientations and actions.

In a follow-up study, bilingual (Spanish–English) children aged 7;0 to 9;9 with language impairment produced personal narratives and narratives in response to a wordless picture book (McCabe et al., 2008). Narratives were analysed using High Point Analysis (Peterson and McCabe, 1983). High-point ratings of personal narratives significantly exceeded those of wordless picture books. There was only a modest significant correlation between performances on the two genres of narrative, accounting for 9 per cent of the variance. While 14 per cent of the personal narratives did not contain even one past tense event, 44.4 per cent of the fictional, wordless picture-book narratives contained no past tense event and, therefore, consisted entirely of picture description – not narratives even given our relaxed definition.

Improving narration at home and at school

While longitudinal investigation of parents talking with children allowed us (e.g. McCabe and Peterson, 1991) to discuss the kind of parental input that predicted child narration, a random assignment intervention was required in order to discuss what caused child narrative prowess (Peterson et al., 1999). Low-income mothers of ENA three- to four-year-olds were randomly assigned to a topic-extension narrative intervention or a control condition. Intervention mothers were shown transcripts taken from the previous longitudinal study, one of which displayed an exemplary topic-extending, elaborative narrative style that we wanted the mothers to emulate. Mothers in the intervention group took turns reading these exemplary conversations aloud with other mothers, who played the child; pairs then switched roles. Mothers were encouraged to do the following:

1 Talk to your child frequently and consistently about past experiences.
2 Spend a lot of time talking about each topic.
3 Ask plenty of 'wh-' questions (who, what, when, where, why) and relatively fewer 'yes/ no' questions (e.g. 'Was Grandpa wearing a red coat?'). Ask questions about where and when events took place – the setting of the experience.
4 Listen carefully to what your child is saying and encourage elaboration.
5 Encourage your child to say more than one sentence at a time by using back-channel responses (e.g. 'I see' or 'Really?') or simply repeating what your child has just said.
6 Follow your child's lead. That is, talk about what your child wants to talk about.

Every month we reminded parents by phone of the importance of reminiscing with their children about past events. At the end of one year, intervention children had significantly increased receptive vocabularies compared to control children despite no explicit attention to vocabulary. At the end of two years, intervention children's narrative skills surpassed those of their peers. Reese and Newcombe (2007) similarly trained mothers of 1½- to 2½-year-olds to engage in elaborate reminiscing (very similar to topic extension, but focused on memory instead of language) and found that one to two years later intervention children had richer and more accurate memories so long as they had high levels of self-awareness to begin with. Reese et al. (2010) assigned low-income white Hispanic and non-Hispanic black parents (half of whom were bilingual) to one of three conditions: (1) elaborative reminiscing, (2) dialogic reading or (3) a control condition. Those authors found that training in elaborative reminiscing boosted the quality of narrative skills compared to dialogic reading and supported story comprehension significantly more than the other two conditions.

A variation on the interventions described in this section was also implemented in pre-school classrooms that served high-risk low-income, primarily bilingual four-year-olds of mixed ethnicity. Children in these classrooms were compared to children in similar classrooms in the same school district who received a standard preschool curriculum. Each child in the intervention classroom received approximately 26 one-on-one sessions in which volunteers elicited, extended (by asking open-ended questions) and took dictation of their narratives, which were also read back to the child on four additional occasions. At the end of a year, children in the intervention programme had significantly higher receptive vocabulary and narrative quality scores.

Conclusion

A keen appreciation of the complexity of a child's narrative confers many benefits upon literacy educators and policy-makers. Knowledge of the typical developmental sequence children follow in narration enables us to determine whether particular children are performing typically for their age, lag behind or excel. Knowledge of how parents influence children's narration, derived from random assignment experiments, not only explains narrative excellence but also offers a route to advance the skills of children who lag behind their peers in this important ability – preferably before these children finish preschool. Parents have been and can be easily informed about the importance of developing their children's ability to talk about past events at length and the means by which to do so. Classroom aids (parent volunteers, paraprofessionals) can easily be taught to do the same with vulnerable children at school (during drop-off and pick-up times, lunch, etc.). Past interventions with personal narrative have demonstrated that it takes a year or two of concentrated, heightened input to improve a child's narration. Thus, attempts to intervene with children who lag in this respect may require recruiting adults both at school and at home. After all, parents have abundantly more access to their children than even the most dedicated professionals. Just as parents will usually speak more and more complexly in their native language than in a second language, and are encouraged by numerous researchers to speak their native language with their children (see McCabe et al., 2013, for review), educators should support parents to encourage their children to narrate in ways family members understand and appreciate. Early childhood educators should thus also be familiar with cultural differences in preferred narrative style.

An appreciation of cultural differences in narration might lead savvy educators to include authentic published stories from children's cultures in their classrooms (see McCabe, 1996, for a full treatment of this endeavour). As noted at the outset, to tell a narrative is to make sense of experience. We understand the narratives we hear and read by means of mapping these on to the kind of narratives we tell. Bilingual students perform better when they are provided with culturally relevant materials in either of their languages, but especially in their native language (Goldenberg et al., 2006). Snow (2006) underlines this fact as key for the success of bilingual students and for understanding how what a student brings to school from their country of origin contrasts with what is expected of such students at school.

One final caveat regarding children's narration. Although parents, other family members and teachers can and usually do encourage a child's ability to narrate, children themselves provide the content of such narration. Parents differ individually and culturally in the extent to which they value asking children to reflect on the meaning of what they have experienced. But when children are carefully listened to, they are the ones who determine that meaning. To demonstrate this issue, consider my informal collections of narratives about children's favourite times at Disneyworld© and Disneyland©. Parents typically take their preschoolers to these parks and spend large sums of money to provide exciting experiences of meeting favourite characters, take thrilling rides, buy toys or delicious food, only to find that when they ask their children to tell their grandparents, say, about their favourite moments, those children reply, 'Two sinks. Our hotel room had two sinks!' or 'blue lights on the floor of the airplane!' or 'crystal rocks in the flower bed' or 'peeing my pants' (and getting a change of clothes). To listen carefully to children's narration of their own lives is to be continually surprised, as well as far more effective, in working with them to succeed.

References

Barra, G. and McCabe, A. (2013). Narrative skills of Chilean preschool children. *Imagination, Cognition and Personality*, *32*(4), 367–391.

Berman, R. A. (1995). Narrative competence and storytelling performance: How children tell stories in different contexts. *Journal of Narrative and Life History*, *5*, 285–314.

Biddle, K. R., McCabe, A. and Bliss, L. S. (1996) Narrative skills following traumatic brain injury in children and adults. *Journal of Communication Disorders*, *29*, 447–469.

Champion, T. B. (1995). Narrative discourse of African America children. *Journal of Narrative and Life History*, 5(4), 333–352.

Champion, T. B. (2003). *Understanding Storytelling among African American Children: A Journey from Africa to America*. Mahwah, NJ: Erlbaum.

Champion, T. B. and McCabe, A. (in press). Narrative structures of African American children: Commonalities and differences. In S. Lanehart, L. Green and J. Bloomquist (eds), *Oxford Handbook of African American Language*. New York: Oxford University Press.

Champion, T. B., McCabe, A. and Colinet, Y. (2003). The whole world could hear: The structure of Haitian American children's narratives. *Imagination, Cognition and Personality*, 22(4), 381–400.

Champion, T. B., McCabe, A. and Cuneo, C. N. (in press). Performative features in adults' Haitian Creole narratives. *Imagination, Cognition & Personality*.

Chang, C. and McCabe, A. (2013). Evaluation in Mandarin Chinese children's personal narratives. In A. McCabe and C. Chang (eds), *Chinese Language Narration: Culture, Cognition, and Emotion* (pp. 33–56). Amsterdam: John Benjamins.

Cristofaro, T. N. and Tamis-LeMonda, C. S. (2008). Lessons in mother–child and father–child personal narratives in Latino families. In A. McCabe, A.L. Bailey and G. Melzi (eds), *Spanish-language Narration and Literacy* (pp. 54–91). Cambridge: Cambridge University Press.

Cuneo, C. N., McCabe, A. and Melzi, G. (2008). Mestizaje: Afro-Caribbean and Indigenous Costa Rican children's narratives and links with other traditions. In A. McCabe, A. L. Bailey and G. Melzi (eds), *Spanish-Language Narration and Literacy* (pp. 237–272). Cambridge: Cambridge University Press.

Dickinson, D. K., Hofer, K. G. and Rivera, B. L. (in press). Narrative, literacy and other skills: Studies in interventions. The Developing Language Foundation for Reading Comprehension: Vocabulary, Complex Syntax and Extended Discourse from Preschool to Grade One. In E. Veneziano and A. Nicolopoulou (eds), *Narrative, Literacy and Other Skills: Studies in Interventions*. New York: John Benjamin.

Ely, R., Gleason, J. B., Narasimhan, B. and McCabe, A. (1995). Family talk about talk: Mothers lead the way. *Discourse Processes*, 19, 201–218.

Ely, R., Gleason, J. B. and McCabe, A. (1996). 'Why didn't you talk to your Mommy, Honey?' Parents' and children's talk about talk. *Research on Language and Social Interaction*, 29, 7–25.

Ely, R. and McCabe, A. (1993). Remembered voices. *Journal of Child Language*, 20(3), 671– 696.

Ely, R. and McCabe, A. (1996). Gender differences in memories for speech. In S. Leydesdorff, L. Passerini and P. Thompson (eds), *International Yearbook of Oral History and Life Stories: Gender and Memory* (pp. 17–30). New York: Oxford University Press.

Fernandez, C. and Melzi, G. (2008). Evaluation in Spanish-speaking mother–child narratives: The social and sense-making function of internal-state references. In A. McCabe, A. L. Bailey and G. Melzi (eds), *Spanish-Language Narration and Literacy* (pp. 92–118). Cambridge: Cambridge University Press.

Fivush, R. and Fromhoff, F. A. (1988). Style and structure in mother–child conversations about the past. *Discourse Processes*, 11, 337–355.

Fivush, R., Haden, C. A. and Reese, E. (2006). Elaborating on elaborations: Role of maternal reminiscing style in cognitive and socioemotional development. *Child Development*, 77(6), 1568–1588.

Goldenberg, C., Rueda, R. S. and August, D. (2006). Sociocultural influences on the literacy attainment of language-minority children and youth. In D. August and T. Shanahan (eds), *Developing Literacy in Second-Language Learners* (pp. 269–318). Mahwah, NJ: Erlbaum.

Guerra, A. W. (2008). The intersection of language and culture among Mexican-heritage children 3 to 7 years old. In A. McCabe, A. Bailey and G. Melzi (eds), *Spanish-Language Narration and Literacy: Culture, Cognition, and Emotion* (pp.146–174). Cambridge: Cambridge University Press.

Hymes, D. (1982). Narrative form as a 'grammar' of experience: Native Americans and a glimpse of English. *Journal of Education*, 2, 121–142.

Janes, H. and Kermani, H. (2001). Caregivers' story reading to young children in family literacy programs: Pleasure or punishment? *Journal of Adolescent and Adult Literacy*, 44, 458–466.

King, K. A. and Gallagher, C. (2008). Love, diminutives, and gender socialization in Andean mother–child narrative conversations. In A. McCabe, A. L. Bailey and G. Melzi (eds), *Spanish-Language Narration and Literacy* (pp. 119–145). Cambridge: Cambridge University Press.

Koh, J. B. K. and Wang, Q. (2013). Narrative self-making during dinnertime conversations in Chinese immigrant families. In A. McCabe and C. Chang (eds), *Chinese Language Narration: Culture, Cognition, and Emotion* (pp. 7–34). Amsterdam: John Benjamins.

Labov, W. and Waletsky, J. (1997). Narrative analysis. *Journal of Narrative and Life History*, 7(1–4), 3–38. (Original work published 1967.)

Lai, W. F. (2013). Socioeconomic differences in Taiwanese children's personal narratives: Conjunctions, internal state terms, and narrative structures. In A. McCabe and C. Chang (eds), *Chinese Language Narration: Culture, Cognition, and Emotion* (pp. 115–142). Amsterdam: John Benjamins.

Leyva, D., Berrocal, M. and Nolivos, V. (2012). Spanish-speaking parent–child emotional narratives and children's social problem-solving skills. *Journal of Cognition & Development*, 15(1), 22–42. doi:10.1080/15248372.2012.725188.

McCabe, A. (1991a). Editorial. *Journal of Narrative and Life History*, 1, 1–2.

McCabe, A. (1991b). Structure as a way of understanding. In A. McCabe and C. Peterson (eds), *Developing Narrative Structure* (pp. ix–xvii). Hillsdale, NJ: L. Erlbaum Associates.

McCabe, A. (1996). *Chameleon Readers: Teaching Children to Appreciate All Kinds of Good Stories.* New York: McGraw Hill.

McCabe, A. and Bliss, L. S. (2003). *Patterns of Narrative Discourse: A Multicultural Life Span Approach.* Boston: Allyn & Bacon.

McCabe, A. and Bliss, L. S. (2005). Narratives from Spanish-speaking children with impaired and typical language development. *Imagination, Cognition, and Personality*, 24(4), 331–346.

McCabe, A., Bliss, L. S., Barra, G. and Bennett, M. B. (2008). Comparison of personal versus fictional narratives of children with language impairment. *American Journal of Speech-Language Pathology*, 17, 1–13.

McCabe, A., Boccia, J., Bennett, M., Lyman, N. and Hagen, R. (2010). Improving oral language skills in preschool children from disadvantaged backgrounds: Remembering, writing, reading (RWR). *Imagination, Cognition and Personality*, 29(4), 363–391.

McCabe, A. and Chang, C. (2013). Introduction. In A. McCabe and C. Chang (eds), *Chinese Language Narration: Culture, Cognition, and Emotion* (pp. 1–6). Amsterdam: John Benjamins.

McCabe, A., Hillier, A. and Shapiro, C. (2012). Brief report: Structure of personal narratives of adults with Autism Spectrum Disorder. *Journal of Autism and Developmental Disorders*, 43(3), 733–738. doi:10.1007/s10803-012=1585-x.

McCabe, A. and Peterson, C. (1991). Getting the story: A longitudinal study of parental styles in eliciting narratives and developing narrative skill. In A. McCabe and C. Peterson (eds), *Developing Narrative Structure* (pp. 217–254). Hillsdale, NJ: L. Erlbaum Associates.

McCabe, A. and Rollins, P. R. (1994). Assessment of preschool narrative skills: Prerequisite for literacy. *American Journal of Speech Language Pathology: A Journal of Clinical Practice*, 3(1), 45–56.

McCabe, A., Tamis-LeMonda, C. S., Bornstein, M. H., Cates, C. B., Golinkoff, R. Hirsh-Pasek, K., Hoff, E., Kuchirko, Y., Melzi, G., Mendelsohn, A., Paez, M., Song, L., Guerra, A. W. (2013). Multilingual children: Beyond myths and towards best practices. *Society for Research in Child Development Social Policy Report*, 27(4), 1–21.

Melzi, G. (2000). Cultural variations in the construction of personal narrative: Central American and ENA mothers' elicitation style. *Discourse Processes*, 30(2), 153–177.

Minami, M. and McCabe, A (1991). Haiku as a discourse regulation device: A stanza analysis of Japanese children's personal narratives. *Language in Society*, 20(4), 577 599.

Minami, M. and McCabe, A. (1995). Rice balls versus bear hunts: Japanese and Caucasian family narrative patterns. *Journal of Child Language*, 22(2), 423–446.

Miranda, A. E., McCabe, A. and Bliss, L. S. (1998). Jumping around and leaving things out: A profile of the narrative abilities of children with specific language impairment. *Applied Psycholinguistics*, 19 (4), 647–668.

Nelson, K. (1989). *Narratives from the Crib.* Cambridge, MA: Harvard University Press.

Okpewho, I. (1992). *African oral Literature.* Bloomington, ID: Indiana University Press.

Peterson, C., Jesso, B. and McCabe, A. (1999). Encouraging narratives in preschoolers: An intervention study. *Journal of Child Language*, 26, 49–67.

Peterson, C. and McCabe, A. (1983). *Developmental Psycholinguistics: Three ways of Looking at a Child's Narrative.* Hillsdale, NJ: Erlbaum.

Peterson, C. and McCabe, A. (1992). Parental styles of narrative elicitation: Effect on children's narrative structure and content. *First Language*, 12, 299–321.

Peterson, C. and McCabe, A. (1994). A social interactionist account of developing decontextualized narrative skill. *Developmental Psychology*, 30(6), 937–948.

Peterson, C. and McCabe, A. (1996). Parental scaffolding of context in children's narratives. In C. E. Johnson and J. H. V. Gilbert (eds), *Children's Language* (vol. 9, pp. 183–196). Mahwah, N.J.: Lawrence Erlbaum Associates.

Propp, W. (1968). *Morphology of the Folktale*. Austin, TX: University of Texas Press. (Originally published 1928.)

Reese, E., Leyva, D., Sparks, A. and Grolnick, W. (2010). Maternal elaborative reminiscing increases low-income children's narrative skills relative to dialogic reading. *Early Education and Development*, *21*(3), 318–342. doi:10.1080/10409289.2010.481552.

Reese, E. and Newcombe, R. (2007). Training mothers in elaborative reminiscing enhances children's autobiographical memory and narrative. *Child Development*, *78*(4), 1153–1170.

Scarborough, H. (2001). Connecting early language and literacy to later reading (dis)abilities: Evidence, theory, and Practice. In S. B. Neuman and D. K. Dickinson (eds), *Handbook of Early Literacy Practice* (pp. 97–110). New York: Guilford.

Silva, M. J. and McCabe, A. (1996). Vignettes of the continuous and family ties. In A. McCabe (ed.), *Chameleon Readers: Teaching Children to Appreciate All Kinds of Good Stories* (pp. 116–136). New York: McGraw-Hill.

Slobin, D. (2011). Remarks made in discussion of 'Language and literacy development through childhood and adolescence: Crosslinguistic and crossmodal perspectives on complex syntax' (convenor: J. S. Reilly), International Association for the Study of Child Language. Montreal.

Snow, C. (2006). Cross-cutting themes and future research directions. In D. August and T. Shanahan (eds), *Developing Literacy in Second-Language Learners* (pp. 631–651). Mahwah, NJ: Erlbaum.

Snow, C. E., Porche, M. V., Tabors, P. O. and Harris, S. R. (2007). *Is Literacy Enough? Pathways to Academic Success for Adolescents*. Baltimore, MD: Brookes Pub. Co.

Sparks, A. (2008). Latino mothers and their preschool children talk about the past: Implications for language and literacy. In A. McCabe, A. L. Bailey and G. Melzi, (eds), *Spanish-Language Narration and Literacy* (pp. 273–295). Cambridge: Cambridge University Press.

Staikova, E., Gomes, H., Tartter, V. McCabe, A. and Halperin, J.M. (2013). Pragmatic deficits and social impairment in children with ADHD. *Journal of Child Psychology and Psychiatry*. doi:10.1111/jcpp.12082.

Stein, N. and Glenn, C. (1979). An analysis of story comprehension in elementary school children. In R. Freedle (ed.), *New Directions in Discourse Processing*. Hillsdale, NJ: Ablex.

Uccelli, P. (2008). Beyond chronicity: Evaluation and temporality in Spanish-speaking children's personal narratives. .In A. McCabe, A. L. Bailey and G. Melzi (eds), *Spanish-Language Narration and Literacy* (pp. 54–91). Cambridge: Cambridge University Press.

Wang, Q. (2013). *The Autobiographical Self in Time and Culture*. Oxford: Oxford University Press.

Zhang, F. (2013). A study of narrative development of young Chinese children with specific language impairment aged four to six years. In A. McCabe and C. Chang (eds), *Chinese Language Narration: Culture, Cognition, and Emotion* (pp. 143–180). Amsterdam: John Benjamins.

26

STORYING AS A SOCIAL CONTEXT FOR LANGUAGE DEVELOPMENT

Kathy G. Short, María V. Acevedo,
Dorea Kleker and Lauren H. Pangle

The complexities of using language in social interactions can be learned in social contexts where young children engage in talk as a social action within everyday interactions to construct meaning through narratives. The role of narratives is especially significant in language development because story is a way of knowing, an instrument of mind that is used to constitute as well as represent reality (Bruner, 1990). Research on storying with young children has emphasized the contexts in families and classrooms that encourage the making and telling of stories, particularly building on the work of Vivian Paley (2004). Within the context of previous research, this study focused on curricular engagements that immerse young children in storying processes and provide spaces for authentic engagement in co-constructing stories with peers and adults. These spaces were examined through a narrative inquiry methodology to identify how these engagements invited particular kinds of talk, stories and language use. The analysis provided insights into how the selection and grouping of books can influence children's storying as well as the ways in which artifacts and play open up spaces for storying and invite the cultural and linguistic practices of families into the classroom in authentic ways.

Elena and her family gather around a family story backpack, pulling out three books on family interactions and a set of finger puppets. *Let's Eat* by Ana Zamorano (2003), about a busy family trying to find time to eat a meal together, catches their attention. Elena snuggles close as her mother reads the book aloud, both enjoying the code-switching in the talk between family members. When the story ends, Elena disappears, returning with scribbled restaurant menus. She hands the menus to her mother, father and brother, and takes their orders, moving between English and Spanish to talk about food as they co-construct a narrative within Elena's pretend restaurant.

The stories and play Elena enters into with her family create a social context that encourages language use within meaningful interactions. This use of language in social contexts is termed pragmatics, the ways people produce and comprehend meanings through language and the rules governing social uses of language within a particular context (Yule, 1996). Pragmatics focuses on what is communicated by the utterance of sentences – not what is said explicitly but how those utterances are interpreted in situational contexts (Burton-Roberts, 2007). A study of pragmatics thus encompasses fields that identify the complex understandings influencing communicative competence.

The complexities of using language in social interactions is challenging for young children, given their age and, therefore, fewer experiences with language in different social contexts. Bridges et al. (2012) argue pragmatics involves young children learning three types of communicative strategies: 'using language for different intentions, changing language according to the needs of a communicative partner, and following rules for conversation, storytelling and narration' (p. 180). They believe these domains should frame language instruction through scaffolding by adults.

Elena's story demonstrates that these communicative strategies can also be learned in authentic social contexts where young children engage in talk as a social action within everyday interactions to co-construct meaning through narratives (Larson and Peterson, 2013). The ability to generate and comprehend narratives is considered a critical language skill, significant for later academic success, but often underemphasized in early childhood settings (Bridges et al., 2012). Botting (2002) argues narratives form the basis of many childhood speech acts and are one of the most 'ecologically valid ways to measure communicative competence' (p. 1), while Paley (2004) believes narrative play is essential to the linguistic, intellectual and social development of children.

This chapter highlights story as a way to make sense of experiences, a role that includes but goes beyond narration as a skill in communicative competence. Within the theoretical and research frame of story as a way of knowing, we position our research on curricular engagements that immerse young children in storying processes and provide space for authentic engagement in co-constructing stories with peers and adults. These spaces are created through books, artifacts and play to offer rich opportunities for young children to explore language use by storying across social contexts.

Story as a mode of knowing

Stories are woven so tightly into the fabric of everyday life that it is easy to overlook their significance in framing how we think about ourselves and the world. Rosen (1986) argues our minds engage in storying to make sense of new experiences and move from the chaotic 'stuff' of daily life into understanding. Storying imposes order and coherence on the endless stream of daily experiences and allows us to work out significance, providing a means of structuring and reflecting on experience (Bruner, 1990). Storying is a cognitive process that can lead to narratives we share with others to invite them to consider our meanings and to better understand those experiences ourselves. We listen to and play out other's stories to try on alternative ways of being in the world.

Storying is thus a mode of knowing – one of the primary ways our minds construct meaning to capture the richness and nuances of human life. Bruner (1990) argues story is an instrument of mind that is used to constitute as well as represent reality. A story accommodates the ambiguity and complexity of situations through a multiplicity of meanings (Short, 2012). Our views of the world are thus a web of interconnected stories; a distillation of all the stories we have shared and an interpretive lens to which we connect in order to understand new experiences.

A story is also a theory of something; what we tell and how we tell it reveals what we believe (Carter, 1993). Our human need to story our experiences may be universal but there is no one way to tell stories across cultures (Lindfors, 1991). Each story is always intertextualized with the stories that exist within a particular culture, both in content and in the style and structure of the telling. While all children come to school with stories, the types of stories and the ways in which they tell those stories may be quite different from school norms (Heath, 1983). The culture of a family or community enters a classroom when that community's stories, and thus the child's way of knowing, are valued as a form of meaning-making.

Research on storying with young children emphasizes the contexts in families and classrooms that encourage the making and telling of stories, in contrast to elicitation of narratives in experimental settings. One such context is the family dinner table, which has been studied to understand the conditions under which children naturally tell stories. Research by Beals and Snow (2002) indicates that the demand characteristics and participation structures of dinner table stories provide a better estimate of children's narrative competence than elicited narratives. Georgakopoulou (2002) studied family stories (events from the past) and child stories (recent events in the child's life) shared at mealtimes of Greek families, arguing these stories are locally situated as well as embedded in broader cultural frameworks of values and conventions. Children's pragmatic socialization occurs through nurturing their competence in the narrative performances valued in that community. Quintero (2010) documents the integration of stories based in family knowledge and cultural practices into classrooms to support learning and critical literacy.

A group of studies in early childhood classrooms focuses on the work of Vivian Paley (2004), who invited children to tell fantasy stories, dictated to a teacher and then acted out in collaboration with peers. Nicolopoulou (1996, 2002) and Nicolopoulou et al. (2015) gathered data in early childhood contexts where children follow their own narrative agendas through storytelling and story-acting to document children's movement toward narrative competence. These studies focus on fantasy narratives, rather than factual narratives of past events, and the influence of peer-group interactions, rather than adult–child interactions. Nicolopoulou (2002) argues children's narrative development is motivated by the interplay of social-relational concerns about peer-group membership and status with aesthetic concerns about constructing powerful stories. Her research indicates children's spontaneous stories are a window into their minds, capturing the interplay of mind and culture.

Our research focused on inviting the stories of families into schools through their memories of past and current events, rather than fantasy stories, and on the process of storying by sharing stories, rather than by storytelling and story-acting. We worked to create spaces that encourage young children to engage in storying about their lives and connections to the world, thus enhancing their communicative competence.

Storying as a context for research

Our research took place within a large project, Community as Resources in Early Childhood Teacher Education (CREATE), a comprehensive re-design of the early childhood teacher education programme at the University of Arizona that is based in a funds of knowledge perspective (Gonzalez et al., 2005). During their two years in the programme, teacher candidates visit families, participate in community events and engage in classroom field experiences to develop sustained relationships with families, community members and teachers across learning contexts. These relationships support them in closely examining the ways in which individual, community and institutional interactions impact the language and literacy development of culturally and linguistically diverse young children (Iddings, in press).

Curricular engagements to encourage storying

Our role in CREATE was to develop engagements that encourage storying as a means for young children to access family funds of knowledge and explore global understandings. These engagements, family story backpacks and cultural community story boxes create an opportunity space for children to engage in different types of talk with peers and adults and to develop their flexibility in social uses of language. These engagements are simultaneously child-regulated and teacher guided, which Nicolopoulou (2002) argues positively influences children's enthusiasm, creativity and learning.

The family story backpacks are a transportable curriculum designed to facilitate the sharing of family stories and to build home/school connections. The increasing emphasis on academic skills in primary classrooms has led many teachers of young children to send school-like activities home to families, but rarely to invite families to share their funds of knowledge with the school as a resource for classroom instruction.

Each backpack is created around a theme significant to families, such as bedtime routines, birthday traditions and the origin of a child's name. The backpacks contain three picture books (one global nonfiction and two fiction stories), a related artifact and a family story journal. Teacher candidates implement the backpacks during their student teaching experience in K-2 classrooms. Four to five families in each classroom receive a backpack each week and are invited to interact with the books and artifacts and to share their family stories. The journals offer a way to record family stories and interactions with the backpacks and to bring these stories back to the classroom. Children are given time to share with peers when returning the backpack to school. The entries stay in the journals so each new family has access to entries from other families.

The cultural community story boxes are a curricular resource designed to immerse young children in exploring books and artifacts that reflect local and global communities. To counter a portrayal of cultures as either 'all the same' or 'exotic', children are invited to identify their connections with these communities as they move towards exploring differences. The boxes are integrated into classrooms of three- to five-year-old children through units of study around a community or the integration of books and artifacts into centres. Young children interact with the materials and each other to share ideas and inquiries through play and story.

The story boxes reflect a specific global or local community and are created around a group of people (Mexican American), a country (India), a region (Southwest) or a group of countries (East Africa). Each box contains eight to ten books representing a variety of experiences within a community, two to three artifacts to encourage story and play connected to that community, and a cloth world map.

Data collection and analysis

We collected data over a three-year period on children's use of language as they engaged with the family story backpacks and cultural community story boxes within the social contexts of school and home. Using narrative inquiry methodology (Clandinin and Connelly, 2000), we gathered focus group interviews with teacher candidates, field notes by teacher candidates and researchers on home and school interactions, and family story journal entries. School contexts were multiple early learning centres and K-2 classrooms in urban settings, ranging from middle-class to high poverty neighbourhoods. Given our location near the border with Mexico, many of the children were Mexican American and bilingual speakers of Spanish and English.

We worked as a team to analyse this data, using constant comparative analysis (Strauss and Corbin, 1998) to develop categories on types of language use in these social contexts. Once we had identified the types of talk, we closely examined the spaces in which this talk occurred to identify which aspects of engagements seemed to encourage storying. We sorted the examples of children's talk and play according to these spaces and then selected examples that provide insights into characteristics of those spaces and represented the types of data in a particular space. We wanted to understand how these engagements invited particular kinds of talk, stories and language use.

This analysis provided insights into the constructions of authentic contexts that create space for children to listen to stories and construct stories with family, teachers and children. We wanted to understand the characteristics of these contexts to examine the role of social context in young children's language development and to more effectively construct these spaces as teachers. This analysis provided insights into how the selection and grouping of books can influence children's storying as well as the ways artifacts and play open up spaces for storying. These spaces, in turn, supported all three major communication strategies identified by Bridges et al. (2012).

The following sections integrate examples from the data organized around four themes identified as important to opening up space for children's storying. These themes highlight the significance of literature, play, artifacts and social interactions as ways to invite children's storying. Because our approach to research involves thinking with theory about data (Jackson and Mazzei, 2012), theory is interwoven with the data and used to both frame and discuss the examples.

Opening spaces for storying through literature

The books in the backpacks and story boxes were carefully chosen not only to represent the theme or culture but to invite connections and stories. The books provided opportunities for children to draw from their lives and share stories about social practices within their homes and communities as well as to use those connections to explore new cultural practices and to recognize differences across cultures. Quintero (2010) found that literature provides voices and perspectives of possibility along with connection.

The books in the backpack highlighted connections to family stories based in their funds of knowledge. As a family read *What Can You Do with a Paleta?* (Tafolla, 2014), from the play backpack, they shared stories about experiences with paleta (popsicle [ice-lolly]) wagons during summers in Mexico. This book created a space to relive their story through a connected experience as did *Back to Bed, Ed* (Braun, 2009) about a child who slips into his parents' bed at night. As a father read the book to his young daughter, Jacelyn's two older sisters joined the reading, laughing because the 'story was about us and our nightly challenges. Jacelyn kept smiling from cheek to cheek because she knew Ed does what she does.' When the book ended, the four storied about their experiences.

Books also created a space for children to co-construct a story with family members. Prompted by a beach picture, Jonah and his mother co-constructed a memory about their ocean experiences in Hawaii:

Mother: Oh, look at the waves, Jonah! You liked to kick and punch the waves.
Jonah: I liked to get them . . . and win!
Mother: But what happened when you didn't win?
Jonah: When I was not looking, the wave came and knocked me down.

Mother: Yes, they did. And what did we learn? What do they always say in Hawaii?
Jonah: Never turn your back on the Ocean.

This joint narrative supported them in recounting a significant event in their family, adding depth to the story.

Wordless books connected to children's lives were particularly rich in creating space for co-construction of stories. As families looked through *Clementina's Cactus* (Keats, 1999), in the rain backpack, the absence of a written text invited diverse storying as young children collaborated with adults in drawing from their experiences of living in the desert to co-construct a narrative around the illustrations and to share their experiences with sudden thunderstorms in the desert (Figure 26.1).

Social interactions around books sometimes created new experiences. The bilingual book *My Tata's Guitar* (Brammer, 2002), in the grandparents' backpack, led to meaningful interactions between Sofia, an English-speaker, and her grandfather, who only spoke Spanish, as they read the book over and over in two languages. This intergenerational connection resulted in a new story about Sofia and her grandfather that she was eager to share with classmates.

Children also used connection to go beyond viewing a global community as 'strange'. Alex selected *Deron Goes to Nursery School* (Onyefulu, 2009), about a young boy's first day of school in Ghana, to read with his teacher. He was unsure initially about the unfamiliar cultural setting but noticed Deron had a sister and dad like he did and recited the rhyme

Figure 26.1   Gerardo's response to *Clementina's Cactus*

'1, 2, Buckle My Shoe' from the wall of Deron's school. He thought it strange that the children in Deron's school wore similar clothing, until his teacher asked him to look at his pants and the clothing of his classmates, leading Alex to realize he also wore a uniform to school. The differences in Deron's school became interesting to explore once Alex made these connections, instead of separating him from Deron's community.

The connections children made to books also enriched their play. One group of children transformed their casita into a healthcare facility with doctors and patients. As 'doctors' attended to a sick teacher, Matias handed the teacher a make-believe cup of blueberry tea, saying, 'Actually, I think this will work instead'. Several children sang to help the teacher feel better, drawing from *My Nana's Remedies* (Rivera-Ashford, 2002), about a grandmother's traditional remedies. The children requested multiple rereadings of this book from the Mexican American story box and used play to connect doctor visits with the remedies offered by elders in their communities.

Lindfors (1991) argues children's early development in oral language is based in holistic experiences at home and in the community. As children, families and teachers interact with books that provide significant points of connection to children's lives, a holistic experience is created, opening up multiple opportunities for continued storying through play and talk that go beyond the initial read aloud of the book. Play also provides a way for children to explore the content of books in order to comprehend, express response and experience the story in affective and kinesthetic ways (Rowe, 1998).

Opening spaces for storying through artifacts

Wohlwend (2009) argues that play around artifacts can open new spaces and lead to rich and diverse literacy and language practices. Pahl and Roswell's (2013) research on artifactual literacies detail how artifacts invite story and serve as a resource for meaning making. Building on this research, the artifacts within the story boxes and backpacks were integrated into children's play to construct spaces from which narratives could be enacted, promoting meaningful interactions and eliciting authentic oral language.

Pahl and Roswell (2013) found artifacts can connect worlds because they travel across different spaces and provide new experiences, thus encouraging children to respect diversity and find points of commonality across communities. Several children used chopsticks from the South Korea story box, exploring how to pick up food items. Marisol situated the chopsticks in her hand to pick up felt dumplings, saying, 'Mmm, I'm going to eat all of these empanadas'. Kylie quickly wove the chopsticks through her fingers, 'Look here's a dumpling; the dumpling is hard to eat because it is fake. If it were real, I would poke the dumpling with one chopstick, and that would be much easier.'

Not only did the artifacts create a space for children to share an inquiry around a new tool, the chopsticks and dumplings encouraged the girls to go beyond interrogative forms of language often associated with school. Talking about artifacts during play provided an entryway into cultural narratives, making them accessible to all involved in the drama. These narratives often connected children's familiar worlds to new cultural practices, such as when children used sari cloth from India for dress-up, which they connected to dressing up in their parents' clothing.

Children used the same artifact in imaginative ways, such as when the sari became a parachute or a tent. Research by Glaubman et al. (2001) indicates that when children free themselves from the constraints of the actual object and move into free and imaginative use of artifacts, the narrative quality of their play increases.

Hurdley (2006) found the same objects can lead to different stories at different times. The cloth world map, an artifact in every story box, elicited a great deal of attention. The map led Armando to ask where New Mexico was because 'my dad lives there'. Several pointed to Tucson, saying 'That's where my house is', and others pointed to places asking what they were. Children were interested in Madagascar because of a recent movie, commenting on the distance from Arizona and wondering how to get there. Diego believed he could go by boat because of the ocean. Gabriela wondered if people there spoke English or Spanish. Locating Mexico on the map led to stories about family members and swimming in oceans.

For some children, the map invited inquiries and for others the map prompted sharing stories. While young children may not fully understand geographic concepts such as countries and distances between places, the map encouraged questions about places and oral sharing of family stories.

Elena, in the opening vignette, used written language inspired by books and artifacts to create a new artifact. These menus opened a space for Elena and her family to co-construct new narratives. Similarly, the dry erase board in the school backpack provided new spaces to story, such as when Melody used the white board and markers as a tool to write family names. Within this action, she created a space to share memories of events she associated with each person.

Research by Pahl and Roswell (2013) indicates that artifacts connected to children's lives bring collective and social memories into new spaces, providing a way into stories that move from the home into classrooms. Artifacts provide connection to lived lives and everyday experiences, while also creating the possibility of new worlds of experiences and common points of connection and diversity across communities.

Opening spaces for storying through play

Through play, children negotiate meaning and co-produce and co-play within live-action spaces to share, reflect and interpret stories. Our understandings of play are based in Wohlwend's (2013) definition of play as a 'social and semiotic practice that facilitates pivots to imagined contexts by recontextualizing classroom realities and maintaining a not-real frame' (p. 80). Her research shows the 'not-real' frame of play creates a safe space for children to explore their own cultural contexts along with unfamiliar cultural communities.

Play provides countless opportunities for language use and inquiry as children make personal connections, talk in role, discuss procedures and ask questions. A play space was created as families independently engaged with artifacts from the backpacks. Sometimes families used the artifacts to story about their social practices as occurred when one family acted out their family shopping trips with the finger puppets. Lotería, a Mexican bingo game from the play backpack, brought strong cultural memories when parents shared stories of playing the game in Mexico as a child. For other families, the game created a new narrative about an unfamiliar cultural practice through playing the game for the first time as depicted in the child's drawing (Figure 26.2).

Teachers created invitations for play from the artifacts, books and map to integrate into play areas, especially the casita and block centres, so children could explore individual and collective inquiries. When allowed to explore freely, children often took artifacts from story boxes in one centre and incorporated them into places where they saw connections, such as bringing chopsticks from the Korea box into the casita or incorporating artifacts from the desert box into their outdoor play. At other times, children brought materials from other

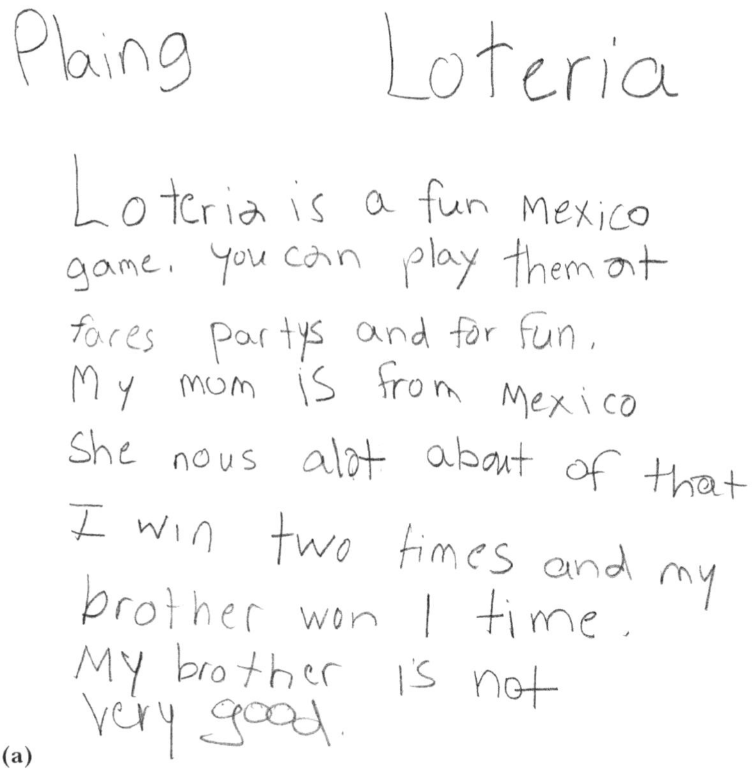

Plaing Loteria

Loteria is a fun Mexico game. You can play them at fares partys and for fun. My mom is from Mexico She nous alot about of that I win two times and my brother won 1 time. My brother is not very good.

(a)

(b)

Figures 26.2a and 26.2b Family journal entries on playing lotería

centres to integrate with story-box artifacts and books. This playful transaction with artifacts and texts supported children in making meaning within a range of social interactions.

One way children made sense of global contexts was to integrate new language into their play, referencing an artifact or book. Sometimes they revisited family stories as when Sofia commented, 'Teacher, you know my mom makes chapati.' The physical similarities between tortillas and chapati, bread from India, encouraged Sofia to story about familiar practices in her home. Other times, children used new vocabulary to consider new practices. Emilia, an expert on the role of a mother in the dramatic play centre, integrated the name of an artifact, commenting 'This is a kanga blanket, where you wrap up your babies' after a read-aloud of a book set in Tanzania. She also stated the purpose of the artifact as she carefully placed a doll on a piece of fabric, wrapping it around her shoulder and back to try out a new way of carrying a baby. The integration of language from global contexts enabled children to make local and global connections as they pursued their inquiries.

Children drew from their knowledge of social discourses in their play. A book set in Ethiopia, *New Shoes for Helen* (Onyefulu, 2011), led to explorations of the different places children buy shoes and the creation of a shoe store. While playing in the store, Sebastian saw Jordan taking four boxes without permission and accused him of stealing. He called the police, saying 'Someone is stealing our shoes', and then asked Nydia to call 911. When another child took on the role of the police officer, Sebastian pointed, 'There he is, get him'. Their familiarity with this emergency protocol and how to ask for assistance created a live-action space to explore each other's perspectives.

Play also provided a space for children to explore philosophical issues. Children's curiosity about a photograph of the Great Wall in a book about China quickly spilled over into building the wall in the block area and talking about the role of the wall in protecting people from 'the bad guys'. Alejandro's question 'What happens to bad guys?' led to an inquiry. Mario replied, 'They go away and get shot in the heart and die and go to heaven and God tells them to be a good person and puts a new heart in them and sends them back.' 'What happens once they are sent back?' Alejandro asked. 'Then they are good people.' Later the children took dolls and animals to determine rooms where each would stay and who would be outside to protect the others, realizing not all of them could sleep in order to watch out for bad guys. Mario's description is a complicated transformation process rooted in his understandings of actions, consequences and punishment along with religious beliefs of God as forgiving. Their play explored the consequences of being a bad guy and the global nature of these consequences.

Children's interactions in the shoe store and block centre reflect Sawyer's (1993) research on young children learning to negotiate multiple interpretations through co-created play frames as well as constantly changing individual play frames. In order to successfully play together, these frames must intersect through children's ability to use implicit and explicit metacommunication.

Children talked frequently about their play, describing what they were doing and planning what to do next. As children examined the Chinese characters in *The Pet Dragon* (Niemann, 2008) and a dragon artifact, they drew their own dragons, saying, 'I am making a cookie Dragon, because I like cookies', 'I need white for the boat', 'It's going to look like that even when it has white. I'm drawing the houses, my water turned green. Now I have to wash it.' Their descriptions and planning moved into storytelling: 'This is the symbol for mountain and this is a Scorpion Dragon and it got hurt. His name is Orange-y. He swims and he gets bubbles in his mouth, and then he gets fired at school and then he goes on a pirate ship and meets new pirates and then he got eaten up!'

Although some story boxes contained books and artifacts that highlighted fantasy, we rarely saw fantasy play such as this dragon story, a reflection of the cultural nature of play. Goncu et al. (1999) argue play is a cultural construction that must be contextualized, instead of considered a universal activity. Kirova (2010) found children enact and acquire knowledge of culturally specific ways of being in the world, with some children using play to try on the roles of adults in their communities and others moving into imaginary characters from mass media, a more Western middle-class stance. The majority of children in our study came from Mexican-American families who were struggling economically, and with strong extended family contexts within which children spent their time. Their play seemed to emphasize interpreting reality and internalizing cultural meanings, rather than inventive self-expression, a distinction noted by Gaskins (2014) in her review of differences in play as cultural activity.

Children often used play as a way to access and deepen their understandings of familiar cultural contexts and stories, but they also played to investigate what was new within a global community. Research by Butler and Weatherall (2009) indicates play provides ways for children to use cultural resources to learn about the world as well as to play with ideas already known about the world. In addition, the children's play provided further evidence of Wohlwend's (2013) findings that pretending opens access to familiar cultural contexts, resources and ways of knowing for young children, while letting them imagine communities to which they hope to belong as they make sense of increasingly complex cultural spaces.

Storying as an invitation for social interaction

The spaces created for children to story also functioned as invitations to develop other communicative skills, including using language for different intentions and changing language according to the needs of a communicative partner. The backpack engagement involved children in first storying with family members and then taking that experience into school contexts to share with teachers and classmates. They moved from a context of co-constructing stories and sharing memories with insiders with whom they shared a cultural context to retelling stories and describing experiences to an outside audience who were not familiar with the events or stories and sometimes did not share cultural contexts. Both purpose and audience shifted in moving from home to school. Nicolopoulou (2002) points out this kind of decontextualized language use has greater demands and is essential to later school success in literacy.

This shift from informal conversation with family to sharing with others moved children to more formal talk to describe their home experiences and family stories. They responded to questions and comments from peers and teachers and used oral language to clarify and expand their thoughts so others could understand and connect to their stories. Jahir and his family used the backpack on family activities to recall their difficult journey from Iraq to Tucson, co-constructing that narrative as Jahir's mother drew pictures in a detailed four-page journal entry. Jahir's recounting of that journey to his classmates was a different and difficult communicative task since children did not know the story nor were they familiar with Iraqi culture.

The name backpack was significant for families in sharing stories about their child's name, often eliciting stories about other family members. Sharing these stories with classmates who did not know the family was a different communicative task and many children chose to only tell the story of their own name, not other family members, recognizing their new audience was most interested in a classmate. In one classroom, this sharing led children to assert their agency as they discussed the names they prefer to be called, rather than the ones used by teachers.

Children also asked and responded to questions from parents during the backpack engagement. As Yaron's mother read aloud a book from the backpack, she asked him to predict what was going to happen and to point to each character as she read. She asked questions such as 'What is happening here?' and 'What kind of things do you see?' which kept Yaron actively engaged.

Classroom sharing often involved questioning as peers asked for more details or clarification out of interest or confusion, When Ana showed a picture of her extended family and talked about what her family meant to her, Michael asked many questions such as 'How old are they? What are their names? What are their jobs?'

In a review of research on talk and social competence, Hutchby (2005) found most research has been restricted to children interacting with adults and interactions in which adults manage or regulate a child's behaviour. In contrast, the sharing around backpacks put children, not the teacher, in the position of authority about their family, and the story boxes encouraged talk during play within children's own imagined social worlds as they built and shared knowledge with peers.

Children offered their knowledge to peers, as when Cameron, who rarely talked due to a speech impediment, told classmates about his favourite place after a read aloud. Children also shared knowledge about how to interact with artifacts, as when Maya exclaimed, 'Look, it is easier to pick up the food with the salad pinchers than with the chopsticks'. In addition, children shared knowledge in responding to questions. Sometimes their answers were based on noticing similarities as when a teacher asked children why they were using a Chinese hand fan to keep cool and they replied, 'It is hot in Tucson like China'. Other times children's answers led to identifying and exploring differences among cultural communities as when children tried to figure out how the foods eaten with chopsticks by Chinese families differed from the foods they eat and which of their foods would work with chopsticks.

Children also shared new knowledge gained from classroom experiences, such as when they learned about islands while exploring the Caribbean story box. Later in a conversation about islands, Maya tried out her new knowledge, describing an island as: 'You can live on it. The island stands on the water and the water stands the island up'.

Creating invitations for children to story adds depth and meaning to their experiences and develops communicative competence through sharing in different social contexts. Siegal and Surlan (2009) found when young children are immersed in conversations they develop the ability to figure out what to attend to in order to distinguish between the literal meaning of a statement and the speaker's intended meaning, an understanding previously considered conceptual rather than attentional in development.

Final reflections

Although this chapter separates the spaces created by books, artifacts and play, our observations of children indicate their intersectionality creates a rich social context for children's storying. The sharing of *Carry Me* (Star Bright, 2010), a global book showing methods of carrying babies, led Emelia to inquiries within her role as a mother in the casita. She first used a long piece of African fabric to tie a doll on her back. Then, because she could not find a basket, she put her arms through the handles of a large purse and wore it like a backpack with the doll inside, saying, 'Look, a basket for the baby'. Drina used the kanga cloth to wrap a doll saying, 'I smushed it around her like a burrito, but I don't want to walk around with her 'cause she'll fall out'. Javier grabbed a rebozo from the Mexican story box and wrapped a baby doll inside, standing in front of a mirror to adjust the baby until he was satisfied. He later explored other uses, tying the rebozo around his neck, saying, 'Hey, about we put it like a scarf?' and then wrapping it around his head, commenting, 'I tied it but it's hurting here a little'. He called out, 'Hey, teacher, I use my imagination', a direct connection to *What Can You Do with a Rebozo?* (Tafolla, 2008).

Dewey (1938) argues the role of the teacher is to create learning environments that have the most *potential* for tension and inquiry for children. In our case, we selected books, artifacts, and play invitations we thought might engage young children in Tucson in storying. The inquiries within that environment were child-driven, not predetermined by adults. The goal was to draw on children's everyday practices and invite them into the official curriculum in authentic ways – not to simply colonize children's practices for school purposes (Larson and Peterson, 2013).

Storying across home and school provides a space for teachers to invite children's cultural and linguistic practices into classrooms and to engage young children in the fluid construction of meaning from their local communities. At the same time, children's talk in authentic interactions provides them with the opportunity to engage in and examine the situated production of their cultural and social worlds through story. Children story their way into communicative competence to powerfully and effectively navigate these worlds.

Note

The Helios Foundation supported the research described in this chapter. A list of the backpacks and story boxes and their contents and related forms can be found online at www.createarizona.org/curricular-experiences/story-interactions.

References

Beal, D. and Snow, C. (2002). Deciding what to tell. In S. Blum-Kulka and C. Snow (ed.), *Talking to Adults* (pp. 15–32). New York: Erlbaum.

Botting, N. (2002). Narrative as a tool for the assessment of linguistic and pragmatic impairments. *Child Language Teaching and Therapy*, *18*, 1–21.

Bridges, M. Justice, L, Hogan, T. and Gray, S. (2012). Promoting lower- and higher-level language skills in early childhood classrooms. In R. Pieanta and S. Barrett (eds), *Handbook of Early Childhood Education* (pp. 177–193). New York: Guilford.

Bruner, J. (1990). *Acts of Meaning*. Cambridge, MA: Harvard University Press.

Burton-Roberts, N. (2007). *Pragmatics*. London: Palgrave.

Butler, C. and Weatherall, A. (2006). 'No, we're not playing families': Membership categorization in children's play. *Research on Language and Social Interaction*, *39*(4), 441–470.

Carter, K. (1993). The place of story in the study of teaching and teacher education. *Educational Researcher*, *22*(1), 5–12.

Clandinin, D. J. and Connelly, F. M. (2000). *Narrative Inquiry: Experience and Story in Qualitative Research*. San Francisco: Jossey-Bass.

Dewey, J. (1938). *Experience and Education*. New York: Collier Books.

Gaskins, S. (2014). Children's play as cultural activity. In L. Brooker, M. Glaise and S. Edwards (eds), *The SAGE Handbook of Play and Learning in Early Childhood* (pp. 31–42). London: Sage.

Georgakopoulou, A. (2002). Greek children and familiar narratives in family contexts. In S. Blum-Kulka and C. Snow (eds), *Talking to Adults* (pp. 33–54). New York: Erlbaum.

Glaubman, R., Kashi, G. and Koresh. R. (2001). Facilitating the narrative quality of sociodramatic play. In A. Göncü and E. Klein (eds), *Children in Play, Story, and School* (pp. 132–157). London: Guilford Press.

Göncü, A., Tuermer, U., Jain, J. and Johnson, D. (1999). Children's play as cultural activity. In A. Göncü (ed.), *Children's Engagement in the World* (pp. 148–170). London: Cambridge.

González, N., Moll, L. and Amanti, C. (2005). *Funds of Knowledge: Theorizing Practices in Households, Communities, and Classroom*s. New York: Erlbaum.

Heath, S. B. (1983). *Ways with Words*. Cambridge, MA: Cambridge University Press.

Hurdley, R. (2006). Dismantling mantelpieces: Narrating identities and materializing culture in the home. *Sociology*, *40*(4): 717–733.

Hutchby, I. (2005). Children's talk and social competence: A research review. *Children and Society*, *19*, 66–73.

Iddings, A. C. (in press). *Communities as Resources in Early Childhood Teacher Education: An Ecological Reform Design*. New York: Routledge.

Jackson, A. and Mazzei, L. (2012). *Thinking with Theory in Qualitative Research*. New York: Routledge.

Kirova, A. (2010). Children's representations of cultural scripts in play. *Diaspora, Indigenous, and Minority Education*, 4, 74–91.

Larson, J. and Peterson, S. (2013). Talk and discourse in formal learning settings. In J. Larson and J. Marsh (eds), *The SAGE Handbook of Early Childhood Literacy* (pp. 501–539). London: SAGE.

Lindfors, J. W. (1991). *Children's Language and Learning* (2nd edn). New York: Allyn & Bacon.

Nicolopoulous, A. (1996). Narrative development in social context. In D. Slob, J. Gerhardt, A. Kyratzis and G. Jiansheng (eds), *Social Interaction, Social Context, and Language* (pp. 369–390). New York: Erlbaum.

Nicolopoulou, A. (2002). Peer-group culture and narrative development. In S. Blum-Kulka and C. Snow (eds), *Talking to Adults* (pp. 117–132). New York: Erlbaum.

Nicolopoulou, A., Cortina, K., Ilgaz, H., Cates, C. and de Sá, A. (2015) Using a narrative- and play-based activity to promote low-income preschoolers' oral language, emergent literacy, and social competence. *Early Childhood Research Quarterly*, 31, 147–162.

Pahl, K. and J. Rowsell (2013). Artifactual literacies. In J. Larson and J. Marsh (eds), *The SAGE Handbook of Early Childhood Literacy* (pp. 263–279). London: Sage.

Paley, V. (2004). *A Child's Work: The Importance of Fantasy Play*. Chicago: University of Chicago Press.

Quintero, W. (2010). Something to say: Children learning through story. *Early Education and Development*, *21*(3), 372–391.

Rosen, H. (1986). *Stories and Meanings*. London: NATE.

Rowe, D. (1998). The literate potentials of book-related dramatic play. *Reading Research Quarterly*, *33*(1), 10–35.

Sawyer, K. (1993). The pragmatics of play: Interactional strategies during children's pretend play. *Pragmatics*, *3*(3): 259–282.

Short, K. (2012). Story as world making. *Language Arts*, *90*(1), 9–17.

Siegel, M. and Surlan, L. (2009). Conversational understanding in young children. In E. Hoff and M. Shatz (eds), *The Blackwell Handbook of Language Development* (pp. 304–323). New York: Wiley-Blackwell.

Strauss, A. and Corbin, J. (1998). *Basics of Qualitative Research* (2nd edn). Thousand Oaks, CA: Sage.

Wohlwend, K. (2013). Play, literacies and the converging cultures of childhood. In J. Larson and J. Marsh (eds), *The SAGE Handbook of Early Childhood Literacy* (pp. 80–110). London: Sage.

Yule, G. (1996). *Pragmatics*. London: Oxford University Press.

Children's literature cited

Brammer, E. (2002). *My Tata's Guitar/La guitarra de mi tata*. Houston, TX: Piñata.

Braun, S. (2014). *Back to Bed, Ed!* Atlanta, GA: Peachtree.

Keats, E. (1999). *Clementina's Cactus*. New York: Viking.

Niemann, C. (2008). *The Pet Dragon*. New York: Greenwillow.

Onyefulu, I. (2009). *Deron Goes to Nursery School*. London: Frances Lincoln.

Onyefulu, I. (2011). *New Shoes for Helen*. London: Frances Lincoln.

Rivera-Ashford, R. (2002). *My Nana's Remedies/Los remedies de mí nana*. Tucson, AZ: ASDM.

Star Bright (2010). *Carry Me*. Cambridge, MA: Star Bright Books.

Tafolla, C. (2009). *What Can You Do with a Paleta?/¿Qué puedes hacer con una paleta?* New York: Dragonfly.

Zamorano, A. (1996). *Let's Eat!* Norwood, Australia: Scholastic.

27

INTERVENTIONS FOR CHILDREN WITH LANGUAGE DIFFICULTIES

K. S. Richard Wong

Helping young children with oral language difficulties is important because oral language skills predict the development of code-related skills (e.g. phonological awareness) in the early grades and reading comprehension in the later grades. Because adults play a vital role in shaping children's language development, this chapter reviews the effectiveness of oral language intervention programmes delivered by different groups of adults: parents, teachers/teaching assistants and speech therapists in the settings of home, classroom and clinics respectively. Home-, classroom- and clinic-based interventions are important for helping children overcome their language difficulties, although the overall effect of any particular intervention on language outcomes may not be strong. Furthermore, receptive language problems appear to be more difficult to address than expressive language problems. Future research should explore alternative strategies for helping children to overcome difficulties in receptive language more effectively, so that these children do not fall behind even more than their peers, first in language and then in literacy development.

Interventions for children with language difficulties

'Language difficulties' refers to the receptive and/or expressive problems that an individual encounters in the areas of vocabulary, morphology, syntax and phonology or in a combination of these areas during the course of language development. These difficulties may represent a primary or secondary condition arising from developmental disorders such as autism, hearing impairment and general developmental difficulties (see Law et al., 2010). Also, the difficulties may originate from different sources, including social deprivation (e.g. poor quality parent–child interaction: Snow et al., 1998) or limitations in working memory (Montgomery, 2002).

Apart from affecting children's communicative capacities, language difficulties may also lead to reading difficulties. Past research has shown that a large part of the variance in reading outcomes can be explained by the individual differences in code-related skills (e.g. phonological awareness: Bowey, 2005; Muter et al., 2004) and oral language skills (e.g. vocabulary knowledge, grammar knowledge and narrative skills: Muter et al., 2004; Storch and Whitehurst, 2002) with which children enter school (see Snowling et al., 2000 and Wagner et al., 1994 for further details). Oral language skills are particularly important because they are associated with the development of code-related skills (Metsala and Walley, 1998; Storch and Whitehurst, 2002; Walley et al., 2003). Also, they have been linked to children's reading comprehension in the later grades (Storch and Whitehurst, 2002). In some studies, the association between oral language skills (in particular, listening comprehension skills) and reading comprehension (Gernsbacher, 1990) was so strong (correlation coefficient $r = .90$) that improvements in one domain were suggested to lead to improvements in the other (see Perfetti et al., 2005). These results underscore the need to enhance young children's oral language development in order to prevent reading difficulties (Snow et al., 1998). Conversely, unresolved difficulties with general oral language skills are likely to pose a barrier to children's literacy development.

Given that adults play a vital role in shaping young children's language development, this chapter focuses on the effectiveness of early interventions (up to grade three) delivered by three groups of adults: parents, teachers/teaching assistants and speech therapists in the settings of home, classroom and clinics respectively. Though varying in their professional knowledge, these three groups of adults can help children overcome language difficulties at different developmental stages. The chapter begins with home-based intervention because home is the setting where adult–child interactions and literacy activities conducive to children's language development occur first (Purcell-Gates, 1996; Strickland and Taylor, 1989; Weigel et al., 2006). Next, classroom-based intervention programmes at the preschool and early primary settings are examined, followed by findings related to the effectiveness of intervention in the clinical setting. There are some key differences between home-based and non-home-based interventions. Non-home based interventions are more likely to be needed by children with more severe difficulties, and/or difficulties that persist into the school years and manifest as literacy problems. In addition, the interventions delivered by teachers/teaching assistants or therapists are likely to be more specialized, focusing on specific aspects of oral language development, reflecting these adults' professional knowledge of, and training in, language development and education. While acknowledging the importance of qualitative research, due to space restrictions this review foregrounds large-scale quantitative studies that provide evidence of efficacy.

Interventions in the home environment

Before children enter preschool, home provides the first social setting for language-supporting adult–child interactions. Research has shown that the quantity of parent–child interaction influences children's oral language development, in particular vocabulary development. This quantity was found to co-vary with the families' socioeconomic status (SES). In the influential study conducted by Hart and Risley (1995), professional families were predicted to utter 30 million more words than their counterparts from welfare families by the time children were five, and this quantitative difference in language input to children translated into an approximate 600-word gap in the children's vocabularies at the age of 36 months. These SES-related differences have resulted in campaigns and research programmes conducted in the USA (e.g. Providence Talks: Hirsh-Pasek et al., 2015) aimed at improving the home literacy environment (HLE). The HLE is an important concept because the experiences, attitudes and materials pertaining to literacy that children encounter and interact with at home impact on their later language and literacy skills (Griffin and Morrison, 1997; Leseman and DeJong, 1998; Lonigan and Whitehurst, 1998; Payne et al., 1994; Sénéchal et al., 1998). Important aspects of HLE include:

Age. Reading to younger preschoolers is even more important than reading to older preschoolers as younger preschoolers are more dependent on oral interactions as a source of language development (Bus and van IJzendoorn, 1994; DeLoache and DeMendoza, 1987; Sénéchal and Cornell, 1993).

Frequency of book reading. Bus and colleagues (1995) found in their meta-analysis that the frequency of joint reading activities with picture books during the preschool years accounted for 7 per cent of the variance in preschool language and literacy outcomes. Before children become readers, parental support in book reading can help children access a wide variety of vocabulary, grammar structures and discourse rules otherwise unavailable in spoken language (Roberts et al., 2005; Weigel et al., 2006).

Quality of book reading activities. Interaction strategies used in book reading were found to be related to early language outcomes (Haden et al., 1996; Leseman and DeJong, 1998; Pellegrini et al., 1990; Reese and Cox, 1999; Roberts et al., 2005; van Kleeck et al., 1997). Important strategies include: encouraging young children to reflect on the meanings of words, to predict, discuss and comment on the content of stories and to relate stories to real life experiences. Scarborough and Dobrich (1994) noted that the quality of book reading accounted for 3 to 8 per cent of the variance of the language and literacy outcomes (see also Lonigan and Whitehurst, 1998; Whitehurst, Arnold et al., 1994; Whitehurst, Epstein et al., 1994; Whitehurst et al., 1988), suggesting the potential of interventions to improve book reading quality.

Parental or maternal sensitivity. The emotional quality of the parent–child interaction (as indexed by factors such as parents' supportive presence, respect for children's autonomy, etc.) was found to be linked to children's receptive vocabulary at age three and at entry to kindergarten (Roberts et al., 2005) and also to language and reading skills during the early elementary school years (Bus et al., 2000; DeJong and Leseman, 2001). This variable is related to parents' SES: lower-income, less educated parents were found to have less stimulating, less responsive and more punitive interaction styles (Hashima and Amato, 1994; Mistry et al., 2004).

Motivation. Scarborough and Dobrich (1994) found that a child's interest in reading (e.g. how often a child asks to be read to) accounted for about 14 per cent of the variance in children's language and literacy outcomes, more than the 7 per cent of variance explained by the frequency of book reading (Bus et al., 1995).

This chapter highlights two intervention studies conducted by Whitehurst and colleagues (Lonigan and Whitehurst, 1998; Whitehurst, Arnold et al., 1994) because of their methodological rigour. Apart from using randomized controlled trials to minimize the influence of pre-existing differences between parents, the studies used a videotape training method (see Arnold et al., 1994) to reduce the effects of trainer differences on the outcome measures. The video contained a list of guidelines and taped vignettes presenting examples of parent–child interactions that conform and do not conform to the guidelines. In addition, both receptive and expressive language skills were measured. It was thus possible to evaluate whether the interventions would lead to across-the-board changes. Furthermore, their studies compared programmes led by parents and by preschool teachers, thereby enabling an evaluation of the unique contribution of parents to children's language development. These studies focussed on a special form of joint reading around picture books called dialogic reading (DR). In DR, the parents are sensitive to the social emotional needs of their children. Instead of simply reading the text, the parents provide models of language, ask the children questions, provide the children with feedback and elicit increasingly sophisticated contributions from the children, with the ultimate goal of facilitating the children to become the storytellers (see McCabe, this volume, for similar findings related to oral narratives).

In Whitehurst, Arnold, et al. (1994), 73 four-year-old children from low-income families, who were delayed approximately ten months on measures of language and literacy, participated in a six-week intervention, and were assigned randomly to either a control group, a teacher-led reading intervention group or a reading intervention group led by both teachers and parents. The teachers and parents in the intervention groups were trained using the aforementioned videotape training method. Comparison of pre- and post-test results showed that both intervention groups made gains in oral language skills compared with the control. Also, the children who were read to by both parents and teachers made greater gains than those who were just read to by their teachers, although the differences between the two groups were not statistically significant.

Lonigan and Whitehurst (1998) added a parent-led intervention group to the design used in Whitehurst, Arnold, et al. (1994), permitting an evaluation of the independent contribution of parents to changes in children's oral language status. Ninety-one three- and four-year-old children from low-income families who were delayed in both receptive and expressive vocabularies (measured by the Peabody Picture Vocabulary Test-Revised, see Dunn and Dunn, 1981, and the Expressive One Word Picture Vocabulary Test, see Gardner, 1990) took part in a six-week intervention. A comparison of pre- and post-test results revealed that all three types of intervention examined (programme led by parents only, teachers only and by both parents and teachers) had a more pronounced influence on expressive language than on receptive language. Furthermore, although there was a difference in the effect size of the three types of intervention on expressive vocabulary (ranging from .30 for the teacher-only condition to .74 for the teacher-plus-parent condition), the differences in gains among the three groups were not statistically significant.

The absence of a strong effect on receptive vocabulary is probably due to this variable being more affected by parental demographic variables and beliefs (e.g. whether the parents have a stronger belief in their own role in promoting literacy) than by joint reading activities (Weigel et al., 2006). Future intervention studies should therefore target both parental beliefs and receptive language, because they show so little improvement in previous intervention studies. In addition, because parental beliefs depend so strongly on culture (e.g. Chen and Stevenson, 1995), further research should explore whether aspects of HLE that are important for English-speaking children are equally important for children from other cultures.

Interventions in the classroom setting

When the home literacy environment is less than optimal for supporting children's language development, both preschools and schools become an important resource to help children lagging in their language skills. Past research has shown that as children become older, the relative importance of home to children's language and literacy development will diminish because the overall school environment and children's growing reading abilities can partially compensate for lack of family reading experiences (Cunningham and Stanovich, 1991, 1997). Four intervention studies in this area are worth highlighting: three are preschool-based (Raver et al., 2012; Weiland et al., 2013; Weiland and Yoshikawa, 2013) and one school-based (Bowyer-Crane et al., 2008), with a specific focus on the issues that schools should consider when implementing oral language interventions for young children.

Weiland and Yoshikawa (2013) examined the efficacy of a language-cum-numeracy prekindergarten programme that combined evidence-based curricula with coaching support for teachers. The study included 2,018 racially, linguistically and socioeconomically diverse four- and five-year-old children (50 per cent being English language learners and 69 per cent from low-income families) who were enrolled in the Boston Public Schools (BPS) public prekindergarten programme in 2008–2009. In the language component of the intervention, the children were exposed to a programme called Opening the World of Learning (OWL) (see Schickedanz and Dickinson, 2005; Dickinson et al., 2011) which serves to integrate young children's language, literacy and socioemotional development. In the lessons, the class would discuss socioemotional issues so as to promote the learning of emotion-related vocabulary. This study was unique in several ways: first, a regression-discontinuity (RD) design was used in order to provide an unbiased estimate of the average effect of assignment to the treatment condition (vs. control) for participants immediately on either side of the birthday cut-off for entry into the programme (see Bloom, 2012; Murnane and Willett, 2010 for further details on RD). Second, the majority of the participating teachers had a master's degree, and were therefore more likely to possess the types of knowledge and skills required for delivering the intervention. Third, coaching was emphasized in the intervention to ensure teachers' faithfulness to the intervention (to ensure a good implementation of the OWL programme by the teachers): an experienced coach was available to model instruction, observe teachers' practice and provide teachers with constructive feedback on their pedagogy (Neuman and Cunningham, 2009). The continual coaching support not only maintained the quality of support provided to teachers but also optimized resource allocation (see Sachs and Weiland, 2010 for further details). Finally, the inclusion of children who varied in both SES and ethnicity permitted an examination of SES-/race-related effects of the public prekindergarten programme. By the end of intervention children across the various SES levels had made significant gains in their language skills, most importantly in receptive vocabulary as measured by PPVT-III (with an effect size of 0.45). The impact on the PPVT was also larger for Hispanic children than for the monolingual English-speaking children. These findings provide initial evidence that a good implementation of the OWL curriculum can promote children's receptive vocabulary, an area that previous studies have found to resist intervention. Also, OWL may be particularly useful in classrooms with a high proportion of Hispanic children.

While it was encouraging that children's receptive vocabulary skills grew as a result of OWL, it was unclear which specific aspect(s) of OWL (curricula, coaching support or the use of highly qualified teachers) contributed to children's improvement in language. Because of this, Weiland and colleagues (Weiland et al., 2013) also explored the longitudinal relationships between children's receptive vocabulary skills and several classroom quality indicators, including the Early Childhood Environment Rating Scale-Revised Edition (ECERS), the Classroom Assessment Scoring System (CLASS) and the Early Language and Literacy Classroom Observation Tool (ELLCO). This study included 414 four-year-old children with profiles similar to the children in Weiland and Yoshikawa (2013). The results showed that although the children exhibited growth in their receptive vocabulary, none of the classroom quality indicators were associated with the children's PPVT standardized scores. These results were, nonetheless, consistent with findings from other studies which found little evidence on the key components of effective early vocabulary intervention for young children (Marualis and Neuman, 2013; see also Burchinal et al., 2010; Burchinal, Kainz et al., 2011). Further research is thus needed to examine whether there are unexplored aspects of this OWL intervention which brought about the children's improvement in receptive vocabulary. One potential candidate concerns the native language proficiency of the English-language learners in Weiland and Yoshikawa (2013) and Weiland et al. (2013). Gámez and Levine (2013) observed that an exposure to high-quality native language was associated with English-language learners' gains in native oral language skills, specifically expressive language, over the kindergarten year. Given the well-documented cross-linguistic relationship between L1 and L2 skills (e.g. Proctor et al., 2006), it is possible that the Hispanic children who had experienced more growth in English receptive vocabulary than their monolingual English-speaking peers in the two studies conducted by Weiland and colleagues had higher than average skills in their native language or had been exposed to high-quality language input in Spanish. Future interventions which include English-language learners should therefore control for the children's native-language proficiency. Alternatively, the studies should test whether strengthening young children's native-language skills would further enhance the impact of OWL on the children's receptive vocabulary in English.

In Raver et al. (2012), the focus was on a different group of disadvantaged children: three-to-five-year-old children with cochlear implants. The pilot study aimed to test the effectiveness of 'parallel talk' in improving the language and pragmatic skills of three preschoolers with cochlear implants who were at least one-year delayed in their receptive/expressive language skills. 'Parallel talk' is a type of intervention in which adult–child joint attention is created through an adult commenting on a child's play by stating what the child is doing, thinking or feeling, rather than requiring the child to answer direct questions or produce particular responses. During the intervention, five-minute parallel-talk sessions were organized three times a week during which an adult (a para-educator) provided between 19 and 30 comments on the child's play. The results showed that the intervention was able to increase the frequency of children's verbal turn-taking. Furthermore, two of the children participating in the study increased their verbal/vocal responses during the course of the intervention. More importantly, all children were able to generalize what they had learned to new situations involving a peer rather than an adult. These results underscore the importance of rich adult talk. Even brief and intermittent exposure was able to help disadvantaged children with persistent difficulties in language and social skills.

In Bowyer-Crane et al. (2008), the efficacy of two teacher-assistant-led intervention programmes for children with poor oral language at school entry were examined. One hundred and fifty-two four-year-old children from 19 schools were randomly assigned to either a Phonology with Reading (P + R) programme or an Oral Language (OL) programme. In the P + R programme, the children received 20 weeks of daily intervention focusing on letter–sound knowledge, phonological awareness and book-level reading skills. In the OL programme, the children received the same intensity of training but the training focused on vocabulary, comprehension, inference generation and narrative skills. The children were tested four times with measures of phoneme awareness, early literacy, vocabulary, grammar and narrative skills. At the end of intervention, the children in the OL group outperformed the P + R group on measures of vocabulary and grammatical skills, while children in the P + R group outperformed the OL group on literacy and phonological measures. In other words, OL programmes can successfully improve young children's vocabulary and grammatical skills, which form the basis for development in reading comprehension. However, the study also found a lack of immediate transfer of OL training to reading skills. This could be because the reading tasks associated with oral language skills are only encountered some time later on (but see Bishop and Snowling, 2004 which argued that language and phonological skills are modular systems that underpin reading development and its difficulties). Taken together, these findings underscore the need to incorporate both language and code-related skills in early language curriculum.

The review above showed that classroom-based intervention was generally effective for improving children's oral language proficiency and in some studies the interventions were even effective for receptive language skills. It is important for school staff to understand what oral-language-based programmes can do and what is needed in order to ensure the programmes' success (e.g. the availability of coaching support). Moreover, teachers should also be aware of the following findings before introducing an intervention. First, there appear to be no statistical differences in the effects on children's language and literacy outcomes between studies using a whole-class setting (e.g. Hatcher et al., 2004) and those using a small group setting (Vellutino et al., 1996) (see Snowling and Hulme, 2011 for a review). Therefore, to save costs, schools might consider delivering intervention in the whole-class rather than small-group setting. Second, about 2 per cent of the Grade 1 population respond poorly to reading comprehension interventions. These 'poor responders' suffered more severe phonological impairments, had poor vocabulary skills and tended to have problems in attention control (Snowling and Hulme, 2011). Schools should be aware that further research is still needed to understand what intervention strategies would work for these 'non-responders'. Finally, teaching assistants rather than classroom teachers were involved in some previous intervention studies. They delivered the intervention outside of the regular school hours. Because of this, it is unclear whether intervention delivered by teachers during school hours will be more effective than, or as effective as, intervention delivered by assistants outside of regular school hours. Also, teaching assistants are unlikely to have the same academic qualifications and enjoy the same salary and fringe benefits as the classroom teachers. If the turnover rate of teaching assistants is high because of a lack of career prospects or other reasons, the quality of intervention they lead can be compromised. In such a situation, schools might even have to invest additional resources and time to ensure that the newly recruited teaching assistants will be able to deliver the intervention appropriately.

Interventions in the clinical setting

When both home- and classroom-based interventions fail, private or public speech and hearing services might serve as yet another resource to help children overcome their language difficulties. Seeing speech and hearing pathologists requires both financial resources and parents' commitment. The fees charged at a private speech and hearing setting are not negligible and could be prohibitive for children from lower SES families, resulting in differential access to speech and hearing services across socioeconomic groups. Moreover, parents will need to invest their time by attending the therapy sessions and also practising suggested strategies with their children regularly. Recognizing the considerable financial and time costs, it is important to evaluate the effectiveness of therapist-led intervention on children's oral language skills.

Law et al. (2010) reviewed 36 high-quality therapist-led interventions that used randomized control trials. However, compared with the classroom-based programmes, the sample size involved is smaller. Twenty-nine out of 36 studies recruited fewer than 50 participants, and the socioeconomic status of the participants was often not described. Law and colleagues noted that interventions were more effective in treating expressive than receptive language problems, echoing findings from home-based interventions. Also, one-to-one interventions appeared to be no more effective than interventions involving small group training. The implication for parents is that when finance is an issue, they could consider enrolling their children in group rather than more expensive individual therapy sessions. Finally, interventions shorter than ten weeks were less effective than training extending over a period of ten months. Since therapist-led interventions of longer duration will be more costly, lower SES children with language difficulties might not be able to afford the type and length of service optimal for treating their problems. If educational authorities agree that therapist-led interventions are an important last resort for children with persistent language difficulties, financial assistance schemes should be introduced to improve lower SES children's access to speech and hearing services.

While therapist-led interventions appear promising, especially for improving children's expressive language skills, there are a few issues with previous studies. Unlike the home- or classroom-based interventions, the intervention procedures used by therapists were often not thoroughly described in the original articles. Law and colleagues attributed this to the space limits in journal articles. Regardless of the validity of this reason, the absence of such information renders the replication of a particular intervention difficult. Furthermore, only 16 of the studies reviewed (less than 50 per cent) provided SES information. It is therefore unclear whether the children's persistent difficulties especially in the area of receptive language were a result of environmental or biological factors or their combination. Finally, it is also unclear whether other variables, such as therapists' characteristics (experience, gender, etc.) and children's motivation, are linked to the outcome variables in the reported studies. All these issues call for more carefully planned intervention studies with better described procedures in the future.

Conclusion and the way forward

This chapter began with a review of how general language skills contributed to children's word-decoding skills and comprehension skills, followed by a description of the effectiveness of interventions conducted in the home, classroom and clinics. The review showed that both home- and classroom-based interventions were important for helping children overcome their language difficulties, although the overall effect on language outcomes may not be as strong as anticipated (e.g. frequency of book reading at home accounted for less than 10 per cent of the variance in language and literacy measures; see Bus et al., 1995). In addition, receptive language problems appeared to be more difficult to treat compared with expressive language issues especially in the home and clinical settings. Finally, apart from having persistent receptive problems, the children who do not respond well to intervention tend to have other behavioural or motivational issues (see Snowling and Hulme, 2011). While it is important to focus on the skills that are important for reading comprehension, future studies should also examine how to best motivate the learning interests of 'poor responders' who have become accustomed to years of falling behind their peers in reading development. Indeed, without enough motivation, it might be very difficult for these children to sustain their interest in programmes that are supposed to be helping them.

References

Arnold, D. H., Lonigan, C. J., Whitehurst, G. J. and Epstein, J. N. (1994) Accelerating language development through picture book reading: Replication and extension to a videotape training format. *Journal of Educational Psychology*, 86, 235–243.

Bishop, D. V. M. and Snowling, M. J. (2004). Developmental dyslexia and specific language impairment: Same or different? *Psychological Bulletin*, 130, 858–888.

Bloom, H. S. (2012). Modern regression discontinuity analysis. *Journal of Research on Educational Effectiveness*, 5, 43–82.

Bowey, J. A. (2005). Predicting individual differences in learning to read. In M. J. Snowling and C. Hulme (eds), *The Science of Reading: A Handbook* (pp. 155–172). Oxford: Blackwell.

Bowyer-Crane, C., Snowling, M. J., Duff, F. J., Fieldsend, E., Carroll, J. M., Miles, J., et al. (2008). Improving early language and literacy skills: Differential effects of an oral language versus a phonology with reading intervention. *Journal of Child Psychology and Psychiatry, 49*(4), 422–432.

Burchinal, M., Kainz, K. and Cai, Y. (2011). How well do our measures of quality predict child outcomes? A meta-analysis and coordinated analysis of data from largescale studies of early childhood settings. In M. Zaslow, I. Martinez-Beck, K. Tout and T. Halle (eds), *Quality Measurement in Early Childhood Settings* (pp. 11–31). Baltimore, MD: Brookes.

Burchinal, M., Vandergrift, N., Pianta, R. and Mashburn, A. (2010). Threshold analysis of association between child care quality and child outcomes for low-income children in pre-kindergarten programs. *Early Childhood Research Quarterly, 25*(2), 166–176.

Burgess, S. R., Hecht, S. A. and Lonigan, C. J. (2002). Relations of the home literacy environment (HLE) to the development of reading-related abilities: a one-year longitudinal study. *Reading Research Quarterly, 37*, 408–426.

Bus, A. G., Leseman, P. P. M. and Keultjes, P. (2000). Joint book reading across cultures: A comparison of Surinamese-Dutch and Dutch parent–child dyads. *Journal of Literacy Research, 32*, 53–76.

Bus, A. G., van Ijzendoorn, M. H. and Pellegrini, A. D. (1995). Joint book reading makes for success in learning to read: A meta-analysis on intergenerational transmission of literacy. *Review of Educational Research, 65*, 1–21.

Chen, C. and Stevenson, H. W. (1995). Motivation and mathematics achievement: A comparative study of Asian-American, Caucasian-American, and East Asian high school students. *Child Development, 66*(4), 1215–1234.

Clarke, P. J., Snowling, M. J., Truelove, E. and Hulme, C. (2010). Ameliorating children's reading comprehension difficulties: A randomised controlled trial. *Psychological Science, 21*(8), 1106–1116.

Cunningham, A. E. and Stanovich, K. E. (1991). Tracking the unique effects of print exposure in children: Associations with vocabulary, general knowledge, and spelling. *Journal of Educational Psychology, 83*, 264–274.

Cunningham, A. E. and Stanovich, K. E. (1997). Early reading acquisition and its relation to reading experience and ability 10 years later. *Developmental Psychology, 33*, 934–945.

DeJong, P. F. and Leseman, P. P. M. (2001). Lasting effects of home literacy on reading achievement in school. *Journal of School Psychology, 39*, 389–414.

DeLoache, J. S. and DeMendoza, O. A. (1987). Joint picturebook interactions of mothers of 1-year-old children. *British Journal of Developmental Psychology, 5*, 111–123.

Dickinson, D. K., Kaiser, A., Roberts, M., Hofer, K. G., Darrow, C. L. and Griffenhagen, J. B. (2011). The effects of two language focused preschool curricula on children's achievement through first grade. Paper presented at the Spring Conference of the Society for Research in Educational Effectiveness, Washington, DC, March.

Dunn, L. M. and Dunn, L. M. (1981). *Peabody Picture Vocabulary Test – Revised*. Circle Pines, MN: American Guidance Service.

Gámez, P. B. and Levine, S. C. (2013). Oral language skills of Spanish-speaking English language learners: The impact of high-quality native language exposure. *Applied Psycholinguistics, 34*(4), 673.

Gardner, M. F. (1990). *Expressive One-Word Picture Vocabulary Test- Revised*. Novato, CA: Academic Therapy.

Gernsbacher, M. A. (1990). *Language Comprehension as Structure Building*. Hillsdale, NJ: Erlbaum.

Griffin, E. A. and Morrison, F. J. (1997). The unique contribution of home literacy environment to differences in early literacy skills. *Early Child Development and Care, 127–128*, 233–243.

Haden, C., Reese, E. and Fivush, R. (1996). Mother's extratextual comments during storybook reading: Stylistic differences over time and across texts. *Discourse Processes, 21*, 135–169.

Hatcher, P. J., Hulme, C. and Snowling, M. J. (2004). Explicit phoneme training combined with phonic reading instruction helps young children at risk of reading failure. *Journal of Child Psychology & Psychiatry, 45*(2), 338–358.

Hart, B. and Risley, T. R. (1995). *Meaningful Differences in the Everyday Experiences of Young American Children*. New York: Brookes.

Hashima, P. Y. and Amato, P. R. (1994). Poverty, social support, and parental behavior. *Child Development, 65*, 394–403.

K. S. Richard Wong

Hirsh-Pasek, K., Adamson, L. B., Bakeman, R., Owen, M. T., Golinkoff, R. M., Pace, A., et al. (2015). The contribution of early communication quality to low income children's language success. *Psychological Science, 26*(7), 1071–1083.

Johnson-Glenberg, M. C. (2000). Training reading comprehension in adequate decoders/poor comprehenders: Verbal versus visual strategies. *Journal of Educational Psychology, 92*(4), 772–782.

Landry, S. H., Smith, K. E., Swank, P. R. and Miller-Loncar, C. L. (2000). Early maternal and child influences on children's later independent cognitive and social functioning. *Child Development, 71*, 358–375.

Law, J., Garrett, Z. and Nye, C. (2010). Speech and language therapy interventions for children with primary speech and language delay or disorder. *Cochrane Database of Systematic Reviews* 2003, Issue 3. Art. No.: CD004110.

Leseman, P. P. and de Jong, P. F. (1998). Home literacy: Opportunity, instruction, cooperation, and social-emotional quality predicting early reading achievement. *Reading Research Quarterly, 33*, 294–319.

Lonigan, C. J. and Whitehurst, G. J. (1998). Relative efficacy of parent and teacher involvement in a shared reading intervention for preschool children from low income backgrounds. *Early Childhood Research Quarterly, 13*, 263–290.

Marulis, L. M. and Neuman, S. B. (2010). The effects of vocabulary intervention on young children's word learning: A meta-analysis. *Review of Educational Research, 80*(3), 300–335.

Mashburn, A. J., Pianta, R. C., Hamre, B. K., Downer, J. T., Barbarin, O. A., Bryant, D. et al. (2008). Measures of classroom quality in prekindergarten and children's development of academic, language, and social skills. *Child Development, 79*(3), 732–749.

McArdle, N., Osypuk, T. and Acevedo-Garcia. (2010). Prospects for equity in Boston Public Schools' school assignment plans. Retrieved from http://diversitydata.sph.harvard.edu/Publications/ Prospects for Equity in%20Boston Schools.pdf.

Metsala, J. L. and Walley, A. C. (1998). Spoken vocabulary growth and the segmental restructuring of lexical representations: Precursors to phonemic awareness and early reading ability. In J. L. Metsala and L. C. Ehri (eds), *Word Recognition in Beginning Literacy* (pp. 89–120). Mahwah, NJ: LEA.

Mistry, R. S., Biesanz, J. C., Taylor, L. C., Burchinal, M. and Cox, M. J. (2004). Family income and its relation to preschool children's adjustment for families in the NICHD study of early child care. *Developmental Psychology, 40*, 727–745.

Montgomery, J. W. (2002). Understanding the language difficulties of children with specific language impairments: Does verbal working memory matter? *American Journal of Speech-Language Pathology, 11*, 77–91.

Murnane, R. and Willett, J. (2010). *Method Matters: Improving Causal Inference in Educational Research.* New York: Oxford University Press.

Muter, V., Hulme, C., Snowling, M. J. and Stevenson, J. (2004). Phonemes, rimes, vocabulary, and grammatical skills as foundations of early reading development: Evidence from a longitudinal study. *Developmental Psychology, 40*, 663–681.

National Institute of Child Health and Human Development, Early Child Care Research Network. (2000). The relation of child care to cognitive and language development. *Child Development, 71*, 960–980.

National Institute of Child Health and Human Development, Early Child Care Research Network. (2002). Early child care and children's development prior to school entry: Results from the NICHD study of early child care. *American Educational Research Journal, 39*, 133–164.

Neuman, S. B. and Cunningham, L. (2009). The impact of professional development and coaching on early language and literacy practices. *American Educational Research Journal, 46*, 532–566.

Payne, A. C., Whitehurst, G. J. and Angell, A. L. (1994). The role of home literacy environment in the development of language ability in preschool children from low-income families. *Early Childhood Research Quarterly, 9*, 427–440.

Perfetti, C. A., Landi, N. and Oakhill, J. (2005). *The Acquisition of Reading Comprehension Skill.* Oxford: Blackwell. http://onlinelibrary.wiley.com/doi/10.1002/9780470757642.ch13/summary.

Proctor, C. P., August, D., Carlo, M. S. and Snow, C. E. (2006). The intriguing role of Spanish vocabulary knowledge in predicting English reading comprehension. *Journal of Educational Psychology, 98*, 159–169.

Purcell-Gates, V. (1996). Stories, coupons, and the TV Guide: Relationships between home literacy experiences and emergent literacy knowledge. *Reading Research Quarterly, 31*, 406–428.

Raver, S. A., Bobzien, J., Richels, C., Hester, P., Michalek, A. and Anthony, N. (2012). Effects of parallel talk on the language and interactional skills of preschoolers with cochlear implants and hearing aids. *Literacy Information and Computer Education Journal*, 3(1), 530–538.

Reese, E. and Cox, A. (1999). Quality of adult book reading affects children's emergent literacy skills. *Developmental Psychology*, 35, 20–28.

Roberts, J., Jurgens, J. and Burchinal, M. (2006). The role of home literacy practices in preschool children's language and emergent literacy skills. *Journal of Speech, Language, and Hearing Research*, 49, 345–359.

Sachs, J. and Weiland, C. (2010). Boston's rapid expansion of public school-based preschool: Promoting quality, lessons learned. *Young Children*, 65, 74–77.

Scarborough, H. S. and Dobrich, W. (1994). On the efficacy of reading to preschoolers. *Developmental Review*, 14, 245–302.

Schickedanz, J. and Dickinson, D. (2005). *Opening the World of Learning*. Iowa City, IA: Pearson Publishing.

Sénéchal, M. and Cornell, E. H. (1993). Vocabulary acquisition through shared reading experiences. *Reading Research Quarterly*, 28, 360–374.

Sénéchal, M., LeFevre, J., Thomas, E. and Daley, K. (1998). Differential effects of home literacy experiences on the development of oral and written language. *Reading Research Quarterly*, 33, 96–116.

Snow, C. E., Burns, M. S. and Griffin, P. (eds) (1998) *Preventing Reading Difficulties in Young Children: Committee on the Prevention of Reading Difficulties in Young Children, National Research Council*. Available online at: www.nap.edu/readingroom/books/prdyc/ (accessed 5 December 2014).

Snowling, M. J., Bishop, D. V. M. and Stothard, S. E. (2000). Is pre-school language impairment a risk factor for dyslexia in adolescence? *Journal of Child Psychology and Psychiatry*, 41, 587–600.

Snowling, M. J. and Hulme, C. (2011). Evidence-based interventions for reading and language difficulties: Creating a virtuous circle. *British Journal of Educational Psychology*, 81(1), 1–23.

Snowling, M. J. and Hulme, C. (2012). Interventions for children's language and literacy difficulties. *International Journal of Language and Communication Disorders*, 47(1): 27–34.

Storch, S. A. and Whitehurst, G. J. (2002). Oral language and code-related precursors to reading: Evidence from a longitudinal structural model. *Developmental Psychology*, 38, 934–947.

Strickland, D. S. and Taylor, D. (1989) Family storybook reading: implications for children, families, and curriculum. In D. S. Strickland and L. Morrow (eds), *Emerging Literacy: Young Children Learn to Read and Write* (pp. 147–159). Newark, DE: International Reading Association.

van Kleeck, A., Gillam, R. B., Hamilton, L. and McGrath, C. (1997). The relationship between middle-class parents' book-sharing discussion and their preschoolers' abstract language. *Journal of Speech, Language, and Hearing Research*, 40, 1261–1271.

Vellutino, F. R., Fletcher, J. M., Snowling, M. J. and Scanlon, D. M. (2004). Specific reading disability (dyslexia): What have we learned in the past four decades? *Journal of Child Psychology and Psychiatry*, 45(1), 2–40.

Wagner, R. K., Torgesen, J. K. and Rashotte, C. A. (1994). Development of reading-related phonological processing abilities: New evidence of bidirectional causality from a latent variable longitudinal study. *Developmental Psychology*, 30, 73–87.

Walley, A. C., Metsala, J. L. and Garlock, V. M. (2003). Spoken vocabulary growth: Its role in the development of phoneme awareness and early reading ability. *Reading and Writing*, 16, 5–20.

Wechsler, D. (2005). *Wechsler Individual Achievement Test – Second UK Edition (WIAT-IIUK)*. London: Harcourt Assessment.

Weigel, D. J., Martin, S. S. and Bennett, K. K. (2006). Contributions of the home literacy environment to preschool-aged children's emerging literacy and language skills. *Early Child Development and Care*, 176(3–4), 357–378.

Weiland, C., Ulvestad, K., Sachs, J. and Yoshikawa, H. (2013). Associations between classroom quality and children's vocabulary and executive function skills in an urban public prekindergarten program. *Early Childhood Research Quarterly*, 28(2), 199–209.

Weiland, C. and Yoshikawa, H. (2013). Impacts of a prekindergarten program on children's mathematics, language, literacy, executive function, and emotional skills. *Child Development*, 84(6), 2112–2130.

Whitehurst, G. J., Arnold, D. S., Epstein, J. N., Angell, A. L., Smith, M. and Fischel, J. E. (1994). A picture book reading intervention in day care and home for children from low-income families. *Developmental Psychology, 30*(5), 679–689.

Whitehurst, G. J., Epstein, J. N., Angell, A. L., Payne, A. C., Crone, D. A. and Fischel, J. E. (1994). Outcomes of an emergent literacy intervention in Head Start. *Journal of Educational Psychology, 86,* 542–555.

Whitehurst, G. J., Falco, F. L., Lonigan, C. J., Fischel, J. E., DeBaryshe, B. D., Valdez-Menchaca, M. C. and Caulfield, M. (1988). Accelerating language development through picture book reading. *Developmental Psychology, 24,* 552–559.

Whitehurst, G. J. and Lonigan, C. J. (1998). Child development and emergent literacy. *Child Development, 69,* 848–872.

28

PROMOTING FIRST-LANGUAGE DEVELOPMENT AND MAINTENANCE AND CAPITALIZING ON 'FUNDS OF KNOWLEDGE' IN FAMILY LITERACY PROGRAMMES

Jim Anderson, Ann Anderson and Harini Rajagopal

Although there is converging evidence that family literacy programmes enhance young children's language and literacy learning and benefit their parents, they have been criticized on the grounds that they privilege the dominant language and fail to capitalize on families' funds of knowledge. Responding to this criticism, educators have developed bilingual family literacy programmes. In this chapter, we first review the empirical literature on bilingual family literacy, revealing that such programmes positively contribute to young children's early literacy learning while promoting families' maintaining their home languages. Then, we report on a collaboratively developed family literacy programme called Parents As Literacy Supporters in Immigrant Communities that was implemented with more than 500 families from four linguistic groups in five communities in a metropolitan area of Canada. We conclude by discussing the implications of the research and raise lingering concerns and issues that need ongoing attention.

The fact that young children acquire considerable knowledge about literacy prior to schooling is now considered axiomatic by most educators and researchers. Ethnographic and socio-linguistic studies reveal that this principle generally holds across social and cultural groups (e.g. Anderson, 1994; Li, 2001; Taylor and Dorsey-Gaines, 1988). A key finding from this body of research is that families play an important mediating role in supporting early literacy development, even though they might be unaware that they are doing so (Taylor, 1983).

Drawing on the research from literacy-rich homes (e.g. Bissex, 1985; Taylor, 1983) in the 1980s and 1990s, educators began developing family literacy programmes that attempted to have participants emulate or replicate the literacy activities, events and practices, and the learning that occurred 'naturally' (e.g. Forrester, 1997) in these homes. However, these programmes were critiqued by Auerbach (1989) and others because of their deficit orientation in that they: were aimed at low-income, minority, immigrant and refugee families; promoted the dominant language (usually English) at the expense of the home languages of the families; ignored the existing practices of the families while promoting school-like literacy practices; and tended not to reflect families' cultural knowledge or *funds of knowledge* (Moll et al., 1992). The critiques by Auerbach and others had a sobering effect and many family literacy programme developers and providers attempted to shift toward a strengths-based orientation by promoting families' home languages and their cultural capital – their funds of knowledge.

The purpose of this chapter is to review critically the emerging literature on bi-lingual family literacy programmes that promote first language maintenance while helping families learn the dominant language of the community, as well as attempting to acknowledge and build on their literacy practices as they expand their repertoires so that they can support their children's transition into school. We first present the framework that informs our work; then review the literature on first language maintenance and loss; next, critically review the emerging literature on bilingual family literacy programmes; share some of the findings from our own work with immigrant and refugee families; and conclude with a discussion and the implications of this work.

Framework

Informing our work is socio-historical theory developed by Vygotsky (1978) and subsequently elaborated upon (e.g. Cole, 1997; Wertsch, 1998). Central to this theory is the notion that learning is social as children learn to use cognitive tools, including language and literacy, in the context of family and community. These tools are first used *inter-psychologically* with the support and mediation of parents and significant others; then, support is gradually withdrawn as children learn to use the tools *intra-psychologically*, or independently without the support of others. However, Rogoff (2003) and other cultural psychologists have documented considerable variation in how learning and development occur across socio-cultural contexts. She points out the cultural nature of development, but reminds us that 'to date, the study of human development has been based largely on research and theory coming from middle class communities in Europe and North America' (p. 4).

We also draw on research in bilingualism, first language maintenance and language loss. Cummins (2013) postulated the notion of *common underlying proficiency* proposing that although there are obviously differences in the surface feature of one's first language and an additional language, *interlinguistic resources* or higher order analytic and cognitive abilities and skills transfer across languages. He refers to *additive bilingualism* to describe the notion that one can maintain one's first language (L1) while acquiring a second language (L2) (Cummins et al., 2006). Researchers have identified several benefits to maintaining one's first or home language. For example, Bialystok's (2011) review illustrates that bilingual individuals consistently outperform their monolingual counterparts on various tasks involving executive control in the brain. She theorized that the effect of bilingualism on cognitive performance exemplifies how everyday experiences accumulate to modify cognitive networks and abilities across the lifespan. In their report to the National Reading Council, Snow et al. (1998) concluded that children's literacy success in a second language is enhanced if their first language is well developed. Tabors and Snow (2001) cautioned against expecting and encouraging parents to interact with their children in English when it was not as well developed as their first language.

Related literature

Although a burgeoning research literature documents the potential effects of family literacy programmes (e.g. Anderson and Morrison, 2007; Brooks et al., 2008; Jordan et al., 2000; Phillips et al., 2006; Prins et al., 2009; Purcell-Gates et al., 2012), only recently have researchers begun to study bilingual family literacy programmes in immigrant, indigenous and refugee communities (Compton-Lilly et al., 2012). We review this emerging literature next.

While cast as an 'English as a Second Language' initiative with less emphasis placed on first language maintenance, Project FLAME (Shanahan et al., 1995) was one of the earliest programmes that attempted to build on families' cultural and linguistic resources. FLAME was designed for Latino families with children aged three to nine in Chicago. Adults attended basic skills/ESL classes twice a week, and twice a month, they attended *parents as teachers* sessions where they learned about selecting and sharing appropriate books and magazines, teaching the letters of the alphabet/letter–sound relationships, and using games and songs with their children. Evaluation of the programme indicated that parents' English proficiency improved and children's knowledge of letter names and print concepts improved significantly, although the programme did not directly teach children. Although the goal of the programme was to increase parents' and children's proficiency in English, it should be noted that parents were also encouraged to read to their children in Spanish if they were more comfortable doing so and Spanish was the language of instruction.

Hirst et al. (2010) evaluated a bilingual preschool family literacy programme involving Pakistani-origin families of three-year old children in the UK. Teachers and a bilingual programme assistant visited the families every three weeks for a year. Each session focused on a particular aspect of early literacy development such as early writing, oral language or reading books with children. In addition to providing suggestions for supporting young children's language and literacy development, the teachers and the bilingual assistants demonstrated respect for the cultural practices and language of the participants and, for example, provided bilingual picture books; encouraged families to use either English or their home language, Mirpuri Punjabi or Urdu, in the activities; and acknowledged and included the children's experiences at the mosque school. The children participating in the programme and a randomly assigned control group were assessed using the Sheffield Early Literacy Development Profile (SELDP), which measures children's knowledge of books, environmental print and writing, as well as letter recognition. Results indicated that the children in the programme made significant gains on the SELDP compared to the control group. As well, take-up and levels of participation in the programme were high. Parents were also interviewed about literacy practices in their homes and about their participation in the project. They viewed their experiences positively; believed that the programme had enhanced their children's literacy development; appreciated more fully the family's role in children's literacy learning; and believed that the programme should be offered to all families with young children.

Working with Karen-speaking refugee families originally from Myanmar living in upstate New York in the United States, Singh et al. (2015) documented the literacy practices within a family literacy programme and a book-sharing programme. Typically, 10–12 families whose children ranged in age from a few months to five years attended weekly, one-and-a-half hour sessions in an intergenerational family literacy programme, 'Storycircles', for ten months. Instruction and directions were in English with simultaneous translation into Karen, the families' home language. In the book-sharing programme – Dolly Parton's Imagination Library Program – families were mailed a free, age-appropriate book each month (Conyer, 2012). Data collection entailed participant observation of sessions where the researchers took field notes of the instruction and families' engagement in the activities, transcription of interactions that occurred within the programme, and interviews with eight families and with the teachers. Because of the shortage of bilingual books and the parents' limited facility in English, parents were unable to read the books to their children. However, the programme teacher taught the families how to do 'picture walks', essentially talking about the pictures in their home language, which according to Singh et al. helped families become familiar with sharing books with young children and early literacy pedagogy of American schools and its emphasis on shared book reading.

Beyond shared book reading in family literacy programmes

Although shared book reading with young children is a practice that is not shared by some cultural and social groups (Anderson et al., 2003; Boyce et al., 2010), it has become nearly synonymous with family literacy programmes (Anderson et al., 2007; Purcell-Gates, this volume). However, some programmes have expanded the repertoires of literacy activities that they promote. For example, Boyce et al. (2010) proposed that *storytelling* is a more universal phenomenon that families engage in *naturally* (Bruner, 1991). They reported on a study of the Storytelling for the Home Enrichment of Language and Literacy Skills (SHELLS) programme. Initially, the SHELLS programme encouraged families to share stories about their everyday experiences in their home language. Then, families were supported in making their own books based on these stories, eventually sharing these books so that children availed of the benefits of repeated readings and language expansion that written texts afford. From 75 three- and four-year-olds attending a Migrant Head Start programme in the United States, Boyce et al. randomly assigned 32 children and their families to the SHELLS programme while they continued to participate in the typical Head Start programme. The other 43 children continued with the Migrant Head Start programme only. The researchers assessed the total number of words children used, the number of different words used and mothers' elicitation strategies during a shared narrative prior to and after the programme. Mothers in the SHELLS programme significantly increased their elicitation strategies compared with the mothers in the control group. Likewise, the children in the SHELLS programme significantly increased the total number of words used and the different words used in the shared narrative task compared to the control group.

Responding to calls for family literacy programmes to become more responsive to local contexts, Hope (2011) undertook an ethnographic study of family learning programmes for refugee families in two schools in South London to document whether or not families' home language and their literacy knowledge and practices were acknowledged and incorporated. Data collection included observations, field notes and interviews, as well as questionnaires and records of attendance. Hope (2011) concluded that the activities and structure of the programme, while offering support, also offered little autonomy to parents and took little regard of refugees' own literacies. The utilization of dual-language books, games or toys made by parents, home language and culture was outweighed by unidirectional transmission of school practices, and a course structure with no focus on social cohesion or connecting parents with each other. While the project strengthened relationships between staff and families at both sites, and participants displayed growing self-esteem in terms of personal development and skills, opportunities for involving families in course design and for empowering parents for the future were, from Hope's perspective, not sufficiently developed. She emphasized the need for programme providers to understand and respond to the specific strengths of immigrant and refugee parents, as well as the needs that they identify. She advocated for leveraging the families' *transcultural capital* (Triandafyllidou, 2009) – their knowledge, skills and social networks from their home country.

Addressing the disconnection between home and school experienced by immigrant families, Iddings (2009) reported on a programme that reflected a more expansive notion of family literacy in an elementary school in the southwestern US. It included an informal Welcome Centre based on the theoretical underpinnings of 'funds of knowledge' (Moll et al., 1992), creating a social and instructional space where recently immigrated families gathered to trade and share a variety of expertise and information, and gather information about their children's education. Activities included exchanging oral narratives about families' homelands, sharing recipes, discussing the linguistic features of Spanish and English, storytelling, creating picture books, and so forth. Iddings (2009) concluded that the participatory nature of the programme couched within participants' knowledge and lived experience contributed to its success. She reiterated the need for schools to provide explicit spaces and planned programmes for newcomers in order to support them in using their home language and literacy practices, and to help them learn respectfully about these practices in their new community.

Some caution in bilingual family literacy programmes

In a study suggesting the need for a more nuanced understanding of bilingual family literacy programmes, Zhang et al. (2010) reported on an initiative with Chinese immigrants in Canada. Forty-two preschool children and their families participated in the programme, at three community centres. The programme consisted of eight two-hour sessions conducted in Chinese and English each focusing on a topic such as oral language, reading Chinese and numeracy. Parents completed a questionnaire prior to commencing the programme to ascertain family demographics, home literacy environment, parents' perceptions of their own and their children's literacy abilities; kept a weekly log of literacy activities engaged in; and participated in a focus group at the completion of the programme. Children completed Chinese and English versions of the *Expressive Vocabulary Test (EPT)* and the *Peabody Picture Vocabulary Test-III (PPVT-III)*. Results indicated that although engagement in literacy activities on average increased across the eight weeks, it was not statistically significant. Pre- and post-test comparisons of children's scores on the Chinese and English versions of the *EPT* indicated significant gains. However, pre- and post-test comparisons of scores on the Chinese and English versions of the *PPVT-III* indicated no significant differences. Zhang et al. disaggregated the data by community site and found that children from socially disadvantaged homes made fewer gains than children from more advantaged families. That children from poor families appeared to benefit less than their more socially advantaged peers from a family literacy programme that capitalized on home language is counter to the assumptions underlying socio-contextual perspectives of family literacy programmes (e.g. Auerbach, 1989), Zang et al. intimate.

As can be seen from the emerging literature on bilingual family literacy programmes, young children's language and literacy learning are generally enhanced as they continue to use their first language. Adult family members also value these programmes and they begin to feel comfortable in schools and with Western curriculum and pedagogy. However, most of the studies to date have involved small numbers of participants, usually from a single language group, and have focused on either qualitative or quantitative data. We now turn to a three-year study of a bilingual family literacy project, Parents As Literacy Supporters in Immigrant Communities, that employed a mixed methods design and involved more than 500 families from four linguistic groups in five communities.

Parents As Literacy Supporters in immigrant communities

The Parents[1] as Literacy Supporters (Anderson and Morrison, 2000) or PALS family literacy programme was developed as part of a multi-agency, community development project in an inner-city neighbourhood at the invitation of the mayor of Langley, a small city in the metropolitan area of Vancouver, Canada. The first author of this chapter and early childhood educator, Fiona Morrison, held focus groups with families, early childhood educators and community members, and drawing on their extensive backgrounds in working with families and the extant literature, they developed and piloted modules of the programme, refining them as necessary. PALS was then implemented in two community schools in Langley and the next year, other school districts, hearing about it through word of mouth, requested that the programme be offered in their district.

PALS is designed for the families of three- to five-year-old children and consists of 10–15 sessions, each about two hours' duration, focusing on topics such as 'learning to read', 'early mathematics' and 'learning and technology'. Some flexibility is built into the programme – for example, at the request of families who were concerned about the amount of television their children were watching, we developed a session, 'Children and television'. Sessions are offered at a time and day convenient for the families; the programme has been offered first thing in the morning, over lunchtime and in the early evening. Sessions begin with the families and the programme facilitators – who are early childhood teachers – eating together, after which the teacher accompanies the children to a classroom while the parents and the facilitator meet for about half an hour to discuss the session planned for that day. For example, if the topic is early writing, parents are asked to share their memories of learning to write as well as their children's drawing, scribbling and writing. The facilitator then reviews the key ideas about that day's topic (e.g. that young children's drawings and scribbling are their attempts to communicate and represent meaning and are important in their literacy development) and describes the age-appropriate activities that have been set up in five or six learning centres in the classroom. Parents then join the children where they and their children circulate through the various centres, engaging in the activities for about an hour after which the children go to recess and the facilitator and parents retreat for an informal, half-hour debriefing session over coffee or tea. The facilitator encourages the parents to share their impressions of, and give feedback on, the session: What worked? What didn't? What did they observe about their children? What did the children learn? What did they learn? The children then rejoin this group and each family is provided with a high-quality children's book and other resources, for example crayons, markers, paper and pencils for drawing and writing and counters, dice, playing cards and shapes for early mathematics, to take home.

The basic principles and structure of the PALS programme were retained in the Parents As Literacy Supporters in Immigrant Communities project but we also made modifications. First, because we would be working with different cultural and linguistic groups, we formed an advisory group of representatives from each community where we would be working. We also formed a working group including the facilitators from each site and the English as a Second Language programme coordinators from the districts in which we worked. We hired a cultural worker from each of the linguistic groups to be co-facilitators alongside the early childhood teachers in the programme. We then translated all of the materials into the four languages represented – Chinese, Farsi, Karen and Punjabi – and purchased high-quality, bilingual children's books in each language.

Evaluation of PALS in immigrant communities

As described by Anderson et al. (2011), the study involved approximately 500 families representing the four different linguistic groups in five communities. We employed a mixed methods design that included: pre- and post-test comparisons of Normal Curve Equivalent Scores on the Test of Early Reading Ability-2 (Reid et al., 1989), a widely used norm-referenced instrument with fairly good psychometric properties designed to measure three- to eight-year-old children's emergent literacy knowledge; pre- and post-test comparisons of the qualitative and quantitative components of the Parents Perceptions of Literacy Interview Schedule (Anderson, 1995); focus group sessions; audio recordings of the debriefing sessions; children's literacy artifacts collected over a two-week period at home; and researchers' field notes.[2]

Children's literacy knowledge

Comparing the aggregated pre- and post-test Normal Curve Equivalent scores on the *TERA*-2, Anderson et al. (2011) found a significant increase in children's literacy knowledge over time with an effect size of .318, which is considered large (Cohen, 1988). Although children's NEC scores increased across all sites, at one site the growth was much more modest than at the other sites and not statistically significant. The reasons for this anomaly were not apparent from the data and may be attributable to measurement error.

Parents' perceptions

In earlier research conducted with immigrant and refugee families in the same metropolitan area as the current study Anderson (1995) and Gunderson and Anderson (2003) found that parents held traditional beliefs about literacy learning, favouring rote memory, and drill and practice, and decrying learning through play and child-centred curriculum and pedagogy. However, the pre-test results of the PPLLIS indicated that parents in the current study held perceptions or beliefs consistent with an emergent literacy or holistic paradigm before they had participated in the programme. For example, on the open-ended question that asked parents 'What are the five most important things you are doing to support your child learning to read and write', the most frequent response across all five sites was 'learning through play', a perspective that was an anathema in the earlier studies with immigrant and refugee parents. Indeed, there were no significant differences in parents' perceptions at the beginning of the programme and at the end, which we did not anticipate.

First-language maintenance

As noted earlier, we aimed to promote first-language maintenance and the notion of additive bilingualism, and in the focus group sessions we asked parents about this issue. In general, they were very supportive for various reasons. Some felt that their home language was an important part of their culture, their identity, and they wanted their children to know their cultural background and to identify with it. Others had pragmatic reasons, indicating that if their children maintained their first language *and* learned English, as bilinguals in an increasingly multi-lingual world, they would be advantaged in terms of employability when they became of working age. Some indicated it was important that children maintain their first language so that they could continue to communicate with grandparents and other relatives, many of whom did not speak or understand English. And still others saw having two languages as a 'good thing' – a form of cultural capital (Bourdieu, 1991).

Notwithstanding their general overall support for L1 maintenance, parents at times experienced the tension of holding on to their own language while ensuring that their children learned English so that they could be successful in school and in their lives (Wong-Fillmore, 1991). For example, at one site, some of the parents feared that children's English learning would be impacted if they continued to use their home language and so we provided them with accessible material on the benefits of home-language maintenance which allayed the concerns somewhat. Likewise, some of the families reported that their four- and five-year-olds were already expressing aversion to their home languages.

Cultural ways of learning and teaching

We also attempted to respect and honour the differing views of learning and teaching that the families held. Whereas from a Western perspective, verbal scaffolding is highly regarded and promoted, in some cultures children learn through more peripheral or guided participation (Rogoff, 2003). For example, we observed parents modelling an art activity for a child in a deliberate, demonstrative way and then hand the brush to the child, all without speaking. On other occasions, we observed the adults carefully guide the child in a hand-over-hand manner as she printed her name on a drawing she had done.

We worked diligently on developing rapport with families and earning and keeping their trust, and they felt comfortable in raising concerns. Occasionally, they expressed concerns with the pedagogical approaches we employed. For example, at one site, parents felt that we were not sufficiently explaining the purpose of the activities we introduced in the sessions and how they could continue these at home; we then provided them with a list of such activities and the key ideas, after each session. At another site, the families indicated that they saw little benefit of the session we called Riddles, Raps and Rhymes that focused on oral language and ways to encourage children's phonemic awareness. Consequently, we adapted a more direct, didactic style explicitly explaining the role of rhyme and rhythm in children's development and their facilitative role in children's early literacy learning (Friedrich et al., 2014).

Although the results of the PALS in Immigrant Communities study were generally positive and the children and their families seemed to benefit, there are lingering issues. While the programme continues and has expanded to include other linguistic groups, its continuation is contingent upon securing yearly grants to fund it, a problem that is endemic to family literacy programmes generally. Fidelity to the structure of the programme is an issue and, for example, there is a tendency to truncate the debriefing segment of the programme where learning is consolidated and reinforced and where feedback from parents can be garnered and used formatively. We have also noticed that there is slippage in using the families' first languages in print such as in messages home, in the agendas posted for each session, and so forth, and we have had to draw facilitators' attention to these issues consistently.

Discussion

In this section, we present some cautions in interpreting the studies on bilingual family literacy programmes, affirm the potential of these programmes in supporting children's language and literacy development and in maintaining their first language, and end with some ongoing concerns. First, many of the studies involved relatively small numbers of participants from one homogeneous group. Second, the studies were short term and it is not known whether the gains in language and literacy that children accrued will be maintained. Furthermore, while some of the studies included comparison or control groups, others did not. Nevertheless, there is converging evidence of the benefits of bilingual family literacy programmes; in the remainder of the chapter, we discuss the findings and their implications. As well, several issues are evident and we address these.

One of the interesting findings is that young children's early literacy learning *in English* is enhanced as they participate in bilingual family literacy programmes. Because of the benefits associated with first language maintenance (and bilingualism), the evidence suggests that children benefit from participating in early literacy activities and experiences in their home language and in English, accruing early literacy knowledge and skills regarded as foundational for literacy learning in school, which, of course, families strongly desire. This finding has implications for policy-makers, programme developers and providers and for families themselves.

Previous research suggests that many immigrant and refugee families tend not to promote their children's retaining their home language – indeed, in some cases they deliberately eschew it – in the belief that it will negatively impact on learning English and therefore their success in school and in life (e.g. Wong-Fillmore, 1991). However, there is evidence that with encouragement, explanation and support, parents do see the value of their children maintaining their first language while learning a second and, for example, the parents in the PALS in Immigrant Communities study identified a number of pragmatic and social and cultural reasons for doing so. Given the cognitive, linguistic, social and psychological benefits of additive bilingualism, this finding is encouraging as it demonstrates a practical way of countering the pervasive, dominant-language-only ideology and the hegemonic positioning of English.

Although the results of most of the studies were positive, several issues also emerged. For example, ensuring that first languages are used as prominently as English in the programme is a challenge and programme providers will need to assume a reflective stance to ensure that the emphasis on both languages is maintained. As well, being able to leverage families' *transcultural capital* (Hope, 2011) for their benefits is challenging. Indeed, even though we were able to adjust pedagogy to fit the cultural models of families as described, we believe that capitalizing on linguistic funds of knowledge is less difficult than is capitalizing on epistemologies and ways of learning and teaching. That is, seeing the value in another's language is much easier than challenging taken-for-granted assumptions that our Western pedagogy is *the way* of supporting children's learning and others are misinformed or wrong.

Conclusion

Although the literature on bilingual family literacy programmes is limited, we believe the results of the empirical studies we reviewed are hopeful in addressing the concerns raised by Auerbach and others about family literacy programmes not valuing home language and literacy, and essentially perpetuating home-language loss. However, more work needs to be done, including large-scale studies that include comparison groups, longitudinal work to ascertain the durability of the gains that children make in literacy achievement, and ethnographic work to document the particularities of programme delivery, so that these can be shared to inform programme development and implementation.

Notes

1 We quickly realized that other adults including grandparents, older siblings and other relatives accompany the children but because families and teachers had taken up using the PALS acronym, we retained it. We use 'parents' as a proxy for any adult who accompanies a child.

2 Obviously, it is beyond the scope of this chapter to report on the findings from all of these data. The complete report of the study is available at http://decoda.ca/wp-content/files_flutter/1314987 684PALSinImmigrantCommunitiesResearchReport-Feb2011.pdf.

References

Anderson, J. (1994). 'Daddy, what's a picket?' One child's emerging knowledge of workplace literacy. *Early Child Development and Care, 98*, 7–20.

Anderson, J. (1995). Listening to parents' voices: Cross cultural perceptions of learning to read and to write. *Reading Horizons, 35*, 394–413.

Anderson, J., Anderson, A., Lynch, J. and Shapiro, J. (2003). Storybook reading in a multicultural society: Critical perspectives. In A. van Kleeck, S. A. Stahl and E. B. Bauer (eds), *On Reading Books to Children: Parents and Teachers* (pp. 203–230). Mahwah, NJ: Lawrence Erlbaum Associates.

Anderson, J., Friedrich, N. and Kim, Ji Eun. (2011). *Implementing a Bilingual Family Literacy Program with Immigrant and Refugee Families: The Case of Parents As Literacy Supporters (PALS)*. Vancouver, BC: Decoda Literacy Solutions. Available at: http://decoda.ca/wpcontent/files_flutter/131498768 4PALSinImmigrantCommunitiesResearchReport-Feb2011.pdf.

Anderson, J. and Morrison, F. (2000). *The PALS Handbook: Creating and Sustaining a Culturally Responsive Family Literacy Program*. Langley, British Columbia: Langley School District.

Anderson, J. and Morrison, F. (2007). 'A great program . . . for me as a Gramma': Caregivers evaluate a family literacy initiative. *Canadian Journal of Education, 30*, 68–89.

Anderson, J., Streelasky, J. and Anderson, T. (2007). Representing and promoting family literacy on the WWW: A critical analysis. *Alberta Journal of Educational Research, 53*, 143–156.

Auerbach, E. R. (1989). Toward a social-contextual approach to family literacy. *Harvard Educational Review, 59*, 165–181.

Bialystok, E. (2011). Reshaping the mind: The benefits of bilingualism. *Canadian Journal of Experimental Psychology, 65*(4), 229–235.

Bissex, G. (1985). *Gyns at Work: A Child Learns to Write and Read*. Cambridge, MA: Harvard University Press.

Bourdieu, P. (1991). *Language and Symbolic Power*. Cambridge: Polity Press.

Boyce, L. K., Innocenti, M. S., Roggman, L. A., Norman, V. K. J. and Ortiz, E. (2010). Telling stories and making books: Evidence for an intervention to help parents in Migrant Head Start families support their children's language and literacy. *Early Education & Development, 21*(3), 343–371.

Brooks, G., Pahl, K., Pollard, A. and Rees, F. (2008) *Effective and Inclusive Practices in Family Literacy, Language and Numeracy: A Review of Programmes and Practice in the UK and Internationally*. Reading: CfBT Education Trust.

Bruner, J. (1991). The narrative construction of reality. *Critical Inquiry, 18*, 1–21.

Cohen, J. W. (1988). *Statistical Power Analysis for the Behavioral Sciences* (2nd edn). Hillsdale, NJ: Lawrence Erlbaum Associates.

Cole, M. (1997). Cultural mechanisms of cognitive development. In E. Amsel and K. A. Renninger (eds), *Change and Development: Issues of Theory, Method, and Application* (pp. 245–263). Mahwah, NJ: Erlbaum.

Compton-Lilly, C. F., Rogers, R. and Lewis, T. Y. (2012). Analyzing epistemological considerations related to diversity: An integrative critical literature review of family literacy scholarship. *Reading Research Quarterly, 47*(1), 33–60.

Conyer, J. (2012). My very own Imagination Library. *Childhood Education, 88*(4), 221–225.

Cummins, J. (2013). BICS and CALP: Empirical support, theoretical status, and policy implications. In M. Hawkins (ed.), *Framing Languages and Literacies* (pp. 10–23). London: Routledge.

Cummins, J., Chow, P. and Schecter, S. R. (2006). Community as curriculum. *Language Arts, 83*, 297–307.

Forrester, A. (1997). What teachers can learn from 'natural readers'. *The Reading Teacher, 31*(2), 160–166.

Friedrich, N., Anderson, J. and Morrison, F. (2014). Culturally appropriate pedagogy in a bilingual family literacy program. *Literacy*, *48*(2), 72–79.

Gunderson, L. and Anderson, J. (2003). Multicultural views of literacy learning and teaching. In A. Willis, G. Garcia, R. Barrera and V. Harris (eds), *Multicultural Issues in Literacy Research and Practice* (pp. 123–144). Mahwah, NJ: Lawrence Erlbaum Associates.

Hirst, K., Hannon, P. and Nutbrown, C. (2010). Effects of preschool bilingual family literacy programme. *Journal of Early Childhood Literacy*, *10*, 183–208.

Hope, J. (2011). New insights into family learning for refugees: Bonding, bridging and building transcultural capital. *Literacy*, *45*(2), 91–97.

Iddings, A. C. D. (2009). Bridging home and school literacy practices: Empowering families of recent immigrant children. *Theory Into Practice*, *48*, 304–311.

Jordan, G., Snow, C. and Porche, M. (2000). Project EASE: The effect of a family literacy project on kindergarten students' early literacy skills. *Reading Research Quarterly*, *35*(4), 524–546.

Li, G. (2001). Literacy as situated practice: The world of a Chinese preschooler. *Canadian Journal of Education*, *26*(1), 57–75.

Moll, L. C., Amanti, C., Neff, D. and Gonzalez, N. (1992). Funds of knowledge for teaching: Using a qualitative approach to connect homes and classrooms. *Theory Into Practice*, *31*(2), 132–141.

Phillips, L., Hayden, R. and Norris, S. (2006). *Family Literacy Matters: A Longitudinal Parent–Child Literacy Intervention Study*. Calgary: Detselig Press.

Prins, E., Toso, B. and Schafft, K. (2009). 'It feels like family to me!' Social interaction and support among women in adult education and family literacy. *Adult Education Quarterly*, *59*(4), 335–352.

Purcell-Gates, V., Anderson, J., Jang, K., Gagne, M., Lenters, K. and McTavish, M. (2012). Measuring situated literacy activity: Challenges and promises. *Journal of Literacy Research*, *44*, 4, 132–141.

Reid, D., Hresko, W., Hammill, D. (1989). *Test of Early Reading Ability-2*. Texas: PRO-ED, Inc.

Rogoff, B. (2003). *The Cultural Nature of Development*. New York: Oxford University Press.

Shanahan, T., Mulhern, V. and Rodriguez-Brown, F. (1995). Project FLAME: Lessons learned from a family literacy program for linguistic minority students. *The Reading Teacher*, *48*(7), 586–593.

Singh, S., Sylvia, M. R. and Ridzi, M. (2015). Exploring the literacy practices of refugee families enrolled in a book distribution program and an intergenerational family literacy program. *Early Childhood Education Journal*, *43*, 37–45.

Snow, C., Burns, M. and Griffins, P. (eds.) (1998). *Preventing Reading Difficulties in Young Children*. Washington, DC: National Academy Press.

Tabors, P. and Snow, C. (2001). Young bilingual children and early literacy development. In S. Neuman and D. Dickinson (eds), *Handbook of Early Literacy Research* (pp. 159–178). New York: The Guilford Press.

Taylor, D. (1983). *Family Literacy: Young Children Learning to Read and to Write*. Portsmouth, NH: Heinemann.

Taylor, D. and Dorsey-Gaines, C. (1988). *Growing up Literate: Learning from Inner-City Families*. Portsmouth, NH: Heinemann.

Triandafyllidou, A. (2009). Sub-Saharan African immigrant activists in Europe: Transcultural capital and transcultural community building. *Ethnic and Racial Studies*, *32*(1), 93–116.

Vygotsky, L. (1978). *Mind in Society*. Cambridge, MA: Harvard University Press.

Wertsch, J. (1998). *Mind as Action*. New York: Oxford University Press.

Wong-Fillmore, L. (1991). When learning a second language means losing the first. *Early Childhood Research Quarterly*, *6*, 323–346.

Zhang, J., Pelletier, J. and Doyle, A. (2010). Promising effects of an intervention: Young children's literacy gains and changes in their home literacy activities from a bilingual family literacy program in Canada. *Frontiers of Education in China*, *5*, 409–429.

29

BREAKING THE BARRIER OF BLAME

Parents as literacy brokers

Victoria Purcell-Gates

Central to this chapter is the concept of *home literacy culture*, which I developed to describe the patterned ways that reading and writing are used within homes as literacy mediates social lives. I illustrate the different ways that home literacy cultures vary across different social, linguistic and geographical groups, and review the research that supports the argument that parents can and do serve as brokers – cultural brokers as well and linguistic brokers – for their young children as they develop early literacy concepts and skills in families and homes, outside of formal instruction. I cover the research on parent–child book reading through this cultural lens and broaden it to include the many additional and different literacy practices to be found in homes and families. The chapter concludes with descriptions of research that is beginning to document the positive effects of family literacy programmes that work dialogically with parents to embed early literacy learning activities within everyday (i.e. culturally congruent) family practices.

'Parents are a child's first teacher.' This belief has become accepted and embedded in how we think about child development, literacy development and school policy and pedagogy in most Western, developed countries. What happens in families during the first five years of a child's life is now seen as critical and foundational to children's success in school. Thus, it becomes important to examine family practices to better understand how they do and do not facilitate development.

Learning to read and write in school is dependent in many ways on emergent literacy development before school. How parents can support and develop that development is the topic of this chapter. The argument I will make with this review of research on family practice and early literacy development is that the scope of literacy practices in homes that can facilitate early learning of foundational concepts goes beyond parent–child book reading to encompass wide varieties of literacy practices that young children experience in their homes.

In this chapter I will develop the construct of *home literacy culture* and, within that frame, I will review the research that supports the argument that parents can and do serve as brokers – cultural brokers as well as linguistic brokers – for their children as they develop early literacy concepts and skills. I will focus on the brokering that takes place within families before formal literacy instruction begins in kindergarten or first grade. This focus will include the thoroughly reviewed research on the cultural practice of reading with young children. It will expand, though, to include literacy practice in homes and families in addition to, or in place of, book sharing. I will conclude with descriptions of research that is beginning to document the effects of family literacy programmes that work dialogically with parents to embed early literacy learning activities within everyday (i.e. culturally congruent) family practices. I begin with a brief description of the theoretical frame for this review.

Theoretical frame for review

I am situating this review within a sociocultural theoretical frame. Within this frame, all human behaviour, including cognition and learning, is understood as socially and culturally situated (Vygotsky, 1980). The construct of literacy practice is central to the sociocultural theoretical frame for behaviour related to literacy. When one considers literacy practice as compared to literacy skill, the focus shifts from individual in-the-head traits to social acts – literacy in use, in practice. This reflects a multiple literacies perspective (Street, 1984). Street argued for a definition of literacy that acknowledges its multiplicity – the ways that literacy is always socially and historically situated and patterned by social institutions and power relationships, resulting not in one, universal, literacy but in many different ones (albeit overlapping in different ways) as social, cultural and political relationships change and develop. Literacy practices are best thought of, according to this perspective, as cultural practices, and are larger than print-based reading and writing events in that they also reflect values, beliefs, attitudes and social relationships (Barton and Hamilton, 1998; Purcell-Gates et al., 2004).

Within frames of power, different socioculturally constructed literacy practices mediate the social lives of people. People who read and write do so to get things done in their lives. They read the news (whether in paper newspapers or online); they purchase items to wear or to eat; they practise their different religions; they conduct business; they pay taxes; they maintain social bonds through cards and letters; they relax over a good book or read movie reviews before going out to a movie, and so on.

Literacy cultures

Researchers like Barton and Hamilton (1998) have introduced the notion of an ecology of written language and literacy (Barton, 2007). Within this I have developed the construct of literacy cultures or literacy worlds to capture the ecology of literacy within homes and home lives of different families (e.g. Purcell-Gates, 2013, 2014). The use of the term literacy culture rests upon a broader definition of culture, a contested term with definitions that have shifted over the years. For purposes of this chapter, I will present the definition of culture that frames my use of the term literacy culture.

Culture as currently defined

Over the years, many anthropologists have shifted the definition of culture from a more essentialized perspective to one that recognizes the fluidity and multiplicity of what can be thought of as culture. At base is the general consensus that cultures involve shared beliefs, values and patterns of behaviour. The current perspective, though, rejects the essentialized view of culture that leads to statements such as 'Mexicans do X' or 'Koreans do Y'. Further, it does not treat culture as 'traits' of individuals (Purcell-Gates et al., 2010). Rather, the current perspective, and the one that I take in this chapter, considers culture as dynamic and patterned ways of organizing everyday life

A culture of literacy

When I use the term literacy culture within families or homes, I am not thinking of the ways that literacy in the home is contextualized by cultures; rather, I am naming the patterned ways that reading and writing are used within the home as a type of culture – a literacy culture. This captures the ways that literacy mediates people's lives (Vygotsky, 1980) and can be thought of as being both a 'culture' present in individual's/family member's lives but also as heavily reflective of community ways of incorporating literacy into everyday lives.

Literacy cultures within family groupings are also fluid and multiple and shift over time as family members move between roles, responsibilities, education and so on (Purcell-Gates et al., 2004; Purcell-Gates et al., 2002). In this way, therefore, just as with broader conceptions of culture, one cannot essentialize literacy cultures according to race, ethnicity, socio-economic status and so on. However, literacy cultures do reflect patterned ways of reading and writing texts, which texts are read and written, by whom and for which purposes within homes and families (Purcell-Gates et al., 2011). Within the theoretical frame presented above, we can explore the variety of literacy cultures within which young children live and grow.

Literacy brokering

Perry defines literacy brokering as 'a complex activity that may involve one aspect of a text, such as translation of word meanings, mediation of cultural content, or explanation of genre aspects of a printed text, or it may involve many of these aspects all at once' (2009: 257). I am appropriating the term for our purposes to apply to the ways that parents, through various means, broker *early literacy concepts* for their children. As literacy brokers they provide informal support (Durkin, 1966) to help their young children learn about the ways that language and meaning are represented in print and the ways that literacy mediates their lives: which texts are read and written and by whom, and the functions that are served by those texts for the people reading and writing them as well as the social purposes that are served by the different literacy events.

Emergent literacy research

Early emergent literacy research was often descriptive in nature. Taylor provided an early ethnographic description of the ways that literacy mediated the lives of six middle- to upper-middle-class families in the United States (1985). She described how children in the families appropriated practices that they had experienced within their homes, using emergent spellings to produce texts for their play in clubhouses, games, pretend scenarios, leave notes to parents and siblings, and so on. They also experienced their parents and literate siblings engaging in a variety of literacy practices such as reading the newspaper, reading books to themselves and to their children, and writing personal letters. While descriptive research continued for other researchers, another line of research began to examine the relationships between types of home literacy and the development of what had by then been described as critical foundational early literacy concepts and skills (Purcell-Gates, 2000).

Foundational early literacy concepts

In a review of the emergent literacy research, Purcell-Gates (2000) concluded that, depending upon their home/community literacy experiences, young children learn about the different levels of decontextualization of written language (Snow, 1983; Sulzby, 1985), the genre-related characteristics and features of written language such as syntax and wording, and the different genre-determined forms (e.g. the forms of personal letters, grocery lists or written stories – Butler and Clay, 1979; Ferreiro and Teberosky, 1982; Goodman, 1984; Harste et al., 1984; Holdaway, 1979; Purcell-Gates, 1988; Sulzby, 1985). Further, according to this analysis, young children, through participating in literacy events within their homes and communities, learn that print is a language signifier and about the ways that print represents meaning – the 'code' – and the conventions of encoding and decoding the print (Clay, 1975; Ferreiro and Teberosky, 1982; Goodman and Altwerger, 1981; Harste et al., 1984; Hiebert, 1980, 1981; Mason, 1980). The emergent literacy research also documented how young children learn values and beliefs about literacy and literacy practice (e.g. Heath, 1983) as well as concepts and cognitive models for how and why literacy is practised and who does and does not do it (Purcell-Gates and Dahl, 1991; Taylor and Dorsey-Gaines, 1988).

Reading to young children

The most thoroughly researched domain of literacy activity involving young children is that of parent–child book sharing/reading (e.g. Bus et al., 1995; Hargrave and Sénéchal, 2000; Isbell et al., 2004; Kassow, 2006; Lonigan and Whitehurst, 1998; Snow, 1983; Snow et al., 1998; Whitehurst et al., 1994). Researchers have consistently found correlations with (e.g. Purcell-Gates, 1988, 1996) and effects on such critical early literacy components as vocabulary (e.g. Hargrave and Sénéchal, 2000; Whitehurst et al., 1994), decontextualized language (e.g. Bus et al., 1995), concepts of print (Newman, 1996) and comprehension of text (e.g. Isbell et al., 2004)

Further, ethnographic research has noted the central presence of parent–child book reading in the literacy cultures of many young children, suggesting that this literacy practice is significant to the development of affective understandings as well as those psycholinguistic literacy concepts noted above (Bissex, 1980; Sonnenschein and Munsterman, 2002; Taylor, 1985; Taylor and Dorsey-Gaines, 1988).

During parent–child book sharing events, parents serve as literacy brokers, demonstrating and sharing the ways that readers make sense of text, reading intonations, wordings (vocabulary) and syntax. They also demonstrate how reading different kinds of stories or information texts can serve as entertainment, relaxation and sources of information.

Research shows that the nature of the brokering during parent–child book reading also reflect differing cultural beliefs, values and traditions (Purcell-Gates, et al., 2010). For example, in many middle-class European-heritage families, book reading is a structured daily routine. Parents ask questions that encourage children to participate in the co-construction of the story, to focus on the print and to move beyond the information presented in the book (Fletcher and Reese, 2005). In contrast, middle-class Peruvian mothers, who also value reading with their children, prefer to be the sole narrator, discouraging child participation (Melzi and Caspe, 2005). As the expert story readers, they expect their children to learn to be attentive and (see also Fung et al., 2004) by not interrupting the reader. Similar book reading routines have been noted with Mexican and Dominican immigrant mothers living in New York City (Caspe, 2007). Finally, in some communities, adult sharing of picture books with children may not be a regular routine at all (Barrueco et al., 2007), but older children might read to younger siblings as part of their work as family translators (Orellana et al., 2003). In this way, they combine the cultural norm emphasizing sibling caretaking with the cultural value their new society places on storybook reading, and they provide exposure to English print that might not always be accessible to their predominantly Spanish-speaking parents (Orellana and Reynolds, 2008).

Parent–child book reading, itself, is a cultural practice and does not reflect the literacy worlds of many young children (Fletcher and Reese, 2005; Yarosz and Barnett, 2001). Unfortunately, much of the research that has been done on literacy in homes, with a focus on young children, has used the presence of books and book reading – both parent reading and parent–child reading – as proxies for home literacy (e.g. Frijters et al., 2000; Kuo et al., 2004; Sénéchal et al., 1998; Weinberger, 1996). The terms *family literacy* and *parent–child book reading* have become conflated, leaving us with a major conundrum: we cannot begin to design culturally relevant early literacy instruction and test its effectiveness if we do not know what home literacy practice actually looks like for many children.

Documenting different literacy cultures

To address this need, Kristen Perry and I established the Cultural Practices of Literacy Study (CPLS) (see http://sites.education.uky.edu/cpls/) with the goal of providing a more complete portrait of literacy practices within different cultural communities, all with an eye on the home–school connection (Purcell-Gates et al., 2011).

The CPLS database for cross-case analyses currently includes coded literacy events in 23 different languages from more than 26 different research studies, representing 23 countries. Common coding across studies, resulting in the documentation of more that 800 different text types, read and/or written for more than 400 functions for more than 300 different social purposes. I present examples of these texts, functions and purposes below.

Texts

Examples of texts, identified with genre theory methods (Hasan, 1989), include manuals, medication labels, membership cards, minutes, names, news stories, newsletters, notes, notice/announcements, official status identifications (e.g. passports, greed cards and so on), order forms, orders of worship, package texts and personal reflection journals.

Functions

Each text is read or written for different reasons, or functions. Examples include: to inform neighbours that children will be alone, to inform of illness of child, to inform public what one is selling, to inform self/family about family, to invite someone to an event, to keep score, to know which keys to hit, to label location, to label object, to learn about activities in community/school/church, to learn about animals, to learn about characters of a game, to learn about houses for sale, to learn about prizes, to learn about an admission decision.

Social purposes

Reading and writing different texts to get things done (functions) are never done in isolation, but rather to achieve different social purposes. Examples include: in order to bless a child, in order to borrow money, in order to budget expenses, in order to build a romantic relationship, in order to buy food, in order to celebrate a special occasion, in order to communicate when speaking would be rude, in order to pass an exam, in order to conduct a meeting, in order to cook a meal and in order to create a poem.

Clearly, data such as those just described help to broaden our knowledge of literacy as it occurs within families. We see literacy – reading and writing – thoroughly mediating the lives of families through the reading and writing of many different textual genres for different functions and social purposes. We do not see family lives bereft of literacy except for the act of reading to young children. Nor do we see family lives bereft of literacy when there is no reading to young children. This allows us much greater latitude to consider ways that parents – all parents – broker early literacy concepts for their children. Below, I will present brief exemplars of what I refer to as literacy cultures, drawn from research into literacy practice in different communities. Within these different literacy worlds, we can see the children learning about different text types, including their forms, language features, vocabulary, functions and purposes. All names are pseudonyms.

Laura's world of print

Laura and her younger brother Thomas live with a mother attending graduate school and a father, a data-processing manager for a large company. The parents are news junkies, and Mom often shares news with the two children as she reads. Mom and Dad also read books to both children several times during each day and always at bedtime from stories and children's information books, and Laura has already made a tape to send to Grandma of *Green Eggs and Ham* (Seuss, 1960), 'read' from memory as she turned each page, with the intonation, syntax and vocabulary reflecting the storybook genre most well-read-to children acquire through experience with this culturally based literacy practice (Purcell-Gates, 1988; Sulzby, 1985). A quick glance through the house reveals such texts as textbooks, journal articles and notebooks as well as magazines, cookbooks, adult novels, children's books, TV guides, newspapers, magazines, music albums, directions for constructing a music system and so on – all reflecting the lives and interests of parents and children.

Robbie's world of print

Three-year-old Robbie's home is one of activity (Purcell-Gates et al., 2004). Mom teaches sewing to adults and she continues to sew all of the clothes for the family. Books of sewing patterns fill nooks and crannies of the house. Robbie's dad sells toys to department stores and is on the road a lot. When he is home, he is often to be found working at a card table set up in the living room, completing order forms, filling out invoices and drawing up travel plans for the following week – all the while watching the news on TV and commenting on it to the family. Robbie's older brother is usually to be found in the garage taking apart an old car his parents gave him for Christmas one year. A few *Reader's Digest* books sit on the shelves that are primarily filled with knick knacks and souvenirs of vacation travels. Cookbooks, whose pages retain traces of flour and other food ingredients collected over the years, line the shelves in the kitchen or are left open on the counters. Family time consists of long discussions around the kitchen dining table or gatherings around the television set. Mom and Dad always stay up for the 11.00 p.m. news.

Cecilia's world of print

Cecelia lives in a migrant farmworker camp in the northern United States for six months and in Texas for the rest of the year. Her parents keep important documents safe in a box in their bedroom. These documents serve official purposes critical to the life and work of the family: visas to allow them to cross borders to work; vaccination papers for their children that need to be shown to avoid the common problem of revaccinating young children each time they enter a new school or programme; pay stubs that allow the family to access social and medical services for the poor, and so on. The Bible is also read and discussed in Cecilia's home and print appears on religiously themed candles and calendars. Cecilia's family receives many donations of food items, all with their own labels and printed instructions. The family also maintains contact with family members in Mexico and in Texas through birthday cards, wedding announcements and letters (Purcell-Gates, 2013).

Oscar's world of print

Oscar is four years old and lives in El Salvador in a small one-room house made of mud bricks and a tin roof. His mother, Esperanza, is learning to read and write and often sits at the table outside the door and practises writing letters to her older son in the United States by the light of the lantern. There is no electricity or plumbing in the community. Oscar listens as his parents discuss the recent war and read the testimonials of the oppression and torture that affected their neighbours and family members. Oscar also observes his parents writing items for the upcoming agendas of the community meetings, common in post-war El Salvador, and reading past minutes and future resolutions for the meetings (Purcell-Gates and Waterman, 2000).

Early literacy concepts and skills are learned by children such as these through observation, apprenticeship and participation. Young children who are repeatedly read to as part of a cultural practice of parenting can demonstrate their knowledge of written story language through pretend readings that contain written syntax and written vocabulary, and that are decontextualized so that the meaning is inherent in the text (Purcell-Gates, 1988). Similarly, Harste et al. (1984) demonstrated how children who had experienced letter writing, grocery lists and other 'everyday' types of literacy practices could demonstrate through invented spellings the genre conventions and wordings of such practices.

Supporting parents as literacy brokers

The research exemplified above points overwhelmingly to the varied roles that parents play in brokering literacy for their young children and to the influence of such brokering on developing early literacy knowledge. However, to this point, there is almost no research on the effects of instruction that reflects the literacy cultures of the children and the brokering of literacy events present in these cultures. In this section I describe the few such studies that I could find listed in online databases. Although they are rare, I feel it is important to mention them in the hope of motivating more such studies in response to calls to honour and incorporate the sociocultural lives of all children (e.g. Guitérrez, et al., 1999). One study is described elsewhere in this handbook by Jim Anderson and colleagues with the IPALS project in Canada.

Another study from Canada employed an action research design to study the effects on early literacy learning of engaging three groups of recently arrived immigrant parents and their young children in culturally congruent literacy activities (Anderson et al., 2012; Purcell-Gates et al., 2012). The Literacy for Life programme included typical early childhood activities such as painting, playing games, making art projects and listening to stories. In addition, embedded into these activities was a meta-focus on print and texts. For each activity, the teacher would either introduce texts that would mediate the activities or create activities that would require the reading or writing of texts. For example, the class at one site was in need of play materials. In response, the teacher devised a plan for the children to make their own play mat where they could stage different games. The children drew pictures of houses, roads and so on. The teacher led them in inserting text such as 'Start', 'Stop' (on a stop sign), the children's names on individual houses, store names on pictures of stores, and others. Children were encouraged to bring familiar literacy practices into the programme. One child from a Muslim family conveyed her father's directive to avoid snack foods that contained gelatin (in some yoghurts) due to religious constraints. This initiated a demonstration of how one could find and read ingredients on food packaging.

The teachers brokered literacy in different ways: explicitly pointing to the print, reading it and explaining its purpose (e.g. 'This word says "start" and it tells us where to begin with our pieces. S-T-A-R-T. "Start".'), pointing out print in the environment, during outside walks or at play as well as in the classrooms; generating menus for snack times with the children and writing them, helping children 'order' from the menus; and supporting the children as they created birthday and get-well cards for family or other class members, complete with emergent writing. Pre- and post-tests on normed emergent literacy knowledge revealed that the children significantly increased their knowledge as compared to the norm. Attendance was significantly related to growth as was the number of times each child engaged in real-life literacy activities.

A study from the United States focused on training parents to broker literacy learning in the process of engaging in everyday activities (Roberts et al., 2015). This study addressed the following questions: (1) In what ways did parent–child home literacy interactions change over the course of five literacy-based family workshops? (2) Did children whose families participated in these workshops show gains that were significantly greater than control group peers on measures of language and literacy?

Three- to five-year-old preschool children (N = 124) and their families were recruited from preschool classrooms representing four districts and two states. Classrooms were randomly assigned to experimental and control conditions. Families assigned to the experimental condition were invited to attend five two-hour workshops over the course of ten weeks during which they were taught literacy strategies to use with their children throughout different areas in the home. These workshops were split into three parts. During the first part, families were provided with a snack or meal, followed by a parent-only segment in which (a) parents were introduced to the session theme (e.g. literacy in the kitchen, literacy in the family room); (b) watched a short video about specific areas of literacy development (e.g. letter–sound knowledge, oral language, phonological awareness), with footage of families engaged in literacy interactions related to the session theme; (c) discussed the focal area(s) of literacy development with session leaders; and (d) learned about specific literacy activities (two for each of the six literacy constructs) they could engage in with their children during and outside the session. The final part of the workshop was the parent–child activity time, in which families actively engaged in at least six literacy activities (one for each of the previously listed areas of literacy) that were provided in the session.

Child language and literacy measures included story comprehension, phonological awareness, vocabulary and a home literacy environment survey. Results showed no statistically significant differences between the experimental and control groups on child early literacy measures at the beginning of the programme. Significant outcomes on all measures at the conclusion of the study for children in the experimental group suggest that the literacy-based workshop has positive effects for children and families. Measures included the *Phonological Awareness Literacy Screening* (Invernizzi et al., 2004); the *Test of Semantic Skills—Primary*. University of Virginia (Bowers et al., 2002); and the *Test of Story Comprehension-Preschool* (Language Dynamics Group).

Conclusion

Research such as the two studies described above offer hope for a new, broader and more inclusive paradigm for understanding literacy in families and how young children can develop early literacy concepts with help from their parents. Cultural practices, including literacy practices, shift and change as circumstances, experiences and educational opportunities offer new and different horizons. Thus, for many children, practices such as adult–child storybook reading may need to wait until formal schooling begins, and, fortunately, many studies support the efficacy of storybook reading in school for development of vocabulary and genre learning related to books (e.g. Hargrave and Sénéchal, 2000; Isbell et al., 2004; Purcell-Gates et al., 1995; Whitehurst et al., 1994). In the meantime, parents can, and do, support early acquisition of foundational concepts by engaging themselves and their children with the multitude of other genres that mediate the social lives of literate people around the world.

References

Anderson, J., Purcell-Gates, V., Lenters, K. and McTavish, M. (2012). Real world literacy activity in preschool. *Community Literacy Journal*, 6(2), 75–95.

Barrueco, S., López, M. L. and Miles, J. C. (2007). Parenting behaviors in the first year of life: A national comparison of Latinos and other cultural communities. *Journal of Latinos and Education, Special Issue: National Task Force on Early Childhood Education for Hispanics*, 6(3), 253–265.

Barton, D. (2007). *Literacy: An Introduction to the Ecology of Written Language* (2nd edn). Wiley-Blackwell.

Barton, D. and Hamilton, M. (1998). *Local Literacies: Reading and Writing in One Community*. New York: Routledge.

Bissex, G. L. (1980). *Gnys (Genius) at Wrk (Work): A Child Learns to Write and Read*. Cambridge, MA: Harvard University Press.

Bowers, L., Huisingh, R., LoGiudice, C. and Orman, J. (2002). *Test of Semantic Skills – Primary*. Austin, TX: Linguisystems.

Bus, A. G., Van Ijzendoorn, M. H. and Pellegrini, A. D. (1995). Joint book reading makes for success in learning to read: A meta-analysis on intergenerational transmission of literacy. *Review of Educational Research*, 65(1), 1–21.

Butler, D. and Clay, M. (1979). *Reading Begins at Home: Preparing Children for Reading Before They Go to School*. Exeter, NH: Heinemann.

Caspe, M. (2007). Family involvement, narrative and literacy practices: Predicting low-income Latino children's literacy development. Unpublished doctoral dissertation. New York University: New York.

Clay, M.M. (1975). *What Did I Write?* Auckland: Heinemann.

Durkin, D. (1966). *Children Who Read Early*. New York: Teachers College Press.

Ferreiro, E. and Teberosky, A. (1982). *Literacy Before Schooling*. Portsmouth, NH: Heinemann.

Fletcher, K. L. and Reese, E. (2005). Picture book reading with young children: A conceptual framework. *Developmental Review*, 25(1), 64–103.

Frijters, J. C., Barron, R. W. and Brunello, M. (2000). Direct and mediated influences of home literacy and literacy interest on prereaders' oral vocabulary and early written language skill. *Journal of Educational Psychology*, 92(3), 466.

Fung, H., Miller, P. J. and Lin, L. (2004). Listening is active: Lessons from the narrative practices of Taiwanese families. In M. W. Pratt and B. H. Fiese (eds), *Family Stories and the Life Course: Across Time and Generations* (pp. 303–323). Mahwah, NJ: Lawrence Erlbaum.

Goodman, Y. (1984). The development of initial literacy. In H. Goelman, A. Oberg and F. Smith (eds), *Awakening to Literacy* (pp. 102–109). Exeter, NH: Heinemann.

Goodman, Y. and Altwerger, B. (1981). Print awareness in preschool children: A working paper. Tucson, AZ: University of Arizona, Program in Language and Literacy.

Guitérrez, K., Baquedano-Lopez, P. and Tejeda, C. (1999). Rethinking diversity: Hybridity and hybrid language practices in the third space. *Mind, Culture and Activity, 6*(4), 286–203. doi:10.1080/10749039909524733.

Hargrave, A. C. and Sénéchal, M. (2000). A book reading intervention with preschool children who have limited vocabularies: The benefits of regular reading and dialogic reading. *Early Childhood Research Quarterly, 15*(1), 75–90.

Harste, J., Woodward, V. and Burke, C. (1984). *Language Stories and Literacy Lessons.* Portsmouth, NH: Heinemann.

Heath, S. B. (1983). *Ways with Words: Language, Life and Work in Communities and Classrooms.* Cambridge: Cambridge University Press.

Hiebert, E. H. (1980). The relationship of logical reasoning ability, oral language comprehension, and home experiences to preschool children's print awareness. *Journal of Reading Behavior, 12*(4), 313–324.

Hiebert, E. H. (1981). Developmental patterns and interrelationships of preschool children's print awareness. *Reading Research Quarterly, 16*(2), 236–260.

Holdaway, D. (1979). *The Foundations of Literacy.* Sydney: Ashton Scholastic.

Invernizzi, M., Sullivan, A., Meier, J. and Swank, L. (2004). *Phonological Awareness Literacy Screening.* Richmond, VA: University of Virginia.

Isbell, R., Sobol, J., Lindauer, L. and Lowrance, A. (2004). The effects of storytelling and story reading on the oral language complexity and story comprehension of young children. *Early Childhood Education Journal, 32*(3), 157–163.

Kassow, D. Z. (2006). Parent–child shared book reading: Quality versus quantity of reading interactions between parents and young children. *Talaris Research Institute, 1*(1), 1–9.

Kuo, A. A., Franke, T. M., Regalado, M. and Halfon, N. (2004). Parent report of reading to young children. *Pediatrics, 113*(Supplement 5), 1944–1951.

Language Dynamics Group. *Test of Story Comprehension – Preschool.* Downloaded from http://shop.languagedynamicsgroup.com/Test-of-Story-Comprehension-Preschool-TSCP-TSCP.htm.

Lonigan, C. J. and Whitehurst, G. J. (1998). Relative efficacy of parent and teacher involvement in a shared-reading intervention for preschool children from low-income backgrounds. *Early Childhood Research Quarterly, 13*(2), 263–290.

Orellana, M. F., Reynolds, J., Dorner, L. and Meza, M. (2003). In other words: Translating or 'paraphrasing' as a family literacy practice in immigrant households. *Reading Research Quarterly, 38*(1), 12–34.

Mason, J. M. (1980). When do children begin to read: An exploration of four year old children's letter and word reading competencies. *Reading Research Quarterly, 15*(2), 203–227.

Melzi, G. and Caspe, M. (2005). Variations in maternal narrative styles during book reading interactions. *Narrative Inquiry, 15*(1), 101–125.

Newman, S. B. (1996). Children engaging in storybook reading: The influence of access to print resources, opportunity, and parental interaction. *Early Childhood Research Quarterly, 11*(4), 495–513.

Orellana, M. F. and Reynolds, J. F. (2008). Cultural modeling: Leveraging bilingual skills for school paraphrasing tasks. *Reading Research Quarterly, 43*(1), 48–65.

Perry, K.H. (2009). Genres, contexts, and literacy practices: Literacy brokering among Sudanese refugee families. *Reading Research Quarterly, 44,* 256–276.

Purcell-Gates, V. (1988). Lexical and syntactic knowledge of written narrative held by well-read-to kindergartners and second graders. *Research in the Teaching of English, 22*(2), 128–160.

Purcell-Gates, V. (1996). Stories, coupons, and the TV guide: Relationships between home literacy experiences and emergent literacy knowledge. *Reading Research Quarterly, 31*(4), 406–428.

Purcell-Gates, V. (2000). Family literacy: A research review. *Handbook of Reading Research,* vol. 3 (pp. 853–870). New York: Erlbaum.

Purcell-Gates, V. (2013). Literacy worlds of children of migrant farmworker communities participating in a migrant Head Start program. *Research in the Teaching of English, 48*(1), 68–97.

Purcell-Gates, V. (2014). Constructions of difference and deficit, a case study: Nicaraguan families and children on the margins in Costa Rica. *Global Education Review, 1*(2), 7–25.

Purcell-Gates, V., Anderson, J., Gagne, M., Jang, K., Lenters, K. A. and McTavish, M. (2012). Measuring situated literacy activity: Challenges and promises. *Journal of Literacy Research, 44*(4), 396–425. doi:10.1177/1086296X12457167.

Purcell-Gates, V. and Dahl, K. L. (1991). Low-SES children's success and failure at early literacy learning in skills-based classrooms. *Journal of Literacy Research, 23*(1), 1–34.

Purcell-Gates, V., Degener, S., Jacobson, E. and Soler, M. (2002). Impact of authentic literacy instruction on adult literacy practices. *Reading Research Quarterly, 37*(1), 70–92.

Purcell-Gates, V., Jacobson, E. and Degener, S. (2004). *Print Literacy Development: Uniting the Cognitive and Social Practice Theories.* Cambridge, MA: Harvard University Press.

Purcell-Gates, V., McIntyre, E. and Freppon, P. (1995). Learning written storybook language in school: A comparison of low-ses children in skill-based and whole language classrooms. *American Educational Research Journal, 30*, 659–685.

Purcell-Gates, V., Melzi, G., Najafi, B. and Orellana, M.F. (2010). Building literacy instruction from children's sociocultural worlds. *Child Development Perspectives, 5*(1), 207–212.

Purcell-Gates, V., Perry, K. H. and Briseño, A. (2011). Analyzing literacy practice: Grounded theory to model. *Research in the Teaching of English, 45*(4), 439–458.

Purcell-Gates, V. and Waterman, R. (2000). *Now We Read, We See, We Speak: Portrait of Literacy Development in a Freirean-Based Adult Class.* Mahwah, NJ: Lawrence Erlbaum.

Roberts, K. L., Jordan, G. E., Duke, N. K. and Rochester, S. (2015). Learning through everyday activities: Improving early language and literacy development in children through literacy-based workshops for families. Paper presented at the Literacy Research Association Annual Conference, Carlsbad, CA, December.

Sénéchal, M., Lefevre, J. A., Thomas, E. M. and Daley, K. E. (1998). Differential effects of home literacy experiences on the development of oral and written language. *Reading Research Quarterly, 33*, 96–116. doi:10.1598/RRQ.33.1.5.

Seuss, Dr. (1960). *Green Eggs and Ham.* New York: Beginner Books: Distributed by Random House.

Snow, C. E. (1983). Literacy and language: Relationships during the preschool years. *Harvard Educational Review, 53*(2), 165–189.

Snow, C. E., Burns, S. and Griffin, P. (eds) (1998). *Preventing Reading Difficulties in Young Children.* Washington, DC: National Academy Press.

Sonnenschein, S. and Munsterman, K. (2002). The influence of home-based reading interactions on 5-year-olds' reading motivations and early literacy development. *Early Childhood Research Quarterly, 17*(3), 318–337.

Street, B. V. (1984). *Literacy in Theory and Practice.* Cambridge University Press.

Sulzby, E. (1985). Children's emergent reading of favorite storybooks: A developmental study. *Reading Research Quarterly,* 458–481.

Taylor, D. (1985). *Family Literacy: Children Learning to Read and Write.* Exeter, NH: Heinemann.

Taylor, D. and Dorsey-Gaines, C. (1988). *Growing Up Literate: Learning from Inner-City Families.* Portsmouth, NH: Heinemann.

Vygotsky, L. S. (1980). *Mind in Society: The Development of Higher Psychological Processes.* Cambridge, MA: Harvard University Press.

Weinberger, J. (1996). A longitudinal study of children's early literacy experiences at home and later literacy development at home and school. *Journal of Research in Reading, 19*, 14–24. doi:10.1111/j.1467-9817.1996.tb00083.x.

Whitehurst, G. J., Arnold, D. S., Epstein, J. N., Angell, A. L., Smith, M. and Fischel, J. E. (1994). A picture book reading intervention in day care and home for children from low-income families. *Developmental Psychology, 30*(5), 679–689.

Yarosz, D. J. and Barnett, W.S. (2001). Who reads to young children? Identifying predictors of family reading activities. *Reading Psychology, 22*(1), 67–81.

30

OLD AND NEW

Reflecting on the enduring key issues in early literacy

Catherine McBride, Catherine E. Snow,
Natalia Kucirkova and Vibeke Grøver

In this chapter, we highlight what we consider to be some of the major issues in early literacy development and education worldwide. These issues have been touched upon in previous chapters, and here we summarize our 'take' on some of the most consistent debates related to literacy learning. One is the tension between a focus in early instruction on learning to read versus learning to write. A second is the issue of skill-focused versus comprehension-/communication-focused reading. Some scholars in the United States might refer to this as phonics versus whole language, though this label does not necessarily do full justice to the issue when considered across cultures (e.g. McBride, 2016). A third is the question of how useful or problematic digital devices are as an aid to early literacy development. The affordances of and limitations on digital media use are greatly influenced by local conditions, so this conversation needs input from many national contexts. Our fourth question is the right degree of focus on oral language in literacy instruction. We know that oral language skills predict literacy outcomes, a fact that creates a challenge when a majority of children in the world attend schools that use what is for them a second language. While we acknowledge the inevitability, and indeed the benefits, of multilingualism for all, we think there are serious questions to be raised about how best to build and exploit children's oral language skills in early years literacy instruction, taking into account both what we know about child development and the constraints of practicality in multilingual settings. Given the robust evidence that children's oral language skills predict their literacy development, a fifth question is related to the forms of oral language instruction in early childhood that may support children's literacy achievements in a long-term perspective. The sixth issue is the nature of literacy across cultures. For example, should we continue to consider early literacy development primarily in the context of book reading, even in cultures where children's books are rare and reading to children uncommon? Or should our thinking about promoting early literacy be broadened to include other literacy-related activities, engaged in both for learning and for pleasure? The seventh and final question is also a definitional one: how are the tasks of learning to read and to write influenced by the specifics of the language and the script in which the child is learning? Given limitations of space, we can only touch on each of these issues briefly. We begin with the first issue, among several, related to definitional aspects of literacy.

Learning to read, learning to write

We have tried, in this volume, to encourage inclusion of work on both reading and writing by scholars describing early literacy instruction and research around the world. However, it is often the case that researchers focus on one or the other of these processes. In fact, reading and writing development are not necessarily strongly associated (e.g. Ahmed et al., 2014; Shanahan, 1984). An extreme example of dissociation comes from children learning Chinese. Children texting one another in Chinese can choose from among several systems. They can write characters, but also have the option of relying on Pinyin skills. Pinyin is an alphabetic system (based on the Roman alphabet) that is used to spell out characters. For example, man means slow (man4 (慢)). Children who use this Pinyin system frequently to write electronically may recognize characters but lack the detailed knowledge of the various strokes required to write them correctly. This situation arises because entering the Pinyin brings up a range of characters to choose from, so the texter's task is just to recognize the correct one. Writing the characters requires recall, a deeper level of memory than recognition (e.g. McBride-Chang and Liu, 2011).

There are entire societies and journals devoted only to the study of reading or the study of writing. And yet, there is evidence that writing can help develop reading skills. For example, invented spelling promotes phonological awareness and early word reading (e.g. Martins and Silva, 2006), and attention to the correct spelling of new vocabulary helps support retention (Ehri and Rosenthal, 2007; Silverman and Hartranft, 2015). Ultimately, though, writing is also an educational goal on its own, so it is unfortunate that there is much less research devoted to what facilitates good spelling or dictation skills, or how best to teach narrative and analytic writing, as compared with how children develop into excellent readers. We know the foundations of early word reading very well and those for reading comprehension moderately well. We know the foundations of spelling a bit less well, and those for writing composition not all that clearly yet. Thus, one research priority is to explore the precursors of writing, as well as relationships between reading and writing developmental trajectories in young children. There is clear evidence that scaffolding of both the writing (Aram and Levin, 2002, 2004) and reading processes by parents or teachers are uniquely helpful for young children's development. There has been an upsurge on studies devoted to invented spelling across languages, for example (e.g. Martins et al., 2014; Sénéchal et al., 2012). At the same time, however, the precise ways in which teachers and parents can be most helpful in supporting early writing skills could be researched much more thoroughly, and we hope to see this as a direction that attracts robust research attention in the coming years. We now turn to an issue that has been the subject of considerable research and long-standing debates; namely what the precise foci should be for facilitating early reading skills.

Skills-focused versus content-focused development

Some researchers have spent considerable resources on the question of how much time and energy to devote to the development of specific reading-related skills as compared with overall comprehension skills (for a review, see Tunmer, 2014). That said, there is some consistency in what early childhood educators consider to be good practices across cultures. Essentially, it is important to teach children the building blocks of reading in their script(s) and also to emphasize that the code gives access to meaning by including rich exposure to stories and other text genres (e.g. McBride, 2016). What we mean by 'the building blocks of reading' varies across orthographies, but in all scripts is key for ensuring that children develop accurate and fluent word-recognition skills. In Chinese, this might involve learning some very simple characters and some radicals, character components that give clues to the meaning and/or sound of given characters. In Korean, children are often exposed to syllable blocks that they memorize from a syllable chart. Although these syllables comprise phonemes, they are first learned as consonant–vowel or consonant–vowel–consonant units. In alphabetic orthographies, the foundational skills typically involve memorizing letter names, letter sounds or both. Other aspects of word recognition are highlighted by culture as well. For example, in Thai, words are initially separated and only later presented in their mature form, that is without spaces between words. In Hebrew and Arabic, children first learn words with short vowels explicitly included in the writing and only later learn to infer the short vowels.

The second aspect, exposure to stories and other text-based genres, as well as confrontations with extended texts, ensures that children get the idea that reading is for the purpose of communication. In addition, it creates positive attitudes, by demonstrating that reading can be fun. Shared book reading gives parents, teachers or other adults a chance to scaffold the child's understanding, pose and answer questions, and familiarize the child with basic print concepts (letters versus illustrations, title and author, the 'shape' of specific repeated words). The language of books exposes children to new vocabulary, to a wider range of grammatical structures than those used in conversation and to information about phenomena, characters and real or hypothetical situations that expand their knowledge base and stimulate their imaginations (Dickinson et al., 2012; Robbins and Ehri, 1994). Motivation for reading is likely to be enhanced by shared book reading as well (Baker et al., 2001), in part because it creates a warm affective bond between child and adult (see Bus et al., 1995).

It is unfortunate that the debates in the area of early childhood literacy have driven participants to extreme positions. Worries about overly academicized early childhood settings have led to banning alphabet friezes or book corners in some places, whereas in others three-year-olds are given worksheets to complete. Fortunately, the phonics versus whole language debate has receded, and most educators embrace a focus both on specific literacy skills and on a rich oral language/literacy environment as prerequisites for solid literacy skills (Tunmer, 2014). Clearly, children need to learn the tricks of the code in order to be able to read and write fluently. At the same time, they require control over language structures and some understanding of how and why reading is useful from the beginning. Books as a source of information and entertainment are key for this.

Digital media as a tool for literacy development?

Another key literacy debate at present involves the utility of digital media as ways of introducing and practising different aspects of literacy. As we have learned from Chapters 4 and 5, digital media can and do serve to enhance literacy skills. Computer games can be successful in facilitating children's mastery of word reading and writing skills. Digital books (or e-books) can also be helpful in probing aspects of reading comprehension. Years ago, some researchers posed the question whether television viewing is good or bad. Others argued that such a question is basically obsolete. Rather, the question should be how television should be used. In what ways is it helpful or detrimental? A similar question should be considered in relation to all digital media. Video games, social media and, for younger children, computer games and e-books are all powerful tools that can facilitate learning in some circumstances and impede learning in others.

Games embedded in technology-enhanced environments are most helpful when they are targeting skills for which children require extensive practice in an engaging yet focused way.

For example, GraphoGame, as described by Richardson and Lyytinen (2014), has yielded remarkable success for children at-risk for reading difficulties (e.g. Kyle et al., 2013; Ojanen et al., 2015; Saine et al., 2011). Different researchers have debated the value of digital media in targeting particular reading-related skills (e.g. Tallal et al., 1996; Wouters et al., 2013), some arguing that particular skills are gatekeepers to fully-fledged literacy. It seems clear that computer games that target specific skills related to fluent word recognition, such as phoneme or syllable recognition (e.g. Kyle et al., 2013; Wouters et al., 2013), tend to yield good results for the skills targeted. Some researchers claim that video games can even help specifically with visual skills in reading (e.g. Franceschini et al., 2013). These games, if targeted to specific skill sets, are fun for everyone and potentially essential for those who are at risk for reading problems or dyslexic, that is lacking in those particular targeted skills. Most typically developing readers, on the other hand, acquire such skills naturally, without the need for support from intensive practice sessions.

Digital books have a somewhat mixed record. On the one hand, there is clear evidence that children sometimes pay good attention to and learn from books that are narrated. They follow along and they comprehend text that is at an appropriate level. On the other hand, stories with many 'bells and whistles' can be distracting. That is, when interesting visual or auditory manipulations occur in the book, children often pay attention to these (e.g. a dog barks, a girl throws a ball, a flower grows) in ways that interfere with comprehending the overall narrative. This is a risk of enhanced (or embellished) e-books (Bus et al., 2015).

Future research in this area needs to concentrate on developing a fuller understanding of the key features of digital books that would enhance or impede children's learning and enjoyment derived from book reading. While early research on children's e-books focused on comparing them with print-based books, more recent research has analysed specific features of e-books such as interactivity (Takacs et al., 2015), personalization (Kucirkova et al., 2013), aesthetic value (including chromatics and colours; see Kao et al., 2016) and high visual representation (Wei and Mia, 2016). There has also been a shift towards the use of e-books in pre- and primary schools, with studies complementing home-based and parent–child e-reading with investigations of e-books' use in traditional literacy teaching (e.g. Roskos et al., 2014). The role of teachers as media mentors in facilitating this transition and their role as co-developers of e-book content is likely to be the primary focus for the next years (Guernsey and Levine, 2015).

Given the international focus of this volume, it seems important to note that digital resources are a potential solution to a major educational challenge in many parts of the developing world: access to books, both in the language of schooling and in local languages. Providing paper-based libraries to all the schools in the developing world is a daunting task, but providing access to digital resources, for reading either on digital devices or for downloading and printing, can greatly expand many children's access to print. Groups such as African Storybook (www.africanstorybook.org/), Pratham (https://storyweaver.org.in/about) and others have created open-source resources to support literacy education around the world.

The role of oral language in literacy development

All fully-fledged theories of literacy development emphasize comprehension and effective written communication as the ultimate goals. Thus, it is impossible to avoid a focus on oral language development in thinking about promoting literacy, as language is the key to both comprehension and to writing. One can legitimately ask, though, to what extent early literacy programmes are and should be focusing on teaching vocabulary, grammar and discourse structures, and whether long-term outcomes from such a focus would be superior to outcomes from a focus on decoding and spelling.

There is robust evidence that children's oral language skills predict their literacy achievement. For example, oral language at age three predicts first grade reading (NICHD Early Child Care Research Network, 2005), kindergarten vocabulary scores predict reading comprehension scores through to at least eighth grade (Snow et al., 1998; Snow et al., 2007), preschool measures of vocabulary (Forget-Dubois et al., 2009) and comprehension (Cristofaro and Tamis-Lemonda, 2011) predict school readiness, and clinical deficits in language skills are associated with poor literacy outcomes (Justice et al., 2009; Lyytinen et al., 2005).

Given the centrality of oral language to reading success, questions arise about situations in which children are being taught to read in a language they do not speak. Immigrants, children from language minority communities, children growing up in highly diglossic situations and the majority of children in post-colonial school systems are confronted with instruction in a language that may be completely unfamiliar to them, or that deviates in various ways from the variety they speak. Such children may also face extra challenges associated with membership in groups at high risk of poor literacy outcomes – low parental education, limited financial and educational resources, and so on. Thus identifying the optimal literacy-learning environments for such children is crucial. There is now ample evidence that a very high proportion of children learning to read in a second language fail (see, e.g., Pretorius and Spaull, 2016), that children can benefit from initial literacy instruction in their first language, but at the same time that many children succeed at learning to read in a second language (August and Shanahan, 2006). The question is how best to introduce literacy to second language learners so as to maximize the likelihood of their success and minimize their risks of failure.

Designing early childhood programmes that support literacy achievement

A fifth debate, following up on the previous topic, is related to instructional implications of the evidence that oral language skills are crucial in literacy development. Early education institutions, even in fairly homogeneous societies, demonstrate huge variability across classrooms in the types of words, complexity of sentences and range of discourse structures children are exposed to in interaction with their teachers and peers. This variability is found to have implications for children's oral language development, documented both in descriptive long-term studies (Dickinson and Porche, 2011; Rydland et al., 2014; Snow et al., 2007) and in short-term experimental intervention studies (Coyne et al., 2007; Silverman, 2007). However, the implications of this evidence for the development of early childhood programmes are not yet clear. We identify two pertinent research topics related to questions of designing early childhood programmes with the purpose of supporting literacy achievement. The first has to do with *whom* programmes are developed for; the second is related to *how* – that is identifying core components of efficient early education programmes.

First, the motivation behind language and literacy programmes is often compensatory; that is to enhance language skills in children who are demographically at risk and expected to lag behind their peers in reading and writing achievements. Some experimental studies of oral language interventions have confirmed the Matthew effect, suggesting that children with more developed language skills benefit the most from language-enriching programmes (Penno et al., 2002). Other studies have concluded that universal programmes serving children from lower and higher income families may be beneficial for children across demographic groups (Weiland and Yoshikawa, 2013). Second, while some intervention results in small-scale trials addressing oral language learning have been encouraging, large-scale studies of programme impacts on young children's language and literacy have produced mixed findings. For example, a study in Chile that incorporated support to teachers found moderate to large impacts on classroom quality, but no universal programme effects on the children's language and literacy outcomes were detected (Yoshikawa et al., 2015). On the other hand, studies on early education curricula designed to ensure an emphasis on children's language and literacy development, in addition to offering support for teachers, have reported positive outcomes (Dickinson et al., 2011; Weiland and Yoshikawa, 2013).

Effective programmes may require a nuanced vocabulary, complex sentences and a wide range of discourse structures embedded in meaningful and engaging content in the classroom. We need more research on the conditions under which a curriculum might support the development of oral language skills in early childhood as preparation for future reading comprehension. For the international readership of this handbook we would particularly like to point out the value and necessity of researching questions of *for whom* and *how* across societies that differ in demographics, language profile and resources.

Beyond these issues that relate primarily to what advice or practices might be advocated for policy-makers, teachers and parents of young children, there are two broader issues that are important to consider across cultures. The first is the culture of literacy. The second is how literacy is manifested in one's culture.

The culture of literacy: what are reading and writing for?

One other pervasive issue in early literacy is how to teach and present literacy skills. This involves an academic conversation about how important it is to emphasize literacy skills for enjoyment and love of the written word versus for academic necessity. Worldwide, many countries are introducing literacy instruction to children at younger and younger ages for the purpose of ensuring that they learn as much as possible as early as possible. There is more and more to learn. Hong Kong is an extreme, with children receiving formal instruction from age 3.5 years. But there is a push in many countries to introduce children to literacy skills relatively early. This issue relates also to how to test children's skills as they grow up. Should we routinely tap all kinds of literacy skills, including making a shopping list, texting a friend or searching for a topic on a search engine on the internet? Should we test children's reading skills not only via traditional narratives or expository texts but also by noting how efficiently they can glean information from a website or play an online game that makes use of text for giving instructions?

Snow's (2002) model of reading comprehension highlights the different types of reading that adult literacy competence requires. We not only read intensively to learn things but also we skim to get the gist of an article or to locate one specific piece of information (e.g. what colour were the boy's high tops?). When we talk about literacy skills, then, and what is important, what should we highlight? The nature of communication these days makes it such that literacy skills need to be more flexible and diverse than previously. The trend appears to be that we are adding more and more skills to be learned, rather than substituting some for others.

Literacy-learning across languages/orthographies

The way forward for literacy development in early childhood also depends somewhat on the culture in which one finds oneself. The varied language environments of Africa and India, for example, ensure that for many parents and teachers the literacy skills that should be taught may be debatable. There are usually official scripts or languages to be learned, but at the same time, most support the idea of teaching children literacy skills first in their mother tongue. This situation is complicated when the teacher or school makes use of a different language than the one that is the child's own. This may be particularly confusing in India, which makes use of at least 20 different scripts and many more languages.

We mention this because many of the current models of literacy learning, whatever their focus, come from places in the world where literacy learning is relatively cut and dry. There is a longer history of research on literacy learning from the USA, UK, Canada or some other countries in Europe than, say, from China, India or Africa. However, in China, India and Africa, it is much more common than, say, in Europe or in English-speaking countries for children to speak one language at home and to have to learn another one in school. Moreover, children in most non-English speaking countries have to learn English fairly early in school as well. In Asia and at least some of Africa, children are learning English as early as second grade even if they began schooling in a local language. The challenge of learning to read perhaps first in a non-native language and possibly also in not one but often two second languages is quite different from the situations that Western models typically highlight. Indeed, it has been estimated that more than 50 per cent of the world population first learn to read in a second language (e.g. McBride, 2016). In addition, the prospect of having to learn two very different scripts seems daunting; there are few models for that as of yet. In China, the scripts are Chinese and English. In India, the scripts are usually Hindi and English. But often in each place, the language at home is different from either of these.

There is not enough space to talk extensively about how models of literacy might differ for these multilingual, multiliterate, multiorthographic learners. However, it is likely that such diversity demands more different cognitive-linguistic skills than would be required for fewer languages or for several languages all using a single script, in particular for word reading. Furthermore, different languages may evoke important, divergent cultural aspects to the reading process. Are motivations to read very different texts in very different scripts divergent? Future research should focus more particularly on the well-populated but under-researched areas of the world vis-à-vis literacy. These should include particularly Africa and Asia.

This chapter has highlighted what we consider to be seven promising domains of exploration that might enhance literacy learning around the globe. We have attempted to explain why more research on learning to write, along with learning to read, is important for future work in early literacy. The second issue we raise, skills-focused versus content-focused teaching, can be extended to writing (word writing versus sentence/essay writing). Our third topic, the status of digital media for literacy, is of great interest around the world. Worldwide, most families have access to either a computer or a cell phone, and aids to literacy can be easily presented on either one. However, teachers and parents should be cautious about how to use these in ways that will benefit children. We also tried to point out that reading and writing represent a wide range of skills. Reading can be undertaken for pleasure, for academic learning, for informal learning, for religious purposes and for many other purposes as well. Writing is similarly complicated. As societies become more complex and students are required to learn more and more in order to compete globally, the issue of the range of literacy components is important to highlight and define. Having expanded our definition of literacy to encompass writing as well as reading, we note that oral language skills are crucial prerequisites to good reading outcomes, and that learning to read in a non-proficient language can pose particular challenges to children, and to the design of early childhood educational programmes. Finally, we noted that given our global emphasis in this volume, we must acknowledge culture fully in understanding early literacy development. The majority of children engaged in early literacy are likely learning to read in a language that is not their mother tongue. Different language environments and different scripts to be learned make early literacy learning more complicated than some Western models of literacy might have us believe. Much more research on this topic is required before researchers can easily isolate all the cognitive and linguistic, not to mention motivational, components required for optimal literacy learning.

References

Ahmed, Y., Wagner, R. K. and Lopez, D. (2014). Developmental relations between reading and writing at the word, sentence, and text levels: A latent change score analysis. *Journal of Educational Psychology*, *106*(2), 419–434.

Aram, D. and Levin, I. (2002). Mother–child joint writing and storybook reading: Relations with literacy among low SES kindergartners. *Merrill-Palmer Quarterly*, *48*(2), 202–224.

Aram, D. and Levin, I. (2004). The role of maternal mediation of writing to kindergartners in promoting literacy in school: A longitudinal perspective. *Reading and Writing*, *17*(4), 387–409.

August, D. and Shanahan, T. (eds). (2006). *Developing Literacy in Second-Language Learners: Report of the National Literacy Panel on Language Minority Children and Youth*. Mahwah, NJ: Erlbaum.

Baker, L., Mackler, K., Sonnenschein, S. and Serpell, R. (2001). Parents' interactions with their first-grade children during storybook reading and relations with subsequent home reading activity and reading achievement. *Journal of School Psychology*, *39*(5), 415–438.

Bus, A. G., Takacs, Z. K. and Kegel, C. A. (2015). Affordances and limitations of electronic storybooks for young children's emergent literacy. *Developmental Review*, *35*, 79–97.

Bus, A. G., Van Ijzendoorn, M. H. and Pellegrini, A. D. (1995). Joint book reading makes for success in learning to read: A meta-analysis on intergenerational transmission of literacy. *Review of Educational Research*, *65*(1), 1–21.

Coyne, M. D., McCoach, B. and Kapp, S. (2007). Vocabulary intervention for kindergarten students: comparing extended instruction to embedded instruction and incidental exposure. *Learning Disability Quarterly*, *30*(2), 74–88. doi:10.2307/30035543.

Cristofaro, T. N. and Tamis-LeMonda, C. S. (2012). Mother–child conversations at 36 months and at pre-kindergarten: Relations to children's school readiness. *Journal of Early Childhood Literacy*, *12*(1), 68–97. doi:10.1177/1468798411416879.

Dickinson, D. K., Freiberg, J. B. and Barnes, E. M. (2011). Why are so few interventions really effective? A call for fine-grained research methodology. In S. B. Neuman and D. K. Dickinson (eds), *Handbook of Early Literacy Research*. New York: The Guilford Press.

Dickinson, D. K., Griffith, J. A., Golinkoff, R. M. and Hirsh-Pasek, K. (2012). How reading books fosters language development around the world. *Child Development Research*, *2012*, 1–15. doi:10.1155/2012/602807.

Dickinson, D. K. and Porche, M. V. (2011). Relation between language experiences in preschool classrooms and children's kindergarten and fourth-grade language and reading abilities. *Child Development*, *82*(3), 870–886. doi:10.1111/j.1467-8624.2011.01576.x.

Ehri, L. and Rosenthal, L. (2007). Spellings of words: A neglected facilitator of vocabulary learning. *Journal of Literacy Research*, *39*, 389–409.

Forget-Dubois, N., Dionne, G., Lemelin, J. P., Perusse, D., Tremblay, R. E. and Boivin, M. (2009). Early child language mediates the relation between home environment and school readiness. *Child Development*, *80*(3), 736–749. doi:10.1111/j.1467-8624.2009.01294.x.

Franceschini, S., Gori, S., Ruffino, M., Viola, S., Molteni, M. and Facoetti, A. (2013). Action video games make dyslexic children read better. *Current Biology*, *23*(6), 462–466.

Guernsey, L. and Levine, M. H. (2015). *Tap, Click, Read: Growing Readers in a World of Screens*. San Francisco, CA: John Wiley & Sons.

Justice, L. M., Bowles, R. P., Pence Turnbull, K. L. and Skibbe, L. E. (2009). School readiness among children with varying histories of language difficulties. *Developmental Psychology*, *45*(2), 460–476. doi:10.1037/a0014324.

Kao, G. Y.-M., TsaiChin-Chung, Liu, C.-Y. and Yang, C.-H. (2016). The effects of high/low interactive electronic storybooks on elementary school students' reading motivation, story comprehension and chromatics concepts. *Computers & Education, 100,* 56–70. doi:10.1016/j.compedu.2016.04.013.

Kucirkova, N., Messer, D., Sheehy, K. and Flewitt, R. (2013). Sharing personalised stories on iPads: A close look at one parent–child interaction. *Literacy, 47*(3), 115–122.

Kyle, F., Kujala, J., Richardson, U., Lyytinen, H. and Goswami, U. (2013). Assessing the effectiveness of two theoretically motivated computer-assisted reading interventions in the United Kingdom: GG rime and GG phoneme. *Reading Research Quarterly, 48*(1), 61–76.

Lyytinen, P., Eklund, K. and Lyytinen, H. (2005). Language development and literacy skills in late-talking toddlers with and without familial risk for dyslexia. *Annals of Dyslexia, 55*(2), 166–192. doi:10.1007/s11881-005-0010-y.

Martins, M. A., Salvador, L., Albuquerque, A. and Silva, C. (2014). Invented spelling activities in small groups and early spelling and reading. *Educational Psychology, 36*(4), 738–752. doi:10.1080/01443410.2014.950947.

Martins, M. A. and Silva, C. (2006). The impact of invented spelling on phonemic awareness. *Learning and Instruction, 16,* 41–56.

McBride, C. (2016). *Children's Literacy Development: A Cross-Cultural Perspective on Learning to Read and Write* (2nd edn). Abingdon: Routledge.

McBride-Chang, C. and Liu, P. D. (2011). Chinese reading development and reading disability: Fundamentals and how they might differ across orthographies. In P. McCardle, B. Miller, J. R. Lee and O. J. Tzeng (eds), *Dyslexia Across Languages: Orthography and the Brain-Gene Behavior Link* (pp. 40–55). Baltimore, MD: Paul H. Books Publishing.

NICHD Early Child Care Research Network (2005). Pathways to reading: The role of oral language in the transition to reading. *Developmental Psychology, 41*(2), 428–442. doi:10.1037/0012-1649.41.2.428,

Ojanen, E., Ronimus, M., Ahonen, T., Chansa-Kabali, T., February, P., Jere-Folotiya, J. et al. (2015). GraphoGame – a catalyst for multi-level promotion of literacy in diverse contexts. *Frontiers in Psychology, 6*(671), 1–13. doi:10.3389/fpsyg.2015.00671.

Penno, J., Wilkinson, I. and Moore, D. (2002). Vocabulary acquisition from teacher explanation and repeated listening to stories: Do they overcome the Matthew effect? *Journal of Educational Psychology, 94*(1), 23–33. doi:10.1037//0022-0663.94.1.23.

Pretorius, E. J. and Spaull, N. (2016). Exploring relationships between oral reading fluency and reading comprehension amongst English second language readers in South Africa. *Reading and Writing, 29*(7), 1–23.

Richardson, U. and Lyytinen, H. (2014). The GraphoGame method: The theoretical and methodological background of the technology-enhanced learning environment for learning to read. *Human Technology: An Interdisciplinary Journal on Humans in ICT Environments, 10*(1), 39–60.

Robbins, C. and Ehri, L. C. (1994). Reading storybooks to kindergartners helps them learn new vocabulary words. *Journal of Educational Psychology, 86*(1), 54–64.

Roskos, K., Burstein, K., Shang, Y. and Gray, E. (2014). Young children's engagement with e-books at school. Retrieved 26 April 2016, from SAGE Open, http://sgo.sagepub.com/content/4/1/2158244013517244.short.

Rydland, V., Grøver, V. and Lawrence, J. (2014). The second-language vocabulary trajectories of Turkish immigrant children in Norway from ages five to ten: The role of preschool talk exposure, maternal education, and co-ethnic concentration in the neighborhood. *Journal of Child Language, 41*(2), 352–381. doi:10.1017/S0305000912000712.

Saine, N. L., Lerkkanen, M. K., Ahonen, T., Tolvanen, A. and Lyytinen, H. (2011). Computer-assisted remedial reading intervention for school beginners at risk for reading disability. *Child Development, 82*(3), 1013–1028.

Sénéchal, M., Ouellette, G., Pagan, S. and Lever, R. (2012). The role of invented spelling on learning to read in low-phoneme awareness kindergartners: A randomized-control-trial study. *Reading and Writing, 25*(4), 917–934.

Shanahan, T. (1984). Nature of the reading–writing relation: An exploratory multivariate analysis. *Journal of Educational Psychology, 76*(3), 466–477.

Silverman, R. (2007). Vocabulary development of English-Language and English-Only learners in kindergarten. *The Elementary School Journal, 107,* 365–383. doi:10.1086/516669.

Silverman, R. and Hartrranft, A. (2015) *Developing Vocabulary and Oral Language in Young Children.* New York: The Guilford Press.

Snow, C. (2002). *Reading for Understanding: Toward a Research and Development Program in Reading Comprehension*. Santa Monica, CA: RAND.

Snow, C. E., Burns, S. and Griffin, P. (eds) (1998). *Preventing Reading Difficulties in Young Children*. Washington, DC: National Academy Press.

Snow, C. E., Porche, M., Tabors, P. and Harris, S. (2007). *Is Literacy Enough? Pathways to Academic Success for Adolescents*. Baltimore, MD: Paul H. Brookes Publishing Co.

Takacs, Z. K., Swart, E. K. and Bus, A. G. (2015). Benefits and pitfalls of multimedia and interactive features in technology-enhanced storybooks, a meta-analysis. *Review of Educational Research, 85*(4), 698–739.

Tallal, P., Miller, S. L., Bedi, G., Byma, G., Wang, X., Nagarajan, S. S. et al. (1996). Language comprehension in language-learning impaired children improved with acoustically modified speech. *Science, 271*(5245), 81–84.

Tunmer, W. E. (2014). How cognitive science has provided the theoretical basis for resolving the 'great debate' over reading methods in alphabetic orthographies. In S. Cooper and K. Ratele (eds), *Psychology Serving Humanity: Proceedings of the 30th International Congress of Psychology, Volume 2: Western Psychology* (pp. 228–239). Hove: Psychology Press.

Wei, C.-C. and Ma, M.-Y. (2016). Influences of visual attention and reading time on children and adults. *Reading & Writing Quarterly*, April, 1–12. doi:10.1080/10573569.2015.1092100.

Weiland, C. and Yoshikawa, H. (2013). Impacts of a prekindergarten program on children's mathematics, language, literacy, executive function, and emotional skills. *Child Development, 84*(6), 2112–2130. doi:10.1111/cdev.12099.

Wouters, P., van Nimwegen, C., van Oostendorp, H. and van der Spek, E. D. (2013). A meta-analysis of the cognitive and motivational effects of serious games. *Journal of Educational Psychology, 105*(2), 249–265.

Yoshikawa, H., Leyva, D., Snow, C. E., Trevino, E., Barata, M. C., Weiland, C. et al. (2015). Experimental impacts of a teacher professional development program in Chile on preschool classroom quality and child outcomes. *Developmental Psychology, 51*(3), 309–322. doi:10.1037/a0038785.

INDEX